# Immigration & Nationality Act
## 2010 Edition

# AILA PUBLICATIONS

## AILA's OCCUPATIONAL GUIDEBOOKS

*Immigration Options for Artists and Entertainers*

*Immigration Options for Essential Workers*

*Immigration Options for Physicians*

*Immigration Options for Nurses & Allied Health Care Professionals*

*Immigration Options for Religious Workers*

*Immigration Options for Academics and Researchers*

*Immigration Options for Investors and Entrepreneurs*

## CORE CURRICULUM

*Code of Federal Regulations*

*Immigration & Nationality Act*

*Navigating the Fundamentals of Immigration Law*

*Immigration Law for Paralegals\**

## TOOLBOX SERIES

*AILA's Immigration Practice Toolbox*

*AILA's Litigation Toolbox*

## FOR YOUR CLIENTS

*Client Brochures (10 Titles)*

*U.S. Tax Guides for Foreign Persons and Those Who Pay Them, 4 volumes— (H-1Bs, L-1s, J-1s, B-1s)\**

## AILA's FOCUS SERIES

*EB-2 & EB-3 Degree Equivalency*
by Ronald Wada

*Waivers Under the INA*
by Julie Ferguson

*Private Bills & Pardons in Immigration*
by Anna Gallagher

*The Child Status Protection Act*
by Charles Wheeler

*Immigration Practice Under AC21*
by A. James Vazquez-Azpiri & Eleanor Pelta

## ONLINE RESEARCH TOOLS

*AILALink Online*

## TREATISES & PRIMERS

*Kurzban's Immigration Law Sourcebook*
by Ira J. Kurzban

*Professionals: A Matter of Degree*
by Martin J. Lawler

*AILA's Asylum Primer*
by Regina Germain

*Immigration Consequences of Criminal Activity*
by Mary E. Kramer

*Representing Clients in Immigration Court*
by CLINIC

*Essentials of Immigration Law*
by Richard A. Boswell

*Litigating Immigration Cases in Federal Court*
by Robert Pauw

*Immigration Law & the Family*
edited and written by Charles Wheeler

*Immigration Law & the Transgender Client*
by Transgender Law Center & Immigration Equality

## OTHER TITLES

*AILA's Guide to Worksite Enforcement and Corporate Compliance*

*David Stanton Manual on Labor Certification*

*Going Global: Trends in Outbound Immigration*

*AILA's Global Immigration Guide: A Country-by-Country Survey*

*Immigration & Nationality Law Handbook*

*The Visa Processing Guide & Consular Posts Handbook*

*Immigration Practice Under NAFTA and Other Free Trade Agreements*

*The International Adoption Sourcebook*

## GOVERNMENT REPRINTS

*BIA Practice Manual*

*Immigration Judge Benchbook*

*Citizenship Laws of the World*

*CBP Inspector's Field Manual*

*EOIR Immigration Court Practice Manual*

*Affirmative Asylum Procedures Manual*

Tables of Contents and other information about these publications can be found at ***www.ailapubs.com***. Orders may be placed at that site or by calling 1-800-982-2839.

\*An AILA-distributed title

# Immigration & Nationality Act

## An AILA Primary Source Reference

### Current through March 1, 2010

**Rizwan Hassan**
*Legal Editor*

**Kathy Jo Frazier**
*Editorial Assistant*

AMERICAN IMMIGRATION LAWYERS ASSOCIATION

1331 G Street NW, Washington, DC 20005 ♦ www.aila.org

## Website for Corrections and Updates

Corrections and other updates to this and other AILA publications can be found on the Internet at *www.aila.org/BookUpdates*. This site will include links to new public laws that amend the INA.

If you have any corrections or updates to the information in this book, please let us know by sending a note to the address below, or a message to *books@aila.org*.

This publication is designed to provide accurate and authoritative information in regard to the subject matter covered. It is distributed with the understanding that the publisher is not engaged in rendering legal, accounting, or other professional service. If legal advice or other expert assistance is required, the services of a competent professional should be sought.

*—from a Declaration of Principles jointly adopted by a Committee of the American Bar Association and a Committee of Publishers*

Requests for permission to make electronic or print copies of any part of this work should be mailed to Director of Publications, American Immigration Lawyers Association, 1331 G Street NW, Suite 300, Washington, DC 20005, or e-mailed to *books@aila.org*.

Printed in the United States of America

ISBN 978-1-57370-293-5

*Stock No. 52-93*

# Summary of Contents

# PREFACE

This 2010 edition of AILA's *Immigration & Nationality Act* incorporates laws enacted through March 1, 2010. It includes provisions to:

- The Department of Homeland Security Appropriations Bill for FY2010 (Pub. L. No. 111-83, amending §§101(a)(27)(C)(ii), 201(b)(2)(A)(i), 204, and 213A(f)(5)). This legislation extends through September 30, 2012: the Special Immigrant Non-Minister Religious Worker Program; the "Conrad 30" waiver for foreign medical graduate physicians; the EB-5 visa program; and the E-Verify program. This law also includes statutory authority for USCIS to complete processing of permanent residence applications for surviving spouses and other relatives of immigration sponsors who die during the adjudication process.

- An Act to Extend Certain Immigrant Programs for 2009 (Pub. L. No. 111-9, amending §101(a)(27)(C)(ii)). This legislation extended to September 30, 2009: the Special Immigrant Non-Minister Religious Worker Program; and the "Conrad 30" waiver for foreign medical graduate physicians. This legislation has since been superseded by The Department of Homeland Security Appropriations Bill for FY2010, which extended both programs to September 30, 2012.

- Human Rights Enforcement Act of 2009 (Pub. L. No. 111-122, amending §§103(h) and 212(a)(3)(E)(ii)). This legislation establishes a section within the Criminal Division of the Department of Justice with responsibility for the enforcement of laws against suspected participants in serious human rights offenses.

Legislative histories are cumulated at the end of the relevant INA section. Other editorial notes, such as sunset provisions, congressional drafting errors, and applicability information, can be found throughout the text.

All the immigration-related statutes codified in title 8 of the U.S. Code that are not part of the INA are included in Appendix A. Other immigration-related statutory provisions not in the INA are set forth in the appendices as well, including the provisions of the USA PATRIOT Act that granted certain benefits to victims of terrorism; other legislation awarding posthumous benefits to 9/11 victims; IIRAIRA §§110, 309, and 641 (as most recently amended or affected by the USA PATRIOT Act); the noncodified portions of AC21 (as amended by the REAL ID Act) and the LIFE Act; the most recently amended versions of NACARA, HRIFA, and the Hmong Veterans' Naturalization Act; the EB-5 amendments contained in the DOJ Appropriations Act; and the House Rules of Procedure and Statement of Policy for Private Immigration Bills. The book also includes a detailed, comprehensive index.

This book is updated electronically as a service to users. See *www.aila.org/BookUpdates* for the latest legislation or any other updates or corrections. Users are invited to submit suggestions and other comments to *books@aila.org*.

AILA is pleased to continue to offer its print INA and CFR publications on a standing order basis, providing users with a convenient way to be sure they have the most current edition of each, as soon as they are available. For further information, please see the order form in this book.

# Perpetual Discount, Immediate Shipment!

# AILA's INA and CFR
## AVAILABLE ON STANDING ORDER

Now you can be sure to receive the *Immigration & Nationality Act* and/or *Immigration Regulations* (Vol. 1 — Title 8  and Vol. 2 — Titles 6, 20, 22, 28, and 42) **automatically** each year, as soon as they are published, **and** get a guaranteed **10% discount**—even off the already-discounted combo price or quantity discounts.

- - - - - - - - - - - - - - - - - - - - - - - - - - - - - - - - - - - - - - - - - - - - - - - - - - - - - - - - -

**PHONE:** 1-800-982-2839     **FAX:** (301) 843-0159

**MAIL:** AILA Publications, P.O. Box 753, Waldorf, MD  20604-0753

☐  **Yes, I have the 2010 edition(s) and I want to be placed on Standing Order for future editions of the following title(s).**

| TITLE | STOCK CODE | MBR PRICE* | REG PRICE | QTY | TOTAL |
|-------|------------|------------|-----------|-----|-------|
| Immigration & Nationality Act, 2010 Edition | 52-93 | $69 | $99 | | |
| Immigration Regulations (CFR), 2010 Editions (2 volumes) | 52-94 | $149 | $195 | | |
| INA/CFR Combo, 2010 Editions (3 volumes) | CINACFR10 | $199 | $269 | | |

| | |
|---|---|
| I understand that I will receive the indicated item(s) automatically each year, as soon as they are published. My credit card will not be charged until the book(s) actually ships. Moreover, each year, I will automatically receive an additional 10% off the list price (before s&h)—even off the already-discounted combo price. I may cancel my Standing Order at any time. And, like all AILA publications, any Standing Order title is returnable within 30 days of receipt for a full refund (must be in resalable condition). | Subtract 10% Standing Order Disc.  — |
| | Add Shipping & Handling** |
| | **SUBTOTAL** |
| | DC (6%) / MD (6%) add sales tax |
| | **TOTAL** |

***All govt agencies, academic institutions, & nonprofit organizations are eligible for the AILA member price.**

Name_____

Title  _____     AILA Member Number _____

Firm/Organization_____

Address_____

City_____

State _____     Zip _____     Country_____

Phone  _____     e-mail _____

**CREDIT CARD ORDERS ONLY** ☐ Visa     ☐ MC     ☐ AmEx

Card # _____

Exp. Date _____

Name on Card _____

Signature _____

| **Shipping & Handling Charges** (Continental U.S.) | | | |
|---|---|---|---|
| 1-2 | books | $12.00 | 7-9   books   $33.00 |
| 3-4 | books | $18.00 | 10 books or more   3% of total |
| 5-6 | books | $25.00 | |

Failure to provide proper shipping may delay your order. International orders & orders outside the continental U.S. must include exact post.  Please contact AILA Publications for fee.

**INACFR**

# ABOUT AILA

The American Immigration Lawyers Association (AILA) is a national bar association of more than 11,000 attorneys who practice immigration law and/or work as teaching professionals. AILA member attorneys represent tens of thousands of U.S. families who have applied for permanent residence for their spouses, children, and other close relatives for lawful entry and residence in the United States. AILA members also represent thousands of U.S. businesses and industries who sponsor highly skilled foreign workers seeking to enter the United States on a temporary or permanent basis. In addition, AILA members represent foreign students, entertainers, athletes, and asylum-seekers, often on a pro bono basis. Founded in 1946, AILA is a nonpartisan, not-for-profit organization that provides its members with continuing legal education, publications, information, professional services, and expertise through its 36 chapters and over 50 national committees. AILA is an affiliated organization of the American Bar Association and is represented in the ABA House of Delegates.

American Immigration Lawyers Association

*www.aila.org*

AILA Publications: *www.ailapubs.org* or (800) 982-2839

# LIST OF SECTIONS

# Title I—General Provisions (§§101–06)

## Sec. 101 Definitions
## [8 U.S.C. 1101]

**(a)** As used in this Act—

(1) The term "administrator" means the official designated by the Secretary of State pursuant to section 104(b) of this Act.

(2) The term "advocates" includes, but is not limited to, advises, recommends, furthers by overt act, and admits belief in.

(3) The term "alien" means any person not a citizen or national of the United States.

(4) The term "application for admission" has reference to the application for admission into the United States and not to the application for the issuance of an immigrant or nonimmigrant visa.

(5) The term "Attorney General" means the Attorney General of the United States.

(6) The term "border crossing identification card" means a document of identity bearing that designation issued to an alien who is lawfully admitted for permanent residence, or to an alien who is a resident in foreign contiguous territory, by a consular officer or an immigration officer for the purpose of crossing over the borders between the United States and foreign contiguous territory in accordance with such conditions for its issuance and use as may be prescribed by regulations. Such regulations shall provide that (A) each such document include a biometric identifier (such as the fingerprint or handprint of the alien) that is machine readable and (B) an alien presenting a border crossing identification is not permitted to cross over the border into the United States unless the biometric identifier card contained on the card matches the appropriate biometric characteristic of the alien.[1]

(7) The term "clerk of court" means a clerk of a naturalization court.

(8) The terms "Commissioner" and "Deputy Commissioner" mean the Commissioner of Immigration and Naturalization and a Deputy Commissioner of Immigration and Naturalization, respectively.

(9) The term "consular officer" means any consular, diplomatic, or other officer or employee of the United States designated under regulations prescribed under authority contained in this Act, for the purpose of issuing immigrant or nonimmigrant visas or, when used in title III, for the purpose of adjudicating nationality.

(10) The term "crewman" means a person serving in any capacity on board a vessel or aircraft.

(11) The term "diplomatic visa" means a nonimmigrant visa bearing that title and issued to a nonimmigrant in accordance with such regulations as the Secretary of State may prescribe.

(12) The term "doctrine" includes, but is not limited to, policies, practices, purposes, aims, or procedures.

(13)[2] (A) The terms "admission" and "admitted" mean, with respect to an alien, the lawful

---

[1] Clause (A) of paragraph (6) applies to documents issued on or after 18 months after the date of the enactment of IIRAIRA, P.L. 104-208, §104(b). Clause (B) applies to cards presented on or after six years after the date of enactment of IIRAIRA, P.L. 107-173, §601.

[2] The effective date (referred to as the title III-A effective date) is established by §309 of IIRAIRA, *reprinted in* Appendix C, *infra*.

entry of the alien into the United States after inspection and authorization by an immigration officer.

(B) An alien who is paroled under section 212(d)(5) or permitted to land temporarily as an alien crewman shall not be considered to have been admitted.

(C) An alien lawfully admitted for permanent residence in the United States shall not be regarded as seeking an admission into the United States for purposes of the immigration laws unless the alien—

(i) has abandoned or relinquished that status,

(ii) has been absent from the United States for a continuous period in excess of 180 days,

(iii) has engaged in illegal activity after having departed the United States,

(iv) has departed from the United States while under legal process seeking removal of the alien from the United States, including removal proceedings under this Act and extradition proceedings,

(v) has committed an offense identified in section 212(a)(2), unless since such offense the alien has been granted relief under section 212(h) or 240A(a), or

(vi) is attempting to enter at a time or place other than as designated by immigration officers or has not been admitted to the United States after inspection and authorization by an immigration officer.

(14) The term "foreign state" includes outlying possessions of a foreign state, but self-governing dominions and territories under mandate or trusteeship shall be regarded as separate foreign states.

(15) The term "immigrant" means every alien except an alien who is within one of the following classes of nonimmigrant aliens—[3]

(A) (i) an ambassador, public minister, or career diplomatic or consular officer who has been accredited by a foreign government recognized de jure by the United States and who is accepted by the President or by the Secretary of State, and the members of the alien's immediate family;

(ii) upon a basis of reciprocity, other officials and employees who have been accredited by a foreign government recognized de jure by the United States, who are accepted by the Secretary of State, and the members of their immediate families; and

(iii) upon a basis of reciprocity, attendants, servants, personal employees, and members of their immediate families, of the officials and employees who have a nonimmigrant status under (i) and (ii) above;

(B) an alien (other than one coming for the purpose of study or of performing skilled or unskilled labor or as a representative of foreign press, radio, film, or other foreign information media coming to engage in such vocation) having a residence in a foreign country

---

[3] Sec. 306 of the Enhanced Border Security and Visa Entry Reform Act of 2002 (EBSVERA), P.L. 107-173 (5/14/02), provides that no nonimmigrant visa under INA §101(a)(15) shall be issued to any alien from a country that is a state sponsor of international terrorism unless the appropriate U.S. agencies determine that such alien does not pose a threat to the safety or national security of the country. EBSVERA §606 requires the State Department to retain, for a period of seven years from date of application, every application for nonimmigrant visa under INA §101(a)(15).

which he has no intention of abandoning and who is visiting the United States temporarily for business or temporarily for pleasure;

(C) an alien in immediate and continuous transit through the United States, or an alien who qualifies as a person entitled to pass in transit to and from the United Nations Headquarters District and foreign countries, under the provisions of paragraphs (3), (4), and (5) of section 11 of the Headquarters Agreement with the United Nations (61 Stat. 758);

(D) (i) an alien crewman serving in good faith as such in a capacity required for normal operation and service on board a vessel, as defined in section 258(a) (other than a fishing vessel having its home port or an operating base in the United States), or aircraft, who intends to land temporarily and solely in pursuit of his calling as a crewman and to depart from the United States with the vessel or aircraft on which he arrived or some other vessel or aircraft;

(ii) an alien crewman serving in good faith as such in any capacity required for normal operations and service aboard a fishing vessel having its home port or an operating base in the United States who intends to land temporarily in Guam or the Commonwealth of the Northern Mariana Islands and solely in pursuit of his calling as a crewman and to depart from Guam or the Commonwealth of the Northern Mariana Islands with the vessel on which he arrived;

(E) an alien entitled to enter the United States under and in pursuance of the provisions of a treaty of commerce and navigation between the United States and the foreign state of which he is a national, and the spouse and children of any such alien if accompanying or following to join him:[4]

(i) solely to carry on substantial trade, including trade in services or trade in technology, principally between the United States and the foreign state of which he is a national;

(ii) solely to develop and direct the operations of an enterprise in which he has invested, or of an enterprise in which he is actively in the process of investing, a substantial amount of capital; or

(iii) solely to perform services in a specialty occupation in the United States if the alien is a national of the Commonwealth of Australia and with respect to whom the Secretary of Labor determines and certifies to the Secretary of Homeland Security and the Secretary of State that the intending employer has filed with the Secretary of Labor an attestation under section 212(t)(1);

(F)[5] (i) an alien having a residence in a foreign country which he has no intention of abandoning, who is a bona fide student qualified to pursue a full course of study and who seeks to enter the United States temporarily and solely for the purpose of pursu-

---

[4] Made applicable to nonimmigrant traders and investors from Jordan, Chile, and Singapore pursuant to P.L. 107-43, §301 (9/28/01), P.L. 108-77, §401 (9/3/03, *effective* 1/1/04, the date U.S.-Chile Free Trade Agreement entered into force), and P.L. 108-78, §401 (9/3/03, *effective* 1/1/04, the date U.S.-Singapore Free Trade Agreement entered into force), respectively.

[5] Amended by §625 of IIRAIRA, effective as to "individuals who obtain the status of a nonimmigrant under §101(a)(15)(F) of the [INA] after the end of the 60-day period beginning on the date of the enactment of this Act, including aliens whose status as such a nonimmigrant is extended after the end of such period."

*See* §501(b) and (c) of the Enhanced Border Security and Visa Entry Reform Act of 2002, P.L. 107-173 (5/14/02), for additional requirements imposed on F, M, and certain J visa applicants, and §502 for additional government recordkeeping and reporting requirements.

ing such a course of study consistent with section 214(*l*)[6] at an established college, university, seminary, conservatory, academic high school, elementary school, or other academic institution or in a language training program in the United States, particularly designated by him and approved by the Attorney General after consultation with the Secretary of Education, which institution or place of study shall have agreed to report to the Attorney General the termination of attendance of each nonimmigrant student, and if any such institution of learning or place of study fails to make reports promptly the approval shall be withdrawn,

(ii) the alien spouse and minor children of any alien described in clause (i) if accompanying or following to join such an alien, and

(iii) an alien who is a national of Canada or Mexico, who maintains actual residence and place of abode in the country of nationality, who is described in clause (i) except that the alien's qualifications for and actual course of study may be full or part-time, and who commutes to the United States institution or place of study from Canada or Mexico;

(G) (i) a designated principal resident representative of a foreign government recognized de jure by the United States, which foreign government is a member of an international organization entitled to enjoy privileges, exemptions, and immunities as an international organization under the International Organizations Immunities Act (59 Stat. 669) 22 U.S.C. 288, note, accredited resident members of the staff of such representatives, and members of his or their immediate family;

(ii) other accredited representatives of such a foreign government to such international organizations, and the members of their immediate families;

(iii) an alien able to qualify under (i) or (ii) above except for the fact that the government of which such alien is an accredited representative is not recognized de jure by the United States, or that the government of which he is an accredited representative is not a member of such international organization, and the members of his immediate family;

(iv) officers, or employees of such international organizations, and the members of their immediate families;

(v) attendants, servants, and personal employees of any such representative, officer, or employee, and the members of the immediate families of such attendants, servants, and personal employees;

(H) an alien

(i) (a) [Repealed].[7]

(b) subject to section 212(j)(2), who is coming temporarily to the United States to perform services (other than services described in subclause (a) during the period in which such subclause applies and other than services described in subclause (ii)(a) or in subparagraph (O) or (P)) in a specialty occupation described in section 214(i)(1) or as a fashion model, who meets the requirements for the occupation specified in section 214(i)(2) or, in the case of a fashion model, is of distinguished

---

[6] *Sic.* Now §214(m).

[7] .Repealed by P.L. 106-95 (11/12/99), §2(c).

merit and ability, and with respect to whom the Secretary of Labor determines and certifies to the Attorney General that the intending employer has filed with the Secretary an application under section 212(n)(1), or

(b1) who is entitled to enter the United States under and in pursuance of the provisions of an agreement listed in section 214(g)(8)(A), who is engaged in a specialty occupation described in section 214(i)(3), and with respect to whom the Secretary of Labor determines and certifies to the Secretary of Homeland Security and the Secretary of State that the intending employer has filed with the Secretary of Labor an attestation under section 212(t)(1), or

(c) who is coming temporarily to the United States to perform services as a registered nurse, who meets the qualifications described in section 212(m)(1), and with respect to whom the Secretary of Labor determines and certifies to the Attorney General that an unexpired attestation is on file and in effect under section 212(m)(2) for the facility (as defined in section 212(m)(6)) for which the alien will perform the services; or

(ii) (a) having a residence in a foreign country which he has no intention of abandoning who is coming temporarily to the United States to perform agricultural labor or services, as defined by the Secretary of Labor in regulations and including agricultural labor defined in section 3121(g) of the Internal Revenue Code of 1986, agriculture as defined in section 3(f) of the Fair Labor Standards Act of 1938 (29 U.S.C. 203(f)), and the pressing of apples for cider on a farm, of a temporary or seasonal nature, or

(b) having a residence in a foreign country which he has no intention of abandoning who is coming temporarily to the United States to perform other temporary service or labor if unemployed persons capable of performing such service or labor cannot be found in this country, but this clause shall not apply to graduates of medical schools coming to the United States to perform services as members of the medical profession; or

(iii) having a residence in a foreign country which he has no intention of abandoning who is coming temporarily to the United States as a trainee, other than to receive graduate medical education or training, in a training program that is not designed primarily to provide productive employment; and the alien spouse and minor children of any such alien specified in this paragraph if accompanying him or following to join him;

(I) upon a basis of reciprocity, an alien who is a bona fide representative of foreign press, radio, film, or other foreign information media, who seeks to enter the United States solely to engage in such vocation, and the spouse and children of such a representative if accompanying or following to join him;

(J) an alien having a residence in a foreign country which he has no intention of abandoning who is a bona fide student, scholar, trainee, teacher, professor, research assistant, specialist, or leader in a field of specialized knowledge or skill, or other person of similar description, who is coming temporarily to the United States as a participant in a program designated by the Director of the United States Information Agency, for the purpose of teaching, instructing or lecturing, studying, observing, conducting research, consulting, demonstrating special skills, or receiving training and who, if he is coming to the United States to participate in a program under which he will receive graduate medical education or training, also meets the requirements of section 212(j), and the alien spouse and minor children of any such alien if accompanying him or following to join him;[8]

(K)[9] subject to subsections (d) and (p)[10] of section 214, an alien who—

(i) is the fiancée or fiancé of a citizen of the United States (other than a citizen described in section 204(a)(1)(A)(viii)(I)) and who seeks to enter the United States solely to conclude a valid marriage with the petitioner within ninety days after admission;

(ii) has concluded a valid marriage with a citizen of the United States (other than a citizen described in section 204(a)(1)(A)(viii)(I)) who is the petitioner, is the beneficiary of a petition to accord a status under section 201(b)(2)(A)(i) that was filed under section 204 by the petitioner, and seeks to enter the United States to await the approval of such petition and the availability to the alien of an immigrant visa; or

(iii) is the minor child of an alien described in clause (i) or (ii) and is accompanying, or following to join, the alien;

(L) subject to section 214(c)(2), an alien who, within 3 years preceding the time of his application for admission into the United States, has been employed continuously for one year by a firm or corporation or other legal entity or an affiliate or subsidiary thereof and who seeks to enter the United States temporarily in order to continue to render his services to the same employer or a subsidiary or affiliate thereof in a capacity that is managerial, executive, or involves specialized knowledge, and the alien spouse and minor children of any such alien if accompanying him or following to join him;

(M)[11](i) an alien having a residence in a foreign country which he has no intention of abandoning who seeks to enter the United States temporarily and solely for the purpose of pursuing a full course of study at an established vocational or other recognized nonacademic institution (other than in a language training program) in the United States particularly designated by him and approved by the Attorney General, after consultation with the Secretary of Education, which institution shall have agreed to report to the Attorney General the termination of attendance of each nonimmigrant nonacademic student and if any such institution fails to make reports promptly the approval shall be withdrawn, and

(ii) the alien spouse and minor children of any alien described in clause (i) if accompanying or following to join such an alien, and

(iii) an alien who is a national of Canada or Mexico, who maintains actual residence and place of abode in the country of nationality, who is described in clause (i) except

---

[8] *See* §501(b) and (c) of the Enhanced Border Security and Visa Entry Reform Act of 2002, P.L. 107-173, for additional requirements imposed on F, M, and certain J visa applicants, and §502 for additional government recordkeeping and reporting requirements.

[9] Sec. 832(b) of P.L. 109-162 (1/6/06) provides: "The fact that an alien described in [INA §101(a)(15)(K)(i) or (ii)] is aware of any information disclosed under the amendments made by this section or under §833 [requiring the government to supply certain domestic violence information and resources, and regulating international marriage brokers] shall not be used to deny the alien eligibility for relief under any other provision of law." Further, §834 of that Act provides that INA §222(f) shall not be construed to prevent the sharing of information regarding a U.S. petitioner for a visa under INA §101(a)(15)(K)(i) or (ii) for the limited purposes of fulfilling disclosure obligations imposed by the amendments made by §§832(a) or 833 of P.L. 109-162.

[10] Redesignated as (r). P.L. 108-193 (12/19/03), §8(a)(3).

[11] *See* note 8, *supra.*

that the alien's course of study may be full or part-time, and who commutes to the United States institution or place of study from Canada or Mexico;

(N) (i) the parent of an alien accorded the status of special immigrant under paragraph (27)(I)(i), (or under analogous authority under paragraph (27)(L)) but only if and while the alien is a child, or

(ii) a child of such parent or of an alien accorded the status of a special immigrant under clause (ii), (iii), or (iv) or paragraph (27)(I) (or under analogous authority under paragraph (27)(L));

(O) an alien who—

(i) has extraordinary ability in the sciences, arts, education, business, or athletics which has been demonstrated by sustained national or international acclaim or, with regard to motion picture and television productions a demonstrated record of extraordinary achievement, and whose achievements have been recognized in the field through extensive documentation, and seeks to enter the United States to continue work in the area of extraordinary ability; or

(ii) (I) seeks to enter the United States temporarily and solely for the purpose of accompanying and assisting in the artistic or athletic performance by an alien who is admitted under clause (i) for a specific event or events,

(II) is an integral part of such actual performance,

(III)(a) has critical skills and experience with such alien which are not of a general nature and which cannot be performed by other individuals, or

(b) in the case of a motion picture or television production, has skills and experience with such alien which are not of a general nature and which are critical either based on a pre-existing longstanding working relationship or, with respect to the specific production, because significant production (including pre- and post-production work) will take place both inside and outside the United States and the continuing participation of the alien is essential to the successful completion of the production, and

(IV) has a foreign residence which the alien has no intention of abandoning; or

(iii) is the alien spouse or child of an alien described in clause (i) or (ii) and is accompanying, or following to join, the alien;

(P) an alien having a foreign residence which the alien has no intention of abandoning who—

(i) (a) is described in section 214(c)(4)(A) (relating to athletes), or

(b) is described in section 214(c)(4)(B) (relating to entertainment groups);

(ii) (I) performs as an artist or entertainer, individually or as part of a group, or is an integral part of the performance of such a group, and

(II) seeks to enter the United States temporarily and solely for the purpose of performing as such an artist or entertainer or with such a group under a reciprocal exchange program which is between an organization or organizations in the United States and an organization or organizations in one or more foreign states and which provides for the temporary exchange of artists and entertainers, or groups of artists and entertainers;

(iii) (I) performs as an artist or entertainer, individually or as part of a group, or is an integral part of the performance of such a group, and

(II) seeks to enter the United States temporarily and solely to perform, teach, or coach as such an artist or entertainer or with such a group under a commercial or noncommercial program that is culturally unique; or

(iv) is the spouse or child of an alien described in clause (i), (ii), or (iii) and is accompanying, or following to join, the alien;

(Q) (i) an alien having a residence in a foreign country which he has no intention of abandoning who is coming temporarily (for a period not to exceed 15 months) to the United States as a participant in an international cultural exchange program approved by the Secretary of Homeland Security for the purpose of providing practical training, employment, and the sharing of the history, culture, and traditions of the country of the alien's nationality and who will be employed under the same wages and working conditions as domestic workers; or

(ii)[12](I) an alien citizen of the United Kingdom or the Republic of Ireland, 21 to 35 years of age, unemployed for not less than 12 months, and having a residence for not less than 18 months in Northern Ireland, or the counties of Louth, Monaghan, Cavan, Leitrim, Sligo, and Donegal within the Republic of Ireland, which the alien has no intention of abandoning who is coming temporarily (for a period not to exceed 24 months) to the United States as a participant in a cultural and training program approved by the Secretary of State and the Secretary of Homeland Security under section 2(a) of the Irish Peace Process Cultural and Training Program Act of 1998 for the purpose of providing practical training, employment, and the experience of coexistence and conflict resolution in a diverse society, and

(II) the alien spouse and minor children of any such alien if accompanying the alien or following to join the alien;

(R) an alien, and the spouse and children of the alien if accompanying or following to join the alien, who—

(i) for the 2 years immediately preceding the time of application for admission, has been a member of a religious denomination having a bona fide nonprofit, religious organization in the United States; and

(ii) seeks to enter the United States for a period not to exceed 5 years to perform the work described in subclause (I), (II), or (III) of paragraph (27)(C)(ii);

(S) subject to section 214(k), an alien—

(i) who the Attorney General determines—

(I) is in possession of critical reliable information concerning a criminal organization or enterprise;

(II) is willing to supply or has supplied such information to Federal or State law enforcement authorities or a Federal or State court; and

---

[12] *Sunset.* Clause (Q)(ii) sunsets on 10/1/08. P.L. 108-449, §1(a)(2)(B).

(III) whose presence in the United States the Attorney General determines is essential to the success of an authorized criminal investigation or the successful prosecution of an individual involved in the criminal organization or enterprise; or

(ii) who the Secretary of State and the Attorney General jointly determine—

(I) is in possession of critical reliable information concerning a terrorist organization, enterprise, or operation;

(II) is willing to supply or has supplied such information to Federal law enforcement authorities or a Federal court;

(III) will be or has been placed in danger as a result of providing such information; and

(IV) is eligible to receive a reward under section 36(a) of the State Department Basic Authorities Act of 1956, and, if the Attorney General (or with respect to clause (ii), the Secretary of State and the Attorney General jointly) considers it to be appropriate, the spouse, married and unmarried sons and daughters, and parents of an alien described in clause (i) or (ii) if accompanying, or following to join, the alien;

(T)[13](i) subject to section 214(o), an alien who the Secretary of Homeland Security, or in the case of subclause (III)(aa) the Secretary of Homeland Security, in consultation with the Attorney General, determines—

(I) is or has been a victim of a severe form of trafficking in persons, as defined in section 103 of the Trafficking Victims Protection Act of 2000;

(II) is physically present in the United States, American Samoa, or the Commonwealth of the Northern Mariana Islands, or at a port of entry thereto, on account of such trafficking, including physical presence on account of the alien having been allowed entry into the United States for participation in investigative or judicial processes associated with an act or a perpetrator of trafficking;

(III)(aa) has complied with any reasonable request for assistance in the Federal, State, or local investigation or prosecution of acts of trafficking or the investigation of crime where acts of trafficking are at least one central reason for the commission of that crime;

(bb) in consultation with the Attorney General, as appropriate, is unable to cooperate with a request described in item (aa) due to physical or psychological trauma; or

(cc) has not attained 18 years of age; and

---

[13] Sec. 813(b) of P.L. 109-162 (VAWA 2005) (1/5/06) provides as follows:

DISCRETION TO CONSENT TO AN ALIEN'S REAPPLICATION FOR ADMISSION.—

(1) IN GENERAL.—The Secretary of Homeland Security, the Attorney General, and the Secretary of State shall continue to have discretion to consent to an alien's reapplication for admission after a previous order of removal, deportation, or exclusion.

(2) SENSE OF CONGRESS.—It is the sense of Congress that the officials described in paragraph (1) should particularly consider exercising this authority in cases under the Violence Against Women Act of 1994, cases involving nonimmigrants described in subparagraph (T) or (U) of §101(a)(15) of the Immigration and Nationality Act (8 U.S.C. 1101(a)(15)), and relief under §240A(b)(2) or 244(a)(3) of such Act (as in effect on March 31, 1997) pursuant to regulations under §212.2 of title 8, Code of Federal Regulations.

(IV) the alien would suffer extreme hardship involving unusual and severe harm upon removal; and

(ii) if accompanying, or following to join, the alien described in clause (i)—

(I) in the case of an alien described in clause (i) who is under 21 years of age, the spouse, children, unmarried siblings under 18 years of age on the date on which such alien applied for status under such clause, and parents of such alien;

(II) in the case of an alien described in clause (i) who is 21 years of age or older, the spouse and children of such alien; or

(III) any parent or unmarried sibling under 18 years of age of an alien described in subclause (I) or (II) who the Secretary of Homeland Security, in consultation with the law enforcement officer investigating a severe form of trafficking, determines faces a present danger of retaliation as a result of the alien's escape from the severe form of trafficking or cooperation with law enforcement.

(iii) if the Secretary of Homeland Security, in his or her discretion and with the consultation of the Attorney General, determines that a trafficking victim, due to psychological or physical trauma, is unable to cooperate with a request for assistance described in clause (i)(III)(aa), the request is unreasonable.

(U)[14](i) subject to section 214(p), an alien who files a petition for status under this subparagraph, if the Secretary of Homeland Security determines that—

(I) the alien has suffered substantial physical or mental abuse as a result of having been a victim of criminal activity described in clause (iii);

(II) the alien (or in the case of an alien child under the age of 16, the parent, guardian, or next friend of the alien) possesses information concerning criminal activity described in clause (iii);

(III) the alien (or in the case of an alien child under the age of 16, the parent, guardian, or next friend of the alien) has been helpful, is being helpful, or is likely to be helpful to a Federal, State, or local law enforcement official, to a Federal, State, or local prosecutor, to a Federal or State judge, to the Service, or to other Federal, State, or local authorities investigating or prosecuting criminal activity described in clause (iii); and

(IV) the criminal activity described in clause (iii) violated the laws of the United States or occurred in the United States (including in Indian country and military installations) or the territories and possessions of the United States;

(ii) if accompanying, or following to join, the alien described in clause (i)—

(I) in the case of an alien described in clause (i) who is under 21 years of age, the spouse, children, unmarried siblings under 18 years of age on the date on which such alien applied for status under such clause, and parents of such alien; or

(II) in the case of an alien described in clause (i) who is 21 years of age or older, the spouse and children of such alien; and

---

[14] *See* note 13, *supra.*

(iii) the criminal activity referred to in this clause is that involving one or more of the following or any similar activity in violation of Federal, State, or local criminal law: rape; torture; trafficking; incest; domestic violence; sexual assault; abusive sexual contact; prostitution; sexual exploitation; female genital mutilation; being held hostage; peonage; involuntary servitude; slave trade; kidnapping; abduction; unlawful criminal restraint; false imprisonment; blackmail; extortion; manslaughter; murder; felonious assault; witness tampering; obstruction of justice; perjury; or attempt, conspiracy, or solicitation to commit any of the above mentioned crimes; or

(V) subject to section 214(q), an alien who is the beneficiary (including a child of the principal alien, if eligible to receive a visa under section 203(d)) of a petition to accord a status under section 203(a)(2)(A) that was filed with the Attorney General under section 204 on or before the date of the enactment of the Legal Immigration Family Equity Act, if—

(i) such petition has been pending for 3 years or more; or

(ii) such petition has been approved, 3 years or more have elapsed since such filing date, and—

(I) an immigrant visa is not immediately available to the alien because of a waiting list of applicants for visas under section 203(a)(2)(A); or

(II) the alien's application for an immigrant visa, or the alien's application for adjustment of status under section 245, pursuant to the approval of such petition, remains pending.

(16) The term "immigrant visa" means an immigrant visa required by this Act and properly issued by a consular officer at his office outside of the United States to an eligible immigrant under the provisions of this Act.

(17) The term "immigration laws" includes this Act and all laws, conventions, and treaties of the United States relating to the immigration, exclusion, deportation, expulsion, or removal of aliens.

(18) The term "immigration officer" means any employee or class of employees of the Service or of the United States designated by the Attorney General, individually or by regulation, to perform the functions of an immigration officer specified by this Act or any section thereof.

(19) The term "ineligible to citizenship," when used in reference to any individual, means, notwithstanding the provisions of any treaty relating to military service, an individual who is, or was at any time, permanently debarred from becoming a citizen of the United States under section 3(a) of the Selective Training and Service Act of 1940, as amended (54 Stat. 885; 55 Stat. 844), or under section 4(a) of the Selective Service Act of 1948, as amended (62 Stat. 605; 65 Stat. 76) 50 U.S.C. App. 454, or under any section of this Act, or any other Act, or under any law amendatory of, supplementary to, or in substitution for, any of such sections or Acts.

(20) The term "lawfully admitted for permanent residence" means the status of having been lawfully accorded the privilege of residing permanently in the United States as an immigrant in accordance with the immigration laws, such status not having changed.

(21) The term "national" means a person owing permanent allegiance to a state.

(22) The term "national of the United States" means (A) a citizen of the United States, or (B) a person who, though not a citizen of the United States, owes permanent allegiance to the United States.

(23) The term "naturalization" means the conferring of nationality of a state upon a person after birth, by any means whatsoever.

(24) [Repealed].[15]

(25) The term "noncombatant service" shall not include service in which the individual is not subject to military discipline, court martial, or does not wear the uniform of any branch of the armed forces.

(26) The term "nonimmigrant visa" means a visa properly issued to an alien as an eligible nonimmigrant by a competent officer as provided in this Act.

(27) The term "special immigrant" means—[16]

(A) an immigrant, lawfully admitted for permanent residence, who is returning from a temporary visit abroad;

(B) an immigrant who was a citizen of the United States and may, under section 324(a) or 327 of title III, apply for reacquisition of citizenship;

(C) an immigrant, and the immigrant's spouse and children if accompanying or following to join the immigrant, who—

(i) for at least 2 years immediately preceding the time of application for admission, has been a member of a religious denomination having a bona fide nonprofit, religious organization in the United States;

(ii) seeks to enter the United States—

(I) solely for the purpose of carrying on the vocation of a minister of that religious denomination,

(II) before September 30, 2012, in order to work for the organization at the request of the organization in a professional capacity in a religious vocation or occupation, or

(III) before September 30, 2012, in order to work for the organization (or for a bona fide organization which is affiliated with the religious denomination and is exempt from taxation as an organization described in section 501(c)(3) of the Internal Revenue Code of 1986) at the request of the organization in a religious vocation or occupation; and

(iii) has been carrying on such vocation, professional work, or other work continuously for at least the 2-year period described in clause (i);

(D) an immigrant who is an employee, or an honorably retired former employee, of the United States Government abroad, or of the American Institute in Taiwan, and who has performed faithful service for a total of fifteen years, or more, and his accompanying spouse and children: *Provided,* That the principal officer of a Foreign Service establishment (or, in the case of the American Institute in Taiwan, the Director thereof), in his discretion, shall have recommended the granting of special immigrant status to such alien

---

[15] Repealed by P.L. 102-232 (12/12/91), title III, §305(m)(1).

[16] *See* §421 of the USA PATRIOT Act, P.L. 107-56 (*reprinted in* Appendix J, *infra*), for provisions relating to immigration benefits for the victims of terrorism. See Omnibus Appropriations Act, 2009, P.L. 111-8 (123 STAT. 524) for Special Immigrant Status for certain Afghanis.

in exceptional circumstances and the Secretary of State approves such recommendation and finds that it is in the national interest to grant such status;

(E) an immigrant, and his accompanying spouse and children, who is or has been an employee of the Panama Canal Company or Canal Zone Government before the date on which the Panama Canal Treaty of 1977 (as described in section 3(a)(1) of the Panama Canal Act of 1979) enters into force, who was resident in the Canal Zone on the effective date of the exchange of instruments of ratification of such Treaty, and who has performed faithful service as such an employee for one year or more;

(F) an immigrant, and his accompanying spouse and children, who is a Panamanian national and

(i) who, before the date on which such Panama Canal Treaty of 1977 enters into force, has been honorably retired from United States Government employment in the Canal Zone with a total of 15 years or more of faithful service, or

(ii) who, on the date on which such Treaty enters into force, has been employed by the United States Government in the Canal Zone with a total of 15 years or more of faithful service and who subsequently is honorably retired from such employment or continues to be employed by the United States Government in an area of the former Canal Zone;

(G) an immigrant, and his accompanying spouse and children, who was an employee of the Panama Canal Company or Canal Zone Government on the effective date of the exchange of instruments of ratification of such Panama Canal Treaty of 1977, who has performed faithful service for five years or more as such an employee, and whose personal safety, or the personal safety of whose spouse or children, as a direct result of such Treaty, is reasonably placed in danger because of the special nature of any of that employment;

(H) an immigrant, and his accompanying spouse and children, who—

(i) has graduated from a medical school or has qualified to practice medicine in a foreign state,

(ii) was fully and permanently licensed to practice medicine in a State on January 9, 1978, and was practicing medicine in a State on that date,

(iii) entered the United States as a nonimmigrant under subsection (a)(15)(H) or (a)(15)(J) before January 10, 1978, and

(iv) has been continuously present in the United States in the practice or study of medicine since the date of such entry;

(I) (i) an immigrant who is the unmarried son or daughter of an officer or employee, or of a former officer or employee, of an international organization described in paragraph (15)(G)(i), and who (I) while maintaining the status of a nonimmigrant under paragraph (15)(G)(iv) or paragraph (15)(N), has resided and been physically present in the United States for periods totaling at least one-half of the seven years before the date of application for a visa or for adjustment of status to a status under this subparagraph and for a period or periods aggregating at least seven years between the ages of five and 21 years, and (II) applies for a visa or adjustment of status under this subparagraph no later than his twenty-fifth birthday or six months after the date of the enactment of the Immigration Technical Corrections Act of 1988, whichever is later;

(ii) an immigrant who is the surviving spouse of a deceased officer or employee of such an international organization, and who (I) while maintaining the status of a nonimmigrant under paragraph (15)(G)(iv) or paragraph (15)(N), has resided and been physically present in the United States for periods totaling at least one-half of the seven years before the date of application for a visa or for adjustment of status to a status under this subparagraph and for a period or periods aggregating at least 15 years before the date of the death of such officer or employee, and (II) files a petition for status under this subparagraph no later than six months after the date of such death or six months after the date of such death or six months after the date of the enactment of the Immigration Technical Corrections Act of 1988, whichever is later;

(iii) an immigrant who is a retired officer or employee of such an international organization, and who (I) while maintaining the status of a nonimmigrant under paragraph (15)(G)(iv), has resided and been physically present in the United States for periods totaling at least one-half of the seven years before the date of application for a visa or for adjustment of status to a status under this subparagraph and for a period or periods aggregating at least 15 years before the date of the officer or employee's retirement from any such international organization, and (II) files a petition for status under this subparagraph no later than six months after the date of such retirement or six months after the date of enactment of the Immigration and Nationality Technical Corrections Act of 1994, whichever is later; or

(iv) an immigrant who is the spouse of a retired officer or employee accorded the status of special immigrant under clause (iii), accompanying or following to join such retired officer or employee as a member of his immediate family;

(J) an immigrant who is present in the United States—

(i) who has been declared dependent on a juvenile court located in the United State, or an individual or entity appointed by a State or juvenile court located in the United States, and whose reunification with 1 or both of the immigrant's parents is not viable due to abuse, neglect, abandonment, or a similar basis found under State law;

(ii) for whom it has been determined in administrative or judicial proceedings that it would not be in the alien's best interest to be returned to the alien's or parent's previous country of nationality or country of last habitual residence; and

(iii) in whose case the Secretary of Homeland Security consents to the grant of special immigrant juvenile status, except that—

(I) no juvenile court has jurisdiction to determine the custody status or placement of an alien in the custody of the Secretary of Health and Human Services unless the Secretary of Health and Human Services specifically consents to such jurisdiction; and

(II) no natural parent or prior adoptive parent of any alien provided special immigrant status under this subparagraph shall thereafter, by virtue of such parentage, be accorded any right, privilege, or status under this Act; or

(K) an immigrant who has served honorably on active duty in the Armed Forces of the United States after October 15, 1978, and after original lawful enlistment outside the United States (under a treaty or agreement in effect on the date of the enactment of this subparagraph) for a period or periods aggregating—

(i) 12 years and who, if separated from such service, was never separated except under honorable conditions, or

(ii) 6 years, in the case of an immigrant who is on active duty at the time of seeking special immigrant status under this subparagraph and who has reenlisted to incur a total active duty service obligation of at least 12 years, and the spouse or child of any such immigrant if accompanying or following to join the immigrant, but only if the executive department under which the immigrant serves or served recommends the granting of special immigrant status to the immigrant;

(L) an immigrant who would be described in clause (i), (ii), (iii), or (iv) of subparagraph (I) if any reference in such a clause—

(i) to an international organization described in paragraph (15)(G)(i) were treated as a reference to the North Atlantic Treaty Organization (NATO);

(ii) to a nonimmigrant under paragraph (15)(G)(iv) were treated as a reference to a nonimmigrant classifiable under NATO-6 (as a member of a civilian component accompanying a force entering in accordance with the provisions of the NATO Status-of-Forces Agreement, a member of a civilian component attached to or employed by an Allied Headquarters under the 'Protocol on the Status of International Military Headquarters' set up pursuant to the North Atlantic Treaty, or as a dependent); and

(iii) to the Immigration Technical Corrections Act of 1988 or to the Immigration and Nationality Technical Corrections Act of 1994 were a reference to the American Competitiveness and Workforce Improvement Act of 1998[; or][17]

(M) subject to the numerical limitations of section 203(b)(4), an immigrant who seeks to enter the United States to work as a broadcaster in the United States for the International Broadcasting Bureau of the Broadcasting Board of Governors, or for a grantee of the Broadcasting Board of Governors, and the immigrant's accompanying spouse and children.

(28) The term "organization" means, but is not limited to, an organization, corporation, company, partnership, association, trust, foundation or fund; and includes a group of persons, whether or not incorporated, permanently or temporarily associated together with joint action on any subject or subjects.

(29) The term "outlying possessions of the United States" means American Samoa and Swains Island.

(30) The term "passport" means any travel document issued by competent authority showing the bearer's origin, identity, and nationality if any, which is valid for the admission of the bearer into a foreign country.

(31) The term "permanent" means a relationship of continuing or lasting nature, as distinguished from temporary, but a relationship may be permanent even though it is one that may be dissolved eventually at the instance either of the United States or of the individual, in accordance with law.

(32) The term "profession" shall include but not be limited to architects, engineers, lawyers, physicians, surgeons, and teachers in elementary or secondary schools, colleges, academies, or seminaries.

---

[17] Semicolon and "or" omitted in original.

(33) The term "residence" means the place of general abode; the place of general abode of a person means his principal, actual dwelling place in fact, without regard to intent.

(34) The term "Service" means the Immigration and Naturalization Service of the Department of Justice.

(35) The term "spouse", "wife", or "husband" does not include a spouse, wife, or husband by reason of any marriage ceremony where the contracting parties thereto are not physically present in the presence of each other, unless the marriage shall have been consummated.

(36) The term "State" includes the District of Columbia, Puerto Rico, Guam, the Virgin Islands of the United States, and the Commonwealth of the Northern Mariana Islands

(37) The term "totalitarian party" means an organization which advocates the establishment in the United States of a totalitarian dictatorship or totalitarianism. The terms "totalitarian dictatorship" and "totalitarianism" mean and refer to systems of government not representative in fact, characterized by

(A) the existence of a single political party, organized on a dictatorial basis, with so close an identity between such party and its policies and the governmental policies of the country in which it exists, that the party and the government constitute an indistinguishable unit, and

(B) the forcible suppression of opposition to such party.

(38) The term "United States", except as otherwise specifically herein provided, when used in a geographical sense, means the continental United States, Alaska, Hawaii, Puerto Rico, Guam, the Virgin Islands of the United States, and the Commonwealth of the Northern Mariana Islands.

(39) The term "unmarried", when used in reference to any individual as of any time, means an individual who at such time is not married, whether or not previously married.

(40) The term "world communism" means a revolutionary movement, the purpose of which is to establish eventually a Communist totalitarian dictatorship in any or all the countries of the world through the medium of an internationally coordinated Communist political movement.

(41) The term "graduates of a medical school" means aliens who have graduated from a medical school or who have qualified to practice medicine in a foreign state, other than such aliens who are of national or international renown in the field of medicine.

(42) The term "refugee" means

(A) any person who is outside any country of such person's nationality or, in the case of a person having no nationality, is outside any country in which such person last habitually resided, and who is unable or unwilling to return to, and is unable or unwilling to avail himself or herself of the protection of, that country because of persecution or a well-founded fear of persecution on account of race, religion, nationality, membership in a particular social group, or political opinion, or

(B) in such special circumstances as the President after appropriate consultation (as defined in section 207(e) of this Act) may specify, any person who is within the country of such person's nationality or, in the case of a person having no nationality, within the country in which such person is habitually residing, and who is persecuted or who has a well-founded fear of persecution on account of race, religion, nationality, membership in a particular social group, or political opinion.

The term "refugee" does not include any person who ordered, incited, assisted, or otherwise participated in the persecution of any person on account of race, religion, nationality, membership in a particular social group, or political opinion. For purposes of determinations under this Act, a person who has been forced to abort a pregnancy or to undergo involuntary sterilization, or who has been persecuted for failure or refusal to undergo such a procedure or for other resistance to a coercive population control program, shall be deemed to have been persecuted on account of political opinion, and a person who has a well founded fear that he or she will be forced to undergo such a procedure or subject to persecution for such failure, refusal, or resistance shall be deemed to have a well founded fear of persecution on account of political opinion.

(43)[18] The term "aggravated felony" means—

(A) murder, rape, or sexual abuse of a minor;

(B) illicit trafficking in a controlled substance (as defined in section 102 of the Controlled Substances Act), including a drug trafficking crime (as defined in section 924(c) of title 18, United States Code);

(C) illicit trafficking in firearms or destructive devices (as defined in section 921 of title 18, United States Code) or in explosive materials (as defined in section 841(c) of that title);

(D) an offense described in section 1956 of title 18, United States Code (relating to laundering of monetary instruments) or section 1957 of that title (relating to engaging in monetary transactions in property derived from specific unlawful activity) if the amount of the funds exceeded $10,000;

(E) an offense described in—

(i) section 842(h) or (i) of title 18, United States Code, or section 844(d), (e), (f), (g), (h), or (i) of that title (relating to explosive materials offenses);

(ii) section 922(g)(1), (2), (3), (4), or (5), (j), (n), (o), (p), or (r) or 924(b) or (h) of title 18, United States Code (relating to firearms offenses); or

(iii) section 5861 of the Internal Revenue Code of 1986 (relating to firearms offenses);

(F) a crime of violence (as defined in section 16 of title 18, United States Code, but not including a purely political offense) for which the term of imprisonment at least[19] 1 year;

(G) a theft offense (including receipt of stolen property) or burglary offense for which the term of imprisonment at least[20] 1 year;

(H) an offense described in section 875, 876, 877, or 1202 of title 18, United States Code (relating to the demand for or receipt of ransom);

(I) an offense described in section 2251, 2251A, or 2252 of title 18, United States Code (relating to child pornography);

---

[18] The amendments made by IIRAIRA §321(a) to this subsection "shall apply to actions taken on or after the date of the enactment of this Act, regardless of when the conviction occurred, and shall apply under [INA §276(b)] only to violations of §276(a) of such Act occurring on or after such date."

[19] *Sic*. Probably should be "… is at least…"

[20] *Sic*. Probably should be "… is at least…"

(J) an offense described in section 1962 of title 18, United States Code (relating to racketeer influenced corrupt organizations), or an offense described in section 1084 (if it is a second or subsequent offense) or 1955 of that title (relating to gambling offenses), for which a sentence of 1 year imprisonment or more may be imposed;

(K) an offense that—

(i) relates to the owning, controlling, managing, or supervising of a prostitution business;

(ii) is described in section 2421, 2422, 2423, of Title 18, United States Code (relating to transportation for the purpose of prostitution) if committed for commercial advantage; or

(iii) is described in any of sections 1581–1585 or 1588–1591 of title 18, United States Code (relating to peonage, slavery, involuntary servitude, and trafficking in persons);

(L) an offense described in—

(i) section 793 (relating to gathering or transmitting national defense information), 798 (relating to disclosure of classified information), 2153 (relating to sabotage) or 2381 or 2382 (relating to treason) of title 18, United States Code;

(ii) section 601 of the National Security Act of 1947 (50 U.S.C. 421) (relating to protecting the identity of undercover intelligence agents); or

(iii) section 601 of the National Security Act of 1947 (relating to protecting the identity of undercover agents);

(M) an offense that—

(i) involves fraud or deceit in which the loss to the victim or victims exceeds $10,000; or

(ii) is described in section 7201 of the Internal Revenue Code of 1986 (relating to tax evasion) in which the revenue loss to the Government exceeds $10,000;

(N) an offense described in paragraph (1)(A) or (2) of section 274(a) (relating to alien smuggling), except in the case of a first offense for which the alien has affirmatively shown that the alien committed the offense for the purpose of assisting, abetting, or aiding only the alien's spouse, child, or parent (and no other individual) to violate a provision of this Act;

(O) an offense described in section 275(a) or 276 committed by an alien who was previously deported on the basis of a conviction for an offense described in another subparagraph of this paragraph[;][21]

(P) an offense (i) which either is falsely making, forging, counterfeiting, mutilating, or altering a passport or instrument in violation of section 1543 of title 18, United States Code, or is described in section 1546(a) of such title (relating to document fraud) and (ii) for which the term of imprisonment is at least 12 months, except in the case of a first offense for which the alien has affirmatively shown that the alien committed the offense for

---

[21] Semicolon omitted in original.

the purpose of assisting, abetting, or aiding only the alien's spouse, child, or parent (and no other individual) to violate a provision of this Act;

(Q) an offense relating to a failure to appear by a defendant for service of sentence if the underlying offense is punishable by imprisonment for a term of 5 years or more;

(R) an offense relating to commercial bribery, counterfeiting, forgery, or trafficking in vehicles the identification numbers of which have been altered for which the term of imprisonment is at least one year;

(S) an offense relating to obstruction of justice, perjury or subornation of perjury, or bribery of a witness, for which the term of imprisonment is at least one year;

(T) an offense relating to a failure to appear before a court pursuant to a court order to answer to or dispose of a charge of a felony for which a sentence of 2 years' imprisonment or more may be imposed; and

(U) an attempt or conspiracy to commit an offense described in this paragraph.

The term applies to an offense described in this paragraph whether in violation of Federal or State law and applies to such an offense in violation of the law of a foreign country for which the term of imprisonment was completed within the previous 15 years. Notwithstanding any other provision of law (including any effective date), the term applies regardless of whether the conviction was entered before, on, or after the date of enactment of this paragraph.

(44)(A) The term "managerial capacity" means an assignment within an organization in which the employee primarily—

(i) manages the organization, or a department, subdivision, function, or component of the organization;

(ii) supervises and controls the work of other supervisory, professional, or managerial employees, or manages an essential function within the organization, or a department or subdivision of the organization;

(iii) if another employee or other employees are directly supervised, has the authority to hire and fire or recommend those as well as other personnel actions (such as promotion and leave authorization) or, if no other employee is directly supervised, functions at a senior level within the organizational hierarchy or with respect to the function managed; and

(iv) exercises discretion over the day-to-day operations of the activity or function for which the employee has authority.

A first-line supervisor is not considered to be acting in a managerial capacity merely by virtue of the supervisor's supervisory duties unless the employees supervised are professional.

(B) The term "executive capacity" means an assignment within an organization in which the employee primarily—

(i) directs the management of the organization or a major component or function of the organization;

(ii) establishes the goals and policies of the organization, component, or function;

(iii) exercises wide latitude in discretionary decision-making; and

(iv) receives only general supervision or direction from higher level executives, the board of directors, or stockholders of the organization.

(C) If staffing levels are used as a factor in determining whether an individual is acting in a managerial or executive capacity, the Attorney General shall take into account the reasonable needs of the organization, component, or function in light of the overall purpose and stage of development of the organization, component, or function. An individual shall not be considered to be acting in a managerial or executive capacity (as previously defined) merely on the basis of the number of employees that the individual supervises or has supervised or directs or has directed.

(45) The term "substantial" means, for purposes of paragraph (15)(E) with reference to trade or capital, such an amount of trade or capital as is established by the Secretary of State, after consultation with appropriate agencies of Government.

(46) The term "extraordinary ability" means, for purposes of section 101(a)(15)(O)(i), in the case of the arts, distinction.

(47)(A) The term "order of deportation" means the order of the special inquiry officer, or other such administrative officer to whom the Attorney General has delegated the responsibility for determining whether an alien is deportable, concluding that the alien is deportable or ordering deportation.

(B) The order described under subparagraph (A) shall become final upon the earlier of—

(i) a determination by the Board of Immigration Appeals affirming such order; or

(ii) the expiration of the period in which the alien is permitted to seek review of such order by the Board of Immigration Appeals.

(48)(A) The term "conviction" means, with respect to an alien, a formal judgment of guilt of the alien entered by a court or, if adjudication of guilt has been withheld, where—

(i) a judge or jury has found the alien guilty or the alien has entered a plea of guilty or nolo contendere or has admitted sufficient facts to warrant a finding of guilt, and

(ii) the judge has ordered some form of punishment, penalty, or restraint on the alien's liberty to be imposed.

(B) Any reference to a term of imprisonment or a sentence with respect to an offense is deemed to include the period of incarceration or confinement ordered by a court of law regardless of any suspension of the imposition or execution of that imprisonment or sentence in whole or in part.

(49) The term "stowaway" means any alien who obtains transportation without the consent of the owner, charterer, master or person in command of any vessel or aircraft through concealment aboard such vessel or aircraft. A passenger who boards with a valid ticket is not to be considered a stowaway.

(50) The term "intended spouse" means any alien who meets the criteria set forth in section 204(a)(1)(A)(iii)(II)(aa)(BB), 204(a)(1)(B)(ii)(II)(aa)(BB), or 240A(b)(2)(A)(i)(III).

(51) The term "VAWA self-petitioner" means an alien, or a child of the alien, who qualifies for relief under—

(A) clause (iii), (iv), or (vii) of section 204(a)(1)(A);

(B) clause (ii) or (iii) of section 204(a)(1)(B);

(C) section 216(c)(4)(C);

(D) the first section of Public Law 89-732 (8 U.S.C. 1255 note) (commonly known as the Cuban Adjustment Act) as a child or spouse who has been battered or subjected to extreme cruelty;

(E) section 902(d)(1)(B) of the Haitian Refugee Immigration Fairness Act of 1998 (8 U.S.C. 1255 note);

(F) section 202(d)(1) of the Nicaraguan Adjustment and Central American Relief Act; or

(G) section 309 of the Illegal Immigration Reform and Immigrant Responsibility Act of 1996 (division C of Public Law 104-208).

**(b)** As used in titles I and II—

(1) The term "child" means an unmarried person under twenty-one years of age who is—

(A) a child born in wedlock;

(B) a stepchild, whether or not born out of wedlock, provided the child had not reached the age of eighteen years at the time the marriage creating the status of stepchild occurred;

(C) a child legitimated under the law of the child's residence or domicile, or under the law of the father's residence or domicile, whether in or outside the United States, if such legitimation takes place before the child reaches the age of eighteen years and the child is in the legal custody of the legitimating parent or parents at the time of such legitimation;

(D) a child born out of wedlock, by, through whom, or on whose behalf a status, privilege, or benefit is sought by virtue of the relationship of the child to its natural mother or to its natural father if the father has or had a bona fide parent-child relationship with the person;

(E) (i) a child adopted while under the age of sixteen years if the child has been in the legal custody of, and has resided with, the adopting parent or parents for at least two years or if the child has been battered or subject to extreme cruelty by the adopting parent or by a family member of the adopting parent residing in the same household: *Provided,* That no natural parent of any such adopted child shall thereafter, by virtue of such parentage, be accorded any right, privilege, or status under this Act; or

(ii) subject to the same proviso as in clause (i), a child who: (I) is a natural sibling of a child described in clause (i) or subparagraph (F)(i); (II) was adopted by the adoptive parent or parents of the sibling described in such clause or subparagraph; and (III) is otherwise described in clause (i), except that the child was adopted while under the age of 18 years;

(F) (i) a child, under the age of sixteen at the time a petition is filed in his behalf to accord a classification as an immediate relative under section 201(b), who is an orphan because of the death or disappearance of, abandonment or desertion by, or separation or loss from, both parents, or for whom the sole or surviving parent is incapable of providing the proper care and has in writing irrevocably released the child for emigration and adoption; who has been adopted abroad by a United States citizen and spouse jointly, or by an unmarried United States citizen at least twenty-five years of age, who personally saw and observed the child prior to or during the adoption proceedings; or who is coming to the United States for adoption by a United States citizen and spouse jointly, or by an unmarried United States citizen at least twenty-five years of age, who have or has complied with the preadoption requirements, if any, of the child's proposed residence: *Provided,* That the Attorney General is satisfied that proper care will be furnished the child if admitted to the United States: *Provided further*, That no natural parent or prior adoptive parent of any such child shall thereafter, by virtue of such parentage, be accorded any right, privilege, or status under this Act; or

(ii) subject to the same provisos as in clause (i), a child who:

(I) is a natural sibling of a child described in clause (i) or subparagraph (E)(i);

(II) has been adopted abroad, or is coming to the United States for adoption, by the adoptive parent (or prospective adoptive parent) or parents of the sibling described in such clause or subparagraph; and

(III) is otherwise described in clause (i), except that the child is under the age of 18 at the time a petition is filed in his or her behalf to accord a classification as an immediate relative under section 201(b); or

(G)[22] a child, under the age of sixteen at the time a petition is filed on the child's behalf to accord a classification as an immediate relative under section 201(b), who has been adopted in a foreign state that is a party to the Convention on Protection of Children and Co-operation in Respect of Intercountry Adoption done at The Hague on May 29, 1993, or who is emigrating from such a foreign state to be adopted in the United States, by a United States citizen and spouse jointly, or by an unmarried United States citizen at least 25 years of age—

(i) if—

(I) the Attorney General is satisfied that proper care will be furnished the child if admitted to the United States;

(II) the child's natural parents (or parent, in the case of a child who has one sole or surviving parent because of the death or disappearance of, abandonment or desertion by, the other parent), or other persons or institutions that retain legal custody of the child, have freely given their written irrevocable consent to the termination of their legal relationship with the child, and to the child's emigration and adoption;

(III) in the case of a child having two living natural parents, the natural parents are incapable of providing proper care for the child;

(IV) the Attorney General is satisfied that the purpose of the adoption is to form a bona fide parent-child relationship, and the parent-child relationship of the child and the natural parents has been terminated (and in carrying out both obligations under this subclause the Attorney General may consider whether there is a petition pending to confer immigrant status on one or both of such natural parents); and

(V) in the case of a child who has not been adopted—

---

[22] ***Delayed effective date.*** Subparagraph (G), which was added by §302(a) of the Intercountry Adoption Act of 2000 (IAA), P.L. 106-279 (10/6/00), takes effect (along with references thereto) upon "the entry into force of the [Hague Convention on Protection of Children and Cooperation in Respect of Intercountry Adoption] for the United States pursuant to Article 46(2)(a) of the Convention." (*See* IAA §505.) This occurs when DHS and DOS publish implementing regulations in the *Federal Register* and the United States deposits the instruments of ratification with the Permanent Bureau of the Hague Conference. The final rule on the Accreditation and Approval of Agencies and Persons (22 CFR Part 96) to implement the Convention and the IAA has been implemented. 71 FR 8063 & 71 FR 8161 (2/15/06, *effective* 3/17/06). For IAA transition rules, see IAA §505(b).

(aa) the competent authority of the foreign state has approved the child's emigration to the United States for the purpose of adoption by the prospective adoptive parent or parents; and

(bb) the prospective adoptive parent or parents has or have complied with any pre-adoption requirements of the child's proposed residence; and

(ii) except that no natural parent or prior adoptive parent of any such child shall thereafter, by virtue of such parentage, be accorded any right, privilege, or status under this Act.

(2) The terms "parent", "father", or "mother" mean a parent, father, or mother only where the relationship exists by reason of any of the circumstances set forth in (1) above, except that, for purposes of paragraph (1)(F) (other than the second proviso therein) and paragraph (1)(G)(i) in the case of a child born out of wedlock described in paragraph (1)(D) (and not described in paragraph (1)(C)), the term "parent" does not include the natural father of the child if the father has disappeared or abandoned or deserted the child or if the father has in writing irrevocably released the child for emigration and adoption.

(3) The term "person" means an individual or an organization.

(4) The term "immigration judge" means an attorney whom the Attorney General appoints as an administrative judge within the Executive Office of Immigration Review, qualified to conduct specified classes of proceedings, including a hearing under section 240. An immigration judge shall be subject to such supervision and shall perform such duties as the Attorney General shall prescribe, but shall not be employed by the Immigration and Naturalization Service.

(5) The term "adjacent islands" includes Saint Pierre, Miquelon, Cuba, the Dominican Republic, Haiti, Bermuda, the Bahamas, Barbados, Jamaica, the Windward and Leeward Islands, Trinidad, Martinique, and other British, French, and Netherlands territory or possessions in or bordering on the Caribbean Sea.

**(c)** As used in title III—

(1) The term "child" means an unmarried person under twenty-one years of age and includes a child legitimated under the law of the child's residence or domicile, or under the law of the father's residence or domicile, whether in the United States or elsewhere, and, except as otherwise provided in sections 320 and 321[23] of title III, a child adopted in the United States, if such legitimation or adoption takes place before the child reaches the age of 16 years (except to the extent that the child is described in subparagraph (E)(ii) or (F)(ii) of subsection (b)(1)), and the child is in the legal custody of the legitimating or adopting parent or parents at the time of such legitimation or adoption.

(2) The terms "parent", "father", and "mother" include in the case of a posthumous child a deceased parent, father, and mother.

**(d)** [Repealed].[24]

**(e)** For the purpose of this Act—

---

[23] Sec. 321 (8 USC §1432) was repealed by P.L. 106-395 (10/30/00), title I, §103(a).

[24] Repealed by P.L. 100-525 (10/24/88), §9(a)(3).

(1) The giving, loaning, or promising of support or of money or any other thing of value to be used for advocating any doctrine shall constitute the advocating of such doctrine; but nothing in this paragraph shall be construed as an exclusive definition of advocating.

(2) The giving, loaning, or promising of support or of money or any other thing of value for any purpose to any organization shall be presumed to constitute affiliation therewith; but nothing in this paragraph shall be construed as an exclusive definition of affiliation.

(3) Advocating the economic, international, and governmental doctrines of world communism means advocating the establishment of a totalitarian Communist dictatorship in any or all of the countries of the world through the medium of an internationally coordinated Communist movement.

**(f) For the purposes of this Act**— No person shall be regarded as, or found to be, a person of good moral character who, during the period for which good moral character is required to be established, is, or was—

(1) a habitual drunkard;

(2) [Repealed].[25]

(3) a member of one or more of the classes of persons, whether inadmissible or not, described in paragraphs (2)(D), (6)(E), and (10)(A)[26] of section 212(a) of this Act; or subparagraphs (A) and (B) of section 212(a)(2) and subparagraph (C) thereof of such section[27] (except as such paragraph relates to a single offense of simple possession of 30 grams or less of marihuana); if the offense described therein, for which such person was convicted or of which he admits the commission, was committed during such period;

(4) one whose income is derived principally from illegal gambling activities;

(5) one who has been convicted of two or more gambling offenses committed during such period;

(6) one who has given false testimony for the purpose of obtaining any benefits under this Act;

(7) one who during such period has been confined, as a result of conviction, to a penal institution for an aggregate period of one hundred and eighty days or more, regardless of whether the offense, or offenses, for which he has been confined were committed within or without such period;

(8) one who at any time has been convicted of an aggravated felony (as defined in subsection (a)(43)); or

(9) one who at any time has engaged in conduct described in section 212(a)(3)(E) (relating to assistance in Nazi persecution, participation in genocide, or commission of acts of torture or extrajudicial killings) or 212(a)(2)(G) (relating to severe violations of religious freedom).

The fact that any person is not within any of the foregoing classes shall not preclude a finding that for other reasons such person is or was not of good moral character. In the case of an alien who makes a false statement or claim of citizenship, or who registers to vote or votes in a Federal, State, or local election (including an initiative, recall, or referendum) in violation of a lawful restriction of

---

[25] Repealed by P.L. 97-116 (12/29/81), §2(c)(1).

[26] The amendment to INA §101(f)(3) made by §822(c)(1) of P.L. 109-162 (VAWA 2005) (1/5/06) [changing "(9)(A)" to "(10)(A)"] is be effective, pursuant to §822(c)(2), "as if included in §603(a)(1) of [IMMACT90, P.L. 101-649]."

[27] *Sic.* The phrase "of such section" probably should not appear.

such registration or voting to citizens, if each natural parent of the alien (or, in the case of an adopted alien, each adoptive parent of the alien) is or was a citizen (whether by birth or naturalization), the alien permanently resided in the United States prior to attaining the age of 16, and the alien reasonably believed at the time of such statement, claim, or violation that he or she was a citizen, no finding that the alien is, or was, not of good moral character may be made based on it.

**(g)** For the purposes of this Act any alien ordered deported or removed (whether before or after the enactment of this Act) who has left the United States, shall be considered to have been deported or removed in pursuance of law, irrespective of the source from which the expenses of his transportation were defrayed or of the place to which he departed.

**(h)** For purposes of section 212(a)(2)(E), the term "serious criminal offense" means—

(1) any felony;

(2) any crime of violence, as defined in section 16 of title 18 of the United States Code; or

(3) any crime of reckless driving or of driving while intoxicated or under the influence of alcohol or of prohibited substances if such crime involves personal injury to another.

**(i)** With respect to each nonimmigrant alien described in subsection (a)(15)(T)(i)—

(1) the Secretary of Homeland Security, the Attorney General, and other Government officials, where appropriate, shall provide the alien with a referral to a nongovernmental organization that would advise the alien regarding the alien's options while in the United States and the resources available to the alien; and

(2) the Secretary of Homeland Security shall, during the period the alien is in lawful temporary resident status under that subsection, grant the alien authorization to engage in employment in the United States and provide the alien with an "employment authorized" endorsement or other appropriate work permit.

(June 27, 1952, ch. 477, title I, §101, 66 Stat. 166; as amended by P.L. 85-316 (9/11/57); P.L. 85-508 (7/7/58); P.L. 86-3 (3/18/59); P.L. 87-256 (9/21/61); P.L. 87-301 (9/26/61); P.L. 89-236 (10/3/65); P.L. 89-710 (11/2/66); P.L. 91-225 (4/7/70); P.L. 94-155 (12/16/75); P.L. 94-484 (10/12/76); P.L. 94-571 (10/20/76); P.L. 94-484 (10/12/76), as added by P.L. 95-83 (8/1/77; P.L. 95-105 (8/17/77); P.L. 96-70 (9/27/79); P.L. 96-212 (3/17/80); P.L. 97-116 (12/29/81), §2(c)(1) [striking (f)(2)]; Priv.L. 98-47 (10/30/84); P.L. 99-505 (10/21/86); P.L. 99-514 (10/22/86); P.L. 99-603 (11/6/86); P.L. 99-653 (11/14/86); P.L. 100-459 (10/1/88); P.L. 100-525 (10/24/88), §(a)(3) [striking (d)]; P.L. 100-690 (11/18/88); P.L. 101-162 (11/21/89); P.L. 101-238 (12/18/89); P.L. 101-246 (2/16/90); P.L. 101-649 (11/29/90); P.L. 102-110 (10/1/91); P.L. 102-232 (12/12/91); P.L. 103-236 (4/30/94); P.L. 103-322 (9/13/94); P.L. 103-337 (10/5/94); P.L. 103-416 (10/25/94); P.L. 104-51 (11/15/95); P.L. 104-132 (AEDPA) (4/24/96), §440(b), [adding (a)(47)]; P.L. 104-208 (IIRAIRA) (9/30/96) §104 [revising (a)(6)]. Clause (A) applies to documents issued on or after 18 months after the date of the enactment of IIRAIRA. Clause (B) applies to cards presented on or after 3 years after the date of enactment of IIRAIRA. §301 [revising (a)(13)]; §321(b) [revising (a)(43)]; §322 [adding (a)(48)]. This section also made several conforming amendments to (a)(43) by striking the term "imposed (regardless of any suspension of imprisonment)" in (a)(43)(F), (G), (N), & (P). These amendments (new (a)(48) and the conforming amendments to (a)(43)) all apply "to convictions and sentences entered before, on, or after the date of the enactment of [IIRAIRA]. Subparagraphs (B) & (C) of §240(c)(3) of [this Act], . . .shall apply to proving such convictions." §322(c); §304(a)(3). §361 [adding (a)(49)], effective on the date of enactment of IIRAIRA §371 [revising (b)(4)], effective on the date of enactment of IIRAIRA. §601 [revising (a)(42)]; §625 [revising (a)(15)(F)]; P.L. 105-54 (10/6/97), §1(a) [revising (a)(27)(C)(ii)]; P.L. 105-119 (11/26/97), title I, §113 [revising (a)(27)(J)]; P.L. 105-277 (10/21/98), (ACWIA) div. C, title IV, §421 [revising (a)(15)(N), (a)(27)(J), (a)(27)(K); adding (a)(27)(L)], div. G, title XXII, §2222(e) [revising (a)(9)]; P.L. 105-319 (10/30/98), §2(b)(1) [revising (a)(15)(Q)]; P.L. 106-95 (11/12/99), §2(a) [repealing (a)(15)(H)(i)(a); adding (a)(15)(H)(i)(c)]; P.L. 106-139 (12/7/99), §1(a) [revising (b)(1)(E)–(F), (c)(1)]; P.L. 106-279 (10/6/00), title III, §302(a) [revising (b)(1); adding (b)(1)(G)]; P.L. 106-386 (10/28/00), div. A, §107(e)(1) [revising (a)(15); adding (a)(15)(T)], div. B, title V, §1503(a) [adding (a)(50), (i)], §1513(b) [adding (a)(15)(U)]; P.L. 106-395 (CCA) (10/30/00, *effective* 2/27/01), title II, §201(a)(1) [revising (f)]; P.L. 106-409 (11/1/00), §2(a) [revising (a)(27)]; P.L. 106-536 (11/22/00), §1(a) [adding (a)(27)(M)]; P.L. 106-553 (LIFE Act) (12/21/00), §1(a)(2), title XI, §1102(a) [adding (a)(15)(V)], §1103(a) [revising (a)(15)(K)]; P.L. 107-125 (1/16/02), §2(b) [revising (a)(15)(L)]; P.L. 107-234 (10/4/02) [revising (a)(15)(Q)]; P.L. 107-274 (11/2/02), §2(a) [revising (a)(15)(F)(ii), (a)(15)(M)(ii); adding (a)(15)(F)(iii), (a)(15)(M)(iii)]; P.L. 108-77 (9/3/03, *effective* 1/1/04), title IV, §402(a)(1), [adding (a)(15)(H)(i)(b1)]; P.L. 108-99 (10/15/03), §1 [revising (a)(27)(C)(ii)]; P.L. 108-193 (12/19/03), §4(b)(1) [revising (a)(15)(T)–(V)], §8(a)(1) [revising (a)(43)]; P.L. 108-449 (12/10/04), §1(a)(2)(B) [revising (a)(15)(Q)]; P.L. 108-458 (12/17/04), title V, §5504 [adding (f)(9)]; P.L. 109-13 (REAL ID) (5/11/05), §501 [adding (a)(15)(E)(iii)]; P.L. 109-90 (10/18/05), §536 [revising (a)(15)(H)(ii)(a)]; P.L. 109-162 (1/5/06), title VIII, §801, §805(d), §811, §822(c)(1) [revising (a)(15)(T)(i)–(ii), (a)(15)(U), (b)(1)(E)(i), (f)(3), (i)(1)–(2); adding (a)(15)(T)(iii), (a)(51)]; P.L. 109-

248 (7/27/06), §402 [revising (a)(15)(K)]; P.L. 110-229 (5/8/08) §702(j) [revising (a)(15)(D)(ii), (a)(36) & (a)(38)]; P.L. 110-391 (10/10/08) [revising (a)(27)(C)(ii)]; P.L. 110-457 (12/23/08) [revising (a)(2)(H)(i)]; P.L. 110-457 (12/23/08) [revising (a)(15)(T) & (a)(27)(J)]; P.L. 111-9 (3/20/09) §1 [revising (a)(27)(C)(ii)]; P.L. 111-83 (10/28/09) §568(a) [revising (a)(27)(C)(ii)].)

## Sec. 102 Diplomatic and Semidiplomatic Immunities
[8 U.S.C. 1102]

Except as otherwise provided in this Act, for so long as they continue in the nonimmigrant classes enumerated in this section, the provisions of this Act relating to ineligibility to receive visas and the removal of aliens shall not be construed to apply to nonimmigrants—

(1) within the class described in paragraph (15)(A)(i) of section 101(a), except those provisions relating to reasonable requirements of passports and visas as a means of identification and documentation necessary to establish their qualifications under such paragraph (15)(A)(i), and, under such rules and regulations as the President may deem to be necessary, the provisions of subparagraphs (A) through (C) of section 212(a)(3);

(2) within the class described in paragraph (15)(G)(i) of section 101(a), except those provisions relating to reasonable requirements of passports and visas as a means of identification and documentation necessary to establish their qualifications under such paragraph (15)(G)(i), and the provisions of subparagraphs (A) through (C) of section 212(a)(3); and

(3) within the classes described in paragraphs (15)(A)(ii), (15)(G)(ii), (15)(G)(iii), or (15)(G)(iv) of section 101(a), except those provisions relating to reasonable requirements of passports and visas as a means of identification and documentation necessary to establish their qualifications under such paragraphs, and the provisions of subparagraphs (A) through (C) of section 212(a)(3).

(June 27, 1952, ch. 477, title I, §102, 66 Stat. 173; as amended by P.L. 100-525 (10/24/88); P.L. 101-649 (IMMACT90) (11/29/90); P.L. 102-232 (MTINA) (12/12/91, *effective* 4/1/92), P.L. 104-208 (IIRAIRA) (9/30/96), §308(d)(4)(B).)

## Sec. 103 Powers and Duties of the Secretary, the Under Secretary, and the Attorney General[28]
[8 U.S.C. 1103]

### (a) Secretary of Homeland Security.

(1) The Secretary of Homeland Security shall be charged with the administration and enforcement of this Act and all other laws relating to the immigration and naturalization of aliens, except insofar as this Act or such laws relate to the powers, functions, and duties conferred upon the President, Attorney General, the Secretary of State, the officers of the Department of State, or diplomatic or consular officers: *Provided, however,* That determination and ruling by the Attorney General with respect to all questions of law shall be controlling.

(2) He shall have control, direction, and supervision of all employees and of all the files and records of the Service.

(3) He shall establish such regulations; prescribe such forms of bond, reports, entries, and other papers; issue such instructions; and perform such other acts as he deems necessary for carrying out his authority under the provisions of this Act.

---

[28] Sec. 1103 of the Homeland Security Act of 2002 (HSA), P.L. 107-296 (11/25/02), provides: "Nothing in [HSA], any amendment made by [HSA], or in [INA §103], as amended by [HSA] §1102, shall be construed to limit judicial deference to regulations, adjudications, interpretations, orders, decisions, judgments, or any other actions of the Secretary of Homeland Security or the Attorney General."

(4) He may require or authorize any employee of the Service or the Department of Justice to perform or exercise any of the powers, privileges, or duties conferred or imposed by this Act or regulations issued thereunder upon any other employee of the Service.

(5) He shall have the power and duty to control and guard the boundaries and borders of the United States against the illegal entry of aliens and shall, in his discretion, appoint for that purpose such number of employees of the Service as to him shall appear necessary and proper.

(6) He is authorized to confer or impose upon any employee of the United States, with the consent of the head of the Department or other independent establishment under whose jurisdiction the employee is serving, any of the powers, privileges, or duties conferred or imposed by this Act or regulations issued thereunder upon officers or employees of the Service.

(7) He may, with the concurrence of the Secretary of State, establish offices of the Service in foreign countries; and, after consultation with the Secretary of State, he may, whenever in his judgment such action may be necessary to accomplish the purposes of this Act, detail employees of the Service for duty in foreign countries.

(8) After consultation with the Secretary of State, the Attorney General may authorize officers of a foreign country to be stationed at preclearance facilities in the United States for the purpose of ensuring that persons traveling from or through the United States to that foreign country comply with that country's immigration and related laws.

(9) Those officers may exercise such authority and perform such duties as United States immigration officers are authorized to exercise and perform in that foreign country under reciprocal agreement, and they shall enjoy such reasonable privileges and immunities necessary for the performance of their duties as the government of their country extends to United States immigration officers.

(10) In the event the Attorney General determines that an actual or imminent mass influx of aliens arriving off the coast of the United States, or near a land border, presents urgent circumstances requiring an immediate Federal response, the Attorney General may authorize any State or local law enforcement officer, with the consent of the head of the department, agency, or establishment under whose jurisdiction the individual is serving, to perform or exercise any of the powers, privileges, or duties conferred or imposed by this Act or regulations issued thereunder upon officers or employees of the Service.

(11) The Attorney General, in support of persons in administrative detention in non-Federal institutions, is authorized—

(A) to make payments from funds appropriated for the administration and enforcement of the laws relating to immigration, naturalization, and alien registration for necessary clothing, medical care, necessary guard hire, and the housing, care, and security of persons detained by the Service pursuant to Federal law under an agreement with a State or political subdivision of a State; and

(B) to enter into a cooperative agreement with any State, territory, or political subdivision thereof, for the necessary construction, physical renovation, acquisition of equipment, supplies or materials required to establish acceptable conditions of confinement and detention services in any State or unit of local government which agrees to provide guaranteed bed space for persons detained by the Service.

**(b) Land acquisition authority.**

(1) The Attorney General may contract for or buy any interest in land, including temporary use rights, adjacent to or in the vicinity of an international land border when the Attorney General deems the land essential to control and guard the boundaries and borders of the United States against any violation of this Act.

(2) The Attorney General may contract for or buy any interest in land identified pursuant to paragraph (1) as soon as the lawful owner of that interest fixes a price for it and the Attorney General considers that price to be reasonable.

(3) When the Attorney General and the lawful owner of an interest identified pursuant to paragraph (1) are unable to agree upon a reasonable price, the Attorney General may commence condemnation proceedings pursuant to the Act of August 1, 1888 (Chapter 728; 25 Stat. 357).

(4) The Attorney General may accept for the United States a gift of any interest in land identified pursuant to paragraph (1).

**(c) Commissioner; appointment.**— The Commissioner shall be a citizen of the United States and shall be appointed by the President, by and with the advice and consent of the Senate. He shall be charged with any and all responsibilities and authority in the administration of the Service and of this Act which are conferred upon the Attorney General as may be delegated to him by the Attorney General or which may be prescribed by the Attorney General. The Commissioner may enter into cooperative agreements with State and local enforcement agencies for the purpose of assisting in the enforcement of the immigration laws.

**(d) Statistical information system.**

(1) The Commissioner, in consultation with interested academicians, government agencies, and other parties, shall provide for a system for collection and dissemination, to Congress and the public, of information (not in individually identifiable form) useful in evaluating the social, economic, environmental, and demographic impact of immigration laws.

(2) Such information shall include information on the alien population in the United States, on the rates of naturalization and emigration of resident aliens, on aliens who have been admitted, paroled, or granted asylum, on nonimmigrants in the United States (by occupation, basis for admission, and duration of stay), on aliens who have not been admitted or have been removed from the United States, on the number of applications filed and granted for cancellation of removal, and on the number of aliens estimated to be present unlawfully in the United States in each fiscal year.

(3) Such system shall provide for the collection and dissemination of such information not less often than annually.

**(e) Annual report.**

(1) The Commissioner shall submit to Congress annually a report which contains a summary of the information collected under subsection (d) and an analysis of trends in immigration and naturalization.

(2) Each annual report shall include information on the number, and rate of denial administratively, of applications for naturalization, for each district office of the Service and by national origin group.

**(f) Minimum number of agents in states.**— The Attorney General shall allocate to each State not fewer than 10 full-time active duty agents of the Immigration and Naturalization Service to carry out the functions of the Service, in order to ensure the effective enforcement of this Act.

**(g) Attorney General.—**

(1) *In general.*— The Attorney General shall have such authorities and functions under this Act and all other laws relating to the immigration and naturalization of aliens as were exercised by the Executive Office for Immigration Review, or by the Attorney General with respect to the Executive Office for Immigration Review, on the day before the effective date of the Immigration Reform, Accountability and Security Enhancement Act of 2002.[29]

(2) *Powers.*— The Attorney General shall establish such regulations, prescribe such forms of bond, reports, entries, and other papers, issue such instructions, review such administrative determinations in immigration proceedings, delegate such authority, and perform such other acts as the Attorney General determines to be necessary for carrying out this section.

**(h)** [Repealed].

(June 27, 1952, ch. 477, title I, §103, 66 Stat. 173; as amended by P.L. 100-525 (10/24/88), §9(c); P.L. 101-649 (IMMACT90) (11/29/90), §142; P.L. 104-208 (IIRAIRA) (9/30/96), §102(d), §125, §134(a), §308(d)(4)(C), §372, §373; P.L. 107-296 (11/25/02), §1102 [revising heading, (a), correcting a misnumbering problem in (a)(8)–(10); adding (g)]; P.L. 108-7 (2/20/03) Div. (L) §105 [revising (a) heading & (a)(1)]; P.L. 108-458 (12/17/04) §5505(a) [adding (h)]; P.L. 111-122 (12/22/09) §2 [repealing (h)].)

## Sec. 104 Powers and Duties of the Secretary of State
[8 U.S.C. 1104]

**(a) Powers and duties.**—[30] The Secretary of State shall be charged with the administration and the enforcement of the provisions of this Act and all other immigration and nationality laws relating to—

(1) the powers, duties and functions of diplomatic and consular officers of the United States, except those powers, duties and functions conferred upon the consular officers relating to the granting or refusal of visas;

(2) the powers, duties and functions of the Administrator; and

(3) the determination of nationality of a person not in the United States.

He shall establish such regulations; prescribe such forms of reports, entries and other papers; issue such instructions; and perform such other acts as he deems necessary for carrying out such provisions. He is authorized to confer or impose upon any employee of the United States, with the consent of the head of the department or independent establishment under whose jurisdiction the employee is serving, any of the powers, functions, or duties conferred or imposed by this Act or regulations issued thereunder upon officers or employees of the Department of State or of the American Foreign Service.

**(b) Designation and duties of Administrator.**— The Secretary of State shall designate an Administrator who shall be a citizen of the United States, qualified by experience. The Administrator shall maintain close liaison with the appropriate committees of Congress in order that they may be advised regarding the administration of this Act by consular officers. The Administrator shall be charged with any and all responsibility and authority in the administration of this Act which are conferred on the Secretary of State as may be delegated to the Administrator by the

---

[29] A bill entitled "The Immigration Reform, Accountability and Security Enhancement Act of 2002," which would have abolished the INS and created an Immigration Affairs Agency within DOJ, was introduced in May 2002 (S. 2444; 107th Cong.), but never passed. Later that session, Congress passed and President Bush signed the Homeland Security Act, P.L. 107-296.

[30] *See* §428(b) of the 2002 Homeland Security Act, P.L. 107-296 (11/25/02), for powers of the Secretary of Homeland Security notwithstanding INA §104(a).

Secretary of State or which may be prescribed by the Secretary of State, and shall perform such other duties as the Secretary of State may prescribe.

**(c) Passport Office, Visa Office, and other offices; directors.—** Within the Department of State there shall be a Passport Office, a Visa Office, and such other offices as the Secretary of State may deem to be appropriate, each office to be headed by a director. The Directors of the Passport Office and the Visa Office shall be experienced in the administration of the nationality and immigration laws.

**(d) Transfer of duties.—** The functions heretofore performed by the Passport Division and the Visa Division of the Department of State shall hereafter be performed by the Passport Office and the Visa Office, respectively.

**(e) General Counsel of Visa Office; appointment and duties.—** There shall be a General Counsel of the Visa Office, who shall be appointed by the Secretary of State and who shall serve under the general direction of the Legal Adviser of the Department of State. The General Counsel shall have authority to maintain liaison with the appropriate officers of the Service with a view to securing uniform interpretations of the provisions of this Act.

(June 27, 1952, ch. 477, title I, §104, 66 Stat. 174; as amended by P.L. 87-510 (6/28/62); P.L. 88-426 (8/14/64); P.L. 95-105 (8/17/77); P.L. 100-525 (10/24/88); P.L. 103-236 (4/30/94).)

## Sec. 105 Liaison with Internal Security Officers
[8 U.S.C. 1105]

**(a) In general.—** The Commissioner and the Administrator shall have authority to maintain direct and continuous liaison with the Directors of the Federal Bureau of Investigation and the Central Intelligence Agency and with other internal security officers of the Government for the purpose of obtaining and exchanging information for use in enforcing the provisions of this Act in the interest of the internal and border security of the United States. The Commissioner and the Administrator shall maintain direct and continuous liaison with each other with a view to a coordinated, uniform, and efficient administration of this Act, and all other immigration and nationality laws.

**(b) National crime information center files.—**

(1) The Attorney General and the Director of the Federal Bureau of Investigation shall provide the Department of State and the Service access to the criminal history record information contained in the National Crime Information Center's Interstate Identification Index (NCIC-III), Wanted Persons File, and to any other files maintained by the National Crime Information Center that may be mutually agreed upon by the Attorney General and the agency receiving the access, for the purpose of determining whether or not a visa applicant or applicant for admission has a criminal history record indexed in any such file.

(2) Such access shall be provided by means of extracts of the records for placement in the automated visa lookout or other appropriate database, and shall be provided without any fee or charge.

(3) The Federal Bureau of Investigation shall provide periodic updates of the extracts at intervals mutually agreed upon with the agency receiving the access. Upon receipt of such updated extracts, the receiving agency shall make corresponding updates to its database and destroy previously provided extracts.

(4) Access to an extract does not entitle the Department of State to obtain the full content of the corresponding automated criminal history record. To obtain the full content of a criminal

history record, the Department of State shall submit the applicant's fingerprints and any appropriate fingerprint processing fee authorized by law to the Criminal Justice Information Services Division of the Federal Bureau of Investigation.

**(c) Reconsideration.—** The provision of the extracts described in subsection (b) may be reconsidered by the Attorney General and the receiving agency upon the development and deployment of a more cost-effective and efficient means of sharing the information.

**(d) Regulations.—** For purposes of administering this section, the Department of State shall, prior to receiving access to NCIC data but not later than 4 months after the date of enactment of this subsection, promulgate final regulations—

(1) to implement procedures for the taking of fingerprints; and

(2) to establish the conditions for the use of the information received from the Federal Bureau of Investigation, in order—

(A) to limit the redissemination of such information;

(B) to ensure that such information is used solely to determine whether or not to issue a visa to an alien or to admit an alien to the United States;

(C) to ensure the security, confidentiality, and destruction of such information; and

(D) to protect any privacy rights of individuals who are subjects of such information.

(June 27, 1952, ch. 477, title I, §105, 66 Stat. 175; as amended by P.L. 95-105 (8/17/77); P.L. 103-236 (4/30/94); P.L. 107-56 (PATRIOT Act) (10/26/01), §403(a) [revising (a)–(d)].)

## Sec. 106 Employment Authorization for Battered Spouses of Certain Nonimmigrants [8 U.S.C. 1105a]

**(a) In general.—** In the case of an alien spouse admitted under subparagraph (A), (E)(iii), (G), or (H) of section 101(a)(15) who is accompanying or following to join a principal alien admitted under subparagraph (A), (E)(iii), (G), or (H) of such section, respectively, the Secretary of Homeland Security may authorize the alien spouse to engage in employment in the United States and provide the spouse with an "employment authorized" endorsement or other appropriate work permit if the alien spouse demonstrates that during the marriage the alien spouse or a child of the alien spouse has been battered or has been the subject of extreme cruelty perpetrated by the spouse of the alien spouse. Requests for relief under this section shall be handled under the procedures that apply to aliens seeking relief under section 204(a)(1)(A)(iii).

**(b) Construction.—** The grant of employment authorization pursuant to this section shall not confer upon the alien any other form of relief.

(June 27, 1952, ch. 477, title I, Sec. 106, original was repealed by P.L. 104-208 (IIRAIRA) (9/30/96), div. C, title III, §306, §371 [revising (a)(2) before repealing], §671 [revising (a)]; as added by P.L. 109-162 (1/5/06), §814.)

# Title II — Immigration (§§201–95)
## Chapter 1 — Selection System

### Sec. 201 Worldwide Level of Immigration
[8 U.S.C. 1151]

**(a) In general.**— Exclusive of aliens described in subsection (b), aliens born in a foreign state or dependent area who may be issued immigrant visas or who may otherwise acquire the status of an alien lawfully admitted to the United States for permanent residence are limited to—

(1) family-sponsored immigrants described in section 203(a) (or who are admitted under section 211(a) on the basis of a prior issuance of a visa to their accompanying parent under section 203(a)) in a number not to exceed in any fiscal year the number specified in subsection (c) for that year, and not to exceed in any of the first 3 quarters of any fiscal year 27 percent of the worldwide level under such subsection for all of such fiscal year;

(2) employment-based immigrants described in section 203(b) (or who are admitted under section 211(a) on the basis of a prior issuance of a visa to their accompanying parent under section 203(b)), in a number not to exceed in any fiscal year the number specified in subsection (d) for that year, and not to exceed in any of the first 3 quarters of any fiscal year 27 percent of the worldwide level under such subsection for all of such fiscal year; and

(3) for fiscal years beginning with fiscal year 1995, diversity immigrants described in section 203(c) (or who are admitted under section 211(a) on the basis of a prior issuance of a visa to their accompanying parent under section 203(c)) in a number not to exceed in any fiscal year the number specified in subsection (e) for that year, and not to exceed in any of the first 3 quarters of any fiscal year 27 percent of the worldwide level under such subsection for all of such fiscal year.

**(b) Aliens not subject to direct numerical limitations.**—[31] Aliens described in this subsection, who are not subject to the worldwide levels or numerical limitations of subsection (a), are as follows:

(1) (A) Special immigrants described in subparagraph (A) or (B) of section 101(a)(27).

(B) Aliens who are admitted under section 207 or whose status is adjusted under section 209.

(C) Aliens whose status is adjusted to permanent residence under section 210, or 245A.

(D) Aliens whose removal is canceled under section 240A(a).

(E) Aliens provided permanent resident status under section 249.

(2) (A) (i) Immediate relatives.— For purposes of this subsection, the term "immediate relatives" means the children, spouses, and parents of a citizen of the United States, except that, in the case of parents, such citizens shall be at least 21 years of age. In the case of an alien who was the spouse of a citizen of the United States and was not legally separated from the citizen at the time of the citizen's death, the alien (and each child of the alien) shall be considered, for purposes of this subsection, to remain an immediate relative after the date of the citizen's death but only if the spouse files a petition under section 204(a)(1)(A)(ii) within 2 years after such date and only until the date the spouse remarries. For purposes of this clause, an alien who has filed a

---

[31] *See* §423(a) of the USA PATRIOT Act, P.L. 107-56 (*reprinted in* Appendix J, *infra*), for provisions relating to immigration benefits for the victims of terrorism.

petition under clause (iii) or (iv) of section 204(a)(1)(A) of this Act remains an immediate relative in the event that the United States citizen spouse or parent loses United States citizenship on account of the abuse.[32]

(ii) Aliens admitted under section 211(a) on the basis of a prior issuance of a visa to their accompanying parent who is such an immediate relative.

(B) Aliens born to an alien lawfully admitted for permanent residence during a temporary visit abroad.

**(c) Worldwide level of family-sponsored immigrants.—**

(1) (A) The worldwide level of family-sponsored immigrants under this subsection for a fiscal year is, subject to subparagraph (B), equal to—

(i) 480,000, minus

(ii) the sum of the number computed under paragraph (2) and the number computed under paragraph (4), plus

(iii) the number (if any) computed under paragraph (3).

(B) (i) For each of fiscal years 1992, 1993, and 1994, 465,000 shall be substituted for 480,000 in subparagraph (A)(i).

(ii) In no case shall the number computed under subparagraph (A) be less than 226,000.

(2) The number computed under this paragraph for a fiscal year is the sum of the number of aliens described in subparagraphs (A) and (B) of subsection (b)(2) who were issued immigrant visas or who otherwise acquired the status of aliens lawfully admitted to the United States for permanent residence in the previous fiscal year.

(3) (A) The number computed under this paragraph for fiscal year 1992 is zero.

(B) The number computed under this paragraph for fiscal year 1993 is the difference (if any) between the worldwide level established under paragraph (1) for the previous fiscal year and the number of visas issued under section 203(a) during that fiscal year.

(C) The number computed under this paragraph for a subsequent fiscal year is the difference (if any) between the maximum number of visas which may be issued under section 203(b) (relating to employment-based immigrants) during the previous fiscal year and the number of visas issued under that section during that year.

(4) The number computed under this paragraph for a fiscal year (beginning with fiscal year 1999) is the number of aliens who were paroled into the United States under section 212(d)(5) in the second preceding fiscal year—

(A) who did not depart from the United States (without advance parole) within 365 days; and

(B) who

---

[32] For related provisions regarding posthumous benefits to surviving spouses, children, and parents of citizens who "served honorably in active duty status in the military, air, or naval forces of the United States and died as a result of injury or disease incurred in or aggravated by by combat," see P.L. 108-136, §§1703(a) and (b), retroactively effective 9/11/01. For related provisions regarding posthumous benefits to surviving spouses, children, and parents of lawful permanent residents, see P.L. 108-136, §§1703(c) and (d). Sec. 1703 is *reprinted in* Appendix M, *infra. See* §568(c)(1) of the P.L. 111-83 (123 STAT. 524), §568(c)(2) contains effective-date and transition-rule provisions for the Surviving Spouse relief.

(i) did not acquire the status of aliens lawfully admitted to the United States for permanent residence in the two preceding fiscal years, or

(ii) acquired such status in such years under a provision of law (other than section 201(b)) which exempts such adjustment from the numerical limitation on the worldwide level of immigration under this section.

(5) If any alien described in paragraph (4) (other than an alien described in paragraph (4)(B)(ii)) is subsequently admitted as an alien lawfully admitted for permanent residence, such alien shall not again be considered for purposes of paragraph (1).

**(d) Worldwide level of employment-based immigrants.—**

(1) The worldwide level of employment-based immigrants under this subsection for a fiscal year is equal to—

(A) 140,000, plus

(B) the number computed under paragraph (2).

(2) (A) The number computed under this paragraph for fiscal year 1992 is zero.

(B) The number computed under this paragraph for fiscal year 1993 is the difference (if any) between the worldwide level established under paragraph (1) for the previous fiscal year and the number of visas issued under section 203(b) during that fiscal year.

(C) The number computed under this paragraph for a subsequent fiscal year is the difference (if any) between the maximum number of visas which may be issued under section 203(a) (relating to family-sponsored immigrants) during the previous fiscal year and the number of visas issued under that section during that year.

**(e) Worldwide level of diversity immigrants.—** The worldwide level of diversity immigrants is equal to 55,000 for each fiscal year.

**(f) Rules for determining whether certain aliens are immediate relatives.—**[33]

(1) *Age on petition filing date.—* Except as provided in paragraphs (2) and (3), for purposes of subsection (b)(2)(A)(i), a determination of whether an alien satisfies the age requirement in the matter preceding subparagraph (A) of section 101(b)(1) shall be made using the age of the alien on the date on which the petition is filed with the Attorney General under section 204 to classify the alien as an immediate relative under subsection (b)(2)(A)(i).

(2) *Age on parent's naturalization date.—* In the case of a petition under section 204 initially filed for an alien child's classification as a family-sponsored immigrant under section 203(a)(2)(A), based on the child's parent being lawfully admitted for permanent residence, if the petition is later converted, due to the naturalization of the parent, to a petition to classify the alien as an immediate relative under subsection (b)(2)(A)(i), the determination described in paragraph (1) shall be made using the age of the alien on the date of the parent's naturalization.

(3) *Age on marriage termination date.—* In the case of a petition under section 204 initially filed for an alien's classification as a family-sponsored immigrant under section 203(a)(3),

---

[33] Added by P.L. 107-208 (CSPA) (8/6/02), and, pursuant to CSPA §8, took effect on 8/6/02 and apply to any alien who is a derivative beneficiary or any other beneficiary of "(1) a petition for classification under [INA §204] approved before such date but only if a final determination has not been made on the beneficiary's application for an immigrant visa or adjustment of status to lawful permanent residence pursuant to such approved petition; (2) a petition for classification under [INA §204] pending on or after such date; or (3) an application pending before the Department of Justice or the Department of State on or after such date."

based on the alien's being a married son or daughter of a citizen, if the petition is later converted, due to the legal termination of the alien's marriage, to a petition to classify the alien as an immediate relative under subsection (b)(2)(A)(i) or as an unmarried son or daughter of a citizen under section 203(a)(1), the determination described in paragraph (1) shall be made using the age of the alien on the date of the termination of the marriage.

(4) *Application to self-petitions.*— Paragraphs (1) through (3) shall apply to self-petitioners and derivatives of self-petitioners.

(June 27, 1952, ch. 477, title II, ch. 1, §201, 66 Stat. 175; as amended by P.L. 89-236 (10/3/65); P.L. 94-571 (10/20/76); P.L. 95-412 (10/5/78); P.L. 96-212 (3/17/80); P.L. 97-116 (12/29/81); P.L. 101-649 (IMMACT90) (11/29/90), §101(a); P.L. 102-232 (MTINA) (12/12/91, *effective* 4/1/92), §302(a)(1); P.L. 103-322 (VAWA) (9/13/94); P.L. 103-416 (INTCA) (10/25/94, *effective* 4/1/95); P.L. 104-208 (IIRAIRA) (9/30/96), §308(e)(5), §603, §671(d)(1)(A); P.L. 106-386 (10/28/00), §1507(a)(3) [revising (b)(2)]; P.L. 107-208 (CSPA) (8/6/02), §2 [adding (f)]; P.L. 109-162 (1/5/06), §805(b)(1) [adding (f)(4)]; P.L. 111-83 (10/28/09) §568(c) [revising (b)(2)(A)(i)].)

## Sec. 202 Numerical Limitations on Individual Foreign States
[8 U.S.C. 1152]

### (a) Per country level.—

(1) *Nondiscrimination.*—

(A) Except as specifically provided in paragraph (2) and in sections 101(a)(27), 201(b)(2)(A)(i), and 203, no person shall receive any preference or priority or be discriminated against in the issuance of an immigrant visa because of the person's race, sex, nationality, place of birth, or place of residence.

(B) Nothing in this paragraph shall be construed to limit the authority of the Secretary of State to determine the procedures for the processing of immigrant visa applications or the locations where such applications will be processed.

(2) *Per country levels for family-sponsored and employment-based immigrants.*— Subject to paragraphs (3), (4), and (5) the total number of immigrant visas made available to natives of any single foreign state or dependent area under subsections (a) and (b) of section 203 in any fiscal year may not exceed 7 percent (in the case of a single foreign state) or 2 percent (in the case of a dependent area) of the total number of such visas made available under such subsections in that fiscal year.

(3) *Exception if additional visas available.*— If because of the application of paragraph (2) with respect to one or more foreign states or dependent areas, the total number of visas available under both subsections (a) and (b) of section 203 for a calendar quarter exceeds the number of qualified immigrants who otherwise may be issued such a visa, paragraph (2) shall not apply to visas made available to such states or areas during the remainder of such calendar quarter.

(4) *Special rules for spouses and children of lawful permanent resident aliens.*—

(A) *75 percent of 2nd preference set-aside for spouses and children not subject to per country limitation.*—

(i) In general.— Of the visa numbers made available under section 203(a) to immigrants described in section 203(a)(2)(A) in any fiscal year, 75 percent of the 2-A floor (as defined in clause (ii)) shall be issued without regard to the numerical limitation under paragraph (2).

(ii) 2-A floor defined.— In this paragraph, the term "2-A floor" means, for a fiscal year, 77 percent of the total number of visas made available under section 203(a) to immigrants described in section 203(a)(2) in the fiscal year.

(B) *Treatment of remaining 25 percent for countries subject to subsection (e).*—

(i) In general.— Of the visa numbers made available under section 203(a) to immigrants described in section 203(a)(2)(A) in any fiscal year, the remaining 25 percent of the 2-A floor shall be available in the case of a state or area that is subject to subsection (e) only to the extent that the total number of visas issued in accordance with subparagraph (A) to natives of the foreign state or area is less than the subsection (e) ceiling (as defined in clause (ii)).

(ii) Subsection (e) ceiling defined.— In clause (i), the term "subsection (e) ceiling" means, for a foreign state or dependent area, 77 percent of the maximum number of visas that may be made available under section 203(a) to immigrants who are natives of the state or area under section 203(a)(2) consistent with subsection (e).

(C) *Treatment of unmarried sons and daughters in countries subject to subsection (e).*— In the case of a foreign state or dependent area to which subsection (e) applies, the number of immigrant visas that may be made available to natives of the state or area under section 203(a)(2)(B) may not exceed—

(i) 23 percent of the maximum number of visas that may be made available under section 203(a) to immigrants of the state or area described in section 203(a)(2) consistent with (subsection (e), or

(ii) the number (if any) by which the maximum number of visas that may be made available under section 203(a) to immigrants of the state or area described in section 203(a)(2) consistent with subsection (e) exceeds the number of visas issued under section 203(a)(2)(A),

whichever is greater.

(D) *Limiting pass down for certain countries subject to subsection (e).*— In the case of a foreign state or dependent area to which subsection (e) applies, if the total number of visas issued under section 203(a)(2) exceeds the maximum number of visas that may be made available to immigrants of the state or area under section 203(a)(2) consistent with (subsection (e) (determined without regard to this paragraph), in applying paragraphs (3) and (4) of section 203(a) under subsection (e)(2) all visas shall be deemed to have been required for the classes specified in paragraphs (1) and (2) of such section.

(5) *Rules for employment-based immigrants.*—

(A) *Employment-based immigrants not subject to per country limitation if additional visas available.*— If the total number of visas available under paragraph (1), (2), (3), (4), or (5) of section 203(b) for a calendar quarter exceeds the number of qualified immigrants who may otherwise be issued such visas, the visas made available under that paragraph shall be issued without regard to the numerical limitation under paragraph (2) of this subsection during the remainder of the calendar quarter.

(B) *Limiting fall across for certain countries subject to subsection (e).*— In the case of a foreign state or dependent area to which subsection (e) applies, if the total number of visas issued under section 203(b) exceeds the maximum number of visas that may be made available to immigrants of the state or area under section 203(b) consistent with subsection

(e) (determined without regard to this paragraph), in applying subsection (e) all visas shall be deemed to have been required for the classes of aliens specified in section 203(b).

**(b) Rules for chargeability.**— Each independent country, self-governing dominion, mandated territory, and territory under the international trusteeship system of the United Nations, other than the United States and its outlying possessions, shall be treated as a separate foreign state for the purposes of a numerical level established under subsection (a)(2) when approved by the Secretary of State. All other inhabited lands shall be attributed to a foreign state specified by the Secretary of State. For the purposes of this Act the foreign state to which an immigrant is chargeable shall be determined by birth within such foreign state except that—

(1) an alien child, when accompanied by or following to join his alien parent or parents, may be charged to the foreign state of either parent if such parent has received or would be qualified for an immigrant visa, if necessary to prevent the separation of the child from the parent or parents, and if immigration charged to the foreign state to which such parent has been or would be chargeable has not reached a numerical level established under subsection (a)(2) for that fiscal year;

(2) if an alien is chargeable to a different foreign state from that of his spouse, the foreign state to which such alien is chargeable may, if necessary to prevent the separation of husband and wife, be determined by the foreign state of the spouse he is accompanying or following to join, if such spouse has received or would be qualified for an immigrant visa and if immigration charged to the foreign state to which such spouse has been or would be chargeable has not reached a numerical level established under subsection (a)(2) for that fiscal year;

(3) an alien born in the United States shall be considered as having been born in the country of which he is a citizen or subject, or, if he is not a citizen or subject of any country, in the last foreign country in which he had his residence as determined by the consular officer; and

(4) an alien born within any foreign state in which neither of his parents was born and in which neither of his parents had a residence at the time of such alien's birth may be charged to the foreign state of either parent.

**(c) Chargeability for dependent areas.**— Any immigrant born in a colony or other component or dependent area of a foreign state overseas from the foreign state, other than an alien described in section 201(b), shall be chargeable for the purpose of the limitation set forth in subsection (a), to the foreign state.

**(d) Changes in territory.**— In the case of any change in the territorial limits of foreign states, the Secretary of State shall, upon recognition of such change, issue appropriate instructions to all diplomatic and consular offices.

**(e) Special rules for countries at ceiling.**— If it is determined that the total number of immigrant visas made available under subsections (a) and (b) of section 203 to natives of any single foreign state or dependent area will exceed the numerical limitation specified in subsection (a)(2) in any fiscal year, in determining the allotment of immigrant visa numbers to natives under subsections (a) and (b) of section 203, visa numbers with respect to natives of that state or area shall be allocated (to the extent practicable and otherwise consistent with this section and section 203) in a manner so that—

(1) the ratio of the visa numbers made available under section 203(a) to the visa numbers made available under section 203(b) is equal to the ratio of the worldwide level of immigration under section 201(c) to such level under section 201(d);

(2) except as provided in subsection (a)(4), the proportion of the visa numbers made available under each of paragraphs (1) through (4) of section 203(a) is equal to the ratio of the total number of visas made available under the respective paragraph to the total number of visas made available under section 203(a), and

(3) except as provided in subsection (a)(5), the proportion of the visa numbers made available under each of paragraphs (1) through (5) of section 203(b) is equal to the ratio of the total number of visas made available under the respective paragraph to the total number of visas made available under section 203(b).

Nothing in this subsection shall be construed as limiting the number of visas that may be issued to natives of a foreign state or dependent area under section 203(a) or 203(b) if there is insufficient demand for visas for such natives under section 203(b) or 203(a), respectively, or as limiting the number of visas that may be issued under section 203(a)(2)(A) pursuant to subsection (a)(4)(A).

(June 27, 1952, ch. 477, title II, ch. 1, §202, 66 Stat. 176; as amended by P.L. 87-301 (9/26/61); P.L. 89-236 (10/3/65); P.L. 94-571 (10/20/76); P.L. 95-412 (10/5/78); P.L. 96-212 (3/17/80); P.L. 97-116 (12/29/81); P.L. 99-603 (IRCA) (11/6/86); P.L. 99-653 (11/14/86); P.L. 100-525 (10/24/88); P.L. 101-649 (IMMACT90) (11/29/90); P.L. 102-232 (MTINA) (12/12/91, *effective* 4/1/92); P.L. 104-208 (IIRAIRA) (9/30/96), §633 [adding (a)(1)]; P.L. 106-313 (AC21) (10/17/00), §104(a)–(b) [revising (a)(2), (e); & adding (a)(5)].)

## Sec. 203 Allocation of Immigrant Visas
[8 U.S.C. 1153]

**(a) Preference allocation for family-sponsored immigrants.**— Aliens subject to the worldwide level specified in section 201(c) for family-sponsored immigrants shall be allotted visas as follows:

(1) *Unmarried sons and daughters of citizens.*— Qualified immigrants who are the unmarried sons or daughters of citizens of the United States shall be allocated visas in a number not to exceed 23,400, plus any visas not required for the class specified in paragraph (4).

(2) *Spouses and unmarried sons and unmarried daughters of permanent resident aliens.*— Qualified immigrants—[34]

(A) who are the spouses or children of an alien lawfully admitted for permanent residence, or

(B) who are the unmarried sons or unmarried daughters (but are not the children) of an alien lawfully admitted for permanent residence,

shall be allocated visas in a number not to exceed 114,200, plus the number (if any) by which such worldwide level exceeds 226,000, plus any visas not required for the class specified in paragraph (1); except that not less than 77 percent of such visa numbers shall be allocated to aliens described in subparagraph (A).

(3) *Married sons and married daughters of citizens.*— Qualified immigrants who are the married sons or married daughters of citizens of the United States shall be allocated visas in a number not to exceed 23,400, plus any visas not required for the classes specified in paragraphs (1) and (2).

(4) *Brothers and sisters of citizens.*— Qualified immigrants who are the brothers or sisters of citizens of the United States, if such citizens are at least 21 years of age, shall be allocated vi-

---

[34] *See* §423(b) of the USA PATRIOT Act, P.L. 107-56, *reprinted in* Appendix J, *infra*, for provisions relating to immigration benefits for the victims of terrorism.

sas in a number not to exceed 65,000, plus any visas not required for the classes specified in paragraphs (1) through (3).

**(b) Preference allocation for employment-based immigrants.—**[35] Aliens subject to the worldwide level specified in section 201(d) for employment-based immigrants in a fiscal year shall be allotted visas as follows:

(1) *Priority workers.—* Visas shall first be made available in a number not to exceed 28.6 percent of such worldwide level, plus any visas not required for the classes specified in paragraphs (4) and (5), to qualified immigrants who are aliens described in any of the following subparagraphs (A) through (C):

(A) *Aliens with extraordinary ability.—* An alien is described in this subparagraph if—

(i) the alien has extraordinary ability in the sciences, arts, education, business, or athletics which has been demonstrated by sustained national or international acclaim and whose achievements have been recognized in the field through extensive documentation,

(ii) the alien seeks to enter the United States to continue work in the area of extraordinary ability, and

(iii) the alien's entry into the United States will substantially benefit prospectively the United States.

(B) *Outstanding professors and researchers.—* An alien is described in this subparagraph if—

(i) the alien is recognized internationally as outstanding in a specific academic area,

(ii) the alien has at least 3 years of experience in teaching or research in the academic area, and

(iii) the alien seeks to enter the United States—

(I) for a tenured position (or tenure-track position) within a university or institution of higher education to teach in the academic area,

(II) for a comparable position with a university or institution of higher education to conduct research in the area, or

(III) for a comparable position to conduct research in the area with a department, division, or institute of a private employer, if the department, division, or institute employs at least 3 persons full-time in research activities and has achieved documented accomplishments in an academic field.

(C) *Certain multinational executives and managers.—* An alien is described in this subparagraph if the alien, in the 3 years preceding the time of the alien's application for classification and admission into the United States under this subparagraph, has been employed for at least 1 year by a firm or corporation or other legal entity or an affiliate or subsidiary thereof and the alien seeks to enter the United States in order to continue to render services to the same employer or to a subsidiary or affiliate thereof in a capacity that is managerial or executive.

(2) *Aliens who are members of the professions holding advanced degrees or aliens of exceptional ability.—*

---

[35] *See also* §11036(c) of P.L. 107-273 for effective date provision.

(A) *In general.*— Visas shall be made available, in a number not to exceed 28.6 percent of such worldwide level, plus any visas not required for the classes specified in paragraph (1), to qualified immigrants who are members of the professions holding advanced degrees or their equivalent or who because of their exceptional ability in the sciences, arts, or business, will substantially benefit prospectively the national economy, cultural or educational interests, or welfare of the United States, and whose services in the sciences, arts, professions, or business are sought by an employer in the United States.

(B) *Waiver of job offer.*

(i) National interest waiver.— Subject to clause (ii), the Attorney General may, when the Attorney General deems it to be in the national interest, waive the requirements of subparagraph (A) that an alien's services in the sciences, arts, professions, or business be sought by an employer in the United States.

(ii) Physicians working in shortage areas or veterans facilities.—

(I) In general.— The Attorney General shall grant a national interest waiver pursuant to clause (i) on behalf of any alien physician with respect to whom a petition for preference classification has been filed under subparagraph (A) if—

(aa) the alien physician agrees to work full time as a physician in an area or areas designated by the Secretary of Health and Human Services as having a shortage of health care professionals or at a health care facility under the jurisdiction of the Secretary of Veterans Affairs; and

(bb) a Federal agency or a department of public health in any State has previously determined that the alien physician's work in such an area or at such facility was in the public interest.

(II) Prohibition.— No permanent resident visa may be issued to an alien physician described in subclause (I) by the Secretary of State under section 204(b), and the Attorney General may not adjust the status of such an alien physician from that of a nonimmigrant alien to that of a permanent resident alien under section 245, until such time as the alien has worked full time as a physician for an aggregate of 5 years (not including the time served in the status of an alien described in section 101(a)(15)(J)), in an area or areas designated by the Secretary of Health and Human Services as having a shortage of health care professionals or at a health care facility under the jurisdiction of the Secretary of Veterans Affairs.

(III) Statutory construction.— Nothing in this subparagraph may be construed to prevent the filing of a petition with the Attorney General for classification under section 204(a), or the filing of an application for adjustment of status under section 245, by an alien physician described in subclause (I) prior to the date by which such alien physician has completed the service described in subclause (II).

(IV) Effective date.— The requirements of this subsection do not affect waivers on behalf of alien physicians approved under section 203(b)(2)(B) before the enactment date of this subsection. In the case of a physician for whom an application for a waiver was filed under section 203(b)(2)(B) prior to November 1, 1998, the Attorney General shall grant a national interest waiver pursuant to section 203(b)(2)(B) except that the alien is required to have worked full time as a physician for an aggregate of 3 years (not including time served in the status of an alien described in section 101(a)(15)(J)) before a visa can be issued to the alien under section 204(b) or the status of the alien is adjusted to permanent resident under section 245.

(C) *Determination of exceptional ability.*— In determining under subparagraph (A) whether an immigrant has exceptional ability, the possession of a degree, diploma, certificate, or similar award from a college, university, school, or other institution of learning or a license to practice or certification for a particular profession or occupation shall not by itself be considered sufficient evidence of such exceptional ability.

(3) *Skilled workers, professionals, and other workers.*—

(A) *In general.*— Visas shall be made available, in a number not to exceed 28.6 percent of such worldwide level, plus any visas not required for the classes specified in paragraphs (1) and (2), to the following classes of aliens who are not described in paragraph (2):

(i) Skilled workers.— Qualified immigrants who are capable, at the time of petitioning for classification under this paragraph, of performing skilled labor (requiring at least 2 years training or experience), not of a temporary or seasonal nature, for which qualified workers are not available in the United States.

(ii) Professionals.— Qualified immigrants who hold baccalaureate degrees and who are members of the professions.

(iii) Other workers.— Other qualified immigrants who are capable, at the time of petitioning for classification under this paragraph, of performing unskilled labor, not of a temporary or seasonal nature, for which qualified workers are not available in the United States.

(B) *Limitation on other workers.*— Not more than 10,000 of the visas made available under this paragraph in any fiscal year may be available for qualified immigrants described in subparagraph (A)(iii).

(C) *Labor certification required.*— An immigrant visa may not be issued to an immigrant under subparagraph (A) until the consular officer is in receipt of a determination made by the Secretary of Labor pursuant to the provisions of section 212(a)(5)(A).

(4) *Certain special immigrants.*— Visas shall be made available, in a number not to exceed 7.1 percent of such worldwide level, to qualified special immigrants described in section 101(a)(27) (other than those described in subparagraphs (A) or (B) thereof), of which not more than 5,000 may be made available in any fiscal year to special immigrants described in subclause (II) or (III) of section 101(a)(27)(C)(ii), and not more than 100 may be made available in any fiscal year to special immigrants, excluding spouses and children, who are described in section 101(a)(27)(M).

(5) *Employment creation.*—

(A) *In general.*— Visas shall be made available, in a number not to exceed 7.1 percent of such worldwide level, to qualified immigrants seeking to enter the United States for the purpose of engaging in a new commercial enterprise (including a limited partnership)—

(i) in which such alien has invested (after the date of the enactment of the Immigration Act of 1990) or, is actively in the process of investing, capital in an amount not less than the amount specified in subparagraph (C), and

(ii) which will benefit the United States economy and create full-time employment for not fewer than 10 United States citizens or aliens lawfully admitted for permanent residence or other immigrants lawfully authorized to be employed in the United States (other than the immigrant and the immigrant's spouse, sons, or daughters).

(B) *Set-aside for targeted employment areas.—*

(i) In general.— Not less than 3,000 of the visas made available under this paragraph in each fiscal year shall be reserved for qualified immigrants who invest in a new commercial enterprise described in subparagraph (A) which will create employment in a targeted employment area.

(ii) Targeted employment area defined.— In this paragraph, the term "targeted employment area" means, at the time of the investment, a rural area or an area which has experienced high unemployment (of at least 150 percent of the national average rate).

(iii) Rural area defined.— In this paragraph, the term "rural area" means any area other than an area within a metropolitan statistical area or within the outer boundary of any city or town having a population of 20,000 or more (based on the most recent decennial census of the United States).

(C) *Amount of capital required.—*

(i) In general.— Except as otherwise provided in this subparagraph, the amount of capital required under subparagraph (A) shall be $1,000,000. The Attorney General, in consultation with the Secretary of Labor and the Secretary of State, may from time to time prescribe regulations increasing the dollar amount specified under the previous sentence.

(ii) Adjustment for targeted employment areas.— The Attorney General may, in the case of investment made in a targeted employment area, specify an amount of capital required under subparagraph (A) that is less than (but not less than ½ of) the amount specified in clause (i).

(iii) Adjustment for high employment areas.— In the case of an investment made in a part of a metropolitan statistical area that at the time of the investment—

(I) is not a targeted employment area, and

(II) is an area with an unemployment rate significantly below the national average unemployment rate, the Attorney General may specify an amount of capital required under subparagraph (A) that is greater than (but not greater than 3 times) the amount specified in clause (i).

(D) *Full-time employment defined.—* In this paragraph, the term "full-time employment" means employment in a position that requires at least 35 hours of service per week at any time, regardless of who fills the position.

(6) *Special rules for "K" special immigrants.—*

(A) *Not counted against numerical limitation in year involved.—* Subject to subparagraph (B), the number of immigrant visas made available to special immigrants under section 101(a)(27)(K) in a fiscal year shall not be subject to the numerical limitations of this subsection or of section 202(a).

(B) *Counted against numerical limitations in following year.—*

(i) Reduction in employment-based immigrant classifications.— The number of visas made available in any fiscal year under paragraphs (1), (2), and (3) shall each be reduced by ⅓ of the number of visas made available in the previous fiscal year to special immigrants described in section 101(a)(27)(K).

(ii) Reduction in per country level.— The number of visas made available in each fiscal year to natives of a foreign state under section 202(a) shall be reduced by the number of visas made available in the previous fiscal year to special immigrants described in section 101(a)(27)(K) who are natives of the foreign state.

(iii) Reduction in employment-based immigrant classifications within per country ceiling.— In the case of a foreign state subject to section 202(e) in a fiscal year (and in the previous fiscal year), the number of visas made available and allocated to each of paragraphs (1) through (3) of this subsection in the fiscal year shall be reduced by ⅓ of the number of visas made available in the previous fiscal year to special immigrants described in section 101(a)(27)(K) who are natives of the foreign state.

**(c) Diversity immigrants.**—[36]

(1) *In general*.— Except as provided in paragraph (2), aliens subject to the worldwide level specified in section 201(e) for diversity immigrants shall be allotted visas each fiscal year as follows:

(A) *Determination of preference immigration*.— The Attorney General shall determine for the most recent previous 5-fiscal-year period for which data are available, the total number of aliens who are natives of each foreign state and who

(i) were admitted or otherwise provided lawful permanent resident status (other than under this subsection) and

(ii) were subject to the numerical limitations of section 201(a) (other than paragraph (3) thereof) or who were admitted or otherwise provided lawful permanent resident status as an immediate relative or other alien described in section 201(b)(2).

(B) *Identification of high-admission and low-admission regions and high-admission and low-admission states*.— The Attorney General—

(i) shall identify—

(I) each region (each in this paragraph referred to as a "high-admission region") for which the total of the numbers determined under subparagraph (A) for states in the region is greater than 1/6 of the total of all such numbers, and

(II) each other region (each in this paragraph referred to as a "low-admission region"); and

(ii) shall identify—

(I) each foreign state for which the number determined under subparagraph (A) is greater than 50,000 (each such state in this paragraph referred to as a "high-admission state"), and

(II) each other foreign state (each such state in this paragraph referred to as a

---

[36] *See* §422(c) of the USA PATRIOT Act, P.L. 107-56, *reprinted in* Appendix J, *infra*, for provisions relating to immigration benefits for the victims of terrorism.

"low-admission state").

(C) *Determination of percentage of worldwide immigration attributable to high-admission regions.*— The Attorney General shall determine the percentage of the total of the numbers determined under subparagraph (A) that are numbers for foreign states in high-admission regions.

(D) *Determination of regional populations excluding high-admission states and ratios of populations of regions within low-admission regions and high-admission regions.*— The Attorney General shall determine—

(i) based on available estimates for each region, the total population of each region not including the population of any high-admission state;

(ii) for each low-admission region, the ratio of the population of the region determined under clause (i) to the total of the populations determined under such clause for all the low-admission regions; and

(iii) for each high-admission region, the ratio of the population of the region determined under clause (i) to the total of the populations determined under such clause for all the high-admission regions.

(E) *Distribution of visas.*—

(i) No visas for natives of high-admission states.— The percentage of visas made available under this paragraph to natives of a high-admission state is 0.

(ii) For low-admission states in low-admission regions.— Subject to clauses (iv) and (v), the percentage of visas made available under this paragraph to natives (other than natives of a high-admission state) in a low-admission region is the product of—

(I) the percentage determined under subparagraph (C), and

(II) the population ratio for that region determined under subparagraph (D)(ii).

(iii) For low-admission states in high-admission regions.— Subject to clauses (iv) and (v), the percentage of visas made available under this paragraph to natives (other than natives of a high-admission state) in a high-admission region is the product of—

(I) 100 percent minus the percentage determined under subparagraph (C), and

(II) the population ratio for that region determined under subparagraph (D)(iii).

(iv) Redistribution of unused visa numbers.— If the Secretary of State estimates that the number of immigrant visas to be issued to natives in any region for a fiscal year under this paragraph is less than the number of immigrant visas made available to such natives under this paragraph for the fiscal year, subject to clause (v), the excess visa numbers shall be made available to natives (other than natives of a high-admission state) of the other regions in proportion to the percentages otherwise specified in clauses (ii) and (iii).

(v) Limitation on visas for natives of a single foreign state.— The percentage of visas made available under this paragraph to natives of any single foreign state for any fiscal year shall not exceed 7 percent.

(F) *Region defined.*— Only for purposes of administering the diversity program under this subsection, Northern Ireland shall be treated as a separate foreign state, each colony or other component or dependent area of a foreign state overseas from the foreign state shall be treated as part of the foreign state, and the areas described in each of the following clauses shall be considered to be a separate region:

(i) Africa.

(ii) Asia.

(iii) Europe.

(iv) North America (other than Mexico).

(v) Oceania.

(vi) South America, Mexico, Central America, and the Caribbean.

(2) *Requirement of education or work experience.*— An alien is not eligible for a visa under this subsection unless the alien—

(A) has at least a high school education or its equivalent, or

(B) has, within 5 years of the date of application for a visa under this subsection, at least 2 years of work experience in an occupation which requires at least 2 years of training or experience.

(3) *Maintenance of information.*— The Secretary of State shall maintain information on the age, occupation, education level, and other relevant characteristics of immigrants issued visas under this subsection.

**(d) Treatment of family members.**— A spouse or child as defined in subparagraph (A), (B), (C), (D), or (E) of section 101(b)(1) shall, if not otherwise entitled to an immigrant status and the immediate issuance of a visa under subsection (a), (b), or (c), be entitled to the same status, and the same order of consideration provided in the respective subsection, if accompanying or following to join, the spouse or parent.

**(e) Order of consideration.—**

(1) Immigrant visas made available under subsection (a) or (b) shall be issued to eligible immigrants in the order in which a petition in behalf of each such immigrant is filed with the Attorney General (or in the case of special immigrants under section 101(a)(27)(D), with the Secretary of State) as provided in section 204(a).

(2) Immigrant visa numbers made available under subsection (c) (relating to diversity immigrants) shall be issued to eligible qualified immigrants strictly in a random order established by the Secretary of State for the fiscal year involved.

(3) Waiting lists of applicants for visas under this section shall be maintained in accordance with regulations prescribed by the Secretary of State.

**(f) Authorization for issuance.**— In the case of any alien claiming in his application for an immigrant visa to be described in section 201(b)(2) or in subsection (a), (b), or (c) of this section, the consular officer shall not grant such status until he has been authorized to do so as provided by section 204.

**(g) Lists.**— For purposes of carrying out the Secretary's responsibilities in the orderly administration of this section, the Secretary of State may make reasonable estimates of the anticipated numbers of visas to be issued during any quarter of any fiscal year within each of the categories under subsections (a), (b), and (c) and to rely upon such estimates in authorizing the issuance of visas. The Secretary of State shall terminate the registration of any alien who fails to apply for an immigrant visa within one year following notification to the alien of the availability of such visa, but the Secretary shall reinstate the registration of any such alien who establishes within 2 years following the date of notification of the availability of such visa that such failure to apply was due to circumstances beyond the alien's control.

### (h) Rules for determining whether certain aliens are children.—[37]

(1) *In general.*— For purposes of subsections (a)(2)(A) and (d), a determination of whether an alien satisfies the age requirement in the matter preceding subparagraph (A) of section 101(b)(1) shall be made using—

(A) the age of the alien on the date on which an immigrant visa number becomes available for such alien (or, in the case of subsection (d), the date on which an immigrant visa number became available for the alien's parent), but only if the alien has sought to acquire the status of an alien lawfully admitted for permanent residence within one year of such availability; reduced by

(B) the number of days in the period during which the applicable petition described in paragraph (2) was pending.

(2) *Petitions described.*— The petition described in this paragraph is—

(A) with respect to a relationship described in subsection (a)(2)(A), a petition filed under section 204 for classification of an alien child under subsection (a)(2)(A); or

(B) with respect to an alien child who is a derivative beneficiary under subsection (d), a petition filed under section 204 for classification of the alien's parent under subsection (a), (b), or (c).

(3) *Retention of priority date.*— If the age of an alien is determined under paragraph (1) to be 21 years of age or older for the purposes of subsections (a)(2)(A) and (d), the alien's petition shall automatically be converted to the appropriate category and the alien shall retain the original priority date issued upon receipt of the original petition.

(4) *Applications to self-petitions.*— Paragraphs (1) through (3) shall apply to self-petitioners and derivatives of self-petitioners.

(June 27, 1952, ch. 477, title II, ch. 1, §203, 66 Stat. 178; as amended by P.L. 85-316 (9/11/57); P.L. 86-363 (9/22/59); P.L. 89-236 (10/3/65); P.L. 94-571 (10/20/76); P.L. 95-412 (10/5/78); P.L. 95-417 (10/5/78); P.L. 96-212 (3/17/80); P.L. 101-649 (IMMACT90) (11/29/90); P.L. 102-110 (10/1/91); P.L. 102-232 (MTINA) (12/12/91, *effective* 4/1/92), §302; P.L. 103-416 (INTCA) (10/25/94, *effective* 4/1/95), §212, §219 [striking (6)(C)]; P.L. 106-95 (11/12/99), §5 [revising (b)(2)(B)]; P.L. 106-113 (11/29/99), §117 [revising (b)(2)(B)]; P.L. 106-536 (11/22/00), §1 [revising (b)(4)]; P.L. 107-208 (CSPA) (8/6/02), §3 [adding (h)]; P.L. 107-273 (11/2/02), div. C, title I, §11035, §11036 [revising (b)(5)]; P.L. 109-162 (1/5/06), title VIII, §805 [adding (h)(4)].)

### Sec. 204 Procedure for Granting Immigrant Status
[8 U.S.C. 1154]

### (a) Petitioning procedure.[38]

(1) (A) (i) Except as provided in clause (viii), any citizen of the United States claiming that an alien is entitled to classification by reason of a relationship described in paragraph (1), (3), or (4) of section 203(a) or to an immediate relative status under section 201(b)(2)(A)(i) may file a petition with the Attorney General for such classification.

---

[37] *See* note 33, *supra.*

[38] *See* note 33, *supra. See* §568(c)(1) of the P.L. 111-83 (123 STAT. 524), §568(c)(2) contains effective-date and transition-rule provisions for the Surviving Spouse relief.

(ii) An alien spouse described in the second sentence of section 201(b)(2)(A)(i) also may file a petition with the Attorney General under this subparagraph for classification of the alien (and the alien's children) under such section.

(iii) (I) An alien who is described in subclause (II) may file a petition with the Attorney General under this clause for classification of the alien (and any child of the alien) if the alien demonstrates to the Attorney General that—

(aa) the marriage or the intent to marry the United States citizen was entered into in good faith by the alien; and

(bb) during the marriage or relationship intended by the alien to be legally a marriage, the alien or a child of the alien has been battered or has been the subject of extreme cruelty perpetrated by the alien's spouse or intended spouse.

(II) For purposes of subclause (I), an alien described in this subclause is an alien—

(aa)(AA) who is the spouse of a citizen of the United States;

(BB) who believed that he or she had married a citizen of the United States and with whom a marriage ceremony was actually performed and who otherwise meets any applicable requirements under this Act to establish the existence of and bona fides of a marriage, but whose marriage is not legitimate solely because of the bigamy of such citizen of the United States; or

(CC) who was a bona fide spouse of a United States citizen within the past 2 years and—

(aaa) whose spouse died within the past 2 years;

(bbb) whose spouse lost or renounced citizenship status within the past 2 years related to an incident of domestic violence; or

(ccc) who demonstrates a connection between the legal termination of the marriage within the past 2 years and battering or extreme cruelty by the United States citizen spouse;

(bb) who is a person of good moral character;

(cc) who is eligible to be classified as an immediate relative under section 201(b)(2)(A)(i) or who would have been so classified but for the bigamy of the citizen of the United States that the alien intended to marry; and

(dd) who has resided with the alien's spouse or intended spouse.

(iv) An alien who is the child of a citizen of the United States, or who was a child of a United States citizen parent who within the past 2 years lost or renounced citizenship status related to an incident of domestic violence, and who is a person of good moral character, who is eligible to be classified as an immediate relative under section 201(b)(2)(A)(i), and who resides, or has resided in the past, with the citizen parent may file a petition with the Attorney General under this subparagraph for classification of the alien (and any child of the alien) under such section if the alien demonstrates to the Attorney General that the alien has been battered by or has been the subject of extreme cruelty perpetrated by the alien's citizen parent. For purposes of this clause, residence includes any period of visitation.

(v) An alien who—

(I) is the spouse, intended spouse, or child living abroad of a citizen who—

(aa) is an employee of the United States Government:

(bb) is a member of the uniformed services (as defined in section 101(a) of title 10, United States Code); or

(cc) has subjected the alien or the alien's child to battery or extreme cruelty in the United States; and

(II) is eligible to file a petition under clause (iii) or (iv),

shall file such petition with the Attorney General under the procedures that apply to self-petitioners under clause (iii) or (iv), as applicable.

(vi) For the purposes of any petition filed under clause (iii) or (iv), the denaturalization, loss or renunciation of citizenship, death of the abuser, divorce, or changes to the abuser's citizenship status after filing of the petition shall not adversely affect the approval of the petition, and for approved petitions shall not preclude the classification of the eligible self-petitioning spouse or child as an immediate relative or affect the alien's ability to adjust status under subsections (a) and (c) of section 245 or obtain status as a lawful permanent resident based on the approved self-petition under such clauses.

(vii) An alien may file a petition with the Secretary of Homeland Security under this subparagraph for classification of the alien under section 201(b)(2)(A)(i) if the alien—

(I) is the parent of a citizen of the United States or was a parent of a citizen of the United States who, within the past 2 years, lost or renounced citizenship status related to an incident of domestic violence or died;

(II) is a person of good moral character;

(III) is eligible to be classified as an immediate relative under section 201(b)(2)(A)(i);

(IV) resides, or has resided, with the citizen daughter or son; and

(V) demonstrates that the alien has been battered or subject to extreme cruelty by the citizen daughter or son.

(viii) (I) Clause (i) shall not apply to a citizen of the United States who has been convicted of a specified offense against a minor, unless the Secretary of Homeland Security, in the Secretary's sole and unreviewable discretion, determines that the citizen poses no risk to the alien with respect to whom a petition described in clause (i) is filed.

(II) For purposes of subclause (I), the term "specified offense against a minor" is defined as in section 111 of the Adam Walsh Child Protection and Safety Act of 2006.

(B) (i) (I) Except as provided in subclause (II), any alien lawfully admitted for permanent residence claiming that an alien is entitled to a classification by reason of the relationship described in section 203(a)(2) may file a petition with the Attorney General for such classification.

(II)[39] Subclause (I) shall not apply in the case of an alien lawfully admitted for permanent residence who has been convicted of a specified offense against a minor (as defined in subparagraph (A)(viii)(II)), unless the Secretary of Homeland Security, in the Secretary's sole and unreviewable discretion, determines that such person poses no risk to the alien with respect to whom a petition described in subclause (I) is filed.

(ii) (I) An alien who is described in subclause (II) may file a petition with the Attorney General under this clause for classification of the alien (and any child of the alien) if such a child has not been classified under clause (iii) of section 203(a)(2)(A) and if the alien demonstrated to the Attorney General that—

(aa) the marriage or the intent to marry the lawful permanent resident was entered into in good faith by the alien; and

(bb) during the marriage or relationship intended by the alien to be legally a marriage, the alien or a child of the alien has been battered or has been the subject of extreme cruelty perpetrated by the alien's spouse or intended spouse.

(II) For purposes of subclause (I), an alien described in this paragraph is an alien—

(aa) (AA) who is the spouse of a lawful permanent resident of the United States; or

(BB) who believed that he or she had married a lawful permanent resident of the United States and with whom a marriage ceremony was actually performed and who otherwise meets any applicable requirements under this Act to establish the existence of and bona fides of a marriage, but whose marriage is not legitimate solely because of the bigamy of such lawful permanent resident of the United States: or

(CC) who was a bona fide spouse of a lawful permanent resident within the past 2 years and—

(aaa) whose spouse lost status within the past 2 years due to an incident of domestic violence; or

(bbb) who demonstrates a connection between the legal termination of the marriage within the past 2 years and battering or extreme cruelty by the lawful permanent resident spouse;

(bb) who is a person of good moral character;

(cc) who is eligible to be classified as a spouse of an alien lawfully admitted for permanent residence under section 203(a)(2)(A) or who would have been so classified but for the bigamy of the lawful permanent resident of the United States that the alien intended to marry; and

(dd) who has resided with the alien's spouse or intended spouse.

(iii) An alien who is the child of an alien lawfully admitted for permanent residence, or who was the child of a lawful permanent resident who within the past 2 years lost

---

[39] *Sic.* P.L. 109-248 (7/27/06), §402(a)(3)(B), which added this subclause, erroneously called it subclause "(I)".

lawful permanent resident status due to an incident of domestic violence, and who is a person of good moral character, who is eligible for classification under section 203(a)(2)(A), and who resides, or has resided in the past, with the alien's permanent resident alien parent may file a petition with the Attorney General under this subparagraph for classification of the alien (and any child of the alien under such section if the alien demonstrates to the Attorney General that the alien has been battered by or has been the subject of extreme cruelty perpetrated by the alien's permanent resident parent.

(iv) An alien who—

(I) is the spouse, intended spouse, or child living abroad of a lawful permanent resident who—

(aa) is an employee of the United States Government;

(bb) is a member of the uniformed services (as defined in section 101(a) of title 10, United States Code); or

(cc) has subjected the alien or the alien's child to battery or extreme cruelty in the Untied States; and

(II) is eligible to file a petition under clause (ii) or (iii), shall file such petition with the Attorney General under the procedures that apply to self-petitioners under clause (ii) or (iii), as applicable.

(v) (I) For the purposes of any petition filed or approved under clause (ii) or (iii), divorce, or the loss of lawful permanent resident status by a spouse or parent after the filing of a petition under that clause shall not adversely affect approval of the petition, and, for an approved petition, shall not affect the alien's ability to adjust status under subsections (a) and (c) of section 245 or obtain status as a lawful permanent resident based on an approved self-petition under clause (ii) or (iii).

(II) Upon the lawful permanent resident spouse or parent becoming or establishing the existence of United States citizenship through naturalization, acquisition of citizenship, or other means, any petition filed with the Immigration and Naturalization Service and pending or approved under clause (ii) or (iii) on behalf of an alien who has been battered or subjected to extreme cruelty shall be deemed reclassified as a petition filed under subparagraph (A) even if the acquisition of citizenship occurs after divorce or termination of parental rights.

(C) Notwithstanding section 101(f), an act or conviction that is waivable with respect to the petitioner for purposes of a determination of the petitioner's admissibility under section 212(a) or deportability under section 237(a) shall not bar the Attorney General from finding the petitioner to be of good moral character under subparagraph (A)(iii), (A)(iv), (B)(ii), or (B)(iii) if the Attorney General finds that the act or conviction was connected to the alien's having been battered or subjected to extreme cruelty.

(D) (i)(I) Any child who attains 21 years of age who has filed a petition under clause (iv) of section 204(a)(1)(A) or section 204(a)(1)(B)(iii) that was filed or approved before the date on which the child attained 21 years of age shall be considered (if the child has not been admitted or approved for lawful permanent residence by the date the child attained 21 years of age) a petitioner for preference status under paragraph (1), (2), or (3) of section 203(a), whichever paragraph is applicable, with the same priority date assigned to the self-petition filed under clause (iv) of section 204(a)(1)(A) or section

204(a)(1)(B)(iii). No new petition shall be required to be filed.

(II) Any individual described in subclause (I) is eligible for deferred action and work authorization.

(III) Any derivative child who attains 21 years of age who is included in a petition described in clause (ii) that was filed or approved before the date on which the child attained 21 years of age shall be considered (if the child has not been admitted or approved for lawful permanent residence by the date the child attained 21 years of age) a VAWA self-petitioner with the same priority date as that assigned to the petitioner in any petition described in clause (ii). No new petition shall be required to be filed.

(IV) Any individual described in subclause (III) and any derivative child of a petition described in clause (ii) is eligible for deferred action and work authorization.

(ii) The petition referred to in clause (i)(III) is a petition filed by an alien under subparagraph (A)(iii), (A)(iv), (B)(ii) or (B)(iii) in which the child is included as a derivative beneficiary.

(iii) Nothing in the amendments made by the Child Status Protection Act shall be construed to limit or deny any right or benefit provided under this subparagraph.[40]

(iv) Any alien who benefits from this subparagraph may adjust status in accordance with subsections (a) and (c) of section 245 as an alien having an approved petition for classification under subparagraph (A)(iii), (A)(iv), (B)(ii) or (B)(iii).

(v) For purposes of this paragraph, an individual who is not less than 21 years of age, who qualified to file a petition under subparagraph (A)(iv) or (B)(iii) as of the day before the date on which the individual attained 21 years of age, and who did not file such a petition before such day, shall be treated as having filed a petition under such subparagraph as of such day if a petition is filed for the status described in such subparagraph before the individual attains 25 years of age and the individual shows that the abuse was at least one central reason for the filing delay. Clauses (i) through (iv) of this subparagraph shall apply to an individual described in this clause in the same manner as an individual filing a petition under subparagraph (A)(iv) or (B)(iii).

(E) Any alien desiring to be classified under section 203(b)(1)(A), or any person on behalf of such an alien, may file a petition with the Attorney General for such classification.

(F) Any employer desiring and intending to employ within the United States an alien entitled to classification under section 203(b)(1)(B), 203(b)(1)(C), 203(b)(2), or 203(b)(3) may file a petition with the Attorney General for such classification.

(G) (i) Any alien (other than a special immigrant under section 101(a)(27)(D)) desiring to be classified under section 203(b)(4), or any person on behalf of such an alien, may file a petition with the Attorney General for such classification.

(ii) Aliens claiming status as a special immigrant under section 101(a)(27)(D) may file a petition only with the Secretary of State and only after notification by the Secretary that such status has been recommended and approved pursuant to such section.

---

[40] *See* note 33, *supra*.

(H) Any alien desiring to be classified under section 203(b)(5) may file a petition with the Attorney General for such classification.

(I)(i) Any alien desiring to be provided an immigrant visa under section 203(c) may file a petition at the place and time determined by the Secretary of State by regulation. Only one such petition may be filed by an alien with respect to any petitioning period established. If more than one petition is submitted all such petitions submitted for such period by the alien shall be voided.

(ii) (I) The Secretary of State shall designate a period for the filing of petitions with respect to visas which may be issued under section 203(c) for the fiscal year beginning after the end of the period.

(II) Aliens who qualify, through random selection, for a visa under section 203(c) shall remain eligible to receive such visa only through the end of the specific fiscal year for which they were selected.

(III) The Secretary of State shall prescribe such regulations as may be necessary to carry out this clause.

(iii) A petition under this subparagraph shall be in such form as the Secretary of State may by regulation prescribe and shall contain such information and be supported by such documentary evidence as the Secretary of State may require.

(J) In acting on petitions filed under clause (iii) or (iv) of subparagraph (A) or clause (ii) or (iii) of subparagraph (B), or in making determinations under subparagraphs (C) and (D), the Attorney General shall consider any credible evidence relevant to the petition. The determination of what evidence is credible and the weight to be given that evidence shall be within the sole discretion of the Attorney General.

(K) Upon the approval of a petition as a VAWA self-petitioner, the alien—

(i) is eligible for work authorization; and

(ii) may be provided an "employment authorized" endorsement or appropriate work permit incidental to such approval.

(L) Notwithstanding the previous provisions of this paragraph, an individual who was a VAWA petitioner or who had the status of a nonimmigrant under subparagraph (T) or (U) of section 101(a)(15) may not file a petition for classification under this section or section 214 to classify any person who committed the battery or extreme cruelty or trafficking against the individual (or the individual's child) which established the individual's (or individual's child) eligibility as a VAWA petitioner or for such nonimmigrant status.

(2) (A) The Attorney General may not approve a spousal second preference petition for the classification of the spouse of an alien if the alien, by virtue of a prior marriage, has been accorded the status of an alien lawfully admitted for permanent residence as the spouse of a citizen of the United States or as the spouse of an alien lawfully admitted for permanent residence, unless—

(i) a period of 5 years has elapsed after the date the alien acquired the status of an alien lawfully admitted for permanent residence, or

(ii) the alien establishes to the satisfaction of the Attorney General by clear and convincing evidence that the prior marriage (on the basis of which the alien obtained the status of an alien lawfully admitted for permanent residence) was not entered into for the purpose of evading any provision of the immigration laws.

In this subparagraph, the term "spousal second preference petition" refers to a petition, seeking preference status under section 203(a)(2), for an alien as a spouse of an alien lawfully admitted for permanent residence.

(B) Subparagraph (A) shall not apply to a petition filed for the classification of the spouse of an alien if the prior marriage of the alien was terminated by the death of his or her spouse.

**(b) Investigation; consultation; approval; authorization to grant preference status.**— After an investigation of the facts in each case, and after consultation with the Secretary of Labor with respect to petitions to accord a status under section 203(b)(2) or 203(b)(3), the Attorney General shall, if he determines that the facts stated in the petition are true and that the alien in behalf of whom the petition is made is an immediate relative specified in section 201(b) or is eligible for preference under subsection (a) or (b) of section 203, approve the petition and forward one copy thereof to the Department of State. The Secretary of State shall then authorize the consular officer concerned to grant the preference status.

**(c) Limitation on orphan petitions approved for a single petitioner; prohibition against approval in cases of marriages entered into in order to evade immigration laws; restriction on future entry of aliens involved with marriage fraud.**— Notwithstanding the provisions of subsection (b) no petition shall be approved if—

(1) the alien has previously been accorded, or has sought to be accorded, an immediate relative or preference status as the spouse of a citizen of the United States or the spouse of an alien lawfully admitted for permanent residence, by reason of a marriage determined by the Attorney General to have been entered into for the purpose of evading the immigration laws or

(2) the Attorney General has determined that the alien has attempted or conspired to enter into a marriage for the purpose of evading the immigration laws.

**(d) Recommendation of valid home-study.**—[41]

(1) Notwithstanding the provisions of subsections (a) and (b) no petition may be approved on behalf of a child defined in subparagraph (F) or (G) of section 101(b)(1) unless a valid home-study has been favorably recommended by an agency of the State of the child's proposed residence, or by an agency authorized by that State to conduct such a study, or, in the case of a child adopted abroad, by an appropriate public or private adoption agency which is licensed in the United States.

(2) Notwithstanding the provisions of subsections (a) and (b), no petition may be approved on behalf of a child defined in section 101(b)(1)(G) unless the Secretary of State has certified that the central authority of the child's country of origin has notified the United States central authority under the convention referred to in such section 101(b)(1)(G) that a United States citizen habitually resident in the United States has effected final adoption of the child, or has been

---

[41] ***Delayed effective date.*** Sec. 302(b) of the Intercountry Adoption Act of 2000 (IAA), P.L. 106-279 (10/6/00), added a (1) in front of the existing text of INA §204(d), and then added a new paragraph (2). This revised INA §204(d) (as well as language referring to it) takes effect upon "the entry into force of the [Hague Convention on Protection of Children and Cooperation in Respect of Intercountry Adoption] for the United States pursuant to Article 46(2)(a) of the Convention." (*See* IAA §505.) This occurs when DHS and DOS publish implementing regulations in the *Federal Register* and the United States deposits the instruments of ratification with the Permanent Bureau of the Hague Conference (71 FR 8063 and 71 FR 8161, 2/15/06, *effective* 3/17/06). For IAA transition rules, see IAA §505(b).

granted custody of the child for the purpose of emigration and adoption, in accordance with such convention and the Intercountry Adoption Act of 2000.

**(e) Subsequent finding of non-entitlement to preference classification.**— Nothing in this section shall be construed to entitle an immigrant, in behalf of whom a petition under this section is approved, to be admitted the United States[42] as an immigrant under subsection (a), (b), or (c) of section 203 or as an immediate relative under section 201(b) if upon his arrival at a port of entry in the United States he is found not to be entitled to such classification.

**(f) Preferential treatment for children fathered by United States citizens and born in Korea, Vietnam, Laos, Kampuchea, or Thailand after 1950 and before October 22, 1982.**—

(1) Any alien claiming to be an alien described in paragraph (2)(A) of this subsection (or any person on behalf of such an alien) may file a petition with the Attorney General for classification under section 201(b), 203(a)(1), or 203(a)(3), as appropriate. After an investigation of the facts of each case the Attorney General shall, if the conditions described in paragraph (2) are met, approve the petition and forward one copy to the Secretary of State.

(2) The Attorney General may approve a petition for an alien under paragraph (1) if—

    (A) he has reason to believe that the alien

        (i) was born in Korea, Vietnam, Laos, Kampuchea, or Thailand after 1950 and before the date of the enactment of this subsection, and

        (ii) was fathered by a United States citizen;

    (B) he has received an acceptable guarantee of legal custody and financial responsibility described in paragraph (4); and

    (C) in the case of an alien under eighteen years of age,

        (i) the alien's placement with a sponsor in the United States has been arranged by an appropriate public, private, or State child welfare agency licensed in the United States and actively involved in the intercountry placement of children and

        (ii) the alien's mother or guardian has in writing irrevocably released the alien for emigration.

(3) In considering petitions filed under paragraph (1), the Attorney General shall—

    (A) consult with appropriate governmental officials and officials of private voluntary organizations in the country of the alien's birth in order to make the determinations described in subparagraphs (A) and (C)(ii) of paragraph (2); and

    (B) consider the physical appearance of the alien and any evidence provided by the petitioner, including birth and baptismal certificates, local civil records, photographs of, and letters or proof of financial support from, a putative father who is a citizen of the United States, and the testimony of witnesses, to the extent it is relevant or probative.

(4) (A) A guarantee of legal custody and financial responsibility for an alien described in paragraph (2) must—

        (i) be signed in the presence of an immigration officer or consular officer by an individual (hereinafter in this paragraph referred to as the "sponsor") who is twenty-

---

[42] *Sic.* This should probably read "… admitted to the United States… "

one years of age or older, is of good moral character, and is a citizen of the United States or alien lawfully admitted for permanent residence, and

(ii) provide that the sponsor agrees—

(I) in the case of an alien under eighteen years of age, to assume legal custody for the alien after the alien's departure to the United States and until the alien becomes eighteen years of age, in accordance with the laws of the State where the alien and the sponsor will reside, and

(II) to furnish, during the five-year period beginning on the date of the alien's acquiring the status of an alien lawfully admitted for permanent residence, or during the period beginning on the date of the alien's acquiring the status of an alien lawfully admitted for permanent residence and ending on the date on which the alien becomes twenty-one years of age, whichever period is longer, such financial support as is necessary to maintain the family in the United States of which the alien is a member at a level equal to at least 125 per centum of the current official poverty line (as established by the Director of the Office of Management and Budget, under section 673(2) of the Omnibus Budget Reconciliation Act of 1981 and as revised by the Secretary of Health and Human Services under the second and third sentences of such section) for a family of the same size as the size of the alien's family.

(B) A guarantee of legal custody and financial responsibility described in subparagraph (A) may be enforced with respect to an alien against his sponsor in a civil suit brought by the Attorney General in the United States district court for the district in which the sponsor resides, except that a sponsor or his estate shall not be liable under such a guarantee if the sponsor dies or is adjudicated a bankrupt under title 11, United States Code.

**(g) Restriction on petitions based on marriages entered while in exclusion or deportation proceedings.**— Notwithstanding subsection (a), except as provided in section 245(e)(3), a petition may not be approved to grant an alien immediate relative status or preference status by reason of a marriage which was entered into during the period described in section 245(e)(2), until the alien has resided outside the United States for a 2-year period beginning after the date of the marriage.

**(h) Survival of rights to petition.**— The legal termination of a marriage may not be the sole basis for revocation under section 205 of a petition filed under subsection (a)(1)(A)(iii) or a petition filed under subsection (a)(1)(B)(ii) pursuant to conditions described in subsection (a)(1)(A)(iii)(I). Remarriage of an alien whose petition was approved under section 204(a)(1)(B)(ii) or 204(a)(1)(A)(iii) or marriage of an alien described in clause (iv) or (vi) of section 204(a)(1)(A) or in section 204(a)(1)(B)(iii) shall not be the basis for revocation of a petition approval under section 205.

**(i) Professional athletes.**—

(1) *In general.*— A petition under subsection (a)(4)(D)[43] for classification of a professional athlete shall remain valid for the athlete after the athlete changes employers, if the new employer is a team in the same sport as the team which was the employer who filed the petition.

(2) *Definition.*— For purposes of paragraph (1), the term "professional athlete" means an individual who is employed as an athlete by—

---

[43] *Sic.* This should probably be subsection (a)(1)(D).

(A) a team that is a member of an association of 6 or more professional sports teams whose total combined revenues exceed $10,000,000 per year, if the association governs the conduct of its members and regulates the contests and exhibitions in which its member teams regularly engage; or

(B) any minor league team that is affiliated with such an association.

**(j) Job flexibility for long delayed applicants for adjustment of status to permanent residence.**— A petition under subsection (a)(1)(D)[44] for an individual whose application for adjustment of status pursuant to section 245 has been filed and remained unadjudicated for 180 days or more shall remain valid with respect to a new job if the individual changes jobs or employers if the new job is in the same or a similar occupational classification as the job for which the petition was filed.

**(k) Procedures for unmarried sons and daughters of citizens.**—[45]

(1) *In general.*— Except as provided in paragraph (2), in the case of a petition under this section initially filed for an alien unmarried son or daughter's classification as a family-sponsored immigrant under section 203(a)(2)(B), based on a parent of the son or daughter being an alien lawfully admitted for permanent residence, if such parent subsequently becomes a naturalized citizen of the United States, such petition shall be converted to a petition to classify the unmarried son or daughter as a family-sponsored immigrant under section 203(a)(1).

(2) *Exception.*— Paragraph (1) does not apply if the son or daughter files with the Attorney General a written statement that he or she elects not to have such conversion occur (or if it has occurred, to have such conversion revoked). Where such an election has been made, any determination with respect to the son or daughter's eligibility for admission as a family-sponsored immigrant shall be made as if such naturalization had not taken place.

(3) *Priority date.*— Regardless of whether a petition is converted under this subsection or not, if an unmarried son or daughter described in this subsection was assigned a priority date with respect to such petition before such naturalization, he or she may maintain that priority date.

(4) *Clarification.*— This subsection shall apply to a petition if it is properly filed, regardless of whether it was approved or not before such naturalization.

**(*l*) Surviving Relative Consideration for Certain Petitions and Applications.**—

(1) In general.— An alien described in paragraph (2) who resided in the United States at the time of the death of the qualifying relative and who continues to reside in the United States shall have such petition described in paragraph (2), or an application for adjustment of status to that of a person admitted for lawful permanent residence based upon the family relationship described in paragraph (2), and any related applications, adjudicated notwithstanding the death of the qualifying relative, unless the Secretary of Homeland Security determines, in the unreviewable discretion of the Secretary, that approval would not be in the public interest.

(2) Alien described.— An alien described in this paragraph is an alien who, immediately prior to the death of his or her qualifying relative, was—

(A) the beneficiary of a pending or approved petition for classification as an immediate relative (as described in section 201(b)(2)(A)(i));

---

[44] *Sic.* This should probably be subsection (a)(1)(F).

[45] *See* note 33, *supra.*

(B) the beneficiary of a pending or approved petition for classification under section 203 (a) or (d);

(C) a derivative beneficiary of a pending or approved petition for classification under section 203(b) (as described in section 203(d));

(D) the beneficiary of a pending or approved refugee/asylee relative petition under section 207 or 208;

(E) an alien admitted in 'T' nonimmigrant status as described in section 101(a)(15)(T)(ii) or in 'U' nonimmigrant status as described in section 101(a)(15)(U)(ii); or

(F) an asylee (as described in section 208(b)(3)).

(June 27, 1952, ch. 477, title II, ch. 1, §204, 66 Stat. 179; as amended by P.L. 87-885 (10/24/62); P.L. 89-236 (10/3/65); P.L. 94-571 (10/20/76); P.L. 95-417 (10/5/78); P.L. 96-470 (10/19/80); P.L. 97-116 (12/29/81); P.L. 97-359 (10/22/82); P.L. 99-639 (11/10/86); P.L. 100-525 (10/24/88); P.L. 101-649 (IMMACT90) (11/29/90); P.L. 102-232 (MTINA) (12/12/91, *effective* 4/1/92); P.L. 103-322 (VAWA) (9/13/94); P.L. 103-416 (INTCA) (10/25/94, *effective* 4/1/95); P.L. 104-208 (IIRAIRA) (9/30/96), div. C, title III, §308, title VI, §624 [adding (i)]; P.L. 106-279 (10/6/00), title III, §302; P.L. 106-313 (AC21) (10/17/00), title I, §106 [adding (j)]; P.L. 106-386 (10/28/00), div. B, title V, §1503, §1507; P.L. 107-208 (CSPA) (8/6/02), §6 [adding (k)], §7 [adding (a)(1)(D)(iii)]; P.L. 109-162 (1/5/06), title VIII, §805, §814, §816 [revising (a)(1)(D)(i) & adding (a)(1)(A)(vii), (a)(1)(D)(iv)–(v), & (a)(1)(K)–(L)]; P.L. 109-248 (7/27/06), §402 [revising (a)(1)(A)(i) & (B)(i); & adding (a)(1)(A)(viii) & (B)(i)(II)]; P.L. 109-271 (8/12/06), §6 [revising (a)(1)(D)(v)]; P.L. 111-83 (10/28/09) §568(d) [adding (*l*)].)

## Sec. 205 Revocation of Approval of Petitions; Notice of Revocation; Effective Date
## [8 U.S.C. 1155]

The Secretary of Homeland Security may, at any time, for what he deems to be good and sufficient cause, revoke the approval of any petition approved by him under section 204. Such revocation shall be effective as of the date of approval of any such petition.[46]

(June 27, 1952, ch. 477, title II, ch. 1, §205, 66 Stat. 180; as amended by P.L. 86-363 (9/22/59); P.L. 87-301 (9/26/61); P.L. 89-236 (10/3/65); P.L. 104-208 (9/30/96), div. C, title III, §308; P.L. 108-458 (12/17/04), §5304.)

## Sec. 206 Unused Immigrant Visas
## [8 U.S.C. 1156]

If an immigrant having an immigrant visa is denied admission to the United States and removed, or does not apply for admission before the expiration of the validity of his visa, or if an alien having an immigrant visa issued to him as a preference immigrant is found not to be a preference immigrant, an immigrant visa or a preference immigrant visa, as the case may be, may be issued in lieu thereof to another qualified alien.

(June 27, 1952, ch. 477, title II, ch. 1, §206, 66 Stat. 181; as amended by P.L. 89-236 (10/3/65); P.L. 104-208 (9/30/96), div. C, title III, §308.)

---

[46] Amended by §5304 of P.L. 108-458 (12/17/04). Amendment applicable to revocations under INA §§205 and 221(i) made before, on, or after 12/17/04.

## Sec. 207 Annual Admission of Refugees and Admission of Emergency Situation Refugees[47]
**[8 U.S.C. 1157]**

**(a) Maximum number of admissions; increases for humanitarian concerns; allocations.—**

(1) Except as provided in subsection (b), the number of refugees who may be admitted under this section in fiscal year 1980, 1981, or 1982, may not exceed fifty thousand unless the President determines, before the beginning of the fiscal year and after appropriate consultation (as defined in subsection (e)), that admission of a specific number of refugees in excess of such number is justified by humanitarian concerns or is otherwise in the national interest.

(2) Except as provided in subsection (b), the number of refugees who may be admitted under this section in any fiscal year after fiscal year 1982 shall be such number as the President determines, before the beginning of the fiscal year and after appropriate consultation, is justified by humanitarian concerns or is otherwise in the national interest.

(3) Admissions under this subsection shall be allocated among refugees of special humanitarian concern to the United States in accordance with a determination made by the President after appropriate consultation.

(4) In the determination made under this subsection for each fiscal year (beginning with fiscal year 1992), the President shall enumerate, with the respective number of refugees so determined, the number of aliens who were granted asylum in the previous year.

**(b) Determinations by President respecting number of admissions for humanitarian concerns.**— If the President determines, after appropriate consultation, that—

(1) an unforeseen emergency refugee situation exists,

(2) the admission of certain refugees in response to the emergency refugee situation is justified by grave humanitarian concerns or is otherwise in the national interest, and

(3) the admission to the United States of these refugees cannot be accomplished under subsection (a), the President may fix a number of refugees to be admitted to the United States during the succeeding period (not to exceed twelve months) in response to the emergency refugee situation and such admissions shall be allocated among refugees of special humanitarian concern to the United States in accordance with a determination made by the President after the appropriate consultation provided under this subsection.

**(c) Admission by Attorney General of refugees; criteria; admission status of spouse or child; applicability of other statutory requirements; termination of refugee status of alien, spouse or child.—**

(1) Subject to the numerical limitations established pursuant to subsections (a) and (b), the Attorney General may, in the Attorney General's discretion and pursuant to such regulations as the Attorney General may prescribe, admit any refugee who is not firmly resettled in any foreign country, is determined to be of special humanitarian concern to the United States, and is admissible (except as otherwise provided under paragraph (3)) as an immigrant under this Act.

(2) (A) A spouse or child (as defined in section 101(b)(1)(A), (B), (C), (D), or (E)) of any refugee who qualifies for admission under paragraph (1) shall, if not otherwise entitled to

---

[47] P.L. 107-185 (5/30/02) extends eligibility for refugee status of unmarried sons and daughters of certain Vietnamese refugees. Sec. 309 of the Enhanced Border Security and Visa Entry Reform Act, 2002, P.L. 107-173 (5/14/02) requires the attorney general, by 180 days after enactment, to ensure that aliens admitted under INA §207 immediately be issued an employment authorization document.

admission under paragraph (1) and if not a person described in the second sentence of section 101(a)(42), be entitled to the same admission status as such refugee if accompanying, or following to join, such refugee and if the spouse or child is admissible (except as otherwise provided under paragraph (3)) as an immigrant under this Act. Upon the spouse's or child's admission to the United States, such admission shall be charged against the numerical limitation established in accordance with the appropriate subsection under which the refugee's admission is charged.

(B) An unmarried alien who seeks to accompany, or follow to join, a parent granted admission as a refugee under this subsection, and who was under 21 years of age on the date on which such parent applied for refugee status under this section, shall continue to be classified as a child for purposes of this paragraph, if the alien attained 21 years of age after such application was filed but while it was pending.[48]

(3) The provisions of paragraphs (4), (5), and (7)(A) of section 212(a) shall not be applicable to any alien seeking admission to the United States under this subsection, and the Attorney General may waive any other provision of such section (other than paragraph (2)(C) or subparagraph (A), (B), (C), or (E) of paragraph (3)) with respect to such an alien for humanitarian purposes, to assure family unity, or when it is otherwise in the public interest. Any such waiver by the Attorney General shall be in writing and shall be granted only on an individual basis following an investigation. The Attorney General shall provide for the annual reporting to Congress of the number of waivers granted under this paragraph in the previous fiscal year and a summary of the reasons for granting such waivers.

(4) The refugee status of any alien (and of the spouse or child of the alien) may be terminated by the Attorney General pursuant to such regulations as the Attorney General may prescribe if the Attorney General determines that the alien was not in fact a refugee within the meaning of section 101(a)(42) at the time of the alien's admission.

**(d) Oversight reporting and consultation requirements.—**

(1) Before the start of each fiscal year the President shall report to the Committees on the Judiciary of the House of Representatives and of the Senate regarding the foreseeable number of refugees who will be in need of resettlement during the fiscal year and the anticipated allocation of refugee admissions during the fiscal year. The President shall provide for periodic discussions between designated representatives of the President and members of such committees regarding changes in the worldwide refugee situation, the progress of refugee admissions, and the possible need for adjustments in the allocation of admissions among refugees.

(2) As soon as possible after representatives of the President initiate appropriate consultation with respect to the number of refugee admissions under subsection (a) or with respect to the admission of refugees in response to an emergency refugee situation under subsection (b), the Committees on the Judiciary of the House of Representatives and of the Senate shall cause to have printed in the Congressional Record the substance of such consultation.

(3) (A) After the President initiates appropriate consultation prior to making a determination under subsection (a), a hearing to review the proposed determination shall be held unless public disclosure of the details of the proposal would jeopardize the lives or safety of individuals.

---

[48] *See* note 33, *supra*.

(B) After the President initiates appropriate consultation prior to making a determination, under subsection (b), that the number of refugee admissions should be increased because of an unforeseen emergency refugee situation, to the extent that time and the nature of the emergency refugee situation permit, a hearing to review the proposal to increase refugee admissions shall be held unless public disclosure of the details of the proposal would jeopardize the lives or safety of individuals.

(e) **"Appropriate consultation" defined.**— For purposes of this section, the term "appropriate consultation" means, with respect to the admission of refugees and allocation of refugee admissions, discussions in person by designated Cabinet-level representatives of the President with members of the Committees on the Judiciary of the Senate and of the House of Representatives to review the refugee situation or emergency refugee situation, to project the extent of possible participation of the United States therein, to discuss the reasons for believing that the proposed admission of refugees is justified by humanitarian concerns or grave humanitarian concerns or is otherwise in the national interest, and to provide such members with the following information:

(1) A description of the nature of the refugee situation.

(2) A description of the number and allocation of the refugees to be admitted and an analysis of conditions within the countries from which they came.

(3) A description of the proposed plans for their movement and resettlement and the estimated cost of their movement and resettlement.

(4) An analysis of the anticipated social, economic, and demographic impact of their admission to the United States.

(5) A description of the extent to which other countries will admit and assist in the resettlement of such refugees.

(6) An analysis of the impact of the participation of the United States in the resettlement of such refugee on the foreign policy interests of the United States.

(7) Such additional information as may be appropriate or requested by such members.

To the extent possible, information described in this subsection shall be provided at least two weeks in advance of discussions in person by designated representatives of the President with such members.

(f) **Training.**—

(1) The Attorney General, in consultation with the Secretary of State, shall provide all United States officials adjudicating refugee cases under this section with the same training as that provided to officers adjudicating asylum cases under section 208.

(2) Such training shall include country-specific conditions, instruction on the internationally recognized right to freedom of religion, instruction on methods of religious persecution practiced in foreign countries, and applicable distinctions within a country between the nature of and treatment of various religious practices and believers.

(June 27, 1952, ch. 477, title II, ch. 1, §207, as added by P.L. 96-212 (3/17/80); as amended by P.L. 100-525 (10/24/88); P.L. 101-649 (IMMACT90) (11/29/90); P.L. 102-232 (MTINA) (12/12/91, *effective* 4/1/92); P.L. 104-208 (IIRAIRA) (9/30/96), div. C, title VI, §601 [adding (a)(5)]; P.L. 105-292 (10/27/98), §602 [adding (f)]; P.L. 107-208 (CSPA) (8/6/02), §5 [adding (c)(2)(B)]; P.L. 109-13 (REAL ID) (5/11/05), title I, §101(g) [removing (a)(5)].)

## Sec. 208 Asylum[49]
**[8 U.S.C. 1158]**

### (a) Authority to apply for asylum.—

(1) *In general.*— Any alien who is physically present in the United States or who arrives in the United States (whether or not at a designated port of arrival and including an alien who is brought to the United States after having been interdicted in international or United States waters), irrespective of such alien's status, may apply for asylum in accordance with this section or, where applicable, section 235(b).

(2) *Exceptions.*—

(A) *Safe third country.*— Paragraph (1) shall not apply to an alien if the Attorney General determines that the alien may be removed, pursuant to a bilateral or multilateral agreement, to a country (other than the country of the alien's nationality or, in the case of an alien having no nationality, the country of the alien's last habitual residence) in which the alien's life or freedom would not be threatened on account of race, religion, nationality, membership in a particular social group, or political opinion, and where the alien would have access to a full and fair procedure for determining a claim to asylum or equivalent temporary protection, unless the Attorney General finds that it is in the public interest for the alien to receive asylum in the United States.

(B) *Time limit.*— Subject to subparagraph (D), paragraph (1) shall not apply to an alien unless the alien demonstrates by clear and convincing evidence that the application has been filed within 1 year after the date of alien's arrival in the United States.

(C) *Previous asylum applications.*— Subject to subparagraph (D), paragraph (1) shall not apply to an alien if the alien has previously applied for asylum and had such application denied.

(D) *Changed circumstances.*— An application for asylum of an alien may be considered, notwithstanding subparagraphs (B) and (C), if the alien demonstrates to the satisfaction of the Attorney General either the existence of changed circumstances which materially affect the applicant's eligibility for asylum or extraordinary circumstances relating to the delay in filing the application within the period specified in subparagraph (B).

(E) *Applicability.*— Subparagraphs (A) and (B) shall not apply to an unaccompanied alien child (as defined in section 462(g) of the Homeland Security Act of 2002 (6 U.S.C. 279(g))).

(3) *Limitation on judicial review.*— No court shall have jurisdiction to review any determination of the Attorney General under paragraph (2).

### (b) Conditions for granting asylum.—

(1) *In general.*—

(A) *Eligibility.*— The Secretary of Homeland Security or the Attorney General may grant asylum to an alien who has applied for asylum in accordance with the requirements and

---

[49] Added by §604(a) of IIRAIRA, effective for "applications for asylum filed on or after the first day of the first month beginning more than 180 days after the date of the enactment of [IIRAIRA]."

Sec. 309 of the Enhanced Border Security and Visa Entry Reform Act, 2002, P.L. 107-173 (5/14/02) requires the attorney general, by 180 days after enactment, to ensure that aliens granted asylum under INA §208 immediately be issued an employment authorization document.

procedures established by the Secretary of Homeland Security or the Attorney General under this section if the Secretary of Homeland Security or the Attorney General determines that such alien is a refugee within the meaning of section 101(a)(42)(A).[50]

(B) *Burden of proof.*—[51]

(i) In general.— The burden of proof is on the applicant to establish that the applicant is a refugee, within the meaning of section 101(a)(42)(A). To establish that the applicant is a refugee within the meaning of such section, the applicant must establish that race, religion, nationality, membership in a particular social group, or political opinion was or will be at least one central reason for persecuting the applicant.

(ii) Sustaining burden.— The testimony of the applicant may be sufficient to sustain the applicant's burden without corroboration, but only if the applicant satisfies the trier of fact that the applicant's testimony is credible, is persuasive, and refers to specific facts sufficient to demonstrate that the applicant is a refugee. In determining whether the applicant has met the applicant's burden, the trier of fact may weigh the credible testimony along with other evidence of record. Where the trier of fact determines that the applicant should provide evidence that corroborates otherwise credible testimony, such evidence must be provided unless the applicant does not have the evidence and cannot reasonably obtain the evidence.

(iii) Credibility determination.— Considering the totality of the circumstances, and all relevant factors, a trier of fact may base a credibility determination on the demeanor, candor, or responsiveness of the applicant or witness, the inherent plausibility of the applicant's or witness's account, the consistency between the applicant's or witness's written and oral statements (whenever made and whether or not under oath, and considering the circumstances under which the statements were made), the internal consistency of each such statement, the consistency of such statements with other evidence of record (including the reports of the Department of State on country conditions), and any inaccuracies or falsehoods in such statements, without regard to whether an inconsistency, inaccuracy, or falsehood goes to the heart of the applicant's claim, or any other relevant factor. There is no presumption of credibility, however, if no adverse credibility determination is explicitly made, the applicant or witness shall have a rebuttable presumption of credibility on appeal.

(2) *Exceptions.*—

(A) *In general.*— Paragraph (1) shall not apply to an alien if the Attorney General determines that—

(i) the alien ordered, incited, assisted, or otherwise participated in the persecution of any person on account of race, religion, nationality, membership in a particular social group, or political opinion;

(ii) the alien, having been convicted by a final judgment of a particularly serious crime, constitutes a danger to the community of the United States;

---

[50] The amendments made by §§101(a)(1)–(2) of REAL ID Act, P.L. 109-13 (5/11/05), took effect as if enacted on 3/1/03.

[51] The amendment made by §101(a)(3) of REAL ID Act, P.L. 109-13, took effect on the date of enactment (5/11/05) and applies to applications for asylum, withholding, or other relief from removal made on or after such date.

(iii) there are serious reasons for believing that the alien has committed a serious nonpolitical crime outside the United States prior to the arrival of the alien in the United States;

(iv) there are reasonable grounds for regarding the alien as a danger to the security of the United States;

(v) the alien is described in subclause (I), (II), (III), (IV), or (VI) of section 212(a)(3)(B)(i) or section 237(a)(4)(B) (relating to terrorist activity), unless, in the case only of an alien described in subclause (IV) of section 212(a)(3)(B)(i), the Attorney General determines, in the Attorney General's discretion, that there are not reasonable grounds for regarding the alien as a danger to the security of the United States; or[52]

(vi) the alien was firmly resettled in another country prior to arriving in the United States.

(B) *Special rules.*—

(i) Conviction of aggravated felony.— For purposes of clause (ii) of subparagraph (A), an alien who has been convicted of an aggravated felony shall be considered to have been convicted of a particularly serious crime.

(ii) Offenses.— The Attorney General may designate by regulation offenses that will be considered to be a crime described in clause (ii) or (iii) of subparagraph (A).

(C) *Additional limitations.*— The Attorney General may by regulation establish additional limitations and conditions, consistent with this section, under which an alien shall be ineligible for asylum under paragraph (1).

(D) *No judicial review.*— There shall be no judicial review of a determination of the Attorney General under subparagraph (A)(v).

(3) *Treatment of spouse and children.*—[53]

(A) *In general.*— A spouse or child (as defined in section 101(b)(1)(A), (B), (C), (D), or (E)) of an alien who is granted asylum under this subsection may, if not otherwise eligible for asylum under this section, be granted the same status as the alien if accompanying, or following to join, such alien.

(B) *Continued classification of certain aliens as children.*— An unmarried alien who seeks to accompany, or follow to join, a parent granted asylum under this subsection, and who was under 21 years of age on the date on which such parent applied for asylum under this section, shall continue to be classified as a child for purposes of this paragraph and section 209(b)(3), if the alien attained 21 years of age after such application was filed but while it was pending.

(C) *Initial jurisdiction.*— An asylum officer (as defined in section 235(b)(1)(E)) shall have initial jurisdiction over any asylum application filed by an unaccompanied alien child (as defined in section 462(g) of the Homeland Security Act of 2002 (6 U.S.C. 279(g))), regardless of whether filed in accordance with this section or section 235(b).

---

[52] The amendment made by §101(b) of REAL ID Act, P.L. 109-13, took effect on the date of enactment (5/11/05) and applies to applications for asylum, withholding, or other relief from removal made on or after such date.

[53] *See* note 33, *supra.*

**(c) Asylum status.—**

(1) *In general.*— In the case of an alien granted asylum under subsection (b), the Attorney General—

(A) shall not remove or return the alien to the alien's country of nationality or, in the case of a person having no nationality, the country of the alien's last habitual residence;

(B) shall authorize the alien to engage in employment in the United States and provide the alien with appropriate endorsement of that authorization; and

(C) may allow the alien to travel abroad with the prior consent of the Attorney General.

(2) *Termination of asylum.*— Asylum granted under subsection (b) does not convey a right to remain permanently in the United States, and may be terminated if the Attorney General determines that—

(A) the alien no longer meets the conditions described in subsection (b)(1) owing to a fundamental change in circumstances;

(B) the alien meets a condition described in subsection (b)(2);

(C) the alien may be removed, pursuant to a bilateral or multilateral agreement, to a country (other than the country of the alien's nationality or, in the case of an alien having no nationality, the country of the alien's last habitual residence) in which the alien's life or freedom would not be threatened on account of race, religion, nationality, membership in a particular social group, or political opinion, and where the alien is eligible to receive asylum or equivalent temporary protection;

(D) the alien has voluntarily availed himself or herself of the protection of the alien's country of nationality or, in the case of an alien having no nationality, the alien's country of last habitual residence, by returning to such country with permanent resident status or the reasonable possibility of obtaining such status with the same rights and obligations pertaining to other permanent residents of that country; or

(E) the alien has acquired a new nationality and enjoys the protection of the country of his or her new nationality.

(3) *Removal when asylum is terminated.*— An alien described in paragraph (2) is subject to any applicable grounds of inadmissibility or deportability under section 212(a) and 237(a), and the alien's removal or return shall be directed by the Attorney General in accordance with sections 240 and 241.

**(d) Asylum procedure.—**

(1) *Applications.*— The Attorney General shall establish a procedure for the consideration of asylum applications filed under subsection (a). The Attorney General may require applicants to submit fingerprints and a photograph at such time and in such manner to be determined by regulation by the Attorney General.

(2) *Employment.*— An applicant for asylum is not entitled to employment authorization, but such authorization may be provided under regulation by the Attorney General. An applicant who is not otherwise eligible for employment authorization shall not be granted such authorization prior to 180 days after the date of filing of the application for asylum.

(3) *Fees.*— The Attorney General may impose fees for the consideration of an application for asylum, for employment authorization under this section, and for adjustment of status under

section 209(b). Such fees shall not exceed the Attorney General's costs in adjudicating the applications. The Attorney General may provide for the assessment and payment of such fees over a period of time or by installments. Nothing in this paragraph shall be construed to require the Attorney General to charge fees for adjudication services provided to asylum applicants, or to limit the authority of the Attorney General to set adjudication and naturalization fees in accordance with section 286(m).

(4) *Notice of privilege of counsel and consequences of frivolous application.*— At the time of filing an application for asylum, the Attorney General shall—

(A) advise the alien of the privilege of being represented by counsel and of the consequences, under paragraph (6), of knowingly filing a frivolous application for asylum; and

(B) provide the alien a list of persons (updated not less often than quarterly) who have indicated their availability to represent aliens in asylum proceedings on a pro bono basis.

(5) *Consideration of asylum applications.*—

(A) *Procedures.*— The procedure established under paragraph (1) shall provide that—

(i) asylum cannot be granted until the identity of the applicant has been checked against all appropriate records or databases maintained by the Attorney General and by the Secretary of State, including the Automated Visa Lookout System, to determine any grounds on which the alien may be inadmissible to or deportable from the United States, or ineligible to apply for or be granted asylum;

(ii) in the absence of exceptional circumstances, the initial interview or hearing on the asylum application shall commence not later than 45 days after the date an application is filed;

(iii) in the absence of exceptional circumstances, final administrative adjudication of the asylum application, not including administrative appeal, shall be completed within 180 days after the date an application is filed;

(iv) any administrative appeal shall be filed within 30 days of a decision granting or denying asylum, or within 30 days of the completion of removal proceedings before an immigration judge under section 240, whichever is later; and

(v) in the case of an applicant for asylum who fails without prior authorization or in the absence of exceptional circumstances to appear for an interview or hearing, including a hearing under section 240, the application may be dismissed or the applicant may be otherwise sanctioned for such failure.

(B) *Additional regulatory conditions.*— The Attorney General may provide by regulation for any other conditions or limitations on the consideration of an application for asylum not inconsistent with this Act.

(6) *Frivolous applications.*— If the Attorney General determines that an alien has knowingly made a frivolous application for asylum and the alien has received the notice under paragraph (4)(A), the alien shall be permanently ineligible for any benefits under this Act, effective as of the date of a final determination on such application.

(7) *No private right of action.*— Nothing in this subsection shall be construed to create any substantive or procedural right or benefit that is legally enforceable by any party against the United States or its agencies or officers or any other person.

**(e) Commonwealth of the Northern Mariana Islands.**— The provisions of this section and section 209(b) shall apply to persons physically present in the Commonwealth of the Northern Mariana Islands or arriving in the Commonwealth (whether or not at a designated port of arrival and including persons who are brought to the Commonwealth after having been interdicted in international or United States waters) only on or after January 1, 2014.

(June 27, 1952, ch. 477, title II, ch. 1, §208, as added by P.L. 96-212 (3/17/80); as amended by P.L. 101-649 (IMMACT90) (11/29/90); P.L. 103-322 (VAWA) (9/13/94); P.L. 104-132 (AEDPA) (4/24/96), title IV, §421; P.L. 104-208 (IIRAIRA) (9/30/96), div. C, title VI, §604; P.L. 107-56 (PATRIOT Act) (10/26/01), title IV, §411(b) [revising (b)(2)(A)(v)]; P.L. 107-208 (CSPA) (8/6/02), §4; P.L. 109-13 (REAL ID) (5/11/05), div. B, title I, §101 [revising (b)(1)(A), (b)(2)(A)(v); & adding (b)(1)(B)]; P.L. 110-229 (5/8/08) §702(j) [adding (e)]; P.L. 110-457 (12/23/08) [adding (a)(2)(E) & (b)(3)(C)].)

## Sec. 209 Adjustment of Status of Refugees
[8 U.S.C. 1159]

**(a) Criteria and procedures applicable for admission as immigrant; effect of adjustment.**

(1) Any alien who has been admitted to the United States under section 207—

(A) whose admission has not been terminated by the Secretary of Homeland Security or the Attorney General pursuant to such regulations as the Secretary of Homeland Security or the Attorney General may prescribe,

(B) who has been physically present in the United States for at least one year, and

(C) who has not acquired permanent resident status,

shall, at the end of such year period, return or be returned to the custody of the Department of Homeland Security for inspection and examination for admission to the United States as an immigrant in accordance with the provisions of sections 235, 240, and 241.

(2) Any alien who is found upon inspection and examination by an immigration officer pursuant to paragraph (1) or after a hearing before an immigration judge to be admissible (except as otherwise provided under subsection (c)) as an immigrant under this Act at the time of the alien's inspection and examination shall, notwithstanding any numerical limitation specified in this Act, be regarded as lawfully admitted to the United States for permanent residence as of the date of such alien's arrival into the United States.

**(b) Maximum number of adjustments; recordkeeping.**— The Secretary of Homeland Security or the Attorney General, in the Secretary's or the Attorney General's discretion and under such regulations as the Secretary or the Attorney General may prescribe, may adjust to the status of an alien lawfully admitted for permanent residence the status of any alien granted asylum who—

(1) applies for such adjustment,

(2) has been physically present in the United States for at least one year after being granted asylum,

(3) continues to be a refugee within the meaning of section 101(a)(42)(A) or a spouse or child of such a refugee,

(4) is not firmly resettled in any foreign country, and

(5) is admissible (except as otherwise provided under subsection (c)) as an immigrant under this Act at the time of examination for adjustment of such alien.

Upon approval of an application under this subsection, the Secretary of Homeland Security or the Attorney General shall establish a record of the alien's admission for lawful permanent residence as of the date one year before the date of the approval of the application.

**(c) Applicability of other federal statutory requirements.**— The provisions of paragraphs (4), (5), and (7)(A) of section 212(a) shall not be applicable to any alien seeking adjustment of status under this section, and the Secretary of Homeland Security or the Attorney General may waive any other provision of such section (other than paragraph (2)(C) or subparagraph (A), (B), (C), or (E) of paragraph (3)) with respect to such an alien for humanitarian purposes, to assure family unity, or when it is otherwise in the public interest.

(June 27, 1952, ch. 477, title II, ch. 1, §209, as added by P.L. 96-212 (3/17/80); as amended by P.L. 101-649 (IMMACT90) (11/29/90); P.L. 102-232 (MTINA) (12/12/91, *effective* 4/1/92); P.L. 104-208 (IIRAIRA) (9/30/96), div. C, title III, §308, §371; P.L. 109-13 (REAL ID) (5/11/05), div. B, title I, §101(g) [revising (a)–(c)].)

## Sec. 210 Special Agricultural Workers
## [8 U.S.C. 1160]

**(a) Lawful residence.—**

(1) *In general.*— The Attorney General shall adjust the status of an alien to that of an alien lawfully admitted for temporary residence if the Attorney General determines that the alien meets the following requirements:

(A) *Application period.*— The alien must apply for such adjustment during the 18-month period beginning on the first day of the seventh month that begins after the date of enactment of this section.

(B) *Performance of seasonal agricultural services and residence in the United States.*— The alien must establish that he has—

(i) resided in the United States, and

(ii) performed seasonal agricultural services in the United States for at least 90 man-days,

during the 12-month period ending on May 1, 1986. For purposes of the previous sentence, performance of seasonal agricultural services in the United States for more than one employer on any one day shall be counted as performance of services for only 1 man-day.

(C) *Admissible as immigrant.*— The alien must establish that he is admissible to the United States as an immigrant, except as otherwise provided under subsection (c)(2).

(2) *Adjustment to permanent residence.*— The Attorney General shall adjust the status of any alien provided lawful temporary resident status under paragraph (1) to that of an alien lawfully admitted for permanent residence on the following date:

(A) *Group 1.*— Subject to the numerical limitation established under subparagraph (C), in the case of an alien who has established, at the time of application for temporary residence under paragraph (1), that the alien performed seasonal agricultural services in the United States for at least 90 man-days during each of the 12-month periods ending on May 1, 1984, 1985, and 1986, the adjustment shall occur on the first day after the end of the one-year period that begins on the later of (I) the date the alien was granted such temporary resident status, or (II) the day after the last day of the application period described in paragraph (1)(A).

(B) *Group 2.*— In the case of aliens to which subparagraph (A) does not apply, the adjustment shall occur on the day after the last day of the two-year period that begins on the later of (I) the date the alien was granted such temporary resident status, or (II) the day after the last day of the application period described in paragraph (1)(A).

(C) *Numerical limitation.*— Subparagraph (A) shall not apply to more than 350,000 aliens. If more than 350,000 aliens meet the requirements of such subparagraph, such subparagraph shall apply to the 350,000 aliens whose applications for adjustment were first filed under paragraph (1) and subparagraph (B) shall apply to the remaining aliens.

(3) *Termination of temporary residence.*—

(A) During the period of temporary resident status granted an alien under paragraph (1), the Attorney General may terminate such status only upon a determination under this Act that the alien is deportable.

(B) Before any alien becomes eligible for adjustment of status under paragraph (2), the Attorney General may deny adjustment to permanent status and provide for termination of the temporary resident status granted such alien under paragraph (1) if—

(i) the Attorney General finds by a preponderance of the evidence that the adjustment to temporary resident status was the result of fraud or willful misrepresentation as set out in section 212(a)(6)(C)(i), or

(ii) the alien commits an act that (I) makes the alien inadmissible to the United States as an immigrant, except as provided under subsection (c)(2), or (II) is convicted of a felony or 3 or more misdemeanors committed in the United States.

(4) *Authorized travel and employment during temporary residence.*— During the period an alien is in lawful temporary resident status granted under this subsection, the alien has the right to travel abroad (including commutation from a residence abroad) and shall be granted authorization to engage in employment in the United States and shall be provided an "employment authorized" endorsement or other appropriate work permit, in the same manner as for aliens lawfully admitted for permanent residence.

(5) *In general.*— Except as otherwise provided in this subsection, an alien who acquires the status of an alien lawfully admitted for temporary residence under paragraph (1), such status not having changed, is considered to be an alien lawfully admitted for permanent residence (as described in section 101(a)(20)), other than under any provision of the immigration laws.

**(b) Applications for adjustment of status.—**

(1) *To whom may be made.*—

(A) *Within the United States.*— The Attorney General shall provide that applications for adjustment of status under subsection (a) may be filed—

(i) with the Attorney General, or

(ii) with a designated entity (designated under paragraph (2)), but only if the applicant consents to the forwarding of the application to the Attorney General.

(B) *Outside the United States.*— The Attorney General, in cooperation with the Secretary of State, shall provide a procedure whereby an alien may apply for adjustment of status under subsection (a)(1) at an appropriate consular office outside the United States. If the alien otherwise qualifies for such adjustment, the Attorney General shall provide such documentation of authorization to enter the United States and to have the alien's status adjusted upon entry as may be necessary to carry out the provisions of this section.

(2) *Designation of entities to receive applications.*— For purposes of receiving applications under this section, the Attorney General—

(A) shall designate qualified voluntary organizations and other qualified State, local, community, farm labor organizations, and associations of agricultural employers, and

(B) may designate such other persons as the Attorney General determines are qualified and have substantial experience, demonstrated competence, and traditional long-term involvement in the preparation and submittal of applications for adjustment of status under section 209 or 245, Public Law 89-732, or Public Law 95-145.

(3) *Proof of eligibility.*—

(A) *In general.*— An alien may establish that he meets the requirement of subsection (a)(1)(B)(ii) through government employment records, records supplied by employers or collective bargaining organizations, and such other reliable documentation as the alien may provide. The Attorney General shall establish special procedures to credit properly work in cases in which an alien was employed under an assumed name.

(B) *Documentation of work history.*—

(i) An alien applying for adjustment of status under subsection (a)(1) has the burden of proving by a preponderance of the evidence that the alien has worked the requisite number of man-days (as required under subsection (a)(1)(B)(ii)).

(ii) If an employer or farm labor contractor employing such an alien has kept proper and adequate records respecting such employment, the alien's burden of proof under clause (i) may be met by securing timely production of those records under regulations to be promulgated by the Attorney General.

(iii) An alien can meet such burden of proof if the alien establishes that the alien has in fact performed the work described in subsection (a)(1)(B)(ii) by producing sufficient evidence to show the extent of that employment as a matter of just and reasonable inference. In such a case, the burden then shifts to the Attorney General to disprove the alien's evidence with a showing which negates the reasonableness of the inference to be drawn from the evidence.

(4) *Treatment of applications by designated entities.*— Each designated entity must agree to forward to the Attorney General applications filed with it in accordance with paragraph (1)(A)(ii) but not to forward to the Attorney General applications filed with it unless the applicant has consented to such forwarding. No such entity may make a determination required by this section to be made by the Attorney General.

(5) *Limitation on access to information.*— Files and records prepared for purposes of this section by designated entities operating under this section are confidential and the Attorney General and the Service shall not have access to such files or records relating to an alien without the consent of the alien, except as allowed by a court order issued pursuant to paragraph (6) of this subsection.

(6) *Confidentiality of information.*—[54]

---

[54] The final sentence of (b)(6) was first amended by §384 of IIRAIRA, which was effective for "offenses occurring on or after
*continued*

(A) *In general.*— Except as provided in this paragraph, neither the Attorney General, nor any other official or employee of the Department of Justice, or bureau or agency thereof, may—

(i) use the information furnished by the applicant pursuant to an application filed under this section for any purpose other than to make a determination on the application, including a determination under subsection (a)(3)(B), or for enforcement of paragraph (7);

(ii) make any publication whereby the information furnished by any particular individual can be identified; or

(iii) permit anyone other than the sworn officers and employees of the Department or bureau or agency or, with respect to applications filed with a designated entity, that designated entity, to examine individual applications.

(B) *Required disclosures.*— The Attorney General shall provide information furnished under this section, and any other information derived from such furnished information, to a duly recognized law enforcement entity in connection with a criminal investigation or prosecution, when such information is requested in writing by such entity, or to an official coroner for purposes of affirmatively identifying a deceased individual (whether or not such individual is deceased as a result of a crime).

(C) *Construction.*—

(i) In general.— Nothing in this paragraph shall be construed to limit the use, or release, for immigration enforcement purposes or law enforcement purposes of information contained in files or records of the Service pertaining to an application filed under this section, other than information furnished by an applicant pursuant to the application, or any other information derived from the application, that is not available from any other source.

(ii) Criminal convictions.— Information concerning whether the applicant has at any time been convicted of a crime may be used or released for immigration enforcement or law enforcement purposes.

(D) *Crime.*— Whoever knowingly uses, publishes, or permits information to be examined in violation of this paragraph shall be fined not more than $10,000.

**(7) *Penalties for false statements in applications.*—**

(A) *Criminal penalty.*— Whoever—

(i) files an application for adjustment of status under this section and knowingly and willfully falsifies, conceals, or covers up a material fact or makes any false, fictitious, or fraudulent statements or representations, or makes or uses any false writing or document knowing the same to contain any false, fictitious, or fraudulent statement or entry, or

(ii) creates or supplies a false writing or document for use in making such an application,

---

the date of the enactment of this Act." However, §623(b) of IIRAIRA rewrote the entire paragraph. The language that was overwritten read as follows: "Anyone who uses, publishes, or permits information to be examined in violation of this paragraph shall be subject to appropriate disciplinary action and subject to a civil money penalty of not more than $5,000 for each violation." *See also,* §245A(c), as amended by §623 of IIRAIRA.

shall be fined in accordance with title 18, United States Code, or imprisoned not more than five years, or both.

(B) *Exclusion.*— An alien who is convicted of a crime under subparagraph (A) shall be considered to be inadmissible to the United States on the ground described in section 212(a)(6)(C)(i).

**(c) Waiver of numerical limitations and certain grounds for exclusion.—**

(1) *Numerical limitations do not apply.*— The numerical limitations of sections 201 and 202 shall not apply to the adjustment of aliens to lawful permanent resident status under this section.

(2) *Waiver of grounds for exclusion.*— In the determination of an alien's admissibility under subsection (a)(1)(C)—

(A) *Grounds of exclusion not applicable.*— The provisions of paragraphs (5) and (7)(A) of section 212(a) shall not apply.

(B) *Waiver of other grounds.*—

(i) In general.— Except as provided in clause (ii), the Attorney General may waive any other provision of section 212(a) in the case of individual aliens for humanitarian purposes, to assure family unity, or when it is otherwise in the public interest.

(ii) Grounds that may not be waived.— The following provisions of section 212(a) may not be waived by the Attorney General under clause (i):

(I) Paragraphs (2)(A) and (2)(B) (relating to criminals).

(II) Paragraph (4) (relating to aliens likely to become public charges).

(III) Paragraph (2)(C) (relating to drug offenses), except for so much of such paragraph as relates to a single offense of simple possession of 30 grams or less of marihuana.

(IV) Paragraph (3) (relating to security and related grounds), other than subparagraph (E) thereof.

(C) *Special rule for determination of public charge.*— An alien is not ineligible for adjustment of status under this section due to being inadmissible under section 212(a)(4) if the alien demonstrates a history of employment in the United States evidencing self-support without reliance on public cash assistance.

**(d) Temporary stay of exclusion or deportation and work authorization for certain applicants.—**

(1) *Before application period.*— The Attorney General shall provide that in the case of an alien who is apprehended before the beginning of the application period described in subsection (a)(1) and who can establish a nonfrivolous case of eligibility to have his status adjusted under subsection (a) (but for the fact that he may not apply for such adjustment until the beginning of such period), until the alien has had the opportunity during the first 30 days of the application period to complete the filing of an application for adjustment, the alien—

(A) may not be excluded or deported, and

(B) shall be granted authorization to engage in employment in the United States and be provided an "employment authorized" endorsement or other appropriate work permit.

(2) *During application period.*— The Attorney General shall provide that in the case of an alien who presents a nonfrivolous application for adjustment of status under subsection (a) during the application period, and until a final determination on the application has been made in accordance with this section, the alien—

(A) may not be excluded or deported, and

(B) shall be granted authorization to engage in employment in the United States and be provided an "employment authorized" endorsement or other appropriate work permit.

(3) No application fees collected by the Service pursuant to this subsection may be used by the Service to offset the costs of the special agricultural worker legalization program until the Service implements the program consistent with the statutory mandate as follows:

(A) During the application period described in subsection (a)(1)(A) the Service may grant temporary admission to the United States, work authorization, and provide an "employment authorized" endorsement or other appropriate work permit to any alien who presents a preliminary application for adjustment of status under subsection (a) at a designated port of entry on the southern land border. An alien who does not enter through a port of entry is subject to deportation and removal as otherwise provided in this Act.

(B) During the application period described in subsection (a)(1)(A) any alien who has filed an application for adjustment of status within the United States as provided in subsection (b)(1)(A) pursuant to the provision of 8 C.F.R. section 210.1(j) is subject to paragraph (2) of this subsection.

(C) A preliminary application is defined as a fully completed and signed application with fee and photographs which contains specific information concerning the performance of qualifying employment in the United States and the documentary evidence which the applicant intends to submit as proof of such employment. The applicant must be otherwise admissible to the United States and must establish to the satisfaction of the examining officer during an interview that his or her claim to eligibility for special agriculture worker status is credible.

**(e) Administrative and judicial review.—**

(1) *Administrative and judicial review.*— There shall be no administrative or judicial review of a determination respecting an application for adjustment of status under this section except in accordance with this subsection.

(2) *Administrative review.—*

(A) *Single level of administrative appellate review.*— The Attorney General shall establish an appellate authority to provide for a single level of administrative appellate review of such a determination.

(B) *Standard for review.*— Such administrative appellate review shall be based solely upon the administrative record established at the time of the determination on the application and upon such additional or newly discovered evidence as may not have been available at the time of the determination.

(3) *Judicial review.—*

(A) *Limitation to review of exclusion or deportation.*— There shall be judicial review of such a denial only in the judicial review of an order of exclusion or deportation under section 106 (as in effect before October 1, 1996).

(B) *Standard for judicial review.*— Such judicial review shall be based solely upon the administrative record established at the time of the review by the appellate authority and the findings of fact and determinations contained in such record shall be conclusive unless the applicant can establish abuse of discretion or that the findings are directly contrary to clear and convincing facts contained in the record considered as a whole.

**(f) Temporary disqualification of newly legalized aliens from receiving aid to families with dependent children.**— During the five-year period beginning on the date an alien was granted lawful temporary resident status under subsection (a), and notwithstanding any other provision of law, the alien is not eligible for assistance under a State program funded under part A of title IV of the Social Security Act. Notwithstanding the previous sentence, in the case of an alien who would be eligible for assistance under a State program funded under part A of title IV of the Social Security Act but for the previous sentence, the provisions of paragraph (3) of section 245A(h) shall apply in the same manner as they apply with respect to paragraph (1) of such section and, for this purpose, any reference in section 245A(h)(3) to paragraph (1) is deemed a reference to the previous sentence.

**(g) Treatment of special agricultural workers.**— For all purposes (subject to subsections (a)(5) and (f)) an alien whose status is adjusted under this section to that of an alien lawfully admitted for permanent residence, such status not having changed, shall be considered to be an alien lawfully admitted for permanent residence (within the meaning of section 101(a)(20)).

**(h) Seasonal agricultural services defined.**— In this section, the term "seasonal agricultural services" means the performance of field work related to planting, cultural practices, cultivating, growing and harvesting of fruits and vegetables of every kind and other perishable commodities, as defined in regulations by the Secretary of Agriculture.

(June 27, 1952, ch. 477, title II, ch. 1, §210; as added by P.L. 99-603 (IRCA) (11/6/86); as amended by P.L. 100-202 (12/22/87); P.L. 100-525 (10/24/88); P.L. 101-238 (12/18/89); P.L. 101-649 (IMMACT90) (11/29/90); P.L. 102-232 (MTINA) (12/12/91, *effective* 4/1/92); P.L. 103-416 (INTCA) (10/25/94, *effective* 4/1/95); P.L. 104-132 (AEDPA) (4/24/96); P.L. 104-193 (8/22/96); P.L. 104-208 (IIRAIRA) (9/30/96), div. C, title III, §§308(g)(2)(B), 384(d)(1), title VI, §623(b).)

**Sec. 210A** [Repealed. P.L. 103-416 (INTCA) (10/25/94), §219(ee)(1).]

## Chapter 2 — Admission Qualifications for Aliens; Travel Control of Citizens and Aliens

### Sec. 211 Admission of Immigrants into the United States
[8 U.S.C. 1181]

**(a) Documents required; admission under quotas before June 30, 1968.**— Except as provided in subsection (b) and subsection (c) no immigrant shall be admitted into the United States unless at the time of application for admission he

(1) has a valid unexpired immigrant visa or was born subsequent to the issuance of such visa of the accompanying parent, and

(2) presents a valid unexpired passport or other suitable travel document, or document of identity and nationality, if such document is required under the regulations issued by the Attorney General.

With respect to immigrants to be admitted under quotas of quota areas prior to June 30, 1968, no immigrant visa shall be deemed valid unless the immigrant is properly chargeable to the quota area under the quota of which the visa is issued.

**(b)  Readmission  without  required  documents;  Attorney  General's  discretion.—**
Notwithstanding the provisions of section 212(a)(7)(A) of this Act in such cases or in such classes
of cases and under such conditions as may be by regulations prescribed, returning resident immigrants, defined in section 101(a)(27)(A), who are otherwise admissible may be readmitted to the
United States by the Attorney General in his discretion without being required to obtain a passport, immigrant visa, reentry permit or other documentation.

**(c) Nonapplicability to aliens admitted as refugees.—** The provisions of subsection (a) shall not
apply to an alien whom the Attorney General admits to the United States under section 207.

(June 27, 1952, ch. 477, title II, ch. 2, §211, 66 Stat. 181; as amended by P.L. 89-236 (10/3/65); P.L. 94-571 (10/20/76); P.L. 96-
212 (3/17/80); P.L. 101-649 (IMMACT90) (11/29/90).)

## Sec. 212 Excludable Aliens
[8 U.S.C. 1182]

**(a)**[55] **Classes of aliens ineligible for visas or admission.—** Except as otherwise provided in this
Act, aliens who are inadmissible under the following paragraphs are ineligible to receive visas
and ineligible to be admitted to the United States:

(1) *Health-related grounds.—*

(A) *In general.—* Any alien—

(i) who is determined (in accordance with regulations prescribed by the Secretary of
Health and Human Services) to have a communicable disease of public health sig-
nificance;

(ii)[56] except as provided in subparagraph (C), who seeks admission as an immigrant, or
who seeks adjustment of status to the status of an alien lawfully admitted for permanent
residence, and who has failed to present documentation of having received vaccination
against vaccine-preventable diseases, which shall include at least the following diseases:
mumps, measles, rubella, polio, tetanus and diphtheria toxoids, pertussis, influenza type
B and hepatitis B, and any other vaccinations against vaccine-preventable diseases recommended by the Advisory Committee for Immunization Practices,

(iii) who is determined (in accordance with regulations prescribed by the Secretary of
Health and Human Services in consultation with the Attorney General)—

(I) to have a physical or mental disorder and behavior associated with the
disorder that may pose, or has posed, a threat to the property, safety, or welfare
of the alien or others, or

(II) to have had a physical or mental disorder and a history of behavior
associated with the disorder, which behavior has posed a threat to the property,
safety, or welfare of the alien or others and which behavior is likely to recur or
to lead to other harmful behavior, or

(iv) who is determined (in accordance with regulations prescribed by the Secretary of
Health and Human Services) to be a drug abuser or addict,

---

[55] *See* §309 IIRAIRA (*reprinted in* Appendix C, *infra*) for effective date and transition provisions.

[56] Effective "with respect to applications for immigrant visas or for adjustment of status filed after Sept. 30, 1996." IIRAIRA
§341(c).

is inadmissible.

(B) *Waiver authorized.*— For provision authorizing waiver of certain clauses of subparagraph (A), see subsection (g).

(C) *Exception from immunization requirement for adopted children 10 years of age of younger.*— Clause (ii) of subparagraph (A) shall not apply to a child who—

(i) is 10 years of age or younger,

(ii) is described in section 101(b)(1)(F), and

(iii) is seeking an immigrant visa as an immediate relative under section 201(b),

if, prior to the admission of the child, an adoptive parent or prospective adoptive parent of the child, who has sponsored the child for admission as an immediate relative, has executed an affidavit stating that the parent is aware of the provisions of subparagraph (A)(ii) and will ensure that, within 30 days of the child's admission, or at the earliest time that is medically appropriate, the child will receive the vaccinations identified in such subparagraph.

(2) *Criminal and related grounds.*—

(A) *Conviction of certain crimes.*—

(i) In general.— Except as provided in clause (ii), any alien convicted of, or who admits having committed, or who admits committing acts which constitute the essential elements of—

(I) a crime involving moral turpitude (other than a purely political offense) or an attempt or conspiracy to commit such a crime, or

(II) a violation of (or a conspiracy or attempt to violate) any law or regulation of a State, the United States, or a foreign country relating to a controlled substance (as defined in section 102 of the Controlled Substances Act (21 U.S.C. 802)),

is inadmissible.

(ii) Exception.— Clause (i)(I) shall not apply to an alien who committed only one crime if—

(I) the crime was committed when the alien was under 18 years of age, and the crime was committed (and the alien released from any confinement to a prison or correctional institution imposed for the crime) more than 5 years before the date of application for a visa or other documentation and the date of application for admission to the United States, or

(II) the maximum penalty possible for the crime of which the alien was convicted (or which the alien admits having committed or of which the acts that the alien admits having committed constituted the essential elements) did not exceed imprisonment for one year and, if the alien was convicted of such crime, the alien was not sentenced to a term of imprisonment in excess of 6 months (regardless of the extent to which the sentence was ultimately executed).

(B) *Multiple criminal convictions.*— Any alien convicted of 2 or more offenses (other than purely political offenses), regardless of whether the conviction was in a single trial or whether the offenses arose from a single scheme of misconduct and regardless of whether the offenses involved moral turpitude, for which the aggregate sentences to confinement[57] were 5 years or more is inadmissible.

(C) *Controlled substance traffickers.*— Any alien who the consular officer or the Attorney General knows or has reason to believe—

(i) is or has been an illicit trafficker in any controlled substance or in any listed chemical (as defined in section 102 of the Controlled Substances Act (21 U.S.C. 802)), or is or has been a knowing aider, abettor, assister, conspirator, or colluder with others in the illicit trafficking in any such controlled or listed substance or chemical, or endeavored to do so; or

(ii) is the spouse, son, or daughter of an alien inadmissible under clause (i), has, within the previous 5 years, obtained any financial or other benefit from the illicit activity of that alien, and knew or reasonably should have known that the financial or other benefit was the product of such illicit activity,

is inadmissible.

(D) *Prostitution and commercialized vice.*— Any alien who—

(i) is coming to the United States solely, principally, or incidentally to engage in prostitution, or has engaged in prostitution within 10 years of the date of application for a visa, admission, or adjustment of status,

(ii) directly or indirectly procures or attempts to procure, or (within 10 years of the date of application for a visa, admission, or adjustment of status) procured or attempted to procure or to import, prostitutes or persons for the purpose of prostitution, or receives or (within such 10-year period) received, in whole or in part, the proceeds of prostitution, or

(iii) is coming to the United States to engage in any other unlawful commercialized vice, whether or not related to prostitution,

is inadmissible.

(E) *Certain aliens involved in serious criminal activity who have asserted immunity from prosecution.*— Any alien—

(i) who has committed in the United States at any time a serious criminal offense (as defined in section 101(h)),

(ii) for whom immunity from criminal jurisdiction was exercised with respect to that offense,

(iii) who as a consequence of the offense and exercise of immunity has departed from the United States, and

(iv) who has not subsequently submitted fully to the jurisdiction of the court in the United States having jurisdiction with respect to that offense,

is inadmissible.

---

[57] The term "actually imposed" was deleted after this word by IIRAIRA §322(a)(2)(B). Change applies to "convictions and sentences entered before, on, or after the date of the enactment of this Act. Subparagraphs (B) and (C) of §240(c)(3) of the Immigration and Nationality Act, as inserted by §304(a)(3) of [IIRAIRA], shall apply to proving such convictions."

(F) *Waiver authorized.*— For provision authorizing waiver of certain subparagraphs of this paragraph, see subsection (h).

(G) *Foreign government officials who have committed particularly severe violations of religious freedom.*— Any alien who, while serving as a foreign government official, was responsible for or directly carried out, at any time, particularly severe violations of religious freedom, as defined in section 3 of the International Religious Freedom Act of 1998 (22 U.S.C. 6402), is inadmissible.

(H) *Significant traffickers in persons.*—

(i) In general.— Any alien who commits or conspires to commit human trafficking offenses in the United States or outside the United States, or who the consular officer, the Secretary of Homeland Security, the Secretary of State, or the Attorney General knows or has reason to believe is or has been a knowing aider, abettor, assister, conspirator, or colluder with such a trafficker in severe forms of trafficking in persons, as defined in the section 103 of such Act, is inadmissible.

(ii) Beneficiaries of trafficking.— Except as provided in clause (iii), any alien who the consular officer or the Attorney General knows or has reason to believe is the spouse, son, or daughter of an alien inadmissible under clause (i), has, within the previous 5 years, obtained any financial or other benefit from the illicit activity of that alien, and knew or reasonably should have known that the financial or other benefit was the product of such illicit activity, is inadmissible.

(iii) Exception for certain sons and daughters.— Clause (ii) shall not apply to a son or daughter who was a child at the time he or she received the benefit described in such clause.

(I) *Money laundering.*— Any alien—

(i) who a consular officer or the Attorney General knows, or has reason to believe, has engaged, is engaging, or seeks to enter the United States to engage, in an offense which is described in section 1956 or 1957 of title 18, United States Code (relating to laundering of monetary instruments); or

(ii) who a consular officer or the Attorney General knows is, or has been, a knowing aider, abettor, assister, conspirator, or colluder with others in an offense which is described in such section;

is inadmissible.

(3)[58] *Security and related grounds.*—

(A) *In general.*— Any alien who a consular officer or the Attorney General knows, or has reasonable ground to believe, seeks to enter the United States to engage solely, principally, or incidentally in—

(i) any activity

(I) to violate any law of the United States relating to espionage or sabotage or

(II) to violate or evade any law prohibiting the export from the United States of goods, technology, or sensitive information,

---

[58] *See also* §411(c) of USA PATRIOT Act, P.L. 107-56, Retroactive Application of Amendments.

(ii) any other unlawful activity, or

(iii) any activity a purpose of which is the opposition to, or the control or overthrow of, the Government of the United States by force, violence, or other unlawful means,

is inadmissible.

(B)[59] *Terrorist activities.*—

(i) In general.— Any alien who—

(I) has engaged in a terrorist activity,

(II) a consular officer, the Attorney General, or the Secretary of Homeland Security knows, or has reasonable ground to believe, is engaged in or is likely to engage after entry in any terrorist activity (as defined in clause (iv)),

(III)[60] has, under circumstances indicating an intention to cause death or serious bodily harm, incited terrorist activity;

(IV) is a representative (as defined in clause (v)) of—

(aa) a terrorist organization (as defined in clause (vi)); or

(bb) a political, social, or other group that endorses or espouses terrorist activity;

(V) is a member of a terrorist organization described in subclause (I) or (II) of clause (vi);

(VI) is a member of a terrorist organization described in clause (vi)(III), unless the alien can demonstrate by clear and convincing evidence that the alien did not know, and should not reasonably have known, that the organization was a terrorist organization;

(VII) endorses or espouses terrorist activity or persuades others to endorse or espouse terrorist activity or support a terrorist organization;

(VIII) has received military-type training (as defined in section 2339D(c)(1) of title 18, United States Code) from or on behalf of any organization that, at the time the training was received, was a terrorist organization (as defined in clause (vi)); or

(IX) is the spouse or child of an alien who is inadmissible under this subparagraph, if the activity causing the alien to be found inadmissible occurred within the last 5 years,

is inadmissible. An alien who is an officer, official, representative, or spokesman of the Palestine Liberation Organization is considered, for purposes of this Act, to be engaged in a terrorist activity.[61]

---

[59] *See* §411(c) of USA PATRIOT Act, P.L. 107-56 (10/26/01) for "Special Rule for Aliens in Exclusion or Deportation Proceedings."

The amendments made by §103 of REAL ID Act, P.L. 109-13 (5/11/05) took effect on the date of enactment. They and §212(a)(3)(B) apply to: (1) removal procedings instituted before, on, or after the date of enactment; and (2) acts and conditions constituting a ground for inadmissibility, excludability, deportation, or removal occurring or existing before, on, or after such date.

[60] *See* §342 of IIRAIRA, effective on the date of the enactment of IIRAIRA. It applies to incitement "regardless of when it occurs."

[61] A literal reading of §103(a) of P.L. 109-13 (REAL ID Act) (5/11/05), which revised INA §212(a)(3)(B)(i), would put the words "is inadmissible" at the end of subclause (IX); however, placement at the beginning of the "outdented" paragraph resum-
*continued*

(ii) Exception— Subclause (IX) of clause (i) does not apply to a spouse or child—

(I) who did not know or should not reasonably have known of the activity causing the alien to be found inadmissible under this section; or

(II) whom the consular officer or Attorney General has reasonable grounds to believe has renounced the activity causing the alien to be found inadmissible under this section.

(iii) "Terrorist activity" defined.— As used in this Act, the term "terrorist activity" means any activity which is unlawful under the laws of the place where it is committed (or which, if it had been committed in the United States, would be unlawful under the laws of the United States or any State) and which involves any of the following:

(I) The highjacking or sabotage of any conveyance (including an aircraft, vessel, or vehicle).

(II) The seizing or detaining, and threatening to kill, injure, or continue to detain, another individual in order to compel a third person (including a governmental organization) to do or abstain from doing any act as an explicit or implicit condition for the release of the individual seized or detained.

(III) A violent attack upon an internationally protected person (as defined in section 1116(b)(4) of title 18, United States Code) or upon the liberty of such a person.

(IV) An assassination.

(V) The use of any—

(a) biological agent, chemical agent, or nuclear weapon or device, or

(b) explosive, firearm, or other weapon or dangerous device (other than for mere personal monetary gain), with intent to endanger, directly or indirectly, the safety of one or more individuals or to cause substantial damage to property.

(VI) A threat, attempt, or conspiracy to do any of the foregoing.

(iv) Engage in terrorist activity defined.— As used in this Act, the term "engage in terrorist activity" means, in an individual capacity or as a member of an organization—

(I) to commit or to incite to commit, under circumstances indicating an intention to cause death or serious bodily injury, a terrorist activity;

(II) to prepare or plan a terrorist activity;

(III) to gather information on potential targets for terrorist activity;

(IV) to solicit funds or other things of value for—

(aa) a terrorist activity;

(bb) a terrorist organization described in clause (vi)(I) or (vi)(II); or

(cc) a terrorist organization described in clause (vi)(III), unless the solicitor can demonstrate by clear and convincing evidence that he did not know, and should not reasonably have known, that the organization was a terrorist organization;

---

ing clause (B)(i) (as here), reflects the likely intention of Congress (and the position of the same words before the amendment).

(V) to solicit any individual—

(aa) to engage in conduct otherwise described in this subsection;

(bb) for membership in a terrorist organization described in clause (vi)(I) or (vi)(II); or

(cc) for membership in a terrorist organization described in clause (vi)(III) unless the solicitor can demonstrate by clear and convincing evidence that he did not know, and should not reasonably have known, that the organization was a terrorist organization; or

(VI) to commit an act that the actor knows, or reasonably should know, affords material support, including a safe house, transportation, communications, funds, transfer of funds or other material financial benefit, false documentation or identification, weapons (including chemical, biological, or radiological weapons), explosives, or training—

(aa) for the commission of a terrorist activity;

(bb) to any individual who the actor knows, or reasonably should know, has committed or plans to commit a terrorist activity;

(cc) to a terrorist organization described in subclause (I) or (II) of clause (vi) or to any member of such an organization; or

(dd) to a terrorist organization described in clause (vi)(III), or to any member of such an organization, unless the actor can demonstrate by clear and convincing evidence that the actor did not know, and should not reasonably have known, that the organization was a terrorist organization.

(v) Representative defined.— As used in this paragraph, the term "representative" includes an officer, official, or spokesman of an organization, and any person who directs, counsels, commands, or induces an organization or its members to engage in terrorist activity.

(vi)[62] Terrorist organization defined.— As used in this section, the term "terrorist organization" means an organization—

(I) designated under section 219;

(II) otherwise designated, upon publication in the *Federal Register*, by the Secretary of State in consultation with or upon the request of the Attorney General or the Secretary of Homeland Security, as a terrorist organization, after finding that the organization engages in the activities described in subclauses (I) through (VI) of clause (iv); or

(III) that is a group of two or more individuals, whether organized or not, which engages in, or has a subgroup which engages in, the activities described in subclauses (I) through (VI) of clause (iv).

(C) *Foreign policy.*—

---

[62] *See* §411(c) of USA PATRIOT Act, P.L. 107-56 (10/26/01) for "Special Rule for §219 Organizations and Organizations Designated Under §212(a)(3)(B)(vi)(II)."

(i) In general.— An alien whose entry or proposed activities in the United States the Secretary of State has reasonable ground to believe would have potentially serious adverse foreign policy consequences for the United States is inadmissible.

(ii) Exception for officials.— An alien who is an official of a foreign government or a purported government, or who is a candidate for election to a foreign government office during the period immediately preceding the election for that office, shall not be excludable or subject to restrictions or conditions on entry into the United States under clause (i) solely because of the alien's past, current, or expected beliefs, statements, or associations, if such beliefs, statements, or associations would be lawful within the United States.

(iii) Exception for other aliens.— An alien, not described in clause (ii), shall not be excludable or subject to restrictions or conditions on entry into the United States under clause (i) because of the alien's past, current, or expected beliefs, statements, or associations, if such beliefs, statements, or associations would be lawful within the United States, unless the Secretary of State personally determines that the alien's admission would compromise a compelling United States foreign policy interest.

(iv) Notification of determinations.— If a determination is made under clause (iii) with respect to an alien, the Secretary of State must notify on a timely basis the chairmen of the Committees on the Judiciary and Foreign Affairs of the House of Representatives and of the Committees on the Judiciary and Foreign Relations of the Senate of the identity of the alien and the reasons for the determination.

(D) *Immigrant membership in totalitarian party.*—

(i) In general.— Any immigrant who is or has been a member of or affiliated with the Communist or any other totalitarian party (or subdivision or affiliate thereof), domestic or foreign, is inadmissible.

(ii) Exception for involuntary membership.— Clause (i) shall not apply to an alien because of membership or affiliation if the alien establishes to the satisfaction of the consular officer when applying for a visa (or to the satisfaction of the Attorney General when applying for admission) that the membership or affiliation is or was involuntary, or is or was solely when under 16 years of age, by operation of law, or for purposes of obtaining employment, food rations, or other essentials of living and whether necessary for such purposes.

(iii) Exception for past membership.— Clause (i) shall not apply to an alien because of membership or affiliation if the alien establishes to the satisfaction of the consular officer when applying for a visa (or to the satisfaction of the Attorney General when applying for admission) that—

(I) the membership or affiliation terminated at least—

(a) 2 years before the date of such application, or

(b) 5 years before the date of such application, in the case of an alien whose membership or affiliation was with the party controlling the government of a foreign state that is a totalitarian dictatorship as of such date, and

(II) the alien is not a threat to the security of the United States.

(iv) Exception for close family members.— The Attorney General may, in the Attorney General's discretion, waive the application of clause (i) in the case of an immigrant who is the parent, spouse, son, daughter, brother, or sister of a citizen of the United States or a spouse, son, or daughter of an alien lawfully admitted for permanent residence for humanitarian purposes, to assure family unity, or when it is otherwise in the public interest if the immigrant is not a threat to the security of the United States.

(E)[63] *Participants in Nazi persecution, genocide, or the commission of any act of torture or extrajudicial killing.*—

(i) Participation in Nazi persecutions.— Any alien who, during the period beginning on March 23, 1933, and ending on May 8, 1945, under the direction of, or in association with—

(I) the Nazi government of Germany,

(II) any government in any area occupied by the military forces of the Nazi government of Germany,

(III) any government established with the assistance or cooperation of the Nazi government of Germany, or

(IV) any government which was an ally of the Nazi government of Germany,

ordered, incited, assisted, or otherwise participated in the persecution of any person because of race, religion, national origin, or political opinion is inadmissible.

(ii) Participation in genocide.— Any alien who ordered, incited, assisted, or otherwise participated in genocide, as defined in section 1091(a) of title 18, United States Code, is inadmissible.

(iii) Commission of acts of torture or extrajudicial killings.— Any alien who, outside the United States, has committed, ordered, incited, assisted, or otherwise participated in the commission of—

(I) any act of torture, as defined in section 2340 of title 18, United States Code; or

(II) under color of law of any foreign nation, any extrajudicial killing, as defined in section 3(a) of the Torture Victim Protection Act of 1991 (28 U.S.C. 1350 note),

is inadmissible.

(F) *Association with terrorist organizations.*— Any alien who the Secretary of State, after consultation with the Attorney General, or the Attorney General, after consultation with the Secretary of State, determines has been associated with a terrorist organization and intends while in the United States to engage solely, principally, or incidentally in activities that could endanger the welfare, safety, or security of the United States is inadmissible.

(G) *Recruitment or use of child soldiers.*— Any alien who has engaged in the recruitment or use of child soldiers in violation of section 2442 of title 18, United States Code, is inadmissible.

(4)[64] *Public charge.*—

---

[63] Changes to INA §212(a)(3)(E) effected by §5501 of P.L. 108-458 (12/17/04) applicable to "offenses committed before, on, or after" 12/17/04.

[64] *See* §423(d) of the USA PATRIOT Act, P.L. 107-56, *reprinted in* Appendix J, *infra*, for provisions relating to immigration benefits for the victims of terrorism.

(A)[65] *In general.*— Any alien who, in the opinion of the consular officer at the time of application for a visa, or in the opinion of the Attorney General at the time of application for admission or adjustment of status, is likely at any time to become a public charge is inadmissible.

(B) *Factors to be taken into account.*—

(i) In determining whether an alien is excludable under this paragraph, the consular officer or the Attorney General shall at a minimum consider the alien's—

(I) age;

(II) health;

(III) family status;

(IV) assets, resources, and financial status; and

(V) education and skills.

(ii) In addition to the factors under clause (i), the consular officer or the Attorney General may also consider any affidavit of support under section 213A for purposes of exclusion under this paragraph.

(C) *Family-sponsored immigrants.*— Any alien who seeks admission or adjustment of status under a visa number issued under section 201(b)(2) or 203(a) is excludable under this paragraph unless—

(i) the alien has obtained—

(I) status as a spouse or a child of a United States citizen pursuant to clause (ii), (iii), or (iv) of section 204(a)(1)(A), or

(II) classification pursuant to clause (ii) or (iii) of section 204(a)(1)(B);

(III) classification or status as a VAWA self-petitioner; or

(ii) the person petitioning for the alien's admission (and any additional sponsor required under section 213A(f) or any alternative sponsor permitted under paragraph (5)(B) of such section) has executed an affidavit of support described in section 213A with respect to such alien.

(D) Certain employment-based immigrants.— Any alien who seeks admission or adjustment of status under a visa number issued under section 203(b) by virtue of a classification petition filed by a relative of the alien (or by an entity in which such relative has a significant ownership interest) is excludable under this paragraph unless such relative has executed an affidavit of support described in section 213A with respect to such alien.

(5)[66] *Labor certification and qualifications for certain immigrants.*—

---

[65] Sec. 308(d)(1)(C) of IIRAIRA changes the term "is excludable" to "is inadmissible." IIRAIRA §531 rewrites the entire paragraph using the term "is excludable." The Office of the Law Revision Counsel, which prepares and published the U.S. Code, uses "is inadmissible."

The amendments made by IIRAIRA §531 "shall apply to applications submitted on or after such date, not earlier than 30 days and not later than 60 days after the date the Attorney General promulgates under §551(c)(2) of [IIRAIRA] a standard form for an affidavit of support, as the Attorney General shall specify, but subparagraphs (C) and (D) of §212(a)(4) of the Immigration and Nationality Act, as so amended, shall not apply to applications with respect to which an official interview with an immigration officer was conducted before such effective date."

[66] For special provisions for citizens of Federated States of Micronesia (FSM) and of the Republic of the Marshall Islands

*continued*

(A) *Labor certification.*—

(i) In general.— Any alien who seeks to enter the United States for the purpose of performing skilled or unskilled labor is inadmissible, unless the Secretary of Labor has determined and certified to the Secretary of State and the Attorney General that—

(I) there are not sufficient workers who are able, willing, qualified (or equally qualified in the case of an alien described in clause (ii)) and available at the time of application for a visa and admission to the United States and at the place where the alien is to perform such skilled or unskilled labor, and

(II) the employment of such alien will not adversely affect the wages and working conditions of workers in the United States similarly employed.

(ii) Certain aliens subject to special rule.— For purposes of clause (i)(I), an alien described in this clause is an alien who—

(I) is a member of the teaching profession, or

(II) has exceptional ability in the sciences or the arts.

(iii) Professional athletes.—

(I) In general.— A certification made under clause (i) with respect to a professional athlete shall remain valid with respect to the athlete after the athlete changes employer, if the new employer is a team in the same sport as the team which employed the athlete when the athlete first applied for certification.

(II) Definition.— For purposes of subclause (I), the term "professional athlete" means an individual who is employed as an athlete by—

(aa) a team that is a member of an association of 6 or more professional sports teams whose total combined revenues exceed $10,000,000 per year, if the association governs the conduct of its members and regulates the contests and exhibitions in which its member teams regularly engage; or

(bb) any minor league team that is affiliated with such an association.

(iv) Long delayed adjustment applicants.— A certification made under clause (i) with respect to an individual whose petition is covered by section 204(j) shall remain valid with respect to a new job accepted by the individual after the individual changes jobs or employers if the new job is in the same or a similar occupational classification as the job for which the certification was issued.

(B) *Unqualified physicians.*— An alien who is a graduate of a medical school not accredited by a body or bodies approved for the purpose by the Secretary of Education (regardless of whether such school of medicine is in the United States) and who is coming to the United States principally to perform services as a member of the medical profession is inadmissible, unless the alien

(i) has passed parts I and II of the National Board of Medical Examiners Examination (or an equivalent examination as determined by the Secretary of Health and Human Services) and

---

(RMI), notwithstanding INA §212(a)(5), see Compacts between the United States and those two governments (Art. IV in each respective Compact), as approved in the Compact of Free Association Amendments Act, 2003, P.L. 108-188 (12/17/03), §§201(a) [FSM] and (b) [RMI]. *See also* §104(b) of that Act.

(ii) is competent in oral and written English. For purposes of the previous sentence, an alien who is a graduate of a medical school shall be considered to have passed parts I and II of the National Board of Medical Examiners if the alien was fully and permanently licensed to practice medicine in a State on January 9, 1978, and was practicing medicine in a State on that date.

(C) *Uncertified foreign health-care workers.*— Subject to subsection (r), any alien who seeks to enter the United States for the purpose of performing labor as a health-care worker, other than a physician, is excludable unless the alien presents to the consular officer, or, in the case of an adjustment of status, the Attorney General, a certificate from the Commission on Graduates of Foreign Nursing Schools, or a certificate from an equivalent independent credentialing organization approved by the Attorney General in consultation with the Secretary of Health and Human Services, verifying that—

(i) the alien's education, training, license, and experience—

(I) meet all applicable statutory and regulatory requirements for entry into the United States under the classification specified in the application;

(II) are comparable with that required for an American health-care worker of the same type; and

(III) are authentic and, in the case of a license, unencumbered;

(ii) the alien has the level of competence in oral and written English considered by the Secretary of Health and Human Services, in consultation with the Secretary of Education, to be appropriate for health care work of the kind in which the alien will be engaged, as shown by an appropriate score on one or more nationally recognized, commercially available, standardized assessments of the applicant's ability to speak and write; and

(iii) if a majority of States licensing the profession in which the alien intends to work recognize a test predicting the success on the profession's licensing or certification examination, the alien has passed such a test, or has passed such an examination.

For purposes of clause (ii), determination of the standardized tests required and of the minimum scores that are appropriate are within the sole discretion of the Secretary of Health and Human Services and are not subject to further administrative or judicial review.

(D) *Application of grounds.*— The grounds for inadmissibility of aliens under subparagraphs (A) and (B) shall apply to immigrants seeking admission or adjustment of status under paragraph (2) or (3) of section 203(b).

(6) *Illegal entrants and immigration violators.*—

(A)[67] *Aliens present without admission or parole.*—

(i) In general.— An alien present in the United States without being admitted or paroled, or who arrives in the United States at any time or place other than as designated by the Attorney General, is inadmissible.

---

[67] Sec. 301(c)(2) of IIRAIRA provides: "Transition for battered spouse or child provision.—The requirements of subclauses (II) and (III) of §212(a)(6)(A)(ii) of the Immigration and Nationality Act, as inserted by paragraph (1), shall not apply to an alien who demonstrates that the alien first arrived in the United States before the title III-A effective date (described in §309(a))." *See* §309 IIRAIRA (*reprinted in* Appendix C, *infra*) for "title III-A" effective date provisions.

(ii) Exception for certain battered women and children.— Clause (i) shall not apply to an alien who demonstrates that—

(I) the alien is a VAWA self-petitioner;

(II) (a) the alien has been battered or subjected to extreme cruelty by a spouse or parent, or by a member of the spouse's or parent's family residing in the same household as the alien and the spouse or parent consented or acquiesced to such battery or cruelty, or

(b) the alien's child has been battered or subjected to extreme cruelty by a spouse or parent of the alien (without the active participation of the alien in the battery or cruelty) or by a member of the spouse's or parent's family residing in the same household as the alien when the spouse or parent consented to or acquiesced in such battery or cruelty and the alien did not actively participate in such battery or cruelty, and

(III) there was a substantial connection between the battery or cruelty described in subclause (I) or (II) and the alien's unlawful entry into the United States.

(B) *Failure to attend removal proceeding.*— Any alien who without reasonable cause fails or refuses to attend or remain in attendance at a proceeding to determine the alien's inadmissibility or deportability and who seeks admission to the United States within 5 years of such alien's subsequent departure or removal is inadmissible.

(C) *Misrepresentation.*—

(i) In general.— Any alien who, by fraud or willfully misrepresenting a material fact, seeks to procure (or has sought to procure or has procured) a visa, other documentation, or admission into the United States or other benefit provided under this Act is inadmissible.

(ii) Falsely claiming citizenship.—

(I) In general.— Any alien who falsely represents, or has falsely represented, himself or herself to be a citizen of the United States for any purpose or benefit under this Act (including section 274A) or any other Federal or State law is inadmissible.

(II)[68] Exception.— In the case of an alien making a representation described in subclause (I), if each natural parent of the alien (or, in the case of an adopted alien, each adoptive parent of the alien) is or was a citizen (whether by birth or naturalization), the alien permanently resided in the United States prior to attaining the age of 16, and the alien reasonably believed at the time of making such representation that he or she was a citizen, the alien shall not be considered to be inadmissible under any provision of this subsection based on such representation.

(iii) Waiver authorized.— For provision authorizing waiver of clause (i), see subsection (i).

(D) *Stowaways.*— Any alien who is a stowaway is inadmissible.

(E) *Smugglers.*—

---

[68] Added by §344(a) of IIRAIRA, effective for "representations made on or after the date of enactment of [IIRAIRA]."

(i) In general.— Any alien who at any time knowingly has encouraged, induced, assisted, abetted, or aided any other alien to enter or to try to enter the United States in violation of law is inadmissible.

(ii) Special rule in the case of family reunification.— Clause (i) shall not apply in the case of alien who is an eligible immigrant (as defined in section 301(b)(1) of the Immigration Act of 1990), was physically present in the United States on May 5, 1988, and is seeking admission as an immediate relative or under section 203(a)(2) (including under section 112 of the Immigration Act of 1990) or benefits under section 301(a) of the Immigration Act of 1990 if the alien, before May 5, 1988, has encouraged, induced, assisted, abetted, or aided only the alien's spouse, parent, son, or daughter (and no other individual) to enter the United States in violation of law.

(iii) Waiver authorized.— For provision authorizing waiver of clause (i), see subsection (d)(11).

(F) *Subject of civil penalty.—*

(i) In general.— An alien who is the subject of a final order for violation of section 274C is inadmissible.

(ii) Waiver authorized.— For provision authorizing waiver of clause (i), see subsection (d)(12).

(G)[69] *Student visa abusers.—* An alien who obtains the status of a nonimmigrant under section 101(a)(15)(F)(i) and who violates a term or condition of such status under section 214(*l*)[70] is excludable until the alien has been outside the United States for a continuous period of 5 years after the date of the violation.

(7) *Documentation requirements.—*

(A) *Immigrants.—*

(i) In general.— Except as otherwise specifically provided in this Act, any immigrant at the time of application for admission—

(I) who is not in possession of a valid unexpired immigrant visa, reentry permit, border crossing identification card, or other valid entry document required by this Act, and a valid unexpired passport, or other suitable travel document, or document of identity and nationality if such document is required under the regulations issued by the Attorney General under section 211(a), or

(II) whose visa has been issued without compliance with the provisions of section 203,

is inadmissible.

(ii) Waiver authorized.— For provision authorizing waiver of clause (i), see subsection (k).

(B) *Nonimmigrants.—*

---

[69] *See* §346 of IIRAIRA, effective for "aliens who obtain the status of a nonimmigrant under §101(a)(15)(F) of the [INA] after the end of the 60-day period beginning on the date of enactment of [IIRAIRA], including aliens whose status as such a nonimmigrant is extended after the end of such period."

[70] Reference is most likey to the §214(*l*) that was redesignated §214(m) by Pub. L. 106-386.

(i) In general.— Any nonimmigrant who—

(I) is not in possession of a passport valid for a minimum of six months from the date of the expiration of the initial period of the alien's admission or contemplated initial period of stay authorizing the alien to return to the country from which the alien came or to proceed to and enter some other country during such period, or

(II)[71] is not in possession of a valid nonimmigrant visa or border crossing identification card at the time of application for admission,

is inadmissible.

(ii) General waiver authorized.— For provision authorizing waiver of clause (i), see subsection (d)(4).

(iii) Guam and northern mariana islands visa waiver.— For provision authorizing waiver of clause (i) in the case of visitors to Guam or the Commonwealth of the Northern Mariana Islands, see subsection (*l*).

(iv) Visa waiver program.— For authority to waive the requirement of clause (i) under a program, see section 217.

(8) *Ineligible for citizenship.—*

(A) *In general.—* Any immigrant who is permanently ineligible to citizenship is inadmissible.

(B) *Draft evaders.—* Any person who has departed from or who has remained outside the United States to avoid or evade training or service in the armed forces in time of war or a period declared by the President to be a national emergency is inadmissible, except that this subparagraph shall not apply to an alien who at the time of such departure was a nonimmigrant and who is seeking to reenter the United States as a nonimmigrant.

(9) *Aliens previously removed.—*

(A) *Certain aliens previously removed.—*

(i) Arriving aliens.— Any alien who has been ordered removed under section 235(b)(1) or at the end of proceedings under section 240 initiated upon the alien's arrival in the United States and who again seeks admission within 5 years of the date of such removal (or within 20 years in the case of a second or subsequent removal or at any time in the case of an alien convicted of an aggravated felony) is inadmissible.

(ii) Other aliens.— Any alien not described in clause (i) who—

(I) has been ordered removed under section 240 or any other provision of law, or

(II) departed the United States while an order of removal was outstanding,

and who seeks admission within 10 years of the date of such alien's departure or removal (or within 20 years of such date in the case of a second or subsequent removal or at any time in the case of an alien convicted of an aggravated felony) is inadmissible.

(iii) Exception.— Clauses (i) and (ii) shall not apply to an alien seeking admission within a period if, prior to the date of the alien's reembarkation at a place outside the

---

[71] *See* note 66, *supra.*

United States or attempt to be admitted from foreign contiguous territory, the Attorney General has consented to the alien's reapplying for admission.

(B)[72] *Aliens unlawfully present.*—

(i) In general.— Any alien (other than an alien lawfully admitted for permanent residence) who—

(I) was unlawfully present in the United States for a period of more than 180 days but less than 1 year, voluntarily departed the United States (whether or not pursuant to section 244(e)[73]) prior to the commencement of proceedings under section 235(b)(1) or section 240, and again seeks admission within 3 years of the date of such alien's departure or removal, or

(II) has been unlawfully present in the United States for one year or more, and who again seeks admission within 10 years of the date of such alien's departure or removal from the United States,

is inadmissible.

(ii) Construction of unlawful presence.— For purposes of this paragraph, an alien is deemed to be unlawfully present in the United States if the alien is present in the United States after the expiration of the period of stay authorized by the Attorney General or is present in the United States without being admitted or paroled.

(iii) Exceptions.—

(I) Minors.— No period of time in which an alien is under 18 years of age shall be taken into account in determining the period of unlawful presence in the United States under clause (i).

(II) Asylees.— No period of time in which an alien has a bona fide application for asylum pending under section 208 shall be taken into account in determining the period of unlawful presence in the United States under clause (i) unless the alien during such period was employed without authorization in the United States.

(III) Family unity.— No period of time in which the alien is a beneficiary of family unity protection pursuant to section 301 of the Immigration Act of 1990 shall be taken into account in determining the period of unlawful presence in the United States under clause (i).

(IV) Battered women and children.— Clause (i) shall not apply to an alien who would be described in paragraph (6)(A)(ii) if "violation of the terms of the alien's nonimmigrant visa" were substituted for "unlawful entry into the United States" in subclause (III) of that paragraph.

(V) Victims of a severe form of trafficking in persons.— Clause (i) shall not apply to an alien who demonstrates that the severe form of trafficking (as that term is defined in section 103 of the Trafficking Victims Protection Act of 2000 (22 U.S.C. 7102)) was at least one central reason for the alien's unlawful presence in the United States.

---

[72] Sec. 301(b)(3) of IIRAIRA provides: "In applying §212(a)(9)(B) of the Immigration and Nationality Act, as inserted by paragraph (1), no period before the title III-A effective date shall be included in a period of unlawful presence in the United States." *See* IIRAIRA §309 (*reprinted in* Appendix C, *infra*) for title III-A effective date provisions.

[73] *Sic.* Probably should be §240B.

(iv) Tolling for good cause.— In the case of an alien who—

(I) has been lawfully admitted or paroled into the United States,

(II) has filed a nonfrivolous application for a change or extension of status before the date of expiration of the period of stay authorized by the Attorney General, and

(III) has not been employed without authorization in the United States before or during the pendency of such application,

the calculation of the period of time specified in clause (i)(I) shall be tolled during the pendency of such application, but not to exceed 120 days.

(v) Waiver.— The Attorney General has sole discretion to waive clause (i) in the case of an immigrant who is the spouse or son or daughter of a United States citizen or of an alien lawfully admitted for permanent residence, if it is established to the satisfaction of the Attorney General that the refusal of admission to such immigrant alien would result in extreme hardship to the citizen or lawfully resident spouse or parent of such alien. No court shall have jurisdiction to review a decision or action by the Attorney General regarding a waiver under this clause.

(C) *Aliens unlawfully present after previous immigration violations.*—

(i) In general.— Any alien who—

(I) has been unlawfully present in the United States for an aggregate period of more than 1 year, or

(II) has been ordered removed under section 235(b)(1), section 240, or any other provision of law,

and who enters or attempts to reenter the United States without being admitted is inadmissible.

(ii) Exception.— Clause (i) shall not apply to an alien seeking admission more than 10 years after the date of the alien's last departure from the United States if, prior to the alien's reembarkation at a place outside the United States or attempt to be readmitted from a foreign contiguous territory, the Secretary of Homeland Security has consented to the alien's reapplying for admission.

(iii) Waiver.— The Secretary of Homeland Security may waive the application of clause (i) in the case of an alien who is a VAWA self-petitioner if there is a connection between—

(I) the alien's battering or subjection to extreme cruelty; and

(II) the alien's removal, departure from the United States, reentry or reentries into the United States; or attempted reentry into the United States.

(10) *Miscellaneous.*—

(A) *Practicing polygamists.*— Any immigrant who is coming to the United States to practice polygamy is inadmissible.

(B) *Guardian required to accompany helpless alien.*— Any alien—

(i) who is accompanying another alien who is inadmissible and who is certified to be helpless from sickness, mental or physical disability, or infancy pursuant to section 232(c), and

(ii) whose protection or guardianship is determined to be required by the alien described in clause (i),

is inadmissible.

(C) *International child abduction.—*

(i) In general.— Except as provided in clause (ii), any alien who, after entry of an order by a court in the United States granting custody to a person of a United States citizen child who detains or retains the child, or withholds custody of the child, outside the United States from the person granted custody by that order, is inadmissible until the child is surrendered to the person granted custody by that order.

(ii) Aliens supporting abductors and relatives of abductors.— Any alien who—

(I) is known by the Secretary of State to have intentionally assisted an alien in the conduct described in clause (i),

(II) is known by the Secretary of State to be intentionally providing material support or safe haven to an alien described in clause (i), or

(III)[74] is a spouse (other than the spouse who is the parent of the abducted child), child (other than the abducted child), parent, sibling, or agent of an alien described in clause (i), if such person has been designated by the Secretary of State at the Secretary's sole and unreviewable discretion, is inadmissible until the child described in clause (i) is surrendered to the person granted custody by the order described in that clause, and such person and child are permitted to return to the United States or such person's place of residence.

(iii) Exceptions.— Clauses (i) and (ii) shall not apply—

(I) to a government official of the United States who is acting within the scope of his or her official duties;

(II) to a government official of any foreign government if the official has been designated by the Secretary of State at the Secretary's sole and unreviewable discretion; or

(III) so long as the child is located in a foreign state that is a party to the Convention on the Civil Aspects of International Child Abduction, done at The Hague on October 25, 1980.

(D) *Unlawful voters.—*

(i) In general.— Any alien who has voted in violation of any Federal, State, or local constitutional provision, statute, ordinance, or regulation is inadmissible.

(ii) Exception.— In the case of an alien who voted in a Federal, State, or local election (including an initiative, recall, or referendum) in violation of a lawful re-

---

[74] Subclause 212(a)(10)(C)(ii)(III), reprinted here as in the original legislation (P.L. 105-277, §2226), most probably should be read as if it ended after the comma after the words "unreviewable discretion," with the remaining text (beginning with "is inadmissible") outdented and applicable to all of clause (10)(C)(ii).

striction of voting to citizens, if each natural parent of the alien (or, in the case of an adopted alien, each adoptive parent of the alien) is or was a citizen (whether by birth or naturalization), the alien permanently resided in the United States prior to attaining the age of 16, and the alien reasonably believed at the time of such violation that he or she was a citizen, the alien shall not be considered to be inadmissible under any provision of this subsection based on such violation.

(E)[75] *Former citizens who renounced citizenship to avoid taxation.*— Any alien who is a former citizen of the United States who officially renounces United States citizenship and who is determined by the Attorney General to have renounced United States citizenship for the purpose of avoiding taxation by the United States is excludable.

**(b) Notices of denials.—**

(1) Subject to paragraphs (2) and (3) if an alien's application for a visa, for admission to the United States, or for adjustment of status is denied by an immigration or consular officer because the officer determines the alien to be inadmissible under subsection (a), the officer shall provide the alien with a timely written notice that—

(A) states the determination, and

(B) lists the specific provision or provisions of law under which the alien is inadmissible or adjustment[76] of status.

(2) The Secretary of State may waive the requirements of paragraph (1) with respect to a particular alien or any class or classes of inadmissible aliens.

(3) Paragraph (1) does not apply to any alien inadmissible under paragraph (2) or (3) of subsection (a).

**(c)** [Repealed][77]

**(d) Temporary admission of nonimmigrants.—**

(1) The Attorney General shall determine whether a ground for inadmissibility exists with respect to a nonimmigrant described in section 101(a)(15)(S). The Attorney General, in the Attorney General's discretion, may waive the application of subsection (a) (other than paragraph (3)(E)) in the case of a nonimmigrant described in section 101(a)(15)(S), if the Attorney General considers it to be in the national interest to do so. Nothing in this section shall be regarded as prohibiting the Immigration and Nationalization Service from instituting removal proceedings against an alien admitted as a nonimmigrant under section 101(a)(15)(S) for

---

[75] Effective for "individuals who renounce United States citizenship on and after the date of the enactment of [P.L. 104-208]." P.L. 104-208 (9/30/96), div. C, §352(b).

[76] *Sic.* Probably should be "... inadmissible or ineligible for adjustment of status."

[77] Sec. 212(c) was repealed by §304(b) of IIRAIRA, effective on the title III-A effective date; however, IIRAIRA §306(d) makes an amendment to AEDPA §440(d), which in turn amends former INA §212(c). [For IIRAIRA effective-date and transition rules, see IIRAIRA §309, *reprinted in* Appendix C, *infra.*] The former §212(c) follows; references to INA §237 have been changed below to §241, to which it had been redesignated.

"(c) Aliens lawfully admitted for permanent residence who temporarily proceeded abroad voluntarily and not under an order of deportation, and who are returning to a lawful unrelinquished domicile of seven consecutive years, may be admitted in the discretion of the Attorney General without regard to the provisions of subsection (a) (other than paragraphs (3) and (9)(C)). Nothing contained in this subsection shall limit the authority of the Attorney General to exercise the discretion vested in him under §211(b). This subsection shall not apply to an alien who is deportable by reason of having committed any criminal offense covered in §241(a)(2)(A)(iii), (B), (C), or (D), or any offense covered by §241(a)(2)(A)(ii) for which both predicate offenses are, without regard to the date of their commission, otherwise covered by §241(a)(2)(A)(i)."

conduct committed after the alien's admission into the United States, or for conduct or a condition that was not disclosed to the Attorney General prior to the alien's admission as a nonimmigrant under section 101(a)(15)(S).

(2) [Repealed.][78]

(3)  (A) Except as provided in this subsection, an alien

(i) who is applying for a nonimmigrant visa and is known or believed by the consular officer to be ineligible for such visa under subsection (a) (other than paragraphs (3)(A)(i)(I), (3)(A)(ii), (3)(A)(iii), (3)(C), and clauses (i) and (ii) of paragraph (3)(E) of such subsection), may, after approval by the Attorney General of a recommendation by the Secretary of State or by the consular officer that the alien be admitted temporarily despite his inadmissibility, be granted such a visa and may be admitted into the United States temporarily as a nonimmigrant in the discretion of the Attorney General, or

(ii) who is inadmissible under subsection (a) (other than paragraphs (3)(A)(i)(I), (3)(A)(ii), (3)(A)(iii), (3)(C), and clauses (i) and (ii) of paragraph (3)(E) of such subsection), but who is in possession of appropriate documents or is granted a waiver thereof and is seeking admission, may be admitted into the United States temporarily as a nonimmigrant in the discretion of the Attorney General. The Attorney General shall prescribe conditions, including exaction of such bonds as may be necessary, to control and regulate the admission and return of inadmissible aliens applying for temporary admission under this paragraph.

(B) (i)[79] The Secretary of State, after consultation with the Attorney General and the Secretary of Homeland Security, or the Secretary of Homeland Security, after consultation with the Secretary of State and the Attorney General, may determine in such Secretary's sole unreviewable discretion that subsection (a)(3)(B) shall not apply with respect to an alien within the scope of that subsection or that subsection (a)(3)(B)(vi)(III) shall not apply to a group within the scope of that subsection, except that no such waiver may be extended to an alien who is within the scope of subsection (a)(3)(B)(i)(II), no such waiver may be extended to an alien who is a member or representative of, has voluntarily and knowingly engaged in or endorsed or espoused or persuaded others to endorse or espouse or support terrorist activity on behalf of, or has voluntarily and knowingly received military-type training from a terrorist organization that is described in subclause (I) or (II) of subsection (a)(3)(B)(vi), and no such waiver may be extended to a group that has engaged terrorist activity against the United States or another democratic country or that has purposefully engaged in a pattern or practice of terrorist activity that is directed at civilians. Such a determination shall neither prejudice the ability of the United States Government to commence criminal or civil proceedings involving a beneficiary of such a determination or any other person, nor create any substantive or procedural right or benefit for a beneficiary of such a determination or any other person. Notwithstanding any other provision of law (statutory or nonstatutory), including section

---

[78] Repealed by P.L. 101-649 (11/29/90), title VI, §601(d)(2)(A).

[79] Subsection (B)(i), as amended by P.L. 110-161, applies to removal proceeding instituted before, on, or after Dec. 26, 2007, and to acts and conditions constituting a ground for inadmissibility, excludability, deportation, or removal occurring or existing before, on, or after Dec. 26, 2007. P.L. 110-161, §691(f).

2241 of title 28, or any other habeas corpus provision, and sections 1361 and 1651 of such title, no court shall have jurisdiction to review such a determination or revocation except in a proceeding for review of a final order of removal pursuant to section 1252 of this title, and review shall be limited to the extent provided in section 1252(a)(2)(D). The Secretary of State may not exercise the discretion provided in this clause with respect to an alien at any time during which the alien is the subject of pending removal proceedings under section 1229a of this title.

(ii) Not later than 90 days after the end of each fiscal year, the Secretary of State and the Secretary of Homeland Security shall each provide to the Committees on the Judiciary of the House of Representatives and of the Senate, the Committee on International Relations of the House of Representatives, the Committee on Foreign Relations of the Senate, and the Committee on Homeland Security of the House of Representatives a report on the aliens to whom such Secretary has applied clause (i). Within one week of applying clause (i) to a group, the Secretary of State or the Secretary of Homeland Security shall provide a report to such Committees.

(4) Either or both of the requirements of paragraph (7)(B)(i) of subsection (a) may be waived by the Attorney General and the Secretary of State acting jointly

(A) on the basis of unforeseen emergency in individual cases, or

(B)[80] on the basis of reciprocity with respect to nationals of foreign contiguous territory or of adjacent islands and residents thereof having a common nationality with such nationals, or

(C)[81] in the case of aliens proceeding in immediate and continuous transit through the United States under contracts authorized in section 238(c).

(5)[82](A) The Attorney General may, except as provided in subparagraph (B) or in section 214(f), in his discretion parole into the United States temporarily under such conditions as he may prescribe only on a case-by-case basis for urgent humanitarian reasons or significant public benefit any alien applying for admission to the United States, but such parole of such alien shall not be regarded as an admission of the alien and when the purposes of such parole shall, in the opinion of the Attorney General, have been served the alien shall forthwith return or be returned to the custody from which he was paroled and thereafter his case shall continue to be dealt with in the same manner as that of any other applicant for admission to the United States.

(B) The Attorney General may not parole into the United States an alien who is a refugee unless the Attorney General determines that compelling reasons in the public interest with respect to that particular alien require that the alien be paroled into the United States rather than be admitted as a refugee under section 207.

---

[80] Sec. 7209 of P.L. 108-458 (12/17/04) mandates the creation of a plan to expedite the travel of certain frequent travelers. Subsection (c)(1) of that section provides that "neither the Secretary of State nor the Secretary of Homeland Security may exercise discretion under [INA §212(d)(4)(B)] to waive documentary requirements for travel into the United States."

[81] Sec. 7209(d) of P.L. 108-458 (12/17/04) provides that "[t]he Secretary of State shall not use any authorities granted under [INA §212(d)(4)(C)] until the Secretary, in conjunction with the Secretary of Homeland Security, completely implements a security plan to fully ensure secure transit passage areas to prevent aliens proceeding in immediate and continuous transit through the United States from illegally entering the United States."

[82] *See* §422(e) of the USA PATRIOT Act, P.L. 107-56, *reprinted in* Appendix J, *infra*, for provisions relating to immigration benefits for the victims of terrorism.

(6) [Repealed.][83]

(7) The provisions of subsection (a) (other than paragraph (7)) shall be applicable to any alien who shall leave Guam the Commonwealth of the Northern Mariana Islands, Puerto Rico, or the Virgin Islands of the United States, and who seeks to enter the continental United States or any other place under the jurisdiction of the United States. The Attorney General shall by regulations provide a method and procedure for the temporary admission to the United States of the aliens described in this proviso. Any alien described in this paragraph, who is denied admission to the United States, shall be immediately removed in the manner provided by section 241(c) of this Act.

(8) Upon a basis of reciprocity accredited officials of foreign governments, their immediate families, attendants, servants, and personal employees may be admitted in immediate and continuous transit through the United States without regard to the provisions of this section except paragraphs (3)(A), (3)(B), (3)(C), and (7)(B) of subsection (a) of this section.

(9) [Repealed.][84]

(10) [Repealed.][85]

(11)[86] The Attorney General may, in his discretion for humanitarian purposes, to assure family unity, or when it is otherwise in the public interest, waive application of clause (i) of subsection (a)(6)(E) in the case of any alien lawfully admitted for permanent residence who temporarily proceeded abroad voluntarily and not under an order of removal, and who is otherwise admissible to the United States as a returning resident under section 211(b) and in the case of an alien seeking admission or adjustment of status as an immediate relative or immigrant under section 203(a) (other than paragraph (4) thereof), if the alien has encouraged, induced, assisted, abetted, or aided only an individual who at the time of the offense was the alien's spouse, parent, son, or daughter (and no other individual) to enter the United States in violation of law.

(12) The Attorney General may, in the discretion of the Attorney General for humanitarian purposes or to assure family unity, waive application of clause (i) of subsection (a)(6)(F)—

   (A) in the case of an alien lawfully admitted for permanent residence who temporarily proceeded abroad voluntarily and not under an order of deportation or removal and who is otherwise admissible to the United States as a returning resident under section 211(b), and

   (B) in the case of an alien seeking admission or adjustment of status under section 201(b)(2)(A) or under section 203(a),

if no previous civil money penalty was imposed against the alien under section 274C and the offense was committed solely to assist, aid, or support the alien's spouse or child (and not another individual). No court shall have jurisdiction to review a decision of the Attorney General to grant or deny a waiver under this paragraph.

(13)(A)[87] The Secretary of Homeland Security shall determine whether a ground for

---

[83] Repealed by P.L. 101-649 (11/29/90), title VI, §601(d)(2)(A).

[84] Repealed by P.L. 101-649 (11/29/90), title VI, §601(d)(2)(A).

[85] Repealed by P.L. 101-649 (11/29/90), title VI, §601(d)(2)(A).

[86] IIRAIRA §351 added the clarifying phrase "an individual who was at the time of the offense was" both here and in §237(a)(1)(E)(iii). Effective "for waivers filed before, on, or after the date of the enactment of [IIRAIRA], but shall not apply to such an application for which a final determination has been made as of the date of the enactment of [IIRAIRA]."

[87] Created by §107(e)(3) of P.L. 106-386 (Victims of Trafficking and Violence Protection Act, 2000 (10/28/00)). A second para-
*continued*

inadmissibility exists with respect to a nonimmigrant described in section 101(a)(15)(T), except that the ground for inadmissibility described in subsection (a)(4) shall not apply with respect to such a nonimmigrant.

(B) In addition to any other waiver that may be available under this section, in the case of a nonimmigrant described in section 101(a)(15)(T), if the Secretary of Homeland Security considers it to be in the national interest to do so, the Secretary of Homeland Security, in the Secretary of Homeland Security's discretion, may waive the application of—

(i) subsection (a)(1); and

(ii) any other provision of subsection (a) (excluding paragraphs (3), (4), (10)(C), and (10)(E))[88] if the activities rendering the alien inadmissible under the provision were caused by, or were incident to, the victimization described in section 101(a)(15)(T)(i)(I).

(14)[89] The Secretary of Homeland Security shall determine whether a ground for inadmissibility exists with respect to a nonimmigrant described in section 101(a)(15)(U). The Secretary of Homeland Security, in the Secretary of Homeland Security's discretion, may waive the application of subsection (a) (other than paragraph (3)(E)) in the case of a nonimmigrant described in section 101(a)(15)(U), if the Secretary of Homeland Security considers it to be in the public or national interest to do so.

**(e) Educational visitor status; foreign residence requirement; waiver.**— No person admitted under section 101(a)(15)(J) or acquiring such status after admission (i) whose participation in the program for which he came to the United States was financed in whole or in part, directly or indirectly, by an agency of the Government of the United States or by the government of the country of his nationality or his last residence, (ii) who at the time of admission or acquisition of status under section 101(a)(15)(J) was a national or resident of a country which the Director of the United States Information Agency pursuant to regulations prescribed by him, had designated as clearly requiring the services of persons engaged in the field of specialized knowledge or skill in which the alien was engaged, or (iii) who came to the United States or acquired such status in order to receive graduate medical education or training, shall be eligible to apply for an immigrant visa, or for permanent residence, or for a nonimmigrant visa under section 101(a)(15)(H) or section 101(a)(15)(L) until it is established that such person has resided and been physically present in the country of his nationality or his last residence for an aggregate of at least two years following departure from the United States: *Provided,* That upon the favorable recommendation of the Director, pursuant to the request of an interested United States Government agency (or, in the case of an alien described in clause (iii), pursuant to the request of a State Department of Public Health, or its equivalent), or of the Commissioner of Immigration and Naturalization after he has determined that departure from the United States would impose exceptional hardship upon the alien's spouse or child (if such spouse or child is a citizen of the United States or a lawfully resident alien), or that the alien cannot return to the country of his nationality or last residence because he would be subject to persecution on account of race, religion, or political opinion, the Attorney General may waive the requirement of such two-year foreign residence abroad in the case of any alien whose admission to the United States is found by the Attorney General to be in

---

graph (13) was created by §1513(e) of the same 2000 Act, but redesignated as (14) by P.L. 108-193 (12/19/03).

[88] Original text omitted the open parenthesis in "(E)."

[89] Created as paragraph (13) by §1513(e) of P.L. 106-386 (Victims of Trafficking and Violence Protection Act, 2000 (10/28/00)); redesignated as (14) by P.L. 108-193 (12/19/03).

the public interest except that in the case of a waiver requested by a State Department of Public Health, or its equivalent, or in the case of a waiver requested by an interested United States government agency on behalf of an alien described in clause (iii), the waiver shall be subject to the requirements of section 214(*l*): *And provided further,* That, except in the case of an alien described in clause (iii), the Attorney General may, upon the favorable recommendation of the Director, waive such two-year foreign residence requirement in any case in which the foreign country of the alien's nationality or last residence has furnished the Director a statement in writing that it has no objection to such waiver in the case of such alien.

**(f) Suspension of entry or imposition of restrictions by President.**— Whenever the President finds that the entry of any aliens or of any class of aliens into the United States would be detrimental to the interests of the United States, he may by proclamation, and for such period as he shall deem necessary, suspend the entry of all aliens or any class of aliens as immigrants or nonimmigrants, or impose on the entry of aliens any restrictions he may deem to be appropriate. Whenever the Attorney General finds that a commercial airline has failed to comply with regulations of the Attorney General relating to requirements of airlines for the detection of fraudulent documents used by passengers traveling to the United States (including the training of personnel in such detection), the Attorney General may suspend the entry of some or all aliens transported to the United States by such airline.

**(g) Bond and conditions for admission of alien excludable on health-related grounds.**— The Attorney General may waive the application of—[90]

(1) subsection (a)(1)(A)(i) in the case of any alien who—

(A) is the spouse or the unmarried son or daughter, or the minor unmarried lawfully adopted child, of a United States citizen, or of an alien lawfully admitted for permanent residence, or of an alien who has been issued an immigrant visa,

(B) has a son or daughter who is a United States citizen, or an alien lawfully admitted for permanent residence, or an alien who has been issued an immigrant visa; or

(C) is a VAWA self-petitioner,

in accordance with such terms, conditions, and controls, if any, including the giving of bond, as the Attorney General, in the discretion of the Attorney General after consultation with the Secretary of Health and Human Services, may by regulation prescribe;

(2) subsection (a)(1)(A)(ii) in the case of any alien—

(A) who receives vaccination against the vaccine-preventable disease or diseases for which the alien has failed to present documentation of previous vaccination,

(B) for whom a civil surgeon, medical officer, or panel physician (as those terms are defined by section 34.2 of title 42 of the Code of Federal Regulations) certifies according to such regulations as the Secretary of Health and Human Services may prescribe, that such vaccination would not be medically appropriate, or

(C) under such circumstances as the Attorney General provides by regulation, with respect to whom the requirement of such a vaccination would be contrary to the alien's religious beliefs or moral convictions; or

---

[90] *See* IIRAIRA §341(b), effective with respect to applications for immigrant visas or for adjustment of status filed after 9/30/96.

(3) subsection (a)(1)(A)(iii) in the case of any alien, in accordance with such terms, conditions, and controls, if any, including the giving of bond, as the Attorney General, in the discretion of the Attorney General after consultation with the Secretary of Health and Human Services, may by regulation prescribe.

**(h) Waiver of subsection (a)(2)(A)(i)(I), (II), (B), (D), and (E).—** The Attorney General may, in his discretion, waive the application of subparagraphs (A)(i)(I), (B), (D), and (E) of subsection (a)(2) and subparagraph (A)(i)(II) of such subsection insofar as it relates to a single offense of simple possession of 30 grams or less of marijuana if—

(1) (A) in the case of any immigrant it is established to the satisfaction of the Attorney General that—

(i) the alien is inadmissible only under subparagraph (D)(i) or (D)(ii) of such subsection or the activities for which the alien is inadmissible occurred more than 15 years before the date of the alien's application for a visa, admission, or adjustment of status,

(ii) the admission to the United States of such alien would not be contrary to the national welfare, safety, or security of the United States, and

(iii) the alien has been rehabilitated; or

(B) in the case of an immigrant who is the spouse, parent, son, or daughter of a citizen of the United States or an alien lawfully admitted for permanent residence if it is established to the satisfaction of the Attorney General that the alien's denial of admission would result in extreme hardship to the United States citizen or lawfully resident spouse, parent, son, or daughter of such alien; or

(C) the alien is a VAWA self-petitioner; and

(2) the Attorney General, in his discretion, and pursuant to such terms, conditions and procedures as he may by regulations prescribe, has consented to the alien's applying or reapplying for a visa, for admission to the United States, or adjustment of status.

No waiver shall be provided under this subsection in the case of an alien who has been convicted of (or who has admitted committing acts that constitute) murder or criminal acts involving torture, or an attempt or conspiracy to commit murder or a criminal act involving torture. No waiver shall be granted under this subsection in the case of an alien who has previously been admitted to the United States as an alien lawfully admitted for permanent residence if either since the date of such admission the alien has been convicted of an aggravated felony or the alien has not lawfully resided continuously in the United States for a period of not less than 7 years immediately preceding the date of initiation of proceedings to remove the alien from the United States. No court shall have jurisdiction to review a decision of the Attorney General to grant or deny a waiver under this subsection.[91]

**(i) Admission of immigrant excludable for fraud or willful misrepresentation of material fact.—**

(1) The Attorney General may, in the discretion of the Attorney General, waive the application of clause (i) of subsection (a)(6)(C) in the case of an immigrant who is the spouse, son, or daughter of a United States citizen or of an alien lawfully admitted for permanent

---

[91] *See* §348 of IIRAIRA, effective on the date of enactment of IIRAIRA. It applies in the case of any alien who is in exclusion or deportation proceedings as of such date unless a final administrative order in such proceedings has been entered as of such date. IIRAIRA §308(g)(10) offers the following amendment to INA §212(h): "(10) *Miscellaneous Cross-Reference Corrections for Newly Added Provisions.*—(A) Sec. 212(h), as amended by §301(h) of this division, is amended by striking "§212(c)" and inserting "paragraphs (1) and (2) of §240A(a)". The amendment makes no sense since there is no §301(h) in IIRAIRA nor is the referenced text in §212(h) of the INA.

residence, if it is established to the satisfaction of the Attorney General that the refusal of admission to the United States of such immigrant alien would result in extreme hardship to the citizen or lawfully resident spouse or parent of such an alien or, in the case of a VAWA self-petitioner, the alien demonstrates extreme hardship to the alien or the alien's United States citizen, lawful permanent resident, or qualified alien parent or child.

(2) No court shall have jurisdiction to review a decision or action of the Attorney General regarding a waiver under paragraph (1).

**(j) Limitation on immigration of foreign medical graduates.—**

(1) The additional requirements referred to in section 101(a)(15)(J) for an alien who is coming to the United States under a program under which he will receive graduate medical education or training are as follows:

(A) A school of medicine or of one of the other health professions, which is accredited by a body or bodies approved for the purpose by the Secretary of Education, has agreed in writing to provide the graduate medical education or training under the program for which the alien is coming to the United States or to assume responsibility for arranging for the provision thereof by an appropriate public or nonprofit private institution or agency, except that, in the case of such an agreement by a school of medicine, any one or more of its affiliated hospitals which are to participate in the provision of the graduate medical education or training must join in the agreement.

(B) Before making such agreement, the accredited school has been satisfied that the alien

(i) is a graduate of a school of medicine which is accredited by a body or bodies approved for the purpose by the Secretary of Education (regardless of whether such school of medicine is in the United States); or

(ii) (I) has passed parts I and II of the National Board of Medical Examiners Examination (or an equivalent examination as determined by the Secretary of Health and Human Services),

(II) has competency in oral and written English,

(III) will be able to adapt to the educational and cultural environment in which he will be receiving his education or training, and

(IV) has adequate prior education and training to participate satisfactorily in the program for which he is coming to the United States. For the purposes of this subparagraph, an alien who is a graduate of a medical school shall be considered to have passed parts I and II of the National Board of Medical Examiners examination if the alien was fully and permanently licensed to practice medicine in a State on January 9, 1978, and was practicing medicine in a State on that date.

(C) The alien has made a commitment to return to the country of his nationality or last residence upon completion of the education or training for which he is coming to the United States, and the government of the country of his nationality or last residence has provided a written assurance, satisfactory to the Secretary of Health and Human Services, that there is a need in that country for persons with the skills the alien will acquire in such education or training.

(D) The duration of the alien's participation in the program of graduate medical education or training for which the alien is coming to the United States is limited to the time typically required to complete such program, as determined by the Director of the United States Information Agency at the time of the alien's admission into the United States, based on criteria which are established in coordination with the Secretary of Health and Human Services and which take into consideration the published requirements of the medical specialty board which administers such education or training program; except that—

(i) such duration is further limited to seven years unless the alien has demonstrated to the satisfaction of the Director that the country to which the alien will return at the end of such specialty education or training has an exceptional need for an individual trained in such specialty, and

(ii) the alien may, once and not later than two years after the date the alien is admitted to the United States as an exchange visitor or acquires exchange visitor status, change the alien's designated program of graduate medical education or training if the Director approves the change and if a commitment and written assurance with respect to the alien's new program have been provided in accordance with subparagraph (C).

(E) The alien furnishes the Attorney General each year with an affidavit (in such form as the Attorney General shall prescribe) that attests that the alien—

(i) is in good standing in the program of graduate medical education or training in which the alien is participating, and

(ii) will return to the country of his nationality or last residence upon completion of the education or training for which he came to the United States.

(2) An alien who is a graduate of a medical school and who is coming to the United States to perform services as a member of the medical profession may not be admitted as a nonimmigrant under section 101(a)(15)(H)(i)(b) unless—

(A) the alien is coming pursuant to an invitation from a public or nonprofit private educational or research institution or agency in the United States to teach or conduct research, or both, at or for such institution or agency, or

(B) (i) the alien has passed the Federation licensing examination (administered by the Federation of State Medical Boards of the United States) or an equivalent examination as determined by the Secretary of Health and Human Services, and

(ii) (I) has competency in oral and written English or

(II) is a graduate of a school of medicine which is accredited by a body or bodies approved for the purpose by the Secretary of Education (regardless of whether such school of medicine is in the United States).

**(k) Attorney General's discretion to admit otherwise inadmissible aliens who possess immigrant visas.**— Any alien, inadmissible from the United States under paragraph (5)(A) or (7)(A)(i) of subsection (a), who is in possession of an immigrant visa may, if otherwise admissible, be admitted in the discretion of the Attorney General if the Attorney General is satisfied that inadmissibility was not known to, and could not have been ascertained by the exercise of reasonable diligence by, the immigrant before the time of departure of the vessel or aircraft from the last port outside the United States and outside foreign contiguous territory or, in the case of an immigrant coming from foreign contiguous territory, before the time of the immigrant's application for admission.

**(l) Guam and Northern Mariana Islands Visa Waiver Program.**—

(1) *In general.*— The requirement of subsection (a)(7)(B)(i) may be waived by the Secretary of Homeland Security, in the case of an alien applying for admission as a nonimmigrant visitor for business or pleasure and solely for entry into and stay in Guam or the Commonwealth of the Northern Mariana Islands for a period not to exceed 45 days, if the Secretary of Homeland Security, after consultation with the Secretary of the Interior, the Secretary of State, the Governor of Guam and the Governor of the Commonwealth of the Northern Mariana Islands, determines that—

(A) an adequate arrival and departure control system has been developed in Guam and the Commonwealth of the Northern Mariana Islands; and

(B) such a waiver does not represent a threat to the welfare, safety, or security of the United States or its territories and commonwealths.

(2) *Alien waiver of rights.*— An alien may not be provided a waiver under this subsection unless the alien has waived any right—

(A) to review or appeal under this Act an immigration officer's determination as to the admissibility of the alien at the port of entry into Guam or the Commonwealth of the Northern Mariana Islands; or

(B) to contest, other than on the basis of an application for withholding of removal under section 241(b)(3) of this Act or under the Convention Against Torture, or an application for asylum if permitted under section 208, any action for removal of the alien.

(3) *Regulations.*— All necessary regulations to implement this subsection shall be promulgated by the Secretary of Homeland Security, in consultation with the Secretary of the Interior and the Secretary of State, on or before the 180th day after the date of enactment of the Consolidated Natural Resources Act of 2008. The promulgation of such regulations shall be considered a foreign affairs function for purposes of section 553(a) of title 5, United States Code. At a minimum, such regulations should include, but not necessarily be limited to—

(A) a listing of all countries whose nationals may obtain the waiver also provided by this subsection, except that such regulations shall provide for a listing of any country from which the Commonwealth has received a significant economic benefit from the number of visitors for pleasure within the one-year period preceding the date of enactment of the Consolidated Natural Resources Act of 2008, unless the Secretary of Homeland Security determines that such country's inclusion on such list would represent a threat to the welfare, safety, or security of the United States or its territories; and

(B) any bonding requirements for nationals of some or all of those countries who may present an increased risk of overstays or other potential problems, if different from such requirements otherwise provided by law for nonimmigrant visitors.

(4) *Factors.*— In determining whether to grant or continue providing the waiver under this subsection to nationals of any country, the Secretary of Homeland Security, in consultation with the Secretary of the Interior and the Secretary of State, hall consider all factors that the Secretary deems relevant, including electronic travel authorizations, procedures for reporting lost and stolen passports, repatriation of aliens, rates of refusal for nonimmigrant visitor visas, overstays, exit systems, and information exchange.

(5) *Suspension.*— The Secretary of Homeland Security shall monitor the admission of nonimmigrant visitors to Guam and the Commonwealth of the Northern Mariana Islands under this subsection. If the Secretary determines that such admissions have resulted in an unacceptable number of visitors from a country remaining unlawfully in Guam or the Common-

wealth of the Northern Mariana Islands, unlawfully obtaining entry to other parts of the United States, or seeking withholding of removal or asylum, or that visitors from a country pose a risk to law enforcement or security interests of Guam or the Commonwealth of the Northern Mariana Islands or of the United States (including the interest in the enforcement of the immigration laws of the United States), the Secretary shall suspend the admission of nationals of such country under this subsection. The Secretary of Homeland Security may in the Secretary's discretion suspend the Guam and Northern Mariana Islands visa waiver program at any time, on a country-by-country basis, for other good cause.

(6) *Addition of countries.*— The Governor of Guam and the Governor of the Commonwealth of the Northern Mariana Islands may request the Secretary of the Interior and the Secretary of Homeland Security to add a particular country to the list of countries whose nationals may obtain the waiver provided by this subsection, and the Secretary of Homeland Security may grant such request after consultation with the Secretary of the Interior and the Secretary of State, and may promulgate regulations with respect to the inclusion of that country and any special requirements the Secretary of Homeland Security, in the Secretary's sole discretion, may impose prior to allowing nationals of that country to obtain the waiver provided by this subsection.

**(m) Requirements for admission of nonimmigrant nurses.—**

(1) The qualifications referred to in section 101(a)(15)(H)(i)(c), with respect to an alien who is coming to the United States to perform nursing services for a facility, are that the alien—

(A) has obtained a full and unrestricted license to practice professional nursing in the country where the alien obtained nursing education or has received nursing education in the United States;

(B) has passed an appropriate examination (recognized in regulations promulgated in consultation with the Secretary of Health and Human Services) or has a full and unrestricted license under State law to practice professional nursing in the State of intended employment; and

(C) is fully qualified and eligible under the laws (including such temporary or interim licensing requirements which authorize the nurse to be employed) governing the place of intended employment to engage in the practice of professional nursing as a registered nurse immediately upon admission to the United States and is authorized under such laws to be employed by the facility.

(2) (A) The attestation referred to in section 101(a)(15)(H)(i)(c), with respect to a facility for which an alien will perform services, is an attestation as to the following:

(i) The facility meets all requirements of paragraph (6).

(ii) The employment of the alien will not adversely affect the wages and working conditions of registered nurses similarly employed.

(iii) The alien employed by the facility will be paid the wage rate for registered nurses similarly employed by the facility.

(iv) The facility has taken and is taking timely and significant steps designed to recruit and retain sufficient registered nurses who are United States citizens or immigrants who are authorized to perform nursing services, in order to remove as quickly as reasonably possible the dependence of the facility on nonimmigrant registered nurses

(v) There is not a strike or lockout in the course of a labor dispute, the facility did not lay off and will not lay off a registered nurse employed by the facility within the period beginning 90 days before and ending 90 days after the date of filing of any visa petition, and the employment of such an alien is not intended or designed to influence an election for a bargaining representative for registered nurses of the facility.

(vi) At the time of the filing of the petition for registered nurses under section 101(a)(15)(H)(i)(c), notice of the filing has been provided by the facility to the bargaining representative of the registered nurses at the facility or, where there is no such bargaining representative, notice of the filing has been provided to the registered nurses employed at the facility through posting in conspicuous locations.

(vii) The facility will not, at any time, employ a number of aliens issued visas or otherwise provided nonimmigrant status under section 101(a)(15)(H)(i)(c) that exceeds 33 percent of the total number of registered nurses employed by the facility.

(viii) The facility will not, with respect to any alien issued a visa or otherwise provided nonimmigrant status under section 101(a)(15)(H)(i)(c)

(I) Authorize the alien to perform nursing services at any worksite other than a worksite controlled by the facility; or

(II) transfer the place of employment of the alien from one worksite to another.

Nothing in clause (iv) shall be construed as requiring a facility to have taken significant steps descried in such clause before the date of the enactment of the Nursing Relief for Disadvantaged Areas Act of 1999. A copy of the attestation shall be provided, within 30 days of the date of filing, to registered nurses employed at the facility on the date of filing.

(B) For purposes of subparagraph (A)(iv), each of the following shall be considered a significant step reasonably designed to recruit and retain registered nurses:

(i) Operating a training program for registered nurses at the facility or financing (or providing participation in) a training program for registered nurses elsewhere.

(ii) Providing career development programs and other methods of facilitating health care workers to become registered nurses.

(iii) Paying registered nurses wages at a rate higher than currently being paid to registered nurses similarly employed in the geographic area.

(iv) Providing reasonable opportunities for meaningful salary advancement by registered nurses.

The steps described in this subparagraph shall not be considered to be an exclusive list of the significant steps that may be taken to meet the conditions of subparagraph (A)(iv). Nothing in this subparagraph shall require a facility to take more than one step if the facility can demonstrate that taking a second step is not reasonable.

(C) Subject to subparagraph (E), an attestation under subparagraph (A)—

(i) shall expire on the date that is the later of—

(I) the end of the one-year period beginning on the date of its filing with the Secretary of Labor; or

(II) the end of the period of admission under section 101(a)(15)(H)(i)(c) of the last alien with respect to whose admission it was applied (in accordance with clause (ii)); and

(ii) shall apply to petitions filed during the one-year period beginning on the date of its filing with the Secretary of Labor if the facility states in each such petition that it continues to comply with the conditions in the attestation.

(D) A facility may meet the requirements under this paragraph with respect to more than one registered nurse in a single petition.

(E) (i) The Secretary of Labor shall compile and make available for public examination in a timely manner in Washington, D.C., a list identifying facilities which have filed petitions for nonimmigrants under section 101(a)(15)(H)(i)(c) and, for each such facility, a copy of the facility's attestation under subparagraph (A) (and accompanying documentation) and each such petition filed by the facility.

(ii) The Secretary of Labor shall establish a process, including reasonable time limits, for the receipt, investigation, and disposition of complaints respecting a facility's failure to meet conditions attested to or a facility's misrepresentation of a material fact in an attestation. Complaints may be filed by any aggrieved person or organization (including bargaining representatives, associations deemed appropriate by the Secretary, and other aggrieved parties as determined under regulations of the Secretary). The Secretary shall conduct an investigation under this clause if there is reasonable cause to believe that a facility fails to meet conditions attested to. Subject to the time limits established under this clause, this subparagraph shall apply regardless of whether an attestation is expired or unexpired at the time a complaint is filed.

(iii) Under such process, the Secretary shall provide, within 180 days after the date such a complaint is filed, for a determination as to whether or not a basis exists to make a finding described in clause (iv). If the Secretary determines that such a basis exists, the Secretary shall provide for notice of such determination to the interested parties and an opportunity for a hearing on the complaint within 60 days of the date of the determination.

(iv) If the Secretary of Labor finds, after notice and opportunity for a hearing, that a facility (for which an attestation is made) has failed to meet a condition attested to or that there was a misrepresentation of material fact in the attestation, the Secretary shall notify the Attorney General of such finding and may, in addition, impose such other administrative remedies (including civil monetary penalties in an amount not to exceed $1,000 per nurse per violation, with the total penalty not to exceed $10,000 per violation) as the Secretary determines to be appropriate. Upon receipt of such notice, the Attorney General shall not approve petitions filed with respect to a facility during a period of at least one year for nurses to be employed by the facility.

(v) In addition to the sanctions provided for under clause (iv), if the Secretary of Labor finds, after notice and an opportunity for a hearing, that a facility has violated the condition attested to under subparagraph (A)(iii) (relating to payment of registered nurses at the prevailing wage rate), the Secretary shall order the facility to provide for payment of such amounts of back pay as may be required to comply with such condition.

(F) (i) The Secretary of Labor shall impose on a facility filing an attestation under subparagraph (A) a filing fee, in an amount prescribed by the Secretary based on the costs of carrying out the Secretary's duties under this subsection, but not exceeding $250.

(ii) Fees collected under this subparagraph shall be deposited in a fund established for this purpose in the Treasury of the United States.

(iii) The collected fees in the fund shall be available to the Secretary of Labor, to the extent and in such amounts as may be provided in appropriations Acts, to cover the costs described in clause (i), in addition to any other funds that are available to the Secretary to cover such costs.

(3) The period of admission of an alien under section 101(a)(15)(H)(i)(c) shall be 3 years.

(4) The total number of nonimmigrant visas issued pursuant to petitions granted under section 101(a)(15)(H)(i)(c) in each fiscal year shall not exceed 500. The number of such visas issued for employment in each State in each fiscal year shall not exceed the following:

(A) For States with populations of less than 9,000,000, based upon the 1990 decennial census of population, 25 visas.

(B) For States with populations of 9,000,000 or more, based upon the 1990 decennial census of population, 50 visas.

(C) If the total number of visas available under this paragraph for a fiscal year quarter exceeds the number of qualified nonimmigrants who may be issued such visas during those quarters, the visas made available under this paragraph shall be issued without regard to the numerical limitation under subparagraph (A) or (B) of this paragraph during the last fiscal year quarter.

(5) A facility that has filed a petition under section 101(a)(15)(H)(i)(c) to employ a nonimmigrant to perform nursing services for the facility—

(A) shall provide the nonimmigrant a wage rate and working conditions commensurate with those of nurses similarly employed by the facility;

(B) shall require the nonimmigrant to work hours commensurate with those of nurses similarly employed by the facility; and

(C) shall not interfere with the right of the nonimmigrant to join or organize a union.

(6) For purposes of this subsection and section 101(a)(15)(H)(i)(c), the term "facility" means a subsection (d) hospital (as defined in section 1886(d)(1)(B) of the Social Security Act (42 U.S.C. 1395ww(d)(1)(B))) that meets the following requirements:

(A) As of March 31, 1997, the hospital was located in a health professional shortage area (as defined in section 332 of the Public Health Service Act (42 U.S.C. 254e)).

(B) Based on its settled cost report filed under title XVIII of the Social Security Act for its cost reporting period beginning during fiscal year 1994—

(i) the hospital has not less than 190 licensed acute care beds;

(ii) the number of the hospital's inpatient days for such period which were made up of patients who (for such days) were entitled to benefits under part A of such title is not less than 35 percent of the total number of such hospital's acute care inpatient days for such period; and

(iii) the number of the hospital's inpatient days for such period which were made up of patients who (for such days) were eligible for medical assistance under a State plan approved under title XIX of the Social Security Act, is not less than 28 percent of the total number of such hospital's acute care inpatient days for such period.

(7) For purposes of paragraph (2)(A)(v), the term "lay off", with respect to a worker—

(A) means to cause the worker's loss of employment, other than through a discharge for inadequate performance, violation of workplace rules, cause, voluntary departure, voluntary retirement, or the expiration of a grant or contract; but

(B) does not include any situation in which the worker is offered, as an alternative to such loss of employment, a similar employment opportunity with the same employer at equivalent or higher compensation and benefits than the position from which the employee was discharged, regardless of whether or not the employee accepts the offer.

Nothing in this paragraph is intended to limit an employee's or an employer's rights under a collective bargaining agreement or other employment contract.

**(n) Labor condition application.—**[92]

(1) No alien may be admitted or provided status as an H-1B nonimmigrant in an occupational classification unless the employer has filed with the Secretary of Labor an application stating the following:

(A) The employer—

(i) is offering and will offer during the period of authorized employment to aliens admitted or provided status as an H-1B nonimmigrant wages that are at least—

(I) the actual wage level paid by the employer to all other individuals with similar experience and qualifications for the specific employment in question, or

(II) the prevailing wage level for the occupational classification in the area of employment,

whichever is greater, based on the best information available as of the time of filing the application, and

(ii) will provide working conditions for such a nonimmigrant that will not adversely affect the working conditions of workers similarly employed.

(B) There is not a strike or lockout in the course of a labor dispute in the occupational classification at the place of employment.

(C) The employer, at the time of filing the application—

(i) has provided notice of the filing under this paragraph to the bargaining representative (if any) of the employer's employees in the occupational classification and area for which aliens are sought, or

(ii) if there is no such bargaining representative, has provided notice of filing in occupational classification through such methods as physical posting in conspicuous locations at the place of employment or electronic notification to employees in the occupational classification for which H-1B nonimmigrants are sought.

(D) The application shall contain a specification of the number of workers sought, the occupational classification in which the workers will be employed, and wage rate and conditions under which they will be employed.

---

[92] *See* P.L. 105-277 (10/21/98) for changes of effective date for applications filed under INA §212(n)(1) on or after the date final regulations are issued to carry out such amendments. *See also* P.L. 108-447 (12/8/04) for varying effective dates—see specific subparagraphs.

(E) (i) In the case of an application described in clause (ii), the employer did not displace and will not displace a United States worker (as defined in paragraph (4)) employed by the employer within the period beginning 90 days before and ending 90 days after the date of filing of any visa petition supported by the application.

(ii)[93] An application described in this clause is an application filed on or after the date final regulations are first promulgated to carry out this subparagraph, and before by an H-1B-dependent employer (as defined in paragraph (3)) or by an employer that has been found, on or after the date of the enactment of the American Competitiveness and Workforce Improvement Act of 1998, under paragraph (2)(C) or (5) to have committed a willful failure or misrepresentation during the 5-year period preceding the filing of the application. An application is not described in this clause if the only H-1B nonimmigrants sought in the application are exempt H-1B nonimmigrants.

(F) In the case of an application described in subparagraph (E)(ii), the employer will not place the nonimmigrant with another employer (regardless of whether or not such other employer is an H-1B-dependent employer) where—

(i) the nonimmigrant performs duties in whole or in part at one or more worksites owned, operated, or controlled by such other employer; and

(ii) there are indicia of an employment relationship between the nonimmigrant and such other employer;

unless the employer has inquired of the other employer as to whether, and has no knowledge that, within the period beginning 90 days before and ending 90 days after the date of the placement of the nonimmigrant with the other employer, the other employer has displaced or intends to displace a United States worker employed by the other employer.

(G) (i) In the case of an application described in subparagraph (E)(ii), subject to clause (ii), the employer, prior to filing the application—

(I) has taken good faith steps to recruit, in the United States using procedures that meet industry-wide standards and offering compensation that is at least as great as that required to be offered to H-1B nonimmigrants under subparagraph (A), United States workers for the job for which the nonimmigrant or nonimmigrants is or are sought; and

(II) has offered the job to any United States worker who applies and is equally or better qualified for the job for which the nonimmigrant or nonimmigrants is or are sought.

(ii) The conditions described in clause (i) shall not apply to an application filed with respect to the employment of an H-1B nonimmigrant who is described in subparagraph (A), (B), or (C) of section 203(b)(1).

The employer shall make available for public examination, within one working day after the date on which an application under this paragraph is filed, at the employer's principal place of business or worksite, a copy of each such application (and such accompanying documents as are necessary). The Secretary shall compile, on a current basis, a list (by employer and by occupational classification) of the applications filed under this subsection. Such list shall in-

---

[93] Amendment striking "October 1, 2003," after "and before" (§422 of the H-1B Visa Reform Act, P.L. 108-447 (12/8/04, *effective* 3/8/05).

clude the wage rate, number of aliens sought, period of intended employment, and date of need. The Secretary shall make such list available for public examination in Washington, D.C. The Secretary of Labor shall review such an application only for completeness and obvious inaccuracies. Unless the Secretary finds that the application is incomplete or obviously inaccurate, the Secretary shall provide the certification described in section 101(a)(15)(H)(i)(b) within 7 days of the date of the filing of the application. The application form shall include a clear statement explaining the liability under subparagraph (F) of a placing employer if the other employer described in such subparagraph displaces a United States worker as described in such subparagraph. Nothing in subparagraph (G) shall be construed to prohibit an employer from using legitimate selection criteria relevant to the job that are normal or customary to the type of job involved, so long as such criteria are not applied in a discriminatory manner.

(2) (A) Subject to paragraph (5)(A), the Secretary shall establish a process for the receipt, investigation, and disposition of complaints respecting a petitioner's failure to meet a condition specified in an application submitted under paragraph (1) or a petitioner's misrepresentation of material facts in such an application. Complaints may be filed by any aggrieved person or organization (including bargaining representatives). No investigation or hearing shall be conducted on a complaint concerning such a failure or misrepresentation unless the complaint was filed not later than 12 months after the date of the failure or misrepresentation, respectively. The Secretary shall conduct an investigation under this paragraph if there is reasonable cause to believe that such a failure or misrepresentation has occurred.

(B) Under such process, the Secretary shall provide, within 30 days after the date such a complaint is filed, for a determination as to whether or not a reasonable basis exists to make a finding described in subparagraph (C). If the Secretary determines that such a reasonable basis exists, the Secretary shall provide for notice of such determination to the interested parties and an opportunity for a hearing on the complaint, in accordance with section 556 of title 5, United States Code, within 60 days after the date of the determination. If such a hearing is requested, the Secretary shall make a finding concerning the matter by not later than 60 days after the date of the hearing. In the case of similar complaints respecting the same applicant, the Secretary may consolidate the hearings under this subparagraph on such complaints.

(C) (i) If the Secretary finds, after notice and opportunity for a hearing, a failure to meet a condition of paragraph (1)(B), (1)(E), or (1)(F), a substantial failure to meet a condition of paragraph (1)(C), (1)(D), or (1)(G)(i)(I), or a misrepresentation of material fact in an application—

(I) the Secretary shall notify the Attorney General of such finding and may, in addition, impose such other administrative remedies (including civil monetary penalties in an amount not to exceed $1,000 per violation) as the Secretary determines to be appropriate; and

(II) the Attorney General shall not approve petitions filed with respect to that employer under section 204 or 214(c) during a period of at least 1 year for aliens to be employed by the employer.

(ii) If the Secretary finds, after notice and opportunity for a hearing, a willful failure to meet a condition of paragraph (1), a willful misrepresentation of material fact in an application, or a violation of clause (iv)—

(I) the Secretary shall notify the Attorney General of such finding and may, in addition, impose such other administrative remedies (including civil monetary penalties in an amount not to exceed $5,000 per violation) as the Secretary determines to be appropriate; and

(II) the Attorney General shall not approve petitions filed with respect to that employer under section 204 or 214(c) during a period of at least 2 years for aliens to be employed by the employer.

(iii) If the Secretary finds, after notice and opportunity for a hearing, a willful failure to meet a condition of paragraph (1) or a willful misrepresentation of material fact in an application, in the course of which failure or misrepresentation the employer displaced a United States worker employed by the employer within the period beginning 90 days before and ending 90 days after the date of filing of any visa petition supported by the application—

(I) the Secretary shall notify the Attorney General of such finding and may, in addition, impose such other administrative remedies (including civil monetary penalties in an amount not to exceed $35,000 per violation) as the Secretary determines to be appropriate; and

(II) the Attorney General shall not approve petitions filed with respect to that employer under section 204 or 214(c) during a period of at least 3 years for aliens to be employed by the employer.

(iv) It is a violation of this clause for an employer who has filed an application under this subsection to intimidate, threaten, restrain, coerce, blacklist, discharge, or in any other manner discriminate against an employee (which term, for purposes of this clause, includes a former employee and an applicant for employment) because the employee has disclosed information to the employer, or to any other person, that the employee reasonably believes evidences a violation of this subsection, or any rule or regulation pertaining to this subsection, or because the employee cooperates or seeks to cooperate in an investigation or other proceeding concerning the employer's compliance with the requirements of this subsection or any rule or regulation pertaining to this subsection.

(v) The Secretary of Labor and the Attorney General shall devise a process under which an H-1B nonimmigrant who files a complaint regarding a violation of clause (iv) and is otherwise eligible to remain and work in the United States may be allowed to seek other appropriate employment in the United States for a period not to exceed the maximum period of stay authorized for such nonimmigrant classification.

(vi) (I) It is a violation of this clause for an employer who has filed an application under this subsection to require an H-1B nonimmigrant to pay a penalty for ceasing employment with the employer prior to a date agreed to by the nonimmigrant and the employer. The Secretary shall determine whether a required payment is a penalty (and not liquidated damages) pursuant to relevant State law.

(II) It is a violation of this clause for an employer who has filed an application under this subsection to require an alien who is the subject of a petition filed under section 214(c)(1), for which a fee is imposed under section 214(c)(9), to reimburse, or otherwise compensate, the employer for part or all of the cost of such fee. It is a violation of this clause for such an employer otherwise to accept such reimbursement or compensation from such an alien.

(III) If the Secretary finds, after notice and opportunity for a hearing, that an employer has committed a violation of this clause, the Secretary may impose a civil monetary penalty of $1,000 for each such violation and issue an administrative order requiring the return to the nonimmigrant of any amount paid in violation of this clause, or, if the nonimmigrant cannot be located, requiring payment of any such amount to the general fund of the Treasury.

(vii)  (I) It is a failure to meet a condition of paragraph (1)(A) for an employer, who has filed an application under this subsection and who places an H-1B nonimmigrant designated as a full-time employee on the petition filed under section 214(c)(1) by the employer with respect to the nonimmigrant, after the nonimmigrant has entered into employment with the employer, in nonproductive status due to a decision by the employer (based on factors such as lack of work), or due to the nonimmigrant's lack of a permit or license, to fail to pay the nonimmigrant full-time wages in accordance with paragraph (1)(A) for all such nonproductive time.

(II) It is a failure to meet a condition of paragraph (1)(A) for an employer, who has filed an application under this subsection and who places an H-1B nonimmigrant designated as a part-time employee on the petition filed under section 214(c)(1) by the employer with respect to the nonimmigrant, after the nonimmigrant has entered into employment with the employer, in nonproductive status under circumstances described in subclause (I), to fail to pay such a nonimmigrant for such hours as are designated on such petition consistent with the rate of pay identified on such petition.

(III) In the case of an H-1B nonimmigrant who has not yet entered into employment with an employer who has had approved an application under this subsection, and a petition under section 214(c)(1), with respect to the nonimmigrant, the provisions of subclauses (I) and (II) shall apply to the employer beginning 30 days after the date the nonimmigrant first is admitted into the United States pursuant to the petition, or 60 days after the date the nonimmigrant becomes eligible to work for the employer (in the case of a nonimmigrant who is present in the United States on the date of the approval of the petition).

(IV) This clause does not apply to a failure to pay wages to an H-1B nonimmigrant for nonproductive time due to non-work-related factors, such as the voluntary request of the nonimmigrant for an absence or circumstances rendering the nonimmigrant unable to work.

(V) This clause shall not be construed as prohibiting an employer that is a school or other educational institution from applying to an H-1B nonimmigrant an established salary practice of the employer, under which the employer pays to H-1B nonimmigrants and United States workers in the same occupational classification an annual salary in disbursements over fewer than 12 months, if—

(aa) the nonimmigrant agrees to the compressed annual salary payments prior to the commencement of the employment; and

(bb) the application of the salary practice to the nonimmigrant does not otherwise cause the nonimmigrant to violate any condition of the nonimmigrant's authorization under this Act to remain in the United States.

(VI) This clause shall not be construed as superseding clause (viii).

(viii) It is a failure to meet a condition of paragraph (1)(A) for an employer who has filed an application under this subsection to fail to offer to an H-1B nonimmigrant, during the nonimmigrant's period of authorized employment, benefits and eligibility for benefits (including the opportunity to participate in health, life, disability, and other insurance plans; the opportunity to participate in retirement and savings plans; and cash bonuses and noncash compensation, such as stock options (whether or not based on performance)) on the same basis, and in accordance with the same criteria, as the employer offers to United States workers.

(D) If the Secretary finds, after notice and opportunity for a hearing, that an employer has not paid wages at the wage level specified under the application and required under paragraph (1), the Secretary shall order the employer to provide for payment of such amounts of back pay as may be required to comply with the requirements of paragraph (1), whether or not a penalty under subparagraph (C) has been imposed.

(E) If an H-1B-dependent employer places a nonexempt H-1B nonimmigrant with another employer as provided under paragraph (1)(F) and the other employer has displaced or displaces a United States worker employed by such other employer during the period described in such paragraph, such displacement shall be considered for purposes of this paragraph a failure, by the placing employer, to meet a condition specified in an application submitted under paragraph (1); except that the Attorney General may impose a sanction described in subclause (II) of subparagraph (C)(i), (C)(ii), or (C)(iii) only if the Secretary of Labor found that such placing employer—

(i) knew or had reason to know of such displacement at the time of the placement of the nonimmigrant with the other employer; or

(ii) has been subject to a sanction under this subparagraph based upon a previous placement of an H-1B nonimmigrant with the same other employer.

(F) The Secretary may, on a case-by-case basis, subject an employer to random investigations for a period of up to 5 years, beginning on the date (on or after the date of the enactment of the American Competitiveness and Workforce Improvement Act of 1998) on which the employer is found by the Secretary to have committed a willful failure to meet a condition of paragraph (1) (or has been found under paragraph (5) to have committed a willful failure to meet the condition of paragraph (1)(G)(i)(II)) or to have made a willful misrepresentation of material fact in an application. The preceding sentence shall apply to an employer regardless of whether or not the employer is an H-1B-dependent employer. The authority of the Secretary under this subparagraph shall not be construed to be subject to, or limited by, the requirements of subparagraph (A).

(G)[94](i) The Secretary of Labor may initiate an investigation of any employer that employs nonimmigrants described in section 101(a)(15)(H)(i)(b) if the Secretary of Labor has reasonable cause to believe that the employer is not in compliance with this subsection. In the case of an investigation under this clause, the Secretary of Labor (or the acting Secretary in the case of the absence of disability of the Secretary of

---

[94] The current INA §212(n)(2)(G) was added by §424 of the H-1B Visa Reform Act, 2004, P.L. 108-447 (12/8/04, *retroactive effective* 10/1/03).

Labor) shall personally certify that reasonable cause exists and shall approve commencement of the investigation. The investigation may be initiated for reasons other than completeness and obvious inaccuracies by the employer in complying with this subsection.

(ii) If the Secretary of Labor receives specific credible information from a source who is likely to have knowledge of an employer's practices or employment conditions, or an employer's compliance with the employer's labor condition application under paragraph (1), and whose identity is known to the Secretary of Labor, and such information provides reasonable cause to believe that the employer has committed a willful failure to meet a condition of paragraph (1)(A), (1)(B), (1)(C), (1)(E), (1)(F), or (1)(G)(i)(I), has engaged in a pattern or practice of failures to meet such a condition, or has committed a substantial failure to meet such a condition that affects multiple employees, the Secretary of Labor may conduct an investigation into the alleged failure or failures. The Secretary of Labor may withhold the identity of the source from the employer, and the source's identity shall not be subject to disclosure under section 552 of title 5, United States Code.

(iii) The Secretary of Labor shall establish a procedure for any person desiring to provide to the Secretary of Labor information described in clause (ii) that may be used, in whole or in part, as the basis for the commencement of an investigation described in such clause, to provide the information in writing on a form developed and provided by the Secretary of Labor and completed by or on behalf of the person. The person may not be an officer or employee of the Department of Labor, unless the information satisfies the requirement of clause (iv)(II) (although an officer or employee of the Department of Labor may complete the form on behalf of the person).

(iv) Any investigation initiated or approved by the Secretary of Labor under clause (ii) shall be based on information that satisfies the requirements of such clause and that—

(I) originates from a source other than an officer or employee of the Department of Labor; or

(II) was lawfully obtained by the Secretary of Labor in the course of lawfully conducting another Department of Labor investigation under this Act of any other Act.

(v) The receipt by the Secretary of Labor of information submitted by an employer to the Attorney General or the Secretary of Labor for purposes of securing the employment of a nonimmigrant described in section 101(a)(15)(H)(i)(b) shall not be considered a receipt of information for purposes of clause (ii).

(vi) No investigation described in clause (ii) (or hearing described in clause (viii) based on such investigation) may be conducted with respect to information about a failure to meet a condition described in clause (ii), unless the Secretary of Labor receives the information not later than 12 months after the date of the alleged failure.

(vii) The Secretary of Labor shall provide notice to an employer with respect to whom there is reasonable cause to initiate an investigation described in clauses (i) or (ii), prior to the commencement of an investigation under such clauses, of the intent to conduct an investigation. The notice shall be provided in such a manner, and shall contain sufficient detail, to permit the employer to respond to the allegations before an investigation is commenced. The Secretary of Labor is not required to comply with this clause if the Secretary of Labor determines that to do so would interfere with an effort by the Secretary of Labor to secure compliance by the employer with the requirements of this subsection. There shall be no judicial review of a determination by the Secretary of Labor under this clause.

(viii) An investigation under clauses (i) or (ii) may be conducted for a period of up to 60 days. If the Secretary of Labor determines after such an investigation that a reasonable basis exists to make a finding that the employer has committed a willful failure to meet a condition of paragraph (1)(A), (1)(B), (1)(C), (1)(E), (1)(F), or (1)(G)(i)(I), has engaged in a pattern or practice of failures to meet such a condition, or has committed a substantial failure to meet such a condition that affects multiple employees, the Secretary of Labor shall provide for notice of such determination to the interested parties and an opportunity for a hearing in accordance with section 556 of title 5, United States Code, within 120 days after the date of the determination. If such a hearing is requested, the Secretary of Labor shall make a finding concerning the matter by not later than 120 days after the date of the hearing.

(H) (i) Except as provided in clauses (ii) and (iii), a person or entity is considered to have complied with the requirements of this subsection, notwithstanding a technical or procedural failure to meet such requirements, if there was a good faith attempt to comply with the requirements.

(ii) Clause (i) shall not apply if—

(I) the Department of Labor (or another enforcement agency) has explained to the person or entity the basis for the failure;

(II) the person or entity has been provided a period of not less than 10 business days (beginning after the date of the explanation) within which to correct the failure; and

(III) the person or entity has not corrected the failure voluntarily within such period.

(iii) A person or entity that, in the course of an investigation, is found to have violated the prevailing wage requirements set forth in paragraph (1)(A), shall not be assessed fines or other penalties for such violation if the person or entity can establish that the manner in which the prevailing wage was calculated was consistent with recognized industry standards and practices.

(iv) Clauses (i) and (iii) shall not apply to a person or entity that has engaged in or is engaging in a pattern or practice of willful violations of this subsection.

(I) Nothing in this subsection shall be construed as superseding or preempting any other enforcement-related authority under this Act (such as the authorities under section 274B), or any other Act.

(3) (A) For purposes of this subsection, the term "H-1B-dependent employer" means an employer that—

(i) (I) has 25 or fewer full-time equivalent employees who are employed in the United States; and

(II) employs more than 7 H-1B nonimmigrants;

    (ii) (I) has at least 26 but not more than 50 full-time equivalent employees who are employed in the United States; and

    (II) employs more than 12 H-1B nonimmigrants; or

    (iii) (I) has at least 51 full-time equivalent employees who are employed in the United States; and

    (II) employs H-1B nonimmigrants in a number that is equal to at least 15 percent of the number of such full-time equivalent employees.

(B) For purposes of this subsection—

    (i) the term "exempt H-1B nonimmigrant" means an H-1B nonimmigrant who—

    (I) receives wages (including cash bonuses and similar compensation) at an annual rate equal to at least $60,000; or

    (II) has attained a master's or higher degree (or its equivalent) in a specialty related to the intended employment; and

    (ii) the term "nonexempt H-1B nonimmigrant" means an H-1B nonimmigrant who is not an exempt H-1B nonimmigrant.

(C) For purposes of subparagraph (A)—

    (i) in computing the number of full-time equivalent employees and the number of H-1B nonimmigrants, exempt H-1B nonimmigrants shall not be taken into account during the longer of—

    (I) the 6-month period beginning on the date of the enactment of the American Competitiveness and Workforce Improvement Act of 1998; or

    (II) the period beginning on the date of the enactment of the American Competitiveness and Workforce Improvement Act of 1998 and ending on the date final regulations are issued to carry out this paragraph; and

    (ii) any group treated as a single employer under subsection (b), (c), (m), or (o) of section 414 of the Internal Revenue Code of 1986 shall be treated as a single employer.

(4) For purposes of this subsection:

(A) The term "area of employment" means the area within normal commuting distance of the worksite or physical location where the work of the H-1B nonimmigrant is or will be performed. If such worksite or location is within a Metropolitan Statistical Area, any place within such area is deemed to be within the area of employment.

(B) In the case of an application with respect to one or more H-1B nonimmigrants by an employer, the employer is considered to "displace" a United States worker from a job if the employer lays off the worker from a job that is essentially the equivalent of the job for which the nonimmigrant or nonimmigrants is or are sought. A job shall not be considered to be essentially equivalent of another job unless it involves essentially the same responsibilities, was held by a United States worker with substantially equivalent qualifications and experience, and is located in the same area of employment as the other job.

(C) The term "H-1B nonimmigrant" means an alien admitted or provided status as a nonimmigrant described in section 101(a)(15)(H)(i)(b).

(D) (i) The term "lays off", with respect to a worker—

(I) means to cause the worker's loss of employment, other than through a discharge for inadequate performance, violation of workplace rules, cause, voluntary departure, voluntary retirement, or the expiration of a grant or contract (other than a temporary employment contract entered into in order to evade a condition described in subparagraph (E) or (F) of paragraph (1)); but

(II) does not include any situation in which the worker is offered, as an alternative to such loss of employment, a similar employment opportunity with the same employer (or, in the case of a placement of a worker with another employer under paragraph (1)(F), with either employer described in such paragraph) at equivalent or higher compensation and benefits than the position from which the employee was discharged, regardless of whether or not the employee accepts the offer.

(ii) Nothing in this subparagraph is intended to limit an employee's rights under a collective bargaining agreement or other employment contract.

(E) The term "United States worker" means an employee who—

(i) is a citizen or national of the United States; or

(ii) is an alien who is lawfully admitted for permanent residence, is admitted as a refugee under section 207, is granted asylum under section 208, or is an immigrant otherwise authorized, by this Act or by the Attorney General, to be employed.

(5) (A) This paragraph shall apply instead of subparagraphs (A) through (E) of paragraph (2) in the case of a violation described in subparagraph (B), but shall not be construed to limit or affect the authority of the Secretary or the Attorney General with respect to any other violation.

(B) The Attorney General shall establish a process for the receipt, initial review, and disposition in accordance with this paragraph of complaints respecting an employer's failure to meet the condition of paragraph (1)(G)(i)(II) or a petitioner's misrepresentation of material facts with respect to such condition. Complaints may be filed by an aggrieved individual who has submitted a resume or otherwise applied in a reasonable manner for the job that is the subject of the condition. No proceeding shall be conducted under this paragraph on a complaint concerning such a failure or misrepresentation unless the Attorney General determines that the complaint was filed not later than 12 months after the date of the failure or misrepresentation, respectively.

(C) If the Attorney General finds that a complaint has been filed in accordance with subparagraph (B) and there is reasonable cause to believe that such a failure or misrepresentation described in such complaint has occurred, the Attorney General shall initiate binding arbitration proceedings by requesting the Federal Mediation and Conciliation Service to appoint an arbitrator from the roster of arbitrators maintained by such Service. The procedure and rules of such Service shall be applicable to the selection of such arbitrator and to such arbitration proceedings. The Attorney General shall pay the fee and expenses of the arbitrator.

(D) (i) The arbitrator shall make findings respecting whether a failure or misrepresentation described in subparagraph (B) occurred. If the arbitrator concludes that failure or misrepresentation was willful, the arbitrator shall make a finding to that effect. The arbitrator may not find such a failure or misrepresentation (or that such a failure or misrepresentation was willful) unless the complainant demonstrates such a failure or misrepresentation (or its willful character) by clear and convincing evidence. The arbitrator shall transmit the findings in the form of a written opinion to the parties to the arbitration and the Attorney General. Such findings shall be final and conclusive, and, except as provided in this subparagraph, no official or court of the United States shall have power or jurisdiction to review any such findings.

(ii) The Attorney General may review and reverse or modify the findings of an arbitrator only on the same bases as an award of an arbitrator may be vacated or modified under section 10 or 11 of title 9, United States Code.

(iii) With respect to the findings of an arbitrator, a court may review only the actions of the Attorney General under clause (ii) and may set aside such actions only on the grounds described in subparagraph (A), (B), or (C) of section 706(a)(2) of title 5, United States Code. Notwithstanding any other provision of law, such judicial review may only be brought in an appropriate United States court of appeals.

(E) If the Attorney General receives a finding of an arbitrator under this paragraph that an employer has failed to meet the condition of paragraph (1)(G)(i)(II) or has misrepresented a material fact with respect to such condition, unless the Attorney General reverses or modifies the finding under subparagraph (D)(ii)—

(i) the Attorney General may impose administrative remedies (including civil monetary penalties in an amount not to exceed $1,000 per violation or $5,000 per violation in the case of a willful failure or misrepresentation) as the Attorney General determines to be appropriate; and

(ii) the Attorney General is authorized to not approve petitions filed, with respect to that employer and for aliens to be employed by the employer, under section 204 or 214(c)—

(I) during a period of not more than 1 year; or

(II) in the case of a willful failure or willful misrepresentation, during a period of not more than 2 years.

(F) The Attorney General shall not delegate, to any other employee or official of the Department of Justice, any function of the Attorney General under this paragraph, until 60 days after the Attorney General has submitted a plan for such delegation to the Committees on the Judiciary of the United States House of Representatives and the Senate.

**(o)** [Expired][95]

**(p) Computation of prevailing wage level.**—[96]

---

[95] Congress allowed §212(o) to sunset on 9/30/97. The following text was §212(o) until 9/30/97:

An alien who has been physically present in the United States shall not be eligible to receive an immigrant visa within ninety days following departure therefrom unless—

(1) the alien was maintaining a lawful nonimmigrant status at the time of such departure, or

(2) The alien is the spouse or unmarried child of an individual who obtained temporary or permanent resident status under §210 or 245A of the Immigration and Nationality Act or §202 of the Immigration Reform and Control Act of 1986 at any date, who—

(A) as of May 5, 1988, was the unmarried child or spouse of the individual who obtained temporary or permanent resident status under §210 or 245A of the Immigration and Nationality Act or §202 of the Immigration Reform and Control Act of 1986;

(B) entered the United States before May 5, 1988, resided in the United States on May 5, 1988, and is not a lawful permanent resident; and

(C) applied for benefits under §301(a) of the Immigration Act of 1990.

(1) In computing the prevailing wage level for an occupational classification in an area of employment for purposes of subsections (a)(5)(A), (n)(1)(A)(i)(II), and (t)(1)(A)(i)(II) in the case of an employee of—

(A) an institution of higher education (as defined in section 101(a) of the Higher Education Act of 1965), or a related or affiliated nonprofit entity; or

(B) a nonprofit research organization or a Governmental research organization, the prevailing wage level shall only take into account employees at such institutions and organizations in the area of employment.

(2) With respect to a professional athlete (as defined in subsection (a)(5)(A)(iii)(II)) when the job opportunity is covered by professional sports league rules or regulations, the wage set forth in those rules or regulations shall be considered as not adversely affecting the wages of United States workers similarly employed and be considered the prevailing wage.

(3) The prevailing wage required to be paid pursuant to subsections (a)(5)(A), (n)(1)(A)(i)(II), and (t)(1)(A)(i)(II) shall be 100 percent of the wage determined pursuant to those sections.

(4) Where the Secretary of Labor uses, or makes available to employers, a governmental survey to determine the prevailing wage, such survey shall provide at least 4 levels of wages commensurate with experience, education, and the level of supervision. Where an existing government survey has only 2 levels, 2 intermediate levels may be created by dividing by 3, the difference between the 2 levels offered, adding the quotient thus obtained to the first level and subtracting that quotient from the second level.

**(q) Academic honoraria.—** Any alien admitted under section 101(a)(15)(B) may accept an honorarium payment and associated incidental expenses for a usual academic activity or activities (lasting not longer than 9 days at any single institution), as defined by the Attorney General in consultation with the Secretary of Education, if such payment is offered by an institution or organization described in subsection (p)(1) and is made for services conducted for the benefit of that institution or entity and if the alien has not accepted such payment or expenses from more than 5 institutions or organizations in the previous 6-month period.

**(r) Certification for certain alien nurses.—** Subsection (a)(5)(C) shall not apply to an alien who seeks to enter the United States for the purpose of performing labor as a nurse who presents to the consular officer (or in the case of an adjustment of status, the Attorney General) a certified statement from the Commission on Graduates of Foreign Nursing Schools (or an equivalent independent credentialing organization approved for the certification of nurses under subsection (a)(5)(C) by the Attorney General in consultation with the Secretary of Health and Human Services) that—

(1) the alien has a valid and unrestricted license as a nurse in a State where the alien intends to be employed and such State verifies that the foreign licenses of alien nurses are authentic and unencumbered;

(2) the alien has passed the National Council Licensure Examination (NCLEX);

(3) the alien is a graduate of a nursing program—

(A) in which the language of instruction was English;

---

[96] *See* P.L. 105-277 (ACWIA) (10/21/98) [applicable to prevailing wage computations made for applications filed on or after 10/21/98 (date of Act enactment) and for applications filed before 10/21/98, but only to the extent that the computation is subject to an administrative or judicial determination that is not final as of such date].

(B) located in a country—

(i) designated by such commission not later than 30 days after the date of the enactment of the Nursing Relief for Disadvantaged Areas Act of 1999, based on such commission's assessment that the quality of nursing education in that country, and the English language proficiency of those who complete such programs in that country, justify the country's designation; or

(ii) designated on the basis of such an assessment by unanimous agreement of such commission and any equivalent credentialing organizations which have been approved under subsection (a)(5)(C) for the certification of nurses under this subsection; and

(C) (i) which was in operation on or before the date of the enactment of the Nursing Relief for Disadvantaged Areas Act of 1999; or

(ii) has been approved by unanimous agreement of such commission and any equivalent credentialing organizations which have been approved under subsection (a)(5)(C) for the certification of nurses under this subsection.

**(s) Consideration of benefits received as battered alien in determination of inadmissibility as likely to become public charge.**— In determining whether an alien described in subsection (a)(4)(C)(i) is inadmissible under subsection (a)(4) or ineligible to receive an immigrant visa or otherwise to adjust to the status of permanent resident by reason of subsection (a)(4), the consular officer or the Attorney General shall not consider any benefits the alien may have received that were authorized under section 501 of the Illegal Immigration Reform and Immigrant Responsibility Act of 1996 (8 U.S.C. 1641(c)).

**(t) [first]**[97] **Labor attestations for nonimmigrant professionals entering under agreement.**—

(1) No alien may be admitted or provided status as a nonimmigrant under section 101(a)(15)(H)(i)(b1) or section 101(a)(15)(E)(iii) in an occupational classification unless the employer has filed with the Secretary of Labor an attestation stating the following:

(A) The employer—

(i) is offering and will offer during the period of authorized employment to aliens admitted or provided status under section 101(a)(15)(H)(i)(b1) or section 101(a)(15)(E)(iii) wages that are at least—

(I) the actual wage level paid by the employer to all other individuals with similar experience and qualifications for the specific employment in question; or

(II) the prevailing wage level for the occupational classification in the area of employment, whichever is greater, based on the best information available as of the time of filing the attestation; and

(ii) will provide working conditions for such a nonimmigrant that will not adversely affect the working conditions of workers similarly employed.

(B) There is not a strike or lockout in the course of a labor dispute in the occupational classification at the place of employment.

(C) The employer, at the time of filing the attestation—

---

[97] Subsection (t) added by P.L. 108-77 (9/3/03, *effective* 1/1/04) (pursuant to §107 of that Act), the date the U.S.-Chile Free Trade Agreement entered into force; however, in P.L. 108-449, Congress added a "new" subsection 212(t), notwithstanding the §212(t) added by P.L. 108-77.

(i) has provided notice of the filing under this paragraph to the bargaining representative (if any) of the employer's employees in the occupational classification and area for which aliens are sought; or

(ii) if there is no such bargaining representative, has provided notice of filing in the occupational classification through such methods as physical posting in conspicuous locations at the place of employment or electronic notification to employees in the occupational classification for which nonimmigrants under section 101(a)(15)(H)(i)(b1) or section 101(a)(15)(E)(iii) are sought.

(D) A specification of the number of workers sought, the occupational classification in which the workers will be employed, and wage rate and conditions under which they will be employed.

(2) (A) The employer shall make available for public examination, within one working day after the date on which an attestation under this subsection is filed, at the employer's principal place of business or worksite, a copy of each such attestation (and such accompanying documents as are necessary).

(B) (i) The Secretary of Labor shall compile, on a current basis, a list (by employer and by occupational classification) of the attestations filed under this subsection. Such list shall include, with respect to each attestation, the wage rate, number of aliens sought, period of intended employment, and date of need.

(ii) The Secretary of Labor shall make such list available for public examination in Washington, D.C.

(C) The Secretary of Labor shall review an attestation filed under this subsection only for completeness and obvious inaccuracies. Unless the Secretary of Labor finds that an attestation is incomplete or obviously inaccurate, the Secretary of Labor shall provide the certification described in section 101(a)(15)(H)(i)(b1) or section 101(a)(15)(E)(iii) within 7 days of the date of the filing of the attestation.

(3) (A) The Secretary of Labor shall establish a process for the receipt, investigation, and disposition of complaints respecting the failure of an employer to meet a condition specified in an attestation submitted under this subsection or misrepresentation by the employer of material facts in such an attestation. Complaints may be filed by any aggrieved person or organization (including bargaining representatives). No investigation or hearing shall be conducted on a complaint concerning such a failure or misrepresentation unless the complaint was filed not later than 12 months after the date of the failure or misrepresentation, respectively. The Secretary of Labor shall conduct an investigation under this paragraph if there is reasonable cause to believe that such a failure or misrepresentation has occurred.

(B) Under the process described in subparagraph (A), the Secretary of Labor shall provide, within 30 days after the date a complaint is filed, for a determination as to whether or not a reasonable basis exists to make a finding described in subparagraph (C). If the Secretary of Labor determines that such a reasonable basis exists, the Secretary of Labor shall provide for notice of such determination to the interested parties and an opportunity for a hearing on the complaint, in accordance with section 556 of title 5, United States Code, within 60 days after the date of the determination. If such a hearing is requested, the Secretary of Labor shall make a finding concerning the matter by not later than 60 days after the date of the hearing. In the case of similar complaints respecting the same applicant, the Secretary of Labor may consolidate the hearings under this subparagraph on such complaints.

(C) (i) If the Secretary of Labor finds, after notice and opportunity for a hearing, a failure to meet a condition of paragraph (1)(B), a substantial failure to meet a condition of paragraph (1)(C) or (1)(D), or a misrepresentation of material fact in an attestation—

(I) the Secretary of Labor shall notify the Secretary of State and the Secretary of Homeland Security of such finding and may, in addition, impose such other administrative remedies (including civil monetary penalties in an amount not to exceed $1,000 per violation) as the Secretary of Labor determines to be appropriate; and

(II) the Secretary of State or the Secretary of Homeland Security, as appropriate, shall not approve petitions or applications filed with respect to that employer under section 204, 214(c), 101(a)(15)(H)(i)(b1), or 101(a)(15)(E)(iii) during a period of at least 1 year for aliens to be employed by the employer.

(ii) If the Secretary of Labor finds, after notice and opportunity for a hearing, a willful failure to meet a condition of paragraph (1), a willful misrepresentation of material fact in an attestation, or a violation of clause (iv)—

(I) the Secretary of Labor shall notify the Secretary of State and the Secretary of Homeland Security of such finding and may, in addition, impose such other administrative remedies (including civil monetary penalties in an amount not to exceed $5,000 per violation) as the Secretary of Labor determines to be appropriate; and

(II) the Secretary of State or the Secretary of Homeland Security, as appropriate, shall not approve petitions or applications filed with respect to that employer under section 204, 214(c), 101(a)(15)(H)(i)(b1), or 101(a)(15)(E)(iii) during a period of at least 2 years for aliens to be employed by the employer.

(iii) If the Secretary of Labor finds, after notice and opportunity for a hearing, a willful failure to meet a condition of paragraph (1) or a willful misrepresentation of material fact in an attestation, in the course of which failure or misrepresentation the employer displaced a United States worker employed by the employer within the period beginning 90 days before and ending 90 days after the date of filing of any visa petition or application supported by the attestation—

(I) the Secretary of Labor shall notify the Secretary of State and the Secretary of Homeland Security of such finding and may, in addition, impose such other administrative remedies (including civil monetary penalties in an amount not to exceed $35,000 per violation) as the Secretary of Labor determines to be appropriate; and

(II) the Secretary of State or the Secretary of Homeland Security, as appropriate, shall not approve petitions or applications filed with respect to that employer under section 204, 214(c), 101(a)(15)(H)(i)(b1), or 101(a)(15)(E)(iii) during a period of at least 3 years for aliens to be employed by the employer.

(iv) It is a violation of this clause for an employer who has filed an attestation under this subsection to intimidate, threaten, restrain, coerce, blacklist, discharge, or in any other manner discriminate against an employee (which term, for purposes of this clause, includes a former employee and an applicant for employment) because the employee has disclosed information to the employer, or to any other person, that the employee reasonably believes evidences a violation of this subsection, or any rule or regulation pertaining to this subsection, or because the employee cooperates or seeks to cooperate in an investigation or other proceeding concerning the employer's compliance with the requirements of this subsection or any rule or regulation pertaining to this subsection.

(v) The Secretary of Labor and the Secretary of Homeland Security shall devise a process under which a nonimmigrant under section 101(a)(15)(H)(i)(b1) or 101(a)(15)(E)(iii) who files a complaint regarding a violation of clause (iv) and is otherwise eligible to remain and work in the United States may be allowed to seek other appropriate employment in the United States for a period not to exceed the maximum period of stay authorized for such nonimmigrant classification.

(vi) (I) It is a violation of this clause for an employer who has filed an attestation under this subsection to require a nonimmigrant under section 101(a)(15)(H)(i)(b1) or 101(a)(15)(E)(iii) to pay a penalty for ceasing employment with the employer prior to a date agreed to by the nonimmigrant and the employer. The Secretary of Labor shall determine whether a required payment is a penalty (and not liquidated damages) pursuant to relevant State law.

(II) If the Secretary of Labor finds, after notice and opportunity for a hearing, that an employer has committed a violation of this clause, the Secretary of Labor may impose a civil monetary penalty of $1,000 for each such violation and issue an administrative order requiring the return to the nonimmigrant of any amount paid in violation of this clause, or, if the nonimmigrant cannot be located, requiring payment of any such amount to the general fund of the Treasury.

(vii)(I) It is a failure to meet a condition of paragraph (1)(A) for an employer who has filed an attestation under this subsection and who places a nonimmigrant under section 101(a)(15)(H)(i)(b1) or 101(a)(15)(E)(iii) designated as a full-time employee in the attestation, after the nonimmigrant has entered into employment with the employer, in nonproductive status due to a decision by the employer (based on factors such as lack of work), or due to the nonimmigrant's lack of a permit or license, to fail to pay the nonimmigrant full-time wages in accordance with paragraph (1)(A) for all such nonproductive time.

(II) It is a failure to meet a condition of paragraph (1)(A) for an employer who has filed an attestation under this subsection and who places a nonimmigrant under section 101(a)(15)(H)(i)(b1) or 101(a)(15)(E)(iii) designated as a part-time employee in the attestation, after the nonimmigrant has entered into employment with the employer, in nonproductive status under circumstances described in subclause (I), to fail to pay such a nonimmigrant for such hours as are designated on the attestation consistent with the rate of pay identified on the attestation.

(III) In the case of a nonimmigrant under section 101(a)(15)(H)(i)(b1) or 101(a)(15)(E)(iii) who has not yet entered into employment with an employer who has had approved an attestation under this subsection with respect to the nonimmigrant, the provisions of subclauses (I) and (II) shall apply to the employer beginning 30 days after the date the nonimmigrant first is admitted into the United States, or 60 days after the date the nonimmigrant becomes eligible to work for the employer in the case of a nonimmigrant who is present in the United States on the date of the approval of the attestation filed with the Secretary of Labor.

(IV) This clause does not apply to a failure to pay wages to a nonimmigrant under section 101(a)(15)(H)(i)(b1) or 101(a)(15)(E)(iii) for nonproductive time due to non-work-related factors, such as the voluntary request of the nonimmigrant for an absence or circumstances rendering the nonimmigrant unable to work.

(V) This clause shall not be construed as prohibiting an employer that is a school or other educational institution from applying to a nonimmigrant under section 101(a)(15)(H)(i)(b1) or 101(a)(15)(E)(iii) an established salary practice of the employer, under which the employer pays to nonimmigrants under section 101(a)(15)(H)(i)(b1) or 101(a)(15)(E)(iii) and United States workers in the same occupational classification an annual salary in disbursements over fewer than 12 months, if—

(aa) the nonimmigrant agrees to the compressed annual salary payments prior to the commencement of the employment; and

(bb) the application of the salary practice to the nonimmigrant does not otherwise cause the nonimmigrant to violate any condition of the nonimmigrant's authorization under this Act to remain in the United States.

(VI) This clause shall not be construed as superseding clause (viii).

(viii) It is a failure to meet a condition of paragraph (1)(A) for an employer who has filed an attestation under this subsection to fail to offer to a nonimmigrant under section 101(a)(15)(H)(i)(b1) or 101(a)(15)(E)(iii), during the nonimmigrant's period of authorized employment, benefits and eligibility for benefits (including the opportunity to participate in health, life, disability, and other insurance plans; the opportunity to participate in retirement and savings plans; and cash bonuses and non-cash compensation, such as stock options (whether or not based on performance)) on the same basis, and in accordance with the same criteria, as the employer offers to United States workers.

(D) If the Secretary of Labor finds, after notice and opportunity for a hearing, that an employer has not paid wages at the wage level specified in the attestation and required under paragraph (1), the Secretary of Labor shall order the employer to provide for payment of such amounts of back pay as may be required to comply with the requirements of paragraph (1), whether or not a penalty under subparagraph (C) has been imposed.

(E) The Secretary of Labor may, on a case-by-case basis, subject an employer to random investigations for a period of up to 5 years, beginning on the date on which the employer is found by the Secretary of Labor to have committed a willful failure to meet a condition of paragraph (1) or to have made a willful misrepresentation of material fact in an attestation. The authority of the Secretary of Labor under this subparagraph shall not be construed to be subject to, or limited by, the requirements of subparagraph (A).

(F) Nothing in this subsection shall be construed as superseding or preempting any other enforcement-related authority under this Act (such as the authorities under section 274B), or any other Act.

(4) For purposes of this subsection:

(A) The term "area of employment" means the area within normal commuting distance of the worksite or physical location where the work of the nonimmigrant under section 101(a)(15)(H)(i)(b1) or 101(a)(15)(E)(iii) is or will be performed. If such worksite or location is within a Metropolitan Statistical Area, any place within such area is deemed to be within the area of employment.

(B) In the case of an attestation with respect to one or more nonimmigrants under section 101(a)(15)(H)(i)(b1) or 101(a)(15)(E)(iii) by an employer, the employer is considered to "displace" a United States worker from a job if the employer lays off the worker from a job that is essentially the equivalent of the job for which the nonimmigrant or nonimmigrants is or are sought. A job shall not be considered to be essentially equivalent of another job unless it involves essentially the same responsibilities, was held by a United States worker with substantially equivalent qualifications and experience, and is located in the same area of employment as the other job.

(C) (i) The term "lays off", with respect to a worker—

(I) means to cause the worker's loss of employment, other than through a discharge for inadequate performance, violation of workplace rules, cause, voluntary departure, voluntary retirement, or the expiration of a grant or contract; but

(II) does not include any situation in which the worker is offered, as an alternative to such loss of employment, a similar employment opportunity with the same employer at equivalent or higher compensation and benefits than the position from which the employee was discharged, regardless of whether or not the employee accepts the offer.

(ii) Nothing in this subparagraph is intended to limit an employee's rights under a collective bargaining agreement or other employment contract.

(D) The term "United States worker" means an employee who—

(i) is a citizen or national of the United States; or

(ii) is an alien who is lawfully admitted for permanent residence, is admitted as a refugee under section 207 of this title, is granted asylum under section 208, or is an immigrant otherwise authorized, by this Act or by the Secretary of Homeland Security, to be employed.

## (t) [second][98]

(1) Except as provided in paragraph (2), no person admitted under section 101(a)(15)(Q)(ii)(I), or acquiring such status after admission, shall be eligible to apply for nonimmigrant status, an immigrant visa, or permanent residence under this Act until it is established that such person has resided and been physically present in the person's country of nationality or last residence for an aggregate of at least 2 years following departure from the United States.

(2) The Secretary of Homeland Security may waive the requirement of such 2-year foreign residence abroad if the Secretary determines that—

(A) departure from the United States would impose exceptional hardship upon the alien's spouse or child (if such spouse or child is a citizen of the United States or an alien lawfully admitted for permanent residence); or

---

[98] This subsection (t) was added by P.L. 108-449 (12/10/04); however, a prior §212(t) was added by P.L. 108-77 (9/3/03, *effective* 1/1/04) (pursuant to §107 of that Act), the date the U.S.-Chile Free Trade Agreement entered into force, thus leaving two subsection (t)s.

(B) the admission of the alien is in the public interest or the national interest of the United States.

(June 27, 1952, ch. 477, title II, ch. 2, §212, 66 Stat. 182; July 18, 1956, ch. 629, title III, §301 (a), 70 Stat. 575; as amended by P.L. 85-508 (7/7/58); P.L. 86-3 (3/18/59); P.L. 86-648 (7/14/60); P.L. 87-256 (9/21/61); P.L. 87-301 (9/26/61); P.L. 89-236 (10/3/65); P.L. 91-225 (4/7/70); P.L. 94-484 (10/12/76); P.L. 94-571 (10/20/76); P.L. 95-83 (8/1/77); P.L. 95-549 (10/30/78); P.L. 96-70 (9/27/79); P.L. 96-212 (3/17/80); P.L. 96-538 (12/17/80); P.L. 97-116 (12/29/81); P.L. 98-454 (10/5/84); P.L. 98-473 (10/12/84); P.L. 99-396 (8/27/86); P.L. 99-570 (10/27/86); P.L. 99-639 (11/10/86); P.L. 99-653 (11/14/86); P.L. 100-204 (12/22/87); P.L. 100-525 (10/24/88); P.L. 100-690 (11/18/88); P.L. 101-238 (12/18/89); P.L. 101-246 (2/16/90); P.L. 101-649 (IMMACT90) (11/29/90), §601(d) [repealing (d)(2), (d)(6), (d)(9), & (d)(10)]; P.L. 102-232 (MTINA) (12/12/91, *effective* 4/1/92); P.L. 103-43 (6/10/93); P.L. 103-317 (8/26/94); P.L. 103-322 (VAWA) (9/13/94); P.L. 103-416 (INTCA) (10/25/94, *effective* 4/1/95); P.L. 104-132 (AEDPA) (4/24/96) [adding (a)(3)(B)(i)(V)]; P.L. 104-208 (IIRAIRA) (9/30/96), div. C, title I, §124(b)(1) [adding (f)]; title III, §301 [revising (a)(6)(A)–(B); redesignating (a)(9) as (a)(10); adding new (a)(9)], §304(b) [repealing (c)], §305(c), §306(d), §308, §322(a)(2)(B), §341(a) [revising (g); adding (a)(1)(A)(ii)], (b), §342(a) [adding (a)(3)(B)(i)(III)], §343, §344(a) [adding (a)(6)(C)(ii)(II)], §345(a) [revising (a)(6)(F)], §346(a) [adding (a)(6)(G)], §347(a), §348(a) [revising (h)], §349, §351(a), §352(a), §355 [revising (a)(3)(B)(i)(V)], title V, §531(a), title VI, §602(a), §622(b), §624(a) [adding (a)(5)(A)(iii)], §671(e)(3); P.L. 105-73 (11/12/97), §1 [revising (a)(1)(A)(ii)]; P.L. 105-277 (10/21/98), (ACWIA) div. C, title IV, §412(a)-(c) [adding (n)(1)(E)–(G), (n)(3)–(5)], §413(a) [revising (n)(2)(A)], §415(a) [adding (p)], §431(a) [adding (q)], div. G, subdiv. B, title XXII, §2226(a) [revising (a)(10)(C)(ii); adding (a)(10)(C)(iii); applies to aliens seeking admission to the U.S. on or after 10/21/98 (date of Act enactment)]; P.L. 105-292 (10/27/98), title VI, §604(a) [adding (a)(2)(G)]; P.L. 106-95 (11/12/99), §2(b) [revising (m)], §4(a) [adding (r)]; P.L. 106-120 (12/3/99), title VIII, §809 [revising (a)(2)(C)]; P.L. 106-313 (AC21) (10/17/00), title I, §106(c)(2) [adding (a)(5)(A)(iv)], §107(a) [revising (n)(1)(E)(ii)]; P.L. 106-386 (10/28/00), div. A, §107(e)(3) [adding two paragraph (13)'s, one by §107(e)(3) of the Act, & a second by §1513(e)], §111(d), div. B, title V, §1505(a) [revising (a)(9)(C)(ii), (g)(1)(C), (i); adding (a)(10)(D) & adding a second (p) without deleting the existing (p)], §1513(e); P.L. 106-395 (CCA) (10/30/00, *effective* 2/27/01), title II, §201 [revising (a)(6)(C)(ii)(II); adding (a)(6)(C)(ii)(I)]; P.L. 106-396 (10/30/00), title I, §101(b)(1); P.L. 107-56 (PATRIOT Act) (10/26/01), title IV, §411(a) [revising (a)(3)], title X, §1006(a); P.L. 107-150 (3/13/02), §2(a)(2) [revising (a)(4)(C)(ii)]; P.L 107-273 (11/2/02), div. C, title I, §11018(c) [revising (e)]; P.L. 108-77 (9/3/03, *effective* 1/1/04), title IV, §402(b) [revising (p); redesignating second (p) added by P.L. 106-386 as (s); & adding (t)]; P.L. 108-193 (12/19/03), §4(b)(4), §8(a)(2) [revising first (13) created by the 2000 Act, & redesignating second (13) created by that Act as (14)]; P.L. 108-447 (12/8/04, *effective* 3/8/05), div. J, title IV, §422(a) [revising (n)(1)(E)(ii)], §423 [adding (p)(3)–(4)], §424(a)(1) [redesignating (n)(2)(H) as (n)(2)(I) & adding new (n)(2)(G), which had expired, & new (n)(2)(H)]; P.L. 108-449 (12/10/04), §1(b)(2) [adding a "new" (t), notwithstanding the §212(t) added by P.L. 108-77]; P.L. 108-458 (12/17/04), title V, §5501(a), §5502(a), §5503 [revising (a)(2)(G), (a)(3)(E)(ii), (a)(4)(D), (d)(3)(A), (d)(3)(B) & (a)(3)(E) heading; adding (a)(3)(E)(iii)]; P.L. 109-13 (REAL ID) (5/11/05), div. B, title I, §103(a)–(c) [revising (a)(3)(B)(i)], §104, title V, §501(d) [revising (a)(3)(B)(i), (a)(3)(B)(iv), & (a)(3)(B)(vi); adding (d)(3)(B)(i)–(ii)]; P.L. 109-162 (1/5/06), title VIII, §802 [revising (a)(9)(B)(iii), (d)(13)–(14); & adding (a)(9)(B)(iii)(V)]; P.L. 109-271 (8/12/06), §6 [revising (a)(6)(A)(ii)(I); (a)(9)(C)(ii); (g)(1)(C); (h)(1)(C); (i)(1); adding (a)(4)(C)(i)(III)]; (a)(9)(C)(iii)]; P.L. 110-161 (12/26/07), §691(a) [revising (d)(3)(B)(i)], §691(c) [revising (a)(3)(B)(ii)]; P.L. 110-229 (5/8/08) §702(b) [revising (a)(7)(B), (d)(7) & (*l*)], §702(d) [revising (d)(7)]; P.L. 110-293 (7/30/08) [revising (a)(1)(A)(i)]; P.L. 110-340 (10/3/08) [adding (a)(3)(G)]; P.L. 110-457 (12/23/08) [revising (a)(2)(H)(i)]; P.L. 111-122 (12/22/09) §3 [revising (a)(3)(E)(ii)].)

## Sec. 213 Admission of Aliens on Giving Bond or Undertaking; Return Upon Permanent Departure
## [8 U.S.C. 1183]

An alien inadmissible under paragraph (4) of section 212(a) may, if otherwise admissible, be admitted in the discretion of the Attorney General (subject to the affidavit of support requirement and attribution of sponsor's income and resources under section 213A) upon the giving of a suitable and proper bond or undertaking approved by the Attorney General, in such amount and containing such conditions as he may prescribe, to the United States, and to all States, territories, counties, towns, municipalities, and districts thereof holding the United States and all States, territories, counties, towns, municipalities, and districts thereof harmless against such alien becoming a public charge. Such bond or undertaking shall terminate upon the permanent departure from the United States, the naturalization, or the death of such alien, and any sums or other security held to secure performance thereof, except to the extent forfeited for violation of the terms thereof, shall be returned to the person by whom furnished, or to his legal representatives. Suit may be brought thereon in the name and by the proper law officers of the United States for the use of the United States, or of any State, territory, district, county, town, or municipality in which such alien becomes a public charge, irrespective of whether a demand for payment of public expenses has been made.

(June 27, 1952, ch. 477, title II, ch. 2, §213, 66 Stat. 188; P.L. 91-313 (7/10/70); P.L. 101-649 (IMMACT90) (11/29/90); P.L. 104-208 (IIRAIRA) (9/30/96), div. C, title III, §308(d)(3)(A), title V, §564(f).)

## Sec. 213A Requirements for Sponsor's Affidavit of Support[99]
[8 U.S.C. 1183a]

### (a) Enforceability.—

(1) *Terms of affidavit.*— No affidavit of support may be accepted by the Attorney General or by any consular officer to establish that an alien is not excludable as a public charge under section 212(a)(4) unless such affidavit is executed by a sponsor of the alien as a contract—

(A) in which the sponsor agrees to provide support to maintain the sponsored alien at an annual income that is not less than 125 percent of the Federal poverty line during the period in which the affidavit is enforceable;

(B) that is legally enforceable against the sponsor by the sponsored alien, the Federal Government, any State (or any political subdivision of such State) or by any other entity that provides any means-tested public benefit (as defined in subsection (e)), consistent with the provisions of this section; and

(C) in which the sponsor agrees to submit to the jurisdiction of any Federal or State court for the purpose of actions brought under subsection (b)(2).

(2) *Period of enforceability.*— An affidavit of support shall be enforceable with respect to benefits provided for an alien before the date the alien is naturalized as a citizen of the United States, or, if earlier, the termination date provided under paragraph (3).

(3) *Termination of period of enforceability upon completion of required period of employment, etc.—*

(A) *In general.*— An affidavit of support is not enforceable after such time as the alien

(i) has worked 40 qualifying quarters of coverage as defined under title II of the Social Security Act or can be credited with such qualifying quarters as provided under subparagraph (B), and

(ii) in the case of any such qualifying quarter creditable for any period beginning after December 31, 1996, did not receive any Federal means-tested public benefit (as provided under section 403 of the Personal Responsibility and Work Opportunity Reconciliation Act of 1996) during any such period.

(B) *Qualifying quarters.*— For purposes of this section, in determining the number of qualifying quarters of coverage under title II of the Social Security Act an alien shall be credited with—

---

[99] Sec. 551(c) of IIRAIRA provides:

(c) *Effective Date; Promulgation of Form—*

(1) In general.—The amendments made by this section shall apply to affidavits of support executed on or after a date specified by the Attorney General, which date shall be not earlier than 60 days (and not later than 90 days) after the date the Attorney General formulates the form for such affidavits under paragraph (2).

(2) Promulgation of form.—Not later than 90 days after the date of the enactment of this Act, the Attorney General, in consultation with the heads of other appropriate agencies, shall promulgate a standard form for an affidavit of support consistent with the provisions of §213A of the Immigration and Nationality Act, as amended by subsection (a).

(i) all of the qualifying quarters of coverage as defined under title II of the Social Security Act worked by a parent of such alien while the alien was under age 18, and

(ii) all of the qualifying quarters worked by a spouse of such alien during their marriage and the alien remains married to such spouse or such spouse is deceased.

No such qualifying quarter of coverage that is creditable under title II of the Social Security Act for any period beginning after December 31, 1996, may be credited to an alien under clause (i) or (ii) if the parent or spouse (as the case may be) of such alien received any Federal means-tested public benefit (as provided under section 403 of the Personal Responsibility and Work Opportunity Reconciliation Act of 1996) during the period for which such qualifying quarter of coverage is so credited.

(C) *Provision of information to save system.*— The Attorney General shall ensure that appropriate information regarding the application of this paragraph is provided to the system for alien verification of eligibility (SAVE) described in section 1137(d)(3) of the Social Security Act.

**(b) Reimbursement of government expenses.**—

(1) *Request for reimbursement.*—

(A) *Requirement.*— Upon notification that a sponsored alien has received any means-tested public benefit, the appropriate nongovernmental entity which provided such benefit or the appropriate entity of the Federal Government, a State, or any political subdivision of a State shall request reimbursement by the sponsor in an amount which is equal to the unreimbursed costs of such benefit.

(B) *Regulations.*— The Attorney General, in consultation with the heads of other appropriate Federal agencies, shall prescribe such regulations as may be necessary to carry out subparagraph (A).

(2) *Actions to compel reimbursement.*—

(A) *In case of nonresponse.*— If within 45 days after a request for reimbursement under paragraph (1)(A), the appropriate entity has not received a response from the sponsor indicating a willingness to commence payment an action may be brought against the sponsor pursuant to the affidavit of support.

(B) *In case of failure to pay.*— If the sponsor fails to abide by the repayment terms established by the appropriate entity, the entity may bring an action against the sponsor pursuant to the affidavit of support.

(C) *Limitation on actions.*— No cause of action may be brought under this paragraph later than 10 years after the date on which the sponsored alien last received any means-tested public benefit to which the affidavit of support applies.

(3) *Use of collection agencies.*— If the appropriate entity under paragraph (1)(A) requests reimbursement from the sponsor or brings an action against the sponsor pursuant to the affidavit of support, the appropriate entity may appoint or hire an individual or other person to act on behalf of such entity acting under the authority of law for purposes of collecting any amounts owed.

**(c) Remedies.**— Remedies available to enforce an affidavit of support under this section include any or all of the remedies described in section 3201, 3203, 3204, or 3205 of title 28, United States Code, as well as an order for specific performance and payment of legal fees and other costs of collection, and include corresponding remedies available under State law. A Federal agency may seek to collect amounts owed under this section in accordance with the provisions of subchapter II of chapter 37 of title 31, United States Code.

**(d) Notification of change of address.—**

(1) *General requirement.*— The sponsor shall notify the Attorney General and the State in which the sponsored alien is currently a resident within 30 days of any change of address of the sponsor during the period in which an affidavit of support is enforceable.

(2) *Penalty.*— Any person subject to the requirement of paragraph (1) who fails to satisfy such requirement shall, after notice and opportunity to be heard, be subject to a civil penalty of—

(A) not less than $250 or more than $2,000, or

(B) if such failure occurs with knowledge that the sponsored alien has received any means-tested public benefits (other than benefits described in section 401(b), 403(c)(2), or 411(b) of the Personal Responsibility and Work Opportunity Reconciliation Act of 1996) not less than $2,000 or more than $5,000.

The Attorney General shall enforce this paragraph under appropriate regulations.

**(e) Jurisdiction.**— An action to enforce an affidavit of support executed under subsection (a) may be brought against the sponsor in any appropriate court—

(1) by a sponsored alien, with respect to financial support; or

(2) by the appropriate entity of the Federal Government, a State or any political subdivision of a State, or by any other nongovernmental entity under subsection (b)(2), with respect to reimbursement.

**(f) Sponsor defined.—**

(1) *In general.*— For purposes of this section the term "sponsor" in relation to a sponsored alien means an individual who executes an affidavit of support with respect to the sponsored alien and who—

(A) is a citizen or national of the United States or an alien who is lawfully admitted to the United States for permanent residence;

(B) is at least 18 years of age;

(C) is domiciled in any of the several States of the United States, the District of Columbia, or any territory or possession of the United States;

(D) is petitioning for the admission of the alien under section 204; and

(E) demonstrates (as provided in paragraph (6)) the means to maintain an annual income equal to at least 125 percent of the Federal poverty line.

(2) *Income requirement case.*— Such term also includes an individual who does not meet the requirement of paragraph (1)(E) but accepts joint and several liability together with an individual under paragraph (5)(A).

(3) *Active duty armed services case.*— Such term also includes an individual who does not meet the requirement of paragraph (1)(E) but is on active duty (other than active duty for training) in the Armed Forces of the United States, is petitioning for the admission of the alien under section 204 as the spouse or child of the individual, and demonstrates (as pro-

vided in paragraph (6)) the means to maintain an annual income equal to at least 100 percent of the Federal poverty line.

(4) *Certain employment-based immigrants case.*— Such term also includes an individual—

(A) who does not meet the requirement of paragraph (1)(D), but is the relative of the sponsored alien who filed a classification petition for the sponsored alien as an employment-based immigrant under section 203(b) or who has a significant ownership interest in the entity that filed such a petition; and

(B) (i) who demonstrates (as provided under paragraph (6)) the means to maintain an annual income equal to at least 125 percent of the Federal poverty line, or

(ii) does not meet the requirement of paragraph (1)(E) but accepts joint and several liability together with an individual under paragraph (5)(A).

(5)[100] *Non-petitioning cases.*— Such term also includes an individual who does not meet the requirement of paragraph (1)(D) but who—

(A) accepts joint and several liability with a petitioning sponsor under paragraph (2) or relative of an employment-based immigrant under paragraph (4) and who demonstrates (as provided under paragraph (6)) the means to maintain an annual income equal to at least 125 percent of the Federal poverty line; or

(B) is a spouse, parent, mother-in-law, father-in-law, sibling, child (if at least 18 years of age), son, daughter, son-in-law, daughter-in-law, sister-in-law, brother-in-law, grandparent, or grandchild of a sponsored alien or a legal guardian of a sponsored alien, meets the requirements of paragraph (1) (other than subparagraph (D)), and executes an affidavit of support with respect to such alien in a case in which—

(i) the individual petitioning under section 204 of this Act for the classification of such alien died after the approval of such petition, and the Secretary of Homeland Security has determined for humanitarian reasons that revocation of such petition under section 205 would be inappropriate; and

(ii) the alien's petition is being adjudicated pursuant to section 204(*l*) (surviving relative consideration).

(6) *Demonstration of means to maintain income.*—

(A) *In general.*—

(i) Method of demonstration.— For purposes of this section, a demonstration of the means to maintain income shall include provision of a certified copy of the individual's Federal income tax return for the individual's 3 most recent taxable years and a written statement, executed under oath or as permitted under penalty of perjury under

---

[100] Sec. 2(b) of the Family Sponsor Immigration Act, P.L. 107-150, which added INA §213A(f)(5), applies with respect to deaths occurring before, on, or after the date of the enactment of this Act [3/13/02], except that, in the case of a death occurring before such date, such amendments shall apply only if—

(1) the sponsored alien—

(A) requests the Attorney General to reinstate the classification petition that was filed with respect to the alien by the deceased and approved under §204 of the Immigration and Nationality Act (8 U.S.C. 1154) before such death; and

(B) demonstrates that he or she is able to satisfy the requirement of §212(a)(4)(C)(ii) of such Act (8 U.S.C. 1182(a)(4)(C)(ii)) by reason of such amendments; and

(2) the Attorney General reinstates such petition after making the determination described in §213A(f)(5)(B)(ii) of such Act (as amended by subsection (a)(1) of this Act).

section 1746 of title 28, United States Code, that the copies are certified copies of such returns.

(ii) Flexibility.— For purposes of this section, aliens may demonstrate the means to maintain income through demonstration of significant assets of the sponsored alien or of the sponsor, if such assets are available for the support of the sponsored alien.

(iii) Percent of poverty.— For purposes of this section, a reference to an annual income equal to at least a particular percentage of the Federal poverty line means an annual income equal to at least such percentage of the Federal poverty line for a family unit of a size equal to the number of members of the sponsor's household (including family and non-family dependents) plus the total number of other dependents and aliens sponsored by that sponsor.

(B) *Limitation.*— The Secretary of State, or the Attorney General in the case of adjustment of status, may provide that the demonstration under subparagraph (A) applies only to the most recent taxable year.

**(g)** [Omitted.]$^{101}$

**(h) Federal poverty line defined.**— For purposes of this section, the term "Federal poverty line" means the level of income equal to the official poverty line (as defined by the Director of the Office of Management and Budget, as revised annually by the Secretary of Health and Human Services, in accordance with section 673(2) of the Omnibus Budget Reconciliation Act of 1981 (42 U.S.C. 9902)) that is applicable to a family of the size involved.

**(i) Sponsor's social security account number required to be provided.**—

(1) An affidavit of support shall include the social security account number of each sponsor.

(2) The Attorney General shall develop an automated system to maintain the social security account number data provided under paragraph (1).

(3) The Attorney General shall submit an annual report to the Committees on the Judiciary of the House of Representatives and the Senate setting forth—

(A) for the most recent fiscal year for which data are available the number of sponsors under this section and the number of sponsors in compliance with the financial obligations of this section; and

(B) a comparison of such numbers with the numbers of such sponsors for the preceding fiscal year.

(June 27, 1952, ch. 477, title II, ch. 2, §213A, as added P.L. 104-193 (8/22/96) as amended by P.L. 104-208 (IIRAIRA) (9/30/96), div. C, title V, §551(a); P.L. 107-150 (3/13/02), §2(a)(1) [revising (f)(5)]; P.L. 111-83 (10/28/09) §568(e) [revising (f)(5)(i)–(ii)].)

## Sec. 214 Admission of Nonimmigrants$^{102}$
[8 U.S.C. 1184]

**(a) Regulations.**—

---

[101] Sec. 213A was enacted without a subsection (g).

[102] *See* §422(a) of the USA PATRIOT Act, P.L. 107-56, *reprinted in* Appendix J, for provisions relating to immigration benefits for the victims of terrorism.

(1) The admission to the United States of any alien as a nonimmigrant shall be for such time and under such conditions as the Attorney General may by regulations prescribe, including when he deems necessary the giving of a bond with sufficient surety in such sum and containing such conditions as the Attorney General shall prescribe, to insure that at the expiration of such time or upon failure to maintain the status under which he was admitted, or to maintain any status subsequently acquired under section 248, such alien will depart from the United States. No alien admitted to Guam or the Commonwealth of the Northern Mariana Islands without a visa pursuant to section 212(*l*) may be authorized to enter or stay in the United States other than in Guam or the Commonwealth of the Northern Mariana Islands or to remain in Guam or the Commonwealth of the Northern Mariana Islands for a period exceeding 45 days from date of admission to Guam or the Commonwealth of the Northern Mariana Islands. No alien admitted to the United States without a visa pursuant to section 217 may be authorized to remain in the United States as a nonimmigrant visitor for a period exceeding 90 days from the date of admission.

(2) (A) The period of authorized status as a nonimmigrant described in section 101(a)(15)(O) shall be for such period as the Attorney General may specify in order to provide for the event (or events) for which the nonimmigrant is admitted.

(B) The period of authorized status as a nonimmigrant described in section 101(a)(15)(P) shall be for such period as the Attorney General may specify in order to provide for the competition, event, or performance for which the nonimmigrant is admitted. In the case of nonimmigrants admitted as individual athletes under section 101(a)(15)(P), the period of authorized status may be for an initial period (not to exceed 5 years) during which the nonimmigrant will perform as an athlete and such period may be extended by the Attorney General for an additional period of up to 5 years.

**(b) Presumption of status; written waiver.**— Every alien (other than a nonimmigrant described in subparagraph (L) or (V) of section 101(a)(15), and other than a nonimmigrant described in any provision of section 101(a)(15)(H)(i) except subclause (b1) of such section) shall be presumed to be an immigrant until he establishes to the satisfaction of the consular officer, at the time of application for a visa, and the immigration officers, at the time of application for admission, that he is entitled to a nonimmigrant status under section 101(a)(15). An alien who is an officer or employee of any foreign government or of any international organization entitled to enjoy privileges, exemptions, and immunities under the International Organizations Immunities Act [22 U.S.C. 288, note], or an alien who is the attendant, servant, employee, or member of the immediate family of any such alien shall not be entitled to apply for or receive an immigrant visa, or to enter the United States as an immigrant unless he executes a written waiver in the same form and substance as is prescribed by section 247(b).

**(c) Petition of importing employer; involvement of departments of labor and agriculture.**—

(1) The question of importing any alien as a nonimmigrant under subparagraph (H), (L), (O), or (P)(i) of section 101(a)(15) (excluding nonimmigrants under section 101(a)(15)(H)(i)(b1)) in any specific case or specific cases shall be determined by the Attorney General, after consultation with appropriate agencies of the Government, upon petition of the importing employer. Such petition shall be made and approved before the visa is granted. The petition shall be in such form and contain such information as the Attorney General shall prescribe. The approval of such a petition shall not, of itself, be construed as establishing that the alien is a nonimmigrant. For purposes of this subsection with respect to nonimmigrants described in section 101(a)(15)(H)(ii)(a), the term "appropriate agencies of Government" means the Department of Labor and includes the Department

of Agriculture. The provisions of section 218 shall apply to the question of importing any alien as a nonimmigrant under section 101(a)(15)(H)(ii)(a).

(2) (A)[103] The Attorney General shall provide for a procedure under which an importing employer which meets requirements established by the Attorney General may file a blanket petition to import aliens as nonimmigrants described in section 101(a)(15)(L) instead of filing individual petitions under paragraph (1) to import such aliens. Such procedure shall permit the expedited processing of visas for admission of aliens covered under such a petition.

(B) For purposes of section 101(a)(15)(L), an alien is considered to be serving in a capacity involving specialized knowledge with respect to a company if the alien has a special knowledge of the company product and its application in international markets or has an advanced level of knowledge of processes and procedures of the company.

(C) The Attorney General shall provide a process for reviewing and acting upon petitions under this subsection with respect to nonimmigrants described in section 101(a)(15)(L) within 30 days after the date a completed petition has been filed.

(D) The period of authorized admission for—

(i) a nonimmigrant admitted to render services in a managerial or executive capacity under section 101(a)(15)(L) shall not exceed 7 years, or

(ii) a nonimmigrant admitted to render services in a capacity that involves specialized knowledge under section 101(a)(15)(L) shall not exceed 5 years.

(E) In the case of an alien spouse admitted under section 101(a)(15)(L), who is accompanying or following to join a principal alien admitted under such section, the Attorney General shall authorize the alien spouse to engage in employment in the United States and provide the spouse with an "employment authorized" endorsement or other appropriate work permit.

(F)[104] An alien who will serve in a capacity involving specialized knowledge with respect to an employer for purposes of section 101(a)(15)(L) and will be stationed primarily at the worksite of an employer other than the petitioning employer or its affiliate, subsidiary, or parent shall not be eligible for classification under section 101(a)(15)(L) if—

(i) the alien will be controlled and supervised principally by such unaffiliated employer; or

(ii) the placement of the alien at the worksite of the unaffiliated employer is essentially an arrangement to provide labor for hire for the unaffiliated employer, rather than a placement in connection with the provision of a product or service for which specialized knowledge specific to the petitioning employer is necessary.

(3) The Attorney General shall approve a petition—

---

[103] Removal of former last sentence ("In the case of an alien seeking admission under §101(a)(15)(L), the 1-year period of continuous employment required under such section is deemed to be reduced to a 6-month period if the importing employer has filed a blanket petition under this subparagraph and met the requirements for expedited processing of aliens covered under such petition.") *effective* 6/6/05 (180 days after enactment of P.L. 108-447); applicable "only to petitions for initial classification filed on or after the effective date of this subtitle." P.L. 108-447 (L-1 Visa Reform Act of 2004), div. J, §413.

[104] Sec. 214(c)(2)(F), added by P.L. 108-447 (L-1 Visa Reform Act of 2004) (12/8/04, *effective* 6/6/05 and is applicable to "petitions filed on or after the effective date of this subtitle, whether for initial, extended, or amended classification."

(A) with respect to a nonimmigrant described in section 101(a)(15)(O)(i) only after consultation in accordance with paragraph (6) or, with respect to aliens seeking entry for a motion picture or television production, after consultation with the appropriate union representing the alien's occupational peers and a management organization in the area of the alien's ability, or

(B) with respect to a nonimmigrant described in section 101(a)(15)(O)(ii) after consultation in accordance with paragraph (6) or, in the case of such an alien seeking entry for a motion picture or television production, after consultation with such a labor organization and a management organization in the area of the alien's ability.

In the case of an alien seeking entry for a motion picture or television production, (i) any opinion under the previous sentence shall only be advisory, (ii) any such opinion that recommends denial must be in writing, (iii) in making the decision the Attorney General shall consider the exigencies and scheduling of the production, and (iv) the Attorney General shall append to the decision any such opinion. The Attorney General shall provide by regulation for the waiver of the consultation requirement under subparagraph (A) in the case of aliens who have been admitted as nonimmigrants under section 101(a)(15)(O)(i) because of extraordinary ability in the arts and who seek readmission to perform similar services within 2 years after the date of a consultation under such subparagraph. Not later than 5 days after the date such a waiver is provided, the Attorney General shall forward a copy of the petition and all supporting documentation to the national office of an appropriate labor organization.

(4) (A) For purposes of section 101(a)(15)(P)(i)(a), an alien is described in this subparagraph if the alien—

    (i) (I) performs as an athlete, individually or as part of a group or team, at an internationally recognized level of performance;

    (II) is a professional athlete, as defined in section 204(i)(2);

    (III) performs as an athlete, or as a coach, as part of a team or franchise that is located in the United States and a member of a foreign league or association of 15 or more amateur sports teams, if—

        (aa) the foreign league or association is the highest level of amateur performance of that sport in the relevant foreign country;

        (bb) participation in such league or association renders players ineligible, whether on a temporary or permanent basis, to earn a scholarship in, or participate in, that sport at a college or university in the United States under the rules of the National Collegiate Athletic Association; and

        (cc) a significant number of the individuals who play in such league or association are drafted by a major sports league or a minor league affiliate of such a sports league; or

    (IV) is a professional athlete or amateur athlete who performs individually or as part of a group in a theatrical ice skating production; and

    (ii) seeks to enter the United States temporarily and solely for the purpose of performing—

        (I) as such an athlete with respect to a specific athletic competition; or

        (II) in the case of an individual described in clause (i)(IV), in a specific theatrical ice skating production or tour.

(B) (i) For purposes of section 101(a)(15)(P)(i)(b), an alien is described in this subparagraph if the alien—

(I) performs with or is an integral and essential part of the performance of an entertainment group that has (except as provided in clause (ii)) been recognized internationally as being outstanding in the discipline for a sustained and substantial period of time,

(II) in the case of a performer or entertainer, except as provided in clause (iii), has had a sustained and substantial relationship with that group (ordinarily for at least one year) and provides functions integral to the performance of the group, and

(III) seeks to enter the United States temporarily and solely for the purpose of performing as such a performer or entertainer or as an integral and essential part of a performance.

(ii) In the case of an entertainment group that is recognized nationally as being outstanding in its discipline for a sustained and substantial period of time, the Attorney General may, in consideration of special circumstances, waive the international recognition requirement of clause (i)(I).

(iii) (I) The one-year relationship requirement of clause (i)(II) shall not apply to 25 percent of the performers and entertainers in a group.

(II) The Attorney General may waive such one-year relationship requirement for an alien who because of illness or unanticipated and exigent circumstances replaces an essential member of the group and for an alien who augments the group by performing a critical role.

(iv) The requirements of subclauses (I) and (II) of clause (i) shall not apply to alien circus personnel who perform as part of a circus or circus group or who constitute an integral and essential part of the performance of such circus or circus group, but only if such personnel are entering the United States to join a circus that has been recognized nationally as outstanding for a sustained and substantial period of time or as part of such a circus.

(C) A person may petition the Attorney General for classification of an alien as a nonimmigrant under section 101(a)(15)(P).

(D) The Attorney General shall approve petitions under this subsection with respect to nonimmigrants described in clause (i) or (iii) of section 101(a)(15)(P) only after consultation in accordance with paragraph (6).

(E) The Attorney General shall approve petitions under this subsection for nonimmigrants described in section 101(a)(15)(P)(ii) only after consultation with labor organizations representing artists and entertainers in the United States.

(F)(i) No nonimmigrant visa under section 101(a)(15)(P)(i)(a) shall be issued to any alien who is a national of a country that is a state sponsor of international terrorism unless the Secretary of State determines, in consultation with the Secretary of Homeland Security and the heads of other appropriate United States agencies, that such alien does not pose a threat to the safety, national security, or national interest of the United States. In making a determination under this subparagraph, the Secretary of State shall apply standards developed by the Secretary of State, in consultation with the Secretary of Homeland Security and the heads of other appropriate United States agencies, that are applicable to the nationals of such states.

(ii) In this subparagraph, the term "state sponsor of inter-national terrorism" means any country the government of which has been determined by the Secretary of State under any of the laws specified in clause (iii) to have repeatedly provided support for acts of international terrorism.

(iii) The laws specified in this clause are the following:

(I) Section 6(j)(1)(A) of the Export Administration Act of 1979 (50 U.S.C. App. 2405(j)(1)(A)) (or successor statute).

(II) Section 40(d) of the Arms Export Control Act (22 U.S.C. 2780(d)).

(III) Section 620A(a) of the Foreign Assistance Act of 1961 (22 U.S.C. 2371(a)).

(G) The Secretary of Homeland Security shall permit a petition under this subsection to seek classification of more than 1 alien as a nonimmigrant under section 101(a)(15)(P)(i)(a).

(H) The Secretary of Homeland Security shall permit an athlete, or the employer of an athlete, to seek admission to the United States for such athlete under a provision of this Act other than section 101(a)(15)(P)(i) if the athlete is eligible under such other provision.

(5) (A) In the case of an alien who is provided nonimmigrant status under section 101(a)(15)(H)(i)(b) or 101(a)(15)(H)(ii)(b) and who is dismissed from employment by the employer before the end of the period of authorized admission, the employer shall be liable for the reasonable costs of return transportation of the alien abroad.

(B) In the case of an alien who is admitted to the United States in nonimmigrant status under section 101(a)(15)(O) or 101(a)(15)(P) and whose employment terminates for reasons other than voluntary resignation, the employer whose offer of employment formed the basis of such nonimmigrant status and the petitioner are jointly and severally liable for the reasonable cost of return transportation of the alien abroad. The petitioner shall provide assurance satisfactory to the Attorney General that the reasonable cost of that transportation will be provided.

(6) (A) (i) To meet the consultation requirement of paragraph (3)(A) in the case of a petition for a nonimmigrant described in section 101(a)(15)(O)(i) (other than with respect to aliens seeking entry for a motion picture or television production), the petitioner shall submit with the petition an advisory opinion from a peer group (or other person or persons of its choosing, which may include a labor organization) with expertise in the specific field involved.

(ii) To meet the consultation requirement of paragraph (3)(B) in the case of a petition for a nonimmigrant described in section 101(a)(15)(O)(ii) (other than with respect to aliens seeking entry for a motion picture or television production), the petitioner shall submit with the petition an advisory opinion from a labor organization with expertise in the skill area involved.

(iii) To meet the consultation requirement of paragraph (4)(D) in the case of a petition for a nonimmigrant described in section 101(a)(15)(P)(i) or 101(a)(15)(P)(iii), the petitioner shall submit with the petition an advisory opinion from a labor organization with expertise in the specific field of athletics or entertainment involved.

(B) To meet the consultation requirements of subparagraph (A), unless the petitioner submits with the petition an advisory opinion from an appropriate labor organization, the Attorney General shall forward a copy of the petition and all supporting documentation to the national office of an appropriate labor organization within 5 days of the date of receipt of the petition. If there is a collective bargaining representative of an employer's employees in the occupational classification for which the alien is being sought, that representative shall be the appropriate labor organization.

(C) In those cases in which a petitioner described in subparagraph (A) establishes that an appropriate peer group (including a labor organization) does not exist, the Attorney General shall adjudicate the petition without requiring an advisory opinion.

(D) Any person or organization receiving a copy of a petition described in subparagraph (A) and supporting documents shall have no more than 15 days following the date of receipt of such documents within which to submit a written advisory opinion or comment or to provide a letter of no objection. Once the 15-day period has expired and the petitioner has had an opportunity, where appropriate, to supply rebuttal evidence, the Attorney General shall adjudicate such petition in no more than 14 days. The Attorney General may shorten any specified time period for emergency reasons if no unreasonable burden would be thus imposed on any participant in the process.

(E) (i) The Attorney General shall establish by regulation expedited consultation procedures in the case of nonimmigrant artists or entertainers described in section 101(a)(15)(O) or 101(a)(15)(P) to accommodate the exigencies and scheduling of a given production or event.

(ii) The Attorney General shall establish by regulation expedited consultation procedures in the case of nonimmigrant athletes described in section 101(a)(15)(O)(i) or 101(a)(15)(P)(i) in the case of emergency circumstances (including trades during a season).

(F) No consultation required under this subsection by the Attorney General with a nongovernmental entity shall be construed as permitting the Attorney General to delegate any authority under this subsection to such an entity. The Attorney General shall give such weight to advisory opinions provided under this section as the Attorney General determines, in his sole discretion, to be appropriate.

(7) If a petition is filed and denied under this subsection, the Attorney General shall notify the petitioner of the determination and the reasons for the denial and of the process by which the petitioner may appeal the determination.

(8) The Attorney General shall submit annually to the Committees on the Judiciary of the House of Representatives and of the Senate a report describing, with respect to petitions under each subcategory of subparagraphs (H), (O), (P), and (Q) of section 101(a)(15) the following:

(A) The number of such petitions which have been filed.

(B) The number of such petitions which have been approved and the number of workers (by occupation) included in such approved petitions.

(C) The number of such petitions which have been denied and the number of workers (by occupation) requested in such denied petitions.

(D) The number of such petitions which have been withdrawn.

(E) The number of such petitions which are awaiting final action.

(9) (A) The Attorney General shall impose a fee on an employer (excluding any employer that is a primary or secondary education institution, an institution of higher education, as defined in section 101(a) of the Higher Education Act of 1965 (20 U.S.C. 1001(a), a nonprofit entity related to or affiliated with any such institution, a nonprofit entity which engages in established curriculum-related clinical training of students registered at any such institution, a nonprofit research organization, or a governmental research organization) filing before a petition under paragraph (1)—

(i) initially to grant an alien nonimmigrant status described in section 101(a)(15)(H)(i)(b);

(ii) to extend the stay of an alien having such status (unless the employer previously has obtained an extension for such alien); or

(iii) to obtain authorization for an alien having such status to change employers.

(B) The amount of the fee shall be $1,500 for each such petition except that the fee shall be half the amount for each such petition by any employer with not more than 25 full-time equivalent employees who are employed in the United States (determined by including any affiliate or subsidiary of such employer).

(C) Fees collected under this paragraph shall be deposited in the Treasury in accordance with section 286(s).

(10) An amended H-1B petition shall not be required where the petitioning employer is involved in a corporate restructuring, including but not limited to a merger, acquisition, or consolidation, where a new corporate entity succeeds to the interests and obligations of the original petitioning employer and where the terms and conditions of employment remain the same but for the identity of the petitioner.

(11)(A) Subject to subparagraph (B), the Secretary of Homeland Security or the Secretary of State, as appropriate, shall impose a fee on an employer who has filed an attestation described in section 212(t)—

(i) in order that an alien may be initially granted nonimmigrant status described in section 101(a)(15)(H)(i)(b1); or

(ii) in order to satisfy the requirement of the second sentence of subsection (g)(8)(C) for an alien having such status to obtain certain extensions of stay.

(B) The amount of the fee shall be the same as the amount imposed by the Secretary of Homeland Security under paragraph (9), except that if such paragraph does not authorize such Secretary to impose any fee, no fee shall be imposed under this paragraph.

(C) Fees collected under this paragraph shall be deposited in the Treasury in accordance with section 286(s).

(12)[105](A) In addition to any other fees authorized by law, the Secretary of Homeland Security shall impose a fraud prevention and detection fee on an employer filing a peti-

---

[105] Sec. 426(c) of P.L. 108-447 (H-1B Visa Reform Act, 2004) states: "The amendments made by this section [including the addition of INA §214(c)(12) by §426(a)] shall take effect on the date of enactment of this Act [12/8/04], and the fees imposed under such amendments shall apply to petitions under §214(c) of the Immigration and Nationality Act, and applications for nonimmigrant visas under §222 of such Act, filed on or after the date that is 90 days after the date of the enactment of this Act [*i.e.*, 3/8/05]." Sec. 430 of the Act also notes that "[t]he amendments made by ... 426(a) ... shall take effect upon date of enactment of this Act."

tion under paragraph (1)—

(i) initially to grant an alien nonimmigrant status described in subparagraph (H)(i)(b) or (L) of section 101(a)(15); or

(ii) to obtain authorization for an alien having such status to change employers.

(B) In addition to any other fees authorized by law, the Secretary of State shall impose a fraud prevention and detection fee on an alien filing an application abroad for a visa authorizing admission to the United States as a nonimmigrant described in section 101(a)(15)(L), if the alien is covered under a blanket petition described in paragraph (2)(A).

(C) The amount of the fee imposed under subparagraph (A) or (B) shall be $500.

(D) The fee imposed under subparagraph (A) or (B) shall only apply to principal aliens and not to the spouses or children who are accompanying or following to join such principal aliens.

(E) Fees collected under this paragraph shall be deposited in the Treasury in accordance with section 286(v).

(13)[106](A) In addition to any other fees authorized by law, the Secretary of Homeland Security shall impose a fraud prevention and detection fee on an employer filing a petition under paragraph (1) for nonimmigrant workers described in section 101(a)(15)(H)(ii)(b).

(B) The amount of the fee imposed under subparagraph (A) shall be $150.

(14)[107](A) If the Secretary of Homeland Security finds, after notice and an opportunity for a hearing, a substantial failure to meet any of the conditions of the petition to admit or otherwise provide status to a nonimmigrant worker under section 101(a)(15)(H)(ii)(b) or a willful misrepresentation of a material fact in such petition—

(i) the Secretary of Homeland Security may, in addition to any other remedy authorized by law, impose such administrative remedies (including civil monetary penalties in an amount not to exceed $10,000 per violation) as the Secretary of Homeland Security determines to be appropriate; and

(ii) the Secretary of Homeland Security may deny petitions filed with respect to that employer under section 204 or paragraph (1) of this subsection during a period of at least 1 year but not more than 5 years for aliens to be employed by the employer.

(B) The Secretary of Homeland Security may delegate to the Secretary of Labor, with the agreement of the Secretary of Labor, any of the authority given to the Secretary of Homeland Security under subparagraph (A)(i).

(C) In determining the level of penalties to be assessed under subparagraph (A), the highest penalties shall be reserved for willful failures to meet any of the conditions of the petition that involve harm to United States workers.

(D) In this paragraph, the term "substantial failure" means the willful failure to comply with the requirements of this section that constitutes a significant deviation from the terms and conditions of a petition.

---

[106] The addition of §214(c)(13) by §403(a) of REAL ID Act (5/11/05) took effect on 5/25/05, and applies to filings "for a fiscal year after fiscal year 2005."

[107] The addition of §214(c)(14) by §404 of REAL ID Act took effect 10/1/05.

**(d)** (1) Issuance of visa to fiancée or fiancé of citizen.— A visa shall not be issued under the provisions of section 101(a)(15)(K)(i) until the consular officer has received a petition filed in the United States by the fiancée or fiancé of the applying alien and approved by the Secretary of Homeland Security. The petition shall be in such form and contain such information as the Secretary of Homeland Security shall, by regulation, prescribe. Such information shall include information on any criminal convictions of the petitioner for any specified crime. It shall be approved only after satisfactory evidence is submitted by the petitioner to establish that the parties have previously met in person within 2 years before the date of filing the petition, have a bona fide intention to marry, and are legally able and actually willing to conclude a valid marriage in the United States within a period of ninety days after the alien's arrival, except that the Secretary of Homeland Security in his discretion may waive the requirement that the parties have previously met in person. In the event the marriage with the petitioner does not occur within three months after the admission of the said alien and minor children, they shall be required to depart from the United States and upon failure to do so shall be removed in accordance with sections 240 and 241.

(2) (A) Subject to subparagraphs (B) and (C), a consular officer may not approve a petition under paragraph (1) unless the officer has verified that—

(i) the petitioner has not, previous to the pending petition, petitioned under paragraph (1) with respect to two or more applying aliens; and

(ii) if the petitioner has had such a petition previously approved, 2 years have elapsed since the filing of such previously approved petition.

(B) The Secretary of Homeland Security may, in the Secretary's discretion, waive the limitations in subparagraph (A) if justification exists for such a waiver. Except in extraordinary circumstances and subject to subparagraph (C), such a waiver shall not be granted if the petitioner has a record of violent criminal offenses against a person or persons.

(C) (i) The Secretary of Homeland Security is not limited by the criminal court record and shall grant a waiver of the condition described in the second sentence of subparagraph (B) in the case of a petitioner described in clause (ii).

(ii) A petitioner described in this clause is a petitioner who has been battered or subjected to extreme cruelty and who is or was not the primary perpetrator of violence in the relationship upon a determination that—

(I) the petitioner was acting in self-defense;

(II) the petitioner was found to have violated a protection order intended to protect the petitioner; or

(III) the petitioner committed, was arrested for, was convicted of, or pled guilty to committing a crime that did not result in serious bodily injury and where there was a connection between the crime and the petitioner's having been battered or subjected to extreme cruelty.

(iii) In acting on applications under this subparagraph, the Secretary of Homeland Security shall consider any credible evidence relevant to the application. The determination of what evidence is credible and the weight to be given that evidence shall be within the sole discretion of the Secretary.

(3) In this subsection:

(A) The terms "domestic violence", "sexual assault", "child abuse and neglect", "dating violence", "elder abuse", and "stalking" have the meaning given such terms in section 3 of the Violence Against Women and Department of Justice Reauthorization Act of 2005.

(B) The term "specified crime" means the following:

(i) Domestic violence, sexual assault, child abuse and neglect, dating violence, elder abuse, and stalking.

(ii) Homicide, murder, manslaughter, rape, abusive sexual contact, sexual exploitation, incest, torture, trafficking, peonage, holding hostage, involuntary servitude, slave trade, kidnapping, abduction, unlawful criminal restraint, false imprisonment, or an attempt to commit any of the crimes described in this clause.

(iii) At least three convictions for crimes relating to a controlled substance or alcohol not arising from a single act.

### (e) Nonimmigrant professionals and annual numerical limit.—

(1) Notwithstanding any other provision of this Act, an alien who is a citizen of Canada and seeks to enter the United States under and pursuant to the provisions of Annex 1502.1 (United States of America), Part C—Professionals, of the United States-Canada Free-Trade Agreement to engage in business activities at a professional level as provided for therein may be admitted for such purpose under regulations of the Attorney General promulgated after consultation with the Secretaries of State and Labor.

(2) An alien who is a citizen of Canada or Mexico, and the spouse and children of any such alien if accompanying or following to join such alien, who seeks to enter the United States under and pursuant to the provisions of Section D of Annex 1603 of the North American Free Trade Agreement (in this subsection referred to as ("NAFTA")) to engage in business activities at a professional level as provided for in such Annex, may be admitted for such purpose under regulations of the Attorney General promulgated after consultation with the Secretaries of State and Labor. For purposes of this Act, including the issuance of entry documents and the application of subsection (b), such alien shall be treated as if seeking classification, or classifiable, as a nonimmigrant under section 101(a)(15). The admission of an alien who is a citizen of Mexico shall be subject to paragraphs (3), (4), and (5). For purposes of this paragraph and paragraphs (3), (4), and (5), the term "citizen of Mexico" means "citizen" as defined in Annex 1608 of NAFTA.

(3) The Attorney General shall establish an annual numerical limit on admissions under paragraph (2) of aliens who are citizens of Mexico, as set forth in Appendix 1603.D.4 of Annex 1603 of the NAFTA. Subject to paragraph (4), the annual numerical limit—

(A) beginning with the second year that NAFTA is in force, may be increased in accordance with the provisions of paragraph 5(a) of Section D of such Annex, and

(B) shall cease to apply as provided for in paragraph 3 of such Appendix.

(4) The annual numerical limit referred to in paragraph (3) may be increased or shall cease to apply (other than by operation of paragraph 3 of such Appendix) only if—

(A) the President has obtained advice regarding the proposed action from the appropriate advisory committees established under section 135 of the Trade Act of 1974 (19 U.S.C. 2155);

(B) the President has submitted a report to the Committee on the Judiciary of the Senate and the Committee on the Judiciary of the House of Representatives that sets forth—

(i) the action proposed to be taken and the reasons therefor, and

(ii) the advice obtained under subparagraph (A);

(C) a period of at least 60 calendar days that begins on the first day on which the President has met the requirements of subparagraphs (A) and (B) with respect to such action has expired; and

(D) the President has consulted with such committees regarding the proposed action during the period referred to in subparagraph (C).

(5) During the period that the provisions of Appendix 1603.D.4 of Annex 1603 of the NAFTA apply, the entry of an alien who is a citizen of Mexico under and pursuant to the provisions of Section D of Annex 1603 of NAFTA shall be subject to the attestation requirement of section 212(m), in the case of a registered nurse, or the application requirement of section 212(n), in the case of all other professions set out in Appendix 1603.D.1 of Annex 1603 of NAFTA, and the petition requirement of subsection (c), to the extent and in the manner prescribed in regulations promulgated by the Secretary of Labor, with respect to sections 212(m) and 212(n), and the Attorney General, with respect to subsection (c).

(6) In the case of an alien spouse admitted under section 101(a)(15)(E), who is accompanying or following to join a principal alien admitted under such section, the Attorney General shall authorize the alien spouse to engage in employment in the United States and provide the spouse with an "employment authorized" endorsement or other appropriate work permit.

**(f) Denial of crewmember status in case of certain labor disputes.—**

(1) Except as provided in paragraph (3), no alien shall be entitled to nonimmigrant status described in section 101(a)(15)(D) if the alien intends to land for the purpose of performing service on board a vessel of the United States (as defined in section 2101(46) of title 46, United States Code) or on an aircraft of an air carrier (as defined in section 40102(a)(2) of title 49, United States Code) during a labor dispute where there is a strike or lockout in the bargaining unit of the employer in which the alien intends to perform such service.

(2) An alien described in paragraph (1)—

(A) may not be paroled into the United States pursuant to section 212(d)(5) unless the Attorney General determines that the parole of such alien is necessary to protect the national security of the United States; and

(B) shall be considered not to be a bona fide crewman for purposes of section 252(b).

(3) Paragraph (1) shall not apply to an alien if the air carrier or owner or operator of such vessel that employs the alien provides documentation that satisfies the Attorney General that the alien—

(A) has been an employee of such employer for a period of not less than 1 year preceding the date that a strike or lawful lockout commenced;

(B) has served as a qualified crewman for such employer at least once in each of 3 months during the 12-month period preceding such date; and

(C) shall continue to provide the same services that such alien provided as such a crewman.

**(g) Temporary workers and trainees; limitation on numbers.—**

(1) The total number of aliens who may be issued visas or otherwise provided nonimmigrant status during any fiscal year (beginning with fiscal year 1992)—

(A) under section 101(a)(15)(H)(i)(b) may not exceed—

(i) 65,000 in each fiscal year before fiscal year 1999;

(ii) 115,000 in fiscal year 1999;

(iii) 115,000 in fiscal year 2000;

(iv) 195,000 in fiscal year 2001;

(v) 195,000 in fiscal year 2002;

(vi) 195,000 in fiscal year 2003; and

(vii) 65,000 in each succeeding fiscal year; or

(B) under section 101(a)(15)(H)(ii)(b) may not exceed 66,000.[108]

(2) The numerical limitations of paragraph (1) shall only apply to principal aliens and not to the spouses or children of such aliens.

(3) Aliens who are subject to the numerical limitations of paragraph (1) shall be issued visas (or otherwise provided nonimmigrant status) in the order in which petitions are filed for such visas or status. If an alien who was issued a visa or otherwise provided nonimmigrant status and counted against the numerical limitations of paragraph (1) is found to have been issued such visa or otherwise provided such status by fraud or willfully misrepresenting a material fact and such visa or nonimmigrant status is revoked, then one number shall be restored to the total number of aliens who may be issued visas or otherwise provided such status under the numerical limitations of paragraph (1) in the fiscal year in which the petition is revoked, regardless of the fiscal year in which the petition was approved.

(4) In the case of a nonimmigrant described in section 101(a)(15)(H)(i)(b), the period of authorized admission as such a nonimmigrant may not exceed 6 years.[109]

(5) The numerical limitations contained in paragraph (1)(A) shall not apply to any nonimmigrant alien issued a visa or otherwise provided status under section 101(a)(15)(H)(i)(b) who—

(A) is employed (or has received an offer of employment) at an institution of higher education (as defined in section 101(a) of the Higher Education Act of 1965 (20 U.S.C. 1001(a))), or a related or affiliated nonprofit entity;

(B) is employed (or has received an offer of employment) at a nonprofit research organization or a governmental research organization; or

(C) has earned a master's or higher degree from a United States institution of higher education (as defined in section 101(a) of the Higher Education Act of 1965 (20 U.S.C. 1001(a))), until the number of aliens who are exempted from such numerical limitation during such year exceeds 20,000.

---

[108] Sec. 14006 of P.L. 108-287 (8/5/04) provides that the numerical limitation contained in INA §214(g)(1)(B) does not apply to any H-2B visaholder "who is employed (or has received an offer of employment) as a fish roe processor, a fish roe technician, or a supervisor of fish roe processing."

[109] *See* §106(a) of AC21 (P.L. 106-313, as amended by P.L. 107-273), *reprinted in* Appendix H, *infra,* for provisions concerning the nonapplicability of this paragraph.

(6) Any alien who ceases to be employed by an employer described in paragraph (5)(A) shall, if employed as a nonimmigrant alien described in section 101(a)(15)(H)(i)(b), who has not previously been counted toward the numerical limitations contained in paragraph (1)(A), be counted toward those limitations the first time the alien is employed by an employer other than one described in paragraph (5).

(7) Any alien who has already been counted, within the 6 years prior to the approval of a petition described in subsection (c), toward the numerical limitations of paragraph (1)(A) shall not again be counted toward those limitations unless the alien would be eligible for a full 6 years of authorized admission at the time the petition is filed. Where multiple petitions are approved for 1 alien, that alien shall be counted only once.

(8)  (A) The agreements referred to in section 101(a)(15)(H)(i)(b1) are—

(i) the United States-Chile Free Trade Agreement; and

(ii) the United States-Singapore Free Trade Agreement.

(B) (i) The Secretary of Homeland Security shall establish annual numerical limitations on approvals of initial applications by aliens for admission under section 101(a)(15)(H)(i)(b1).

(ii) The annual numerical limitations described in clause (i) shall not exceed—

(I) 1,400 for nationals of Chile (as defined in article 14.9 of the United States-Chile Free Trade Agreement) for any fiscal year; and

(II) 5,400 for nationals of Singapore (as defined in Annex 1A of the United States-Singapore Free Trade Agreement) for any fiscal year.

(iii) The annual numerical limitations described in clause (i) shall only apply to principal aliens and not to the spouses or children of such aliens.

(iv) The annual numerical limitation described in paragraph (1)(A) is reduced by the amount of the annual numerical limitations established under clause (i). However, if a numerical limitation established under clause (i) has not been exhausted at the end of a given fiscal year, the Secretary of Homeland Security shall adjust upwards the numerical limitation in paragraph (1)(A) for that fiscal year by the amount remaining in the numerical limitation under clause (i). Visas under section 101(a)(15)(H)(i)(b) may be issued pursuant to such adjustment within the first 45 days of the next fiscal year to aliens who had applied for such visas during the fiscal year for which the adjustment was made.

(C) The period of authorized admission as a nonimmigrant under section 101(a)(15)(H)(i)(b1) shall be 1 year, and may be extended, but only in 1-year increments. After every second extension, the next following extension shall not be granted unless the Secretary of Labor had determined and certified to the Secretary of Homeland Security and the Secretary of State that the intending employer has filed with the Secretary of Labor an attestation under section 212(t)(1) for the purpose of permitting the nonimmigrant to obtain such extension.

(D) The numerical limitation described in paragraph (1)(A) for a fiscal year shall be reduced by one for each alien granted an extension under subparagraph (C) during such year who has obtained 5 or more consecutive prior extensions.

(9)[110](A) Subject to subparagraphs (B) and (C), an alien who has already been counted toward the numerical limitation of paragraph (1)(B) during fiscal year 2004, 2005, or 2006 shall not again be counted toward such limitation during fiscal year 2007.

(B) A petition to admit or otherwise provide status under section 101(a)(15)(H)(ii)(b) shall include, with respect to a returning worker—

(i) all information and evidence that the Secretary of Homeland Security determines is required to support a petition for status under section 101(a)(15)(H)(ii)(b);

(ii) the full name of the alien; and

(iii) a certification to the Department of Homeland Security that the alien is a returning worker.

(C) An H-2B visa or grant of nonimmigrant status for a returning worker shall be approved only if the alien is confirmed to be a returning worker by—

(i) the Department of State; or

(ii) if the alien is visa exempt or seeking to change to status under section 101(a)(15)(H)(ii)(b), the Department of Homeland Security.

(10) The numerical limitations of paragraph (1)(B) shall be allocated for a fiscal year so that the total number of aliens subject to such numerical limits who enter the United States pursuant to a visa or are accorded nonimmigrant status under section 101(a)(15)(H)(ii)(b) during the first 6 months of such fiscal year is not more than 33,000.

(11)(A) The Secretary of State may not approve a number of initial applications submitted for aliens described in section 101(a)(15)(E)(iii) that is more than the applicable numerical limitation set out in this paragraph.

(B) The applicable numerical limitation referred to in subparagraph (A) is 10,500 for each fiscal year.

(C) The applicable numerical limitation referred to in subparagraph (A) shall only apply to principal aliens and not to the spouses or children of such aliens.

**(h) Intention to abandon foreign residence.**— The fact that an alien is the beneficiary of an application for a preference status filed under section 204 or has otherwise sought permanent residence in the United States shall not constitute evidence of an intention to abandon a foreign residence for purposes of obtaining a visa as a nonimmigrant described in subparagraph (H)(i)(b) or (c), (L), or (V) of section 101(a)(15) or otherwise obtaining or maintaining the status of a nonimmigrant described in such subparagraph, if the alien had obtained a change of status under section 248 to a classification as such a nonimmigrant before the alien's most recent departure from the United States.

**(i) "Specialty occupation" defined.—**

(1) Except as provided in paragraph (3), for purposes of section 101(a)(15)(H)(i)(b), section 101(a)(15)(E)(iii), and paragraph (2), the term "specialty occupation" means an occupation that requires—

(A) theoretical and practical application of a body of highly specialized knowledge, and

---

[110] Effective as if enacted on 10/1/04; sunset provision removed by P.L. 109-364. *See* §402 of REAL ID Act for more on implementation.

(B) attainment of a bachelor's or higher degree in the specific specialty (or its equivalent) as a minimum for entry into the occupation in the United States.

(2) For purposes of section 101(a)(15)(H)(i)(b), the requirements of this paragraph, with respect to a specialty occupation, are—

(A) full state licensure to practice in the occupation, if such licensure is required to practice in the occupation,

(B) completion of the degree described in paragraph (1)(B) for the occupation, or

(C) (i) experience in the specialty equivalent to the completion of such degree, and

(ii) recognition of expertise in the specialty through progressively responsible positions relating to the specialty.

(3) For purposes of section 101(a)(15)(H)(i)(b1), the term "specialty occupation" means an occupation that requires—

(A) theoretical and practical application of a body of specialized knowledge; and

(B) attainment of a bachelor's or higher degree in the specific specialty (or its equivalent) as a minimum for entry into the occupation in the United States.

**(j) Labor disputes.—**

(1) Notwithstanding any other provision of this Act, an alien who is a citizen of Canada or Mexico who seeks to enter the United States under and pursuant to the provisions of Section B, Section C, or Section D of Annex 1603 of the North American Free Trade Agreement, shall not be classified as a nonimmigrant under such provisions if there is in progress a strike or lockout in the course of a labor dispute in the occupational classification at the place or intended place of employment, unless such alien establishes, pursuant to regulations promulgated by the Attorney General, that the alien's entry will not affect adversely the settlement of the strike or lockout. Notice of a determination under this paragraph shall be given as may be required by paragraph 3 of article 1603 of such Agreement. For purposes of this paragraph, the term "citizen of Mexico" means "citizen" as defined in Annex 1608 of such Agreement.

(2) Notwithstanding any other provision of this Act except section 212(t)(1), and subject to regulations promulgated by the Secretary of Homeland Security, an alien who seeks to enter the United States under and pursuant to the provisions of an agreement listed in subsection (g)(8)(A), and the spouse and children of such an alien if accompanying or following to join the alien, may be denied admission as a nonimmigrant under subparagraph (E), (L), or (H)(i)(b1) of section 101(a)(15) if there is in progress a labor dispute in the occupational classification at the place or intended place of employment, unless such alien establishes, pursuant to regulations promulgated by the Secretary of Homeland Security after consultation with the Secretary of Labor, that the alien's entry will not affect adversely the settlement of the labor dispute or the employment of any person who is involved in the labor dispute. Notice of a determination under this paragraph shall be given as may be required by such agreement.

**(k) Numerical limitations; period of admission; conditions for admission and stay; annual report.—**

(1) The number of aliens who may be provided a visa as nonimmigrants under section 101(a)(15)(S)(i) in any fiscal year may not exceed 200. The number of aliens who may be provided a visa as nonimmigrants under section 101(a)(15)(S)(ii) in any fiscal year may not exceed 50.

(2) The period of admission of an alien as such a nonimmigrant may not exceed 3 years. Such period may not be extended by the Attorney General.

(3) As a condition for the admission, and continued stay in lawful status, of such a nonimmigrant, the nonimmigrant—

(A) shall report not less often than quarterly to the Attorney General such information concerning the alien's whereabouts and activities as the Attorney General may require;

(B) may not be convicted of any criminal offense punishable by a term of imprisonment of 1 year or more after date of such admission;

(C) must have executed a form that waives the nonimmigrant's right to contest, other than on the basis of an application for withholding of removal, any action for removal of the alien instituted before the alien obtains lawful permanent resident status; and

(D) shall abide by any other condition, limitation, or restriction imposed by the Attorney General.

(4) The Attorney General shall submit a report annually to the Committee on the Judiciary of the House of Representatives and the Committee on the Judiciary of the Senate concerning—

(A) the number of such nonimmigrants admitted;

(B) the number of successful criminal prosecutions or investigations resulting from cooperation of such aliens;

(C) the number of terrorist acts prevented or frustrated resulting from cooperation of such aliens;

(D) the number of such nonimmigrants whose admission or cooperation has not resulted in successful criminal prosecution or investigation or the prevention or frustration of a terrorist act; and

(E) the number of such nonimmigrants who have failed to report quarterly (as required under paragraph (3)) or who have been convicted of crimes in the United States after the date of their admission as such a nonimmigrant.

**(*l*) Restrictions on waiver.—**[111]

(1) In the case of a request by an interested State agency, or by an interested Federal agency, for a waiver of the 2-year foreign residence requirement under section 212(e) on behalf of an alien described in clause (iii) of such section, the Attorney General shall not grant such waiver unless—

(A) in the case of an alien who is otherwise contractually obligated to return to a foreign country, the government of such country furnishes the Director of the United States Information Agency with a statement in writing that it has no objection to such waiver; and

(B) in the case of a request by an interested State agency, the grant of such waiver would not cause the number of waivers allotted for that State for that fiscal year to exceed 30;

---

[111] P.L. 103-416 (10/25/94) §220(c), adding this subsection, noted that "The amendments made by this section shall apply to aliens admitted [under INA §101(a)(15)(J)], or acquiring such status after admission to the United States, before, on, or after the date of enactment of this Act and before June 1, 1996." The latter date has been extended numerous times, most recently to June 1, 2008, by P.L. 109-477 §2.

(C) in the case of a request by an interested Federal agency or by an interested State agency—

(i) the alien demonstrates a bona fide offer of full-time employment, at a health care organization, which employment has been determined by the Attorney General to be in the public interest; and

(ii) the alien agrees to begin employment with the health facility or health care organization within 90 days of receiving such waiver, and agrees to continue to work for a total of not less than 3 years (unless the Attorney General determines that extenuating circumstances exist, such as closure of the facility or hardship to the alien, which would justify a lesser period of employment at such health facility or health care organization, in which case the alien must demonstrate another bona fide offer of employment at a health facility or health care organization for the remainder of such 3-year period); and

(D) in the case of a request by an interested Federal agency (other than a request by an interested Federal agency to employ the alien full-time in medical research or training) or by an interested State agency, the alien agrees to practice primary care or specialty medicine in accordance with paragraph (2) for a total of not less than 3 years only in the geographic area or areas which are designated by the Secretary of Health and Human Services as having a shortage of health care professionals, except that—

(i) in the case of a request by the Department of Veterans Affairs, the alien shall not be required to practice medicine in a geographic area designated by the Secretary;

(ii) in the case of a request by an interested State agency, the head of such State agency determines that the alien is to practice medicine under such agreement in a facility that serves patients who reside in one or more geographic areas so designated by the Secretary of Health and Human Services (without regard to whether such facility is located within such a designated geographic area), and the grant of such waiver would not cause the number of the waivers granted on behalf of aliens for such State for a fiscal year (within the limitation in subparagraph (B)) in accordance with the conditions of this clause to exceed 10; and

(iii) in the case of a request by an interested Federal agency or by an interested State agency for a waiver for an alien who agrees to practice specialty medicine in a facility located in a geographic area so designated by the Secretary of Health and Human Services, the request shall demonstrate, based on criteria established by such agency, that there is a shortage of health care professionals able to provide services in the appropriate medical specialty to the patients who will be served by the alien.

(2) (A) Notwithstanding section 248(a)(2), the Attorney General may change the status of an alien who qualifies under this subsection and section 212(e) to that of an alien described in section 101(a)(15)(H)(i)(b). The numerical limitations contained in subsection (g)(1)(A) shall not apply to any alien whose status is changed under the preceding sentence, if the alien obtained a waiver of the 2-year foreign residence requirement upon a request by an interested Federal agency or an interested State agency.

(B) No person who has obtained a change of status under subparagraph (A) and who has failed to fulfill the terms of the contract with the health facility or health care organization named in the waiver application shall be eligible to apply for an immigrant visa, for permanent residence, or for any other change of nonimmigrant status until it is established that such person has resided and been physically present in the country of his nationality or his last residence for an aggregate of at least 2 years following departure from the United States.

(3) Notwithstanding any other provisions of this subsection, the 2-year foreign residence requirement under section 212(e) shall apply with respect to an alien described in clause (iii) of such section, who has not otherwise been accorded status under section 101(a)(27)(H), if—

(A) at any time the alien ceases to comply with any agreement entered into under subparagraph (C) or (D) of paragraph (1); or

(B) the alien's employment ceases to benefit the public interest at any time during the 3-year period described in paragraph (1)(C).

**(m) Nonimmigrant elementary and secondary school students.—**

(1) An alien may not be accorded status as a nonimmigrant under clause (i) or (iii) of section 101(a)(15)(F) in order to pursue a course of study—

(A) at a public elementary school or in a publicly funded adult education program; or

(B) at a public secondary school unless—

(i) the aggregate period of such status at such a school does not exceed 12 months with respect to any alien, and

(ii) the alien demonstrates that the alien has reimbursed the local educational agency that administers the school for the full, unsubsidized per capita cost of providing education at such school for the period of the alien's attendance.

(2) An alien who obtains the status of a nonimmigrant under clause (i) or (iii) of section 101(a)(15)(F) in order to pursue a course of study at a private elementary or secondary school or in a language training program that is not publicly funded shall be considered to have violated such status, and the alien's visa under section 101(a)(15)(F) shall be void, if the alien terminates or abandons such course of study at such a school and undertakes a course of study at a public elementary school, in a publicly funded adult education program, in a publicly funded adult education language training program, or at a public secondary school (unless the requirements of paragraph (1)(B) are met).

**(n) Increased portability of H-1B status.—**

(1) A nonimmigrant alien described in paragraph (2) who was previously issued a visa or otherwise provided nonimmigrant status under section 101(a)(15)(H)(i)(b) is authorized to accept new employment upon the filing by the prospective employer of a new petition on behalf of such nonimmigrant as provided under subsection (a). Employment authorization shall continue for such alien until the new petition is adjudicated. If the new petition is denied, such authorization shall cease.

(2) A nonimmigrant alien described in this paragraph is a nonimmigrant alien—

(A) who has been lawfully admitted into the United States;

(B) on whose behalf an employer has filed a nonfrivolous petition for new employment before the date of expiration of the period of stay authorized by the Attorney General; and

(C) who, subsequent to such lawful admission, has not been employed without authorization in the United States before the filing of such petition.

**(o) Nonimmigrants guilty of trafficking in persons.—**

(1) No alien shall be eligible for admission to the United States under section 101(a)(15)(T) if there is substantial reason to believe that the alien has committed an act of a severe form of trafficking in persons (as defined in section 103 of the Trafficking Victims Protection Act of 2000).

(2) The total number of aliens who may be issued visas or otherwise provided nonimmigrant status during any fiscal year under section 101(a)(15)(T) may not exceed 5,000.

(3) The numerical limitation of paragraph (2) shall only apply to principal aliens and not to the spouses, sons, daughters, siblings, or parents of such aliens.

(4) An unmarried alien who seeks to accompany, or follow to join, a parent granted status under section 101(a)(15)(T)(i), and who was under 21 years of age on the date on which such parent applied for such status, shall continue to be classified as a child for purposes of section 101(a)(15)(T)(ii), if the alien attains 21 years of age after such parent's application was filed but while it was pending.

(5) An alien described in clause (i) of section 101(a)(15)(T) shall continue to be treated as an alien described in clause (ii)(I) of such section if the alien attains 21 years of age after the alien's application for status under such clause (i) is filed but while it is pending.

(6) In making a determination under section 101(a)(15)(T)(i)(III)(aa) with respect to an alien, statements from State and local law enforcement officials that the alien has complied with any reasonable request for assistance in the investigation or prosecution of crimes such as kidnapping, rape, slavery, or other forced labor offenses, where severe forms of trafficking in persons (as defined in section 103 of the Trafficking Victims Protection Act of 2000) appear to have been involved, shall be considered.

(7) (A) Except as provided in subparagraph (B), an alien who is issued a visa or otherwise provided nonimmigrant status under section 101(a)(15)(T) may be granted such status for a period of not more than 4 years.

(B) An alien who is issued a visa or otherwise provided nonimmigrant status under section 101(a)(15)(T) may extend the period of such status beyond the period described in subparagraph (A) if—

(i) a Federal, State, or local law enforcement official, prosecutor, judge, or other authority investigating or prosecuting activity relating to human trafficking or certifies that the presence of the alien in the United States is necessary to assist in the investigation or prosecution of such activity;

(ii) the alien is eligible for relief under section 245(*l*) and is unable to obtain such relief because regulations have not been issued to implement such section; or

(iii) the Secretary of Homeland Security determines that an extension of the period of such nonimmigrant status is warranted due to exceptional circumstances.

(C) Nonimmigrant status under section 101(a)(15)(T) shall be extended during the pendency of an application for adjustment of status under section 245(*l*).

**(p) Requirements applicable to section 101(a)(15)(U) visas.—**

(1) *Petitioning procedures for section 101(a)(15)(U) visas.—* The petition filed by an alien under section 101(a)(15)(U)(i) shall contain a certification from a Federal, State, or local law enforcement official, prosecutor, judge, or other Federal, State, or local authority investigating criminal activity described in section 101(a)(15)(U)(iii). This certification may also be provided by an official of the Service whose ability to provide such certification is not limited

to information concerning immigration violations. This certification shall state that the alien "has been helpful, is being helpful, or is likely to be helpful" in the investigation or prosecution of criminal activity described in section 101(a)(15)(U)(iii).

(2) *Numerical limitations.*—

(A) The number of aliens who may be issued visas or otherwise provided status as nonimmigrants under section 101(a)(15)(U) in any fiscal year shall not exceed 10,000.

(B) The numerical limitations in subparagraph (A) shall only apply to principal aliens described in section 101(a)(15)(U)(i), and not to spouses, children, or, in the case of alien children, the alien parents of such children.

(3) *Duties of the Attorney General with respect to "U" visa nonimmigrants.*— With respect to nonimmigrant aliens described in subsection (a)(15)(U)—

(A) the Attorney General and other government officials, where appropriate, shall provide those aliens with referrals to nongovernmental organizations to advise the aliens regarding their options while in the United States and the resources available to them; and

(B) the Attorney General shall, during the period those aliens are in lawful temporary resident status under that subsection, provide the aliens with employment authorization.

(4) *Credible evidence considered.*— In acting on any petition filed under this subsection, the consular officer or the Attorney General, as appropriate, shall consider any credible evidence relevant to the petition.

(5) *Nonexclusive relief.*— Nothing in this subsection limits the ability of aliens who qualify for status under section 101(a)(15)(U) to seek any other immigration benefit or status for which the alien may be eligible.

(6) *Duration of status.*— The authorized period of status of an alien as a nonimmigrant under section 101(a)(15)(U) shall be for a period of not more than 4 years, but shall be extended upon certification from a Federal, State, or local law enforcement official, prosecutor, judge, or other Federal, State, or local authority investigating or prosecuting criminal activity described in section 101(a)(15)(U)(iii) that the alien's presence in the United States is required to assist in the investigation or prosecution of such criminal activity. The Secretary of Homeland Security may extend, beyond the 4-year period authorized under this section, the authorized period of status of an alien as a nonimmigrant under section 101(a)(15)(U) if the Secretary determines that an extension of such period is warranted due to exceptional circumstances. Such alien's nonimmigrant status shall be extended beyond the 4-year period authorized under this section if the alien is eligible for relief under section 245(m) and is unable to obtain such relief because regulations have not been issued to implement such section and shall be extended during the pendency of an application for adjustment of status under section 245(m). The Secretary may grant work authorization to any alien who has a pending, bona fide application for nonimmigrant status under section 101(a)(15)(U).

(q) **Employment of nonimmigrants described in section 101(a)(15)(V).**—

(1) In the case of a nonimmigrant described in section 101(a)(15)(V)—

(A) the Attorney General shall authorize the alien to engage in employment in the United States during the period of authorized admission and shall provide the alien with an "employment authorized" endorsement or other appropriate document signifying authorization of employment; and

(B) the period of authorized admission as such a nonimmigrant shall terminate 30 days after the date on which any of the following is denied:

(i) The petition filed under section 204 to accord the alien a status under section 203(a)(2)(A) (or, in the case of a child granted nonimmigrant status based on eligibility to receive a visa under section 203(d), the petition filed to accord the child's parent a status under section 203(a)(2)(A)).

(ii) The alien's application for an immigrant visa pursuant to the approval of such petition.

(iii) The alien's application for adjustment of status under section 245 pursuant to the approval of such petition.

(2) In determining whether an alien is eligible to be admitted to the United States as a nonimmigrant under section 101(a)(15)(V), the grounds for inadmissibility specified in section 212(a)(9)(B) shall not apply.

(3) The status of an alien physically present in the United States may be adjusted by the Attorney General, in the discretion of the Attorney General and under such regulations as the Attorney General may prescribe, to that of a nonimmigrant under section 101(a)(15)(V), if the alien—

(A) applies for such adjustment;

(B) satisfies the requirements of such section; and

(C) is eligible to be admitted to the United States, except in determining such admissibility, the grounds for inadmissibility specified in paragraphs (6)(A), (7), and (9)(B) of section 212(a) shall not apply.

**(r) Visas of nonimmigrants described in section 101(a)(15)(K)(ii).—**[112]

(1) A visa shall not be issued under the provisions of section 101(a)(15)(K)(ii) until the consular officer has received a petition filed in the United States by the spouse of the applying alien and approved by the Attorney General. The petition shall be in such form and contain such information as the Attorney General shall, by regulation, prescribe. Such information shall include information on any criminal convictions of the petitioner for any specified crime.

(2) In the case of an alien seeking admission under section 101(a)(15)(K)(ii) who concluded a marriage with a citizen of the United States outside the United States, the alien shall be considered inadmissible under section 212(a)(7)(B) if the alien is not at the time of application for admission in possession of a valid nonimmigrant visa issued by a consular officer in the foreign state in which the marriage was concluded.

(3) In the case of a nonimmigrant described in section 101(a)(15)(K)(ii), and any child of such a nonimmigrant who was admitted as accompanying, or following to join, such a nonimmigrant, the period of authorized admission shall terminate 30 days after the date on which any of the following is denied:

(A) The petition filed under section 204 to accord the principal alien status under section 201(b)(2)(A)(i).

---

[112] Sec. 832(a)(2) of P.L. 109-162 (1/5/06), which added INA §§214(r)(4) and (5), as well as the second sentence in (r)(1), took effect 60 days after the Act's effective date, *i.e.,* on 3/6/06.

(B) The principal alien's application for an immigrant visa pursuant to the approval of such petition.

(C) The principal alien's application for adjustment of status under section 245 pursuant to the approval of such petition.

(4) (A) The Secretary of Homeland Security shall create a database for the purpose of tracking multiple visa petitions filed for fiancé(e)s and spouses under clauses (i) and (ii) of section 101(a)(15)(K). Upon approval of a second visa petition under section 101(a)(15)(K) for a fiancé(e) or spouse filed by the same United States citizen petitioner, the petitioner shall be notified by the Secretary that information concerning the petitioner has been entered into the multiple visa petition tracking database. All subsequent fiancé(e) or spouse nonimmigrant visa petitions filed by that petitioner under such section shall be entered in the database.

(B) (i) Once a petitioner has had two fiancé(e) or spousal petitions approved under clause (i) or (ii) of section 101(a)(15)(K), if a subsequent petition is filed under such section less than 10 years after the date the first visa petition was filed under such section, the Secretary of Homeland Security shall notify both the petitioner and beneficiary of any such subsequent petition about the number of previously approved fiancé(e) or spousal petitions listed in the database.

(ii) A copy of the information and resources pamphlet on domestic violence developed under section 833(a) of the International Marriage Broker Regulation Act of 2005 shall be mailed to the beneficiary along with the notification required in clause (i).

(5) In this subsection:

(A) The terms "domestic violence", "sexual assault", "child abuse and neglect", "dating violence", "elder abuse", and "stalking" have the meaning given such terms in section 3 of the Violence Against Women and Department of Justice Reauthorization Act of 2005.

(B) The term "specified crime" means the following:

(i) Domestic violence, sexual assault, child abuse and neglect, dating violence, elder abuse, and stalking.

(ii) Homicide, murder, manslaughter, rape, abusive sexual contact, sexual exploitation, incest, torture, trafficking, peonage, holding hostage, involuntary servitude, slave trade, kidnapping, abduction, unlawful criminal restraint, false imprisonment, or an attempt to commit any of the crimes described in this clause.

(iii) At least three convictions for crimes relating to a controlled substance or alcohol not arising from a single act.

(June 27, 1952, ch. 477, title II, ch. 2, §214, 66 Stat. 189; as amende by P.L. 91-225 (4/7/70); P.L. 98-454 (10/5/84); P.L. 99-603 (IRCA) (11/6/86); P.L. 99-639 (11/10/86); P.L. 100-449 (9/28/88); P.L. 100-525 (10/24/88); P.L. 101-649 (IMMACT90) (11/29/90); P.L. 102-232 (MTINA) (12/12/91, *effective* 4/1/92) [repealing (g)(1)(C)]; P.L. 103-182 (12/8/93); P.L. 103-322 (VAWA) (9/13/94); P.L. 103-416 (INTCA) (10/25/94, *effective* 4/1/95) [adding (k)]; P.L. 104-208 (IIRAIRA) (9/30/96), div. C, title III, §308(e), title VI, §621, §622(c) [revising (k)], §625(a)(1) [adding (m)], §671(a) [redesignating (k) as (*l*)]; P.L. 105-65 (10/27/97), title I, §108 [revising (*l*)(1)(D)]; P.L. 105-277 (10/21/98), (ACWIA) div. C, title IV, §411(a) [revising (g)(1)(A)], §414(a) [adding (c)(9)]; P.L. 106-104 (11/13/99), §2; P.L. 106-311 (10/17/00), §1 [revising (c)]; P.L. 106-313 (AC21) (10/17/00), title I, §102(a) [redesignating (g)(1)(A)(v) as (g)(1)(A)(vii); removing (g)(1)(A)(iv); & adding (g)(1)(A)(iv)–(vi)], §103 [adding (g)(5)–(7)], §105(a) [adding (m)], §108; P.L. 106-386 (10/28/00), div. A, §107(e)(2) [redesignating second (*l*) as (m), resulting in two subsection (m)'s; adding (n)], div. B, title V, §1513(c) [adding (o)]; P.L. 106-396 (10/30/00), title IV, §401 [adding (c)(10)]; P.L. 106-553 (LIFE Act) (12/21/00), §1a(2), title XI, §1102(b) [revising (b), (d); adding second (o)], §1103(b) [revising (d); adding (p)]; P.L. 107-45 (10/1/01), §1 [revising (k)]; P.L. 107-124 (1/16/02); P.L. 107-125 (1/16/02), §1,

§2(a) [revising (c)(2)(A); adding (c)(2)(E)]; P.L. 107-273 (11/2/02, *effective* 5/31/02), div. C, title I, §11018(a) [revising (*l*)(1)(B)]; P.L. 107-274 (11/2/02), §2(c) [revising (m)]; P.L. 108-77 (9/3/03, *effective* 1/1/04), title IV, §402(a)(2) [adding (c)(11), (g)(8), (i)], §403 [revising (j)], §404 [revising (b), (c), (h)]; P.L. 108-78 (9/3/03), title IV, §402 [revising (g)(8)]; P.L. 108-193 (12/19/03), §4(b)(2) [revising (o)(3), adding (o)(4)–(6)], §8(a)(3) [redesignating (m) added by P.L. 106-313 §105, (n) added by P.L. 106-386 §107(e), (o) added by P.L. 106-386 §1513(c), (o) added by P.L. 106-553 §1102(b), & (p) added by P.L. 106-553 §1103(b) as (n), (o), (p), (q), & (r), respectively]; P.L. 108-441 (12/3/04), §1(b) [revising (*l*)(1)(D) & (*l*)(2)(A)]; P.L. 108-447 (12/8/04, varying effective dates—see notes in specific paragraphs), div. J, title IV, §412(a) [adding (c)(2)(F)], §413(a) [revising (c)(2)(A)], §422(b) [revising (c)(9)], §425(a) [revising (g)(5); adding (g)(5)(C)], §426(a) [adding (c)(12)]; P.L. 109-13 (REAL ID) (5/11/05, varying effective dates—see notes in specific paragraphs), div. B, title IV, §402(a) [adding (g)(9)], §403, §404, §405 [adding (g)(10)], title V, §501 [adding (c)(13)–(14), (g)(11), (i)]; P.L. 109-162 (1/5/06), §821 [revising (*l*)(2)(A); adding (o)(7) & (p)(6)]; §832 [revising (d)(1); adding (d)(2)–(3)]; §832(a)(2) [*effective* 3/6/06, revising (r)(1) & adding (r)(4)–(5)]; P.L. 109-364 (10/17/06), §1074 [revising (g)(9)(A)–(B)]; P.L. 109-463 (12/22/06) §2 [revising (c)(4)(A)(i)–(ii); adding (c)(4)(F)–(H)]; P.L. 110-229 (5/8/08) §702(b) [revising (a)(1)]; P.L. 110-362 (10/8/08) [revising (l)(1)(D)(ii)]; P.L. 110-457 (12/23/08) [revising (o)(7)(B) & (p)(6), adding (o)(7)(B)(i)–(ii)].)

## Sec. 215 Travel Control of Citizens and Aliens
[8 U.S.C. 1185]

**(a) Restrictions and prohibitions.**— Unless otherwise ordered by the President, it shall be unlawful—

(1) for any alien to depart from or enter or attempt to depart from or enter the United States except under such reasonable rules, regulations, and orders, and subject to such limitations and exceptions as the President may prescribe;

(2) for any person to transport or attempt to transport from or into the United States another person with knowledge or reasonable cause to believe that the departure or entry of such other person is forbidden by this section;

(3) for any person knowingly to make any false statement in an application for permission to depart from or enter the United States with intent to induce or secure the granting of such permission either for himself or for another;

(4) for any person knowingly to furnish or attempt to furnish or assist in furnishing to another a permit or evidence of permission to depart or enter not issued and designed for such other person's use;

(5) for any person knowingly to use or attempt to use any permit or evidence of permission to depart or enter not issued and designed for his use;

(6) for any person to forge, counterfeit, mutilate, or alter, or cause or procure to be forged, counterfeited, mutilated, or altered, any permit or evidence of permission to depart from or enter the United States;

(7) for any person knowingly to use or attempt to use or furnish to another for use any false, forged, counterfeited, mutilated, or altered permit, or evidence of permission, or any permit or evidence of permission which, though originally valid, has become or been made void or invalid.

**(b) Citizens.**— Except as otherwise provided by the President and subject to such limitations and exceptions as the President may authorize and prescribe, it shall be unlawful for any citizen of the United States to depart from or enter, or attempt to depart from or enter, the United States unless he bears a valid United States passport.[113]

---

[113] Sec. 7209 of P.L. 108-458 (12/17/04) mandates the creation of a plan to expedite the travel of certain frequent travelers. Subsection (c)(2) of that section provides that "the President may not exercise discretion under [INA §215(b)] to waive documentary requirements for United States citizens departing from or entering, or attempting to depart from or enter, the United States except (A) where the Secretary of Homeland Security determines that the alternative documentation that is the basis for the waiver

*continued*

**(c) Definition.—** The term "United States" as used in this section includes the Canal Zone, and all territory and waters, continental or insular, subject to the jurisdiction of the United States. The term "person" as used in this section shall be deemed to mean any individual, partnership, association, company, or other incorporated body of individuals, or corporation, or body politic.

**(d) Nonadmission of certain aliens.—** Nothing in this section shall be construed to entitle an alien to whom a permit to enter the United States has been issued to enter the United States, if, upon arrival in the United States, he is found to be inadmissible under any of the provisions of this Act, or any other law, relating to the entry of aliens into the United States.

**(e) Revocation of proclamation as affecting penalties.—** The revocation of any rule, regulation, or order issued in pursuance of this section shall not prevent prosecution for any offense committed, or the imposition of any penalties or forfeitures, liability for which was incurred under this section prior to the revocation of such rule, regulation, or order.

**(f) Permits to enter.—** Passports, visas, reentry permits, and other documents required for entry under this Act may be considered as permits to enter for the purposes of this section.

(June 27, 1952, ch. 477, title II, ch. 2, §215, 66 Stat. 190; P.L. 95-426 (10/7/78); P.L. 103-416 (INTCA) (10/25/94, *effective* 4/1/95).)

## Sec. 216 Conditional Permanent Resident Status for Certain Alien Spouses and Sons and Daughters
[8 U.S.C. 1186a]

**(a) In general.—**

(1) *Conditional basis for status.—* Notwithstanding any other provision of this Act, an alien spouse (as defined in subsection (g)(1)) and an alien son or daughter (as defined in subsection (g)(2)) shall be considered, at the time of obtaining the status of an alien lawfully admitted for permanent residence, to have obtained such status on a conditional basis subject to the provisions of this section.

(2) *Notice of requirements.—*

(A) *At time of obtaining permanent residence.—* At the time an alien spouse or alien son or daughter obtains permanent resident status on a conditional basis under paragraph (1), the Attorney General shall provide for notice to such a spouse, son, or daughter respecting the provisions of this section and the requirements of subsection (c)(1) to have the conditional basis of such status removed.

(B) *At time of required petition.—* In addition, the Attorney General shall attempt to provide notice to such a spouse, son, or daughter, at or about the beginning of the 90-day period described in subsection (d)(2)(A), of the requirements of subsection (c)(1).

(C) *Effect of failure to provide notice.—* The failure of the Attorney General to provide a notice under this paragraph shall not affect the enforcement of the provisions of this section with respect to such a spouse, son, or daughter.

**(b) Termination of status if finding that qualifying marriage improper.—**

---

of the documentary requirement is sufficient to denote identity and citizenship; (B) in the case of an unforeseen emergency in individual cases; or (C) in the case of humanitarian or national interest reasons in individual cases."

(1) *In general.*— In the case of an alien with permanent resident status on a conditional basis under subsection (a), if the Attorney General determines, before the second anniversary of the alien's obtaining the status of lawful admission for permanent residence, that—

(A) the qualifying marriage—

(i) was entered into for the purpose of procuring an alien's admission as an immigrant, or

(ii) has been judicially annulled or terminated, other than through the death of a spouse; or

(B) a fee or other consideration was given (other than a fee or other consideration to an attorney for assistance in preparation of a lawful petition) for the filing of a petition under section 204(a) or subsection (d) or (p) of subsection 214 with respect to the alien;

the Attorney General shall so notify the parties involved and, subject to paragraph (2), shall terminate the permanent resident status of the alien (or aliens) involved as of the date of the determination.

(2) *Hearing in removal proceeding.*— Any alien whose permanent resident status is terminated under paragraph (1) may request a review of such determination in a proceeding to remove the alien. In such proceeding, the burden of proof shall be on the Attorney General to establish, by a preponderance of the evidence, that a condition described in paragraph (1) is met.

**(c) Requirements of timely petition and interview for removal of condition.—**

(1) *In general.*— In order for the conditional basis established under subsection (a) for an alien spouse or an alien son or daughter to be removed—

(A) the alien spouse and the petitioning spouse (if not deceased) jointly must submit to the Attorney General, during the period described in subsection (d)(2), a petition which requests the removal of such conditional basis and which states, under penalty of perjury, the facts and information described in subsection (d)(1), and

(B) in accordance with subsection (d)(3), the alien spouse and the petitioning spouse (if not deceased) must appear for a personal interview before an officer or employee of the Service respecting the facts and information described in subsection (d)(1).

(2) *Termination of permanent resident status for failure to file petition or have personal interview.—*

(A) *In general.*— In the case of an alien with permanent resident status on a conditional basis under subsection (a), if—

(i) no petition is filed with respect to the alien in accordance with the provisions of paragraph (1)(A), or

(ii) unless there is good cause shown, the alien spouse and petitioning spouse fail to appear at the interview described in paragraph (1)(B),

the Attorney General shall terminate the permanent resident status of the alien as of the second anniversary of the alien's lawful admission for permanent residence.

(B) *Hearing in removal proceeding.*— In any removal proceeding with respect to an alien whose permanent resident status is terminated under subparagraph (A), the burden of proof shall be on the alien to establish compliance with the conditions of paragraphs (1)(A) and (1)(B).

(3) *Determination after petition and interview.*—

(A) *In general.*— If—

(i) a petition is filed in accordance with the provisions of paragraph (1)(A), and

(ii) the alien spouse and petitioning spouse appear at the interview described in paragraph (1)(B),

the Attorney General shall make a determination, within 90 days of the date of the interview, as to whether the facts and information described in subsection (d)(1) and alleged in the petition are true with respect to the qualifying marriage.

(B) *Removal of conditional basis if favorable determination.*— If the Attorney General determines that such facts and information are true, the Attorney General shall so notify the parties involved and shall remove the conditional basis of the parties effective as of the second anniversary of the alien's obtaining the status of lawful admission for permanent residence.

(C) *Termination if adverse determination.*— If the Attorney General determines that such facts and information are not true, the Attorney General shall so notify the parties involved and, subject to subparagraph (D), shall terminate the permanent resident status of an alien spouse or an alien son or daughter as of the date of the determination.

(D) *Hearing in removal proceeding.*— Any alien whose permanent resident status is terminated under subparagraph (C) may request a review of such determination in a proceeding to remove the alien. In such proceeding, the burden of proof shall be on the Attorney General to establish, by a preponderance of the evidence, that the facts and information described in subsection (d)(1) and alleged in the petition are not true with respect to the qualifying marriage.

(4) *Hardship waiver.*— The Attorney General, in the Attorney General's discretion, may remove the conditional basis of the permanent resident status for an alien who fails to meet the requirements of paragraph (1) if the alien demonstrates that—

(A) extreme hardship would result if such alien is removed,

(B) the qualifying marriage was entered into in good faith by the alien spouse, but the qualifying marriage has been terminated (other than through the death of the spouse) and the alien was not at fault in failing to meet the requirements of paragraph (1), or

(C) the qualifying marriage was entered into in good faith by the alien spouse and during the marriage the alien spouse or child was battered by or was the subject of extreme cruelty perpetrated by his or her spouse or citizen or permanent resident parent and the alien was not at fault in failing to meet the requirements of paragraph (1).

In determining extreme hardship, the Attorney General shall consider circumstances occurring only during the period that the alien was admitted for permanent residence on a conditional basis. In acting on applications under this paragraph, the Attorney General shall consider any credible evidence relevant to the application. The determination of what evidence is credible and the weight to be given that evidence shall be within the sole discretion of the Attorney General. The Attorney General shall, by regulation, establish measures to protect the confidentiality of information concerning any abused alien spouse or child, including information regarding the whereabouts of such spouse or child.

**(d) Details of petition and interview.**—

(1) *Contents of petition.*— Each petition under subsection (c)(1)(A) shall contain the following facts and information:

(A) *Statement of proper marriage and petitioning process.*— The facts are that—

(i) the qualifying marriage—

(I) was entered into in accordance with the laws of the place where the marriage took place,

(II) has not been judicially annulled or terminated, other than through the death of a spouse, and

(III) was not entered into for the purpose of procuring an alien's admission as an immigrant; and

(ii) no fee or other consideration was given (other than a fee or other consideration to an attorney for assistance in preparation of a lawful petition) for the filing of a petition under section 204(a) or subsection (d) or (p) of section 214 with respect to the alien spouse or alien son or daughter.

(B) *Statement of additional information.*— The information is a statement of—

(i) the actual residence of each party to the qualifying marriage since the date the alien spouse obtained permanent resident status on a conditional basis under subsection (a), and

(ii) the place of employment (if any) of each such party since such date, and the name of the employer of such party.

(2) *Period for filing petition.*—

(A) *90-day period before second anniversary.*— Except as provided in subparagraph (B), the petition under subsection (c)(1)(A) must be filed during the 90-day period before the second anniversary of the alien's obtaining the status of lawful admission for permanent residence.

(B) *Date[114] petitions for good cause.*— Such a petition may be considered if filed after such date, but only if the alien establishes to the satisfaction of the Attorney General good cause and extenuating circumstances for failure to file the petition during the period described in subparagraph (A).

(C) *Filing of petitions during removal.*— In the case of an alien who is the subject of removal hearings as a result of failure to file a petition on a timely basis in accordance with subparagraph (A), the Attorney General may stay such removal proceedings against an alien pending the filing of the petition under subparagraph (B).

(3) *Personal interview.*— The interview under subsection (c)(1)(B) shall be conducted within 90 days after the date of submitting a petition under subsection (c)(1)(A) and at a local office of the Service, designated by the Attorney General, which is convenient to the parties involved. The Attorney General, in the Attorney General's discretion, may waive the deadline for such an interview or the requirement for such an interview in such cases as may be appropriate.

**(e) Treatment of period for purposes of naturalization.**— For purposes of title III, in the case of an alien who is in the United States as a lawful permanent resident on a conditional basis under

---

[114] *Sic.* Probably should be "Late petitions …"

this section, the alien shall be considered to have been admitted as an alien lawfully admitted for permanent residence and to be in the United States as an alien lawfully admitted to the United States for permanent residence.

**(f) Treatment of certain waivers.—** In the case of an alien who has permanent residence status on a conditional basis under this section, if, in order to obtain such status, the alien obtained a waiver under subsection (h) or (i) of section 212 of certain grounds of inadmissibility, such waiver terminates upon the termination of such permanent residence status under this section.

**(g) Definitions.—** In this section:

(1) The term "alien spouse" means an alien who obtains the status of an alien lawfully admitted for permanent residence (whether on a conditional basis or otherwise)—

(A) as an immediate relative (described in section 201(b)) as the spouse of a citizen of the United States,

(B) under section 214(d) as the fiancée or fiancé of a citizen of the United States, or

(C) under section 203(a)(2) as the spouse of an alien lawfully admitted for permanent residence,

by virtue of a marriage which was entered into less than 24 months before the date the alien obtains such status by virtue of such marriage, but does not include such an alien who only obtains such status as a result of section 203(d).

(2) The term "alien son or daughter" means an alien who obtains the status of an alien lawfully admitted for permanent residence (whether on a conditional basis or otherwise) by virtue of being the son or daughter of an individual through a qualifying marriage.

(3) The term "qualifying marriage" means the marriage described to in paragraph (1).

(4) The term "petitioning spouse" means the spouse of a qualifying marriage, other than the alien.

(June 27, 1952, ch. 477, title II, ch. 2, §216, as added by P.L. 99-639 (11/10/86); as amended by P.L. 100-525 (10/24/88); P.L. 101-649 (IMMACT90) (11/29/90); P.L. 102-232 (MTINA) (12/12/91, *effective* 4/1/92); P.L. 103-322 (VAWA) (9/13/94); P.L. 104-208 (IIRAIRA) (9/30/96), div. C, title III, §308; P.L. 106-553 (LIFE Act) (12/21/00), §1, title XI, §1103 [revising (b)(1), (d)(1)].)

## Sec. 216A Conditional Permanent Resident Status for Certain Alien Entrepreneurs, Spouses, and Children[115]
**[8 U.S.C. 1186b]**

**(a) In general.—**

(1) *Conditional basis for status.—* Notwithstanding any other provision of this Act, an alien entrepreneur (as defined in subsection (f)(1)), alien spouse, and alien child (as defined in subsection (f)(2)) shall be considered, at the time of obtaining the status of an alien lawfully admitted for permanent residence, to have obtained such status on a conditional basis subject to the provisions of this section.

(2) *Notice of requirements.—*

---

[115] Sec. 11036 of P.L. 107-73, eliminating the enterprise establishment requirement for alien entrepreneurs, applies to "aliens having any of the following petitions pending on or after the date of the enactment of this Act: (1) A petition under [INA §204(a)(1)(H)] (or any predecessor provision), with respect to status under [§203(b)(5);] (2) A petition under [INA §216A(c)(1)(A)] to remove the conditional basis of an alien's permanent resident status." *See also* Division C, Title I, Subtitle B of the same Act, *reprinted in* Appendix J, *infra,* for additional provisions concerning EB-5 immigrants. In particular, §11031 of the Act sets out provisions that can apply in lieu of INA §216A(c)(3).

(A) *At time of obtaining permanent residence.*— At the time an alien entrepreneur, alien spouse, or alien child obtains permanent resident status on a conditional basis under paragraph (1), the Attorney General shall provide for notice to such an entrepreneur, spouse, or child respecting the provisions of this section and the requirements of subsection (c)(1) to have the conditional basis of such status removed.

(B) *At time of required petition.*— In addition, the Attorney General shall attempt to provide notice to such an entrepreneur, spouse, or child, at or about the beginning of the 90-day period described in subsection (d)(2)(A), of the requirements of subsection (c)(1).

(C) *Effect of failure to provide notice.*— The failure of the Attorney General to provide a notice under this paragraph shall not affect the enforcement of the provisions of this section with respect to such an entrepreneur, spouse, or child.

**(b) Termination of status if finding that qualifying entrepreneurship improper.—**

(1) *In general.*— In the case of an alien entrepreneur with permanent resident status on a conditional basis under subsection (a), if the Attorney General determines, before the second anniversary of the alien's obtaining the status of lawful admission for permanent residence, that—

(A) the investment in the commercial enterprise was intended solely as a means of evading the immigration laws of the United States,

(B) (i) the alien did not invest, or was not actively in the process of investing, the requisite capital; or

(ii) the alien was not sustaining the actions described in clause (i) throughout the period of the alien's residence in the United States, or

(C) the alien was otherwise not conforming to the requirements of section 203(b)(5),

then the Attorney General shall so notify the alien involved and, subject to paragraph (2), shall terminate the permanent resident status of the alien (and the alien spouse and alien child) involved as of the date of the determination.

(2) *Hearing in removal proceeding.*— Any alien whose permanent resident status is terminated under paragraph (1) may request a review of such determination in a proceeding to remove the alien. In such proceeding, the burden of proof shall be on the Attorney General to establish, by a preponderance of the evidence, that a condition described in paragraph (1) is met.

**(c) Requirements of timely petition and interview for removal of condition.—**

(1) *In general.*— In order for the conditional basis established under subsection (a) for an alien entrepreneur, alien spouse, or alien child to be removed—

(A) the alien entrepreneur must submit to the Attorney General, during the period described in subsection (d)(2), a petition which requests the removal of such conditional basis and which states, under penalty of perjury, the facts and information described in subsection (d)(1), and

(B) in accordance with subsection (d)(3), the alien entrepreneur must appear for a personal interview before an officer or employee of the Service respecting the facts and information described in subsection (d)(1).

(2) *Termination of permanent resident status for failure to file petition or have personal interview.—*

(A) *In general.*— In the case of an alien with permanent resident status on a conditional basis under subsection (a), if—

(i) no petition is filed with respect to the alien in accordance with the provisions of paragraph (1)(A), or

(ii) unless there is good cause shown, the alien entrepreneur fails to appear at the interview described in paragraph (1)(B) (if required under subsection (d)(3)),

the Attorney General shall terminate the permanent resident status of the alien (and the alien's spouse and children if it was obtained on a conditional basis under this section or section 216) as of the second anniversary of the alien's lawful admission for permanent residence.

(B) *Hearing in removal proceeding.*— In any removal proceeding with respect to an alien whose permanent resident status is terminated under subparagraph (A), the burden of proof shall be on the alien to establish compliance with the conditions of paragraphs (1)(A) and (1)(B).

(3) *Determination after petition and interview.*—

(A) *In general.*— If—

(i) a petition is filed in accordance with the provisions of paragraph (1)(A), and

(ii) the alien entrepreneur appears at any interview described in paragraph (1)(B),

the Attorney General shall make a determination, within 90 days of the date of the such filing[116] or interview (whichever is later), as to whether the facts and information described in subsection (d)(1) and alleged in the petition are true with respect to the qualifying commercial enterprise.

(B) *Removal of conditional basis if favorable determination.*— If the Attorney General determines that such facts and information are true, the Attorney General shall so notify the alien involved and shall remove the conditional basis of the alien's status effective as of the second anniversary of the alien's lawful admission for permanent residence.

(C) *Termination if adverse determination.*— If the Attorney General determines that such facts and information are not true, the Attorney General shall so notify the alien involved and, subject to subparagraph (D), shall terminate the permanent resident status of an alien entrepreneur, alien spouse, or alien child as of the date of the determination.

(D) *Hearing in removal proceeding.*— Any alien whose permanent resident status is terminated under subparagraph (C) may request a review of such determination in a proceeding to remove the alien. In such proceeding, the burden of proof shall be on the Attorney General to establish, by a preponderance of the evidence, that the facts and information described in subsection (d)(1) and alleged in the petition are not true with respect to the qualifying commercial enterprise.

**(d) Details of petition and interview.**—

(1) *Contents of petition.*— Each petition under subsection (c)(1)(A) shall contain facts and information demonstrating that the alien—

(A) (i) invested, or is actively in the process of investing, the requisite capital; and

---

[116] *Sic.* Should probably read "of such filing."

(ii) sustained the actions described in clause (i) throughout the period of the alien's residence in the United States; and

(B) is otherwise conforming to the requirements of section 203(b)(5).

(2) *Period for filing petition.*—

(A) *90-day period before second anniversary.*— Except as provided in subparagraph (B), the petition under subsection (c)(1)(A) must be filed during the 90-day period before the second anniversary of the alien's lawful admission for permanent residence.

(B) *Date petitions for good cause.*— Such a petition may be considered if filed after such date, but only if the alien establishes to the satisfaction of the Attorney General good cause and extenuating circumstances for failure to file the petition during the period described in subparagraph (A).

(C) *Filing of petitions during removal.*— In the case of an alien who is the subject of removal hearings as a result of failure to file a petition on a timely basis in accordance with subparagraph (A), the Attorney General may stay such removal proceedings against an alien pending the filing of the petition under subparagraph (B).

(3) *Personal interview.*— The interview under subsection (c)(1)(B) shall be conducted within 90 days after the date of submitting a petition under subsection (c)(1)(A) and at a local office of the Service, designated by the Attorney General, which is convenient to the parties involved. The Attorney General, in the Attorney General's discretion, may waive the deadline for such an interview or the requirement for such an interview in such cases as may be appropriate.

**(e) Treatment of period for purposes of naturalization.**— For purposes of title III, in the case of an alien who is in the United States as a lawful permanent resident on a conditional basis under this section, the alien shall be considered to have been admitted as an alien lawfully admitted for permanent residence and to be in the United States as an alien lawfully admitted to the United States for permanent residence.

**(f) Definitions.**— In this section:

(1) The term "alien entrepreneur" means an alien who obtains the status of an alien lawfully admitted for permanent residence (whether on a conditional basis or otherwise) under section 203(b)(5).

(2) The term "alien spouse" and the term "alien child" mean an alien who obtains the status of an alien lawfully admitted for permanent residence (whether on a conditional basis or otherwise) by virtue of being the spouse or child, respectively, of an alien entrepreneur.

(3) The term "commercial enterprise" includes a limited partnership.

(June 27, 1952, ch. 477, title II, ch. 2, §216A, as added by P.L. 101-649 (IMMACT90) (11/29/90); as amended by P.L. 102-232 (MTINA) (12/12/91, *effective* 4/1/92); P.L. 104-208 (IIRAIRA) (9/30/96), div. C, title III, §308(e)(8); P.L. 107-273 (11/2/02), div. C, title I, §11036(b)).)

## Sec. 217 Visa Waiver Program for Certain Visitors[117]
**[8 U.S.C. 1187]**

**(a) Establishment of program.**— The Attorney General and the Secretary of State are authorized to establish a program (hereinafter in this section referred to as the "program") under which the requirement of paragraph (7)(B)(i)(II) of section 212(a) may be waived by the Attorney General, in consultation with the Secretary of State, and in accordance with this section, in the case of an alien who meets the following requirements:

(1) *Seeking entry as tourist for 90 days or less.*— The alien is applying for admission during the program as a nonimmigrant visitor (described in section 101(a)(15)(B)) for a period not exceeding 90 days.

(2) *National of program country.*— The alien is a national of, and presents a passport issued by, a country which—

(A) extends (or agrees to extend), either on its own or in conjunction with one or more other countries that are described in subparagraph (B) and that have established with it a common area for immigration admissions, reciprocal privileges to citizens and nationals of the United States, and

(B) is designated as a pilot program country under subsection (c).

(3) *Machine readable passport.*—

(A) *In general.*— Except as provided in subparagraph (B), on or after October 1, 2003, the alien at the time of application for admission is in possession of a valid unexpired machine-readable passport that satisfies the internationally accepted standard for machine readability.

(B) *Limited waiver authority.*— For the period beginning October 1, 2003, and ending September 30, 2007, the Secretary of State may waive the requirement of subparagraph (A) with respect to nationals of a program country (as designated under subsection (c)), if the Secretary of State finds that the program country—

(i) is making progress toward ensuring that passports meeting the requirement of subparagraph (A) are generally available to its nationals; and

(ii) has taken appropriate measures to protect against misuse of passports the country has issued that do not meet the requirement of subparagraph (A).

(4) *Executes immigration forms.*— The alien before the time of such admission completes such immigration form as the Attorney General shall establish.

(5) *Entry into the United States.*— If arriving by sea or air, the alien arrives at the port of entry into the United States on a carrier, including any carrier conducting operations under part 135 of title 14, Code of Federal Regulations, or a noncommerical aircraft that is owned or operated by a domestic corporation conducting operations under part 91 of title 14, Code of Federal Regulations, which has entered into an agreement with the Attorney General pursuant to subsection (e) of this section. The Attorney General is authorized to require a carrier conducting operations under part 135 of title 14, Code of Federal Regulations, or a domestic corporation conducting operations under part 91 of that title, to give suitable and proper bond,

---

[117] Sec. 303(c)(2) of the Enhanced Border Security and Visa Entry Reform Act of 2002, P.L. 107-173, required VWP travelers to have a biometric passport by 10/26/04. That deadline was extended to 10/26/05 by P.L. 108-299.

in such reasonable amount and containing such conditions as the Attorney General may deem sufficient to ensure compliance with the indemnification requirements of this section, as a term of such an agreement.

(6) *Not a safety threat.*— The alien has been determined not to represent a threat to the welfare, health, safety, or security of the United States.

(7) *No previous violation.*— If the alien previously was admitted without a visa under this section, the alien must not have failed to comply with the conditions of any previous admission as such a nonimmigrant.

(8) *Round-trip ticket.*— The alien is in possession of a round-trip transportation ticket (unless this requirement is waived by the Attorney General under regulations) or the alien is arriving at the port of entry on an aircraft operated under part 135 of title 14, Code of Federal Regulations, or a noncommercial aircraft that is owned or operated by a domestic corporation conducting operations under part 91 of title 14, Code of Federal Regulations.

(9) *Automated system check.*— The identity of the alien has been checked using an automated electronic database containing information about the inadmissibility of aliens to uncover any grounds on which the alien may be inadmissible to the United States, and no such ground has been found.

(10) *Electronic transmission of identification information.*— Operators of aircraft under part 135 of title 14, Code of Federal Regulations, or operators of noncommercial aircraft that are owned or operated by a domestic corporation conducting operations under part 91 of title 14, Code of Federal Regulations, carrying any alien passenger who will apply for admission under this section shall furnish such information as the Attorney General by regulation shall prescribe as necessary for the identification of any alien passenger being transported and for the enforcement of the immigration laws. Such information shall be electronically transmitted not less than one hour prior to arrival at the port of entry for purposes of checking for inadmissibility using the automated electronic database.

(11) *Eligibility determination under the electronic travel authorization system.*—[118] Beginning on the date on which the electronic travel authorization system developed under subsection (h)(3) is fully operational, each alien traveling under the program shall, before applying for admission to the United States, electronically provide to the system biographical information and such other information as the Secretary of Homeland Security shall determine necessary to determine the eligibility of, and whether there exists a law enforcement or security risk in permitting, the alien to travel to the United States. Upon review of such biographical information, the Secretary of Homeland Security shall determine whether the alien is eligible to travel to the United States under the program.

(b) **Waiver of rights.**— An alien may not be provided a waiver under the program unless the alien has waived any right—

(1) to review or appeal under this Act of an immigration officer's determination as to the admissibility of the alien at the port of entry into the United States, or

(2) to contest, other than on the basis of an application for asylum, any action for removal of the alien.

---

[118] INA §217(a)(11), as added by P.L. 110-53, §711(d)(1)(A)(ii) (8/3/07), shall take effect on the date that is 60 days after the date on which the Secretary of Homeland Security publishes notice in the *Federal Register* of the requirement under such paragraph. P.L. 110-53, §711(d)(2)

**(c) Designation of program countries.—**

(1) *In general.*— The Attorney General, in consultation with the Secretary of State may designate any country as a program country if it meets the requirements of paragraph (2).

(2) *Qualifications.*— Except as provided in subsection (f), a country may not be designated as a program country unless the following requirements are met:

(A) *Low nonimmigrant visa refusal rate.*— Either—

(i) the average number of refusals of nonimmigrant visitor visas for nationals of that country during—

(I) the two previous full fiscal years was less than 2.0 percent of the total number of nonimmigrant visitor visas for nationals of that country which were granted or refused during those years; and

(II) either of such two previous full fiscal years was less than 2.5 percent of the total number of nonimmigrant visitor visas for nationals of that country which were granted or refused during that year; or

(ii) such refusal rate for nationals of that country during the previous full fiscal year was less than 3.0 percent.

(B) *Machine readable passport program.*—[119]

(i) In general.— Subject to clause (ii), the government of the country certifies that it issues to its citizens machine-readable passports that satisfy the internationally accepted standard for machine readability.

(ii) Deadline for compliance for certain countries.— In the case of a country designated as a program country under this subsection prior to May 1, 2000, as a condition on the continuation of that designation, the country—

(I) shall certify, not later than October 1, 2000, that it has a program to issue machine-readable passports to its citizens not later than October 1, 2003; and

(II) shall satisfy the requirement of clause (i) not later than October 1, 2003.

(C) *Law enforcement and security interests.*— The Attorney General, in consultation with the Secretary of State—

(i) evaluates the effect that the country's designation would have on the law enforcement and security interests of the United States (including the interest in enforcement of the immigration laws of the United States and the existence and effectiveness of its agreements and procedures for extraditing to the United States individuals, including its own nationals, who commit crimes that violate United States law);

(ii) determines that such interests would not be compromised by the designation of the country; and

(iii) submits a written report to the Committee on the Judiciary and the Committee on International Relations of the House of Representatives and the Committee on the Judiciary and the Committee on Foreign Relations of the Senate regarding the country's qualification for designation that includes an explanation of such determination.

---

[119] *See also* §417 of the USA PATRIOT Act, P.L. 107-56.

(D) *Reporting lost and stolen passports.*— The government of the country enters into an agreement with the United States to report, or make available through Interpol or other means as designated by the Secretary of Homeland Security, to the United States Government information about the theft or loss of passports within a strict time limit and in a manner specified in the agreement.

(E) *Repatriation of aliens.*— The government of the country accepts for repatriation any citizen, former citizen, or national of the country against whom a final executable order of removal is issued not later than three weeks after the issuance of the final order of removal. Nothing in this subparagraph creates any duty for the United States or any right for any alien with respect to removal or release. Nothing in this subparagraph gives rise to any cause of action or claim under this paragraph or any other law against any official of the United States or of any State to compel the release, removal, or consideration for release or removal of any alien.

(F) *Passenger information exchange.*— The government of the country enters into an agreement with the United States to share information regarding whether citizens and nationals of that country traveling to the United States represent a threat to the security or welfare of the United States or its citizens.

(3) *Continuing and subsequent qualifications.*— For each fiscal year after the initial period—

(A) *Continuing qualification.*— In the case of a country which was a program country in the previous fiscal year, a country may not be designated as a program country unless the sum of—

   (i) the total of the number of nationals of that country who were denied admission at the time of arrival or withdrew their application for admission during such previous fiscal year as a nonimmigrant visitor, and

   (ii) the total number of nationals of that country who were admitted as nonimmigrant visitors during such previous fiscal year and who violated the terms of such admission,

was less than 2 percent of the total number of nationals of that country who applied for admission as nonimmigrant visitors during such previous fiscal year.

(B) *New countries.*— In the case of another country, the country may not be designated as a program country unless the following requirements are met:

   (i) Low nonimmigrant visa refusal rate in previous 2-year period.— The average number of refusals of nonimmigrant visitor visas for nationals of that country during the two previous full fiscal years was less than 2 percent of the total number of nonimmigrant visitor visas for nationals of that country which were granted or refused during those years.

   (ii) Low nonimmigrant visa refusal rate in each of the 2 previous years.— The average number of refusals of nonimmigrant visitor visas for nationals of that country during either of such two previous full fiscal years was less than 2.5 percent of the total number of nonimmigrant visitor visas for nationals of that country which were granted or refused during that year.

(4) *Initial period.*— For purposes of paragraphs (2) and (3), the term "initial period" means the period beginning at the end of the 30-day period described in subsection (b)(1) and ending on the last day of the first fiscal year which begins after such 30-day period.

**(5)** *Written reports on continuing qualification; designation terminations.—*

(A) *Periodic evaluations.—*

(i) In general.— The Secretary of Homeland Security, in consultation with the Secretary of State, periodically (but not less than once every 2 years)—

(I) shall evaluate the effect of each program country's continued designation on the law enforcement and security interests of the United States (including the interest in enforcement of the immigration laws of the United States and the existence and effectiveness of its agreements and procedures for extraditing to the United States individuals, including its own nationals, who commit crimes that violate United States law);

(II) shall determine, based upon the evaluation in subclause (I), whether any such designation ought to be continued or terminated under subsection (d);

(III) shall submit a written report to the Committee on the Judiciary, the Committee on Foreign Affairs, and the Committee on Homeland Security, of the House of Representatives and the Committee on the Judiciary, the Committee on Foreign Relations, and the Committee on Homeland Security and Governmental Affairs of the Senate regarding the continuation or termination of the country's designation that includes an explanation of such determination and the effects described in subclause (I); and

(IV) shall submit to Congress a report regarding the implementation of the electronic travel authorization system under subsection (h)(3) and the participation of new countries in the program through a waiver under paragraph (8).

(ii) Effective date.— A termination of the designation of a country under this subparagraph shall take effect on the date determined by the Secretary of Homeland Security, in consultation with the Secretary of State.

(iii) Redesignation.— In the case of a termination under this subparagraph, the Secretary of Homeland Security shall redesignate the country as a program country, without regard to subsection (f) or paragraph (2) or (3), when the Secretary of Homeland Security, in consultation with the Secretary of State, determines that all causes of the termination have been eliminated.

(B) *Emergency termination.—*

(i) In general.— In the case of a program country in which an emergency occurs that the Secretary of Homeland Security, in consultation with the Secretary of State, determines threatens the law enforcement or security interests of the United States (including the interest in enforcement of the immigration laws of the United States), the Secretary of Homeland Security shall immediately terminate the designation of the country as a program country.

(ii) Definition.— For purposes of clause (i), the term "emergency" means—

(I) the overthrow of a democratically elected government;

(II) war (including undeclared war, civil war, or other military activity) on the territory of the program country;

(III) a severe breakdown in law and order affecting a significant portion of the program country's territory;

(IV) a severe economic collapse in the program country; or

(V) any other extraordinary event in the program country that threatens the law enforcement or security interests of the United States (including the interest in enforcement of the immigration laws of the United States) and where the country's participation in the program could contribute to that threat.

(iii) Redesignation.— The Secretary of Homeland Security may redesignate the country as a program country, without regard to subsection (f) or paragraph (2) or (3), when the Secretary of Homeland Security, in consultation with the Secretary of State, determines that—

(I) at least 6 months have elapsed since the effective date of the termination;

(II) the emergency that caused the termination has ended; and

(III) the average number of refusals of nonimmigrant visitor visas for nationals of that country during the period of termination under this subparagraph was less than 3.0 percent of the total number of nonimmigrant visitor visas for nationals of that country which were granted or refused during such period.

(iv) Program suspension authority.— The Director of National Intelligence shall immediately inform the Secretary of Homeland Security of any current and credible threat which poses an imminent danger to the United States or its citizens and originates from a country participating in the visa waiver program. Upon receiving such notification, the Secretary, in consultation with the Secretary of State—

(I) may suspend a country from the visa waiver program without prior notice;

(II) shall notify any country suspended under subclause (I) and, to the extent practicable without disclosing sensitive intelligence sources and methods, provide justification for the suspension; and

(III) shall restore the suspended country's participation in the visa waiver program upon a determination that the threat no longer poses an imminent danger to the United States or its citizens.

(C) *Treatment of nationals after termination.*— For purposes of this paragraph—

(i) nationals of a country whose designation is terminated under subparagraph (A) or (B) shall remain eligible for a waiver under subsection (a) until the effective date of such termination; and

(ii) a waiver under this section that is provided to such a national for a period described in subsection (a)(1) shall not, by such termination, be deemed to have been rescinded or otherwise rendered invalid, if the waiver is granted prior to such termination.

(6) *Computation of visa refusal rates.*— For purposes of determining the eligibility of a country to be designated as a program country, the calculation of visa refusal rates shall not include any visa refusals which incorporate any procedures based on, or are otherwise based on, race, sex, or disability, unless otherwise specifically authorized by law or regulation. No court shall have jurisdiction under this paragraph to review any visa refusal, the denial of admission to the United States of any alien by the Attorney General, the Secretary's computation of the visa refusal rate, or the designation or nondesignation of any country.

(7) *Visa waiver information.*—

(A) *In general.*— In refusing the application of nationals of a program country for United States visas, or the applications of nationals of a country seeking entry into the visa waiver program, a consular officer shall not knowingly or intentionally classify the refusal of the visa under a category that is not included in the calculation of the visa refusal rate only so that the percentage of that country's visa refusals is less than the percentage limitation applicable to qualification for participation in the visa waiver program.

(B) *Reporting requirement.*— On May 1 of each year, for each country under consideration for inclusion in the visa waiver program, the Secretary of State shall provide to the appropriate congressional committees—

(i) the total number of nationals of that country that applied for United States visas in that country during the previous calendar year;

(ii) the total number of such nationals who received United States visas during the previous calendar year;

(iii) the total number of such nationals who were refused United States visas during the previous calendar year;

(iv) the total number of such nationals who were refused United States visas during the previous calendar year under each provision of this Act under which the visas were refused; and

(v) the number of such nationals that were refused under section 214(b) as a percentage of the visas that were issued to such nationals.

(C) *Certification.*— Not later than May 1 of each year, the United States chief of mission, acting or permanent, to each country under consideration for inclusion in the visa waiver program shall certify to the appropriate congressional committees that the information described in subparagraph (B) is accurate and provide a copy of that certification to those committees.

(D) *Consideration of countries in the visa waiver program.*— Upon notification to the Attorney General that a country is under consideration for inclusion in the visa waiver program, the Secretary of State shall provide all of the information described in subparagraph (B) to the Attorney General.

(E) *Definition.*— In this paragraph, the term "appropriate congressional committees" means the Committee on the Judiciary and the Committee on Foreign Relations of the Senate and the Committee on the Judiciary and the Committee on International Relations of the House of Representatives.

(8) *Nonimmigrant visa refusal rate flexibility.*—

(A) *Certification.*—

(i) In general.— On the date on which an air exit system is in place that can verify the departure of not less than 97 percent of foreign nationals who exit through airports of the United States and the electronic travel authorization system required under subsection (h)(3) is fully operational, the Secretary of Homeland Security shall certify to Congress that such air exit system and electronic travel authorization system are in place.

(ii) Notification to congress.— The Secretary shall notify Congress in writing of the date on which the air exit system under clause (i) fully satisfies the biometric requirements specified in subsection (i).

(iii) Temporary suspension of waiver authority.— Notwithstanding any certification made under clause (i), if the Secretary has not notified Congress in accordance with clause (ii) by June 30, 2009, the Secretary's waiver authority under subparagraph (B) shall be suspended beginning on July 1, 2009, until such time as the Secretary makes such notification.

(iv) Rule of construction.— Nothing in this paragraph shall be construed as in any way abrogating the reporting requirements under subsection (i)(3).

(B) *Waiver.*— After certification by the Secretary under subparagraph (A), the Secretary, in consultation with the Secretary of State, may waive the application of paragraph (2)(A) for a country if—

(i) the country meets all security requirements of this section;

(ii) the Secretary of Homeland Security determines that the totality of the country's security risk mitigation measures provide assurance that the country's participation in the program would not compromise the law enforcement, security interests, or enforcement of the immigration laws of the United States;

(iii) there has been a sustained reduction in the rate of refusals for nonimmigrant visas for nationals of the country and conditions exist to continue such reduction;

(iv) the country cooperated with the Government of the United States on counterterrorism initiatives, information sharing, and preventing terrorist travel before the date of its designation as a program country, and the Secretary of Homeland Security and the Secretary of State determine that such cooperation will continue; and

(v) (I) the rate of refusals for nonimmigrant visitor visas for nationals of the country during the previous full fiscal year was not more than ten percent; or

(II) the visa overstay rate for the country for the previous full fiscal year does not exceed the maximum visa overstay rate, once such rate is established under subparagraph (C).

(C) Maximum visa overstay rate.—

(i) Requirement to establish.— After certification by the Secretary under subparagraph (A), the Secretary and the Secretary of State jointly shall use information from the air exit system referred to in such subparagraph to establish a maximum visa overstay rate for countries participating in the program pursuant to a waiver under subparagraph (B). The Secretary of Homeland Security shall certify to Congress that such rate would not compromise the law enforcement, security interests, or enforcement of the immigration laws of the United States.

(ii) Visa overstay rate defined.— In this paragraph the term "visa overstay rate" means, with respect to a country, the ratio of—

(I) the total number of nationals of that country who were admitted to the United States on the basis of a nonimmigrant visa whose periods of authorized stays ended during a fiscal year but who remained unlawfully in the United States beyond such periods; to

(II) the total number of nationals of that country who were admitted to the United States on the basis of a nonimmigrant visa during that fiscal year.

(iii) Report and publication.— The Secretary of Homeland Security shall on the same date submit to Congress and publish in the *Federal Register* information relating to the maximum visa overstay rate established under clause (i). Not later than 60 days after such date, the Secretary shall issue a final maximum visa overstay rate above which a country may not participate in the program.

(9) *Discretionary security-related considerations.*— In determining whether to waive the application of paragraph (2)(A) for a country, pursuant to paragraph (8), the Secretary of Homeland Security, in consultation with the Secretary of State, shall take into consideration other factors affecting the security of the United States, including—

(A) airport security standards in the country;

(B) whether the country assists in the operation of an effective air marshal program;

(C) the standards of passports and travel documents issued by the country; and

(D) other security-related factors, including the country's cooperation with the United States' initiatives toward combating terrorism and the country's cooperation with the United States intelligence community in sharing information regarding terrorist threats.

(10) *Technical assistance.*— The Secretary of Homeland Security, in consultation with the Secretary of State, shall provide technical assistance to program countries to assist those countries in meeting the requirements under this section. The Secretary of Homeland Security shall ensure that the program office within the Department of Homeland Security is adequately staffed and has resources to be able to provide such technical assistance, in addition to its duties to effectively monitor compliance of the countries participating in the program with all the requirements of the program.

(11) *Independent review.*—

(A) *In general.*— Prior to the admission of a new country into the program under this section, and in conjunction with the periodic evaluations required under subsection (c)(5)(A), the Director of National Intelligence shall conduct an independent intelligence assessment of a nominated country and member of the program.

(B) *Reporting requirement.*— The Director shall provide to the Secretary of Homeland Security, the Secretary of State, and the Attorney General the independent intelligence assessment required under subparagraph (A).

(C) *Contents.*— The independent intelligence assessment conducted by the Director shall include—

(i) a review of all current, credible terrorist threats of the subject country;

(ii) an evaluation of the subject country's counterterrorism efforts;

(iii) an evaluation as to the extent of the country's sharing of information beneficial to suppressing terrorist movements, financing, or actions;

(iv) an assessment of the risks associated with including the subject country in the program; and

(v) recommendations to mitigate the risks identified in clause (iv).

**(d) Authority.**— Notwithstanding any other provision of this section, the Secretary of Homeland Security, in consultation with the Secretary of State, may for any reason (including national security) refrain from waiving the visa requirement in respect to nationals of any country which may otherwise qualify for designation or may, at any time, rescind any waiver or designation previously granted under this section. The Secretary of Homeland Security may not waive any eligibility requirement under this section unless the Secretary notifies, with respect to the House of Representatives, the Committee on Homeland Security, the Committee on the Judiciary, the Committee on Foreign Affairs, and the Committee on Appropriations, and with respect to the Senate, the Committee on Homeland Security and Governmental Affairs, the Committee on the Judiciary, the Committee on Foreign Relations, and the Committee on Appropriations not later than 30 days before the effective date of such waiver.

**(e) Carrier agreements.**—

(1) *In general.*— The agreement referred to in subsection (a)(4) is an agreement between a carrier (including any carrier conducting operations under part 135 of title 14, Code of Federal Regulations) or a domestic corporation conducting operations under part 91 of that title and the Attorney General under which the carrier (including any carrier conducting operations under part 135 of title 14, Code of Federal Regulations) or a domestic corporation conducting operations under part 91 of that title agrees, in consideration of the waiver of the visa requirement with respect to a nonimmigrant visitor under the program—

(A) to indemnify the United States against any costs for the transportation of the alien from the United States if the visitor is refused admission to the United States or remains in the United States unlawfully after the 90-day period described in subsection (a)(1)(A),

(B) to submit daily to immigration officers any immigration forms received with respect to nonimmigrant visitors provided a waiver under the program,

(C) to be subject to the imposition of fines resulting from the transporting into the United States of a national of a designated country without a passport pursuant to regulations promulgated by the Attorney General, and

(D) to collect, provide and share passenger data as required under subsection (h)(1)(B).

(2) *Termination of agreements.*— The Attorney General may terminate an agreement under paragraph (1) with five days' notice to the carrier (including any carrier conducting operations under part 135 of title 14, Code of Federal Regulations) or a domestic corporation conducting operations under part 91 of that title for the failure by a carrier (including any carrier conducting operations under part 135 of title 14, Code of Federal Regulations) or a domestic corporation conducting operations under part 91 of that title to meet the terms of such agreement.

(3) *Business aircraft requirements.*—

(A) *In general.*— For purposes of this section, a domestic corporation conducting operations under part 91 of title 14, Code of Federal Regulations that owns or operates a noncommercial aircraft is a corporation that is organized under the laws of any of the States of the United States or the District of Columbia and is accredited by or a member of a national organization that sets business aviation standards. The Attorney General shall prescribe by regulation the provision of such information as the Attorney General deems necessary to identify the domestic corporation, its officers, employees, shareholders, its place of business, and its business activities.

(B) *Collections.*— In addition to any other fee authorized by law, the Attorney General is authorized to charge and collect, on a periodic basis, an amount from each domestic corporation conducting operations under part 91 of title 14, Code of Federal Regulations, for nonimmigrant visa waiver admissions on noncommercial aircraft owned or operated by such domestic corporation equal to the total amount of fees assessed for issuance of nonimmigrant visa waiver arrival/departure forms at land border ports of entry. All fees collected under this paragraph shall be deposited into the Immigration User Fee Account established under section 286(h).

**(f) Duration and termination of designation.—**

(1) *In general.—*

(A) *Determination and notification of disqualification rate.—* Upon determination by the Attorney General that a program country's disqualification rate is 2 percent or more, the Attorney General shall notify the Secretary of State.

(B) *Probationary status.—* If the program country's disqualification rate is greater than 2 percent but less than 3.5 percent, the Attorney General shall place the program country in probationary status for a period not to exceed 2 full fiscal years following the year in which the determination under subparagraph (A) is made.

(C) *Termination of designation.—* Subject to paragraph (3), if the program country's disqualification rate is 3.5 percent or more, the Attorney General shall terminate the country's designation as a program county effective at the beginning of the second fiscal year following the fiscal year in which the determination under subparagraph (A) is made.

(2) *Termination of probationary status.—*

(A) *In general.—* If the Attorney General determines at the end of the probationary period described in paragraph (1)(B) that the program country placed in probationary status under such paragraph has failed to develop a machine-readable passport program as required by section (c)(2)(C), or has a disqualification rate of 2 percent or more, the Attorney General shall terminate the designation of the country as a program country. If the Attorney General determines that the program country has developed a machine-readable passport program and has a disqualification rate of less than 2 percent, the Attorney General shall redesignate the country as a program country.

(B) *Effective date.—* A termination of the designation of a country under subparagraph (A) shall take effect on the first day of the first fiscal year following the fiscal year in which the determination under such paragraph is made. Until such date, nationals of the country shall remain eligible for a waiver under subsection (a).

(3) *Nonapplicability of certain provisions.—* Paragraph (1)(C) shall not apply unless the total number of nationals of a program country described in paragraph (4)(A) exceeds 100.

(4) *Definition.—* For purposes of this subsection, the term "disqualification rate" means the percentage which—

(A) the total number of nationals of the program country who were—

(i) excluded from admission or withdrew their application for admission during the most recent fiscal year for which data are available; and

(ii) admitted as nonimmigrant visitors during such fiscal year and who violated the terms of such admission; bears to

(B) the total number of nationals of such country who applied for admission as nonimmigrant visitors during such fiscal year.

(5) *Failure to report passport thefts.*— If the Secretary of Homeland Security and the Secretary of State jointly determine that the program country is not reporting the theft or loss of passports, as required by subsection (c)(2)(D), the Secretary of Homeland Security shall terminate the designation of the country as a program country.

**(g) Visa application sole method to dispute denial of waiver based on ground of inadmissibility.**— In the case of an alien denied a waiver under the program by reason of a ground of inadmissibility described in section 212(a) that is discovered at the time of the alien's application for the waiver or through the use of an automated electronic database required under subsection (a)(9), the alien may apply for a visa at an appropriate consular office outside the United States. There shall be no other means of administrative or judicial review of such a denial, and no court or person otherwise shall have jurisdiction to consider any claim attacking the validity of such a denial.

**(h) Use of information technology systems.**—

(1) *Automated entry-exit control system.*—

(A) *System.*— Not later than October 1, 2001, the Attorney General shall develop and implement a fully automated entry and exit control system that will collect a record of arrival and departure for every alien who arrives and departs by sea or air at a port of entry into the United States and is provided a waiver under the program.

(B) *Requirements.*— The system under subparagraph (A) shall satisfy the following requirements:

(i) Data collection by carriers.— Not later than October 1, 2001, the records of arrival and departure described in subparagraph (A) shall be based, to the maximum extent practicable, on passenger data collected and electronically transmitted to the automated entry and exit control system by each carrier that has an agreement under subsection (a)(4).

(ii) Data provision by carriers.— Not later than October 1, 2002, no waiver may be provided under this section to an alien arriving by sea or air at a port of entry into the United States on a carrier unless the carrier is electronically transmitting to the automated entry and exit control system passenger data determined by the Attorney General to be sufficient to permit the Attorney General to carry out this paragraph.

(iii) Calculation.— The system shall contain sufficient data to permit the Attorney General to calculate, for each program country and each fiscal year, the portion of nationals of that country who are described in subparagraph (A) and for whom no record of departure exists, expressed as a percentage of the total number of such nationals who are so described.

(C) *Reporting.*—

(i) Percentage of nationals lacking departure record.— As part of the annual report required to be submitted under section 110(e)(1) of the Illegal Immigration Reform and Immigrant Responsibility Act of 1996, the Attorney General shall include a section containing the calculation described in subparagraph (B)(iii) for each program country for the previous fiscal year, together with an analysis of that information.

(ii) System effectiveness.— Not later than December 31, 2004, the Attorney General shall submit a written report to the Committee on the Judiciary of the United States House of Representatives and of the Senate containing the following:

(I) The conclusions of the Attorney General regarding the effectiveness of the automated entry and exit control system to be developed and implemented under this paragraph.

(II) The recommendations of the Attorney General regarding the use of the calculation described in subparagraph (B)(iii) as a basis for evaluating whether to terminate or continue the designation of a country as a program country.

The report required by this clause may be combined with the annual report required to be submitted on that date under section 110(e)(1) of the Illegal Immigration Reform and Immigrant Responsibility Act of 1996.

(2) *Automated data sharing system.*—

(A) *System.*— The Attorney General and the Secretary of State shall develop and implement an automated data sharing system that will permit them to share data in electronic form from their respective records systems regarding the admissibility of aliens who are nationals of a program country.

(B) *Requirements.*— The system under subparagraph (A) shall satisfy the following requirements:

(i) Supplying information to immigration officers conducting inspections at ports of entry.— Not later than October 1, 2002, the system shall enable immigration officers conducting inspections at ports of entry under section 235 to obtain from the system, with respect to aliens seeking a waiver under the program—

(I) any photograph of the alien that may be contained in the records of the Department of State or the Service; and

(II) information on whether the alien has ever been determined to be ineligible to receive a visa or ineligible to be admitted to the United States.

(ii) Supplying photographs of inadmissible aliens.— The system shall permit the Attorney General electronically to obtain any photograph contained in the records of the Secretary of State pertaining to an alien who is a national of a program country and has been determined to be ineligible to receive a visa.

(iii) Maintaining records on applications for admission.— The system shall maintain, for a minimum of 10 years, information about each application for admission made by an alien seeking a waiver under the program, including the following:

(I) The name or Service identification number of each immigration officer conducting the inspection of the alien at the port of entry.

(II) Any information described in clause (i) that is obtained from the system by any such officer.

(III) The results of the application.

(3) *Electronic travel authorization system.*—

(A) *System.*— The Secretary of Homeland Security, in consultation with the Secretary of State, shall develop and implement a fully automated electronic travel authorization system (referred to in this paragraph as the 'System') to collect such biographical and other information as the Secretary of Homeland Security determines necessary to determine, in advance of travel, the eligibility of, and whether there exists a law enforcement or security risk in permitting, the alien to travel to the United States.

(B) *Fees.*— The Secretary of Homeland Security may charge a fee for the use of the System, which shall be—

(i) set at a level that will ensure recovery of the full costs of providing and administering the System; and

(ii) available to pay the costs incurred to administer the System.

(C) *Validity.*—

(i) Period.— The Secretary of Homeland Security, in consultation with the Secretary of State, shall prescribe regulations that provide for a period, not to exceed three years, during which a determination of eligibility to travel under the program will be valid. Notwithstanding any other provision under this section, the Secretary of Homeland Security may revoke any such determination at any time and for any reason.

(ii) Limitation.— A determination by the Secretary of Homeland Security that an alien is eligible to travel to the United States under the program is not a determination that the alien is admissible to the United States.

(iii) Not a determination of visa eligibility.— A determination by the Secretary of Homeland Security that an alien who applied for authorization to travel to the United States through the System is not eligible to travel under the program is not a determination of eligibility for a visa to travel to the United States and shall not preclude the alien from applying for a visa.

(iv) Judicial review.— Notwithstanding any other provision of law, no court shall have jurisdiction to review an eligibility determination under the System.

(D) *Report.*— Not later than 60 days before publishing notice regarding the implementation of the System in the *Federal Register*, the Secretary of Homeland Security shall submit a report regarding the implementation of the system to—

(i) the Committee on Homeland Security of the House of Representatives;

(ii) the Committee on the Judiciary of the House of Representatives;

(iii) the Committee on Foreign Affairs of the House of Representatives;

(iv) the Permanent Select Committee on Intelligence of the House of Representatives;

(v) the Committee on Appropriations of the House of Representatives;

(vi) the Committee on Homeland Security and Governmental Affairs of the Senate;

(vii) the Committee on the Judiciary of the Senate;

(viii) the Committee on Foreign Relations of the Senate;

(ix) the Select Committee on Intelligence of the Senate; and

(x) the Committee on Appropriations of the Senate.

**(i) Exit System.—**

(1) *In general.*— Not later than one year after the date of the enactment of this subsection, the Secretary of Homeland Security shall establish an exit system that records the departure

on a flight leaving the United States of every alien participating in the visa waiver program established under this section.

(2) *System requirements.*— The system established under paragraph (1) shall—

(A) match biometric information of the alien against relevant watch lists and immigration information; and

(B) compare such biometric information against manifest information collected by air carriers on passengers departing the United States to confirm such aliens have departed the United States.

(3) *Report.*— Not later than 180 days after the date of the enactment of this subsection, the Secretary shall submit to Congress a report that describes—

(A) the progress made in developing and deploying the exit system established under this subsection; and

(B) the procedures by which the Secretary shall improve the method of calculating the rates of nonimmigrants who overstay their authorized period of stay in the United States.

(June 27, 1952, ch. 477, title II, ch. 2, §217, as added by P.L. 99-603 (IRCA) (11/6/86); as amended by P.L. 100-525 (10/24/88); P.L. 101-649 (IMMACT90) (11/29/90); P.L. 102-232 (MTINA) (12/12/91, *effective* 4/1/92); P.L. 103-415 (10/25/94); P.L. 103-416 (INTCA) (10/25/94, *effective* 4/1/95); P.L. 104-208 (IIRAIRA) (9/30/96), div. C, title III, §308(d)(4), title VI, §635(a) [revising (c)–(d)]; P.L. 105-119 (11/26/97), §125; P.L. 105-173 (4/27/98), §1, §3 [revising (c)]; P.L. 106-396 (10/30/00), §101(a) [revising (a)–(c), striking (f), redesignating & revising (g) as (f)], §201–207 [adding (a)(9); (c)(2)(B)–(C), (c)(5)–(7)], §403(a) [revising (e); adding (e)(3), (h)]; P.L. 107-56 (PATRIOT Act) (10/26/01), §417(c) [revising (a)(3)(A); adding (a)(3)(B)]; P.L. 107-173 (EBSVERA) (5/14/02), §307(a) [revising (c)(5)(A)(i); adding (c)(2)(D), (f)(5)]; P.L. 110-53 (8/3/07) §711(c) [adding (c)(8)–(9)], §711(d) [revising (a)(9), (c)(2)(D), (c)(5)(A)–(B), (d), (f)(5) adding (a)(10)–(11), (c)(2)(E)–(F), (c)(10)–(11), (h)(3), & (i)].)

## Sec. 218 Admission of Temporary H-2A Workers
## [8 U.S.C. 1188]

### (a) Conditions for approval of H-2A petitions.—

(1) A petition to import an alien as an H-2A worker (as defined in subsection (i)(2)) may not be approved by the Attorney General unless the petitioner has applied to the Secretary of Labor for a certification that—

(A) there are not sufficient workers who are able, willing, and qualified, and who will be available at the time and place needed, to perform the labor or services involved in the petition, and

(B) the employment of the alien in such labor or services will not adversely affect the wages and working conditions of workers in the United States similarly employed.

(2) The Secretary of Labor may require by regulation, as a condition of issuing the certification, the payment of a fee to recover the reasonable costs of processing applications for certification.

### (b) Conditions for denial of labor certification.— The Secretary of Labor may not issue a certification under subsection (a) with respect to an employer if the conditions described in that subsection are not met or if any of the following conditions are met:

(1) There is a strike or lockout in the course of a labor dispute which, under the regulations, precludes such certification.

(2) (A) The employer during the previous two-year period employed H-2A workers and the Secretary of Labor has determined, after notice and opportunity for a hearing, that the

employer at any time during that period substantially violated a material term or condition of the labor certification with respect to the employment of domestic or nonimmigrant workers.

(B) No employer may be denied certification under subparagraph (A) for more than three years for any violation described in such subparagraph.

(3) The employer has not provided the Secretary with satisfactory assurances that if the employment for which the certification is sought is not covered by State workers' compensation law, the employer will provide, at no cost to the worker, insurance covering injury and disease arising out of and in the course of the worker's employment which will provide benefits at least equal to those provided under the State workers' compensation law for comparable employment.

(4) The Secretary determines that the employer has not made positive recruitment efforts within a multi-state region of traditional or expected labor supply where the Secretary finds that there are a significant number of qualified United States workers who, if recruited, would be willing to make themselves available for work at the time and place needed. Positive recruitment under this paragraph is in addition to, and shall be conducted within the same time period as, the circulation through the interstate employment service system of the employer's job offer. The obligation to engage in positive recruitment under this paragraph shall terminate on the date the H-2A workers depart for the employer's place of employment.

**(c) Special rules for consideration of applications.**— The following rules shall apply in the case of the filing and consideration of an application for a labor certification under this section:

(1) *Deadline for filing applications.*— The Secretary of Labor may not require that the application be filed more than 45 days before the first date the employer requires the labor or services of the H-2A worker.

(2) *Notice within seven days of deficiencies.*—

(A) The employer shall be notified in writing within seven days of the date of filing if the application does not meet the standards (other than that described in subsection (a)(1)(A)) for approval.

(B) If the application does not meet such standards, the notice shall include the reasons therefor and the Secretary shall provide an opportunity for the prompt resubmission of a modified application.

(3) *Issuance of certification.*—

(A) The Secretary of Labor shall make, not later than 30 days before the date such labor or services are first required to be performed, the certification described in subsection (a)(1) if—

(i) the employer has complied with the criteria for certification (including criteria for the recruitment of eligible individuals as prescribed by the Secretary), and

(ii) the employer does not actually have, or has not been provided with referrals of, qualified eligible individuals who have indicated their availability to perform such labor or services on the terms and conditions of a job offer which meets the requirements of the Secretary.

In considering the question of whether a specific qualification is appropriate in a job offer, the Secretary shall apply the normal and accepted qualifications required by non-H-2A-employers in the same or comparable occupations and crops.

(B) (i) For a period of 3 years subsequent to the effective date of this section, labor certifications shall remain effective only if, from the time the foreign worker departs for the employer's place of employment, the employer will provide employment to any qualified United States worker who applies to the employer until 50 percent of the period of the work contract, under which the foreign worker who is in the job was hired, has elapsed. In addition, the employer will offer to provide benefits, wages and working conditions required pursuant to this section and regulations.

(ii) The requirement of clause (i) shall not apply to any employer who—

(I) did not, during any calendar quarter during the preceding calendar year, use more than 500 man-days of agricultural labor, as defined in section 3(u) of the Fair Labor Standards Act of 1938 (29 U.S.C. 203(u)),

(II) is not a member of an association which has petitioned for certification under this section for its members, and

(III) has not otherwise associated with other employers who are petitioning for temporary foreign workers under this section.

(iii) Six months before the end of the 3-year period described in clause (i), the Secretary of Labor shall consider the findings of the report mandated by section 403(a)(4)(D) of the Immigration Reform and Control Act of 1986 as well as other relevant materials, including evidence of benefits to United States workers and costs to employers, addressing the advisability of continuing a policy which requires an employer, as a condition for certification under this section, to continue to accept qualified, eligible United States workers for employment after the date the H-2A workers depart for work with the employer. The Secretary's review of such findings and materials shall lead to the issuance of findings in furtherance of the Congressional policy that aliens not be admitted under this section unless there are not sufficient workers in the United States who are able, willing, and qualified to perform the labor or service needed and that the employment of the aliens in such labor or services will not adversely affect the wages and working conditions of workers in the United States similarly employed. In the absence of the enactment of Federal legislation prior to three months before the end of the 3-year period described in clause (i) which addresses the subject matter of this subparagraph, the Secretary shall immediately publish the findings required by this clause, and shall promulgate, on an interim or final basis, regulations based on his findings which shall be effective no later than three years from the effective date of this section.

(iv) In complying with clause (i) of this subparagraph, an association shall be allowed to refer or transfer workers among its members: *Provided*, That for purposes of this section an association acting as an agent for its members shall not be considered a joint employer merely because of such referral or transfer.

(v) United States workers referred or transferred pursuant to clause (iv) of this subparagraph shall not be treated disparately.

(vi) An employer shall not be liable for payments under section 655.202(b)(6) of title 20, Code of Federal Regulations (or any successor regulation) with respect to an H-

2A worker who is displaced due to compliance with the requirement of this subparagraph, if the Secretary of Labor certifies that the H-2A worker was displaced because of the employer's compliance with clause (i) of this subparagraph.

(vii)(I) No person or entity shall willfully and knowingly withhold domestic workers prior to the arrival of H-2A workers in order to force the hiring of domestic workers under clause (i).

(II) Upon the receipt of a complaint by an employer that a violation of subclause (I) has occurred the Secretary shall immediately investigate. He shall within 36 hours of the receipt of the complaint issue findings concerning the alleged violation. Where the Secretary finds that a violation has occurred, he shall immediately suspend the application of clause (i) of this subparagraph with respect to that certification for that date of need.

(4) *Housing.*— Employers shall furnish housing in accordance with regulations. The employer shall be permitted at the employer's option to provide housing meeting applicable Federal standards for temporary labor camps or to secure housing which meets the local standards for rental and/or public accommodations or other substantially similar class of habitation: *Provided*, That in the absence of applicable local standards, State standards for rental and/or public accommodations or other substantially similar class of habitation shall be met: *Provided further*, That in the absence of applicable local or State standards, Federal temporary labor camp standards shall apply: *Provided further*, That the Secretary of Labor shall issue regulations which address the specific requirements of housing for employees principally engaged in the range production of livestock: *Provided further*, That when it is the prevailing practice in the area and occupation of intended employment to provide family housing, family housing shall be provided to workers with families who request it: *And provided further*, That nothing in this paragraph shall require an employer to provide or secure housing for workers who are not entitled to it under the temporary labor certification regulations in effect on June 1, 1986. The determination a s to whether the housing furnished by an employer for an H-2A worker meets the requirements imposed by this paragraph must be made prior to the date specified in paragraph (3)(A) by which the Secretary of Labor is required to make a certification described in subsection (a)(1) with respect to a petition for the importation of such worker.

**(d) Roles of agricultural associations.—**

(1) *Permitting filing by agricultural associations.*— A petition to import an alien as a temporary agricultural worker, and an application for a labor certification with respect to such a worker, may be filed by an association of agricultural producers which use agricultural services.

(2) *Treatment of associations acting as employers.*— If an association is a joint or sole employer of temporary agricultural workers, the certifications granted under this section to the association may be used for the certified job opportunities of any of its producer members and such workers may be transferred among its producer members to perform agricultural services of a temporary or seasonal nature for which the certifications were granted.

(3) *Treatment of violations.—*

(A) *Member's violation does not necessarily disqualify association or other members.—* If an individual producer member of a joint employer association is determined to have committed an act that under subsection (b)(2) results in the denial of certification with respect to the member, the denial shall apply only to that member of the association unless the Secretary determines that the association or other member participated in, had knowledge of, or reason to know of, the violation.

(B) *Association's violation does not necessarily disqualify members.—*

(i) If an association representing agricultural producers as a joint employer is determined to have committed an act that under subsection (b)(2) results in the denial of certification with respect to the association, the denial shall apply only to the association and does not apply to any individual producer member of the association unless the Secretary determines that the member participated in, had knowledge of, or reason to know of, the violation.

(ii) If an association of agricultural producers certified as a sole employer is determined to have committed an act that under subsection (b)(2) results in the denial of certification with respect to the association, no individual producer member of such association may be the beneficiary of the services of temporary alien agricultural workers admitted under this section in the commodity and occupation in which such aliens were employed by the association which was denied certification during the period such denial is in force, unless such producer member employs such aliens in the commodity and occupation in question directly or through an association which is a joint employer of such workers with the producer member.

**(e) Expedited administrative appeals of certain determinations.—**

(1) Regulations shall provide for an expedited procedure for the review of a denial of certification under subsection (a)(1) or a revocation of such a certification or, at the applicant's request, for a de novo administrative hearing respecting the denial or revocation.

(2) The Secretary of Labor shall expeditiously, but in no case later than 72 hours after the time a new determination is requested, make a new determination on the request for certification in the case of an H-2A worker if able, willing, and qualified eligible individuals are not actually available at the time such labor or services are required and a certification was denied in whole or in part because of the availability of qualified workers. If the employer asserts that any eligible individual who has been referred is not able, willing, or qualified, the burden of proof is on the employer to establish that the individual referred is not able, willing, or qualified because of employment-related reasons.

**(f) Violators disqualified for 5 years.—** An alien may not be admitted to the United States as a temporary agricultural worker if the alien was admitted to the United States as such a worker within the previous five-year period and the alien during that period violated a term or condition of such previous admission.

**(g) Authorizations of appropriations.—**

(1) There are authorized to be appropriated for each fiscal year, beginning with fiscal year 1987, $10,000,000 for the purposes—

(A) of recruiting domestic workers for temporary labor and services which might otherwise be performed by nonimmigrants described in section 101(a)(15)(H)(ii)(a), and

(B) of monitoring terms and conditions under which such nonimmigrants (and domestic workers employed by the same employers) are employed in the United States.

(2) The Secretary of Labor is authorized to take such actions, including imposing appropriate penalties and seeking appropriate injunctive relief and specific performance of contractual

obligations, as may be necessary to assure employer compliance with terms and conditions of employment under this section.

(3) There are authorized to be appropriated for each fiscal year, beginning with fiscal year 1987, such sums as may be necessary for the purpose of enabling the Secretary of Labor to make determinations and certifications under this section and under section 212(a)(5)(A)(i).

(4) There are authorized to be appropriated for each fiscal year, beginning with fiscal year 1987, such sums as may be necessary for the purposes of enabling the Secretary of Agriculture to carry out the Secretary's duties and responsibilities under this section.

**(h) Miscellaneous provisions.—**

(1) The Attorney General shall provide for such endorsement of entry and exit documents of nonimmigrants described in section 101(a)(15)(H)(ii) as may be necessary to carry out this section and to provide notice for purposes of section 274A.

(2) The provisions of subsections (a) and (c) of section 214 and the provisions of this section preempt any State or local law regulating admissibility of nonimmigrant workers.

**(i) Definitions.—** For purposes of this section:

(1) The term "eligible individual" means, with respect to employment, an individual who is not an unauthorized alien (as defined in section 274A(h)(3) with respect to that employment.

(2) The term "H-2A worker" means a nonimmigrant described in section 101(a)(15)(H)(ii)(a).

(June 27, 1952, ch. 477, title II, ch. 2, §216, as added by P.L. 99-603 (IRCA) (11/6/86); P.L. 100-525 (10/24/88) [revising & redesignating as §218]; P.L. 102-232 (MTINA) (12/12/91, *effective* 4/1/92); P.L. 103-416 (INTCA) (10/25/94, *effective* 4/1/95); P.L. 106-78 (10/22/99), title VII, §748 [revising (c)]; P.L. 106-554 (12/21/00), §1(a)(1), title I, §105 [revising (c)(4)].)

## Sec. 219 Designation of Foreign Terrorist Organizations[120]
### [8 U.S.C. 1189]

**(a) Designation.—**

(1) *In general.—* The Secretary is authorized to designate an organization as a foreign terrorist organization in accordance with this subsection if the Secretary finds that—

(A) the organization is a foreign organization;

(B) the organization engages in terrorist activity (as defined in section 212(a)(3)(B)) or terrorism (as defined in section 140(d)(2) of the Foreign Relations Authorization Act, Fiscal Years 1988 and 1989 (22 U.S.C. 2656f(d)(2)), or retains the capability and intent to engage in terrorist activity or terrorism;[121] and

---

[120] Sec. 7119(d) of the Intelligence Reform and Terrorism Prevention Act of 2004, P.L. 108-458 (12/17/04) provides: "For purposes of applying [INA §219] on or after [12/17/04], the term "designation", as used in that section, includes all redesignations made pursuant to [INA §219(a)(4)(B)] prior to [12/17/04], and such redesignations shall continue to be effective until revoked as provided in paragraph (5) or (6) of [INA §219(a)]."

*See also* "Special Rule for §219 Organizations and Organizations Designated Under §212(a)(3)(B)(vi)(II)," §411(c) [first] of the USA PATRIOT Act, P.L. 107-56 (10/26/01), [The PATRIOT Act created two paragraphs designated §411(c). The second one amended INA §219(a).]

[121] According to the strict instructions of USA PATRIOT Act §411(c), which amended this clause, the language following the parenthetical with "§212(a)(3)(B)" should also be in the parenthetical. That is probably a technical error, however; the statute should most likely be read as set out herein.

(C) the terrorist activity or terrorism of the organization threatens the security of United States nationals or the national security of the United States.

(2) *Procedure.—*

(A) *Notice.—*

(i) To congressional leaders.— Seven days before making a designation under this subsection, the Secretary shall, by classified communication, notify the Speaker and Minority Leader of the House of Representatives, the President pro tempore, Majority Leader, and Minority Leader of the Senate, and the members of the relevant committees of the House of Representatives and the Senate, in writing, of the intent to designate an organization under this subsection, together with the findings made under paragraph (1) with respect to that organization, and the factual basis therefor.

(ii) Publication in *Federal Register.*— The Secretary shall publish the designation in the *Federal Register* seven days after providing the notification under clause (i).

(B) *Effect of designation.—*

(i) For purposes of section 2339B of title 18, United States Code, a designation under this subsection shall take effect upon publication under subparagraph (A)(ii).

(ii) Any designation under this subsection shall cease to have effect upon an Act of Congress disapproving such designation.

(C) *Freezing of assets.*— Upon notification under paragraph (2)(A)(i), the Secretary of the Treasury may require United States financial institutions possessing or controlling any assets of any foreign organization included in the notification to block all financial transactions involving those assets until further directive from either the Secretary of the Treasury, Act of Congress, or order of court.

(3) *Record.—*

(A) *In general.*— In making a designation under this subsection, the Secretary shall create an administrative record.

(B) *Classified information.*— The Secretary may consider classified information in making a designation under this subsection. Classified information shall not be subject to disclosure for such time as it remains classified, except that such information may be disclosed to a court ex parte and in camera for purposes of judicial review under subsection (c).

(4) *Period of designation.—*

(A) *In general.*— A designation under this subsection shall be effective for all purposes until revoked under paragraph (5) or (6) or set aside pursuant to subsection (c).

(B) *Review of designation upon petition.—*

(i) In general.— The Secretary shall review the designation of a foreign terrorist organization under the procedures set forth in clauses (iii) and (iv) if the designated organization files a petition for revocation within the petition period described in clause (ii).

(ii) Petition period.— For purposes of clause (i)—

(I) if the designated organization has not previously filed a petition for revocation under this subparagraph, the petition period begins 2 years after the date on which the designation was made; or

(II) if the designated organization has previously filed a petition for revocation under this subparagraph, the petition period begins 2 years after the date of the determination made under clause (iv) on that petition.

(iii) Procedures.— Any foreign terrorist organization that submits a petition for revocation under this subparagraph must provide evidence in that petition that the relevant circumstances described in paragraph (1) are sufficiently different from the circumstances that were the basis for the designation such that a revocation with respect to the organization is warranted.

(iv) Determination.—

(I) In general.— Not later than 180 days after receiving a petition for revocation submitted under this subparagraph, the Secretary shall make a determination as to such revocation.

(II) Classified information.— The Secretary may consider classified information in making a determination in response to a petition for revocation. Classified information shall not be subject to disclosure for such time as it remains classified, except that such information may be disclosed to a court ex parte and in camera for purposes of judicial review under subsection (c).

(III) Publication of determination.— A determination made by the Secretary under this clause shall be published in the *Federal Register*.

(IV) Procedures.— Any revocation by the Secretary shall be made in accordance with paragraph (6).

(C) *Other review of designation.*—

(i) In general.— If in a 5-year period no review has taken place under subparagraph (B), the Secretary shall review the designation of the foreign terrorist organization in order to determine whether such designation should be revoked pursuant to paragraph (6).

(ii) Procedures.— If a review does not take place pursuant to subparagraph (B) in response to a petition for revocation that is filed in accordance with that subparagraph, then the review shall be conducted pursuant to procedures established by the Secretary. The results of such review and the applicable procedures shall not be reviewable in any court.

(iii) Publication of results of review.— The Secretary shall publish any determination made pursuant to this subparagraph in the *Federal Register*.

(5) *Revocation by act of Congress.*— The Congress, by an Act of Congress, may block or revoke a designation made under paragraph (1).

(6) *Revocation based on change in circumstances.*—

(A) *In general.*— The Secretary may revoke a designation made under paragraph (1) at any time, and shall revoke a designation upon completion of a review conducted pursuant to subparagraphs (B) and (C) of paragraph (4) if the Secretary finds that—

(i) the circumstances that were the basis for the designation have changed in such a manner as to warrant revocation; or

(ii) the national security of the United States warrants a revocation.

(B) *Procedure.*— The procedural requirements of paragraphs (2) and (3) shall apply to a revocation under this paragraph. Any revocation shall take effect on the date specified in the revocation or upon publication in the *Federal Register* if no effective date is specified.

(7) **Effect of revocation.**— The revocation of a designation under paragraph (5) or (6) shall not affect any action or proceeding based on conduct committed prior to the effective date of such revocation.

(8) **Use of designation in trial or hearing.**— If a designation under this subsection has become effective under paragraph (2)(B) a defendant in a criminal action or an alien in a removal proceeding shall not be permitted to raise any question concerning the validity of the issuance of such designation as a defense or an objection at any trial or hearing.

**(b) Amendments to a designation.—**

(1) **In general.**— The Secretary may amend a designation under this subsection if the Secretary finds that the organization has changed its name, adopted a new alias, dissolved and then reconstituted itself under a different name or names, or merged with another organization.

(2) **Procedure.**— Amendments made to a designation in accordance with paragraph (1) shall be effective upon publication in the *Federal Register*. Subparagraphs (B) and (C) of subsection (a)(2) shall apply to an amended designation upon such publication. Paragraphs (2)(A)(i), (4), (5), (6), (7), and (8) of subsection (a) shall also apply to an amended designation.

(3) **Administrative record.**— The administrative record shall be corrected to include the amendments as well as any additional relevant information that supports those amendments.

(4) **Classified information.**— The Secretary may consider classified information in amending a designation in accordance with this subsection. Classified information shall not be subject to disclosure for such time as it remains classified, except that such information may be disclosed to a court ex parte and in camera for purposes of judicial review under subsection (c).

**(c) Judicial review of designation.—**

(1) **In general.**— Not later than 30 days after publication in the *Federal Register* of a designation, an amended designation, or a determination in response to a petition for revocation, the designated organization may seek judicial review in the United States Court of Appeals for the District of Columbia Circuit.

(2) **Basis of review.**— Review under this subsection shall be based solely upon the administrative record, except that the Government may submit, for ex parte and in camera review, classified information used in making the designation, amended designation, or determination in response to a petition for revocation.

(3) **Scope of review.**— The Court shall hold unlawful and set aside a designation, amended designation, or determination in response to a petition for revocation the court finds to be—

(A) arbitrary, capricious, an abuse of discretion, or otherwise not in accordance with law;

(B) contrary to constitutional right, power, privilege, or immunity;

(C) in excess of statutory jurisdiction, authority, or limitation, or short of statutory right;

(D) lacking substantial support in the administrative record taken as a whole or in classified information submitted to the court under paragraph (2), or

(E) not in accord with the procedures required by law.

(4) *Judicial review invoked.*— The pendency of an action for judicial review of a designation, amended designation, or determination in response to a petition for revocation shall not affect the application of this section, unless the court issues a final order setting aside the designation, amended designation, or determination in response to a petition for revocation.

**(d) Definitions.**— As used in this section—

(1) the term "classified information" has the meaning given that term in section 1(a) of the Classified Information Procedures Act (18 U.S.C. App.);

(2) the term "national security" means the national defense, foreign relations, or economic interests of the United States;

(3) the term "relevant committees" means the Committees on the Judiciary, Intelligence, and Foreign Relations of the Senate and the Committees on the Judiciary, Intelligence, and International Relations of the House of Representatives; and

(4) the term "Secretary" means the Secretary of State, in consultation with the Secretary of the Treasury and the Attorney General.

(June 27, 1952, ch. 477, title II, ch. 2, §219, as added by P.L. 104-132 (AEDPA) (4/24/96), title III, §302(a); as amended by P.L. 104-208 (IIRAIRA) (9/30/96), div. C, title III, §356 [adding (c)(3)(D)–(E)], title VI, §671(c)(1); P.L. 107-56 (PATRIOT Act) (10/26/01), title IV, §411(c) [second] (The PATRIOT Act created two paragraphs designated §411(c). Reference above links to the appropriate paragraph.) [revising (a)]; P.L. 108-458 (12/17/04), title VII, §7119(a) [revising (a)(4)(A)–(B); adding (a)(4)(C); redesignating (b)–(c) as (c)–(d), respectively; adding new (b)].)

# Chapter 3 — Issuance of Entry Documents

## Sec. 221 Issuance of Visas
[8 U.S.C. 1201]

**(a) Immigrants; nonimmigrants.—**

(1) Under the conditions hereinafter prescribed and subject to the limitations prescribed in this Act or regulations issued thereunder, a consular officer may issue

(A) to an immigrant who has made proper application therefor, an immigrant visa which shall consist of the application provided for in section 222, visaed by such consular officer, and shall specify the foreign state, if any, to which the immigrant is charged, the immigrant's particular status under such foreign state, the preference, immediate relative, or special immigrant classification to which the alien is charged, the date on which the validity of the visa shall expire, and such additional information as may be required; and

(B) a nonimmigrant who has made proper application therefor, a nonimmigrant visa, which shall specify the classification under section 101(a)(15) of the nonimmigrant, the period during which the nonimmigrant visa shall be valid, and such additional information as may be required.

(2) The Secretary of State shall provide to the Service an electronic version of the visa file of each alien who has been issued a visa to ensure that the data in that visa file is available to immigration inspectors at the United States ports of entry before the arrival of the alien at such a port of entry.

**(b) Registration; photographs; waiver of requirement.**— Each alien who applies for a visa shall be registered in connection with his application, and shall furnish copies of his photograph signed by him for such use as may be by regulations required. The requirements of this subsection may be waived in the discretion of the Secretary of State in the case of any alien who is within that class of nonimmigrants enumerated in sections 101(a)(15)(A), and 101(a)(15)(G), or in the case of any alien who is granted a diplomatic visa on a diplomatic passport or on the equivalent thereof.

**(c) Period of validity; requirement of visa.**— An immigrant visa shall be valid for such period, not exceeding six months, as shall be by regulations prescribed, except that any visa issued to a child lawfully adopted by a United States citizen and spouse while such citizen is serving abroad in the United States Armed Forces, or is employed abroad by the United States Government, or is temporarily abroad on business, shall be valid until such time, for a period not to exceed three years, as the adoptive citizen parent returns to the United States in due course of his service, employment, or business. A nonimmigrant visa shall be valid for such periods as shall be by regulations prescribed. In prescribing the period of validity of a nonimmigrant visa in the case of nationals of any foreign country who are eligible for such visas, the Secretary of State shall, insofar as practicable, accord to such nationals the same treatment upon a reciprocal basis as such foreign country accords to nationals of the United States who are within a similar class; except that in the case of aliens who are nationals of a foreign country and who either are granted refugee status and firmly resettled in another foreign country or are granted permanent residence and residing in another foreign country, the Secretary of State may prescribe the period of validity of such a visa based upon the treatment granted by that other foreign country to alien refugees and permanent residents, respectively, in the United States. An immigrant visa may be replaced under the original number during the fiscal year in which the original visa was issued for an immigrant who establishes to the satisfaction of the consular officer that he was unable to use the original immigrant visa during the period of its validity because of reasons beyond his control and for which he was not responsible: *Provided,* That the immigrant is found by the consular officer to be eligible for an immigrant visa and the immigrant pays again the statutory fees for an application and an immigrant visa.[122]

**(d) Physical examination.**— Prior to the issuance of an immigrant visa to any alien, the consular officer shall require such alien to submit to a physical and mental examination in accordance with such regulations as may be prescribed. Prior to the issuance of a nonimmigrant visa to any alien, the consular officer may require such alien to submit to a physical or mental examination, or both, if in his opinion such examination is necessary to ascertain whether such alien is eligible to receive a visa.

**(e) Surrender of visa.**— Each immigrant shall surrender his immigrant visa to the immigration officer at the port of entry, who shall endorse on the visa the date and the port of arrival, the identity of the vessel or other means of transportation by which the immigrant arrived, and such other endorsements as may be by regulations required.

**(f) Surrender of documents.**— Each nonimmigrant shall present or surrender to the immigration officer at the port of entry such documents as may be by regulation required. In the case of an alien crewman not in possession of any individual documents other than a passport and until such time as it becomes practicable to issue individual documents, such alien crewman may be admitted, subject to the provisions of this title, if his name appears in the crew list of the vessel or aircraft on which he arrives and the crew list is visaed by a consular officer, but the consular officer shall have the right to deny admission to any alien crewman from the crew list visa.

---

[122] *See* §422(d) of the USA PATRIOT Act, P.L. 107-56, *reprinted in* Appendix J, for provisions relating to immigration benefits for the victims of terrorism.

**(g)**[123] **Nonissuance of visas or other documents.**— No visa or other documentation shall be issued to an alien if

(1) it appears to the consular officer, from statements in the application, or in the papers submitted therewith, that such alien is ineligible to receive a visa or such other documentation under section 212, or any other provision of law,

(2) the application fails to comply with the provisions of this Act, or the regulations issued thereunder, or

(3) the consular officer knows or has reason to believe that such alien is ineligible to receive a visa or such other documentation under section 212, or any other provision of law: *Provided*, That a visa or other documentation may be issued to an alien who is within the purview of section 212(a)(4), if such alien is otherwise entitled to receive a visa or other documentation, upon receipt of notice by the consular officer from the Attorney General of the giving of a bond or undertaking providing indemnity as in the case of aliens admitted under section 213; *Provided further*, That a visa may be issued to an alien defined in section 101(a)(15)(B) or (F), if such alien is otherwise entitled to receive a visa, upon receipt of a notice by the consular officer from the Attorney General of the giving of a bond with sufficient surety in such sum and containing such conditions as the consular officer shall prescribe, to insure that at the expiration of the time for which such alien has been admitted by the Attorney General, as provided in section 214(a), or upon failure to maintain the status under which he was admitted, or to maintain any status subsequently acquired under section 248 of the Act, such alien will depart from the United States.

**(h) Nonadmission upon arrival.**— Nothing in this Act shall be construed to entitle any alien, to whom a visa or other documentation has been issued, to be admitted the United States,[124] if, upon arrival at a port of entry in the United States, he is found to be inadmissible under this Act, or any other provision of law. The substance of this subsection shall appear upon every visa application.

**(i) Revocation of visas or documents.**— After the issuance of a visa or other documentation to any alien, the consular officer or the Secretary of State may at any time, in his discretion, revoke such visa or other documentation. Notice of such revocation shall be communicated to the Attorney General, and such revocation shall invalidate the visa or other documentation from the date of issuance: *Provided,* That carriers or transportation companies, and masters, commanding officers, agents, owners, charterers, or consignees, shall not be penalized under section 273(b) for action taken in reliance on such visas or other documentation, unless they received due notice of such revocation prior to the alien's embarkation. There shall be no means of judicial review (including review pursuant to section 2241 of title 28, United States Code, or any other habeas corpus provision, and sections 1361 and 1651 of such title) of a revocation under this subsection, except in the context of a removal proceeding if such revocation provides the sole ground for removal under section 237(a)(1)(B).[125]

(June 27, 1952, ch. 477, title II, ch. 3, §221, 66 Stat. 191; as amended by P.L. 87-301 (9/26/61); P.L. 89-236 (10/3/65); P.L. 97-116 (12/29/81); P.L. 99-653 (11/14/86), §5(a), formerly §5(a)(a)-(c), renumbered P.L. 100-525 (10/24/88); P.L. 101-649 (IMMACT90) (11/29/90); P.L. 102-232 (MTINA) (12/12/91, *effective* 4/1/92); P.L. 104-208 (IIRAIRA) (9/30/96), div. C, title III, §308(d)(4)(G),

---

[123] Sec. 406 of P.L. 108-199 (1/23/04) provides that "[a]n application for a visa shall be denied without prejudice under §221(g) ... if the application is delayed for a period of more than 60 days from the date of application due to administrative processing by any agency in making a determination of inadmissibility under §212(a)(3)."

[124] *Sic.* Probably should read "... admitted to the United States ..."

[125] Amendment made by P.L. 108-458 (12/17/04) [adding last sentence (beginning "There shall be no means of judicial review...")] is applicable to revocations under INA §§205 and 221(i) made on or before 12/17/04.

title VI, §631 [revising (c) by striking "four months" & inserting "six months"]; P.L. 107-173 (5/14/02), title III, §301 [adding (a)(2); redesignating (a)(1)–(2) as (a)(1)(A)–(B)]; P.L. 108-458 (12/17/04), title V, §5304(a) [revising (i)].)

## Sec. 222 Application for Visas
## [8 U.S.C. 1202]

**(a) Immigrant visas.**— Every alien applying for an immigrant visa and for alien registration shall make application therefor in such form and manner and at such place as shall be by regulations prescribed. In the application the alien shall state his full and true name, and any other name which he has used or by which he has been known; age and sex; the date and place of his birth; and such additional information necessary to the identification of the applicant and the enforcement of the immigration and nationality laws as may be by regulations prescribed.

**(b) Other documentary evidence for immigrant visa.**— Every alien applying for an immigrant visa shall present a valid unexpired passport or other suitable travel document, or document of identity and nationality, if such document is required under the regulations issued by the Secretary of State. The immigrant shall furnish to the consular officer with his application a copy of a certification by the appropriate police authorities stating what their records show concerning the immigrant; a certified copy of any existing prison record, military record, and record of his birth; and a certified copy of all other records or documents concerning him or his case which may be required by the consular officer. The copy of each document so furnished shall be permanently attached to the application and become a part thereof. In the event that the immigrant establishes to the satisfaction of the consular officer that any document or record required by this subsection is unobtainable, the consular officer may permit the immigrant to submit in lieu of such document or record other satisfactory evidence of the fact to which such document or record would, if obtainable, pertain. All immigrant visa applications shall be reviewed and adjudicated by a consular officer.

**(c) Nonimmigrant visas; nonimmigrant registration; form, manner and contents of application.**— Every alien applying for a nonimmigrant visa and for alien registration shall make application therefor in such form and manner as shall be by regulations prescribed. In the application the alien shall state his full and true name, the date and place of birth, his nationality, the purpose and length of his intended stay in the United States; his marital status; and such additional information necessary to the identification of the applicant, the determination of his eligibility for a nonimmigrant visa, and the enforcement of the immigration and nationality laws as may be by regulations prescribed. The alien shall provide complete and accurate information in response to any request for information contained in the application. At the discretion of the Secretary of State, application forms for the various classes of nonimmigrant admissions described in section 101(a)(15) may vary according to the class of visa being requested.

**(d) Other documentary evidence for nonimmigrant visa.**— Every alien applying for a nonimmigrant visa and alien registration shall furnish to the consular officer, with his application, a certified copy of such documents pertaining to him as may be by regulations required. All nonimmigrant visa applications shall be reviewed and adjudicated by a consular officer.

**(e) Signing and verification of application.**— Except as may be otherwise prescribed by regulations, each application for an immigrant visa shall be signed by the applicant in the presence of the consular officer, and verified by the oath of the applicant administered by the consular officer. The application for an immigrant visa, when visaed by the consular officer, shall become the immigrant visa. The application for a nonimmigrant visa or other documentation as a nonimmigrant shall be disposed of as may be by regulations prescribed. The issuance of a nonimmigrant visa shall, except as may be otherwise by regulations prescribed, be evidenced by a stamp, or other placed in the alien's passport.

**(f)**[126] **Confidential nature of records.**— The records of the Department of State and of diplomatic and consular offices of the United States pertaining to the issuance or refusal of visas or permits to enter the United States shall be considered confidential and shall be used only for the formulation, amendment, administration, or enforcement of the immigration, nationality, and other laws of the United States, except that—

(1) in the discretion of the Secretary of State certified copies of such records may be made available to a court which certifies that the information contained in such records is needed by the court in the interest of the ends of justice in a case pending before the court.

(2) the Secretary of State, in the Secretary's discretion and on the basis of reciprocity, may provide to a foreign government information in the Department of State's computerized visa lookout database and, when necessary and appropriate, other records covered by this section related to information in the database—

(A) with regard to individual aliens, at any time on a case-by-case basis for the purpose of preventing, investigating, or punishing acts that would constitute a crime in the United States, including, but not limited to, terrorism or trafficking in controlled substances, persons, or illicit weapons; or

(B) with regard to any or all aliens in the database, pursuant to such conditions as the Secretary of State shall establish in an agreement with the foreign government in which that government agrees to use such information and records for the purposes described in subparagraph (A) or to deny visas to persons who would be inadmissible to the United States.

**(g) Nonimmigrant visa void at conclusion of authorized period of stay.—**

(1) In the case of an alien who has been admitted on the basis of a nonimmigrant visa and remained in the United States beyond the period of stay authorized by the Attorney General, such visa shall be void beginning after the conclusion of such period of stay.

(2) An alien described in paragraph (1) shall be ineligible to be readmitted to the United States as a nonimmigrant, except—

(A) on the basis of a visa (other than the visa described in paragraph (1)) issued in a consular office located in the country of the alien's nationality (or, if there is no office in such country, in such other consular office as the Secretary of State shall specify); or

(B) where extraordinary circumstances are found by the Secretary of State to exist.

**(h)** Notwithstanding any other provision of this Act, the Secretary of State shall require every alien applying for a nonimmigrant visa—

(1) who is at least 14 years of age and not more than 79 years of age to submit to an in person interview with a consular officer unless the requirement for such interview is waived—

(A) by a consular official and such alien is—

(i) within that class of nonimmigrants enumerated in subparagraph (A) or (G) of section 101(a)(15);

(ii) within the NATO visa category;

---

[126] Sec. 834 of of P.L. 109-162 (1/6/06) provides that INA §222(f) shall not be construed to prevent the sharing of information regarding a U.S. petitioner for a visa under INA §101(a)(15)(K)(i) or (ii) for the limited purposes of fulfilling disclosure obligations imposed by the amendments made by §§832(a) or 833 of that Act.

(iii) within that class of nonimmigrants enumerated in section 101(a)(15)(C)(iii) (referred to as the "C-3 visa" category); or

(iv) granted a diplomatic or official visa on a diplomatic or official passport or on the equivalent thereof;

(B) by a consular official and such alien is applying for a visa—

(i) not more than 12 months after the date on which such alien's prior visa expired;

(ii) for the visa classification for which such prior visa was issued;

(iii) from the consular post located in the country of such alien's usual residence, unless otherwise prescribed in regulations that require an applicant to apply for a visa in the country of which such applicant is a national; and

(iv) the consular officer has no indication that such alien has not complied with the immigration laws and regulations of the United States; or

(C) by the Secretary of State if the Secretary determines that such waiver is—

(i) in the national interest of the United States; or

(ii) necessary as a result of unusual or emergent circumstances; and

(2) notwithstanding paragraph (1), to submit to an in person interview with a consular officer if such alien—

(A) is not a national or resident of the country in which such alien is applying for a visa;

(B) was previously refused a visa, unless such refusal was overcome or a waiver of ineligibility has been obtained;

(C) is listed in the Consular Lookout and Support System (or successor system at the Department of State);

(D) is a national of a country officially designated by the Secretary of State as a state sponsor of terrorism, except such nationals who possess nationalities of countries that are not designated as state sponsors or terrorism;

(E) requires a security advisory opinion or other Department of State clearance, unless such alien is—

(i) within that class of nonimmigrants enumerated in subparagraph (A) or (G) of section 101(a)(15);

(ii) within the NATO visa category;

(iii) within that class of nonimmigrants enumerated in section 101(a)(15)(C)(iii) (referred to as the "C-3 visa" category); or

(iv) an alien who qualifies for a diplomatic or official visa, or its equivalent; or

(F) is identified as a member of a group or sector that the Secretary of State determines—

(i) poses a substantial risk of submitting inaccurate information in order to obtain a visa;

(ii) has historically had visa applications denied at a rate that is higher than the average rate of such denials; or

(iii) poses a security threat to the United States.

(June 27, 1952, ch. 477, title II, ch. 3, §222, 66 Stat. 193; as amended by P.L. 87-301 (9/26/61); P.L. 89-236 (10/3/65); P.L. 99-653 (11/14/86); P.L. 100-525 (10/24/88); P.L. 103-416 (INTCA) (10/25/94, *effective* 4/1/95); P.L. 104-208 (IIRAIRA) (9/30/96), div. C, title VI, §632(a) [adding (g)], §634 [revising (e)]; P.L. 107-56 (PATRIOT Act) (10/26/01), title IV, §413 [revising (f)]; P.L. 108-458 (12/17/04, *effective* 3/17/05), title V, §5301(a) [adding (h)], §5302 [revising (c)] title VII, §7203(b) [revising (b) & (d)].)

## Sec. 223 Reentry Permits
[8 U.S.C. 1203]

**(a) Application; contents.—**

(1) Any alien lawfully admitted for permanent residence, or

(2) any alien lawfully admitted to the United States pursuant to clause 6 of section 3 of the Immigration Act of 1924, between July 1, 1924, and July 5, 1932, both dates inclusive, who intends to depart temporarily from the United States may make application to the Attorney General for a permit to reenter the United States, stating the length of his intended absence or absences, and the reasons therefor. Such applications shall be made under oath, and shall be in such form, contain such information, and be accompanied by such photographs of the applicant as may be by regulations prescribed.

**(b) Issuance of permit; nonrenewability.—** If the Attorney General finds

(1) that the applicant under subsection (a)(1) has been lawfully admitted to the United States for permanent residence, or that the applicant under subsection (a)(2) has since admission maintained the status required of him at the time of his admission and such applicant desires to visit abroad and to return to the United States to resume the status existing at the time of his departure for such visit,

(2) that the application is made in good faith, and

(3) that the alien's proposed departure from the United States would not be contrary to the interests of the United States, the Attorney General may, in his discretion, issue the permit, which shall be valid for not more than two years from the date of issuance and shall not be renewable. The permit shall be in such form as shall be by regulations prescribed for the complete identification of the alien.

**(c) Multiple reentries.—** During the period of validity, such permit may be used by the alien in making one or more applications for reentry into the United States.

**(d) Presented and surrendered.—** Upon the return of the alien to the United States the permit shall be presented to the immigration officer at the port of entry, and upon the expiration of its validity, the permit shall be surrendered to the Service.

**(e) Permit in lieu of visa.—** A permit issued under this section in the possession of the person to whom issued, shall be accepted in lieu of any visa which otherwise would be required from such person under this Act. Otherwise a permit issued under this section shall have no effect under the immigration laws except to show that the alien to whom it was issued is returning from a temporary visit abroad; but nothing in this section shall be construed as making such permit the exclusive means of establishing that the alien is so returning.

(June 27, 1952, ch. 477, title II, ch. 3, §223, 66 Stat. 194; as amended by P.L. 97-116 (12/29/81).)

### Sec. 224 Immediate Relative and Special Immigrant Visas
### [8 U.S.C. 1204]

A consular officer may, subject to the limitations provided in section 221, issue an immigrant visa to a special immigrant or immediate relative as such upon satisfactory proof, under regulations prescribed under this Act, that the applicant is entitled to special immigrant or immediate relative status.

(June 27, 1952, ch. 477, title II, ch. 3, §224, 66 Stat. 195; as amended by Pub. L. 89-236, §11(d), Oct. 3, 1965, 79 Stat. 918.)

## Chapter 4 — Inspection, Apprehension, Examination, Exclusion, and Removal

### Sec. 231 Lists of Persons Arriving and Departing[127]
### [8 U.S.C. 1221]

**(a) Arrival manifests.**— For each commercial vessel or aircraft transporting any person to any seaport or airport of the United States from any place outside the United States, it shall be the duty of an appropriate official specified in subsection (d) to provide to any United States border officer (as defined in subsection (i)) at that port manifest information about each passenger, crew member, and other occupant transported on such vessel or aircraft prior to arrival at that port.

**(b) Departure manifests.**— For each commercial vessel or aircraft taking passengers on board at any seaport or airport of the United States, who are destined to any place outside the United States, it shall be the duty of an appropriate official specified in subsection (d) to provide any United States border officer (as defined in subsection (i)) before departure from such port manifest information about each passenger, crew member, and other occupant to be transported.

**(c) Contents of manifest.**— The information to be provided with respect to each person listed on a manifest required to be provided under subsection (a) or (b) shall include—

(1) complete name;

(2) date of birth;

(3) citizenship;

(4) sex;

(5) passport number and country of issuance;

(6) country of residence;

(7) United States visa number, date, and place of issuance, where applicable;

(8) alien registration number, where applicable;

(9) United States address while in the United States; and

(10) such other information the Attorney General, in consultation with the Secretary of State, and the Secretary of Treasury determines as being necessary for the identification of the persons transported and for the enforcement of the immigration laws and to protect safety and national security.

---

[127] *See also* §402 of the Enhanced Border Security and Visa Entry Reform Act, 2002, P.L. 107-173, which required a study regarding the feasibility of extending the requirements of §231(a)–(b) to commercial land carriers, and a report to Congress by 5/14/04.

**(d) Appropriate officials specified.—** An appropriate official specified in this subsection is the master or commanding officer, or authorized agent, owner, or consignee, of the commercial vessel or aircraft concerned.

**(e) Deadline for requirement of electronic transmission of manifest information.—** Not later than January 1, 2003, manifest information required to be provided under subsection (a) or (b) shall be transmitted electronically by the appropriate official specified in subsection (d) to an immigration officer.

**(f) Prohibition.—** No operator of any private or public carrier that is under a duty to provide manifest information under this section shall be granted clearance papers until the appropriate official specified in subsection (d) has complied with the requirements of this subsection, except that, in the case of commercial vessels or aircraft that the Attorney General determines are making regular trips to the United States, the Attorney General may, when expedient, arrange for the provision of manifest information of persons departing the United States at a later date.

**(g) Penalties against noncomplying shipments, aircraft, or carriers.—** If it shall appear to the satisfaction of the Attorney General that an appropriate official specified in subsection (d), any public or private carrier, or the agent of any transportation line, as the case may be, has refused or failed to provide manifest information required by subsection (a) or (b), or that the manifest information provided is not accurate and full based on information provided to the carrier, such official, carrier, or agent, as the case may be, shall pay to the Commissioner the sum of $1,000 for each person with respect to whom such accurate and full manifest information is not provided, or with respect to whom the manifest information is not prepared as prescribed by this section or by regulations issued pursuant thereto. No commercial vessel or aircraft shall be granted clearance pending determination of the question of the liability to the payment of such penalty, or while it remains unpaid, and no such penalty shall be remitted or refunded, except that clearance may be granted prior to the determination of such question upon the deposit with the Commissioner of a bond or undertaking approved by the Attorney General or a sum sufficient to cover such penalty.

**(h) Waiver.—** The Attorney General may waive the requirements of subsection (a) or (b) upon such circumstances and conditions as the Attorney General may by regulation prescribe.

**(i) United States border officer defined.—** In this section, the term "United States border officer" means, with respect to a particular port of entry into the United States, any United States official who is performing duties at that port of entry.

**(j) Record of citizens and resident aliens leaving permanently for foreign countries.—** The Attorney General may authorize immigration officers to record the following information regarding every resident person leaving the United States by way of the Canadian or Mexican borders for permanent residence in a foreign country: Names, age, and sex; whether married or single; calling or occupation; whether able to read or write; nationality; country of birth; country of which citizen or subject; race; last permanent residence in the United States; intended future permanent residence; and time and port of last arrival in the United States; and if a United States citizen or national, the facts on which claim to that status is based.

(June 27, 1952, ch. 477, title II, ch. 4, §231, 66 Stat. 195; as amended by P.L. 97-116 (12/29/81), §18(g); P.L. 101-649 (IMMACT90) (11/29/90), title V, §543; P.L. 102-232 (MTINA) (12/12/91, *effective* 4/1/92), title III, §306(c)(4)(A); P.L. 104-208 (IIRAIRA) (9/30/96), div. C, title III, §308; P.L. 107-77 (11/28/01), title I, §115; P.L. 107-173 (5/14/02), title IV, §402(a) [revising (a)].)

## Sec. 232 Detention of Aliens for Physical and Mental Examination
## [8 U.S.C. 1222]

**(a) Detention of aliens.**— For the purpose of determining whether aliens (including alien crewmen) arriving at ports of the United States belong to any of the classes inadmissible under this Act, by reason of being afflicted with any of the diseases or mental or physical defects or disabilities set forth in section 212(a), or whenever the Attorney General has received information showing that any aliens are coming from a country or have embarked at a place where any of such diseases are prevalent or epidemic, such aliens shall be detained by the Attorney General for a sufficient time to enable the immigration officers and medical officers to subject such aliens to observation and an examination sufficient to determine whether or not they belong to inadmissible classes.

**(b) Physical and mental examination.**— The physical and mental examination of arriving aliens (including alien crewmen) shall be made by medical officers of the United States Public Health Service, who shall conduct all medical examinations and shall certify, for the information of the immigration officers and the immigration judges, any physical and mental defect or disease observed by such medical officers in any such alien. If medical officers of the United States Public Health Service are not available, civil surgeons of not less than four years' professional experience may be employed for such service upon such terms as may be prescribed by the Attorney General. Aliens (including alien crewmen) arriving at ports of the United States shall be examined by at least one such medical officer or civil surgeon under such administrative regulations as the Attorney General may prescribe, and under medical regulations prepared by the Secretary of Health and Human Services. Medical officers of the United States Public Health Service who have had special training in the diagnosis of insanity and mental defects shall be detailed for duty or employed at such ports of entry as the Attorney General may designate, and such medical officers shall be provided with suitable facilities for the detention and examination of all arriving aliens who it is suspected may be inadmissible under paragraph (1) of section 212(a), and the services of interpreters shall be provided for such examination. Any alien certified under paragraph (1) of section 212(a) may appeal to a board of medical officers of the United States Public Health Service, which shall be convened by the Secretary of Health and Human Services, and any such alien may introduce before such board one expert medical witness at his own cost and expense.

**(c) Certification of certain helpless aliens.**— If an examining medical officer determines that an alien arriving in the United States is inadmissible, is helpless from sickness, mental or physical disability, or infancy, and is accompanied by another alien whose protection or guardianship may be required, the officer may certify such fact for purposes of applying section 212(a)(10)(B) with respect to the other alien.

(June 27, 1952, ch. 477, title II, ch. 4, §232, 66 Stat. 196; as amended by P.L. 99-500 (10/18/86), P.L. 99-591 (10/30/86); as renumbered by P.L. 100-525 (10/24/88); P.L. 104-208 (IIRAIRA) (9/30/96), div. C, title III, §308(b)(2) [revising (a); redesignating §234 as §232(b)].)

## Sec. 233 Entry through or from Foreign Territory and Adjacent Islands
## [8 U.S.C. 1223]

**(a) Necessity of transportation contract.**— The Attorney General shall have power to enter into contracts with transportation lines for the inspection and admission of aliens coming to the United States from foreign territory or from adjacent islands. No such transportation line shall be allowed to land any such alien in the United States until and unless it has entered into any such contracts which may be required by the Attorney General.

**(b) Landing stations.**— Every transportation line engaged in carrying alien passengers for hire to the United States from foreign territory or from adjacent islands shall provide and maintain at its expense suitable landing stations, approved by the Attorney General, conveniently located at the point or points of entry. No such transportation line shall be allowed to land any alien passengers in the United States until such landing stations are provided, and unless such stations are thereafter maintained to the satisfaction of the Attorney General.

**(c) Landing agreements.**— The Attorney General shall have power to enter into contracts including bonding agreements with transportation lines to guarantee the passage through the United States in immediate and continuous transit of aliens destined to foreign countries. Notwithstanding any other provision of this Act, such aliens may not have their classification changed under section 248.

**(d) Definitions.**— As used in this section the terms "transportation line" and "transportation company" include, but are not limited to, the owner, charterer, consignee, or authorized agent operating any vessel or aircraft or railroad train bringing aliens to the United States, to foreign territory, or to adjacent islands.

(June 27, 1952, ch. 477, title II, ch. 4, §238, 66 Stat. 202; as amended by P.L. 99-653 (11/14/86); P.L. 104-208 (IIRAIRA) (9/30/96), div. C, title III, §308(b)(4) [redesignating §238 as §233], §362 [revising (a)–(d)].)

## Sec. 234 Designation of Ports of Entry for Aliens Arriving by Aircraft
**[8 U.S.C. 1224]**

The Attorney General is authorized

**(1)** by regulation to designate as ports of entry for aliens arriving by aircraft any of the ports of entry for civil aircraft designated as such in accordance with law;

**(2)** by regulation to provide such reasonable requirements for aircraft in civil air navigation with respect to giving notice of intention to land in advance of landing, or notice of landing, as shall be deemed necessary for purposes of administration and enforcement of this Act; and

**(3)** by regulation to provide for the application to civil air navigation of the provisions of this Act where not expressly so provided in this Act to such extent and upon such conditions as he deems necessary.

Any person who violates any regulation made under this section shall be subject to a civil penalty of $2,000 which may be remitted or mitigated by the Attorney General in accordance with such proceedings as the Attorney General shall by regulation prescribe. In case the violation is by the owner or person in command of the aircraft, the penalty shall be a lien upon the aircraft, and such aircraft may be libeled therefor in the appropriate United States court. The determination by the Attorney General and remission or mitigation of the civil penalty shall be final. In case the violation is by the owner or person in command of the aircraft, the penalty shall be a lien upon the aircraft and may be collected by proceedings in rem which shall conform as nearly as may be to civil suits in admiralty. The Supreme Court of the United States, and under its direction other courts of the United States, are authorized to prescribe rules regulating such proceedings against aircraft in any particular not otherwise provided by law. Any aircraft made subject to a lien by this section may be summarily seized by, and placed in the custody of such persons as the Attorney General may by regulation prescribe. The aircraft may be released from such custody upon deposit of such amount not exceeding $2,000 as the Attorney General may prescribe, or of a bond in such sum and with such sureties as the Attorney General may prescribe, conditioned upon the payment of the penalty which may be finally determined by the Attorney General.

(June 27, 1952, ch. 477, title II, ch. 4, §239, 66 Stat. 203; as amended by P.L. 101-649 (IMMACT90) (11/29/90); P.L. 102-232 (MTINA) (12/12/91, *effective* 4/1/92); P.L. 104-208 (IIRAIRA) (9/30/96), div. C, title III, §304(a)(1) [redesignating §239 as §234].)

## Sec. 235 Inspection by Immigration Officers; Expedited Removal of Inadmissible Arriving Aliens; Referral for Hearing[128]
[8 U.S.C. 1225]

### (a) Inspection.—

(1) *Aliens treated as applicants for admission.*— An alien present in the United States who has not been admitted or who arrives in the United States (whether or not at a designated port of arrival and including an alien who is brought to the United States after having been interdicted in international or United States waters) shall be deemed for purposes of this Act an applicant for admission.

(2) *Stowaways.*— An arriving alien who is a stowaway is not eligible to apply for admission or to be admitted and shall be ordered removed upon inspection by an immigration officer. Upon such inspection if the alien indicates an intention to apply for asylum under section 208 or a fear of persecution, the officer shall refer the alien for an interview under subsection (b)(1)(B). A stowaway may apply for asylum only if the stowaway is found to have a credible fear of persecution under subsection (b)(1)(B). In no case may a stowaway be considered an applicant for admission or eligible for a hearing under section 240.

(3) *Inspection.*— All aliens (including alien crewmen) who are applicants for admission or otherwise seeking admission or readmission to or transit through the United States shall be inspected by immigration officers.

(4) *Withdrawal of application for admission.*— An alien applying for admission may, in the discretion of the Attorney General and at any time, be permitted to withdraw the application for admission and depart immediately from the United States.

(5) *Statements.*— An applicant for admission may be required to state under oath any information sought by an immigration officer regarding the purposes and intentions of the applicant in seeking admission to the United States, including the applicant's intended length of stay and whether the applicant intends to remain permanently or become a United States citizen, and whether the applicant is inadmissible.

### (b) Inspection of applicants for admission.—

(1) *Inspection of aliens arriving in the United States and certain other aliens who have not been admitted or paroled.*—

  (A) *Screening.*—

   (i) In general.— If an immigration officer determines that an alien (other than an alien described in subparagraph (F)) who is arriving in the United States or is described in clause (iii) is inadmissible under section 212(a)(6)(C) or 212(a)(7), the officer shall order the alien removed from the United States without further hearing or review unless the alien indicates either an intention to apply for asylum under section 208 or a fear of persecution.

   (ii) Claims for asylum.— If an immigration officer determines that an alien (other than an alien described in subparagraph (F)) who is arriving in the United States or is described in clause (iii) is inadmissible under section 212(a)(6)(C) or 212(a)(7) and

---

[128] All references to "special inquiry officer" in former §235 were changed to "immigration judge" *after* section was stricken by rewrite. Former §235 remained in effect during transition period (until 4/1/97). New §235 was added by §302 of IIRAIRA. *See* IIRAIRA §309 (*reprinted in* Appendix B, *infra*) for effective date provisions.

the alien indicates either an intention to apply for asylum under section 208 or a fear of persecution, the officer shall refer the alien for an interview by an asylum officer under subparagraph (B).

(iii) Application to certain other aliens.—

(I) In general.— The Attorney General may apply clauses (i) and (ii) of this subparagraph to any or all aliens described in subclause (II) as designated by the Attorney General. Such designation shall be in the sole and unreviewable discretion of the Attorney General and may be modified at any time.

(II) Aliens described.— An alien described in this clause is an alien who is not described in subparagraph (F), who has not been admitted or paroled into the United States, and who has not affirmatively shown, to the satisfaction of an immigration officer, that the alien has been physically present in the United States continuously for the 2-year period immediately prior to the date of the determination of inadmissibility under this subparagraph.

(B) *Asylum interviews.*—

(i) Conduct by asylum officers.— An asylum officer shall conduct interviews of aliens referred under subparagraph (A)(ii), either at a port of entry or at such other place designated by the Attorney General.

(ii) Referral of certain aliens.— If the officer determines at the time of the interview that an alien has a credible fear of persecution (within the meaning of clause (v)), the alien shall be detained for further consideration of the application for asylum.

(iii) Removal without further review if no credible fear of persecution.—

(I) In general.— Subject to subclause (III), if the officer determines that an alien does not have a credible fear of persecution, the officer shall order the alien removed from the United States without further hearing or review.

(II) Record of determination.— The officer shall prepare a written record of a determination under subclause (I). Such record shall include a summary of the material facts as stated by the applicant, such additional facts (if any) relied upon by the officer, and the officer's analysis of why, in the light of such facts, the alien has not established a credible fear of persecution. A copy of the officer's interview notes shall be attached to the written summary.

(III) Review of determination.— The Attorney General shall provide by regulation and upon the alien's request for prompt review by an immigration judge of a determination under subclause (I) that the alien does not have a credible fear of persecution. Such review shall include an opportunity for the alien to be heard and questioned by the immigration judge, either in person or by telephonic or video connection. Review shall be concluded as expeditiously as possible, to the maximum extent practicable within 24 hours, but in no case later than 7 days after the date of the determination under subclause (I).

(IV) Mandatory Detention.— Any alien subject to the procedures under this clause shall be detained pending a final determination of credible fear of persecution and, if found not to have such a fear, until removed.

(iv) Information about interviews.— The Attorney General shall provide information concerning the asylum interview described in this subparagraph to aliens who may be eligible. An alien who is eligible for such interview may consult with a person or persons of the alien's choosing prior to the interview or any review thereof, according to regulations prescribed by the Attorney General. Such consultation shall be at no expense to the Government and shall not unreasonably delay the process.

(v) Credible fear of persecution defined.— For purposes of this subparagraph, the term "credible fear of persecution" means that there is a significant possibility, taking into account the credibility of the statements made by the alien in support of the alien's claim and such other facts as are known to the officer, that the alien could establish eligibility for asylum under section 208.

(C) *Limitation on administrative review.*— Except as provided in subparagraph (B)(iii)(III), a removal order entered in accordance with subparagraph (A)(i) or (B)(iii)(I) is not subject to administrative appeal, except that the Attorney General shall provide by regulation for prompt review of such an order under subparagraph (A)(i) against an alien who claims under oath, or as permitted under penalty of perjury under section 1746 of title 28, United States Code, after having been warned of the penalties for falsely making such claim under such conditions, to have been lawfully admitted for permanent residence, to have been admitted as a refugee under section 207, or to have been granted asylum under section 208.

(D) *Limit on collateral attacks.*— In any action brought against an alien under section 275(a) or section 276, the court shall not have jurisdiction to hear any claim attacking the validity of an order of removal entered under subparagraph (A)(i) or (B)(iii).

(E) *Asylum officer defined.*— As used in this paragraph, the term "asylum officer" means an immigration officer who—

(i) has had professional training in country conditions, asylum law, and interview techniques comparable to that provided to full-time adjudicators of applications under section 208, and

(ii) is supervised by an officer who meets the condition described in clause (i) and has had substantial experience adjudicating asylum applications.

(F) *Exception.*— Subparagraph (A) shall not apply to an alien who is a native or citizen of a country in the Western Hemisphere with whose government the United States does not have full diplomatic relations and who arrives by aircraft at a port of entry.

(G) *Commonwealth of the northern mariana islands.*— Nothing in this subsection shall be construed to authorize or require any person described in section 208(e) to be permitted to apply for asylum under section 208 at any time before January 1, 2014.

(2) *Inspection of other aliens.*—

(A) *In general.*— Subject to subparagraphs (B) and (C), in the case of an alien who is an applicant for admission, if the examining immigration officer determines that an alien seeking admission is not clearly and beyond a doubt entitled to be admitted, the alien shall be detained for a proceeding under section 240.

(B) *Exception.*— Subparagraph (A) shall not apply to an alien—

(i) who is a crewman,

(ii) to whom paragraph (1) applies, or

(iii) who is a stowaway.

(C) *Treatment of aliens arriving from contiguous territory.*— In the case of an alien described in subparagraph (A) who is arriving on land (whether or not at a designated port of arrival) from a foreign territory contiguous to the United States, the Attorney General may return the alien to that territory pending a proceeding under section 240.

(3) *Challenge of decision.*— The decision of the examining immigration officer, if favorable to the admission of any alien, shall be subject to challenge by any other immigration officer and such challenge shall operate to take the alien whose privilege to be admitted is so challenged, before an immigration judge for a proceeding under section 240.

**(c) Removal of aliens inadmissible on security and related grounds.—**

(1) *Removal without further hearing.*— If an immigration officer or an immigration judge suspects that an arriving alien may be inadmissible under subparagraph (A) (other than clause (ii)), (B), or (C) of section 212(a)(3), the officer or judge shall—

(A) order the alien removed, subject to review under paragraph (2);

(B) report the order of removal to the Attorney General; and

(C) not conduct any further inquiry or hearing until ordered by the Attorney General.

(2) *Review of order.*—

(A) The Attorney General shall review orders issued under paragraph (1).

(B) If the Attorney General—

(i) is satisfied on the basis of confidential information that the alien is inadmissible under subparagraph (A) (other than clause (ii)), (B), or (C) of section 212(a)(3), and

(ii) after consulting with appropriate security agencies of the United States Government, concludes that disclosure of the information would be prejudicial to the public interest, safety, or security,

the Attorney General may order the alien removed without further inquiry or hearing by an immigration judge.

(C) If the Attorney General does not order the removal of the alien under subparagraph (B), the Attorney General shall specify the further inquiry or hearing that shall be conducted in the case.

(3) *Submission of statement and information.*— The alien or the alien's representative may submit a written statement and additional information for consideration by the Attorney General.

**(d) Authority relating to inspections.—**

(1) *Authority to search conveyances.*— Immigration officers are authorized to board and search any vessel, aircraft, railway car, or other conveyance or vehicle in which they believe aliens are being brought into the United States.

(2) *Authority to order detention and delivery of arriving aliens.*— Immigration officers are authorized to order an owner, agent, master, commanding officer, person in charge, purser, or consignee of a vessel or aircraft bringing an alien (except an alien crewmember) to the United States—

(A) to detain the alien on the vessel or at the airport of arrival, and

(B) to deliver the alien to an immigration officer for inspection or to a medical officer for examination.

(3) *Administration of oath and consideration of evidence.*— The Attorney General and any immigration officer shall have power to administer oaths and to take and consider evidence of or from any person touching the privilege of any alien or person he believes or suspects to be an alien to enter, reenter, transit through, or reside in the United States or concerning any matter which is material and relevant to the enforcement of this Act and the administration of the Service.

(4) *Subpoena authority.*—

(A) The Attorney General and any immigration officer shall have power to require by subpoena the attendance and testimony of witnesses before immigration officers and the production of books, papers, and documents relating to the privilege of any person to enter, reenter, reside in, or pass through the United States or concerning any matter which is material and relevant to the enforcement of this Act and the administration of the Service, and to that end may invoke the aid of any court of the United States.

(B) Any United States district court within the jurisdiction of which investigations or inquiries are being conducted by an immigration officer may, in the event of neglect or refusal to respond to a subpoena issued under this paragraph or refusal to testify before an immigration officer, issue an order requiring such persons to appear before an immigration officer, produce books, papers, and documents if demanded, and testify, and any failure to obey such order of the court may be punished by the court as a contempt thereof.

(June 27, 1952, ch. 477, title II, ch. 4, §235, 66 Stat. 198; as amended by P.L. 101-649 (IMMACT90) (11/29/90); P.L. 104-132 (AEDPA) (4/24/96), title IV, §422(a), 423(b); P.L. 104-208 (IIRAIRA) (9/30/96), div. C, title III, §302(a) [revising in its entirety], §308(d)(5), §371(b)(4); P.L. 110-229 (5/8/08) §702(j) [adding (b)(1)(G)].)

## Sec. 235A Preinspection at Foreign Airports
## [8 U.S.C. 1225a]

### (a) Establishment of preinspection stations.—

(1) *New stations.*— Subject to paragraph (5), not later than October 31, 1998, the Attorney General, in consultation with the Secretary of State, shall establish and maintain preinspection stations in at least 5 of the foreign airports that are among the 10 foreign airports which the Attorney General identifies as serving as last points of departure for the greatest numbers of inadmissible alien passengers who arrive from abroad by air at ports of entry within the United States. Such preinspection stations shall be in addition to any preinspection stations established prior to the date of the enactment of such Act.

(2) *Report.*— Not later than October 31, 1998, the Attorney General shall report to the Committees on the Judiciary of the House of Representatives and of the Senate on the implementation of paragraph (1).

(3) *Data collection.*— Not later than November 1, 1997, and each subsequent November 1, the Attorney General shall compile data identifying—

(A) the foreign airports which served as last points of departure for aliens who arrived by air at United States ports of entry without valid documentation during the preceding fiscal years;

(B) the number and nationality of such aliens arriving from each such foreign airport; and

(C) the primary routes such aliens followed from their country of origin to the United States.

(4) *Additional stations.*— Subject to paragraph (5), not later than January 1, 2008, the Secretary of Homeland Security, in consultation with the Secretary of State, shall establish preinspection stations in at least 25 additional foreign airports, which the Secretary of Homeland Security, in consultation with the Secretary of State, determines, based on the data compiled under paragraph (3) and such other information as may be available, would most effectively facilitate the travel of admissible aliens and reduce the number of inadmissible aliens, especially aliens who are potential terrorists, who arrive from abroad by air at points of entry within the United States. Such preinspection stations shall be in addition to those established before September 30, 1996, or pursuant to paragraph (1).

(5) *Conditions.*— Prior to the establishment of a preinspection station the Attorney General, in consultation with the Secretary of State, shall ensure that—

(A) employees of the United States stationed at the preinspection station and their accompanying family members will receive appropriate protection;

(B) such employees and their families will not be subject to unreasonable risks to their welfare and safety; and

(C) the country in which the preinspection station is to be established maintains practices and procedures with respect to asylum seekers and refugees in accordance with the Convention Relating to the Status of Refugees (done at Geneva, July 28, 1951), or the Protocol Relating to the Status of Refugees (done at New York, January 31, 1967), or that an alien in the country otherwise has recourse to avenues of protection from return to persecution.

**(b) Establishment of carrier consultant program and immigration security initiative.**— The Secretary of Homeland Security shall assign additional immigration officers to assist air carriers in the detection of fraudulent documents at foreign airports which, based on the records maintained pursuant to subsection (a)(3), served as a point of departure for a significant number of arrivals at United States ports of entry without valid documentation, but where no preinspection station exists. Beginning not later than December 31, 2006, the number of airports selected for an assignment under this subsection shall be at least 50.

(June 27, 1952, ch. 477, title II, ch. 4, §235A, as added by P.L. 104-208 (IIRAIRA) (9/30/96), div. C, title I, §123(a); as amended by P.L. 108-458 (12/17/04), title VII, §7206(a) [revising (b)], §7210(d)(1) [revising (a)(4)].)

## Sec. 236 Apprehension and Detention of Aliens[129]
[8 U.S.C. 1226]

**(a) Arrest, detention, and release.**— On a warrant issued by the Attorney General, an alien may be arrested and detained pending a decision on whether the alien is to be removed from the United States. Except as provided in subsection (c) and pending such decision, the Attorney General—

(1) may continue to detain the arrested alien; and

(2) may release the alien on—

(A) bond of at least $1,500 with security approved by, and containing conditions prescribed by, the Attorney General; or

---

[129] Effective on "title III-A" effective date. *See* IIRAIRA §309, *reprinted in* Appendix B, *infra*. Sec. 303(b)(2) of IIRAIRA provides the attorney general with an optional delay of the effective date of the custody provisions of this section if the attorney general notifies in writing the Committees on the Judiciary of the House and Senate regarding custody space and personnel deficiencies. On 10/9/96, the Commissioner so notified the committees. *See* P.L. 104-302. Sec. 303(b)(3) provides for transition for aliens regarding mandatory custody. *See* IIRAIRA §303(b) for full text of §303(b)(2) and (3).

(B) conditional parole; but

(3) may not provide the alien with work authorization (including an "employment authorized" endorsement or other appropriate work permit), unless the alien is lawfully admitted for permanent residence or otherwise would (without regard to removal proceedings) be provided such authorization.

**(b) Revocation of bond or parole.**— The Attorney General at any time may revoke a bond or parole authorized under subsection (a), rearrest the alien under the original warrant, and detain the alien.

**(c) Detention of criminal aliens.**—

(1) *Custody.*— The Attorney General shall take into custody any alien who—

(A) is inadmissible by reason of having committed any offense covered in section 212(a)(2),

(B) is deportable by reason of having committed any offense covered in section 237(a)(2)(A)(ii), (A)(iii), (B), (C), or (D),

(C) is deportable under section 237(a)(2)(A)(i) on the basis of an offense for which the alien has been sentence[130] to a term of imprisonment of at least 1 year, or

(D) is inadmissible under section 212(a)(3)(B) or deportable under section 237(a)(4)(B),

when the alien is released, without regard to whether the alien is released on parole, supervised release, or probation, and without regard to whether the alien may be arrested or imprisoned again for the same offense.

(2) *Release.*— The Attorney General may release an alien described in paragraph (1) only if the Attorney General decides pursuant to section 3521 of title 18, United States Code, that release of the alien from custody is necessary to provide protection to a witness, a potential witness, a person cooperating with an investigation into major criminal activity, or an immediate family member or close associate of a witness, potential witness, or person cooperating with such an investigation, and the alien satisfies the Attorney General that the alien will not pose a danger to the safety of other persons or of property and is likely to appear for any scheduled proceeding. A decision relating to such release shall take place in accordance with a procedure that considers the severity of the offense committed by the alien.

**(d) Identification of criminal aliens.**—

(1) The Attorney General shall devise and implement a system—

(A) to make available, daily (on a 24-hour basis), to Federal, State, and local authorities the investigative resources of the Service to determine whether individuals arrested by such authorities for aggravated felonies are aliens;

(B) to designate and train officers and employees of the Service to serve as a liaison to Federal, State, and local law enforcement and correctional agencies and courts with respect to the arrest, conviction, and release of any alien charged with an aggravated felony; and

(C) which uses computer resources to maintain a current record of aliens who have been convicted of an aggravated felony, and indicates those who have been removed.

---

[130] *Sic.* Probably should be "sentenced."

(2) The record under paragraph (1)(C) shall be made available—

(A) to inspectors at ports of entry and to border patrol agents at sector headquarters for purposes of immediate identification of any alien who was previously ordered removed and is seeking to reenter the United States, and

(B) to officials of the Department of State for use in its automated visa lookout system.

(3) Upon request of the governor or chief executive officer of any State, the Service shall provide assistance to State courts in the identification of aliens unlawfully present in the United States pending criminal prosecution.

**(e) Judicial review.**— The Attorney General's discretionary judgment regarding the application of this section shall not be subject to review. No court may set aside any action or decision by the Attorney General under this section regarding the detention or release of any alien or the grant, revocation, or denial of bond or parole.

(June 27, 1952, ch. 477, title II, ch. 4, §236, 66 Stat. 200; as amended by P.L. 101-649 (IMMACT90) (11/29/90); P.L. 102-232 (MTINA) (12/12/91, *effective* 4/1/92); P.L. 104-208 (IIRAIRA) (9/30/96), div. C, title III, §303(a) [revising in its entirety], §371(b)(5).)

## Sec. 236A Mandatory Detention of Suspected Terrorists; Habeas Corpus; Judicial Review [8 U.S.C. 1226a]

**(a) Detention of terrorist aliens.**—

(1) *Custody.*— The Attorney General shall take into custody any alien who is certified under paragraph (3).

(2) *Release.*— Except as provided in paragraphs (5) and (6), the Attorney General shall maintain custody of such an alien until the alien is removed from the United States. Except as provided in paragraph (6), such custody shall be maintained irrespective of any relief from removal for which the alien may be eligible, or any relief from removal granted the alien, until the Attorney General determines that the alien is no longer an alien who may be certified under paragraph (3). If the alien is finally determined not to be removable, detention pursuant to this subsection shall terminate.

(3) *Certification.*— The Attorney General may certify an alien under this paragraph if the Attorney General has reasonable grounds to believe that the alien—

(A) is described in section 212(a)(3)(A)(i), 212(a)(3)(A)(iii), 212(a)(3)(B), 237(a)(4)(A)(i), 237(a)(4)(A)(iii), or 237(a)(4)(B); or

(B) is engaged in any other activity that endangers the national security of the United States.

(4) *Nondelegation.*— The Attorney General may delegate the authority provided under paragraph (3) only to the Deputy Attorney General. The Deputy Attorney General may not delegate such authority.

(5) *Commencement of proceedings.*— The Attorney General shall place an alien detained under paragraph (1) in removal proceedings, or shall charge the alien with a criminal offense, not later than 7 days after the commencement of such detention. If the requirement of the preceding sentence is not satisfied, the Attorney General shall release the alien.

(6) *Limitation on indefinite detention.*— An alien detained solely under paragraph (1) who has not been removed under section 241(a)(1)(A), and whose removal is unlikely in the reasonably foreseeable future, may be detained for additional periods of up to six months only if

the release of the alien will threaten the national security of the United States or the safety of the community or any person.

(7) *Review of certification.*— The Attorney General shall review the certification made under paragraph (3) every 6 months. If the Attorney General determines, in the Attorney General's discretion, that the certification should be revoked, the alien may be released on such conditions as the Attorney General deems appropriate, unless such release is otherwise prohibited by law. The alien may request each 6 months in writing that the Attorney General reconsider the certification and may submit documents or other evidence in support of that request.

**(b) Habeas corpus and judicial review.—**

(1) *In general.*— Judicial review of any action or decision relating to this section (including judicial review of the merits of a determination made under subsection (a)(3) or (a)(6)) is available exclusively in habeas corpus proceedings consistent with this subsection. Except as provided in the preceding sentence, no court shall have jurisdiction to review, by habeas corpus petition or otherwise, any such action or decision.

(2) *Application.*—

(A) *In general.*— Notwithstanding any other provision of law, including section 2241(a) of title 28, United States Code, habeas corpus proceedings described in paragraph (1) may be initiated only by an application filed with—

(i) the Supreme Court;

(ii) any justice of the Supreme Court;

(iii) any circuit judge of the United States Court of Appeals for the District of Columbia Circuit; or

(iv) any district court otherwise having jurisdiction to entertain it.

(B) *Application transfer.*— Section 2241(b) of title 28, United States Code, shall apply to an application for a writ of habeas corpus described in subparagraph (A).

(3) *Appeals.*— Notwithstanding any other provision of law, including section 2253 of title 28, in habeas corpus proceedings described in paragraph (1) before a circuit or district judge, the final order shall be subject to review, on appeal, by the United States Court of Appeals for the District of Columbia Circuit. There shall be no right of appeal in such proceedings to any other circuit court of appeals.

(4) *Rule of decision.*— The law applied by the Supreme Court and the United States Court of Appeals for the District of Columbia Circuit shall be regarded as the rule of decision in habeas corpus proceedings described in paragraph (1).

**(c) Statutory construction.**— The provisions of this section shall not be applicable to any other provision of this Act.

(June 27, 1952, ch. 477, title II, ch. 4, §236A, as added by P.L. 107-56 (PATRIOT Act) (10/26/01), title IV, §412(a).)

**Sec. 237 Deportable Aliens**
**[8 U.S.C. 1227]**

**(a) Classes of deportable aliens.**— Any alien (including an alien crewman) in and admitted to the United States shall, upon the order of the Attorney General, be removed if the alien is within one or more of the following classes of deportable aliens:

(1) *Inadmissible at time of entry or of adjustment of status or violates status.*—

(A) *Inadmissible aliens.*— Any alien who at the time of entry or adjustment of status was within one or more of the classes of aliens inadmissible by the law existing at such time is deportable.

(B)[131] *Present in violation of law.*— Any alien who is present in the United States in violation of this Act or any other law of the United States, or whose nonimmigrant visa (or other documentation authorizing admission into the United States as a nonimmigrant) has been revoked under section 221(i), is deportable.

(C) *Violated nonimmigrant status or condition of entry.*—

(i) Nonimmigrant status violators.— Any alien who was admitted as a nonimmigrant and who has failed to maintain the nonimmigrant status in which the alien was admitted or to which it was changed under section 248, or to comply with the conditions of any such status, is deportable.

(ii) Violators of conditions of entry.— Any alien whom the Secretary of Health and Human Services certifies has failed to comply with terms, conditions, and controls that were imposed under section 212(g) is deportable.

(D) *Termination of conditional permanent residence.*—

(i) In general.— Any alien with permanent resident status on a conditional basis under section 216 (relating to conditional permanent resident status for certain alien spouses and sons and daughters) or under section 216A (relating to conditional permanent resident status for certain alien entrepreneurs, spouses, and children) who has had such status terminated under such respective section is deportable.

(ii) Exception.— Clause (i) shall not apply in the cases described in section 216(c)(4) (relating to certain hardship waivers).

(E) *Smuggling.*—

(i) In general.— Any alien who (prior to the date of entry, at the time of any entry, or within 5 years of the date of any entry) knowingly has encouraged, induced, assisted, abetted, or aided any other alien to enter or to try to enter the United States in violation of law is deportable.

(ii) Special rule in the case of family reunification.— Clause (i) shall not apply in the case of alien who is an eligible immigrant (as defined in section 301(b)(1) of the Immigration Act of 1990), was physically present in the United States on May 5, 1988, and is seeking admission as an immediate relative or under section 203(a)(2) (including under section 112 of the Immigration Act of 1990) or benefits under section 301(a) of the Immigration Act of 1990 if the alien, before May 5, 1988, has encouraged, induced, assisted, abetted, or aided only the alien's spouse, parent, son, or daughter (and no other individual) to enter the United States in violation of law.

(iii) Waiver authorized.— The Attorney General may, in his discretion for humanitarian purposes, to assure family unity, or when it is otherwise in the public interest, waive application of clause (i) in the case of any alien lawfully admitted for permanent residence if the alien has encouraged, induced, assisted, abetted, or aided

---

[131] *See* note 46, *supra.*

only an individual who at the time of the offense was the alien's spouse, parent, son, or daughter (and no other individual) to enter the United States in violation of law.

(F) [Repealed. P.L. 104-208 (IIRAIRA) (9/30/96), div. C, title VI, §671(d)(1)(C).]

(G) *Marriage fraud.*— An alien shall be considered to be deportable as having procured a visa or other documentation by fraud (within the meaning of section 212(a)(6)(C)(i)) and to be in the United States in violation of this Act (within the meaning of subparagraph (B)) if—

(i) the alien obtains any admission into the United States with an immigrant visa or other documentation procured on the basis of a marriage entered into less than 2 years prior to such entry of the alien and which, within 2 years subsequent to any admission of the alien in the United States, shall be judicially annulled or terminated, unless the alien establishes to the satisfaction of the Attorney General that such marriage was not contracted for the purpose of evading any provisions of the immigration laws, or

(ii) it appears to the satisfaction of the Attorney General that the alien has failed or refused to fulfill the alien's marital agreement which in the opinion of the Attorney General was made for the purpose of procuring the alien's admission as an immigrant.

(H) *Waiver authorized for certain misrepresentations.*— The provisions of this paragraph relating to the removal of aliens within the United States on the ground that they were inadmissible at the time of admission as aliens described in section 212(a)(6)(C)(i), whether willful or innocent, may, in the discretion of the Attorney General, be waived for any alien (other than an alien described in paragraph (4)(D)) who—

(i) (I) is the spouse, parent, son, or daughter of a citizen of the United States or of an alien lawfully admitted to the United States for permanent residence; and

(II) was in possession of an immigrant visa or equivalent document and was otherwise admissible to the United States at the time of such admission except for those grounds of inadmissibility specified under paragraphs (5)(A) and (7)(A) of section 212(a) which were a direct result of that fraud or misrepresentation.

(ii) is a VAWA self-petitioner.

A waiver of deportation for fraud or misrepresentation granted under this subparagraph shall also operate to waive removal based on the grounds of inadmissibility directly resulting from such fraud or misrepresentation.

(2) *Criminal offenses.*—

(A) *General crimes.*—

(i) Crimes of moral turpitude.— Any alien who—

(I) is convicted of a crime involving moral turpitude committed within five years (or 10 years in the case of an alien provided lawful permanent resident status under section 245(j)) after the date of admission, and

(II) is convicted of a crime for which a sentence of one year or longer may be imposed,

is deportable.

(ii) Multiple criminal convictions.— Any alien who at any time after admission is convicted of two or more crimes involving moral turpitude, not arising out of a single scheme of criminal misconduct, regardless of whether confined therefor and regardless of whether the convictions were in a single trial, is deportable.

(iii) Aggravated felony.— Any alien who is convicted of an aggravated felony at any time after admission is deportable.

(iv) High Speed Flight.— Any alien who is convicted of a violation of section 758 of title 18, United States Code, (relating to high speed flight from an immigration checkpoint) is deportable.

(v) Failure to register as a sex offender.— Any alien who is convicted under section 2250 of title 18, United States Code, is deportable.

(vi) Waiver authorized.— Clauses (i), (ii), (iii), and (iv) shall not apply in the case of an alien with respect to a criminal conviction if the alien subsequent to the criminal conviction has been granted a full and unconditional pardon by the President of the United States or by the Governor of any of the several States.

(B) *Controlled substances.*—

(i) Conviction.— Any alien who at any time after admission has been convicted of a violation of (or a conspiracy or attempt to violate) any law or regulation of a State, the United States, or a foreign country relating to a controlled substance (as defined in section 102 of the Controlled Substances Act (21 U.S.C. 802)), other than a single offense involving possession for one's own use of 30 grams or less of marijuana, is deportable.

(ii) Drug abusers and addicts.— Any alien who is, or at any time after admission has been, a drug abuser or addict is deportable.

(C) *Certain firearm offenses.*— Any alien who at any time after admission is convicted under any law of purchasing, selling, offering for sale, exchanging, using, owning, possessing, or carrying, or of attempting or conspiring to purchase, sell, offer for sale, exchange, use, own, possess, or carry, any weapon, part, or accessory which is a firearm or destructive device (as defined in section 921(a) of title 18, United States Code) in violation of any law is deportable.

(D) *Miscellaneous crimes.*— Any alien who at any time has been convicted (the judgment on such conviction becoming final) of, or has been so convicted of a conspiracy or attempt to violate—

(i) any offense under chapter 37 (relating to espionage), chapter 105 (relating to sabotage), or chapter 115 (relating to treason and sedition) of title 18, United States Code, for which a term of imprisonment of five or more years may be imposed;

(ii) any offense under section 871 or 960 of title 18, United States Code;

(iii) a violation of any provision of the Military Selective Service Act (50 U.S.C. App. 451 *et seq.*) or the Trading With the Enemy Act (50 U.S.C. App. 1 *et seq.*); or

(iv) a violation of section 215 or 278 of this Act,

is deportable.

(E) *Crimes of Domestic violence, stalking, or violation of protection order, crimes against children and—*

(i) Domestic violence, stalking, and child abuse.— Any alien who at any time after admission is convicted of a crime of domestic violence, a crime of stalking, or a crime of child abuse, child neglect, or child abandonment is deportable. For purposes of this clause, the term "crime of domestic violence" means any crime of violence (as defined in section 16 of title 18, United States Code) against a person committed by a current or former spouse of the person, by an individual with whom the person shares a child in common, by an individual who is cohabiting with or has cohabited with the person as a spouse, by an individual similarly situated to a spouse of the person under the domestic or family violence laws of the jurisdiction where the offense occurs, or by any other individual against a person who is protected from that individual's acts under the domestic or family violence laws of the United States or any State, Indian tribal government, or unit of local government.

(ii) Violators of protection orders.— Any alien who at any time after entry is enjoined under a protection order issued by a court and whom the court determines has engaged in conduct that violates the portion of a protection order that involves protection against credible threats of violence, repeated harassment, or bodily injury to the person or persons for whom the protection order was issued is deportable. For purposes of this clause, the term "protection order" means any injunction issued for the purpose of preventing violent or threatening acts of domestic violence, including temporary or final orders issued by civil or criminal courts (other than support or child custody orders or provisions) whether obtained by filing an independent action or as a pendente lite order in another proceeding.

(F) *Trafficking.*— Any alien described in section 212(a)(2)(H) is deportable.

(3) ***Failure to register and falsification of documents.—***

(A) *Change of address.*— An alien who has failed to comply with the provisions of section 265 is deportable, unless the alien establishes to the satisfaction of the Attorney General that such failure was reasonably excusable or was not willful.

(B) *Failure to register or falsification of documents.*— Any alien who at any time has been convicted—

(i) under section 266(c) of this Act or under section 36(c) of the Alien Registration Act, 1940,

(ii) of a violation of, or an attempt or a conspiracy to violate, any provision of the Foreign Agents Registration Act of 1938 (22 U.S.C. 611 *et seq.*), or

(iii) of a violation of, or an attempt or a conspiracy to violate, section 1546 of title 18, United States Code (relating to fraud and misuse of visas, permits, and other entry documents),

is deportable.

(C) *Document fraud.—*

(i) In general.— An alien who is the subject of a final order for violation of section 274C is deportable.

(ii) Waiver authorized.— The Attorney General may waive clause (i) in the case of an alien lawfully admitted for permanent residence if no previous civil money penalty was imposed against the alien under section 274C and the offense was incurred solely to assist, aid, or support the alien's spouse or child (and no other individual). No court shall have jurisdiction to review a decision of the Attorney General to grant or deny a waiver under this clause.

(D) *Falsely claiming citizenship.*—

(i) In general.— Any alien who falsely represents, or has falsely represented, himself to be a citizen of the United States for any purpose or benefit under this Act (including section 274A) or any Federal or State law is deportable.

(ii) Exception.— In the case of an alien making a representation described in clause (i), if each natural parent of the alien (or, in the case of an adopted alien, each adoptive parent of the alien) is or was a citizen (whether by birth or naturalization), the alien permanently resided in the United States prior to attaining the age of 16, and the alien reasonably believed at the time of making such representation that he or she was a citizen, the alien shall not be considered to be deportable under any provision of this subsection based on such representation.

(4) *Security and related grounds.*—[132]

(A) *In general.*— Any alien who has engaged, is engaged, or at any time after admission engages in—

(i) any activity to violate any law of the United States relating to espionage or sabotage or to violate or evade any law prohibiting the export from the United States of goods, technology, or sensitive information,

(ii) any other criminal activity which endangers public safety or national security, or

(iii) any activity a purpose of which is the opposition to, or the control or overthrow of, the Government of the United States by force, violence, or other unlawful means,

is deportable.

(B)[133] *Terrorist activities.*— Any alien who is described in subparagraph (B) or (F) of section 212(a)(3) is deportable.

(C) *Foreign policy.*—

(i) In general.— An alien whose presence or activities in the United States the Secretary of State has reasonable ground to believe would have potentially serious adverse foreign policy consequences for the United States is deportable.

(ii) Exceptions.— The exceptions described in clauses (ii) and (iii) of section 212(a)(3)(C) shall apply to deportability under clause (i) in the same manner as they apply to inadmissibility under section 212(a)(3)(C)(i).

---

[132] Amended by §5501 of P.L. 108-458 (12/17/04) applicable to "offenses committed before, on, or after" 12/17/04.

[133] *See* §411(c) USA PATRIOT Act, P.L. 107-56, for "Special Rule for Aliens in Exclusion or Deportation Proceedings."

The amendment to INA §237(a)(4)(B) made by §105 of REAL ID Act, P.L. 109-13 (5/11/05), applies to (A) removal proceedings instituted before, on, or after the date of the enactment; and (B) acts and conditions consitituting a ground for inadmissibility, excludability, deportation, or removal occurring or existing before, on, or after such date.

(D) *Participated in Nazi persecution, genocide, or the commission of any act of torture or extrajudicial killing.*— Any alien described in clause (i), (ii), or (iii) of section 212(a)(3)(E) is deportable.

(E) [first][134] *Recipient of Military-Type Training.*—

(i) In general.— Any alien who has received military-type training from or on behalf of any organization that, at the time the training was received, was a terrorist organization (as defined in subclause (I) or (II) of section 212(a)(3)(B)(vi)), is deportable.

(ii) Definition.— As used in this subparagraph, the term "military-type training" includes training in means or methods that can cause death or serious bodily injury, destroy or damage property, or disrupt services to critical infrastructure, or training on the use, storage, production, or assembly of any explosive, firearm, or other weapon, including any weapon of mass destruction (as defined in section 2332a(c)(2) of title 18, United States Code).

(E) [second][135] *Participated in the commission of severe violations of religious freedom.*— Any alien described in section 212(a)(2)(G) is deportable.

(F) *Recruitment or use of child soldiers*— Any alien who has engaged in the recruitment or use of child soldiers in violation of section 2442 of title 18, United States Code, is deportable.

(5) *Public charge.*—[136] Any alien who, within five years after the date of entry, has become a public charge from causes not affirmatively shown to have arisen since entry is deportable.

(6) *Unlawful voters.*—

(A) *In general.*— Any alien who has voted in violation of any Federal, State, or local constitutional provision, statute, ordinance, or regulation is deportable.

(B) *Exception.*— In the case of an alien who voted in a Federal, State, or local election (including an initiative, recall, or referendum) in violation of a lawful restriction of voting to citizens, if each natural parent of the alien (or, in the case of an adopted alien, each adoptive parent of the alien) is or was a citizen (whether by birth or naturalization), the alien permanently resided in the United States prior to attaining the age of 16, and the alien reasonably believed at the time of such violation that he or she was a citizen, the alien shall not be considered to be deportable under any provision of this subsection based on such violation.

(7) *Waiver for victims of domestic violence.*—

(A) *In general.*— The Attorney General is not limited by the criminal court record and may waive the application of paragraph (2)(E)(i) (with respect to crimes of domestic violence and crimes of stalking) and (ii) in the case of an alien who has been battered or sub-

---

[134] Added by §5402 of P.L. 108-458 (12/17/04) and designated §237(a)(4)(E). That same public law, at §5502(b), added another provision with same §237(a)(4)(E) designation.

[135] Added by §5502(b) of P.L. 108-458 (12/17/04) and designated §237(a)(4)(E). That same public law, at §5402, added another provision with same §237(a)(4)(E) designation.

[136] Compacts between the United States and the Federated States of Micronesia (FSM) and the Republic of the Marshall Islands (RMI) provide (in Art. IV, §141(f) in each respective Compact) that, with respect to persons admitted or seeking admission under the Compacts, INA §237(a)(5) "shall be construed and applied as if it reads as follows: 'any alien who has been admitted under the Compact, or the Compact, as amended, who cannot show that he or she has sufficient means of support in the United States, is deportable.'" The Compacts were approved by P.L. 108-188 (12/17/03), §§201(a) [FSM] and (b) [RMI].

jected to extreme cruelty and who is not and was not the primary perpetrator of violence in the relationship—

(i) upon a determination that—

(I) the alien was acting is self-defense;[137]

(II) the alien was found to have violated a protection order intended to protect the alien; or

(III) the alien committed, was arrested for, was convicted of, or pled guilty to committing a crime—

(aa) that did not result in serious bodily injury; and

(bb) where there was a connection between the crime and the alien's having been battered or subjected to extreme cruelty.

(B) *Credible evidence considered.*— In acting on applications under this paragraph, the Attorney General shall consider any credible evidence relevant to the application. The determination of what evidence is credible and the weight to be given that evidence shall be within the sole discretion of the Attorney General.

**(b) Deportation of certain nonimmigrants.**— An alien, admitted as an nonimmigrant under the provisions of either section 101(a)(15)(A)(i) or 101(a)(15)(G)(i), and who fails to maintain a status under either of those provisions, shall not be required to depart from the United States without the approval of the Secretary of State, unless such alien is subject to deportation under paragraph (4) of subsection (a).

**(c) Waiver of grounds for deportation.**— Paragraphs (1)(A), (1)(B), (1)(C), (1)(D), and (3)(A) of subsection (a) (other than so much of paragraph (1) as relates to a ground of inadmissibility described in paragraph (2) or (3) of section 212(a)) shall not apply to a special immigrant described in section 101(a)(27)(J) based upon circumstances that existed before the date the alien was provided such special immigrant status.

(d) (1) If the Secretary of Homeland Security determines that an application for nonimmigrant status under subparagraph (T) or (U) of section 101(a)(15) filed for an alien in the United States sets forth a prima facie case for approval, the Secretary may grant the alien an administrative stay of a final order of removal under section 241(c)(2) until—

(A) the application for nonimmigrant status under such subparagraph (T) or (U) is approved; or

(B) there is a final administrative denial of the application for such nonimmigrant status after the exhaustion of administrative appeals.

(2) The denial of a request for an administrative stay of removal under this subsection shall not preclude the alien from applying for a stay of removal, deferred action, or a continuance or abeyance of removal proceedings under any other provision of the immigration laws of the United States.

(3) During any period in which the administrative stay of removal is in effect, the alien shall not be removed.

(4) Nothing in this subsection may be construed to limit the authority of the Secretary of

---

[137] *Sic.* Probably should be "acting in self-defense;".

Homeland Security or the Attorney General to grant a stay of removal or deportation in any case not described in this subsection.

(June 27, 1952, ch. 477, title II, ch. 5, §241, 66 Stat. 204; July 18, 1956, ch. 629, title III, §301(b), (c), 70 Stat. 575; as amended by P.L. 86-648 (7/14/60); P.L. 87-301 (9/26/61); P.L. 89-236 (10/3/65); P.L. 94-571 (10/20/76); P.L. 95-549 (10/30/78); P.L. 97-116 (12/29/81); P.L. 99-570 (10/27/86); P.L. 99-603 (IRCA) (11/6/86); P.L. 99-639 (11/10/86); P.L. 99-653 (11/14/86); P.L. 100-525 (10/24/88); P.L. 100-690 (11/18/88); P.L. 101-649 (IMMACT90) (11/29/90); P.L. 102-232 (MTINA) (12/12/91, *effective* 4/1/92) [repealing (d)]; P.L. 103-322 (VAWA) (9/13/94); P.L. 103-416 (INTCA) (10/25/94, *effective* 4/1/95); P.L. 104-132 (AEDPA) (4/24/96), title IV, §414(a), §435(a) [adding (d) which read: "(d) Notwithstanding any other provision of this title, an alien found in the United States who has not been admitted to the United States after inspection in accordance with section 235 is deemed for purposes of this Act to be seeking entry and admission to the United States and shall be subject to examination and exclusion by the Attorney General under chapter 4. In the case of such an alien the Attorney General shall provide by regulation an opportunity for the alien to establish that the alien was so admitted."]; P.L. 104-208 (IIRAIRA) (9/30/96), div. C, title I, §108(c), title III, §301(d), §305(a)(2) [redesignating §241 as §237], §308(d)(2) [revising (a)(2)(E); repealing (d) before §241 is redesignated as §237; repealing §422 of AEDPA effective as of the date of enactment of AEDPA], §344(b) [adding (a)(3)(D)], §345(b), §347(b) [adding (a)(6)(B)], §350(a) [adding (a)(2)(E)], §351(b), title VI, §671(a)(4)(B) [revising (a)(1)(E)(iii); repealing (a)(1)(F)]; P.L. 106-386 (10/28/00), div. B, title V, §1505(b)(1) [revising (a)(1)(H); adding (a)(7)]; P.L. 106-395 (CCA) (10/30/00, *effective* 2/27/01), title II, §201(c)(1) [revising (a)(3)(D) & (a)(6)]; P.L. 107-56 (PATRIOT Act) (10/26/01), title IV, §411(b)(1) [revising (a)(4)(B)]; P.L. 108-458 (12/17/04), title V, §5304(b) [revising (a)(1)(B)], §5402 [adding *two* subparagraphs (a)(4)(E)], §5501(b) [revising (a)(4)(D)], §5502(b) [adding *two* subparagraphs (a)(4)(E)]; P.L. 109-13 (REAL ID) (5/11/05), div. B, title I, §105(a)(1) [revising (a)(4)(B)]; P.L. 109-248 (7/27/06), §401 [redesignating (a)(2)(A)(v) as (a)(2)(A)(vi) & adding new (a)(2)(A)(v)]; P.L. 109-271 (8/12/06), §6 [revising (a)(1)(H)(ii)]; P.L. 110-340 (10/3/08) [adding (a)(4)(F)]; P.L. 110-457 (12/23/08) [adding (d)(1)–(4)].)

## Sec. 238 Expedited Removal of Aliens Convicted of Committing Aggravated Felonies [8 U.S.C. 1228]

### (a) Removal of criminal aliens.—

(1) *In general.*— The Attorney General shall provide for the availability of special removal proceedings at certain Federal, State, and local correctional facilities for aliens convicted of any criminal offense covered in section 237(a)(2)(A)(iii), (B), (C), or (D), or any offense covered by section 237(a)(2)(A)(ii) for which both predicate offenses are, without regard to the date of their commission, otherwise covered by section 237(a)(2)(A)(i). Such proceedings shall be conducted in conformity with section 240 (except as otherwise provided in this section), and in a manner which eliminates the need for additional detention at any processing center of the Service and in a manner which assures expeditious removal following the end of the alien's incarceration for the underlying sentence. Nothing in this section shall be construed to create any substantive or procedural right or benefit that is legally enforceable by any party against the United States or its agencies or officers or any other person.

(2) *Implementation.*— With respect to an alien convicted of an aggravated felony who is taken into custody by the Attorney General pursuant to section 236(c), the Attorney General shall, to the maximum extent practicable, detain any such felon at a facility at which other such aliens are detained. In the selection of such facility, the Attorney General shall make reasonable efforts to ensure that the alien's access to counsel and right to counsel under section 292 are not impaired.

(3) *Expedited proceedings.*—

(A) Notwithstanding any other provision of law, the Attorney General shall provide for the initiation and, to the extent possible, the completion of removal proceedings, and any administrative appeals thereof, in the case of any alien convicted of an aggravated felony before the alien's release from incarceration for the underlying aggravated felony.

(B) Nothing in this section shall be construed as requiring the Attorney General to effect the removal of any alien sentenced to actual incarceration, before release from the penitentiary or correctional institution where such alien is confined.

(4) *Review.—*

(A) The Attorney General shall review and evaluate removal proceedings conducted under this section.

(B) The Comptroller General shall monitor, review, and evaluate removal proceedings conducted under this section. Within 18 months after the effective date of this section, the Comptroller General shall submit a report to such Committees concerning the extent to which removal proceedings conducted under this section may adversely affect the ability of such aliens to contest removal effectively.

**(b) Removal of aliens who are not permanent residents.—**

(1) The Attorney General may, in the case of an alien described in paragraph (2), determine the deportability of such alien under section 237(a)(2)(A)(iii) (relating to conviction of an aggravated felony) and issue an order of removal pursuant to the procedures set forth in this subsection or section 240.

(2) An alien is described in this paragraph if the alien—

(A) was not lawfully admitted for permanent residence at the time at which proceedings under this section commenced; or

(B) had permanent resident status on a conditional basis (as described in section 216) at the time that proceedings under this section commenced.

(3) The Attorney General may not execute any order described in paragraph (1) until 14 calendar days have passed from the date that such order was issued, unless waived by the alien, in order that the alien has an opportunity to apply for judicial review under section 242.

(4) Proceedings before the Attorney General under this subsection shall be in accordance with such regulations as the Attorney General shall prescribe. The Attorney General shall provide that—

(A) the alien is given reasonable notice of the charges and of the opportunity described in subparagraph (C);

(B) the alien shall have the privilege of being represented (at no expense to the government) by such counsel, authorized to practice in such proceedings, as the alien shall choose;

(C) the alien has a reasonable opportunity to inspect the evidence and rebut the charges;

(D) a determination is made for the record that the individual upon whom the notice for the proceeding under this section is served (either in person or by mail) is, in fact, the alien named in such notice;[138]

(E) a record is maintained for judicial review; and

(F) the final order of removal is not adjudicated by the same person who issues the charges.

---

[138] *See* §304(c) of IIRAIRA. Changes are effective "as if included in the enactment of §442(a) of Public Law 104-132" [AEDPA].

(5) No alien described in this section shall be eligible for any relief from removal that the Attorney General may grant in the Attorney General's discretion.

**(c) [first]**[139] **Presumption of deportability.**— An alien convicted of an aggravated felony shall be conclusively presumed to be deportable from the United States.

**(c) [second]**[140] **Judicial removal.**—

(1) *Authority.*— Notwithstanding any other provision of this Act, a United States district court shall have jurisdiction to enter a judicial order of removal at the time of sentencing against an alien who is deportable, if such an order has been requested by the United States Attorney with the concurrence of the Commissioner and if the court chooses to exercise such jurisdiction.

(2) *Procedure.*—

(A) The United States Attorney shall file with the United States district court, and serve upon the defendant and the Service, prior to commencement of the trial or entry of a guilty plea a notice of intent to request judicial removal.

(B) Notwithstanding section 242B, the United States Attorney, with the concurrence of the Commissioner, shall file at least 30 days prior to the date set for sentencing a charge containing factual allegations regarding the alienage of the defendant and identifying the crime or crimes which make the defendant deportable under section 237(a)(2)(A).

(C) If the court determines that the defendant has presented substantial evidence to establish prima facie eligibility for relief from removal under this Act, the Commissioner shall provide the court with a recommendation and report regarding the alien's eligibility for relief. The court shall either grant or deny the relief sought.

(D) (i) The alien shall have a reasonable opportunity to examine the evidence against him or her, to present evidence on his or her own behalf, and to cross-examine witnesses presented by the Government.

(ii) The court, for the purposes of determining whether to enter an order described in paragraph (1), shall only consider evidence that would be admissible in proceedings conducted pursuant to section 240.

(iii) Nothing in this subsection shall limit the information a court of the United States may receive or consider for the purposes of imposing an appropriate sentence.

(iv) The court may order the alien removed if the Attorney General demonstrates that the alien is deportable under this Act.

(3) *Notice, appeal, and execution of judicial order of removal.*—

(A) (i) A judicial order of removal or denial of such order may be appealed by either party to the court of appeals for the circuit in which the district court is located.

(ii) Except as provided in clause (iii), such appeal shall be considered consistent with the requirements described in section 242.

---

[139] Sec. 671(b)(13) of IIRAIRA redesignated the prior subsection (d), relating to judicial review, as (c). IIRAIRA §442(c), however, added a new subsection (c) (Judicial removal), thus creating two subsections 238(c)s.

[140] *See* note 139, *supra.*

(iii) Upon execution by the defendant of a valid waiver of the right to appeal the conviction on which the order of removal is based, the expiration of the period described in section 242(b)(1), or the final dismissal of an appeal from such conviction, the order of removal shall become final and shall be executed at the end of the prison term in accordance with the terms of the order. If the conviction is reversed on direct appeal, the order entered pursuant to this section shall be void.

(B) As soon as is practicable after entry of a judicial order of removal, the Commissioner shall provide the defendant with written notice of the order of removal, which shall designate the defendant's country of choice for removal and any alternate country pursuant to section 243(a).

(4) *Denial of judicial order.*— Denial of a request for a judicial order of removal shall not preclude the Attorney General from initiating removal proceedings pursuant to section 240 upon the same ground of deportability or upon any other ground of deportability provided under section 241(a).[141]

(5) *Stipulated judicial order of deportation.*— The United States Attorney, with the concurrence of the Commissioner, may, pursuant to Federal Rule of Criminal Procedure 11, enter into a plea agreement which calls for the alien, who is deportable under this Act, to waive the right to notice and a hearing under this section, and stipulate to the entry of a judicial order of deportation from the United States as a condition of the plea agreement or as a condition of probation or supervised release, or both. The United States district court, in both felony and misdemeanor cases, and a United States magistrate judge in misdemeanor cases, may accept such a stipulation and shall have jurisdiction to enter a judicial order of deportation pursuant to the terms of such stipulation.

(June 27, 1952, ch. 477, title II, ch. 5, §242A, as added by P.L. 100-690 (11/18/88); as amended by P.L. 101-649 (IMMACT90) (11/29/90); P.L. 102-232 (MTINA) (12/12/91, *effective* 4/1/92); P.L. 103-322 (VAWA) (9/13/94); P.L. 103-416 (INTCA) (10/25/94, *effective* 4/1/95); P.L. 104-132 (AEDPA) (4/24/96), title IV, §440, 442; P.L. 104-208 (IIRAIRA) (9/30/96), div. C, title III, §304(c)(1) [adding (b)(4)(D)], §306(d) [revising §440(g) (among others) of AEDPA which in turn amends this section as shown. This amendment is effective "as if included in the enactment of [AEDPA]."], §308(b)(5) [redesignating original §242A as new §238; changing references to §241 to §237], §374(a) [revising second (c)], title VI, §442(c) [adding a new (c)], §671(b)(13) [redesignating (d) as (c), thus creating *two* §238(c).].)

## Sec. 239 Initiation of Removal Proceedings[142]
[8 U.S.C. 1229]

(a) Notice to appear.—

(1) *In general.*— In removal proceedings under section 240, written notice (in this section referred to as a "notice to appear") shall be given in person to the alien (or, if personal service is not practicable, through service by mail to the alien or to the alien's counsel of record, if any) specifying the following:

(A) The nature of the proceedings against the alien.

(B) The legal authority under which the proceedings are conducted.

(C) The acts or conduct alleged to be in violation of law.

---

[141] Amendment striking language "without a decision on the merits" was made effective "as if included in the enactment of §224(a) of the Immigration and Nationality Technical Corrections Act of 1994." IIRAIRA §374(d).

[142] *See* note 55, supra.

(D) The charges against the alien and the statutory provisions alleged to have been violated.

(E) The alien may be represented by counsel and the alien will be provided

(i) a period of time to secure counsel under subsection (b)(1) and

(ii) a current list of counsel prepared under subsection (b)(2).

(F) (i) The requirement that the alien must immediately provide (or have provided) the Attorney General with a written record of an address and telephone number (if any) at which the alien may be contacted respecting proceedings under section 240.

(ii) The requirement that the alien must provide the Attorney General immediately with a written record of any change of the alien's address or telephone number.

(iii) The consequences under section 240(b)(5) of failure to provide address and telephone information pursuant to this subparagraph.

(G) (i) The time and place at which the proceedings will be held.

(ii) The consequences under section 240(b)(5) of the failure, except under exceptional circumstances, to appear at such proceedings.

(2) *Notice of change in time or place of proceedings.*—

(A) *In general.*— In removal proceedings under section 240, in the case of any change or postponement in the time and place of such proceedings, subject to subparagraph (B) a written notice shall be given in person to the alien (or, if personal service is not practicable, through service by mail to the alien or to the alien's counsel of record, if any) specifying—

(i) the new time or place of the proceedings, and

(ii) the consequences under section 240(b)(5) of failing, except under exceptional circumstances, to attend such proceedings.

(B) *Exception.*— In the case of an alien not in detention, a written notice shall not be required under this paragraph if the alien has failed to provide the address required under paragraph (1)(F).

(3) *Central address files.*— The Attorney General shall create a system to record and preserve on a timely basis notices of addresses and telephone numbers (and changes) provided under paragraph (1)(F).

**(b) Securing of counsel.—**

(1) *In general.*— In order that an alien be permitted the opportunity to secure counsel before the first hearing date in proceedings under section 240, the hearing date shall not be scheduled earlier than 10 days after the service of the notice to appear, unless the alien requests in writing an earlier hearing date.

(2) *Current lists of counsel.*— The Attorney General shall provide for lists (updated not less often than quarterly) of persons who have indicated their availability to represent pro bono aliens in proceedings under section 240. Such lists shall be provided under subsection (a)(1)(E) and otherwise made generally available.

(3) *Rule of construction.*— Nothing in this subsection may be construed to prevent the Attorney General from proceeding against an alien pursuant to section 240 if the time period described in paragraph (1) has elapsed and the alien has failed to secure counsel.

**(c) Service by mail.**— Service by mail under this section shall be sufficient if there is proof of attempted delivery to the last address provided by the alien in accordance with subsection (a)(1)(F).

**(d) Prompt initiation of removal.**—

(1) In the case of an alien who is convicted of an offense which makes the alien deportable, the Attorney General shall begin any removal proceeding as expeditiously as possible after the date of the conviction.

(2) Nothing in this subsection shall be construed to create any substantive or procedural right or benefit that is legally enforceable by any party against the United States or its agencies or officers or any other person.

**(e) Certification of compliance with restrictions on disclosure.**—[143]

(1) *In general.*— In cases where an enforcement action leading to a removal proceeding was taken against an alien at any of the locations specified in paragraph (2), the Notice to Appear shall include a statement that the provisions of section 384 of the Illegal Immigration Reform and Immigrant Responsibility Act of 1996 (8 U.S.C. 1367) have been complied with.

(2) *Locations.*— The locations specified in this paragraph are as follows:

(A) At a domestic violence shelter, a rape crisis center, supervised visitation center, family justice center, a victim services, or victim services provider, or a community-based organization.

(B) At a courthouse (or in connection with that appearance of the alien at a courthouse) if the alien is appearing in connection with a protection order case, child custody case, or other civil or criminal case relating to domestic violence, sexual assault, trafficking, or stalking in which the alien has been battered or subject to extreme cruelty or if the alien is described in subparagraph (T) or (U) of section 101(a)(15).

(June 27, 1952, ch. 477, title II, ch. 4, §239, as added by P.L. 104-208 (IIRAIRA) (9/30/96), div. C, title III, §304 [redesignating §239 as §234]; P.L. 109-162 (1/5/06, *effective* 2/4/06), §825 [adding (e)]; P.L. 109-271 (8/12/06), §6 [revising (e)(2)(B)].)

## Sec. 240 Removal Proceedings[144]
[8 U.S.C. 1229a]

**(a) Proceeding.**—

(1) *In general.*— An immigration judge shall conduct proceedings for deciding the inadmissibility or deportability of an alien.

(2) *Charges.*— An alien placed in proceedings under this section may be charged with any applicable ground of inadmissibility under section 212(a) or any applicable ground of deportability under section 237(a).

(3) *Exclusive procedures.*— Unless otherwise specified in this Act, a proceeding under this section shall be the sole and exclusive procedure for determining whether an alien may be admitted to the United States or, if the alien has been so admitted, removed from the United States. Nothing in this section shall affect proceedings conducted pursuant to section 238.

---

[143] Sec. 825(c) of P.L. 109-162 (1/5/06), which added INA §239(e), took effect 30 days after the date of enactment, *i.e.,* on Feb. 4, 2006. The amendment "shall apply to apprehensions occurring on or after such date."

[144] *See* note 55, *supra.*

## (b) Conduct of proceeding.—

(1) *Authority of immigration judge.*— The immigration judge shall administer oaths, receive evidence, and interrogate, examine, and cross-examine the alien and any witnesses. The immigration judge may issue subpoenas for the attendance of witnesses and presentation of evidence. The immigration judge shall have authority (under regulations prescribed by the Attorney General) to sanction by civil money penalty any action (or inaction) in contempt of the judge's proper exercise of authority under this Act.

(2) *Form of proceeding.*—

(A) *In general.*— The proceeding may take place—

(i) in person,

(ii) where agreed to by the parties, in the absence of the alien,

(iii) through video conference, or

(iv) subject to subparagraph (B), through telephone conference.

(B) *Consent required in certain cases.*— An evidentiary hearing on the merits may only be conducted through a telephone conference with the consent of the alien involved after the alien has been advised of the right to proceed in person or through video conference.

(3) *Presence of alien.*— If it is impracticable by reason of an alien's mental incompetency for the alien to be present at the proceeding, the Attorney General shall prescribe safeguards to protect the rights and privileges of the alien.

(4) *Aliens rights in proceeding.*— In proceedings under this section, under regulations of the Attorney General—

(A) the alien shall have the privilege of being represented, at no expense to the Government, by counsel of the alien's choosing who is authorized to practice in such proceedings,

(B) the alien shall have a reasonable opportunity to examine the evidence against the alien, to present evidence on the alien's own behalf, and to cross-examine witnesses presented by the Government but these rights shall not entitle the alien to examine such national security information as the Government may proffer in opposition to the alien's admission to the United States or to an application by the alien for discretionary relief under this Act, and

(C) a complete record shall be kept of all testimony and evidence produced at the proceeding.

(5) *Consequences of failure to appear.*—

(A) *In general.*— Any alien who, after written notice required under paragraph (1) or (2) of section 239(a) has been provided to the alien or the alien's counsel of record, does not attend a proceeding under this section, shall be ordered removed in absentia if the Service establishes by clear, unequivocal, and convincing evidence that the written notice was so provided and that the alien is removable (as defined in subsection (e)(2)). The written notice by the Attorney General shall be considered sufficient for purposes of this subparagraph if provided at the most recent address provided under section 239(a)(1)(F).

(B) *No notice if failure to provide address information.*— No written notice shall be required under subparagraph (A) if the alien has failed to provide the address required under section 239(a)(1)(F).

(C) *Rescission of order.*— Such an order may be rescinded only—

(i) upon a motion to reopen filed within 180 days after the date of the order of removal if the alien demonstrates that the failure to appear was because of exceptional circumstances (as defined in subsection (e)(1)), or

(ii) upon a motion to reopen filed at any time if the alien demonstrates that the alien did not receive notice in accordance with paragraph (1) or (2) of section 239(a) or the alien demonstrates that the alien was in Federal or State custody and the failure to appear was through no fault of the alien.

The filing of the motion to reopen described in clause (i) or (ii) shall stay the removal of the alien pending disposition of the motion by the immigration judge.

(D) *Effect on judicial review.*— Any petition for review under section 242 of an order entered in absentia under this paragraph shall (except in cases described in section 242(b)(5)) be confined to

(i) the validity of the notice provided to the alien,

(ii) the reasons for the alien's not attending the proceeding, and

(iii) whether or not the alien is removable.

(E) *Additional application to certain aliens in contiguous territory.*— The preceding provisions of this paragraph shall apply to all aliens placed in proceedings under this section, including any alien who remains in a contiguous foreign territory pursuant to section 235(b)(2)(C).

(6) **Treatment of frivolous behavior.**— The Attorney General shall, by regulation—

(A) define in a proceeding before an immigration judge or before an appellate administrative body under this title, frivolous behavior for which attorneys may be sanctioned,

(B) specify the circumstances under which an administrative appeal of a decision or ruling will be considered frivolous and will be summarily dismissed, and

(C) impose appropriate sanctions (which may include suspension and disbarment) in the case of frivolous behavior.

Nothing in this paragraph shall be construed as limiting the authority of the Attorney General to take actions with respect to inappropriate behavior.

(7) **Limitation on discretionary relief for failure to appear.**— Any alien against whom a final order of removal is entered in absentia under this subsection and who, at the time of the notice described in paragraph (1) or (2) of section 239(a), was provided oral notice, either in the alien's native language or in another language the alien understands, of the time and place of the proceedings and of the consequences under this paragraph of failing, other than because of exceptional circumstances (as defined in subsection (e)(1)) to attend a proceeding under this section, shall not be eligible for relief under section 240A, 240B, 245, 248, or 249 for a period of 10 years after the date of the entry of the final order of removal.

**(c) Decision and burden of proof.—**

(1) *Decision.—*

(A) *In general.*— At the conclusion of the proceeding the immigration judge shall decide whether an alien is removable from the United States. The determination of the immigration judge shall be based only on the evidence produced at the hearing.

(B) *Certain medical decisions.*— If a medical officer or civil surgeon or board of medical officers has certified under section 232(b) that an alien has a disease, illness, or addiction which would make the alien inadmissible under paragraph (1) of section 212(a), the decision of the immigration judge shall be based solely upon such certification.

(2) *Burden on alien.*— In the proceeding the alien has the burden of establishing—

(A) if the alien is an applicant for admission, that the alien is clearly and beyond doubt entitled to be admitted and is not inadmissible under section 212; or

(B) by clear and convincing evidence, that the alien is lawfully present in the United States pursuant to a prior admission.

In meeting the burden of proof under subparagraph (B), the alien shall have access to the alien's visa or other entry document, if any, and any other records and documents, not considered by the Attorney General to be confidential, pertaining to the alien's admission or presence in the United States.

(3) *Burden on service in cases of deportable aliens.*—

(A) *In general.*— In the proceeding the Service has the burden of establishing by clear and convincing evidence that, in the case of an alien who has been admitted to the United States, the alien is deportable. No decision on deportability shall be valid unless it is based upon reasonable, substantial, and probative evidence.

(B) *Proof of convictions.*— In any proceeding under this Act, any of the following documents or records (or a certified copy of such an official document or record) shall constitute proof of a criminal conviction:

(i) An official record of judgment and conviction.

(ii) An official record of plea, verdict, and sentence.

(iii) A docket entry from court records that indicates the existence of the conviction.

(iv) Official minutes of a court proceeding or a transcript of a court hearing in which the court takes notice of the existence of the conviction.

(v) An abstract of a record of conviction prepared by the court in which the conviction was entered, or by a State official associated with the State's repository of criminal justice records, that indicates the charge or section of law violated, the disposition of the case, the existence and date of conviction, and the sentence.

(vi) Any document or record prepared by, or under the direction of, the court in which the conviction was entered that indicates the existence of a conviction.

(vii) Any document or record attesting to the conviction that is maintained by an official of a State or Federal penal institution, which is the basis for that institution's authority to assume custody of the individual named in the record.

(C) *Electronic records.*— In any proceeding under this Act, any record of conviction or abstract that has been submitted by electronic means to the Service from a State or court shall be admissible as evidence to prove a criminal conviction if it is—

(i) certified by a State official associated with the State's repository of criminal justice records as an official record from its repository or by a court official from the court in which the conviction was entered as an official record from its repository, and

(ii) certified in writing by a Service official as having been received electronically from the State's record repository or the court's record repository.

A certification under clause (i) may be by means of a computer-generated signature and statement of authenticity.

(4) *Applications for relief from removal.*—[145]

(A) *In general.*— An alien applying for relief or protection from removal has the burden of proof to establish that the alien—

(i) satisfies the applicable eligibility requirements; and

(ii) with respect to any form of relief that is granted in the exercise of discretion, that the alien merits a favorable exercise of discretion.

(B) *Sustaining burden.*— The applicant must comply with the applicable requirements to submit information or documentation in support of the applicant's application for relief or protection as provided by law or by regulation or in the instructions for the application form. In evaluating the testimony of the applicant or other witness in support of the application, the immigration judge will determine whether or not the testimony is credible, is persuasive, and refers to specific facts sufficient to demonstrate that the applicant has satisfied the applicant's burden of proof. In determining whether the applicant has met such burden, the immigration judge shall weigh the credible testimony along with other evidence of record. Where the immigration judge determines that the applicant should provide evidence which corroborates otherwise credible testimony, such evidence must be provided unless the applicant demonstrates that the applicant does not have the evidence and cannot reasonably obtain the evidence.

(C) *Credibility determination.*— Considering the totality of the circumstances, and all relevant factors, the immigration judge may base a credibility determination on the demeanor, candor, or responsiveness of the applicant or witness, the inherent plausibility of the applicant's or witness's account, the consistency between the applicant's or witness's written and oral statements (whenever made and whether or not under oath, and considering the circumstances under which the statements were made), the internal consistency of each such statement, the consistency of such statements with other evidence of record (including the reports of the Department of State on country conditions), and any inaccuracies or falsehoods in such statements, without regard to whether an inconsistency, inaccuracy, or falsehood goes to the heart of the applicant's claim, or any other relevant factor. There is no presumption of credibility, however, if no adverse credibility determination is explicitly made, the applicant or witness shall have a rebuttable presumption of credibility on appeal.

(5) *Notice.*— If the immigration judge decides that the alien is removable and orders the alien to be removed, the judge shall inform the alien of the right to appeal that decision and of the

---

[145] The amendment made to INA §240(c) by §101(d) of REAL ID Act, P.L. 109-13 [redesignating (4)–(6) as (5)–(7) and adding a new (4)] took effect on the date of enactment (5/11/05) and applies to applications for asylum, withholding, or other relief from removal made on or after such date.

consequences for failure to depart under the order of removal, including civil and criminal penalties.

(6) *Motions to reconsider.*—

(A) *In general.*— The alien may file one motion to reconsider a decision that the alien is removable from the United States.

(B) *Deadline.*— The motion must be filed within 30 days of the date of entry of a final administrative order of removal.

(C) *Contents.*— The motion shall specify the errors of law or fact in the previous order and shall be supported by pertinent authority.

(7) *Motions to reopen.*—

(A) *In general.*— An alien may file one motion to reopen proceedings under this section, except that this limitation shall not apply so as to prevent the filing of one motion to reopen described in subparagraph (C)(iv).

(B) *Contents.*— The motion to reopen shall state the new facts that will be proven at a hearing to be held if the motion is granted, and shall be supported by affidavits or other evidentiary material.

(C) *Deadline.*—

(i) In general.— Except as provided in this subparagraph, the motion to reopen shall be filed within 90 days of the date of entry of a final administrative order of removal.

(ii) Asylum.— There is no time limit on the filing of a motion to reopen if the basis of the motion is to apply for relief under sections 208 or 241(b)(3) and is based on changed country conditions arising in the country of nationality or the country to which removal has been ordered, if such evidence is material and was not available and would not have been discovered or presented at the previous proceeding.

(iii) Failure to appear.— The filing of a motion to reopen an order entered pursuant to subsection (b)(5) is subject to the deadline specified in subparagraph (C) of such subsection.

(iv) Special rule for battered spouses, children, and parents.— Any limitation under this section on the deadlines for filing such motions shall not apply—

(I) if the basis for the motion is to apply for relief under clause (iii) or (iv) of section 204(a)(1)(A), clause (ii) or (iii) of section 204(a)(1)(B), section 240A(b)(2), or section 244(a)(3) (as in effect on March 31, 1997),

(II) if the motion is accompanied by a cancellation of removal application to be filed with the Attorney General or by a copy of the self-petition that has been or will be filed with the Immigration and Naturalization Service upon the granting of the motion to reopen;

(III) if the motion to reopen is filed within 1 year of the entry of the final order of removal, except that the Attorney General may, in the Attorney General's discretion, waive this time limitation in the case of an alien who demonstrates extraordinary circumstances or extreme hardship to the alien's child; and

(IV) if the alien is physically present in the United States at the time of filing the motion.

The filing of a motion to reopen under this clause shall only stay the removal of a qualified alien (as defined in section 431(c)(1)(B) of the Personal Responsibility and Work Opportunity Reconciliation Act of 1996 (8 U.S.C. 1641(c)(1)(B)) pending the final disposition of the motion, including exhaustion of all appeals if the motion establishes that the alien is a qualified alien.

**(d) Stipulated removal.**— The Attorney General shall provide by regulation for the entry by an immigration judge of an order of removal stipulated to by the alien (or the alien's representative) and the Service. A stipulated order shall constitute a conclusive determination of the alien's removability from the United States.

**(e) Definitions.**— In this section and section 240A:

(1) *Exceptional circumstances.*— The term "exceptional circumstances" refers to exceptional circumstances (such as battery or extreme cruelty to the alien or any child or parent of the alien, serious illness of the alien, or serious illness or death of the spouse, child, or parent of the alien, but not including less compelling circumstances) beyond the control of the alien.[146]

(2) *Removable.*— The term "removable" means—

(A) in the case of an alien not admitted to the United States, that the alien is inadmissible under section 212, or

(B) in the case of an alien admitted to the United States, that the alien is deportable under section 237.

(June 27, 1952, ch. 477, title II, ch. 4, §240, as amended by P.L. 104-208 (IIRAIRA) (9/30/96), div. C, title III, §304(a)(3) [redesignating original §240 as §240C; adding new §240]; P.L. 106-386 (10/28/00), div. B, title V, §1506(c)(1)(A) [revising (c)]; P.L. 109-13 (REAL ID) (5/11/05), div. B, title I, §101(d) [redesignating (c)(4)–(6) as (c)(5)–(7); & adding new (c)(4)]; P.L. 109-162 (1/5/06), §§813 & 825 [revising (c)(7)(A), (c)(7)(C), (e)(1)].)

## Sec. 240A Cancellation of Removal; Adjustment of Status[147]
## [8 U.S.C. 1229b]

**(a) Cancellation of removal for certain permanent residents.**— The Attorney General may cancel removal in the case of an alien who is inadmissible or deportable from the United States if the alien—

(1) has been an alien lawfully admitted for permanent residence for not less than 5 years,

(2) has resided in the United States continuously for 7 years after having been admitted in any status, and

(3) has not been convicted of any aggravated felony.

**(b) Cancellation of removal and adjustment of status for certain nonpermanent residents.**—

(1) *In general.*— The Attorney General may cancel removal of, and adjust to the status of an alien lawfully admitted for permanent residence, an alien who is inadmissible or deportable from the United States if the alien—

(A) has been physically present in the United States for a continuous period of not less than 10 years immediately preceding the date of such application;

(B) has been a person of good moral character during such period;

---

[146] Amendment to INA §240(e)(1) made by P.L. 109-162 (1/5/06) (adding "battery or extreme cruelty to the alien or any child or parent of the alien") applies to a failure to appear that occurs "before, on, or after the date of the enactment of this Act [1/5/06]."

[147] *See* note 55, *supra.*

(C) has not been convicted of an offense under section 212(a)(2), 237(a)(2), or 237(a)(3), subject to paragraph (5); and

(D) establishes that removal would result in exceptional and extremely unusual hardship to the alien's spouse, parent, or child, who is a citizen of the United States or an alien lawfully admitted for permanent residence.

(2)[148] *Special rule for battered spouse or child.*—

(A) *Authority.*— The Attorney General may cancel removal of, and adjust to the status of an alien lawfully admitted for permanent residence, an alien who is inadmissible or deportable from the United States if the alien demonstrates that—

(i) (I) the alien has been battered or subjected to extreme cruelty by a spouse or parent who is or was a United States citizen (or is the parent of a child of a United States citizen and the child has been battered or subjected to extreme cruelty by such citizen parent);

(II) the alien has been battered or subjected to extreme cruelty by a spouse or parent who is or was a lawful permanent resident (or is the parent of a child of an alien who is or was a lawful permanent resident and the child has been battered or subjected to extreme cruelty by such permanent resident parent); or

(III) the alien has been battered or subjected to extreme cruelty by a United States citizen or lawful permanent resident whom the alien intended to marry, but whose marriage is not legitimate because of that United States citizen's or lawful permanent resident's bigamy;

(ii) the alien has been physically present in the United States for a continuous period of not less than 3 years immediately preceding the date of such application, and the issuance of a charging document for removal proceedings shall not toll the 3-year period of continuous physical presence in the United States;

(iii) the alien has been a person of good moral character during such period, subject to the provisions of subparagraph (C);

(iv) the alien is not inadmissible under paragraph (2) or (3) of section 212(a), is not deportable under paragraphs (1)(G) or (2) through (4) of section 237(a), subject to paragraph (5), and has not been convicted of an aggravated felony; and

(v) the removal would result in extreme hardship to the alien, the alien's child, or the alien's parent.

(B) *Physical presence.*— Notwithstanding subsection (d)(2), for purposes of subparagraph (A)(ii) or for purposes of section 244(a)(3) (as in effect before the title III-A effective date in section 309 of the Illegal Immigration Reform and Immigrant Re-

---

[148] Sec. 813(b) of P.L. 109-162 (1/5/06) provides as follows:

Discretion to Consent to an Alien's Reapplication for Admission.—

(1) In general.—The Secretary of Homeland Security, the Attorney General, and the Secretary of State shall continue to have discretion to consent to an alien's reapplication for admission after a previous order of removal, deportation, or exclusion.

(2) Sense of Congress.—It is the sense of Congress that the officials described in paragraph (1) should particularly consider exercising this authority in cases under the Violence Against Women Act of 1994, cases involving nonimmigrants described in subparagraph (T) or (U) of §101(a)(15) of the Immigration and Nationality Act (8 U.S.C. 1101(a)(15)), and relief under §240A(b)(2) or 244(a)(3) of such Act (as in effect on March 31, 1997) pursuant to regulations under §212.2 of title 8, Code of Federal Regulations.

sponsibility Act of 1996), an alien shall not be considered to have failed to maintain continuous physical presence by reason of an absence if the alien demonstrates a connection between the absence and the battering or extreme cruelty perpetrated against the alien. No absence or portion of an absence connected to the battering or extreme cruelty shall count toward the 90-day or 180-day limits established in subsection (d)(2). If any absence or aggregate absences exceed 180 days, the absences or portions of the absences will not be considered to break the period of continuous presence. Any such period of time excluded from the 180-day limit shall be excluded in computing the time during which the alien has been physically present for purposes of the 3-year requirement set forth in this subparagraph, subparagraph (A)(ii), and section 244(a)(3) (as in effect before the title III-A effective date in section 309 of the Illegal Immigration Reform and Immigrant Responsibility Act of 1996).

(C) *Good moral character.*— Notwithstanding section 101(f), an act or conviction that does not bar the Attorney General from granting relief under this paragraph by reason of subparagraph (A)(iv) shall not bar the Attorney General from finding the alien to be of good moral character under subparagraph (A)(iii) or section 244(a)(3) (as in effect before the title III-A effective date in section 309 of the Illegal Immigration Reform and Immigrant Responsibility Act of 1996), if the Attorney General finds that the act or conviction was connected to the alien's having been battered or subjected to extreme cruelty and determines that a waiver is otherwise warranted.

(D) *Credible evidence considered.*— In acting on applications under this paragraph, the Attorney General shall consider any credible evidence relevant to the application. The determination of what evidence is credible and the weight to be given that evidence shall be within the sole discretion of the Attorney General.

(3) **Recordation of date.**— With respect to aliens who the Attorney General adjusts to the status of an alien lawfully admitted for permanent residence under paragraph (1) or (2), the Attorney General shall record the alien's lawful admission for permanent residence as of the date of the Attorney General's cancellation of removal under paragraph (1) or (2).

(4) **Children of battered aliens and parents of battered alien children.**—

(A) *In general.*— The Attorney General shall grant parole under section 212(d)(5) to any alien who is a—

(i) child of an alien granted relief under section 240A(b)(2) or 244(a)(3) (as in effect before the title III-A effective date in section 309 of the Illegal Immigration Reform and Immigrant Responsibility Act of 1996); or

(ii) parent of a child alien granted relief under section 240A(b)(2) or 244(a)(3) (as in effect before the title III-A effective date in section 309 of the Illegal Immigration Reform and Immigrant Responsibility Act of 1996).

(B) *Duration of parole.*— The grant of parole shall extend from the time of the grant of relief under section 240A(b)(2) or section 244(a)(3) (as in effect before the title III-A effective date in section 309 of the Illegal Immigration Reform and Immigrant Responsibility Act of 1996) to the time the application for adjustment of status filed by aliens covered under this paragraph has been finally adjudicated. Applications for adjustment of status filed by aliens covered under this paragraph shall be treated as if the applicants were VAWA self-petitioners. Failure by the alien granted relief under section 240A(b)(2) or section 244(a)(3) (as in effect before the title III-A effective date in section 309 of the

Illegal Immigration Reform and Immigrant Responsibility Act of 1996) to exercise due diligence in filing a visa petition on behalf of an alien described in clause (i) or (ii) may result in revocation of parole.

(5) *Application of domestic violence waiver authority.*— The authority provided under section 237(a)(7) may apply under paragraphs (1)(B), (1)(C), and (2)(A)(iv) in a cancellation of removal and adjustment of status proceeding.

(6) *Relatives of trafficking victims.*—

(A) *In general.*— Upon written request by a law enforcement official, the Secretary of Homeland Security may parole under section 212(d)(5) any alien who is a relative of an alien granted continued presence under section 107(c)(3)(A) of the Trafficking Victims Protection Act (22 U.S.C. 7105(c)(3)(A)), if the relative—

(i) was, on the date on which law enforcement applied for such continued presence—

(I) in the case of an alien granted continued presence who is under 21 years of age, the spouse, child, parent, or unmarried sibling under 18 years of age, of the alien; or

(II) in the case of an alien granted continued presence who is 21 years of age or older, the spouse or child of the alien; or

(ii) is a parent or sibling of the alien who the requesting law enforcement official, in consultation with the Secretary of Homeland Security, as appropriate, determines to be in present danger of retaliation as a result of the alien's escape from the severe form of trafficking or cooperation with law enforcement, irrespective of age.

(B) *Duration of parole.*—

(i) In general.— The Secretary may extend the parole granted under subparagraph (A) until the final adjudication of the application filed by the principal alien under section 101(a)(15)(T)(ii).

(ii) Other limits on duration.— If an application described in clause (i) is not filed, the parole granted under subparagraph (A) may extend until the later of—

(I) the date on which the principal alien's authority to remain in the United States under section 107(c)(3)(A) of the Trafficking Victims Protection Act (22 U.S.C. 7105(c)(3)(A)) is terminated; or

(II) the date on which a civil action filed by the principal alien under section 1595 of title 18, United States Code, is concluded.

(iii) Due diligence.— Failure by the principal alien to exercise due diligence in filing a visa petition on behalf of an alien described in clause (i) or (ii) of subparagraph (A), or in pursuing the civil action described in clause (ii)(II) (as determined by the Secretary of Homeland Security in consultation with the Attorney General), may result in revocation of parole.

(C) *Other limitations.*— A relative may not be granted parole under this paragraph if—

(i) the Secretary of Homeland Security or the Attorney General has reason to believe that the relative was knowingly complicit in the trafficking of an alien permitted to remain in the United States under section 107(c)(3)(A) of the Trafficking Victims Protection Act (22 U.S.C. 7105(c)(3)(A)); or

(ii) the relative is an alien described in paragraph (2) or (3) of section 212(a) or paragraph (2) or (4) of section 237(a).

**(c) Aliens ineligible for relief.**— The provisions of subsections (a) and (b)(1) shall not apply to any of the following aliens:

(1) An alien who entered the United States as a crewman subsequent to June 30, 1964.

(2) An alien who was admitted to the United States as a nonimmigrant exchange alien as defined in section 101(a)(15)(J), or has acquired the status of such a nonimmigrant exchange alien after admission, in order to receive graduate medical education or training, regardless of whether or not the alien is subject to or has fulfilled the two-year foreign residence requirement of section 212(e).

(3) An alien who—

(A) was admitted to the United States as a nonimmigrant exchange alien as defined in section 101(a)(15)(J) or has acquired the status of such a nonimmigrant exchange alien after admission other than to receive graduate medical education or training,

(B) is subject to the two-year foreign residence requirement of section 212(e), and

(C) has not fulfilled that requirement or received a waiver thereof.

(4) An alien who is inadmissible under section 212(a)(3) or deportable under of section 237(a)(4).

(5) An alien who is described in section 241(b)(3)(B)(i).

(6) An alien whose removal has previously been canceled under this section or whose deportation was suspended under section 244(a) or who has been granted relief under section 212(c), as such sections were in effect before the date of the enactment of the Illegal Immigration Reform and Immigrant Responsibility Act of 1996.

**(d) Special rules relating to continuous residence or physical presence.**—

(1) *Termination of continuous period.*— For purposes of this section, any period of continuous residence or continuous physical presence in the United States shall be deemed to end

(A) except in the case of an alien who applies for cancellation of removal under subsection (b)(2), when the alien is served a notice to appear under section 239(a), or

(B) when the alien has committed an offense referred to in section 212(a)(2) that renders the alien inadmissible to the United States under section 212(a)(2) or removable from the United States under section 237(a)(2) or 237(a)(4), whichever is earliest.

(2) *Treatment of certain breaks in presence.*— An alien shall be considered to have failed to maintain continuous physical presence in the United States under subsections (b)(1) and (b)(2) if the alien has departed from the United States for any period in excess of 90 days or for any periods in the aggregate exceeding 180 days.

(3) *Continuity not required because of honorable service in armed forces and presence upon entry into service.*— The requirements of continuous residence or continuous physical presence in the United States under subsections (a) and (b) shall not apply to an alien who—

(A) has served for a minimum period of 24 months in an active-duty status in the Armed Forces of the United States and, if separated from such service, was separated under honorable conditions, and

(B) at the time of the alien's enlistment or induction was in the United States.

**(e) Annual limitation.—**

(1) *Aggregate limitation.*— Subject to paragraphs (2) and (3), the Attorney General may not cancel the removal and adjust the status under this section, nor suspend the deportation and adjust the status under section 244(a) (as in effect before the enactment of the Illegal Immigration Reform and Immigrant Responsibility Act of 1996), of a total of more than 4,000 aliens in any fiscal year. The previous sentence shall apply regardless of when an alien applied for such cancellation and adjustment, or such suspension and adjustment, and whether such an alien had previously applied for suspension of deportation under such section 244(a). The numerical limitation under this paragraph shall apply to the aggregate number of decisions in any fiscal year to cancel the removal (and adjust the status) of an alien, or suspend the deportation (and adjust the status) of an alien, under this section or such section 244(a).

(2) *Fiscal Year 1997.*— For fiscal year 1997, paragraph (1) shall only apply to decisions to cancel the removal of an alien, or suspend the deportation of an alien, made after April 1, 1997. Notwithstanding any other provision of law, the Attorney General may cancel the removal or suspend the deportation, in addition to the normal allotment for fiscal year 1998, of a number of aliens equal to 4,000 less the number of such cancellations of removal and suspensions of deportation granted in fiscal year 1997 after April 1, 1997.

(3) *Exception for certain aliens.*— Paragraph (1) shall not apply to the following:

(A) Aliens described in section 309(c)(5)(C)(i) of the Illegal Immigration Reform and Immigrant Responsibility Act of 1996 (as amended by the Nicaraguan Adjustment and Central American Relief Act).

(B) Aliens in deportation proceedings prior to April 1, 1997, who applied for suspension of deportation under section 244(a)(3) (as in effect before the date of the enactment of the Illegal Immigration Reform and Immigrant Responsibility Act of 1996).

(June 27, 1952, ch. 477, title II, ch. 4, §240A, as added by P.L. 104-208 (IIRAIRA) (9/30/96), div. C, title III, §304(a)(3); as amended by P.L. 105-100 (NACARA) (11/19/97), title II, §204(a) [revising (b)(1)–(3), (e)]; P.L. 106-386 (10/28/00), div. B, title V, §1504(a) [revising (b)(2)], §1505(b)(2) [revising (b)(1)(C)], §1506(b)(1) [revising (d)(1)]; P.L. 109-162 (1/5/06), title VIII, §813(c)(1), §822(a) [revising (b)(1)–(2) & adding (b)(5)]; P.L. 109-271 (8/12/06), §6 [revising (b)(4)(B)]; P.L. 110-457 (12/23/08) [adding (b)(6)(A)–(C)].)

## Sec. 240B Voluntary Departure[149]
## [8 U.S.C. 1229c]

**(a) Certain conditions.—**

(1) *In general.*— The Attorney General may permit an alien voluntarily to depart the United States at the alien's own expense under this subsection, in lieu of being subject to proceedings under section 240 or prior to the completion of such proceedings, if the alien is not deportable under section 237(a)(2)(A)(iii) or section 237(a)(4)(B).

(2) *Period.—*

(A) *In general.*— Subject to subparagraph (B), permission to depart voluntarily under this subsection shall not be valid for a period exceeding 120 days.

(B) *Three-year pilot program waiver.*— During the period October 1, 2000, through September 30, 2003, and subject to subparagraphs (C) and (D)(ii), the Attorney General

---

[149] *See* note 55, *supra.*

may, in the discretion of the Attorney General for humanitarian purposes, waive application of subparagraph (A) in the case of an alien—

(i) who was admitted to the United States as a nonimmigrant visitor (described in section 101(a)(15)(B)) under the provisions of the visa waiver pilot program established pursuant to section 217, seeks the waiver for the purpose of continuing to receive medical treatment in the United States from a physician associated with a health care facility, and submits to the Attorney General—

(I) a detailed diagnosis statement from the physician, which includes the treatment being sought and the expected time period the alien will be required to remain in the United States;

(II) a statement from the health care facility containing an assurance that the alien's treatment is not being paid through any Federal or State public health assistance, that the alien's account has no outstanding balance, and that such facility will notify the Service when the alien is released or treatment is terminated; and

(III) evidence of financial ability to support the alien's day-to-day expenses while in the United States (including the expenses of any family member described in clause (ii)) and evidence that any such alien or family member is not receiving any form of public assistance; or

(ii) who—

(I) is a spouse, parent, brother, sister, son, daughter, or other family member of a principal alien described in clause (i); and

(II) entered the United States accompanying, and with the same status as, such principal alien.

(C) *Waiver limitations.*—

(i) Waivers under subparagraph (B) may be granted only upon a request submitted by a Service district office to Service headquarters.

(ii) Not more than 300 waivers may be granted for any fiscal year for a principal alien under subparagraph (B)(i).

(iii) (I) Except as provided in subclause (II), in the case of each principal alien described in subparagraph (B)(i) not more than one adult may be granted a waiver under subparagraph (B)(ii).

(II) Not more than two adults may be granted a waiver under subparagraph (B)(ii) in a case in which—

(aa) the principal alien described in subparagraph (B)(i) is a dependent under the age of 18; or

(bb) one such adult is age 55 or older or is physically handicapped.

(D) *Report to congress; suspension of waiver authority.*—

(i) Not later than March 30 of each year, the Commissioner shall submit to the Congress an annual report regarding all waivers granted under subparagraph (B) during the preceding fiscal year.

(ii) Notwithstanding any other provision of law, the authority of the Attorney General under subparagraph (B) shall be suspended during any period in which an annual report under clause (i) is past due and has not been submitted.

(3) *Bond.*— The Attorney General may require an alien permitted to depart voluntarily under this subsection to post a voluntary departure bond, to be surrendered upon proof that the alien has departed the United States within the time specified.

(4) *Treatment of aliens arriving in the United States.*— In the case of an alien who is arriving in the United States and with respect to whom proceedings under section 240 are (or would otherwise be) initiated at the time of such alien's arrival, paragraph (1) shall not apply. Nothing in this paragraph shall be construed as preventing such an alien from withdrawing the application for admission in accordance with section 235(a)(4).

**(b) At conclusion of proceedings.**—

(1) *In general.*— The Attorney General may permit an alien voluntarily to depart the United States at the alien's own expense if, at the conclusion of a proceeding under section 240, the immigration judge enters an order granting voluntary departure in lieu of removal and finds that—

(A) the alien has been physically present in the United States for a period of at least one year immediately preceding the date the notice to appear was served under section 239(a);

(B) the alien is, and has been, a person of good moral character for at least 5 years immediately preceding the alien's application for voluntary departure;

(C) the alien is not deportable under section 237(a)(2)(A)(iii) or section 237(a)(4); and

(D) the alien has established by clear and convincing evidence that the alien has the means to depart the United States and intends to do so.

(2) *Period.*— Permission to depart voluntarily under this subsection shall not be valid for a period exceeding 60 days.

(3) *Bond.*— An alien permitted to depart voluntarily under this subsection shall be required to post a voluntary departure bond, in an amount necessary to ensure that the alien will depart, to be surrendered upon proof that the alien has departed the United States within the time specified.

**(c) Aliens not eligible.**— The Attorney General shall not permit an alien to depart voluntarily under this section if the alien was previously permitted to so depart after having been found inadmissible under section 212(a)(6)(A).

**(d) Civil penalty for failure to depart.**—

(1) *In general.*— Subject to paragraph (2), if an alien is permitted to depart voluntarily under this section and voluntarily fails to depart the United States within the time period specified, the alien—

(A) shall be subject to a civil penalty of not less than $1,000 and not more than $5,000; and

(B) shall be ineligible, for a period of 10 years, to receive any further relief under this section and sections 240A, 245, 248, and 249.

(2) *Applications of VAWA protections.*— The restrictions on relief under paragraph (1) shall not apply to relief under sections 240A or 245 on the basis of a petition filed by a VAWA self-petitioner, or a petition filed under section 240A(b)(2), or under section 244(a)(3) (as in effect prior to March 31, 1997), if the extreme cruelty or battery was at least one central reason for the alien's overstaying the grant of voluntary departure.

(3) *Notice of penalties.*— The order permitting an alien to depart voluntarily shall inform the alien of the penalties under this subsection.

**(e) Additional conditions.**— The Attorney General may by regulation limit eligibility for voluntary departure under this section for any class or classes of aliens. No court may review any regulation issued under this subsection.

**(f) Judicial review.**— No court shall have jurisdiction over an appeal from denial of a request for an order of voluntary departure under subsection (b), nor shall any court order a stay of an alien's removal pending consideration of any claim with respect to voluntary departure.

(June 27, 1952, ch. 477, title II, ch. 4, §240B, as added by P.L. 104-208 (IIRAIRA) (9/30/96), div. C, title III, §304(a)(3); as amended by P.L. 106-406 (11/1/00), §2 [revising (a)(2); adding (a)(2)(C)–(D)]; P.L. 109-162 (1/5/06), title VIII, §812 [adding (d)(1)].)

## Sec. 240C Records of Admission
## [8 U.S.C. 1230]

**(a)** The Attorney General shall cause to be filed, as a record of admission of each immigrant, the immigrant visa required by section 221(e) to be surrendered at the port of entry by the arriving alien to an immigration officer.

**(b)** The Attorney General shall cause to be filed such record of the admission into the United States of each immigrant admitted under section 211(b) and of each nonimmigrant as the Attorney General deems necessary for the enforcement of the immigration laws.

(June 27, 1952, ch. 477, title II, ch. 4, §240; as amended by P.L. 104-208 (IIRAIRA) (9/30/96), div. C, title III, §304(a)(2) [redesignating original §240 as §240C], §308 [revising (b)].)

## Sec. 241 Detention and Removal of Aliens Ordered Removed
## [8 U.S.C. 1231]

**(a) Detention, release, and removal of aliens ordered removed.—**

(1) *Removal period.—*

(A) *In general.*— Except as otherwise provided in this section, when an alien is ordered removed, the Attorney General shall remove the alien from the United States within a period of 90 days (in this section referred to as the "removal period").

(B) *Beginning of period.*— The removal period begins on the latest of the following:

(i) The date the order of removal becomes administratively final.

(ii) If the removal order is judicially reviewed and if a court orders a stay of the removal of the alien, the date of the court's final order.

(iii) If the alien is detained or confined (except under an immigration process), the date the alien is released from detention or confinement.

(C) *Suspension of period.*— The removal period shall be extended beyond a period of 90 days and the alien may remain in detention during such extended period if the alien fails or refuses to make timely application in good faith for travel or other documents necessary to the alien's departure or conspires or acts to prevent the alien's removal subject to an order of removal.

(2) *Detention.*— During the removal period, the Attorney General shall detain the alien. Under no circumstances during the removal period shall the Attorney General release an alien

who has been found inadmissible under section 212(a)(2) or 212(a)(3)(B) or deportable under section 237(a)(2) or 237(a)(4)(B).

(3) *Supervision after 90-day period.*— If the alien does not leave or is not removed within the removal period, the alien, pending removal, shall be subject to supervision under regulations prescribed by the Attorney General. The regulations shall include provisions requiring the alien—

(A) to appear before an immigration officer periodically for identification;

(B) to submit, if necessary, to a medical and psychiatric examination at the expense of the United States Government;

(C) to give information under oath about the alien's nationality, circumstances, habits, associations, and activities, and other information the Attorney General considers appropriate; and

(D) to obey reasonable written restrictions on the alien's conduct or activities that the Attorney General prescribes for the alien.

(4) *Aliens imprisoned, arrested, or on parole, supervised release, or probation.*—

(A) *In general.*— Except as provided in section 343(a) of the Public Health Service Act (42 U.S.C. 259(a)) and paragraph (2), the Attorney General may not remove an alien who is sentenced to imprisonment until the alien is released from imprisonment. Parole, supervised release, probation, or possibility of arrest or further imprisonment is not a reason to defer removal.

(B) *Exception for removal of nonviolent offenders prior to completion of sentence of imprisonment.*— The Attorney General is authorized to remove an alien in accordance with applicable procedures under this Act before the alien has completed a sentence of imprisonment—

(i) in the case of an alien in the custody of the Attorney General, if the Attorney General determines that (I) the alien is confined pursuant to a final conviction for a nonviolent offense (other than an offense related to smuggling or harboring of aliens or an offense described in section 101(a)(43)(B), (C), (E), (I), or (L)[150] and (II) the removal of the alien is appropriate and in the best interest of the United States; or

(ii) in the case of an alien in the custody of a State (or a political subdivision of a State), if the chief State official exercising authority with respect to the incarceration of the alien determines that (I) the alien is confined pursuant to a final conviction for a nonviolent offense (other than an offense described in section 101(a)(43)(C) or (E)), (II) the removal is appropriate and in the best interest of the State, and (III) submits a written request to the Attorney General that such alien be so removed.

(C) *Notice.*— Any alien removed pursuant to this paragraph shall be notified of the penalties under the laws of the United States relating to the reentry of deported aliens, particularly the expanded penalties for aliens removed under subparagraph (B).

(D) *No private right.*— No cause or claim may be asserted under this paragraph against any official of the United States or of any State to compel the release, removal, or consideration for release or removal of any alien.

---

[150] *Sic.* Probably should contain a close parenthesis after "(L)".

(5) *Reinstatement of removal orders against aliens illegally reentering.*— If the Attorney General finds that an alien has reentered the United States illegally after having been removed or having departed voluntarily, under an order of removal, the prior order of removal is reinstated from its original date and is not subject to being reopened or reviewed, the alien is not eligible and may not apply for any relief under this Act, and the alien shall be removed under the prior order at any time after the reentry.

(6) *Inadmissible or criminal aliens.*— An alien ordered removed who is inadmissible under section 212, removable under section 237(a)(1)(C), 237(a)(2), or 237(a)(4) or who has been determined by the Attorney General to be a risk to the community or unlikely to comply with the order of removal, may be detained beyond the removal period and, if released, shall be subject to the terms of supervision in paragraph (3).

(7) *Employment authorization.*— No alien ordered removed shall be eligible to receive authorization to be employed in the United States unless the Attorney General makes a specific finding that—

(A) the alien cannot be removed due to the refusal of all countries designated by the alien or under this section to receive the alien, or

(B) the removal of the alien is otherwise impracticable or contrary to the public interest.

**(b) Countries to which aliens may be removed.**—

(1) *Aliens arriving at the United States.*— Subject to paragraph (3)—

(A) *In general.*— Except as provided by subparagraphs (B) and (C), an alien who arrives at the United States and with respect to whom proceedings under section 240 were initiated at the time of such alien's arrival shall be removed to the country in which the alien boarded the vessel or aircraft on which the alien arrived in the United States.

(B) *Travel from contiguous territory.*— If the alien boarded the vessel or aircraft on which the alien arrived in the United States in a foreign territory contiguous to the United States, an island adjacent to the United States, or an island adjacent to a foreign territory contiguous to the United States, and the alien is not a native, citizen, subject, or national of, or does not reside in, the territory or island, removal shall be to the country in which the alien boarded the vessel that transported the alien to the territory or island.

(C) *Alternative countries.*— If the government of the country designated in subparagraph (A) or (B) is unwilling to accept the alien into that country's territory, removal shall be to any of the following countries, as directed by the Attorney General:

(i) The country of which the alien is a citizen, subject, or national.

(ii) The country in which the alien was born.

(iii) The country in which the alien has a residence.

(iv) A country with a government that will accept the alien into the country's territory if removal to each country described in a previous clause of this subparagraph is impracticable, inadvisable, or impossible.

(2) *Other aliens.*— Subject to paragraph (3)—

(A) *Selection of country by alien.*— Except as otherwise provided in this paragraph—

(i) any alien not described in paragraph (1) who has been ordered removed may designate one country to which the alien wants to be removed, and

(ii) the Attorney General shall remove the alien to the country the alien so designates.

(B) *Limitation on designation.*— An alien may designate under subparagraph (A)(i) a foreign territory contiguous to the United States, an adjacent island, or an island adjacent to a foreign territory contiguous to the United States as the place to which the alien is to be removed only if the alien is a native, citizen, subject, or national of, or has resided in, that designated territory or island.

(C) *Disregarding designation.*— The Attorney General may disregard a designation under subparagraph (A)(i) if—

(i) the alien fails to designate a country promptly;

(ii) the government of the country does not inform the Attorney General finally, within 30 days after the date the Attorney General first inquires, whether the government will accept the alien into the country;

(iii) the government of the country is not willing to accept the alien into the country; or

(iv) the Attorney General decides that removing the alien to the country is prejudicial to the United States.

(D) *Alternative country.*— If an alien is not removed to a country designated under subparagraph (A)(i), the Attorney General shall remove the alien to a country of which the alien is a subject, national, or citizen unless the government of the country—

(i) does not inform the Attorney General or the alien finally, within 30 days after the date the Attorney General first inquires or within another period of time the Attorney General decides is reasonable, whether the government will accept the alien into the country; or

(ii) is not willing to accept the alien into the country.

(E) *Additional removal countries.*— If an alien is not removed to a country under the previous subparagraphs of this paragraph, the Attorney General shall remove the alien to any of the following countries:

(i) The country from which the alien was admitted to the United States.

(ii) The country in which is located the foreign port from which the alien left for the United States or for a foreign territory contiguous to the United States.

(iii) A country in which the alien resided before the alien entered the country from which the alien entered the United States.

(iv) The country in which the alien was born.

(v) The country that had sovereignty over the alien's birthplace when the alien was born.

(vi) The country in which the alien's birthplace is located when the alien is ordered removed.

(vii) If impracticable, inadvisable, or impossible to remove the alien to each country described in a previous clause of this subparagraph, another country whose government will accept the alien into that country.

(F) *Removal country when United States is at war.*— When the United States is at war and the Attorney General decides that it is impracticable, inadvisable, inconvenient, or impossible to remove an alien under this subsection because of the war, the Attorney General may remove the alien—

(i) to the country that is host to a government in exile of the country of which the alien is a citizen or subject if the government of the host country will permit the alien's entry; or

(ii) if the recognized government of the country of which the alien is a citizen or subject is not in exile, to a country, or a political or territorial subdivision of a country, that is very near the country of which the alien is a citizen or subject, or, with the consent of the government of the country of which the alien is a citizen or subject, to another country.

(3) *Restriction on removal to a country where alien's life or freedom would be threatened.*—

(A) *In general.*— Notwithstanding paragraphs (1) and (2), the Attorney General may not remove an alien to a country if the Attorney General decides that the alien's life or freedom would be threatened in that country because of the alien's race, religion, nationality, membership in a particular social group, or political opinion.

(B) *Exception.*— Subparagraph (A) does not apply to an alien deportable under section 237(a)(4)(D) or if the Attorney General decides that—

(i) the alien ordered, incited, assisted, or otherwise participated in the persecution of an individual because of the individual's race, religion, nationality, membership in a particular social group, or political opinion;

(ii) the alien, having been convicted by a final judgment of a particularly serious crime, is a danger to the community of the United States;

(iii) there are serious reasons to believe that the alien committed a serious nonpolitical crime outside the United States before the alien arrived in the United States; or

(iv) there are reasonable grounds to believe that the alien is a danger to the security of the United States.

For purposes of clause (ii), an alien who has been convicted of an aggravated felony (or felonies) for which the alien has been sentenced to an aggregate term of imprisonment of at least 5 years shall be considered to have committed a particularly serious crime. The previous sentence shall not preclude the Attorney General from determining that, notwithstanding the length of sentence imposed, an alien has been convicted of a particularly serious crime. For purposes of clause (iv), an alien who is described in section 237(a)(4)(B) shall be considered to be an alien with respect to whom there are reasonable grounds for regarding as a danger to the security of the United States.

(C) *Sustaining burden of proof; credibility determinations.*— In determining whether an alien has demonstrated that the alien's life or freedom would be threatened for a reason described in subparagraph (A), the trier of fact shall determine whether the alien has sustained the alien's burden of proof, and shall make credibility determinations, in the manner described in clauses (ii) and (iii) of section 208(b)(1)(B).[151]

---

[151] The amendment made to INA §241(b)(3) by §101(c) of the REAL ID Act, P.L. 109-13 [adding (C)] took effect on the date of enactment (5/11/05) and applies to applications for asylum, withholding, or other relief from removal made on or after such date.

**(c) Removal of aliens arriving at port of entry.—**

(1) *Vessels and aircraft.—* An alien arriving at a port of entry of the United States who is ordered removed either without a hearing under section 235(b)(1) or 235(c) or pursuant to proceedings under section 240 initiated at the time of such alien's arrival shall be removed immediately on a vessel or aircraft owned by the owner of the vessel or aircraft on which the alien arrived in the United States, unless—

(A) it is impracticable to remove the alien on one of those vessels or aircraft within a reasonable time, or

(B) the alien is a stowaway—

(i) who has been ordered removed in accordance with section 235(a)(1),

(ii) who has requested asylum, and

(iii) whose application has not been adjudicated or whose asylum application has been denied but who has not exhausted all appeal rights.

(2) *Stay of removal.—*

(A) *In general.—* The Attorney General may stay the removal of an alien under this subsection if the Attorney General decides that—

(i) immediate removal is not practicable or proper; or

(ii) the alien is needed to testify in the prosecution of a person for a violation of a law of the United States or of any State.

(B) *Payment of detention costs.—* During the period an alien is detained because of a stay of removal under subparagraph (A)(ii), the Attorney General may pay from the appropriation "Immigration and Naturalization Service—Salaries and Expenses"—

(i) the cost of maintenance of the alien; and

(ii) a witness fee of $1 a day.

(C) *Release during stay.—* The Attorney General may release an alien whose removal is stayed under subparagraph (A)(ii) on—

(i) the alien's filing a bond of at least $500 with security approved by the Attorney General;

(ii) condition that the alien appear when required as a witness and for removal; and

(iii) other conditions the Attorney General may prescribe.

(3) *Costs of detention and maintenance pending removal.—*

(A) *In general.—* Except as provided in subparagraph (B) and subsection (d), an owner of a vessel or aircraft bringing an alien to the United States shall pay the costs of detaining and maintaining the alien—

(i) while the alien is detained under subsection (d)(1), and

(ii) in the case of an alien who is a stowaway, while the alien is being detained pursuant to—

(I) subsection (d)(2)(A) or (d)(2)(B)(i),

(II) subsection (d)(2)(B)(ii) or (iii) for the period of time reasonably necessary for the owner to arrange for repatriation or removal of the stowaway, including obtaining necessary travel documents, but not to extend beyond the date on which it is ascertained that such travel documents cannot be obtained from the country to which the stowaway is to be returned, or

(III) section 235(b)(1)(B)(ii), for a period not to exceed 15 days (excluding Saturdays, Sundays, and holidays) commencing on the first such day which begins on the earlier of 72 hours after the time of the initial presentation of the stowaway for inspection or at the time the stowaway is determined to have a credible fear of persecution.

(B) *Nonapplication.*— Subparagraph (A) shall not apply if—

(i) the alien is a crewmember;

(ii) the alien has an immigrant visa;

(iii) the alien has a nonimmigrant visa or other documentation authorizing the alien to apply for temporary admission to the United States and applies for admission not later than 120 days after the date the visa or documentation was issued;

(iv) the alien has a reentry permit and applies for admission not later than 120 days after the date of the alien's last inspection and admission;

(v) (I) the alien has a nonimmigrant visa or other documentation authorizing the alien to apply for temporary admission to the United States or a reentry permit;

(II) the alien applies for admission more than 120 days after the date the visa or documentation was issued or after the date of the last inspection and admission under the reentry permit; and

(III) the owner of the vessel or aircraft satisfies the Attorney General that the existence of the condition relating to inadmissibility could not have been discovered by exercising reasonable care before the alien boarded the vessel or aircraft; or

(vi) the individual claims to be a national of the United States and has a United States passport.

## (d) Requirements of persons providing transportation.—

(1) *Removal at time of arrival.*— An owner, agent, master, commanding officer, person in charge, purser, or consignee of a vessel or aircraft bringing an alien (except an alien crewmember) to the United States shall—

(A) receive an alien back on the vessel or aircraft or another vessel or aircraft owned or operated by the same interests if the alien is ordered removed under this part; and

(B) take the alien to the foreign country to which the alien is ordered removed.

(2) *Alien stowaways.*— An owner, agent, master, commanding officer, charterer, or consignee of a vessel or aircraft arriving in the United States with an alien stowaway—

(A) shall detain the alien on board the vessel or aircraft, or at such place as the Attorney General shall designate, until completion of the inspection of the alien by an immigration officer;

(B) may not permit the stowaway to land in the United States, except pursuant to regulations of the Attorney General temporarily—

(i) for medical treatment,

(ii) for detention of the stowaway by the Attorney General, or

(iii) for departure or removal of the stowaway; and

(C) if ordered by an immigration officer, shall remove the stowaway on the vessel or aircraft or on another vessel or aircraft.

The Attorney General shall grant a timely request to remove the stowaway under subparagraph (C) on a vessel or aircraft other than that on which the stowaway arrived if the requester has obtained any travel documents necessary for departure or repatriation of the stowaway and removal of the stowaway will not be unreasonably delayed.

(3) *Removal upon order.*— An owner, agent, master, commanding officer, person in charge, purser, or consignee of a vessel, aircraft, or other transportation line shall comply with an order of the Attorney General to take on board, guard safely, and transport to the destination specified any alien ordered to be removed under this Act.

**(e) Payment of expenses of removal.—**

(1) *Costs of removal at time of arrival.*— In the case of an alien who is a stowaway or who is ordered removed either without a hearing under section 235(a)(1) or 235(c) or pursuant to proceedings under section 240 initiated at the time of such alien's arrival, the owner of the vessel or aircraft (if any) on which the alien arrived in the United States shall pay the transportation cost of removing the alien. If removal is on a vessel or aircraft not owned by the owner of the vessel or aircraft on which the alien arrived in the United States, the Attorney General may—

(A) pay the cost from the appropriation "Immigration and Naturalization Service— Salaries and Expenses"; and

(B) recover the amount of the cost in a civil action from the owner, agent, or consignee of the vessel or aircraft (if any) on which the alien arrived in the United States.

(2) *Costs of removal to port of removal for aliens admitted or permitted to land.*— In the case of an alien who has been admitted or permitted to land and is ordered removed, the cost (if any) of removal of the alien to the port of removal shall be at the expense of the appropriation for the enforcement of this Act.

(3) *Costs of removal from port of removal for aliens admitted or permitted to land.*—

(A) *Through appropriation.*— Except as provided in subparagraph (B), in the case of an alien who has been admitted or permitted to land and is ordered removed, the cost (if any) of removal of the alien from the port of removal shall be at the expense of the appropriation for the enforcement of this Act.

(B) *Through owner.*—

(i) In general.— In the case of an alien described in clause (ii), the cost of removal of the alien from the port of removal may be charged to any owner of the vessel, aircraft, or other transportation line by which the alien came to the United States.

(ii) Aliens described.— An alien described in this clause is an alien who—

(I) is admitted to the United States (other than lawfully admitted for permanent residence) and is ordered removed within 5 years of the date of admission based on a ground that existed before or at the time of admission, or

(II) is an alien crewman permitted to land temporarily under section 252 and is ordered removed within 5 years of the date of landing.

(C) *Costs of removal of certain aliens granted voluntary departure.*— In the case of an alien who has been granted voluntary departure under section 240B and who is financially unable to depart at the alien's own expense and whose removal the Attorney General deems to be in the best interest of the United States, the expense of such removal may be paid from the appropriation for the enforcement of this Act.

### (f) Aliens requiring personal care during removal.—

(1) *In general.*— If the Attorney General believes that an alien being removed requires personal care because of the alien's mental or physical condition, the Attorney General may employ a suitable person for that purpose who shall accompany and care for the alien until the alien arrives at the final destination.

(2) *Costs.*— The costs of providing the service described in paragraph (1) shall be defrayed in the same manner as the expense of removing the accompanied alien is defrayed under this section.

### (g) Places of detention.—

(1) *In general.*— The Attorney General shall arrange for appropriate places of detention for aliens detained pending removal or a decision on removal. When United States Government facilities are unavailable or facilities adapted or suitably located for detention are unavailable for rental, the Attorney General may expend from the appropriation "Immigration and Naturalization Service—Salaries and Expenses", without regard to section 3709 of the Revised Statutes (41 U.S.C. 5), amounts necessary to acquire land and to acquire, build, remodel, repair, and operate facilities (including living quarters for immigration officers if not otherwise available) necessary for detention.

(2) *Detention facilities of the immigration and naturalization service.*— Prior to initiating any project for the construction of any new detention facility for the Service, the Commissioner shall consider the availability for purchase or lease of any existing prison, jail, detention center, or other comparable facility suitable for such use.

### (h) Statutory construction.— Nothing in this section shall be construed to create any substantive or procedural right or benefit that is legally enforceable by any party against the United States or its agencies or officers or any other person.

### (i) Incarceration.—

(1) If the chief executive officer of a State (or, if appropriate, a political subdivision of the State) exercising authority with respect to the incarceration of an undocumented criminal alien submits a written request to the Attorney General, the Attorney General shall, as determined by the Attorney General—

(A) enter into a contractual arrangement which provides for compensation to the State or a political subdivision of the State, as may be appropriate, with respect to the incarceration of the undocumented criminal alien; or

(B) take the undocumented criminal alien into the custody of the Federal Government and incarcerate the alien.

(2) Compensation under paragraph (1)(A) shall be the average cost of incarceration of a prisoner in the relevant State as determined by the Attorney General.

(3) For purposes of this subsection, the term "undocumented criminal alien" means an alien who—

(A) has been convicted of a felony or two or more misdemeanors; and

(B) (i) entered the United States without inspection or at any time or place other than as designated by the Attorney General;

(ii) was the subject of exclusion or deportation proceedings at the time he or she was taken into custody by the State or a political subdivision of the State; or

(iii) was admitted as a nonimmigrant and at the time he or she was taken into custody by the State or a political subdivision of the State has failed to maintain the nonimmigrant status in which the alien was admitted or to which it was changed under section 248, or to comply with the conditions of any such status.

(4) (A) In carrying out paragraph (1), the Attorney General shall give priority to the Federal incarceration of undocumented criminal aliens who have committed aggravated felonies.

(B) The Attorney General shall ensure that undocumented criminal aliens incarcerated in Federal facilities pursuant to this subsection are held in facilities which provide a level of security appropriate to the crimes for which they were convicted.

(5) There are authorized to be appropriated to carry out this subsection—

(A) $750,000,000 for fiscal year 2006;

(B) $850,000,000 for fiscal year 2007; and

(C) $950,000,000 for each of the fiscal years 2008 through 2011.

(6) Amounts appropriated pursuant to the authorization of appropriations in paragraph (5) that are distributed to a State or political subdivision of a State, including a municipality, may be used only for correctional purposes.

(June 27, 1952, ch. 477, title II, ch. 4, §241; as amended by P.L. 104-208 (IIRAIRA) (9/30/96), div. C, title III, §305(a)(3) [redesignating original §241 as §237], §306(a)(1) [redesignating §242(j) as §241(i)], §328(a)(1) [revising (i)]; P.L. 107-273 (11/2/02), div. C, title I, §11014 [revising (i)(5)]; P.L. 109-13 (REAL ID) (5/11/05), div. B, title I, §101(c) [adding (b)(3)(C)]; P.L. 109-162 (1/5/06), title XI, §1196(a) [revising (i)(5)–(6)].)

## Sec. 242 Judicial Review of Orders of Removal[152]
## [8 U.S.C. 1252]

### (a) Applicable provisions.—

(1) *General orders of removal.*— Judicial review of a final order of removal (other than an order of removal without a hearing pursuant to section 235(b)(1)) is governed only by chapter 158 of title 28 of the United States Code, except as provided in subsection (b) and except that the court may not order the taking of additional evidence under section 2347(c) of such title.

(2) *Matters not subject to judicial review.*—

(A) *Review relating to section 235(b)(1).*— Notwithstanding any other provision of law (statutory or nonstatutory), including section 2241 of title 28, United States Code, or any other habeas corpus provision, and sections 1361 and 1651 of such title, no court shall have jurisdiction to review—

---

[152] The effective date of INA §242 is provided by §306(c) of IIRAIRA.

(i) except as provided in subsection (e), any individual determination or to entertain any other cause or claim arising from or relating to the implementation or operation of an order of removal pursuant to section 235(b)(1),

(ii) except as provided in subsection (e), a decision by the Attorney General to invoke the provisions of such section,

(iii) the application of such section to individual aliens, including the determination made under section 235(b)(1)(B), or

(iv) except as provided in subsection (e), procedures and policies adopted by the Attorney General to implement the provisions of section 235(b)(1).

(B) *Denials of discretionary relief.*— Notwithstanding any other provision of law (statutory or nonstatutory), including section 2241 of title 28, United States Code, or any other habeas corpus provision, and sections 1361 and 1651 of such title, and except as provided in subparagraph (D), and regardless of whether the judgment, decision, or action is made in removal proceedings, no court shall have jurisdiction to review—[153]

(i) any judgment regarding the granting of relief under section 212(h), 212(i), 240A, 240B, or 245, or

(ii) any other decision or action of the Attorney General or the Secretary of Homeland Security the authority for which is specified under this title to be in the discretion of the Attorney General or the Secretary of Homeland Security, other than the granting of relief under section 208(a).

(C) *Orders against criminal aliens.*— Notwithstanding any other provision of law (statutory or nonstatutory), including section 2241 of title 28, United States Code, or any other habeas corpus provision, and sections 1361 and 1651 of such title, and except as provided in subparagraph (D), no court shall have jurisdiction to review any final order of removal against an alien who is removable by reason of having committed a criminal offense covered in section 212(a)(2) or 237(a)(2)(A)(iii), (B), (C), or (D), or any offense covered by section 237(a)(2)(A)(ii) for which both predicate offenses are, without regard to their date of commission, otherwise covered by section 237(a)(2)(A)(i).

(D) *Judicial review of certain legal claims.*— Nothing in subparagraph (B) or (C), or in any other provision of this Act (other than this section) which limits or eliminates judicial review, shall be construed as precluding review of constitutional claims or questions of law raised upon a petition for review filed with an appropriate court of appeals in accordance with this section.

(3) *Treatment of certain decisions.*— No alien shall have a right to appeal from a decision of an immigration judge which is based solely on a certification described in section 240(c)(1)(B).

(4) *Claims under the United Nations Convention.*— Notwithstanding any other provision of law (statutory or nonstatutory), including section 2241 of title 28, United States Code, or any other habeas corpus provision, and sections 1361 and 1651 of such title, a petition for review filed with an appropriate court of appeals in accordance with this section shall be the sole and exclusive means for judicial review of any cause or claim under the United Nations Conven-

---

[153] The amendment made to INA §242(a)(2)(B) by §101(f) of the REAL ID Act, P.L. 109-13, took effect on the date of enactment (5/11/05) and applies to all cases pending before any court on or after such date.

tion Against Torture and Other Forms of Cruel, Inhuman, or Degrading Treatment or Punishment, except as provided in subsection (e).

(5) *Exclusive means of review.*— Notwithstanding any other provision of law (statutory or nonstatutory), including section 2241 of title 28, United States Code, or any other habeas corpus provision, and sections 1361 and 1651 of such title, a petition for review filed with an appropriate court of appeals in accordance with this section shall be the sole and exclusive means for judicial review of an order of removal entered or issued under any provision of this Act, except as provided in subsection (e). For purposes of this Act, in every provision that limits or eliminates judicial review or jurisdiction to review, the terms "judicial review" and "jurisdiction to review" include habeas corpus review pursuant to section 2241 of title 28, United States Code, or any other habeas corpus provision, sections 1361 and 1651 of such title, and review pursuant to any other provision of law (statutory or nonstatutory).

**(b) Requirements for review of orders of removal.**— With respect to review of an order of removal under subsection (a)(1), the following requirements apply:

(1) *Deadline.*— The petition for review must be filed not later than 30 days after the date of the final order of removal.

(2) *Venue and forms.*— The petition for review shall be filed with the court of appeals for the judicial circuit in which the immigration judge completed the proceedings. The record and briefs do not have to be printed. The court of appeals shall review the proceeding on a typewritten record and on typewritten briefs.[154]

(3) *Service.*—

(A) *In general.*— The respondent is the Attorney General. The petition shall be served on the Attorney General and on the officer or employee of the Service in charge of the Service district in which the final order of removal under section 240 was entered.

(B) *Stay of order.*— Service of the petition on the officer or employee does not stay the removal of an alien pending the court's decision on the petition, unless the court orders otherwise.

(C) *Alien's brief.*— The alien shall serve and file a brief in connection with a petition for judicial review not later than 40 days after the date on which the administrative record is available, and may serve and file a reply brief not later than 14 days after service of the brief of the Attorney General, and the court may not extend these deadlines except upon motion for good cause shown. If an alien fails to file a brief within the time provided in this paragraph, the court shall dismiss the appeal unless a manifest injustice would result.

(4) *Scope and standard for review.*— Except as provided in paragraph (5)(B)—

(A) the court of appeals shall decide the petition only on the administrative record on which the order of removal is based,

---

[154] Sec. §106(c) of the REAL ID Act, P.L. 109-13 (5/11/05), provides:

Transfer of cases—If an alien's case, brought under [28 USC §2241], and challenging a final administrative order of removal, deportation, or exclusion, is pending in a district court on the date of the enactment of this division, then the district court shall transfer the case (or the part of the case that challenges the order of removal, deportation, or exclusion) to the court of appeals for the circuit in which a petition for review could have been properly filed under [INA §242(b)(2)], as amended by this section, or under [IIRAIRA §309(c)(4)(D) (*reprinted in* Appendix C, *infra*)]. The court of appeals shall treat the transferred case as if it had been filed pursuant to a petition for review under such §242, except that subsection (b)(1) of such section shall not apply.

(B) the administrative findings of fact are conclusive unless any reasonable adjudicator would be compelled to conclude to the contrary,

(C) a decision that an alien is not eligible for admission to the United States is conclusive unless manifestly contrary to law, and

(D) the Attorney General's discretionary judgment whether to grant relief under section 208(a) shall be conclusive unless manifestly contrary to the law and an abuse of discretion.

No court shall reverse a determination made by a trier of fact with respect to the availability of corroborating evidence, as described in section 208(b)(1)(B), 240(c)(4)(B), or 241(b)(3)(C), unless the court finds, pursuant to section 242(b)(4)(B), that a reasonable trier of fact is compelled to conclude that such corroborating evidence is unavailable.

(5) *Treatment of nationality claims.*—

(A) Court determination if no issue of fact.— If the petitioner claims to be a national of the United States and the court of appeals finds from the pleadings and affidavits that no genuine issue of material fact about the petitioner's nationality is presented, the court shall decide the nationality claim.

(B) Transfer if issue of fact.— If the petitioner claims to be a national of the United States and the court of appeals finds that a genuine issue of material fact about the petitioner's nationality is presented, the court shall transfer the proceeding to the district court of the United States for the judicial district in which the petitioner resides for a new hearing on the nationality claim and a decision on that claim as if an action had been brought in the district court under section 2201 of title 28, United States Code.

(C) Limitation on determination.— The petitioner may have such nationality claim decided only as provided in this paragraph.

(6) *Consolidation with review of motions to reopen or reconsider.*— When a petitioner seeks review of an order under this section, any review sought of a motion to reopen or reconsider the order shall be consolidated with the review of the order.

(7) *Challenge to validity of orders in certain criminal proceedings.*—

(A) *In general.*— If the validity of an order of removal has not been judicially decided, a defendant in a criminal proceeding charged with violating section 243(a) may challenge the validity of the order in the criminal proceeding only by filing a separate motion before trial. The district court, without a jury, shall decide the motion before trial.

(B) *Claims of United States nationality.*— If the defendant claims in the motion to be a national of the United States and the district court finds that—

(i) no genuine issue of material fact about the defendant's nationality is presented, the court shall decide the motion only on the administrative record on which the removal order is based and the administrative findings of fact are conclusive if supported by reasonable, substantial, and probative evidence on the record considered as a whole; or

(ii) a genuine issue of material fact about the defendant's nationality is presented, the court shall hold a new hearing on the nationality claim and decide that claim as if an action had been brought under section 2201 of title 28, United States Code.

The defendant may have such nationality claim decided only as provided in this subparagraph.

(C) *Consequence of invalidation.*— If the district court rules that the removal order is invalid, the court shall dismiss the indictment for violation of section 243(a). The United States Government may appeal the dismissal to the court of appeals for the appropriate circuit within 30 days after the date of the dismissal.

(D) *Limitation on filing petitions for review.*— The defendant in a criminal proceeding under section 243(a) may not file a petition for review under subsection (a) during the criminal proceeding.

(8) *Construction.*— This subsection—

(A) does not prevent the Attorney General, after a final order of removal has been issued, from detaining the alien under section 241(a);

(B) does not relieve the alien from complying with section 241(a)(4) and section 243(g); and

(C) does not require the Attorney General to defer removal of the alien.

(9) *Consolidation of issues for judicial review.*— Application Judicial review of all questions of law and fact, including interpretation and application of constitutional and statutory provisions, arising from any action taken or proceeding brought to remove an alien from the United States under this title shall be available only in judicial review of a final order under this section. Except as otherwise provided in this section, no court shall have jurisdiction, by habeas corpus under section 2241 of title 28, United States Code, or any other habeas corpus provision, by section 1361 or 1651 of such title, or by any other provision of law (statutory or nonstatutory), to review such an order or such questions of law or fact.

**(c) Requirements for petition.**— A petition for review or for habeas corpus of an order of removal—

(1) shall attach a copy of such order, and

(2) shall state whether a court has upheld the validity of the order, and, if so, shall state the name of the court, the date of the court's ruling, and the kind of proceeding.

**(d) Review of final orders.**— A court may review a final order of removal only if—

(1) the alien has exhausted all administrative remedies available to the alien as of right, and

(2) another court has not decided the validity of the order, unless the reviewing court finds that the petition presents grounds that could not have been presented in the prior judicial proceeding or that the remedy provided by the prior proceeding was inadequate or ineffective to test the validity of the order.

**(e) Judicial review of orders under section 235(b)(1).**—

(1) *Limitations on relief.*— Without regard to the nature of the action or claim and without regard to the identity of the party or parties bringing the action, no court may—

(A) enter declaratory, injunctive, or other equitable relief in any action pertaining to an order to exclude an alien in accordance with section 235(b)(1) except as specifically authorized in a subsequent paragraph of this subsection, or

(B) certify a class under Rule 23 of the Federal Rules of Civil Procedure in any action for which judicial review is authorized under a subsequent paragraph of this subsection.

(2) *Habeas corpus proceedings.*— Judicial review of any determination made under section 235(b)(1) is available in habeas corpus proceedings, but shall be limited to determinations of—

(A) whether the petitioner is an alien,

(B) whether the petitioner was ordered removed under such section, and

(C) whether the petitioner can prove by a preponderance of the evidence that the petitioner is an alien lawfully admitted for permanent residence, has been admitted as a refugee under section 207, or has been granted asylum under section 208, such status not having been terminated, and is entitled to such further inquiry as prescribed by the Attorney General pursuant to section 235(b)(1)(C).

(3) *Challenges on validity of the system.*—

(A) *In general.*— Judicial review of determinations under section 235(b) and its implementation is available in an action instituted in the United States District Court for the District of Columbia, but shall be limited to determinations of—

(i) whether such section, or any regulation issued to implement such section, is constitutional; or

(ii) whether such a regulation, or a written policy directive, written policy guideline, or written procedure issued by or under the authority of the Attorney General to implement such section, is not consistent with applicable provisions of this title or is otherwise in violation of law.

(B) *Deadlines for bringing actions.*— Any action instituted under this paragraph must be filed no later than 60 days after the date the challenged section, regulation, directive, guideline, or procedure described in clause (i) or (ii) of subparagraph (A) is first implemented.

(C) *Notice of appeal.*— A notice of appeal of an order issued by the District Court under this paragraph may be filed not later than 30 days after the date of issuance of such order.

(D) *Expeditious consideration of cases.*— It shall be the duty of the District Court, the Court of Appeals, and the Supreme Court of the United States to advance on the docket and to expedite to the greatest possible extent the disposition of any case considered under this paragraph.

(4) *Decision.*— In any case where the court determines that the petitioner—

(A) is an alien who was not ordered removed under section 235(b)(1), or

(B) has demonstrated by a preponderance of the evidence that the alien is an alien lawfully admitted for permanent residence, has been admitted as a refugee under section 207, or has been granted asylum under section 208,

the court may order no remedy or relief other than to require that the petitioner be provided a hearing in accordance with section 240. Any alien who is provided a hearing under section 240 pursuant to this paragraph may thereafter obtain judicial review of any resulting final order of removal pursuant to subsection (a)(1).

(5) *Scope of inquiry.*— In determining whether an alien has been ordered removed under section 235(b)(1), the court's inquiry shall be limited to whether such an order in fact was issued and whether it relates to the petitioner. There shall be no review of whether the alien is actually inadmissible or entitled to any relief from removal.

**(f) Limit on injunctive relief.**—

(1) *In general.*— Regardless of the nature of the action or claim or of the identity of the party or parties bringing the action, no court (other than the Supreme Court) shall have jurisdiction

or authority to enjoin or restrain the operation of the provisions of chapter 4 of title II, as amended by the Illegal Immigration Reform and Immigrant Responsibility Act of 1996, other than with respect to the application of such provisions to an individual alien against whom proceedings under such chapter have been initiated.

(2) *Particular cases.*— Notwithstanding any other provision of law, no court shall enjoin the removal of any alien pursuant to a final order under this section unless the alien shows by clear and convincing evidence that the entry or execution of such order is prohibited as a matter of law.

**(g) Exclusive jurisdiction.**— Except as provided in this section and notwithstanding any other provision of law (statutory or nonstatutory), including section 2241 of title 28, United States Code, or any other habeas corpus provision, and sections 1361 and 1651 of such title, no court shall have jurisdiction to hear any cause or claim by or on behalf of any alien arising from the decision or action by the Attorney General to commence proceedings, adjudicate cases, or execute removal orders against any alien under this Act.

(June 27, 1952, ch. 477, title II, ch. 5, §242, 66 Stat. 208; Sept. 3, 1954, ch. 1263, §17, 68 Stat. 1232; as amended by P.L. 97-116 (12/29/81); P.L. 98-473 (10/12/84); P.L. 99-603 (IRCA) (11/6/86); P.L. 100-525 (10/24/88); P.L. 100-690 (11/18/88); P.L. 101-649 (IMMACT90) (11/29/90); P.L. 102-232 (MTINA) (12/12/91, *effective* 4/1/92); P.L. 103-322 (VAWA) (9/13/94); P.L. 103-416 (INTCA) (10/25/94, *effective* 4/1/95); P.L. 104-132 (AEDPA) (4/24/96), title IV, §436(a), §438(a), §440(c); P.L. 104-208 (IIRAIRA) (9/30/96), div. C, title III, §306(a) [revising in its entirety; redesignating §242(j) as §241(i); effective date provided by IIRAIRA §306(c)], §308(g)(10)(H), §371(b)(6); P.L. 109-13 (REAL ID) (5/11/05), div. B, title I, §101(e) [revising (b)(4); applicable to all cases in which the final administrative removal order is or was issued before, on, or the date of enactment], §106(a) [revising (a)(2)(A)–(C), adding (a)(2)(D); (a)(4)–(5), & revising (b)(9) & (g); applicable to cases in which the final administrative order of removal, deportation, or exclusion was issued before, on, or after the date of enactment].)

## Sec. 243 Penalties Related to Removal
## [8 U.S.C. 1253]

**(a) Penalty for failure to depart.—**

(1) *In general.*— Any alien against whom a final order of removal is outstanding by reason of being a member of any of the classes described in section 237(a), who—

(A) willfully fails or refuses to depart from the United States within a period of 90 days from the date of the final order of removal under administrative processes, or if judicial review is had, then from the date of the final order of the court,

(B) willfully fails or refuses to make timely application in good faith for travel or other documents necessary to the alien's departure,

(C) connives or conspires, or takes any other action, designed to prevent or hamper or with the purpose of preventing or hampering the alien's departure pursuant to such, or

(D) willfully fails or refuses to present himself or herself for removal at the time and place required by the Attorney General pursuant to such order,

shall be fined under title 18, United States Code, or imprisoned not more than four years (or 10 years if the alien is a member of any of the classes described in paragraph (1)(E), (2), (3), or (4) of section 237(a)), or both.

(2) *Exception.*— It is not a violation of paragraph (1) to take any proper steps for the purpose of securing cancellation of or exemption from such order of removal or for the purpose of securing the alien's release from incarceration or custody.

(3) *Suspension.*— The court may for good cause suspend the sentence of an alien under this subsection and order the alien's release under such conditions as the court may prescribe. In

determining whether good cause has been shown to justify releasing the alien, the court shall take into account such factors as—

(A) the age, health, and period of detention of the alien;

(B) the effect of the alien's release upon the national security and public peace or safety;

(C) the likelihood of the alien's resuming or following a course of conduct which made or would make the alien deportable;

(D) the character of the efforts made by such alien himself and by representatives of the country or countries to which the alien's removal is directed to expedite the alien's departure from the United States;

(E) the reason for the inability of the Government of the United States to secure passports, other travel documents, or removal facilities from the country or countries to which the alien has been ordered removed; and

(F) the eligibility of the alien for discretionary relief under the immigration laws.

**(b) Willful failure to comply with terms of release under supervision.**— An alien who shall willfully fail to comply with regulations or requirements issued pursuant to section 241(a)(3) or knowingly give false information in response to an inquiry under such section shall be fined not more than $1,000 or imprisoned for not more than one year, or both.

**(c) Penalties relating to vessels and aircraft.**—

(1) *Civil penalties.*—

(A) *Failure to carry out certain orders.*— If the Attorney General is satisfied that a person has violated subsection (d) or (e) of section 241, the person shall pay to the Commissioner the sum of $2,000 for each violation.

(B) *Failure to remove alien stowaways.*— If the Attorney General is satisfied that a person has failed to remove an alien stowaway as required under section 241(d)(2), the person shall pay to the Commissioner the sum of $5,000 for each alien stowaway not removed.

(C) *No compromise.*— The Attorney General may not compromise the amount of such penalty under this paragraph.

(2) *Clearing vessels and aircraft.*—

(A) *Clearance before decision on liability.*— A vessel or aircraft may be granted clearance before a decision on liability is made under paragraph (1) only if a bond approved by the Attorney General or an amount sufficient to pay the civil penalty is deposited with the Commissioner.

(B) *Prohibition on clearance while penalty unpaid.*— A vessel or aircraft may not be granted clearance if a civil penalty imposed under paragraph (1) is not paid.

**(d) Discontinuing granting visas to nationals of country denying or delaying accepting alien.**— On being notified by the Attorney General that the government of a foreign country denies or unreasonably delays accepting an alien who is a citizen, subject, national, or resident of that country after the Attorney General asks whether the government will accept the alien under this section, the Secretary of State shall order consular officers in that foreign country to discontinue granting immigrant visas or nonimmigrant visas, or both, to citizens, subjects, nationals, and residents of that country until the Attorney General notifies the Secretary that the country has accepted the alien.

(June 27, 1952, ch. 477, title II, ch. 5, §243, 66 Stat. 212; as amended by P.L. 89-236 (10/3/65); P.L. 95-549 (10/30/78); P.L. 96-212 (3/17/80); P.L. 97-116 (12/29/81); P.L. 101-649 (IMMACT90) (11/29/90); P.L. 104-132 (AEDPA) (4/24/96), title IV, §413(a); P.L. 104-208 (IIRAIRA) (9/30/96), div. C, title III, §307(a) [rewriting in its entirety].)

## Sec. 244 Temporary Protected Status
## [8 U.S.C. 1254a]

### (a) Granting of status.—

(1) *In general.*— In the case of an alien who is a national of a foreign state designated under subsection (b) (or in the case of an alien having no nationality, is a person who last habitually resided in such designated state) and who meets the requirements of subsection (c), the Attorney General, in accordance with this section—

(A) may grant the alien temporary protected status in the United States and shall not remove the alien from the United States during the period in which such status is in effect, and

(B) shall authorize the alien to engage in employment in the United States and provide the alien with an "employment authorized" endorsement or other appropriate work permit.

(2) *Duration of work authorization.*— Work authorization provided under this section shall be effective throughout the period the alien is in temporary protected status under this section.

(3) *Notice.*—

(A) Upon the granting of temporary protected status under this section, the Attorney General shall provide the alien with information concerning such status under this section.

(B) If, at the time of initiation of a removal proceeding against an alien, the foreign state (of which the alien is a national) is designated under subsection (b), the Attorney General shall promptly notify the alien of the temporary protected status that may be available under this section.

(C) If, at the time of designation of a foreign state under subsection (b), an alien (who is a national of such state) is in a removal proceeding under this title, the Attorney General shall promptly notify the alien of the temporary protected status that may be available under this section.

(D) Notices under this paragraph shall be provided in a form and language that the alien can understand.

(4) *Temporary treatment for eligible aliens.*—

(A) In the case of an alien who can establish a prima facie case of eligibility for benefits under paragraph (1), but for the fact that the period of registration under subsection (c)(1)(A)(iv) has not begun, until the alien has had a reasonable opportunity to register during the first 30 days of such period, the Attorney General shall provide for the benefits of paragraph (1).

(B) In the case of an alien who establishes a prima facie case of eligibility for benefits under paragraph (1), until a final determination with respect to the alien's eligibility for such benefits under paragraph (1) has been made, the alien shall be provided such benefits.

(5) *Clarification.*— Nothing in this section shall be construed as authorizing the Attorney General to deny temporary protected status to an alien based on the alien's immigration status or to require any alien, as a condition of being granted such status, either to relinquish non-immigrant or other status the alien may have or to execute any waiver of other rights under this Act. The granting of temporary protected status under this section shall not be considered to be inconsistent with the granting of nonimmigrant status under this Act.

**(b) Designations.**—

(1) *In general.*— The Attorney General, after consultation with appropriate agencies of the Government, may designate any foreign state (or any part of such foreign state) under this subsection only if—

(A) the Attorney General finds that there is an ongoing armed conflict within the state and, due to such conflict, requiring the return of aliens who are nationals of that state to that state (or to the part of the state) would pose a serious threat to their personal safety;

(B) the Attorney General finds that—

(i) there has been an earthquake, flood, drought, epidemic, or other environmental disaster in the state resulting in a substantial, but temporary, disruption of living conditions in the area affected,

(ii) the foreign state is unable, temporarily, to handle adequately the return to the state of aliens who are nationals of the state, and

(iii) the foreign state officially has requested designation under this subparagraph; or

(C) the Attorney General finds that there exist extraordinary and temporary conditions in the foreign state that prevent aliens who are nationals of the state from returning to the state in safety, unless the Attorney General finds that permitting the aliens to remain temporarily in the United States is contrary to the national interest of the United States.

A designation of a foreign state (or part of such foreign state) under this paragraph shall not become effective unless notice of the designation (including a statement of the findings under this paragraph and the effective date of the designation) is published in the *Federal Register*. In such notice, the Attorney General shall also state an estimate of the number of nationals of the foreign state designated who are (or within the effective period of the designation are likely to become) eligible for temporary protected status under this section and their immigration status in the United States.

(2) *Effective period of designation for foreign states.*— The designation of a foreign state (or part of such foreign state) under paragraph (1) shall—

(A) take effect upon the date of publication of the designation under such paragraph, or such later date as the Attorney General may specify in the notice published under such paragraph, and

(B) shall remain in effect until the effective date of the termination of the designation under paragraph (3)(B).

For purposes of this section, the initial period of designation of a foreign state (or part thereof) under paragraph (1) is the period, specified by the Attorney General, of not less than 6 months and not more than 18 months.

(3) *Periodic review, terminations, and extensions of designations.*—

(A) *Periodic review.*— At least 60 days before end of the initial period of designation, and any extended period of designation, of a foreign state (or part thereof) under this section the Attorney General, after consultation with appropriate agencies of the Government, shall review the conditions in the foreign state (or part of such foreign state) for which a designation is in effect under this subsection and shall determine whether the conditions for such designation under this subsection continue to be met. The Attorney General shall provide on a timely basis for the publication of notice of each such determination (including the basis for the determination, and, in the case of an affirmative determination, the period of extension of designation under subparagraph (C)) in the *Federal Register*.

(B) *Termination of designation.*— If the Attorney General determines under subparagraph (A) that a foreign state (or part of such foreign state) no longer continues to meet the conditions for designation under paragraph (1), the Attorney General shall terminate the designation by publishing notice in the *Federal Register* of the determination under this subparagraph (including the basis for the determination). Such termination is effective in accordance with subsection (d)(3), but shall not be effective earlier than 60 days after the date the notice is published or, if later, the expiration of the most recent previous extension under subparagraph (C).

(C) *Extension of designation.*— If the Attorney General does not determine under subparagraph (A) that a foreign state (or part of such foreign state) no longer meets the conditions for designation under paragraph (1), the period of designation of the foreign state is extended for an additional period of 6 months (or, in the discretion of the Attorney General, a period of 12 or 18 months).

(4) ***Information concerning protected status at time of designations.***— At the time of a designation of a foreign state under this subsection, the Attorney General shall make available information respecting the temporary protected status made available to aliens who are nationals of such designated foreign state.

(5) ***Review.***—

(A) *Designations.*— There is no judicial review of any determination of the Attorney General with respect to the designation, or termination or extension of a designation, of a foreign state under this subsection.

(B) *Application to individuals.*— The Attorney General shall establish an administrative procedure for the review of the denial of benefits to aliens under this subsection. Such procedure shall not prevent an alien from asserting protection under this section in removal proceedings if the alien demonstrates that the alien is a national of a state designated under paragraph (1).

**(c) Aliens eligible for temporary protected status.—**

(1) ***In general.***—

(A) *Nationals of designated foreign states.*— Subject to paragraph (3), an alien, who is a national of a state designated under subsection (b)(1) (or in the case of an alien having no nationality, is a person who last habitually resided in such designated state), meets the requirements of this paragraph only if—

(i) the alien has been continuously physically present in the United States since the effective date of the most recent designation of that state;

(ii) the alien has continuously resided in the United States since such date as the Attorney General may designate;

(iii) the alien is admissible as an immigrant, except as otherwise provided under paragraph (2)(A), and is not ineligible for temporary protected status under paragraph (2)(B); and

(iv) to the extent and in a manner which the Attorney General establishes, the alien registers for the temporary protected status under this section during a registration period of not less than 180 days.

(B) *Registration fee.*— The Attorney General may require payment of a reasonable fee as a condition of registering an alien under subparagraph (A)(iv) (including providing an alien with an "employment authorized" endorsement or other appropriate work permit under this section). The amount of any such fee shall not exceed $50. In the case of aliens registered pursuant to a designation under this section made after July 17, 1991, the Attorney General may impose a separate, additional fee for providing an alien with documentation of work authorization. Notwithstanding section 3302 of title 31, United States Code, all fees collected under this subparagraph shall be credited to the appropriation to be used in carrying out this section.[155]

(2) *Eligibility standards.*—

(A) *Waiver of certain grounds for inadmissibility.*— In the determination of an alien's admissibility for purposes of subparagraph (A)(iii) of paragraph (1)—

(i) the provisions of paragraphs (5) and (7)(A) of section 212(a) shall not apply;

(ii) except as provided in clause (iii), the Attorney General may waive any other provision of section 212(a) in the case of individual aliens for humanitarian purposes, to assure family unity, or when it is otherwise in the public interest; but

(iii) the Attorney General may not waive—

(I) paragraphs (2)(A) and (2)(B) (relating to criminals) of such section,

(II) paragraph (2)(C) of such section (relating to drug offenses), except for so much of such paragraph as relates to a single offense of simple possession of 30 grams or less of marijuana, or

(III) paragraphs (3)(A), (3)(B), (3)(C), and (3)(E) of such section (relating to national security and participation in the Nazi persecutions or those who have engaged in genocide).

(B) *Aliens ineligible.*— An alien shall not be eligible for temporary protected status under this section if the Attorney General finds that—

(i) the alien has been convicted of any felony or 2 or more misdemeanors committed in the United States, or

(ii) the alien is described in section 208(b)(2)(A).

(3) *Withdrawal of temporary protected status.*— The Attorney General shall withdraw temporary protected status granted to an alien under this section if—

---

[155] *See* §549 of the P.L. 111-83 (123 STAT. 524), authorizes the collection of fees for fingerprinting services, biometric services, and other necessary services for TPS registrants.

(A) the Attorney General finds that the alien was not in fact eligible for such status under this section,

(B) except as provided in paragraph (4) and permitted in subsection (f)(3), the alien has not remained continuously physically present in the United States from the date the alien first was granted temporary protected status under this section, or

(C) the alien fails, without good cause, to register with the Attorney General annually, at the end of each 12-month period after the granting of such status, in a form and manner specified by the Attorney General.

(4) *Treatment of brief, casual, and innocent departures and certain other absences.*—

(A) For purposes of paragraphs (1)(A)(i) and (3)(B), an alien shall not be considered to have failed to maintain continuous physical presence in the United States by virtue of brief, casual, and innocent absences from the United States, without regard to whether such absences were authorized by the Attorney General.

(B) For purposes of paragraphs (1)(A)(ii), an alien shall not be considered to have failed to maintain continuous residence in the United States by reason of a brief, casual, and innocent absence described in subparagraph (A) or due merely to a brief temporary trip abroad required by emergency or extenuating circumstances outside the control of the alien.

(5) *Construction.*— Nothing in this section shall be construed as authorizing an alien to apply for admission to, or to be admitted to, the United States in order to apply for temporary protected status under this section.

(6) *Confidentiality of information.*— The Attorney General shall establish procedures to protect the confidentiality of information provided by aliens under this section.

**(d) Documentation.**—

(1) *Initial issuance.*— Upon the granting of temporary protected status to an alien under this section, the Attorney General shall provide for the issuance of such temporary documentation and authorization as may be necessary to carry out the purposes of this section.

(2) *Period of validity.*— Subject to paragraph (3), such documentation shall be valid during the initial period of designation of the foreign state (or part thereof) involved and any extension of such period. The Attorney General may stagger the periods of validity of the documentation and authorization in order to provide for an orderly renewal of such documentation and authorization and for an orderly transition (under paragraph (3)) upon the termination of a designation of a foreign state (or any part of such foreign state).

(3) *Effective date of terminations.*— If the Attorney General terminates the designation of a foreign state (or part of such foreign state) under subsection (b)(3)(B), such termination shall only apply to documentation and authorization issued or renewed after the effective date of the publication of notice of the determination under that subsection (or, at the Attorney General's option, after such period after the effective date of the determination as the Attorney General determines to be appropriate in order to provide for an orderly transition).

(4) *Detention of the alien.*— An alien provided temporary protected status under this section shall not be detained by the Attorney General on the basis of the alien's immigration status in the United States.

**(e) Relation of period of temporary protected status to cancellation of removal.**— With respect to an alien granted temporary protected status under this section, the period of such status shall not be counted as a period of physical presence in the United States for purposes of section 240A(a), unless the Attorney General determines that extreme hardship exists. Such period shall not cause a break in the continuity of residence of the period before and after such period for purposes of such section.

**(f) Benefits and status during period of temporary protected status.**— During a period in which an alien is granted temporary protected status under this section—

(1) the alien shall not be considered to be permanently residing in the United States under color of law;

(2) the alien may be deemed ineligible for public assistance by a State (as defined in section 101(a)(36)) or any political subdivision thereof which furnishes such assistance;

(3) the alien may travel abroad with the prior consent of the Attorney General; and

(4) for purposes of adjustment of status under section 245 and change of status under section 248, the alien shall be considered as being in, and maintaining, lawful status as a nonimmigrant.

**(g) Exclusive remedy.**— Except as otherwise specifically provided, this section shall constitute the exclusive authority of the Attorney General under law to permit aliens who are or may become otherwise deportable or have been paroled into the United States to remain in the United States temporarily because of their particular nationality or region of foreign state of nationality.

**(h) Limitation on consideration in the Senate of Legislation adjusting status.**—

(1) *In general.*— Except as provided in paragraph (2), it shall not be in order in the Senate to consider any bill, resolution, or amendment that—

(A) provides for adjustment to lawful temporary or permanent resident alien status for any alien receiving temporary protected status under this section, or

(B) has the effect of amending this subsection or limiting the application of this subsection.

(2) *Supermajority required.*— Paragraph (1) may be waived or suspended in the Senate only by the affirmative vote of three-fifths of the Members duly chosen and sworn. An affirmative vote of three-fifths of the Members of the Senate duly chosen and sworn shall be required in the Senate to sustain an appeal of the ruling of the Chair on a point of order raised under paragraph (1).

(3) *Rules.*— Paragraphs (1) and (2) are enacted—

(A) as an exercise of the rulemaking power of the Senate and as such they are deemed a part of the rules of the Senate, but applicable only with respect to the matters described in paragraph (1) and supersede other rules of the Senate only to the extent that such paragraphs are inconsistent therewith; and

(B) with full recognition of the constitutional right of the Senate to change such rules at any time, in the same manner as in the case of any other rule of the Senate.

**(i) Annual report and review.**—

(1) *Annual report.*— Not later than March 1 of each year (beginning with 1992), the Attorney General, after consultation with the appropriate agencies of the Government, shall submit a report to the Committees on the Judiciary of the House of Representatives and of the Senate on the operation of this section during the previous year. Each report shall include—

(A) a listing of the foreign states or parts thereof designated under this section,

(B) the number of nationals of each such state who have been granted temporary protected status under this section and their immigration status before being granted such status, and

(C) an explanation of the reasons why foreign states or parts thereof were designated under subsection (b)(1) and, with respect to foreign states or parts thereof previously designated, why the designation was terminated or extended under subsection (b)(3).

(2) *Committee report.*— No later than 180 days after the date of receipt of such a report, the Committee on the Judiciary of each House of Congress shall report to its respective House such oversight findings and legislation as it deems appropriate.

(June 27, 1952, ch. 477, title II, ch. 5, §244A; as amended by P.L. 101-649 (IMMACT90) (11/29/90); P.L. 102-232 (MTINA) (12/12/91, *effective* 4/1/92); P.L. 103-416 (INTCA) (10/25/94, *effective* 4/1/95); P.L. 104-208 (IIRAIRA) (9/30/96), div. C, title III, §308 [repealing original §244 & redesignating §244A as §244].)

# Chapter 5 — Deportation; Adjustment of Status

## Sec. 245 Adjustment of Status of Nonimmigrant to that of Person Admitted for Permanent Residence
## [8 U.S.C. 1255]

(a)[156] **Status as person admitted for permanent residence on application and eligibility for immigrant visa.**— The status of an alien who was inspected and admitted or paroled into the United States or the status of any other alien having an approved petition for classification as a VAWA self-petitioner may be adjusted by the Attorney General, in his discretion and under such regulations as he may prescribe, to that of an alien lawfully admitted for permanent residence if

(1) the alien makes an application for such adjustment,

(2) the alien is eligible to receive an immigrant visa and is admissible to the United States for permanent residence, and

(3) an immigrant visa is immediately available to him at the time his application is filed.

(b) **Record of lawful admission for permanent residence; reduction of preference visas.**— Upon the approval of an application for adjustment made under subsection (a), the Attorney General shall record the alien's lawful admission for permanent residence as of the date the order of the Attorney General approving the application for the adjustment of status is made, and the Secretary of State shall reduce by one the number of the preference visas authorized to be issued under sections 202 and 203 within the class to which the alien is chargeable for the fiscal year then current.

(c)[157] **Alien crewmen, aliens continuing or accepting unauthorized employment, and aliens admitted in transit without visa.**— Other than an alien having an approved petition for classification as a VAWA self-petitioner, subsection (a) shall not be applicable to

(1) an alien crewman;

(2) subject to subsection (k), an alien (other than an immediate relative as defined in section 201(b) or a special immigrant described in section 101(a)(27)(H), (I), (J), or (K)) who hereaf-

---

[156] Sec. 1703(b) of the 2004 National Defense Authorization Act, P.L. 108-136 (*reprinted in* Appendix M), provides for certain benefits (*retroactively effective* 9/11/01, per §1705 of P.L. 108-136), notwithstanding §245(a) and (c), for surviving spouses, children, and parents of certain deceased military personnel.

[157] *See* note 156, *supra.*

ter continues in or accepts unauthorized employment prior to filing an application for adjustment of status or who is in unlawful immigration status on the date of filing the application for adjustment of status or who has failed (other than through no fault of his own or for technical reasons) to maintain continuously a lawful status since entry into the United States;

(3) any alien admitted in transit without visa under section 212(d)(4)(C);

(4) an alien (other than an immediate relative as defined in section 201(b)) who was admitted as a nonimmigrant visitor without a visa under section 212(*l*) or section 217;

(5) an alien who was admitted as a nonimmigrant described in section 101(a)(15)(S);

(6) an alien who is deportable under section 237(a)(4)(B);

(7) any alien who seeks adjustment of status to that of an immigrant under section 203(b) and is not in a lawful nonimmigrant status; or

(8) any alien who was employed while the alien was an unauthorized alien, as defined in section 274A(h)(3), or who has otherwise violated the terms of a nonimmigrant visa.

**(d) Alien admitted for permanent residence on conditional basis; fiancée or fiancé of citizen.**— The Attorney General may not adjust, under subsection (a), the status of an alien lawfully admitted to the United States for permanent residence on a conditional basis under section 216. The Attorney General may not adjust, under subsection (a), the status of a nonimmigrant alien described in section 101(a)(15)(K) except to that of an alien lawfully admitted to the United States on a conditional basis under section 216 as a result of the marriage of the nonimmigrant (or, in the case of a minor child, the parent) to the citizen who filed the petition to accord that alien's nonimmigrant status under section 101(a)(15)(K).

**(e) Restriction on adjustment of status based on marriages entered while in admissibility or deportation proceedings; bona fide marriage exception.**—

(1) Except as provided in paragraph (3), an alien who is seeking to receive an immigrant visa on the basis of a marriage which was entered into during the period described in paragraph (2) may not have the alien's status adjusted under subsection (a).

(2) The period described in this paragraph is the period during which administrative or judicial proceedings are pending regarding the alien's right to be admitted or remain in the United States.

(3) Paragraph (1) and section 204(g) shall not apply with respect to a marriage if the alien establishes by clear and convincing evidence to the satisfaction of the Attorney General that the marriage was entered into in good faith and in accordance with the laws of the place where the marriage took place and the marriage was not entered into for the purpose of procuring the alien's admission as an immigrant and no fee or other consideration was given (other than a fee or other consideration to an attorney for assistance in preparation of a lawful petition) for the filing of a petition under section 204(a) or subsection (d) or (p) of subsection 214 with respect to the alien spouse or alien son or daughter. In accordance with regulations, there shall be only one level of administrative appellate review for each alien under the previous sentence.

**(f) Limitation on adjustment of status.**— The Attorney General may not adjust, under subsection (a), the status of an alien lawfully admitted to the United States for permanent residence on a conditional basis under section 216A.

**(g) Special immigrants.**— In applying this section to a special immigrant described in section 101(a)(27)(K), such an immigrant shall be deemed, for purposes of subsection (a), to have been paroled into the United States.

**(h) Application with respect to special immigrants.**— In applying this section to a special immigrant described in section 101(a)(27)(J)—

(1) such an immigrant shall be deemed, for purposes of subsection (a), to have been paroled into the United States; and

(2) in determining the alien's admissibility as an immigrant—

(A) paragraphs (4), (5)(A), (6)(A), (6)(C), (6)(D), (7)(A), and (9)(B) of section 212(a) shall not apply; and

(B) the Attorney General may waive other paragraphs of section 212(a) (other than paragraphs (2)(A), (2)(B), (2)(C) (except for so much of such paragraph as related to a single offense of simple possession of 30 grams or less of marijuana), (3)(A), (3)(B), (3)(C), and (3)(E)) in the case of individual aliens for humanitarian purposes, family unity, or when it is otherwise in the public interest.

The relationship between an alien and the alien's natural parents or prior adoptive parents shall not be considered a factor in making a waiver under paragraph (2)(B). Nothing in this subsection or section 101(a)(27)(J) shall be construed as authorizing an alien to apply for admission or be admitted to the United States in order to obtain special immigrant status described in such section.

**(i)[158] Adjustment in status of certain aliens physically present in United States.**

(1) Notwithstanding the provisions of subsections (a) and (c) of this section, an alien physically present in the United States—

(A) who—

(i) entered the United States without inspection; or

(ii) is within one of the classes enumerated in subsection (c) of this section;

(B) who is the beneficiary (including a spouse or child of the principal alien, if eligible to receive a visa under section 203(d)) of—

(i) a petition for classification under section 204 that was filed with the Attorney General on or before April 30, 2001; or

(ii) an application for a labor certification under section 212(a)(5)(A) that was filed pursuant to the regulations of the Secretary of Labor on or before such date; and

(C) who, in the case of a beneficiary of a petition for classification, or an application for labor certification, described in subparagraph (B) that was filed after January 14, 1998, is physically present in the United States on the date of the enactment of the LIFE Act Amendments of 2000;[159]

---

[158] The original §245(i) took effect on 10/1/94 and was scheduled to sunset on 9/30/97. The provision was extended until 11/26/97 by a series of continuing resolutions. P.L. 105-119. The revised §245(i) provides that an individual who is ineligible to adjust under §245(a) may still adjust under §245(i), but in order to be eligible, he or she must either be the beneficiary of a visa petition filed by the attorney general on or before 1/14/98, or a labor certification filed with a state labor office on or before 1/14/98. The LIFE Act Amendments, 2000, P.L. 106-554, changed the date in (i)(1)(B) to 4/30/01, and also added (i)(1)(C).

[159] Sec. 1506 of the LIFE Act Amendments, 2000, P.L. 106-554, provided that the Act took effect "as if included in the enact-
*continued*

may apply to the Attorney General for the adjustment of his or her status to that of an alien lawfully admitted for permanent residence. The Attorney General may accept such application only if the alien remits with such application a sum equaling $1,000 as of the date of receipt of the application, but such sum shall not be required from a child under the age of seventeen, or an alien who is the spouse or unmarried child of an individual who obtained temporary or permanent resident status under section 210 or 245A of the Immigration and Nationality Act or section 202 of the Immigration Reform and Control Act of 1986 at any date, who (i) as of May 5, 1988, was the unmarried child or spouse of the individual who obtained temporary or permanent resident status under section 210 or 245A of the Immigration and Nationality Act or section 202 of the Immigration Reform and Control Act of 1986; (ii) entered the United States before May 5, 1988, resided in the United States on May 5, 1988, and is not a lawful permanent resident; and (iii) applied for benefits under section 301(a) of the Immigration Act of 1990. The sum specified herein shall be in addition to the fee normally required for the processing of an application under this section.

(2) Upon receipt of such an application and the sum hereby required, the Attorney General may adjust the status of the alien to that of an alien lawfully admitted for permanent residence if—

(A) the alien is eligible to receive an immigrant visa and is admissible to the United States for permanent residence; and

(B) an immigrant visa is immediately available to the alien at the time the application is filed.

(3)[160](A) The portion of each application fee (not to exceed $200) that the Attorney General determines is required to process an application under this section and is remitted to the Attorney General pursuant to paragraphs (1) and (2) of this subsection shall be disposed of by the Attorney General as provided in subsections (m), (n), and (o) of section 286.

(B) Any remaining portion of such fees remitted under such paragraphs shall be deposited by the Attorney General into the Breached Bond/Detention Fund established under section 286(r), except that in the case of fees attributable to applications for a beneficiary with respect to whom a petition for classification, or an application for labor certification, described in paragraph (1)(B) was filed after January 14, 1998, one-half of such remaining portion shall be deposited by the Attorney General into the Immigration Examinations Fee Account established under section 286(m).

**(j) Adjustment to permanent resident status.—**

(1) If, in the opinion of the Attorney General—

(A) a nonimmigrant admitted into the United States under section 101(a)(15)(S)(i) has supplied information described in subclause (I) of such section; and

(B) the provision of such information has substantially contributed to the success of an authorized criminal investigation or the prosecution of an individual described in subclause (III) of that section,

the Attorney General may adjust the status of the alien (and the spouse, married and unmarried sons and daughters, and parents of the alien if admitted under that section) to that of an

---

ment of the Legal Immigration Family Equity Act," *i.e.*, 12/21/00.

[160] *See* §376(b) of IIRAIRA, effective for all applications "made on or after the end of the 90-day period beginning on the date of the enactment of this Act."

alien lawfully admitted for permanent residence if the alien is not described in section 212(a)(3)(E).

(2) If, in the sole discretion of the Attorney General—

(A) a nonimmigrant admitted into the United States under section 101(a)(15)(S)(ii) has supplied information described in subclause (I) of such section, and

(B) the provision of such information has substantially contributed to—

(i) the prevention or frustration of an act of terrorism against a United States person or United States property, or

(ii) the success of an authorized criminal investigation of, or the prosecution of, an individual involved in such an act of terrorism, and

(C) the nonimmigrant has received a reward under section 36(a) of the State Department Basic Authorities Act of 1956, the Attorney General may adjust the status of the alien (and the spouse, married and unmarried sons and daughters, and parents of the alien if admitted under such section) to that of an alien lawfully admitted for permanent residence if the alien is not described in section 212(a)(3)(E).

(3) Upon the approval of adjustment of status under paragraph (1) or (2),[161] the Attorney General shall record the alien's lawful admission for permanent residence as of the date of such approval and the Secretary of State shall reduce by one the number of visas authorized to be issued under sections 201(d) and 203(b)(4) for the fiscal year then current.

**(k) Inapplicability of certain provisions for certain employment-based immigrants.**— An alien who is eligible to receive an immigrant visa under paragraph (1), (2), or (3) of section 203(b) (or, in the case of an alien who is an immigrant described in section 101(a)(27)(C), under section 203(b)(4)) may adjust status pursuant to subsection (a) and notwithstanding subsection (c)(2), (c)(7), and (c)(8), if—

(1) the alien, on the date of filing an application for adjustment of status, is present in the United States pursuant to a lawful admission;

(2) the alien, subsequent to such lawful admission has not, for an aggregate period exceeding 180 days—

(A) failed to maintain, continuously, a lawful status;

(B) engaged in unauthorized employment; or

(C) otherwise violated the terms and conditions of the alien's admission.

**(***l***) Adjustment of status for victims of trafficking.**—

(1) If, in the opinion of the Secretary of Homeland Security, or in the case of subparagraph (C)(i), in the opinion of the Secretary of Homeland Security, in consultation with the Attorney General, as appropriate a nonimmigrant admitted into the United States under section 101(a)(15)(T)(i)—

(A) has been physically present in the United States for a continuous period of at least 3 years since the date of admission as a nonimmigrant under section 101(a)(15)(T)(i), or has been physically present in the United States for a continuous period during the inves-

---

[161] Amended by §671(a)(5) of IIRAIRA. Effective as if included in the Violent Crime Control and Law Enforcement Act, 1994 (VCCLEA).

tigation or prosecution of acts of trafficking and that, in the opinion of the Attorney General, the investigation or prosecution is complete, whichever period of time is less;

(B) subject to paragraph (6), has, throughout such period, been a person of good moral character; and

(C) (i) has, during such period, complied with any reasonable request for assistance in the investigation or prosecution of acts of trafficking;

(ii) the alien would suffer extreme hardship involving unusual and severe harm upon removal from the United States, the Secretary of Homeland Security may adjust the status of the alien (and any person admitted under section 101(a)(15)(T)(ii) as the spouse, parent, sibling, or child of the alien) to that of an alien lawfully admitted for permanent residence; or

(iii) was younger than 18 years of age at the time of the victimization qualifying the alien for relief under section 101(a)(15)(T).

(2) Paragraph (1) shall not apply to an alien admitted under section 101(a)(15)(T) who is inadmissible to the United States by reason of a ground that has not been waived under section 212, except that, if the Secretary of Homeland Security considers it to be in the national interest to do so, the Secretary of Homeland Security, in the Secretary of Homeland Security's discretion, may waive the application of—

(A) paragraphs (1) and (4) of section 212(a); and

(B) any other provision of such section (excluding paragraphs (3), (10)(C), and (10)(E)), if the activities rendering the alien inadmissible under the provision were caused by, or were incident to, the victimization described in section 101(a)(15)(T)(i)(I).

(3) An alien shall be considered to have failed to maintain continuous physical presence in the United States under paragraph (1)(A) if the alien has departed from the United States for any period in excess of 90 days or for any periods in the aggregate exceeding 180 days, unless—

(A) the absence was necessary to assist in the investigation or prosecution described in paragraph (1)(A); or

(B) an official involved in the investigation or prosecution certifies that the absence was otherwise justified.

(4) (A) The total number of aliens whose status may be adjusted under paragraph (1) during any fiscal year may not exceed 5,000.

(B) The numerical limitation of subparagraph (A) shall only apply to principal aliens and not to the spouses, sons, daughters, siblings, or parents of such aliens.

(5) Upon the approval of adjustment of status under paragraph (1), the Secretary of Homeland Security shall record the alien's lawful admission for permanent residence as of the date of such approval.

(6) For purposes of paragraph (1)(B), the Secretary of Homeland Security may waive consideration of a disqualification from good moral character with respect to an alien if the disqualification was caused by, or incident to, the trafficking described in section 101(a)(15)(T)(i)(I).

(7) The Secretary of Homeland Security shall permit aliens to apply for a waiver of any fees associated with filing an application for relief through final adjudication of the adjustment of status for a VAWA self-petitioner and for relief under sections 101(a)(15)(T), 101(a)(15)(U), 106, 240A(b)(2), and 244(a)(3) (as in effect on March 31, 1997).

**(m) Adjustment of status for victims of crimes against women.—**

(1) The Secretary of Homeland Security may adjust the status of an alien admitted into the United States (or otherwise provided nonimmigrant status) under section 101(a)(15)(U) to that of an alien lawfully admitted for permanent residence if the alien is not described in section 212(a)(3)(E), unless the Secretary determines based on affirmative evidence that the alien unreasonably refused to provide assistance in a criminal investigation or prosecution, if—

(A) the alien has been physically present in the United States for a continuous period of at least 3 years since the date of admission as a nonimmigrant under clause (i) or (ii) of section 101(a)(15)(U); and

(B) in the opinion of the Secretary of Homeland Security, the alien's continued presence in the United States is justified on humanitarian grounds, to ensure family unity, or is otherwise in the public interest.

(2) An alien shall be considered to have failed to maintain continuous physical presence in the United States under paragraph (1)(A) if the alien has departed from the United States for any period in excess of 90 days or for any periods in the aggregate exceeding 180 days unless the absence is in order to assist in the investigation or prosecution or unless an official involved in the investigation or prosecution certifies that the absence was otherwise justified.

(3) Upon approval of adjustment of status under paragraph (1) of an alien described in section 101(a)(15)(U)(i) the Secretary of Homeland Security may adjust the status of or issue an immigrant visa to a spouse, a child, or, in the case of an alien child, a parent who did not receive a nonimmigrant visa under section 101(a)(15)(U)(ii) if the Secretary considers the grant of such status or visa necessary to avoid extreme hardship.

(4) Upon the approval of adjustment of status under paragraph (1) or (3), the Secretary of Homeland Security shall record the alien's lawful admission for permanent residence as of the date of such approval.

(5) (A) The Secretary of Homeland Security shall consult with the Attorney General, as appropriate, in making a determination under paragraph (1) whether affirmative evidence demonstrates that the alien unreasonably refused to provide assistance to a Federal law enforcement official, Federal prosecutor, Federal judge, or other Federal authority investigating or prosecuting criminal activity described in section 101(a)(15)(U)(iii).

(B) Nothing in paragraph (1)(B) may be construed to prevent the Secretary from consulting with the Attorney General in making a determination whether affirmative evidence demonstrates that the alien unreasonably refused to provide assistance to a State or local law enforcement official, State or local prosecutor, State or local judge, or other State or local authority investigating or prosecuting criminal activity described in section 101(a)(15)(U)(iii).

(June 27, 1952, ch. 477, title II, ch. 5, §245, 66 Stat. 217; as amended by P.L. 85-700 (8/21/58); P.L. 86-648 (7/14/60); P.L. 89-236 (10/3/65); P.L. 94-571 (10/20/76); P.L. 97-116 (12/29/81); P.L. 99-603 (IRCA) (11/6/86); P.L. 99-639 (11/10/86); P.L. 100-525 (10/24/88); P.L. 101-649 (IMMACT90) (11/29/90); P.L. 102-110 (10/1/91); P.L. 102-232 (MTINA) (12/12/91, *effective* 4/1/92); P.L. 103-317 (8/26/94); P.L. 103-322 (VAWA) (9/13/94); P.L. 103-416 (INTCA) (10/25/94, *effective* 4/1/95); P.L. 104-132 (AEDPA) (4/24/96), title IV, §413(d); P.L. 104-208 (IIRAIRA) (9/30/96), div. C, title III, §308(f) [revising (c)(6)], §375 [revising (c)(7)], §376(a) [revising (i)], title VI, §671(a)(4)(A) [revising & redesignating (i) as (j)]; P.L. 105-119 (11/26/97), title

I, §110(3) [revising (i); adding (k)], §111(a) [revising (c)]; P.L. 106-386 (10/28/00), div. A, §107(f) [adding (*l*)], div. B, title V, §1506(a)(1) [revising (a) & (c)], §1513(f) [adding a second (*l*)]; P.L. 106-553 (LIFE Act) (12/21/00), §1(a)(2), title XI, §1102(c) [adding (m)], §1103(c)(3) [revising (d)–(f)]; P.L. 106-554 (12/21/00), §1(a)(4) [revising (d)–(f), div. B, title XV, §1502 [revising (i); repealing original (m)]; P.L. 108-193 (12/19/03), §4(b)(3) [revising (*l*)], §8(a)(4) [redesignating (2), (3), & (4) as (3), (4), & (5) respectively; redesignating second (*l*) as (m)]; P.L. 109-162 (1/5/06), title VIII, §803 [revising (*l*)(1), (*l*)(2), (*l*)(5), (m)(1), (m)(3), & (m)(4)]; P.L. 109-271 (8/12/06), §6 [revising (a) & (c)]; P.L. 110-457 (12/23/08) [revising (h)(2)(A), (*l*)(1), (*l*)(1)(B)–(C), (m)(1); adding (*l*)(1)(C)(iii) & (m)(5)(A)–(B)].)

## Sec. 245A Adjustment of Status of Certain Entrants before January 1, 1982, to that of Person Admitted for Lawful Residence
[8 U.S.C. 1255a]

**(a) Temporary resident status.**— The Attorney General shall adjust the status of an alien to that of an alien lawfully admitted for temporary residence if the alien meets the following requirements:

(1) *Timely application.*—

(A) *During application period.*— Except as provided in subparagraph (B), the alien must apply for such adjustment during the 12-month period beginning on a date (not later than 180 days after the date of enactment of this section) designated by the Attorney General.

(B) *Application within 30 days of show-cause order.*— An alien who, at any time during the first 11 months of the 12-month period described in subparagraph (A), is the subject of an order to show cause issued under section 242 (as in effect before October 1, 1996), must make application under this section not later than the end of the 30-day period beginning either on the first day of such 12-month period or on the date of the issuance of such order, whichever day is later.

(C) *Information included in application.*— Each application under this subsection shall contain such information as the Attorney General may require, including information on living relatives of the applicant with respect to whom a petition for preference or other status may be filed by the applicant at any later date under section 204(a).

(2) *Continuous unlawful residence since 1982.*—

(A) *In general.*— The alien must establish that he entered the United States before January 1, 1982, and that he has resided continuously in the United States in an unlawful status since such date and through the date the application is filed under this subsection.

(B) *Nonimmigrants.*— In the case of an alien who entered the United States as a nonimmigrant before January 1, 1982, the alien must establish that the alien's period of authorized stay as a nonimmigrant expired before such date through the passage of time or the alien's unlawful status was known to the Government as of such date.

(C) *Exchange visitors.*— If the alien was at any time a nonimmigrant exchange alien (as defined in section 101(a)(15)(J)), the alien must establish that the alien was not subject to the two-year foreign residence requirement of section 212(e) or has fulfilled that requirement or received a waiver thereof.

(3) *Continuous physical presence since enactment.*—

(A) *In general.*— The alien must establish that the alien has been continuously physically present in the United States since the date of the enactment of this section.

(B) *Treatment of brief, casual, and innocent absences.*— An alien shall not be considered to have failed to maintain continuous physical presence in the United States for purposes of subparagraph (A) by virtue of brief, casual, and innocent absences from the United States.

(C) *Admissions.*— Nothing in this section shall be construed as authorizing an alien to apply for admission to, or to be admitted to, the United States in order to apply for adjustment of status under this subsection.

(4) *Admissible as immigrant.*— The alien must establish that he—

(A) is admissible to the United States as an immigrant, except as otherwise provided under subsection (d)(2),

(B) has not been convicted of any felony or of three or more misdemeanors committed in the United States,

(C) has not assisted in the persecution of any person or persons on account of race, religion, nationality, membership in a particular social group, or political opinion, and

(D) is registered or registering under the Military Selective Service Act, if the alien is required to be so registered under that Act.

For purposes of this subsection, an alien in the status of a Cuban and Haitian entrant described in paragraph (1) or (2)(A) of section 501(e) of Public Law 96-422 shall be considered to have entered the United States and to be in an unlawful status in the United States.

**(b) Subsequent adjustment to permanent residence and nature of temporary resident status.—**

(1) *Adjustment to permanent residence.*— The Attorney General shall adjust the status of any alien provided lawful temporary resident status under subsection (a) to that of an alien lawfully admitted for permanent residence if the alien meets the following requirements:

(A) *Timely application after one year's residence.*— The alien must apply for such adjustment during the 2-year period beginning with the nineteenth month that begins after the date the alien was granted such temporary resident status.

(B) *Continuous residence.*—

(i) In general.— The alien must establish that he has continuously resided in the United States since the date the alien was granted such temporary resident status.

(ii) Treatment of certain absences.— An alien shall not be considered to have lost the continuous residence referred to in clause (i) by reason of an absence from the United States permitted under paragraph (3)(A).

(C) *Admissible as immigrant.*— The alien must establish that he—

(i) is admissible to the United States as an immigrant, except as otherwise provided under subsection (d)(2), and

(ii) has not been convicted of any felony or three or more misdemeanors committed in the United States.

(D) *Basic citizenship skills.*—

(i) In general.— The alien must demonstrate that he either—

(I) meets the requirements of section 312(a) (relating to minimal understanding of ordinary English and a knowledge and understanding of the history and government of the United States), or

(II) is satisfactorily pursuing a course of study (recognized by the Attorney General) to achieve such an understanding of English and such a knowledge and understanding of the history and government of the United States.

(ii) Exception for elderly or developmentally disabled individuals.— The Attorney General may, in his discretion, waive all or part of the requirements of clause (i) in the case of an alien who is 65 years of age or older or who is developmentally disabled.

(iii) Relation to naturalization examination.— In accordance with regulations of the Attorney General, an alien who has demonstrated under clause (i)(I) that the alien meets the requirements of section 312(a) may be considered to have satisfied the requirements of that section for purposes of becoming naturalized as a citizen of the United States under title III.

(2) *Termination of temporary residence.*— The Attorney General shall provide for termination of temporary resident status granted an alien under subsection (a)—

(A) if it appears to the Attorney General that the alien was in fact not eligible for such status;

(B) if the alien commits an act that (i) makes the alien inadmissible to the United States as an immigrant, except as otherwise provided under subsection (d)(2), or (ii) is convicted of any felony or three or more misdemeanors committed in the United States; or

(C) at the end of the 43rd month beginning after the date the alien is granted such status, unless the alien has filed an application for adjustment of such status pursuant to paragraph (1) and such application has not been denied.

(3) *Authorized travel and employment during temporary residence.*— During the period an alien is in lawful temporary resident status granted under subsection (a)—

(A) *Authorization of travel abroad.*— The Attorney General shall, in accordance with regulations, permit the alien to return to the United States after such brief and casual trips abroad as reflect an intention on the part of the alien to adjust to lawful permanent resident status under paragraph (1) and after brief temporary trips abroad occasioned by a family obligation involving an occurrence such as the illness or death of a close relative or other family need.

(B) *Authorization of employment.*— The Attorney General shall grant the alien authorization to engage in employment in the United States and provide to that alien an "employment authorized" endorsement or other appropriate work permit.

**(c) Applications for adjustment of status.—**

(1) *To whom may be made.*— The Attorney General shall provide that applications for adjustment of status under subsection (a) may be filed—

(A) with the Attorney General, or

(B) with a qualified designated entity, but only if the applicant consents to the forwarding of the application to the Attorney General.

As used in this section, the term "qualified designated entity" means an organization or person designated under paragraph (2).

(2) *Designation of qualified entities to receive applications.*— For purposes of assisting in the program of legalization provided under this section, the Attorney General—

(A) shall designate qualified voluntary organizations and other qualified State, local, and community organizations, and

(B) may designate such other persons as the Attorney General determines are qualified and have substantial experience, demonstrated competence, and traditional long-term involvement in the preparation and submittal of applications for adjustment of status under section 209 or 245, Public Law 89-732, or Public Law 95-145.

(3) *Treatment of applications by designated entities.*— Each qualified designated entity must agree to forward to the Attorney General applications filed with it in accordance with paragraph (1)(B) but not to forward to the Attorney General applications filed with it unless the applicant has consented to such forwarding. No such entity may make a determination required by this section to be made by the Attorney General.

(4) *Limitation on access to information.*— Files and records of qualified designated entities relating to an alien's seeking assistance or information with respect to filing an application under this section are confidential and the Attorney General and the Service shall not have access to such files or records relating to an alien without the consent of the alien.

(5) *Confidentiality of information.*—

(A) *In general.*— Except as provided in this paragraph, neither the Attorney General, nor any other official or employee of the Department of Justice, or bureau or agency thereof, may—

(i) use the information furnished by the applicant pursuant to an application filed under this section for any purpose other than to make a determination on the application, for enforcement of paragraph (6), or for the preparation of reports to Congress under section 404 of the Immigration Reform and Control Act of 1986;

(ii) make any publication whereby the information furnished by any particular applicant can be identified; or

(iii) permit anyone other than the sworn officers and employees of the Department or bureau or agency or, with respect to applications filed with a designated entity, that designated entity, to examine individual applications.

(B) *Required disclosures.*— The Attorney General shall provide the information furnished under this section, and any other information derived from such furnished information, to a duly recognized law enforcement entity in connection with a criminal investigation or prosecution, when such information is requested in writing by such entity, or to an official coroner for purposes of affirmatively identifying a deceased individual (whether or not such individual is deceased as a result of a crime).

(C) *Authorized disclosures.*— The Attorney General may provide, in the Attorney General's discretion, for the furnishing of information furnished under this section in the same manner and circumstances as census information may be disclosed by the Secretary of Commerce under section 8 of title 13, United States Code.

(D) *Construction.*—

(i) In general.— Nothing in this paragraph shall be construed to limit the use, or release, for immigration enforcement purposes or law enforcement purposes of information contained in files or records of the Service pertaining to an application filed under this section, other than information furnished by an applicant pursuant to the application, or any other information derived from the application, that is not available from any other source.

(ii) Criminal convictions.— Information concerning whether the applicant has at any time been convicted of a crime may be used or released for immigration enforcement or law enforcement purposes.

(E) *Crime.*— Whoever knowingly uses, publishes, or permits information to be examined in violation of this paragraph shall be fined not more than $10,000.

(6) ***Penalties for false statements in applications.***— Whoever files an application for adjustment of status under this section and knowingly and willfully falsifies, misrepresents, conceals, or covers up a material fact or makes any false, fictitious, or fraudulent statements or representations, or makes or uses any false writing or document knowing the same to contain any false, fictitious, or fraudulent statement or entry, shall be fined in accordance with title 18, United States Code, or imprisoned not more than five years, or both.

(7) ***Application fees.***—

(A) *Fee schedule.*— The Attorney General shall provide for a schedule of fees to be charged for the filing of applications for adjustment under subsection (a) or (b)(1). The Attorney General shall provide for an additional fee for filing an application for adjustment under subsection (b)(1) after the end of the first year of the 2-year period described in subsection (b)(1)(A).

(B) *Use of fees.*— The Attorney General shall deposit payments received under this paragraph in a separate account and amounts in such account shall be available, without fiscal year limitation, to cover administrative and other expenses incurred in connection with the review of applications filed under this section.

(C) *Immigration-related unfair employment practices.*— Not to exceed $3,000,000 of the unobligated balances remaining in the account established in subparagraph (B) shall be available in fiscal year 1992 and each fiscal year thereafter for grants, contracts, and cooperative agreements to community-based organizations for outreach programs, to be administered by the Office of Special Counsel for Immigration-Related Unfair Employment Practices: *Provided,* That such amounts shall be in addition to any funds appropriated to the Office of Special Counsel for such purposes: *Provided further,* That none of the funds made available by this section shall be used by the Office of Special Counsel to establish regional offices.

**(d) Waiver of numerical limitations and certain grounds for exclusion.—**

(1) ***Numerical limitations do not apply.***— The numerical limitations of sections 201 and 202 shall not apply to the adjustment of aliens to lawful permanent resident status under this section.

(2) ***Waiver of grounds for exclusion.***— In the determination of an alien's admissibility under subsections (a)(4)(A), (b)(1)(C)(i), and (b)(2)(B)—

(A) *Grounds of exclusion not applicable.*— The provisions of paragraphs (5) and (7)(A) of section 212(a) shall not apply.

(B) *Waiver of other grounds.*—

(i) In general.— Except as provided in clause (ii), the Attorney General may waive any other provision of section 212(a) in the case of individual aliens for humanitarian purposes, to assure family unity, or when it is otherwise in the public interest.

(ii) Grounds that may not be waived.— The following provisions of section 212(a) may not be waived by the Attorney General under clause (i):

(I) Paragraphs (2)(A) and (2)(B) (relating to criminals).

(II) Paragraph (2)(C) (relating to drug offenses), except for so much of such paragraph as relates to a single offense of simple possession of 30 grams or less of marihuana.

(III) Paragraph (3) (relating to security and related grounds).

(IV) Paragraph (4) (relating to aliens likely to become public charges) insofar as it relates to an application for adjustment to permanent residence.

Subclause (IV) (prohibiting the waiver of section 212(a)(4)) shall not apply to an alien who is or was an aged, blind, or disabled individual (as defined in section 1614(a)(1) of the Social Security Act).

(iii) *Special rule for determination of public charge.*— An alien is not ineligible for adjustment of status under this section due to being inadmissible under section 212(a)(4) if the alien demonstrates a history of employment in the United States evidencing self-support without receipt of public cash assistance.

(C) *Medical examination.*— The alien shall be required, at the alien's expense, to undergo such a medical examination (including a determination of immunization status) as is appropriate and conforms to generally accepted professional standards of medical practice.

**(e) Temporary stay of deportation and work authorization for certain applicants.—**

(1) *Before application period.*— The Attorney General shall provide that in the case of an alien who is apprehended before the beginning of the application period described in subsection (a)(1)(A) and who can establish a prima facie case of eligibility to have his status adjusted under subsection (a) (but for the fact that he may not apply for such adjustment until the beginning of such period), until the alien has had the opportunity during the first 30 days of the application period to complete the filing of an application for adjustment, the alien—

(A) may not be deported, and

(B) shall be granted authorization to engage in employment in the United States and be provided an "employment authorized" endorsement or other appropriate work permit.

(2) *During application period.*— The Attorney General shall provide that in the case of an alien who presents a prima facie application for adjustment of status under subsection (a) during the application period, and until a final determination on the application has been made in accordance with this section, the alien—

(A) may not be deported, and

(B) shall be granted authorization to engage in employment in the United States and be provided an "employment authorized" endorsement or other appropriate work permit.

**(f) Administrative and judicial review.—**

(1) *Administrative and judicial review.*— There shall be no administrative or judicial review of a determination respecting an application for adjustment of status under this section except in accordance with this subsection.

(2) *No review for late filings.*— No denial of adjustment of status under this section based on a late filing of an application for such adjustment may be reviewed by a court of the United States or of any State or reviewed in any administrative proceeding of the United States Government.

(3) *Administrative review.*—

(A) *Single level of administrative appellate review.*— The Attorney General shall establish an appellate authority to provide for a single level of administrative appellate review of a determination described in paragraph (1).

(B) *Standard for review.*— Such administrative appellate review shall be based solely upon the administrative record established at the time of the determination on the application and upon such additional or newly discovered evidence as may not have been available at the time of the determination.

(4) *Judicial review.*—

(A) *Limitation to review of deportation.*— There shall be judicial review of such a denial only in the judicial review of an order of deportation under section 106 (as in effect before October 1, 1996).[162]

(B) *Standard for judicial review.*— Such judicial review shall be based solely upon the administrative record established at the time of the review by the appellate authority and the findings of fact and determinations contained in such record shall be conclusive unless the applicant can establish abuse of discretion or that the findings are directly contrary to clear and convincing facts contained in the record considered as a whole.

(C) *Jurisdiction of courts.*— Notwithstanding any other provision of law, no court shall have jurisdiction of any cause of action or claim by or on behalf of any person asserting an interest under this section unless such person in fact filed an application under this section within the period specified by subsection (a)(1), or attempted to file a complete application and application fee with an authorized legalization officer of the Service but had the application and fee refused by that officer.[163]

**(g) Implementation of section.—**

(1) *Regulations.*— The Attorney General, after consultation with the Committees on the Judiciary of the House of Representatives and of the Senate, shall prescribe—

(A) regulations establishing a definition of the term "resided continuously", as used in this section, and the evidence needed to establish that an alien has resided continuously in the United States for purposes of this section, and

(B) such other regulations as may be necessary to carry out this section.

(2) *Considerations.*— In prescribing regulations described in paragraph (1)(A)—

(A) *Periods of continuous residence.*— The Attorney General shall specify individual periods, and aggregate periods, of absence from the United States which will be considered to break a period of continuous residence in the United States and shall take into account absences due merely to brief and casual trips abroad.

(B) *Absences caused by deportation or advanced parole.*— The Attorney General shall provide that—

---

[162] *See* §377(b) of IIRAIRA.

[163] *See* §377(a) of IIRAIRA, effective as if included in the enactment of the Immigration Reform and Control Act, 1986.

(i) an alien shall not be considered to have resided continuously in the United States, if, during any period for which continuous residence is required, the alien was outside the United States as a result of a departure under an order of deportation, and

(ii) any period of time during which an alien is outside the United States pursuant to the advance parole procedures of the Service shall not be considered as part of the period of time during which an alien is outside the United States for purposes of this section.

(C) *Waivers of certain absences.*— The Attorney General may provide for a waiver, in the discretion of the Attorney General, of the periods specified under subparagraph (A) in the case of an absence from the United States due merely to a brief temporary trip abroad required by emergency or extenuating circumstances outside the control of the alien.

(D) *Use of certain documentation.*— The Attorney General shall require that—

(i) continuous residence and physical presence in the United States must be established through documents, together with independent corroboration of the information contained in such documents, and

(ii) the documents provided under clause (i) be employment-related if employment-related documents with respect to the alien are available to the applicant.

(3) *Interim final regulations.*— Regulations prescribed under this section may be prescribed to take effect on an interim final basis if the Attorney General determines that this is necessary in order to implement this section in a timely manner.

**(h) Temporary disqualification of newly legalized aliens from receiving certain public welfare assistance.—**

(1) *In general.*— During the five-year period beginning on the date an alien was granted lawful temporary resident status under subsection (a), and notwithstanding any other provision of law—

(A) except as provided in paragraphs (2) and (3), the alien is not eligible for—

(i) any program of financial assistance furnished under Federal law (whether through grant, loan, guarantee, or otherwise) on the basis of financial need, as such programs are identified by the Attorney General in consultation with other appropriate heads of the various departments and agencies of Government (but in any event including the State program of assistance under part A of title IV of the Social Security Act),

(ii) medical assistance under a State plan approved under title XIX of the Social Security Act, and

(iii) assistance under the Food and Nutrition Act of 2008; and

(B) a State or political subdivision therein may, to the extent consistent with subparagraph (A) and paragraphs (2) and (3), provide that the alien is not eligible for the programs of financial assistance or for medical assistance described in subparagraph (A)(ii) furnished under the law of that State or political subdivision.

Unless otherwise specifically provided by this section or other law, an alien in temporary lawful residence status granted under subsection (a) shall not be considered (for purposes of any law of a State or political subdivision providing for a program of financial assistance) to be permanently residing in the United States under color of law.

(2) *Exceptions.*— Paragraph (1) shall not apply—

(A) to a Cuban and Haitian entrant (as defined in paragraph (1) or (2)(A) of section 501(e) of Public Law 96-422, as in effect on April 1, 1983), or

(B) in the case of assistance (other than assistance under a State program funded under part A of title IV of the Social Security Act) which is furnished to an alien who is an aged, blind, or disabled individual (as defined in section 1614(a)(1) of the Social Security Act).

(3) *Restricted Medicaid benefits.*—

(A) *Clarification of entitlement.*— Subject to the restrictions under subparagraph (B), for the purpose of providing aliens with eligibility to receive medical assistance—

(i) paragraph (1) shall not apply,

(ii) aliens who would be eligible for medical assistance but for the provisions of paragraph (1) shall be deemed, for purposes of title XIX of the Social Security Act, to be so eligible, and

(iii) aliens lawfully admitted for temporary residence under this section, such status not having changed, shall be considered to be permanently residing in the United States under color of law.

(B) *Restriction of benefits.*—

(i) Limitation to emergency services and services for pregnant women.— Notwithstanding any provision of title XIX of the Social Security Act (including subparagraphs (B) and (C) of section 1902(a)(10) of such Act), aliens who, but for subparagraph (A), would be ineligible for medical assistance under paragraph (1), are only eligible for such assistance with respect to—

(I) emergency services (as defined for purposes of section 1916(a)(2)(D) of the Social Security Act), and

(II) services described in section 1916(a)(2)(B) of such Act (relating to service for pregnant women).

(ii) No restriction for exempt aliens and children.— The restrictions of clause (i) shall not apply to aliens who are described in paragraph (2) or who are under 18 years of age.

(C) *Definition of medical assistance.*— In this paragraph, the term "medical assistance" refers to medical assistance under a State plan approved under title XIX of the Social Security Act.

(4) *Treatment of certain programs.*— Assistance furnished under any of the following provisions of law shall not be construed to be financial assistance described in paragraph (1)(A)(i):

(A) The Richard B. Russell National School Lunch Act.

(B) The Child Nutrition Act of 1966.

(C) The Carl D. Perkins Career and Technical Education Act of 2006.

(D) Title I of the Elementary and Secondary Education Act of 1965.

(E) The Headstart-Follow Through Act.

(F) The Job Training Partnership Act or title I of the Workforce Investment Act of 1998.

(G) Title IV of the Higher Education Act of 1965.

(H) The Public Health Service Act.

(I) Titles V, XVI, and XX, and parts B, D, and E of title IV, of the Social Security Act (and titles I, X, XIV, and XVI of such Act as in effect without regard to the amendment made by section 301 of the Social Security Amendments of 1972).

(5) *Adjustment not affecting Fascell-Stone benefits.*— For the purpose of section 501 of the Refugee Education Assistance Act of 1980 (Public Law 96-122),[164] assistance shall be continued under such section with respect to an alien without regard to the alien's adjustment of status under this section.

**(i) Dissemination of information on legalization program.**— Beginning not later than the date designated by the Attorney General under subsection (a)(1)(A), the Attorney General, in cooperation with qualified designated entities, shall broadly disseminate information respecting the benefits which aliens may receive under this section and the requirements to obtain such benefits.

(June 27, 1952, ch. 477, title II, ch. 5, §245A, as added by P.L. 99-603 (IRCA) (11/6/86); as amended by P.L. 100-525 (10/24/88); P.L. 101-649 (IMMACT90) (11/29/90); P.L. 102-140 (10/28/91); P.L. 102-232 (MTINA) (12/12/91, *effective* 4/1/92); P.L. 103-382 (10/20/94); P.L. 103-416 (INTCA) (10/25/94, *effective* 4/1/95); P.L. 104-132 (AEDPA) (4/24/96), title IV, §431(a); P.L. 104-193 (8/22/96), title I, §110(s)(2); P.L. 104-208 (IIRAIRA) (9/30/96), div. C, title III, §308(g)(2)(B), §377(a) [adding (f)(4)(C)], §384(d)(1) [revising (c)(5)], title VI, §623(a) [revising (c)(5)]; P.L. 105-277 (10/21/98), (HRIFA) div. A, §101(f), title VIII, §405(d)(4); P.L. 105-332 (10/31/98), §3(a); P.L. 106-78 (10/22/99), title VII, §752(b)(5); P.L. 109-270 (8/12/06), §2 [revising (h)(4)(C)]; P.L. 110-234 (5/22/08) §4002(b) [revising (h)(1)(A)(iii)].)

## Sec. 246 Rescission of Adjustment of Status; Effect upon Naturalized Citizen [8 U.S.C. 1256]

**(a)** If, at any time within five years after the status of a person has been otherwise adjusted under the provisions of section 245 or 249 of this Act or any other provision of law to that of an alien lawfully admitted for permanent residence, it shall appear to the satisfaction of the Attorney General that the person was not in fact eligible for such adjustment of status, the Attorney General shall rescind the action taken granting an adjustment of status to such person and cancelling removal in the case of such person if that occurred and the person shall thereupon be subject to all provisions of this Act to the same extent as if the adjustment of status had not been made. Nothing in this subsection shall require the Attorney General to rescind the alien's status prior to commencement of procedures to remove the alien under section 240, and an order of removal issued by an immigration judge shall be sufficient to rescind the alien's status.[165]

**(b)** Any person who has become a naturalized citizen of the United States upon the basis of a record of a lawful admission for permanent residence, created as a result of an adjustment of status for which such person was not in fact eligible, and which is subsequently rescinded under subsection (a) of this section, shall be subject to the provisions of section 340 of this Act as a person whose naturalization was procured by concealment of a material fact or by willful misrepresentation.

(June 27, 1952, ch. 477, title II, ch. 5, §246, 66 Stat. 217; as amended by P.L. 103-416 (INTCA) (10/25/94, *effective* 4/1/95); P.L. 104-208 (IIRAIRA) (9/30/96), div. C, title III, §308(e)(1)(H), §378(a) [revising (a)].)

---

[164] *Sic.* Probably should be Public Law 96-422.

[165] *See* note 55, *supra*.

## Sec. 247 Adjustment of Status of Certain Resident Aliens to Nonimmigrant Status; Exceptions
[8 U.S.C. 1257]

**(a)** The status of an alien lawfully admitted for permanent residence shall be adjusted by the Attorney General, under such regulations as he may prescribe, to that of a nonimmigrant under paragraph (15)(A), (15)(E), or (15)(G) of section 101(a), if such alien had at the time of admission or subsequently acquires an occupational status which would, if he were seeking admission to the United States, entitle him to a nonimmigrant status under such sections. As of the date of the Attorney General's order making such adjustment of status, the Attorney General shall cancel the record of the alien's admission for permanent residence, and the immigrant status of such alien shall thereby be terminated.

**(b)** The adjustment of status required by subsection (a) shall not be applicable in the case of any alien who requests that he be permitted to retain his status as an immigrant and who, in such form as the Attorney General may require, executes and files with the Attorney General a written waiver of all rights, privileges, exemptions, and immunities under any law or any executive order which would otherwise accrue to him because of the acquisition of an occupational status entitling him to a nonimmigrant status under paragraph (15)(A), (15)(E), or (15)(G) of section 101(a).

(June 27, 1952, ch. 477, title II, ch. 5, §247; as amended by P.L. 104-208 (IIRAIRA) (9/30/96), div. C, title III, §308 [revising (a)].)

## Sec. 248 Change of Nonimmigrant Classification
[8 U.S.C. 1258]

**(a)** The Secretary of Homeland Security may, under such conditions as he may prescribe, authorize a change from any nonimmigrant classification to any other nonimmigrant classification in the case of any alien lawfully admitted to the United States as a nonimmigrant who is continuing to maintain that status and who is not inadmissible under section 212(a)(9)(B)(i) (or whose inadmissibility under such section is waived under section 212(a)(9)(B)(v)), except (subject to subsection (b)) in the case of—

(1) an alien classified as a nonimmigrant under subparagraph (C), (D), (K), or (S) of section 101(a)(15),

(2) an alien classified as a nonimmigrant under subparagraph (J) of section 101(a)(15) who came to the United States or acquired such classification in order to receive graduate medical education or training,

(3) an alien (other than an alien described in paragraph (2)) classified as a nonimmigrant under subparagraph (J) of section 101(a)(15) who is subject to the two-year foreign residence requirement of section 212(e) and has not received a waiver thereof, unless such alien applies to have the alien's classification changed from classification under subparagraph (J) of section 101(a)(15) to a classification under subparagraph (A) or (G) of such section, and

(4) an alien admitted as a nonimmigrant visitor without a visa under section 212(*l*) or section 217.

**(b)** The exceptions specified in paragraphs (1) through (4) of subsection (a) shall not apply to a change of nonimmigrant classification to that of a nonimmigrant under subparagraph (T) or (U) of section 101(a)(15).

(June 27, 1952, ch. 477, title II, ch. 5, §248, 66 Stat. 218; as amended by P.L. 87-256 (9/21/61); P.L. 97-116 (12/29/81); P.L. 99-603 (IRCA) (11/6/86); P.L. 103-322 (VAWA) (9/13/94); P.L. 104-208 (IIRAIRA) (9/30/96), div. C, title III, §301(b)(2) [revising (a)], title VI, §671(a)(2); P.L. 109-162 (1/5/06), title VIII, §821(c)(1) [revising (a) & adding (b)].)

## Sec. 249 Record of Admission for Permanent Residence in the Case of Certain Aliens Who

## Entered the United States Prior to January 1, 1972
[8 U.S.C. 1259]

A record of lawful admission for permanent residence may, in the discretion of the Attorney General and under such regulations as he may prescribe, be made in the case of any alien, as of the date of the approval of his application or, if entry occurred prior to July 1, 1924, as of the date of such entry, if no such record is otherwise available and such alien shall satisfy the Attorney General that he is not inadmissible under section 212(a)(3)(E) or under section 212(a) insofar as it relates to criminals, procurers and other immoral persons, subversives, violators of the narcotic laws or smugglers of aliens, and he establishes that he—

**(a)** entered the United States prior to January 1, 1972;

**(b)** has had his residence in the United States continuously since such entry;

**(c)** is a person of good moral character; and

**(d)** is not ineligible to citizenship and is not deportable under section 237(a)(4)(B).

(June 27, 1952, ch. 477, title II, ch. 5, §249, 66 Stat. 219; as amended by P.L. 85-616 (8/8/58); P.L. 89-236 (10/3/65); P.L. 99-603 (IRCA) (11/6/86); P.L. 100-525 (10/24/88); P.L. 101-649 (IMMACT90) (11/29/90); P.L. 104-132 (AEDPA) (4/24/96), title IV, §413(e); P.L. 104-208 (IIRAIRA) (9/30/96), div. C, title III, §308(g)(10)(C) [revising (d)].)

## Sec. 250 Removal of Aliens Falling into Distress
[8 U.S.C. 1260]

The Attorney General may remove from the United States any alien who falls into distress or who needs public aid from causes arising subsequent to his entry, and is desirous of being so removed, to the native country of such alien, or to the country from which he came, or to the country of which he is a citizen or subject, or to any other country to which he wishes to go and which will receive him, at the expense of the appropriation for the enforcement of this Act. Any alien so removed shall be ineligible to apply for or receive a visa or other documentation for readmission, or to apply for admission to the United States except with the prior approval of the Attorney General.

(June 27, 1952, ch. 477, title II, ch. 5, §250.)

# Chapter 6 — Special Provisions Relating to Alien Crewman

## Sec. 251 Alien Crewmen
[8 U.S.C. 1281]

**(a) Arrival; submission of list; exceptions.**— Upon arrival of any vessel or aircraft in the United States from any place outside the United States it shall be the duty of the owner, agent, consignee, master, or commanding officer thereof to deliver to an immigration officer at the port of arrival

(1) a complete, true, and correct list containing the names of all aliens employed on such vessel or aircraft, the positions they respectively hold in the crew of the vessel or aircraft, when and where they were respectively shipped or engaged, and those to be paid off or discharged in the port of arrival; or

(2) in the discretion of the Attorney General, such a list containing so much of such information, or such additional or supplemental information, as the Attorney General shall by regulations prescribe. In the case of a vessel engaged solely in traffic on the Great Lakes, Saint Lawrence River, and connecting waterways, such lists shall be furnished at such times as the Attorney General may require.

**(b) Reports of illegal landings.—** It shall be the duty of any owner, agent, consignee, master, or commanding officer of any vessel or aircraft to report to an immigration officer, in writing, as soon as discovered, all cases in which any alien crewman has illegally landed in the United States from the vessel or aircraft, together with a description of such alien and any information likely to lead to his apprehension.

**(c) Departure; submission of list; exceptions.—** Before the departure of any vessel or aircraft from any port in the United States, it shall be the duty of the owner, agent, consignee, master, or commanding officer thereof, to deliver to an immigration officer at that port (1) a list containing the names of all alien employees who were not employed thereon at the time of the arrival at that port but who will leave such port thereon at the time of the departure of such vessel or aircraft and the names of those, if any, who have been paid off or discharged, and of those, if any, who have deserted or landed at that port, or (2) in the discretion of the Attorney General, such a list containing so much of such information, or such additional or supplemental information, as the Attorney General shall by regulations prescribe. In the case of a vessel engaged solely in traffic on the Great Lakes, Saint Lawrence River, and connecting waterways, such lists shall be furnished at such times as the Attorney General may require.

**(d) Violations.—** In case any owner, agent, consignee, master, or commanding officer shall fail to deliver complete, true, and correct lists or reports of aliens, or to report cases of desertion or landing, as required by subsections (a), (b), and (c), such owner, agent, consignee, master, or commanding officer shall, if required by the Attorney General, pay to the Commissioner the sum of $200 for each alien concerning whom such lists are not delivered or such reports are not made as required in the preceding subsections. In the case that any owner, agent, consignee, master, or commanding officer of a vessel shall secure services of an alien crewman described in section 101(a)(15)(D)(i) to perform longshore work not included in the normal operation and service on board the vessel under section 258, the owner, agent, consignee, master, or commanding officer shall pay to the Commissioner the sum of $5,000, and such fine shall be a lien against the vessel. No such vessel or aircraft shall be granted clearance from any port at which it arrives pending the determination of the question of the liability to the payment of such fine, and if such fine is imposed, while it remains unpaid. No such fine shall be remitted or refunded. Clearance may be granted prior to the determination of such question upon deposit of a bond or a sum sufficient to cover such fine.

**(e) Regulations.—** The Attorney General is authorized to prescribe by regulations the circumstances under which a vessel or aircraft shall be deemed to be arriving in, or departing from the United States or any port thereof within the meaning of any provision of this chapter.

(June 27, 1952, ch. 477, title II, ch. 6, §251, 66 Stat. 219; as amended by P.L. 101-649, title II, §203(b) (11/29/90); P.L. 102-232, title III, §303(a)(3) (12/12/91).)

## Sec. 252 Conditional Permits to Land Temporarily
[8 U.S.C. 1282]

**(a) Period of time.—** No alien crewman shall be permitted to land temporarily in the United States except as provided in this section, section 212(d)(3), section 212(d)(5), and section 253. If an immigration officer finds upon examination that an alien crewman is a nonimmigrant under paragraph (15)(D) of section 101(a) and is otherwise admissible and has agreed to accept such permit, he may, in his discretion, grant the crewman a conditional permit to land temporarily pursuant to regulations prescribed by the Attorney General, subject to revocation in subsequent proceedings as provided in subsection (b), and for a period of time, in any event, not to exceed—

(1) the period of time (not exceeding twenty-nine days) during which the vessel or aircraft on which he arrived remains in port, if the immigration officer is satisfied that the crewman intends to depart on the vessel or aircraft on which he arrived; or

(2) twenty-nine days, if the immigration officer is satisfied that the crewman intends to depart, within the period for which he is permitted to land, on a vessel or aircraft other than the one on which he arrived.

**(b) Revocation; expenses of detention.**— Pursuant to regulations prescribed by the Attorney General, any immigration officer may, in his discretion, if he determines that an alien is not a bona fide crewman, or does not intend to depart on the vessel or aircraft which brought him, revoke the conditional permit to land which was granted such crewman under the provisions of subsection (a)(1), take such crewman into custody, and require the master or commanding officer of the vessel or aircraft on which the crewman arrived to receive and detain him on board such vessel or aircraft, if practicable, and such crewman shall be removed from the United States at the expense of the transportation line which brought him to the United States. Until such alien is so removed, any expenses of his detention shall be borne by such transportation company. Nothing in this section shall be construed to require the procedure prescribed in section 240 of this Act to cases falling within the provisions of this subsection.

**(c) Penalties.**— Any alien crewman who willfully remains in the United States in excess of the number of days allowed in any conditional permit issued under subsection (a) shall be fined under title 18, United States Code, or imprisoned not more than 6 months, or both.

(June 27, 1952, ch. 477, title II, ch. 6, §252, 66 Stat. 220; as amended by P.L. 101-649 (11/29/90), title V, §543; P.L. 102-232 (12/12/91), title III, §306; P.L. 104-208 (IIRAIRA) (9/30/96), div. C, title III, §308 [revising (b)].)

## Sec. 253 Hospital Treatment of Alien Crewmen Afflicted with Certain Diseases
[8 U.S.C. 1283]

An alien crewman, including an alien crewman ineligible for a conditional permit to land under section 252(a), who is found on arrival in a port of the United States to be afflicted with any of the disabilities or diseases mentioned in section 255, shall be placed in a hospital designated by the immigration officer in charge at the port of arrival and treated, all expenses connected therewith, including burial in the event of death, to be borne by the owner, agent, consignee, commanding officer, or master of the vessel or aircraft, and not to be deducted from the crewman's wages. No such vessel or aircraft shall be granted clearance until such expenses are paid, or their payment appropriately guaranteed, and the collector of customs is so notified by the immigration officer in charge. An alien crewman suspected of being afflicted with any such disability or disease may be removed from the vessel or aircraft on which he arrived to an immigration station, or other appropriate place, for such observation as will enable the examining surgeons to determine definitely whether or not he is so afflicted, all expenses connected therewith to be borne in the manner hereinbefore prescribed. In cases in which it appears to the satisfaction of the immigration officer in charge that it will not be possible within a reasonable time to effect a cure, the return of the alien crewman shall be enforced on, or at the expense of, the transportation line on which he came, upon such conditions as the Attorney General shall prescribe, to insure that the alien shall be properly cared for and protected, and that the spread of contagion shall be guarded against.

(June 27, 1952, ch. 477, title II, ch. 6, §253, 66 Stat. 221.)

## Sec. 254 Control of Alien Crewmen
## [8 U.S.C. 1284]

**(a) Penalties for failure.**— The owner, agent, consignee, charterer, master, or commanding officer of any vessel or aircraft arriving in the United States from any place outside thereof who fails

(1) to detain on board the vessel, or in the case of an aircraft to detain at a place specified by an immigration officer at the expense of the airline, any alien crewman employed thereon until an immigration officer has completely inspected such alien crewman, including a physical examination by the medical examiner, or

(2) to detain any alien crewman on board the vessel, or in the case of an aircraft at a place specified by an immigration officer at the expense of the airline, after such inspection unless a conditional permit to land temporarily has been granted such alien crewman under section 252 or unless an alien crewman has been permitted to land temporarily under section 212(d)(5) or 253 for medical or hospital treatment, or

(3) to remove such alien crewman if required to do so by an immigration officer, whether such removal requirement is imposed before or after the crewman is permitted to land temporarily under section 212(d)(5), 252, or 253, shall pay to the Commissioner the sum of $3,000 for each alien crewman in respect of whom any such failure occurs. No such vessel or aircraft shall be granted clearance pending the determination of the liability to the payment of such fine, or while the fine remains unpaid, except that clearance may be granted prior to the determination of such question upon the deposit of a sum sufficient to cover such fine, or of a bond with sufficient surety to secure the payment thereof approved by the Commissioner. The Attorney General may, upon application in writing therefor, mitigate such penalty to not less than $500 for each alien crewman in respect of whom such failure occurs, upon such terms as he shall think proper.

**(b) Prima facie evidence against transportation line.**— Except as may be otherwise prescribed by regulations issued by the Attorney General, proof that an alien crewman did not appear upon the outgoing manifest of the vessel or aircraft on which he arrived in the United States from any place outside thereof, or that he was reported by the master or commanding officer of such vessel or aircraft as a deserter, shall be prima facie evidence of a failure to detain or remove such alien crewman.

**(c) Removal on other than arriving vessel or aircraft; expenses.**— If the Attorney General finds that removal of an alien crewman under this section on the vessel or aircraft on which he arrived is impracticable or impossible, or would cause undue hardship to such alien crewman, he may cause the alien crewman to be removed from the port of arrival or any other port on another vessel or aircraft of the same transportation line, unless the Attorney General finds this to be impracticable. All expenses incurred in connection with such removal, including expenses incurred in transferring an alien crewman from one place in the United States to another under such conditions and safeguards as the Attorney General shall impose, shall be paid by the owner or owners of the vessel or aircraft on which the alien arrived in the United States. The vessel or aircraft on which the alien arrived shall not be granted clearance until such expenses have been paid or their payment guaranteed to the satisfaction of the Attorney General. An alien crewman who is transferred within the United States in accordance with this subsection shall not be regarded as having been landed in the United States.

(June 27, 1952, ch. 477, title II, ch. 6, §254, 66 Stat. 221; as amended by P.L. 101-649 (11/29/90), §543(a)(4) ; P.L. 102-232 (12/12/91), title III, §306; P.L. 104-208 (IIRAIRA) (9/30/96), div. C, title III, §308(e)(12) [revising in its entirety.].)

## Sec. 255 Employment on Passenger Vessels of Aliens Afflicted with Certain Disabilities
[8 U.S.C. 1285]

It shall be unlawful for any vessel or aircraft carrying passengers between a port of the United States and a port outside thereof to have employed on board upon arrival in the United States any alien afflicted with feeble-mindedness, insanity, epilepsy, tuberculosis in any form, leprosy, or any dangerous contagious disease. If it appears to the satisfaction of the Attorney General, from an examination made by a medical officer of the United States Public Health Service, and is so certified by such officer, that any such alien was so afflicted at the time he was shipped or engaged and taken on board such vessel or aircraft and that the existence of such affliction might have been detected by means of a competent medical examination at such time, the owner, commanding officer, agent, consignee, or master thereof shall pay for each alien so afflicted to the Commissioner the sum of $1,000. No vessel or aircraft shall be granted clearance pending the determination of the question of the liability to the payment of such sums, or while such sums remain unpaid, except that clearance may be granted prior to the determination of such question upon the deposit of an amount sufficient to cover such sums or of a bond approved by the Commissioner with sufficient surety to secure the payment thereof. Any such fine may, in the discretion of the Attorney General, be mitigated or remitted.

(June 27, 1952, ch. 477, title II, ch. 6, §255, 66 Stat. 222; as amended by P.L. 101-649, title V, §543(a)(5) (11/29/90).)

## Sec. 256 Discharge of Alien Crewmen; Penalties
[8 U.S.C. 1286]

It shall be unlawful for any person, including the owner, agent, consignee, charterer, master, or commanding officer of any vessel or aircraft, to pay off or discharge any alien crewman, except an alien lawfully admitted for permanent residence, employed on board a vessel or aircraft arriving in the United States without first having obtained the consent of the Attorney General. If it shall appear to the satisfaction of the Attorney General that any alien crewman has been paid off or discharged in the United States in violation of the provisions of this section, such owner, agent, consignee, charterer, master, commanding officer, or other person, shall pay to the Commissioner the sum of $3,000 for each such violation. No vessel or aircraft shall be granted clearance pending the determination of the question of the liability to the payment of such sums, or while such sums remain unpaid, except that clearance may be granted prior to the determination of such question upon the deposit of an amount sufficient to cover such sums, or of a bond approved by the Commissioner with sufficient surety to secure the payment thereof. Such fine may, in the discretion of the Attorney General, be mitigated to not less than $1,500 for each violation, upon such terms as he shall think proper.

(June 27, 1952, ch. 477, title II, ch. 6, §256, 66 Stat. 223; as amended by P.L. 101-649, title V, §543(a)(6) (11/29/90).)

## Sec. 257 Alien Crewmen Brought into the United States with Intent to Evade Immigration Laws; Penalties
[8 U.S.C. 1287]

Any person, including the owner, agent, consignee, master, or commanding officer of any vessel or aircraft arriving in the United States from any place outside thereof, who shall knowingly sign on the vessel's articles, or bring to the United States as one of the crew of such vessel or aircraft, any alien, with intent to permit or assist such alien to enter or land in the United States in violation of law, or who shall falsely and knowingly represent to a consular officer at the time of application for visa, or to the immigration officer at the port of arrival in the United States, that such alien is a bona fide member of the crew employed in any capacity regularly required for normal operation and services aboard such vessel or aircraft, shall be liable to a penalty not exceeding $10,000 for each such violation, for which sum such vessel or aircraft shall be liable and may be seized and proceeded against by way of libel in any district court of the United States having jurisdiction of the offense.

(June 27, 1952, ch. 477, title II, ch. 6, §257, 66 Stat. 223; as amended by P.L. 101-649, title V, §543(a)(7) (11/29/90).)

### Sec. 258 Limitations on Performance of Longshore Work by Alien Crewmen
[8 U.S.C. 1288]

**(a) In general.**— For purposes of section 101(a)(15)(D)(i), the term "normal operation and service on board a vessel" does not include any activity that is longshore work (as defined in subsection (b)), except as provided under subsection (c), (d), or (e).

**(b) Longshore work defined.**—

(1) *In general.*— In this section, except as provided in paragraph (2), the term "longshore work" means any activity relating to the loading or unloading of cargo, the operation of cargo-related equipment (whether or not integral to the vessel), and the handling of mooring lines on the dock when the vessel is made fast or let go, in the United States or the coastal waters thereof.

(2) *Exception for safety and environmental protection.*— The term "longshore work" does not include the loading or unloading of any cargo for which the Secretary of Transportation has, under the authority contained in chapter 37 of title 46, United States Code (relating to Carriage of Liquid Bulk Dangerous Cargoes), section 311 of the Federal Water Pollution Control Act (33 U.S.C. 1321), section 4106 of the Oil Pollution Act of 1990, or section 5103(b), 5104, 5106, 5107, or 5110 of title 49, United States Code prescribed regulations which govern—

(A) the handling or stowage of such cargo,

(B) the manning of vessels and the duties, qualifications, and training of the officers and crew of vessels carrying such cargo, and

(C) the reduction or elimination of discharge during ballasting, tank cleaning, handling of such cargo.

(3) *Construction.*— Nothing in this section shall be construed as broadening, limiting, or otherwise modifying the meaning or scope of longshore work for purposes of any other law, collective bargaining agreement, or international agreement.

**(c) Prevailing practice exception.**—

(1) Subsection (a) shall not apply to a particular activity of longshore work in and about a local port if—

(A) (i) there is in effect in the local port one or more collective bargaining agreements each covering at least 30 percent of the number of individuals employed in performing longshore work and

(ii) each such agreement (covering such percentage of longshore workers) permits the activity to be performed by alien crewmen under the terms of such agreement; or

(B) there is no collective bargaining agreement in effect in the local port covering at least 30 percent of the number of individuals employed in performing longshore work, and an employer of alien crewmen (or the employer's designated agent or representative) has filed with the Secretary of Labor at least 14 days before the date of performance of the activity (or later, if necessary due to an unanticipated emergency, but not later than the date of performance of the activity) an attestation setting forth facts and evidence to show that—

(i) the performance of the activity by alien crewmen is permitted under the prevailing practice of the particular port as of the date of filing of the attestation and that the use of alien crewmen for such activity—

(I) is not during a strike or lockout in the course of a labor dispute, and

(II) is not intended or designed to influence an election of a bargaining representative for workers in the local port; and

(ii) notice of the attestation has been provided by the owner, agent, consignee, master, or commanding officer to the bargaining representative of longshore workers in the local port, or, where there is no such bargaining representative, notice of the attestation has been provided to longshore workers employed at the local port.

In applying subparagraph (B) in the case of a particular activity of longshore work consisting of the use of an automated self-unloading conveyor belt or vacuum-actuated system on a vessel, the attestation shall be required to be filed only if the Secretary of Labor finds, based on a preponderance of the evidence which may be submitted by any interested party, that the performance of such particular activity is not described in clause (i) of such subparagraph.

(2) Subject to paragraph (4), an attestation under paragraph (1) shall—

(A) expire at the end of the 1-year period beginning on the date of its filing with the Secretary of Labor, and

(B) apply to aliens arriving in the United States during such 1-year period if the owner, agent, consignee, master, or commanding officer states in each list under section 251 that it continues to comply with the conditions in the attestation.

(3) An owner, agent, consignee, master, or commanding officer may meet the requirements under this subsection with respect to more than one alien crewman in a single list.

(4) (A) The Secretary of Labor shall compile and make available for public examination in a timely manner in Washington, D.C., a list identifying owners, agents, consignees, masters, or commanding officers which have filed lists for nonimmigrants described in section 101(a)(15)(D)(i) with respect to whom an attestation under paragraph (1) or subsection (d)(1) is made and, for each such entity, a copy of the entity's attestation under paragraph (1) or subsection (d)(1) (and accompanying documentation) and each such list filed by the entity.

(B) (i) The Secretary of Labor shall establish a process for the receipt, investigation, and disposition of complaints respecting an entity's failure to meet conditions attested to, an entity's misrepresentation of a material fact in an attestation, or, in the case described in the last sentence of paragraph (1), whether the performance of the particular activity is or is not described in paragraph (1)(B)(i).

(ii) Complaints may be filed by any aggrieved person or organization (including bargaining representatives, associations deemed appropriate by the Secretary, and other aggrieved parties as determined under regulations of the Secretary).

(iii) The Secretary shall promptly conduct an investigation under this subparagraph if there is reasonable cause to believe that an entity fails to meet conditions attested to, an entity has misrepresented a material fact in the attestation, or, in the case described in the last sentence of paragraph (1), the performance of the particular activity is not described in paragraph (1)(B)(i).

(C) (i) If the Secretary determines that reasonable cause exists to conduct an investigation with respect to an attestation, a complaining party may request that the activities attested to by the employer cease during the hearing process described in subparagraph (D). If such a request is made, the attesting employer shall be issued notice of such request and shall respond within 14 days to the notice. If the Secretary makes an initial determination that the complaining party's position is supported by a preponderance of the evidence submitted, the Secretary shall require immediately that the employer cease and desist from such activities until completion of the process described in subparagraph (D).

(ii) If the Secretary determines that reasonable cause exists to conduct an investigation with respect to a matter under the last sentence of paragraph (1), a complaining party may request that the activities of the employer cease during the hearing process described in subparagraph (D) unless the employer files with the Secretary of Labor an attestation under paragraph (1). If such a request is made, the employer shall be issued notice of such request and shall respond within 14 days to the notice. If the Secretary makes an initial determination that the complaining party's position is supported by a preponderance of the evidence submitted, the Secretary shall require immediately that the employer cease and desist from such activities until completion of the process described in subparagraph (D) unless the employer files with the Secretary of Labor an attestation under paragraph (1).

(D) Under the process established under subparagraph (B), the Secretary shall provide, within 180 days after the date a complaint is filed (or later for good cause shown), for a determination as to whether or not a basis exists to make a finding described in subparagraph (E). The Secretary shall provide notice of such determination to the interested parties and an opportunity for a hearing on the complaint within 60 days of the date of the determination.

(E) (i) If the Secretary of Labor finds, after notice and opportunity for a hearing, that an entity has failed to meet a condition attested to or has made a misrepresentation of material fact in the attestation, the Secretary shall notify the Attorney General of such finding and may, in addition, impose such other administrative remedies (including civil monetary penalties in an amount not to exceed $5,000 for each alien crewman performing unauthorized longshore work) as the Secretary determines to be appropriate. Upon receipt of such notice, the Attorney General shall not permit the vessels owned or chartered by such entity to enter any port of the United States during a period of up to 1 year.

(ii) If the Secretary of Labor finds, after notice and opportunity for a hearing, that, in the case described in the last sentence of paragraph (1), the performance of the particular activity is not described in subparagraph (B)(i), the Secretary shall notify the Attorney General of such finding and, thereafter, the attestation described in paragraph (1) shall be required of the employer for the performance of the particular activity.

(F) A finding by the Secretary of Labor under this paragraph that the performance of an activity by alien crewmen is not permitted under the prevailing practice of a local port shall preclude for one year the filing of a subsequent attestation concerning such activity in the port under paragraph (1).

(5) Except as provided in paragraph (5) of subsection (d), this subsection shall not apply to longshore work performed in the State of Alaska.

**(d) State of Alaska exception.—**

(1) Subsection (a) shall not apply to a particular activity of longshore work at a particular location in the State of Alaska if an employer of alien crewmen has filed an attestation with the Secretary of Labor at least 30 days before the date of the first performance of the activity (or anytime up to 24 hours before the first performance of the activity, upon a showing that the employer could not have reasonably anticipated the need to file an attestation for that location at that time) setting forth facts and evidence to show that—

(A) the employer will make a bona fide request for United States longshore workers who are qualified and available in sufficient numbers to perform the activity at the particular time and location from the parties to whom notice has been provided under clauses (ii) and (iii) of subparagraph (D), except that—

(i) wherever two or more contract stevedoring companies have signed a joint collective bargaining agreement with a single labor organization described in subparagraph (D)(i), the employer may request longshore workers from only one of such contract stevedoring companies, and

(ii) a request for longshore workers to an operator of a private dock may be made only for longshore work to be performed at that dock and only if the operator meets the requirements of section 32 of the Longshoremen's and Harbor Workers' Compensation Act (33 U.S.C. 932);

(B) the employer will employ all those United States longshore workers made available in response to the request made pursuant to subparagraph (A) who are qualified and available in sufficient numbers and who are needed to perform the longshore activity at the particular time and location;

(C) the use of alien crewmembers for such activity is not intended or designed to influence an election of a bargaining representative for workers in the State of Alaska; and

(D) notice of the attestation has been provided by the employer to—

(i) labor organizations which have been recognized as exclusive bargaining representatives of United States longshore workers within the meaning of the National Labor Relations Act and which make available or intend to make available workers to the particular location where the longshore work is to be performed,

(ii) contract stevedoring companies which employ or intend to employ United States longshore workers at that location, and

(iii) operators of private docks at which the employer will use longshore workers.

(2) (A) An employer filing an attestation under paragraph (1) who seeks to use alien crewmen to perform longshore work shall be responsible while at[166] the attestation is valid to make bona fide requests for United States longshore workers under paragraph (1)(A) and to employ United States longshore workers, as provided in paragraph (1)(B), before using alien crewmen to perform the activity or activities specified in the attestation, except that an employer shall not be required to request longshore workers from a

---

[166] *Sic.* The word "at" probably should not appear.

party if that party has notified the employer in writing that it does not intend to make available United States longshore workers to the location at which the longshore work is to be performed.

(B) If a party that has provided such notice subsequently notifies the employer in writing that it is prepared to make available United States longshore workers who are qualified and available in sufficient numbers to perform the longshore activity to the location at which the longshore work is to be performed, then the employer's obligations to that party under subparagraphs (A) and (B) of paragraph (1) shall begin 60 days following the issuance of such notice.

(3) (A) In no case shall an employer filing an attestation be required—

(i) to hire less than a full work unit of United States longshore workers needed to perform the longshore activity;

(ii) to provide overnight accommodations for the longshore workers while employed; or

(iii) to provide transportation to the place of work, except where—

(I) surface transportation is available;

(II) such transportation may be safely accomplished;

(III) travel time to the vessel does not exceed one-half hour each way; and

(IV) travel distance to the vessel from the point of embarkation does not exceed 5 miles.

(B) In the cases of Wide Bay, Alaska, and Klawock/Craig, Alaska, the travel times and travel distances specified in subclauses (III) and (IV) of subparagraph (A)(iii) shall be extended to 45 minutes and 7½ miles, respectively, unless the party responding to the request for longshore workers agrees to the lesser time and distance limitations specified in those subclauses.

(4) Subject to subparagraphs (A) through (D) of subsection (c)(4), attestations filed under paragraph (1) of this subsection shall—

(A) expire at the end of the 1-year period beginning on the date the employer anticipates the longshore work to begin, as specified in the attestation filed with the Secretary of Labor, and

(B) apply to aliens arriving in the United States during such 1-year period if the owner, agent, consignee, master, or commanding officer states in each list under section 251 that it continues to comply with the conditions in the attestation.

(5) (A) Except as otherwise provided by subparagraph (B), subsection (c)(3) and subparagraphs (A) through (E) of subsection (c)(4) shall apply to attestations filed under this subsection.

(B) The use of alien crewmen to perform longshore work in Alaska consisting of the use of an automated self-unloading conveyor belt or vacuum-actuated system on a vessel shall be governed by the provisions of subsection (c).

(6) For purposes of this subsection—

(A) the term "contract stevedoring companies" means those stevedoring companies licensed to do business in the State of Alaska that meet the requirements of section 32 of the Longshoremen's and Harbor Workers' Compensation Act (33 U.S.C. 932);

(B) the term "employer" includes any agent or representative designated by the employer; and

(C) the terms "qualified" and "available in sufficient numbers" shall be defined by reference to industry standards in the State of Alaska, including safety considerations.

**(e) Reciprocity exception.—**

(1) *In general.*— Subject to the determination of the Secretary of State pursuant to paragraph (2), the Attorney General shall permit an alien crewman to perform an activity constituting longshore work if—

(A) the vessel is registered in a country that by law, regulation, or in practice does not prohibit such activity by crewmembers aboard United States vessels; and

(B) nationals of a country (or countries) which by law, regulation, or in practice does not prohibit such activity by crewmembers aboard United States vessels hold a majority of the ownership interest in the vessel.

(2) *Establishment of list.*— The Secretary of State shall, in accordance with section 553 of title 5, United States Code, compile and annually maintain a list, of longshore work by particular activity, of countries where performance of such a particular activity by crewmembers aboard United States vessels is prohibited by law, regulation, or in practice in the country. By not later than 90 days after the date of the enactment of this section, the Secretary shall publish a notice of proposed rulemaking to establish such list. The Secretary shall first establish such list by not later than 180 days after the date of the enactment of this section.

(3) *In practice defined.*— For purposes of this subsection, the term "in practice" refers to an activity normally performed in such country during the one-year period preceding the arrival of such vessel into the United States or coastal waters thereof.

(June 27, 1952, ch. 477, title II, ch. 6, §258, as added by P.L. 101-649 (IMMACT90) (11/29/90); as amended by P.L. 102-232 (MTINA) (12/12/91, *effective* 4/1/92); P.L. 103-198, (12/17/93); P.L. 103-206 (12/20/93); P.L. 103-416 (INTCA) (10/25/94, *effective* 4/1/95); P.L. 104-208 (IIRAIRA) (9/30/96), div. C, title VI, §671(e)(4)(B) [revising (b)(2)].)

# Chapter 7 — Registration of Aliens

## Sec. 261 Aliens Seeking Entry; Contents
## [8 U.S.C. 1301]

No visa shall be issued to any alien seeking to enter the United States until such alien has been registered in accordance with section 221(b).

(June 27, 1952, ch. 477, title II, ch. 7, §261, 66 Stat. 223; as amended by P.L. 99-653 (11/14/86); P.L. 100-525 (10/24/88).)

## Sec. 262 Registration of Aliens
## [8 U.S.C. 1302]

(a) It shall be the duty of every alien now or hereafter in the United States, who—

(1) is fourteen years of age or older,

(2) has not been registered and fingerprinted under section 221(b) of this Act or section 30 or 31 of the Alien Registration Act, 1940, and

(3) remains in the United States for thirty days or longer,

to apply for registration and to be fingerprinted before the expiration of such thirty days.

**(b)** It shall be the duty of every parent or legal guardian of any alien now or hereafter in the United States, who—

(1) is less than fourteen years of age,

(2) has not been registered under section 221(b) of this Act or section 30 or 31 of the Alien Registration Act, 1940, and

(3) remains in the United States for thirty days or longer,

to apply for the registration of such alien before the expiration of such thirty days. Whenever any alien attains his fourteenth birthday in the United States he shall, within thirty days thereafter, apply in person for registration and to be fingerprinted.

**(c)** The Attorney General may, in his discretion and on the basis of reciprocity pursuant to such regulations as he may prescribe, waive the requirement of fingerprinting specified in subsections (a) and (b) in the case of any nonimmigrant.

(June 27, 1952, ch. 477, title II, ch. 7, §262, 66 Stat. 224; as amended by P.L. 99-653 (11/14/86); P.L. 100-525 (10/24/88); P.L. 103-416 (INTCA) (10/25/94, *effective* 4/1/95), §219.)

## Sec. 263 Registration of Special Groups
[8 U.S.C. 1303]

**(a)** Notwithstanding the provisions of sections 261 and 262, the Attorney General is authorized to prescribe special regulations and forms for the registration and fingerprinting of

(1) alien crewmen,

(2) holders of border-crossing identification cards,

(3) aliens confined in institutions within the United States,

(4) aliens under order of removal,

(5) aliens who are or have been on criminal probation or criminal parole within the United States, and

(6) aliens of any other class not lawfully admitted to the United States for permanent residence.

**(b)** The provisions of section 262 and of this section shall not be applicable to any alien who is in the United States as a nonimmigrant under section 101(a)(15)(A) or 101(a)(15)(G) until the alien ceases to be entitled to such a nonimmigrant status.

(June 27, 1952, ch. 477, title II, ch. 7, §263, 66 Stat. 224; as amended by P.L. 104-208 (IIRAIRA) (9/30/96), div. C, title III, §308(e)(1)(J) [revising (a)(4)], §323 [revising (a)(5)].)

## Sec. 264 Forms for Registration and Fingerprinting
[8 U.S.C. 1304]

**(a) Preparation; contents.**— The Attorney General and the Secretary of State jointly are authorized and directed to prepare forms for the registration of aliens under section 261 of this title, and the Attorney General is authorized and directed to prepare forms for the registration and fingerprinting of aliens under section 262 of this title. Such forms shall contain inquiries with respect to

(1) the date and place of entry of the alien into the United States;

(2) activities in which he has been and intends to be engaged;

(3) the length of time he expects to remain in the United States;

(4) the police and criminal record, if any, of such alien; and

(5) such additional matters as may be prescribed.

**(b) Confidential nature.**— All registration and fingerprint records made under the provisions of this title shall be confidential, and shall be made available only (1) pursuant to section 287(f)(2), and (2) to such persons or agencies as may be designated by the Attorney General.

**(c) Information under oath.**— Every person required to apply for the registration of himself or another under this title shall submit under oath the information required for such registration. Any person authorized under regulations issued by the Attorney General to register aliens under this title shall be authorized to administer oaths for such purpose.

**(d) Certificate of alien registration or alien receipt card.**— Every alien in the United States who has been registered and fingerprinted under the provisions of the Alien Registration Act, 1940, or under the provisions of this Act shall be issued a certificate of alien registration or an alien registration receipt card in such form and manner and at such time as shall be prescribed under regulations issued by the Attorney General.

**(e) Personal possession of registration or receipt card; penalties.**— Every alien, eighteen years of age and over, shall at all times carry with him and have in his personal possession any certificate of alien registration or alien registration receipt card issued to him pursuant to subsection (d). Any alien who fails to comply with the provisions of this subsection shall be guilty of a misdemeanor and shall upon conviction for each offense be fined not to exceed $100 or be imprisoned not more than thirty days, or both.

**(f) Alien's social security account number.**— Notwithstanding any other provision of law, the Attorney General is authorized to require any alien to provide the alien's social security account number for purposes of inclusion in any record of the alien maintained by the Attorney General or the Service.

(June 27, 1952, ch. 477, title II, ch. 7, §264, 66 Stat. 224; as amended by P.L. 99-653 (11/14/86); P.L. 100-525 (10/24/88); P.L. 101-649 (IMMACT90) (11/29/90); P.L. 104-208 (IIRAIRA) (9/30/96), div. C, title IV, §415 [revising (f)].)

**Sec. 265 Notices of Change of Address**
**[8 U.S.C. 1305]**

**(a) Notification of change.**— Each alien required to be registered under this title who is within the United States shall notify the Attorney General in writing of each change of address and new address within ten days from the date of such change and furnish with such notice such additional information as the Attorney General may require by regulation.

**(b) Current address of natives of any one or more foreign states.**— The Attorney General may in his discretion, upon ten days notice, require the natives of any one or more foreign states, or any class or group thereof, who are within the United States and who are required to be registered under this title, to notify the Attorney General of their current addresses and furnish such additional information as the Attorney General may require.

**(c) Notice to parent or legal guardian.**— In the case of an alien for whom a parent or legal guardian is required to apply for registration, the notice required by this section shall be given to such parent or legal guardian.

(June 27, 1952, ch. 477, title II, ch. 7, §265, 66 Stat. 225; as amended by P.L. 97-116 (12/29/81); P.L. 100-525 (10/24/88).)

## Sec. 266 Penalties
[8 U.S.C. 1306]

**(a) Willful failure to register.**— Any alien required to apply for registration and to be fingerprinted in the United States who willfully fails or refuses to make such application or to be fingerprinted, and any parent or legal guardian required to apply for the registration of any alien who willfully fails or refuses to file application for the registration of such alien shall be guilty of a misdemeanor and shall, upon conviction thereof, be fined not to exceed $1,000 or be imprisoned not more than six months, or both.

**(b) Failure to notify change of address.**— Any alien or any parent or legal guardian in the United States of any alien who fails to give written notice to the Attorney General, as required by section 265 of this title, shall be guilty of a misdemeanor and shall, upon conviction thereof, be fined not to exceed $200 or be imprisoned not more than thirty days, or both. Irrespective of whether an alien is convicted and punished as herein provided, any alien who fails to give written notice to the Attorney General, as required by section 265, shall be taken into custody and removed in the manner provided by chapter 4 of this title, unless such alien establishes to the satisfaction of the Attorney General that such failure was reasonably excusable or was not willful.

**(c) Fraudulent statements.**— Any alien or any parent or legal guardian of any alien, who files an application for registration containing statements known by him to be false, or who procures or attempts to procure registration of himself or another person through fraud, shall be guilty of a misdemeanor and shall, upon conviction thereof, be fined not to exceed $1,000, or be imprisoned not more than six months, or both; and any alien so convicted shall, upon the warrant of the Attorney General, be taken into custody and be removed in the manner provided in chapter 4 of this title.

**(d) Counterfeiting.**— Any person who with unlawful intent photographs, prints, or in any other manner makes, or executes, any engraving, photograph, print, or impression in the likeness of any certificate of alien registration or an alien registration receipt card or any colorable imitation thereof, except when and as authorized under such rules and regulations as may be prescribed by the Attorney General, shall upon conviction be fined not to exceed $5,000 or be imprisoned not more than five years, or both.

(June 27, 1952, ch. 477, title II, ch. 7, §266, 66 Stat. 225; as amended by P.L. 104-208 (IIRAIRA) (9/30/96), div. C, title III, §308 [revising (b)–(c)].)

# Chapter 8 — General Penalty Provisions

## Sec. 271 Prevention of Unauthorized Landing of Aliens
[8 U.S.C. 1321]

**(a) Failure to report; penalties.**— It shall be the duty of every person, including the owners, masters, officers, and agents of vessels, aircraft, transportation lines, or international bridges or toll roads, other than transportation lines which may enter into a contract as provided in section 233, bringing an alien to, or providing a means for an alien to come to, the United States (including an alien crewman whose case is not covered by section 254(a)) to prevent the landing of such alien in the United States at a port of entry other than as designated by the Attorney General or at any time or place other than as designated by the immigration officers. Any such person, owner, master, officer, or agent who fails to comply with the foregoing requirements shall be liable to a penalty to be imposed by the Attorney General of $3,000 for each such violation, which may, in the discretion of the Attorney General, be remitted or mitigated by him in accordance with such proceedings as he shall by regulation prescribe. Such penalty shall be a lien upon the vessel or aircraft whose owner, master, officer, or agent violates the provisions of this section, and such vessel or aircraft may be libeled therefor in the appropriate United States court.

**(b) Prima facie evidence.**— Proof that the alien failed to present himself at the time and place designated by the immigration officers shall be prima facie evidence that such alien has landed in the United States at a time or place other than as designated by the immigration officers.

**(c) Liability of owners and operators of international bridges and toll roads.**—

(1) Any owner or operator of a railroad line, international bridge, or toll road who establishes to the satisfaction of the Attorney General that the person has acted diligently and reasonably to fulfill the duty imposed by subsection (a) shall not be liable for the penalty described in such subsection, notwithstanding the failure of the person to prevent the unauthorized landing of any alien.

(2) (A) At the request of any person described in paragraph (1), the Attorney General shall inspect any facility established, or any method utilized, at a point of entry into the United States by such person for the purpose of complying with subsection (a). The Attorney General shall approve any such facility or method (for such period of time as the Attorney General may prescribe) which the Attorney General determines is satisfactory for such purpose.

(B) Proof that any person described in paragraph (1) has diligently maintained any facility, or utilized any method, which has been approved by the Attorney General under subparagraph (A) (within the period for which the approval is effective) shall be prima facie evidence that such person acted diligently and reasonably to fulfill the duty imposed by subsection (a) (within the meaning of paragraph (1) of this subsection).

(June 27, 1952, ch. 477, title II, ch. 8, §271, 66 Stat. 226; as amended by P.L. 99-603 (11/6/86); P.L. 101-649 (IMMACT90) (11/29/90), §543; Pub. L. 104-208 (IIRAIRA) (9/30/96), div. C, title III, §308.)

## Sec. 272 Bringing in Aliens Subject to Exclusion on a Health-Related Ground; Persons Liable; Clearance Papers; Exceptions; "Person" Defined
## [8 U.S.C. 1322]

**(a)** Any person who shall bring to the United States an alien (other than an alien crewman) who is inadmissible under section 212(a)(1) shall pay to the Commissioner for each and every alien so afflicted the sum of $3,000 unless (1) the alien was in possession of a valid, unexpired immigrant visa, or (2) the alien was allowed to land in the United States, or (3) the alien was in possession of a valid unexpired nonimmigrant visa or other document authorizing such alien to apply for temporary admission to the United States or an unexpired reentry permit issued to him, and (A) such application was made within one hundred and twenty days of the date of issuance of the visa or other document, or in the case of an alien in possession of a reentry permit, within one hundred and twenty days of the date on which the alien was last examined and admitted by the Service, or (B) in the event the application was made later than one hundred and twenty days of the date of issuance of the visa or other document or such examination and admission, if such person establishes to the satisfaction of the Attorney General that the existence of the condition causing inadmissibility could not have been detected by the exercise of due diligence prior to the alien's embarkation.

**(b)** No vessel or aircraft shall be granted clearance papers pending determination of the question of liability to the payment of any fine under this section, or while the fines remain unpaid, nor shall such fines be remitted or refunded; but clearance may be granted prior to the determination of such question upon the deposit of a sum sufficient to cover such fines or of a bond with sufficient surety to secure the payment thereof, approved by the Commissioner.

**(c)** Nothing contained in this section shall be construed to subject transportation companies to a fine for bringing to ports of entry in the United States aliens who are entitled by law to exemption from the provisions of section 212(a).

**(d)** As used in this section, the term "person" means the owner, master, agent, commanding officer, charterer, or consignee of any vessel or aircraft.

(June 27, 1952, ch. 477, title II, ch. 8, §272, 66 Stat. 226; as amended by P.L. 89-236, (10/3/65); P.L. 101-649 (11/29/90), title V, §543(a)(9), title VI, §603(a)(15); P.L. 102-232 (12/12/91), title III, §307(l)(7); P.L. 103-416 (10/25/94), title II, §219(o); P.L. 104-208 (IIRAIRA) (9/30/96), §308 [revising (a) & (c)].)

## Sec. 273 Unlawful Bringing of Aliens into United States
[8 U.S.C. 1323]

**(a) Persons liable.—**

(1) It shall be unlawful for any person, including any transportation company, or the owner, master, commanding officer, agent, charterer, or consignee of any vessel or aircraft, to bring to the United States from any place outside thereof (other than from foreign contiguous territory) any alien who does not have a valid passport and an unexpired visa, if a visa was required under this Act or regulations issued thereunder.

(2) It is unlawful for an owner, agent, master, commanding officer, person in charge, purser, or consignee of a vessel or aircraft who is bringing an alien (except an alien crewmember) to the United States to take any consideration to be kept or returned contingent on whether an alien is admitted to, or ordered removed from, the United States

**(b) Evidence.—** If it appears to the satisfaction of the Attorney General that any alien has been so brought, such person, or transportation company, or the master, commanding officer, agent, owner, charterer, or consignee of any such vessel or aircraft, shall pay to the Commissioner a fine of $3,000 for each alien so brought and, except in the case of any such alien who is admitted, or permitted to land temporarily, in addition, an amount equal to that paid by such alien for his transportation from the initial point of departure, indicated in his ticket, to the port of arrival, such latter fine to be delivered by the Commissioner to the alien on whose account the assessment is made. No vessel or aircraft shall be granted clearance pending the determination of the liability to the payment of such fine or while such fine remains unpaid, except that clearance may be granted prior to the determination of such question upon the deposit of an amount sufficient to cover such fine, or of a bond with sufficient surety to secure the payment thereof approved by the Commissioner.

**(c) Remission or refund.—** Except as provided in subsection (e), such fine shall not be remitted or refunded, unless it appears to the satisfaction of the Attorney General that such person, and the owner, master, commanding officer, agent, charterer, and consignee of the vessel or aircraft, prior to the departure of the vessel or aircraft from the last port outside the United States, did not know, and could not have ascertained by the exercise of reasonable diligence, that the individual transported was an alien and that a valid passport or visa was required.

**(d)** [Repealed. P.L. 104-208 (IIRAIRA) (9/30/96), div. C, title III, §308(e)(13).]

**(e) Reduction, refund, or waiver.—** A fine under this section may be reduced, refunded, or waived under such regulations as the Attorney General shall prescribe in cases in which—

(1) the carrier demonstrates that it had screened all passengers on the vessel or aircraft in accordance with procedures prescribed by the Attorney General, or

(2) circumstances exist that the Attorney General determines would justify such reduction, refund, or waiver.

(June 27, 1952, ch. 477, title II, ch. 8, §273, 66 Stat. 227; as amended by P.L. 101-649 (IMMACT90) (11/29/90); P.L. 102-232 (MTINA) (12/12/91, *effective* 4/1/92); P.L. 103-416 (INTCA) (10/25/94, *effective* 4/1/95); P.L. 104-208 (IIRAIRA) (9/30/96), div. C, title III, §§308(c)(3) [adding (a)(2)], (e)(13) [repealing (d)], 371(b)(8) [revising (d) before its repeal], title VI, 671(b)(6) [revising (b)].)

## Sec. 274 Bringing in and Harboring Certain Aliens
## [8 U.S.C. 1324]

### (a) Criminal penalties.—

(1) (A) Any person who—

(i) knowing that a person is an alien, brings to or attempts to bring to the United States in any manner whatsoever such person at a place other than a designated port of entry or place other than as designated by the Commissioner, regardless of whether such alien has received prior official authorization to come to, enter, or reside in the United States and regardless of any future official action which may be taken with respect to such alien;

(ii) knowing or in reckless disregard of the fact that an alien has come to, entered, or remains in the United States in violation of law, transports, or moves or attempts to transport or move such alien within the United States by means of transportation or otherwise, in furtherance of such violation of law;

(iii) knowing or in reckless disregard of the fact that an alien has come to, entered, or remains in the United States in violation of law, conceals, harbors, or shields from detection, or attempts to conceal, harbor, or shield from detection, such alien in any place, including any building or any means of transportation;

(iv) encourages or induces an alien to come to, enter, or reside in the United States, knowing or in reckless disregard of the fact that such coming to, entry, or residence is or will be in violation of law; or

(v) (I) engages in any conspiracy to commit any of the preceding acts, or

(II) aids or abets the commission of any of the preceding acts,

shall be punished as provided in subparagraph (B)

(B) A person who violates subparagraph (A) shall, for each alien in respect to whom such a violation occurs—

(i) in the case of a violation of subparagraph (A)(i) or (v)(I) or in the case of a violation of subparagraph (A)(ii), (iii), or (iv) in which the offense was done for the purpose of commercial advantage or private financial gain, be fined under title 18, United States Code, imprisoned not more than 10 years, or both;

(ii) in the case of a violation of subparagraph (A)(ii), (iii), (iv), or (v)(II), be fined under title 18, United States Code, imprisoned not more than 5 years, or both;

(iii) in the case of a violation of subparagraph (A)(i), (ii), (iii), (iv), or (v) during and in relation to which the person causes serious bodily injury (as defined in section 1365 of title 18, United States Code) to, or places in jeopardy the life of, any person, be fined under title 18, United States Code, imprisoned not more than 20 years, or both; and

(iv) in the case of a violation of subparagraph (A)(i), (ii), (iii), (iv), or (v) resulting in the death of any person, be punished by death or imprisoned for any term of years or for life, fined under title 18, United States Code, or both.

(C) It is not a violation of clauses (ii) or (iii) of subparagraph (A), or of clause (iv) of subparagraph (A) except where a person encourages or induces an alien to come to or enter the United States, for a religious denomination having a bona fide nonprofit, religious organization in the United States, or the agents or officers of such denomination or organization, to encourage, invite, call, allow, or enable an alien who is present in the United States to perform the vocation of a minister or missionary for the denomination or organization in the United States as a volunteer who is not compensated as an employee, notwithstanding the provision of room, board, travel, medical assistance, and other basic living expenses, provided the minister or missionary has been a member of the denomination for at least one year.

(2) Any person who, knowing or in reckless disregard of the fact that an alien has not received prior official authorization to come to, enter, or reside in the United States, brings to or attempts to bring to the United States in any manner whatsoever, such alien, regardless of any official action which may later be taken with respect to such alien shall, for each alien in respect to whom a violation of this paragraph occurs—

(A) be fined in accordance with title 18, United States Code, or imprisoned not more than one year, or both; or

(B) in the case of—

(i) an offense committed with the intent or with reason to believe that the alien unlawfully brought into the United States will commit an offense against the United States or any State punishable by imprisonment for more than 1 year,

(ii) an offense done for the purpose of commercial advantage or private financial gain, or

(iii) an offense in which the alien is not upon arrival immediately brought and presented to an appropriate immigration officer at a designated port of entry,

be fined under title 18, United States Code, and shall be imprisoned, in the case of a first or second violation of subparagraph (B)(iii), not more than 10 years, in the case of a first or second violation of subparagraph (B)(i) or (B)(ii), not less than 3 nor more than 10 years, and for any other violation, not less than 5 nor more than 15 years.

(3) (A) Any person who, during any 12-month period, knowingly hires for employment at least 10 individuals with actual knowledge that the individuals are aliens described in subparagraph (B) shall be fined under title 18, United States Code, or imprisoned for not more than 5 years, or both.

(B) An alien described in this subparagraph is an alien who—

(i) is an unauthorized alien (as defined in section 274A(h)(3)), and

(ii) has been brought into the United States in violation of this subsection.

(4) In the case of a person who has brought aliens into the United States in violation of this subsection, the sentence otherwise provided for may be increased by up to 10 years if—

(A) the offense was part of an ongoing commercial organization or enterprise;

(B) aliens were transported in groups of 10 or more; and

(C) (i) aliens were transported in a manner that endangered their lives; or

(ii) the aliens presented a life-threatening health risk to people in the United States.

**(b) Seizure and forfeiture.—**

(1) *In general.—* Any conveyance, including any vessel, vehicle, or aircraft, which has been or is being used in the commission of a violation of subsection (a), the gross proceeds of such violation, and any property traceable to such conveyance or proceeds, shall be seized and subject to forfeiture.

(2) *Applicable procedures.—* Seizures and forfeitures under this subsection shall be governed by the provisions of Chapter 46 of title 18, United States Code, relating to civil forfeitures, including section 981(d) of such title, except that such duties as are imposed upon the Secretary of the Treasury under the customs laws described in that section shall be performed by such officers, agents, and other persons as may be designated for that purpose by the Attorney General.

(3) *Prima facie evidence in determinations of violations.—* In determining whether a violation of subsection (a) has occurred, any of the following shall be prima facie evidence that an alien involved in the alleged violation had not received prior official authorization to come to, enter, or reside in the United States:

(A) Records of any judicial or administrative proceeding in which that alien's status was an issue and in which it was determined that the alien had not received prior official authorization to come to, enter, or reside in the United States or that such alien had come to, entered, or remained in the United States in violation of law.

(B) Official records of the Service or of the Department of State showing that the alien had not received prior official authorization to come to, enter, or reside in the United States or that such alien had come to, entered, or remained in the United States in violation of law.

(C) Testimony, by an immigration officer having personal knowledge of the facts concerning that alien's status, that the alien had not received prior official authorization to come to, enter, or reside in the United States of that such alien had come to, entered, or remained in the United States in violation of law.

**(c) Authority to arrest.—** No officer or person shall have authority to make any arrest for a violation of any provision of this section except officers and employees of the Service designated by the Attorney General, either individually or as a member of a class, and all other officers whose duty it is to enforce criminal laws.

**(d) Admissibility of videotaped witness testimony.—** Notwithstanding any provision of the Federal Rules of Evidence, the videotaped (or otherwise audiovisually preserved) deposition of a witness to a violation of subsection (a) who has been deported or otherwise expelled from the United States, or is otherwise unable to testify, may be admitted into evidence in an action brought for that violation if the witness was available for cross examination and the deposition otherwise complies with the Federal Rules of Evidence.

**(e) Outreach program.—** The Secretary of Homeland Security, in consultation with the Attorney General and the Secretary of State, as appropriate, shall develop and implement an outreach program to educate the public in the United States and abroad about the penalties for bringing in and harboring aliens in violation of this section.

(June 27, 1952, ch. 477, title II, ch. 8, §274, 66 Stat. 228; as amended by P.L. 95-582 (11/2/78); P.L. 97-116 (12/29/81); P.L. 99-603 (IRCA) (11/6/86); P.L. 100-525 (10/24/88); P.L. 103-322 (VAWA) (9/13/94); P.L. 104-208 (IIRAIRA) (9/30/96), div. C, title II, §203(a) [revising (a)], §219 [adding (d)], title VI, §671(a)(1); P.L. 106-185 (4/25/00), §18(a) [revising (b)]; P.L. 108-458 (12/17/04), title V, §5401 [adding (a)(4), (e)]; P.L. 109-97 (11/10/05), title VII, §796 [adding (a)(1)(C)].)

## Sec. 274A Unlawful Employment of Aliens
## [8 U.S.C. 1324a]

### (a) Making employment of unauthorized aliens unlawful.—

(1) *In general.*— It is unlawful for a person or other entity—

(A) to hire, or to recruit or refer for a fee, for employment in the United States an alien knowing the alien is an unauthorized alien (as defined in subsection (h)(3)) with respect to such employment, or

(B) (i) to hire for employment in the United States an individual without complying with the requirements of subsection (b) or

(ii) if the person or entity is an agricultural association, agricultural employer, or farm labor contractor (as defined in section 3 of the Migrant and Seasonal Agricultural Worker Protection Act), to hire, or to recruit or refer for a fee, for employment in the United States an individual without complying with the requirements of subsection (b).

(2) *Continuing employment.*— It is unlawful for a person or other entity, after hiring an alien for employment in accordance with paragraph (1), to continue to employ the alien in the United States knowing the alien is (or has become) an unauthorized alien with respect to such employment.

(3) *Defense.*— A person or entity that establishes that it has complied in good faith with the requirements of subsection (b) with respect to the hiring, recruiting, or referral for employment of an alien in the United States has established an affirmative defense that the person or entity has not violated paragraph (1)(A) with respect to such hiring, recruiting, or referral.

(4) *Use of labor through contract.*— For purposes of this section, a person or other entity who uses a contract, subcontract, or exchange, entered into, renegotiated, or extended after the date of the enactment of this section, to obtain the labor of an alien in the United States knowing that the alien is an unauthorized alien (as defined in subsection (h)(3)) with respect to performing such labor, shall be considered to have hired the alien for employment in the United States in violation of paragraph (1)(A).

(5) *Use of state employment agency documentation.*— For purposes of paragraphs (1)(B) and (3), a person or entity shall be deemed to have complied with the requirements of subsection (b) with respect to the hiring of an individual who was referred for such employment by a State employment agency (as defined by the Attorney General), if the person or entity has and retains (for the period and in the manner described in subsection (b)(3)) appropriate documentation of such referral by that agency, which documentation certifies that the agency has complied with the procedures specified in subsection (b) with respect to the individual's referral.

(6) *Treatment of documentation for certain employees.*—[167]

(A) *In general.*— For purposes of this section, if—

(i) an individual is a member of a collective-bargaining unit and is employed, under a collective bargaining agreement entered into between one or more employee organizations and an association of two or more employers, by an employer that is a member of such association, and

(ii) within the period specified in subparagraph (B), another employer that is a member of the association (or an agent of such association on behalf of the em-

---

[167] *See* §412(b) of IIRAIRA, effective as "to individuals hired on or after 60 days after the date of enactment of this Act."

ployer) has complied with the requirements of subsection (b) with respect to the employment of the individual,

the subsequent employer shall be deemed to have complied with the requirements of subsection (b) with respect to the hiring of the employee and shall not be liable for civil penalties described in subsection (e)(5).

(B) *Period.*— The period described in this subparagraph is 3 years, or, if less, the period of time that the individual is authorized to be employed in the United States.

(C) *Liability.*—

(i) In general.— If any employer that is a member of an association hires for employment in the United States an individual and relies upon the provisions of subparagraph (A) to comply with the requirements of subsection (b) and the individual is an alien not authorized to work in the United States, then for the purposes of paragraph (1)(A), subject to clause (ii), the employer shall be presumed to have known at the time of hiring or afterward that the individual was an alien not authorized to work in the United States.

(ii) Rebuttal of presumption.— The presumption established by clause (i) may be rebutted by the employer only through the presentation of clear and convincing evidence that the employer did not know (and could not reasonably have known) that the individual at the time of hiring or afterward was an alien not authorized to work in the United States.

(iii) Exception.— Clause (i) shall not apply in any prosecution under subsection (f)(1).

(7) *Application to Federal Government.*— For purposes of this section, the term "entity" includes an entity in any branch of the Federal Government.[168]

**(b) Employment verification system.**— The requirements referred to in paragraphs (1)(B) and (3) of subsection (a) are, in the case of a person or other entity hiring, recruiting, or referring an individual for employment in the United States, the requirements specified in the following three paragraphs:

(1) *Attestation after examination of documentation.*—

(A) *In general.*— The person or entity must attest, under penalty of perjury and on a form designated or established by the Attorney General by regulation, that it has verified that the individual is not an unauthorized alien by examining—

(i) a document described in subparagraph (B), or

(ii) a document described in subparagraph (C) and a document described in subparagraph (D). Such attestation may be manifested by either a hand-written or an electronic signature. A person or entity has complied with the requirement of this paragraph with respect to examination of a document if the document reasonably appears on its face to be genuine. If an individual provides a document or combination of documents that reasonably appears on its face to be genuine and that is sufficient to meet the requirements of the first sentence of this paragraph, nothing in this paragraph shall be construed as requiring the person or entity to solicit the production of any other document or as requiring the individual to produce such another document.

---

[168] *See* §412(d) of IIRAIRA, effective for "hiring occurring before, on, or after the date of the enactment of [IIRAIRA], but no penalty shall be imposed under subsection (e) or (f) of §274A of the Immigration and Nationality Act for such hiring occurring before such date."

(B) *Documents establishing both employment authorization and identity.*— A document described in this subparagraph is an individual's—

(i) United States passport;

(ii) resident alien card, alien registration card, or other document designated by the Attorney General, if the document—

(I) contains a photograph of the individual and such other personal identifying information relating to the individual as the Attorney General finds, by regulation, sufficient for purposes of this subsection,

(II) is evidence of authorization of employment in the United States, and

(III) contains security features to make it resistant to tampering, counterfeiting, and fraudulent use.

(C) *Documents evidencing employment authorization.*— A document described in this subparagraph is an individual's—

(i) social security account number card (other than such a card which specifies on the face that the issuance of the card does not authorize employment in the United States); or

(ii) other documentation evidencing authorization of employment in the United States which the Attorney General finds, by regulation, to be acceptable for purposes of this section.

(D) *Documents establishing identity of individual.*— A document described in this subparagraph is an individual's—

(i) driver's license or similar document issued for the purpose of identification by a State, if it contains a photograph of the individual or such other personal identifying information relating to the individual as the Attorney General finds, by regulation, sufficient for purposes of this section; or

(ii) in the case of individuals under 16 years of age or in a State which does not provide for issuance of an identification document (other than a driver's license) referred to in clause (i), documentation of personal identity of such other type as the Attorney General finds, by regulation, provides a reliable means of identification.

(E) *Authority to prohibit use of certain documents.*— If the Attorney General finds, by regulation, that any document described in subparagraph (B), (C), or (D) as establishing employment authorization or identity does not reliably establish such authorization or identity or is being used fraudulently to an unacceptable degree, the Attorney General may prohibit or place conditions on its use for purposes of this subsection.[169]

(2) *Individual attestation of employment authorization.*— The individual must attest, under penalty of perjury on the form designated or established for purposes of paragraph (1), that the individual is a citizen or national of the United States, an alien lawfully admitted for permanent residence, or an alien who is authorized under this Act or by the Attorney General to be hired, recruited, or referred for such employment. Such attestation may be manifested by either a hand-written or an electronic signature.

---

[169] *See* §412(a) of IIRAIRA, effective "with respect to hiring (or recruitment or referral) occurring on or after such date (not later than 12 months after the date of enactment of [IIRAIRA]) as the Attorney shall designate."

**(3) *Retention of verification form.*—** After completion of such form in accordance with paragraphs (1) and (2), the person or entity must retain a paper, microfiche, microfilm, or electronic version of the form and make it available for inspection by officers of the Service, the Special Counsel for Immigration-Related Unfair Employment Practices, or the Department of Labor during a period beginning on the date of the hiring, recruiting, or referral of the individual and ending—

(A) in the case of the recruiting or referral for a fee (without hiring) of an individual, three years after the date of the recruiting or referral, and

(B) in the case of the hiring of an individual—

(i) three years after the date of such hiring, or

(ii) one year after the date the individual's employment is terminated, whichever is later.

**(4) *Copying of documentation permitted.*—** Notwithstanding any other provision of law, the person or entity may copy a document presented by an individual pursuant to this subsection and may retain the copy, but only (except as otherwise permitted under law) for the purpose of complying with the requirements of this subsection.

**(5) *Limitation on use of attestation form.*—** A form designated or established by the Attorney General under this subsection and any information contained in or appended to such form, may not be used for purposes other than for enforcement of this Act and sections 1001, 1028, 1546, and 1621 of title 18, United States Code.

**(6) *Good faith compliance.*—**[170]

(A) *In general.*— Except as provided in subparagraphs (B) and (C), a person or entity is considered to have complied with a requirement of this subsection notwithstanding a technical or procedural failure to meet such requirement if there was a good faith attempt to comply with the requirement.

(B) *Exception if failure to correct after notice.*— Subparagraph (A) shall not apply if—

(i) the Service (or another enforcement agency) has explained to the person or entity the basis for the failure,

(ii) the person or entity has been provided a period of not less than 10 business days (beginning after the date of the explanation) within which to correct the failure, and

(iii) the person or entity has not corrected the failure voluntarily within such period.

(C) *Exception for pattern or practice violators.*— Subparagraph (A) shall not apply to a person or entity that has or is engaging in a pattern or practice of violations of subsection (a)(1)(A) or (a)(2).

**(c) No authorization of national identification cards.—** Nothing in this section shall be construed to authorize, directly or indirectly, the issuance or use of national identification cards or the establishment of a national identification card.

**(d) Evaluation and changes in employment verification system.—**

**(1) *Presidential monitoring and improvements in system.*—**

---

[170] *See* §411 of IIRAIRA, effective for "failures occurring on or after the date of the enactment of [IIRAIRA]."

(A) *Monitoring.*— The President shall provide for the monitoring and evaluation of the degree to which the employment verification system established under subsection (b) provides a secure system to determine employment eligibility in the United States and shall examine the suitability of existing Federal and State identification systems for use for this purpose.

(B) *Improvements to establish secure system.*— To the extent that the system established under subsection (b) is found not to be a secure system to determine employment eligibility in the United States, the President shall, subject to paragraph (3) and taking into account the results of any demonstration projects conducted under paragraph (4), implement such changes in (including additions to) the requirements of subsection (b) as may be necessary to establish a secure system to determine employment eligibility in the United States. Such changes in the system may be implemented only if the changes conform to the requirements of paragraph (2).

(2) ***Restrictions on changes in system.***— Any change the President proposes to implement under paragraph (1) in the verification system must be designed in a manner so the verification system, as so changed, meets the following requirements:

(A) *Reliable determination of identity.*— The system must be capable of reliably determining whether—

(i) a person with the identity claimed by an employee or prospective employee is eligible to work, and

(ii) the employee or prospective employee is claiming the identity of another individual.

(B) *Using of counterfeit-resistant documents.*— If the system requires that a document be presented to or examined by an employer, the document must be in a form which is resistant to counterfeiting and tampering.

(C) *Limited use of system.*— Any personal information utilized by the system may not be made available to Government agencies, employers, and other persons except to the extent necessary to verify that an individual is not an unauthorized alien.

(D) *Privacy of information.*— The system must protect the privacy and security of personal information and identifiers utilized in the system.

(E) *Limited denial of verification.*— A verification that an employee or prospective employee is eligible to be employed in the United States may not be withheld or revoked under the system for any reason other than that the employee or prospective employee is an unauthorized alien.

(F) *Limited use for law enforcement purposes.*— The system may not be used for law enforcement purposes, other than for enforcement of this Act or sections 1001, 1028, 1546, and 1621 of title 18, United States Code.

(G) *Restriction on use of new documents.*— If the system requires individuals to present a new card or other document (designed specifically for use for this purpose) at the time of hiring, recruitment, or referral, then such document may not be required to be presented for any purpose other than under this Act (or enforcement of sections 1001, 1028, 1546, and 1621 of title 18, United States Code) nor to be carried on one's person.

(3) ***Notice to congress before implementing changes.***—

(A) *In general.*— The President may not implement any change under paragraph (1) unless at least—

(i) 60 days,

(ii) one year, in the case of a major change described in subparagraph (D)(iii), or

(iii) two years, in the case of a major change described in clause (i) or (ii) of subparagraph (D),

before the date of implementation of the change, the President has prepared and transmitted to the Committee on the Judiciary of the House of Representatives and to the Committee on the Judiciary of the Senate a written report setting forth the proposed change. If the President proposes to make any change regarding social security account number cards, the President shall transmit to the Committee on Ways and Means of the House of Representatives and to the Committee on Finance of the Senate a written report setting forth the proposed change. The President promptly shall cause to have printed in the *Federal Register* the substance of any major change (described in subparagraph (D)) proposed and reported to Congress.

(B) *Contents of report.*— In any report under subparagraph (A) the President shall include recommendations for the establishment of civil and criminal sanctions for unauthorized use or disclosure of the information or identifiers contained in such system.

(C) *Congressional review of major changes.*—

(i) Hearings and review.— The Committees on the Judiciary of the House of Representatives and of the Senate shall cause to have printed in the Congressional Record the substance of any major change described in subparagraph (D), shall hold hearings respecting the feasibility and desirability of implementing such a change, and, within the two year period before implementation, shall report to their respective Houses findings on whether or not such a change should be implemented.

(ii) Congressional action.— No major change may be implemented unless the Congress specifically provides, in an appropriations or other Act, for funds for implementation of the change.

(D) *Major changes defined.*— As used in this paragraph, the term "major change" means a change which would—

(i) require an individual to present a new card or other document (designed specifically for use for this purpose) at the time of hiring, recruitment, or referral,

(ii) provide for a telephone verification system under which an employer, recruiter, or referrer must transmit to a Federal official information concerning the immigration status of prospective employees and the official transmits to the person, and the person must record, a verification code, or

(iii) require any change in any card used for accounting purposes under the Social Security Act, including any change requiring that the only social security account number cards which may be presented in order to comply with subsection (b)(1)(C)(i) are such cards as are in a counterfeit-resistant form consistent with the second sentence of section 205(c)(2)(D) of the Social Security Act.

(E) *General revenue funding of social security card changes.*— Any costs incurred in developing and implementing any change describe]d in subparagraph (D)(iii) for purposes of this subsection shall not be paid for out of any trust fund established under the Social Security Act.

(4) *Demonstration projects.*—

(A) *Authority.*— The President may undertake demonstration projects (consistent with paragraph (2)) of different changes in the requirements of subsection (b). No such project may extend over a period of longer than five years.

(B) *Reports on projects.*— The President shall report to the Congress on the results of demonstration projects conducted under this paragraph.

**(e) Compliance.**—

(1) *Complaints and investigations.*— The Attorney General shall establish procedures—

(A) for individuals and entities to file written, signed complaints respecting potential violations of subsection (a) or (g)(1),

(B) for the investigation of those complaints which, on their face, have a substantial probability of validity,

(C) for the investigation of such other violations of subsection (a) or (g)(1) as the Attorney General determines to be appropriate, and

(D) for the designation in the Service of a unit which has, as its primary duty, the prosecution of cases of violations of subsection (a) or (g)(1) under this subsection.

(2) *Authority in investigations.*— In conducting investigations and hearings under this subsection—

(A) immigration officers and administrative law judges shall have reasonable access to examine evidence of any person or entity being investigated,

(B) administrative law judges, may, if necessary, compel by subpoena the attendance of witnesses and the production of evidence at any designated place or hearing, and

(C) immigration officers designated by the Commissioner may compel by subpoena the attendance of witnesses and the production of evidence at any designated place prior to the filing of a complaint in a case under paragraph (2).

In case of contumacy or refusal to obey a subpoena lawfully issued under this paragraph and upon application of the Attorney General, an appropriate district court of the United States may issue an order requiring compliance with such subpoena and any failure to obey such order may be punished by such court as a contempt thereof.

(3) *Hearing.*—

(A) *In general.*— Before imposing an order described in paragraph (4), (5), or (6) against a person or entity under this subsection for a violation of subsection (a) or (g)(1), the Attorney General shall provide the person or entity with notice and, upon request made within a reasonable time (of not less than 30 days, as established by the Attorney General) of the date of the notice, a hearing respecting the violation.

(B) *Conduct of hearing.*— Any hearing so requested shall be conducted before an administrative law judge. The hearing shall be conducted in accordance with the requirements of section 554 of title 5, United States Code. The hearing shall be held at the nearest practicable place to the place where the person or entity resides or of the place where the alleged violation occurred. If no hearing is so requested, the Attorney General's imposition of the order shall constitute a final and unappealable order.

(C) *Issuance of orders.*— If the administrative law judge determines, upon the preponderance of the evidence received, that a person or entity named in the complaint has violated subsection (a) or (g)(1), the administrative law judge shall state his findings of fact and issue and cause to be served on such person or entity an order described in paragraph (4), (5), or (6).

(4) ***Cease and desist order with civil money penalty for hiring, recruiting, and referral violations.***— With respect to a violation of subsection (a)(1)(A) or (a)(2), the order under this subsection—

(A) shall require the person or entity to cease and desist from such violations and to pay a civil penalty in an amount of—

(i) not less than $250 and not more than $2,000 for each unauthorized alien with respect to whom a violation of either such subsection occurred,

(ii) not less than $2,000 and not more than $5,000 for each such alien in the case of a person or entity previously subject to one order under this paragraph, or

(iii) not less than $3,000 and not more than $10,000 for each such alien in the case of a person or entity previously subject to more than one order under this paragraph; and

(B) may require the person or entity—

(i) to comply with the requirements of subsection (b) (or subsection (d) if applicable) with respect to individuals hired (or recruited or referred for employment for a fee) during a period of up to three years, and

(ii) to take such other remedial action as is appropriate.

In applying this subsection in the case of a person or entity composed of distinct, physically separate subdivisions each of which provides separately for the hiring, recruiting, or referring for employment, without reference to the practices of, and not under the control of or common control with, another subdivision, each such subdivision shall be considered a separate person or entity.

(5) ***Order for civil money penalty for paperwork violations.***— With respect to a violation of subsection (a)(1)(B), the order under this subsection shall require the person or entity to pay a civil penalty in an amount of not less than $100 and not more than $1,000 for each individual with respect to whom such violation occurred. In determining the amount of the penalty, due consideration shall be given to the size of the business of the employer being charged, the good faith of the employer, the seriousness of the violation, whether or not the individual was an unauthorized alien, and the history of previous violations.

(6) ***Order for prohibited indemnity bonds.***— With respect to a violation of subsection (g)(1), the order under this subsection may provide for the remedy described in subsection (g)(2).

(7) ***Administrative appellate review.***— The decision and order of an administrative law judge shall become the final agency decision and order of the Attorney General unless either (A) within 30 days, an official delegated by regulation to exercise review authority over the decision and order modifies or vacates the decision and order, or (B) within 30 days of the date of such a modification or vacation (or within 60 days of the date of decision and order of an administrative law judge if not so modified or vacated) the decision and order is referred to the

Attorney General pursuant to regulations, in which case the decision and order of the Attorney General shall become the final agency decision and order under this subsection. The Attorney General may not delegate the Attorney General's authority under this paragraph to any entity which has review authority over immigration-related matters.[171]

(8) *Judicial review.*— A person or entity adversely affected by a final order respecting an assessment may, within 45 days after the date the final order is issued, file a petition in the Court of Appeals for the appropriate circuit for review of the order.

(9) *Enforcement of orders.*— If a person or entity fails to comply with a final order issued under this subsection against the person or entity, the Attorney General shall file a suit to seek compliance with the order in any appropriate district court of the United States. In any such suit, the validity and appropriateness of the final order shall not be subject to review.

**(f) Criminal penalties and injunctions for pattern or practice violations.**—

(1) *Criminal penalty.*— Any person or entity which engages in a pattern or practice of violations of subsection (a)(1)(A) or (a)(2) shall be fined not more than $3,000 for each unauthorized alien with respect to whom such a violation occurs, imprisoned for not more than six months for the entire pattern or practice, or both, notwithstanding the provisions of any other Federal law relating to fine levels.

(2) *Enjoining of pattern or practice violations.*— Whenever the Attorney General has reasonable cause to believe that a person or entity is engaged in a pattern or practice of employment, recruitment, or referral in violation of paragraph (1)(A) or (2) of subsection (a), the Attorney General may bring a civil action in the appropriate district court of the United States requesting such relief, including a permanent or temporary injunction, restraining order, or other order against the person or entity, as the Attorney General deems necessary.

**(g) Prohibition of indemnity bonds.**—

(1) *Prohibition.*— It is unlawful for a person or other entity, in the hiring, recruiting, or referring for employment of any individual, to require the individual to post a bond or security, to pay or agree to pay an amount, or otherwise to provide a financial guarantee or indemnity, against any potential liability arising under this section relating to such hiring, recruiting, or referring of the individual.

(2) *Civil penalty.*— Any person or entity which is determined, after notice and opportunity for an administrative hearing under subsection (e), to have violated paragraph (1) shall be subject to a civil penalty of $1,000 for each violation and to an administrative order requiring the return of any amounts received in violation of such paragraph to the employee or, if the employee cannot be located, to the general fund of the Treasury.

**(h) Miscellaneous provisions.**—

(1) *Documentation.*— In providing documentation or endorsement of authorization of aliens (other than aliens lawfully admitted for permanent residence) authorized to be employed in the United States, the Attorney General shall provide that any limitations with respect to the period or type of employment or employer shall be conspicuously stated on the documentation or endorsement.

---

[171] Amended by §379(a)(1) and (2) of IIRAIRA, effective for "orders issued on or after the date of the enactment of this Act."

(2) *Preemption.*— The provisions of this section preempt any State or local law imposing civil or criminal sanctions (other than through licensing and similar laws) upon those who employ, or recruit or refer for a fee for employment, unauthorized aliens.

(3) *Definition of unauthorized alien.*— As used in this section, the term "unauthorized alien" means, with respect to the employment of an alien at a particular time, that the alien is not at that time either (A) an alien lawfully admitted for permanent residence, or (B) authorized to be so employed by this Act or by the Attorney General.

**(i)–(n)** [removed]

(June 27, 1952, ch. 477, title II, ch. 8, §274A, as added by P.L. 99-603 (IRCA) (11/6/86); as amended by P.L. 100-525 (10/24/88); P.L. 101-649 (IMMACT90) (11/29/90); P.L. 102-232 (MTINA) (12/12/91, *effective* 4/1/92), title III, §306(b)(2), §309(b)(11); P.L. 103-416 (INTCA) (10/25/94, *effective* 4/1/95), title II, §213, §219(z)(4); P.L. 104-208 (IIRAIRA) (9/30/96), div. C, title III, §379(a) [revising (e)(7)], title IV, §411(a) [adding (b)(6)], §412(a) [adding (a)(6)–(7), (b)(1)(B)(ii); striking (i)–(n)], §416 [revising (e)(2); adding (e)(2)(C)]; P.L. 108-390 (10/30/04, *effective* "the earlier of (1) the date on which the final regulations implementing such amendments take effect; or (2) 180 days after the date of the enactment of this Act"), §1(a) [revising (b)(1)–(3)].)

## Sec. 274B Unfair Immigration-Related Employment Practices
## [8 U.S.C. 1324b]

**(a) Prohibition of discrimination based on national origin or citizenship status.**—

(1) *General rule.*— It is an unfair immigration-related employment practice for a person or other entity to discriminate against any individual (other than an unauthorized alien, as defined in section 274A(h)(3)) with respect to the hiring, or recruitment or referral for a fee, of the individual for employment or the discharging of the individual from employment—

(A) because of such individual's national origin, or

(B) in the case of a protected individual (as defined in paragraph (3)), because of such individual's citizenship status.

(2) *Exceptions.*— Paragraph (1) shall not apply to—

(A) a person or other entity that employs three or fewer employees,

(B) a person's or entity's discrimination because of an individual's national origin if the discrimination with respect to that person or entity and that individual is covered under section 703 of the Civil Rights Act of 1964, or

(C) discrimination because of citizenship status which is otherwise required in order to comply with law, regulation, or executive order, or required by Federal, State, or local government contract, or which the Attorney General determines to be essential for an employer to do business with an agency or department of the Federal, State, or local government.

(3) *"Protected individual" defined.*— As used in paragraph (1), the term "protected individual" means an individual who—

(A) is a citizen or national of the United States, or

(B) is an alien who is lawfully admitted for permanent residence, is granted the status of an alien lawfully admitted for temporary residence under section 210(a) or 245A(a)(1), is admitted as a refugee under section 207, or is granted asylum under section 208; but does not include (i) an alien who fails to apply for naturalization within six months of the date the alien first becomes eligible (by virtue of period of lawful permanent residence) to apply for naturalization or, if later, within six months after the date of the enactment of this section and (ii) an alien who has applied on a timely basis, but has not been naturalized as a citizen within 2 years after the date of the application, unless the alien can establish that the alien is actively pursuing naturalization, except that time consumed in the Service's processing the application shall not be counted toward the 2-year period.

(4) *Additional exception providing right to prefer equally qualified citizens.*— Notwithstanding any other provision of this section, it is not an unfair immigration-related employment practice for a person or other entity to prefer to hire, recruit, or refer an individual who is a citizen or national of the United States over another individual who is an alien if the two individuals are equally qualified.

(5) *Prohibition of intimidation or retaliation.*— It is also an unfair immigration-related employment practice for a person or other entity to intimidate, threaten, coerce, or retaliate against any individual for the purpose of interfering with any right or privilege secured under this section or because the individual intends to file or has filed a charge or a complaint, testified, assisted, or participated in any manner in an investigation, proceeding, or hearing under this section. An individual so intimidated, threatened, coerced, or retaliated against shall be considered, for purposes of subsections (d) and (g), to have been discriminated against.

(6) *Treatment of certain documentary practices as employment practices.*— A person's or other entity's request, for purposes of satisfying the requirements of section 274A(b), for more or different documents than are required under such section or refusing to honor documents tendered that on their face reasonably appear to be genuine shall be treated as an unfair immigration-related employment practice if made for the purpose or with the intent of discriminating against an individual in violation of paragraph (1).[172]

**(b) Charges of violations.**—

(1) *In general.*— Except as provided in paragraph (2), any person alleging that the person is adversely affected directly by an unfair immigration-related employment practice (or a person on that person's behalf) or an officer of the Service alleging that an unfair immigration-related employment practice has occurred or is occurring may file a charge respecting such practice or violation with the Special Counsel (appointed under subsection (c)). Charges shall be in writing under oath or affirmation and shall contain such information as the Attorney General requires. The Special Counsel by certified mail shall serve a notice of the charge (including the date, place, and circumstances of the alleged unfair immigration-related employment practice) on the person or entity involved within 10 days.

(2) *No overlap with EEOC complaints.*— No charge may be filed respecting an unfair immigration-related employment practice described in subsection (a)(1)(A) if a charge with respect to that practice based on the same set of facts has been filed with the Equal Employment Opportunity Commission under title VII of the Civil Rights Act of 1964, unless the charge is dismissed as being outside the scope of such title. No charge respecting an employment practice may be filed with the Equal Employment Opportunity Commission under such title if a charge with respect to such practice based on the same set of facts has been filed under this subsection, unless the charge is dismissed under this section as being outside the scope of this section.

**(c) Special counsel.**—

(1) *Appointment.*— The President shall appoint, by and with the advice and consent of the Senate, a Special Counsel for Immigration-Related Unfair Employment Practices (hereinafter in

---

[172] *See* §421 of IIRAIRA, effective as to requests made on or after the date of the enactment of IIRAIRA.

this section referred to as the "Special Counsel") within the Department of Justice to serve for a term of four years. In the case of a vacancy in the office of the Special Counsel the President may designate the officer or employee who shall act as Special Counsel during such vacancy.

(2) *Duties.*— The Special Counsel shall be responsible for investigation of charges and issuance of complaints under this section and in respect of the prosecution of all such complaints before administrative law judges and the exercise of certain functions under subsection (j)(1).

(3) *Compensation.*— The Special Counsel is entitled to receive compensation at a rate not to exceed the rate now or hereafter provided for grade GS-17 of the General Schedule, under section 5332 of title 5, United States Code.

(4) *Regional offices.*— The Special Counsel, in accordance with regulations of the Attorney General, shall establish such regional offices as may be necessary to carry out his duties.

## (d) Investigation of charges.—

(1) *By special counsel.*— The Special Counsel shall investigate each charge received and, within 120 days of the date of the receipt of the charge, determine whether or not there is reasonable cause to believe that the charge is true and whether or not to bring a complaint with respect to the charge before an administrative law judge. The Special Counsel may, on his own initiative, conduct investigations respecting unfair immigration-related employment practices and, based on such an investigation and subject to paragraph (3), file a complaint before such a judge.

(2) *Private actions.*— If the Special Counsel, after receiving such a charge respecting an unfair immigration-related employment practice which alleges knowing and intentional discriminatory activity or a pattern or practice of discriminatory activity, has not filed a complaint before an administrative law judge with respect to such charge within such 120-day period, the Special Counsel shall notify the person making the charge of the determination not to file such a complaint during such period and the person making the charge may (subject to paragraph (3)) file a complaint directly before such a judge within 90 days after the date of receipt of the notice. The Special Counsel's failure to file such a complaint within such 120-day period shall not affect the right of the Special Counsel to investigate the charge or to bring a complaint before an administrative law judge during such 90-day period.

(3) *Time limitations on complaints.*— No complaint may be filed respecting any unfair immigration-related employment practice occurring more than 180 days prior to the date of the filing of the charge with the Special Counsel. This subparagraph shall not prevent the subsequent amending of a charge or complaint under subsection (e)(1).

## (e) Hearings.—

(1) *Notice.*— Whenever a complaint is made that a person or entity has engaged in or is engaging in any such unfair immigration-related employment practice, an administrative law judge shall have power to issue and cause to be served upon such person or entity a copy of the complaint and a notice of hearing before the judge at a place therein fixed, not less than five days after the serving of the complaint. Any such complaint may be amended by the judge conducting the hearing, upon the motion of the party filing the complaint, in the judge's discretion at any time prior to the issuance of an order based thereon. The person or entity so complained of shall have the right to file an answer to the original or amended complaint and to appear in person or otherwise and give testimony at the place and time fixed in the complaint.

(2) *Judges hearing cases.*— Hearings on complaints under this subsection shall be considered before administrative law judges who are specially designated by the Attorney

General as having special training respecting employment discrimination and, to the extent practicable, before such judges who only consider cases under this section.

(3) *Complainant as party.*— Any person filing a charge with the Special Counsel respecting an unfair immigration-related employment practice shall be considered a party to any complaint before an administrative law judge respecting such practice and any subsequent appeal respecting that complaint. In the discretion of the judge conducting the hearing, any other person may be allowed to intervene in the proceeding and to present testimony.

**(f) Testimony and authority of hearing officers.**—

(1) *Testimony.*— The testimony taken by the administrative law judge shall be reduced to writing. Thereafter, the judge, in his discretion, upon notice may provide for the taking of further testimony or hear argument.

(2) *Authority of administrative law judges.*— In conducting investigations and hearings under this subsection[173] and in accordance with regulations of the Attorney General, the Special Counsel and administrative law judges shall have reasonable access to examine evidence of any person or entity being investigated. The administrative law judges by subpoena may compel the attendance of witnesses and the production of evidence at any designated place or hearing. In case of contumacy or refusal to obey a subpoena lawfully issued under this paragraph and upon application of the administrative law judge, an appropriate district court of the United States may issue an order requiring compliance with such subpoena and any failure to obey such order may be punished by such court as a contempt thereof.

**(g) Determinations.**—

(1) *Order.*— The administrative law judge shall issue and cause to be served on the parties to the proceeding an order, which shall be final unless appealed as provided under subsection (i).

(2) *Orders finding violations.*—

(A) *In general.*— If, upon the preponderance of the evidence, an administrative law judge determines that any person or entity named in the complaint has engaged in or is engaging in any such unfair immigration-related employment practice, then the judge shall state his findings of fact and shall issue and cause to be served on such person or entity an order which requires such person or entity to cease and desist from such unfair immigration-related employment practice.

(B) *Contents of order.*— Such an order also may require the person or entity—

(i) to comply with the requirements of section 274A(b) with respect to individuals hired (or recruited or referred for employment for a fee) during a period of up to three years;

(ii) to retain for the period referred to in clause (i) and only for purposes consistent with section 274A(b)(5), the name and address of each individual who applies, in person or in writing, for hiring for an existing position, or for recruiting or referring for a fee, for employment in the United States;

(iii) to hire individuals directly and adversely affected, with or without back pay;

(iv) (I) except as provided in subclauses (II) through (IV), to pay a civil penalty of not less than $250 and not more than $2,000 for each individual discriminated against,

---

[173] *Sic.* Probably should be "section."

(II) except as provided in subclauses (III) and (IV), in the case of a person or entity previously subject to a single order under this paragraph, to pay a civil penalty of not less than $2,000 and not more than $5,000 for each individual discriminated against,

(III) except as provided in subclause (IV), in the case of a person or entity previously subject to more than one order under this paragraph, to pay a civil penalty of not less than $3,000 and not more than $10,000 for each individual discriminated against, and

(IV) in the case of an unfair immigration-related employment practice described in subsection (a)(6), to pay a civil penalty of not less than $100 and not more than $1,000 for each individual discriminated against;

(v) to post notices to employees about their rights under this section and employers' obligations under section 274A;

(vi) to educate all personnel involved in hiring and complying with this section or section 274A about the requirements of this section or such section;

(vii) to remove (in an appropriate case) a false performance review or false warning from an employee's personnel file; and

(viii) to lift (in an appropriate case) any restrictions on an employee's assignments, work shifts, or movements.

(C) *Limitation on back pay remedy.*— In providing a remedy under subparagraph (B)(iii), back pay liability shall not accrue from a date more than two years prior to the date of the filing of a charge with the Special Counsel. Interim earnings or amounts earnable with reasonable diligence by the individual or individuals discriminated against shall operate to reduce the back pay otherwise allowable under such subparagraph. No order shall require the hiring of an individual as an employee or the payment to an individual of any back pay, if the individual was refused employment for any reason other than discrimination on account of national origin or citizenship status.

(D) *Treatment of distinct entities.*— In applying this subsection in the case of a person or entity composed of distinct, physically separate subdivisions each of which provides separately for the hiring, recruiting, or referring for employment, without reference to the practices of, and not under the control of or common control with, another subdivision, each such subdivision shall be considered a separate person or entity.

(3) **Orders not finding violations.**— If upon the preponderance of the evidence an administrative law judge determines that the person or entity named in the complaint has not engaged and is not engaging in any such unfair immigration-related employment practice, then the judge shall state his findings of fact and shall issue an order dismissing the complaint.

(h) **Awarding of attorney's fees.**— In any complaint respecting an unfair immigration-related employment practice, an administrative law judge, in the judge's discretion, may allow a prevailing party, other than the United States, a reasonable attorney's fee, if the losing party's argument is without reasonable foundation in law and fact.

(i) **Review of final orders.**—

(1) *In general.*— Not later than 60 days after the entry of such final order, any person aggrieved by such final order may seek a review of such order in the United States court of

appeals for the circuit in which the violation is alleged to have occurred or in which the employer resides or transacts business.

(2) *Further review.*— Upon the filing of the record with the court, the jurisdiction of the court shall be exclusive and its judgment shall be final, except that the same shall be subject to review by the Supreme Court of the United States upon writ of certiorari or certification as provided in section 1254 of title 28, United States Code.

**(j) Court enforcement of administrative orders.—**

(1) *In general.*— If an order of the agency is not appealed under subsection (i)(1), the Special Counsel (or, if the Special Counsel fails to act, the person filing the charge) may petition the United States district court for the district in which a violation of the order is alleged to have occurred, or in which the respondent resides or transacts business, for the enforcement of the order of the administrative law judge, by filing in such court a written petition praying that such order be enforced.

(2) *Court enforcement order.*— Upon the filing of such petition, the court shall have jurisdiction to make and enter a decree enforcing the order of the administrative law judge. In such a proceeding, the order of the administrative law judge shall not be subject to review.

(3) *Enforcement decree in original review.*— If, upon appeal of an order under subsection (i)(1), the United States court of appeals does not reverse such order, such court shall have the jurisdiction to make and enter a decree enforcing the order of the administrative law judge.

(4) *Awarding of attorney's fees.*— In any judicial proceeding under subsection (i) or this subsection, the court, in its discretion, may allow a prevailing party, other than the United States, a reasonable attorney's fee as part of costs but only if the losing party's argument is without reasonable foundation in law and fact.

**(k) Termination dates.—**

(1) This section shall not apply to discrimination in hiring, recruiting, or referring, or discharging of individuals occurring after the date of any termination of the provisions of section 274A, under subsection (*l*) of that section.

(2) The provisions of this section shall terminate 30 calendar days after receipt of the last report required to be transmitted under section 274A(j) if—

> (A) the Comptroller General determines, and so reports in such report that—

>> (i) no significant discrimination has resulted, against citizens or nationals of the United States or against any eligible workers seeking employment, from the implementation of section 274A, or

>> (ii) such section has created an unreasonable burden on employers hiring such workers; and

> (B) there has been enacted, within such period of 30 calendar days, a joint resolution stating in substance that the Congress approves the findings of the Comptroller General contained in such report.

The provisions of subsections (m) and (n) of section 274A shall apply to any joint resolution under subparagraph (B) in the same manner as they apply to a joint resolution under subsection (*l*) of such section.

**(*l*) Dissemination of information concerning anti-discrimination provisions.—**

(1) Not later than 3 months after the date of the enactment of this subsection, the Special Counsel, in cooperation with the chairman of the Equal Employment Opportunity Commission, the Secretary of Labor, and the Administrator of the Small Business Administration, shall conduct a campaign to disseminate information respecting the rights and remedies prescribed under this section and under title VII of the Civil Rights Act of 1964 in connection with unfair immigration-related employment practices. Such campaign shall be aimed at increasing the knowledge of employers, employees, and the general public concerning employer and employee rights, responsibilities, and remedies under this section and such title.

(2) In order to carry out the campaign under this subsection, the Special Counsel—

(A) may, to the extent deemed appropriate and subject to the availability of appropriations, contract with public and private organizations for outreach activities under the campaign, and

(B) shall consult with the Secretary of Labor, the chairman of the Equal Employment Opportunity Commission, and the heads of such other agencies as may be appropriate.

(3) There are authorized to be appropriated to carry out this subsection $10,000,000 for each fiscal year (beginning with fiscal year 1991).

(June 27, 1952, ch. 477, title II, ch. 8, §274B, as added by P.L. 99-603 (IRCA) (11/6/86); as amended by P.L. 100-525 (10/24/88); P.L. 101-649 (IMMACT90) (11/29/90); P.L. 102-232 (MTINA) (12/12/91, *effective* 4/1/92); P.L. 103-416 (INTCA) (10/25/94, *effective* 4/1/95); P.L. 104-208 (IIRAIRA) (9/30/96), div. C, title IV, §421 [revising (a)(6)], title VI, §671 [revising (a)(3)(B)].)

## Sec. 274C Penalties for Document Fraud
## [8 U.S.C. 1324c]

(a) **Activities prohibited.**— It is unlawful for any person or entity knowingly—

(1) to forge, counterfeit, alter, or falsely make any document for the purpose of satisfying a requirement of this Act or to obtain a benefit under this Act,

(2) to use, attempt to use, possess, obtain, accept, or receive or to provide any forged, counterfeit, altered, or falsely made document in order to satisfy any requirement of this Act or to obtain a benefit under this Act,

(3) to use or attempt to use or to provide or attempt to provide any document lawfully issued to or with respect to a person other than the possessor (including a deceased individual) for the purpose of satisfying a requirement of this Act or obtaining a benefit under this Act,

(4) to accept or receive or to provide any document lawfully issued to or with respect to a person other than the possessor (including a deceased individual) for the purpose of complying with section 274A(b) or obtaining a benefit under this Act, or

(5) to prepare, file, or assist another in preparing or filing, any application for benefits under this Act, or any document required under this Act, or any document submitted in connection with such application or document, with knowledge or in reckless disregard of the fact that such application or document was falsely made or, in whole or in part, does not relate to the person on whose behalf it was or is being submitted, or

(6) (A) to present before boarding a common carrier for the purpose of coming to the United States a document which relates to the alien's eligibility to enter the United States, and

(B) to fail to present such document to an immigration officer upon arrival at a United States port of entry.

**(b) Exception.**— This section does not prohibit any lawfully authorized investigative, protective, or intelligence activity of a law enforcement agency of the United States, a State, or a subdivision of a State, or of an intelligence agency of the United States, or any activity authorized under chapter 224 of title 18, United States Code.

**(c) Construction.**— Nothing in this section shall be construed to diminish or qualify any of the penalties available for activities prohibited by this section but proscribed as well in title 18, United States Code.

**(d) Enforcement.**—

(1) *Authority in investigations.*— In conducting investigations and hearings under this subsection—

(A) immigration officers and administrative law judges shall have reasonable access to examine evidence of any person or entity being investigated,

(B) administrative law judges, may, if necessary, compel by subpoena the attendance of witnesses and the production of evidence at any designated place or hearing, and

(C) immigration officers designated by the Commissioner may compel by subpoena the attendance of witnesses and the production of evidence at any designated place prior to the filing of a complaint in a case under paragraph (2).

In case of contumacy or refusal to obey a subpoena lawfully issued under this paragraph and upon application of the Attorney General, an appropriate district court of the United States may issue an order requiring compliance with such subpoena and any failure to obey such order may be punished by such court as a contempt thereof.

(2) *Hearing.*—

(A) *In general.*— Before imposing an order described in paragraph (3) against a person or entity under this subsection for a violation of subsection (a), the Attorney General shall provide the person or entity with notice and, upon request made within a reasonable time (of not less than 30 days, as established by the Attorney General) of the date of the notice, a hearing respecting the violation.

(B) *Conduct of hearing.*— Any hearing so requested shall be conducted before an administrative law judge. The hearing shall be conducted in accordance with the requirements of section 554 of title 5, United States Code. The hearing shall be held at the nearest practicable place to the place where the person or entity resides or of the place where the alleged violation occurred. If no hearing is so requested, the Attorney General's imposition of the order shall constitute a final and unappealable order.

(C) *Issuance of orders.*— If the administrative law judge determines, upon the preponderance of the evidence received, that a person or entity has violated subsection (a), the administrative law judge shall state his findings of fact and issue and cause to be served on such person or entity an order described in paragraph (3).

(3) *Cease and desist order with civil money penalty.*— With respect to a violation of subsection (a), the order under this subsection shall require the person or entity to cease and desist from such violations and to pay a civil penalty in an amount of—

(A) not less than $250 and not more than $2,000 for each document that is the subject of a violation under subsection (a), or

(B) in the case of a person or entity previously subject to an order under this paragraph, not less than $2,000 and not more than $5,000 for each document that is the subject of a violation under subsection (a).

In applying this subsection in the case of a person or entity composed of distinct, physically separate subdivisions each of which provides separately for the hiring, recruiting, or referring for employment, without reference to the practices of, and not under the control of or common control with, another subdivision, each such subdivision shall be considered a separate person or entity.

(4) *Administrative appellate review.*— The decision and order of an administrative law judge shall become the final agency decision and order of the Attorney General unless either (A) within 30 days, an official delegated by regulation to exercise review authority over the decision and order modifies or vacates the decision and order, or (B) within 30 days of the date of such a modification or vacation (or within 60 days of the date of decision and order of an administrative law judge if not so modified or vacated) the decision and order is referred to the Attorney General pursuant to regulations, in which case the decision and order of the Attorney General shall become the final agency decision and order under this subsection.[174]

(5) *Judicial review.*— A person or entity adversely affected by a final order under this section may, within 45 days after the date the final order is issued, file a petition in the Court of Appeals for the appropriate circuit for review of the order.

(6) *Enforcement of orders.*— If a person or entity fails to comply with a final order issued under this section against the person or entity, the Attorney General shall file a suit to seek compliance with the order in any appropriate district court of the United States. In any such suit, the validity and appropriateness of the final order shall not be subject to review

(7) *Waiver by Attorney General.*— The Attorney General may waive the penalties imposed by this section with respect to an alien who knowingly violates subsection (a)(6) if the alien is granted asylum under section 208 or withholding of removal under section 241(b)(3).

**(e) Criminal penalties for failure to disclose role as document preparer.—**

(1) Whoever, in any matter within the jurisdiction of the Service, knowingly and willfully fails to disclose, conceals, or covers up the fact that they have, on behalf of any person and for a fee or other remuneration, prepared or assisted in preparing an application which was falsely made (as defined in subsection (f)) for immigration benefits, shall be fined in accordance with title 18, United States Code, imprisoned for not more than 5 years, or both, and prohibited from preparing or assisting in preparing, whether or not for a fee or other remuneration, any other such application.

(2) Whoever, having been convicted of a violation of paragraph (1), knowingly and willfully prepares or assists in preparing an application for immigration benefits pursuant to this Act, or the regulations promulgated thereunder, whether or not for a fee or other remuneration and regardless of whether in any matter within the jurisdiction of the Service, shall be fined in accordance with title 18, United States Code, imprisoned for not more than 15 years, or both, and prohibited from preparing or assisting in preparing any other such application.

**(f) Falsely make.**— For purposes of this section, the term "falsely make" means to prepare or provide an application or document, with knowledge or in reckless disregard of the fact that the application or document contains a false, fictitious, or fraudulent statement or material representa-

---

[174] *See* §379 of IIRAIRA, effective for "orders issued on or after the date of the enactment of this Act."

tion, or has no basis in law or fact, or otherwise fails to state a fact which is material to the purpose for which it was submitted.[175]

(June 27, 1952, ch. 477, title II, ch. 8, §274C, as added by P.L. 101-649 (IMMACT90) (11/29/90); as amended by P.L. 102-232 (MTINA) (12/12/91, *effective* 4/1/92); P.L. 103-416 (INTCA) (10/25/94, *effective* 4/1/95); P.L. 104-208 (IIRAIRA) (9/30/96), div. C, title II, §212(a) [revising (d)(3)(A)–(B), (d)(7); adding (a)(5)–(6), (f)], §213 [adding (e)], §220 [adding (d)(1)(C)], title III, §308(g)(10)(D) [revising (d)(7)], §379(a) [revising (d)(4)].)

### Sec. 274D Civil Penalties for Failure to Depart[176]
[8 U.S.C. 1324d]

**(a) In general.**— Any alien subject to a final order of removal who—

(1) willfully fails or refuses to—

(A) depart from the United States pursuant to the order,

(B) make timely application in good faith for travel or other documents necessary for departure, or

(C) present for removal at the time and place required by the Attorney General; or

(2) conspires to or takes any action designed to prevent or hamper the alien's departure pursuant to the order,

shall pay a civil penalty of not more than $500 to the Commissioner for each day the alien is in violation of this section.

**(b) Construction.**— Nothing in this section shall be construed to diminish or qualify any penalties to which an alien may be subject for activities proscribed by section 243(a) or any other section of this Act.

(June 27, 1952, ch. 477, title II, ch. 8, §274D, as added by P.L. 104-208 (IIRAIRA) (9/30/96), div. C, title III, §380(a).)

### Sec. 275 Improper Entry by Alien
[8 U.S.C. 1325]

**(a) Improper time or place; avoidance of examination or inspection; misrepresentation and concealment of facts.**— Any alien who

(1) enters or attempts to enter the United States at any time or place other than as designated by immigration officers, or

(2) eludes examination or inspection by immigration officers, or

(3) attempts to enter or obtains entry to the United States by a willfully false or misleading representation or the willful concealment of a material fact,

shall, for the first commission of any such offense, be fined under title 18, United States Code, or imprisoned not more than 6 months, or both, and, for a subsequent commission of any such offense, be fined under title 18, United States Code, or imprisoned not more than 2 years, or both.

---

[175] Subsection (f) and conforming amendments to §274C(d)(3) were added by §212(b) of IIRAIRA and are applicable to the preparation of applications before, on, or after the date of enactment of IIRAIRA.

[176] *See* §380 of IIRAIRA, effective for actions occurring on or after the title III-A effective date. (For title III-A effective date, see IIRAIRA §309, *reprinted in* Appendix C, *infra*).

**(b) Improper time or place; civil penalties.—** Any alien who is apprehended while entering (or attempting to enter) the United States at a time or place other than as designated by immigration officers shall be subject to a civil penalty of—[177]

(1) at least $50 and not more than $250 for each such entry (or attempted entry); or

(2) twice the amount specified in paragraph (1) in the case of an alien who has been previously subject to a civil penalty under this subsection.

Civil penalties under this subsection are in addition to, and not in lieu of, any criminal or other civil penalties that may be imposed.

**(c) Marriage fraud.—** Any individual who knowingly enters into a marriage for the purpose of evading any provision of the immigration laws shall be imprisoned for not more than 5 years, or fined not more than $250,000, or both.

**(d) Immigration-related entrepreneurship fraud.—** Any individual who knowingly establishes a commercial enterprise for the purpose of evading any provision of the immigration laws shall be imprisoned for not more than 5 years, fined in accordance with title 18, United States Code, or both.

(June 27, 1952, ch. 477, title II, ch. 8, §275, 66 Stat. 229; as amended by P.L. 99-639 (11/10/86); P.L. 101-649 (IMMACT90) (11/29/90); P.L. 102-232 (MTINA) (12/12/91, *effective* 4/1/92); P.L. 104-208 (IIRAIRA) (9/30/96), div. C, title I, §105(a) [adding (b)].)

## Sec. 276 Reentry of Removed Alien
## [8 U.S.C. 1326]

**(a) In general.—** Subject to subsection (b) any alien who—

(1) has been denied admission, excluded, deported, or removed or has departed the United States while an order of exclusion, deportation, or removal is outstanding, and thereafter[178]

(2) enters, attempts to enter, or is at any time found in, the United States, unless

(A) prior to his reembarkation at a place outside the United States or his application for admission from foreign contiguous territory, the Attorney General has expressly consented to such alien's reapplying for admission; or

(B) with respect to an alien previously denied admission and removed, unless such alien shall establish that he was not required to obtain such advance consent under this or any prior Act,

shall be fined under title 18, United States Code, or imprisoned not more than 2 years, or both.

**(b) Criminal penalties for reentry of certain removed aliens.—** Notwithstanding subsection (a), in the case of any alien described in such subsection—

(1) whose removal was subsequent to a conviction for commission of three or more misdemeanors involving drugs, crimes against the person, or both, or a felony (other than an aggravated felony), such alien shall be fined under title 18, United States Code, imprisoned not more than 10 years, or both;

---

[177] *See* §105 of IIRAIRA, applicable "to illegal entries or attempts to enter occurring on or after the first day of the sixth month beginning after the date of the enactment of this Act."

[178] Sec. 308's amendments went into effect on 4/1/97, at which time the amendment by §324 was overwritten. (*See* IIRAIRA §309, *reprinted in* Appendix C, *infra.*)

(2) whose removal was subsequent to a conviction for commission of an aggravated felony, such alien shall be fined under such title, imprisoned not more than 20 years, or both;

(3) who has been excluded from the United States pursuant to section 235(c) because the alien was excludable under section 212(a)(3)(B) or who has been removed from the United States pursuant to the provisions of title V, and who thereafter, without the permission of the Attorney General, enters the United States, or attempts to do so, shall be fined under title 18, United States Code, and imprisoned for a period of 10 years, which sentence shall not run concurrently with any other sentence[;] or

(4) who was removed from the United States pursuant to section 241(a)(4)(B) who thereafter, without the permission of the Attorney General, enters, attempts to enter, or is at any time found in, the United States (unless the Attorney General has expressly consented to such alien's reentry) shall be fined under title 18, United States Code, imprisoned for not more than 10 years, or both.[179]

For the purposes of this subsection, the term "removal" includes any agreement in which an alien stipulates to removal during (or not during) a criminal trial under either Federal or State law.

**(c) Reentry of alien deported prior to completion of term of imprisonment.—** Any alien deported pursuant to section 242(h)(2)[180] who enters, attempts to enter, or is at any time found in, the United States (unless the Attorney General has expressly consented to such alien's reentry) shall be incarcerated for the remainder of the sentence of imprisonment which was pending at the time of deportation without any reduction for parole or supervised release. Such alien shall be subject to such other penalties relating to the reentry of deported aliens as may be available under this section or any other provision of law.

**(d)** Limitation on collateral attack on underlying deportation order.— In a criminal proceeding under this section, an alien may not challenge the validity of the deportation order described in subsection (a)(1) or subsection (b) unless the alien demonstrates that—

(1) the alien exhausted any administrative remedies that may have been available to seek relief against the order;

(2) the deportation proceedings at which the order was issued improperly deprived the alien of the opportunity for judicial review; and

(3) the entry of the order was fundamentally unfair.

(June 27, 1952, ch. 477, title II, ch. 8, §276, 66 Stat. 229; as amended by P.L. 100-690 (11/18/88); P.L. 101-649 (IMMACT90) (11/29/90); P.L. 103-322 (VAWA) (9/13/94); P.L. 104-132 (AEDPA) (4/24/96), title IV, §401(c) [adding (b)(3)], §438(b) [adding (c)], §441(a) [adding (d)]; P.L. 104-208 (IIRAIRA) (9/30/96), div. C, title III, §305(b) [adding (b)(4)], §308(d)(4)(J) [revising (a)(1)], §324(a) [revising (a)(1)].)

### Sec. 277 Aiding or Assisting Certain Aliens to Enter
[8 U.S.C. 1327]

Any person who knowingly aids or assists any alien inadmissible under section 212(a)(2) (insofar as an alien inadmissible under such section has been convicted of an aggravated felony) or 212(a)(3) (other than subparagraph (E) thereof) to enter the United States, or who connives or conspires with any person or persons to allow, procure, or permit any such alien to enter the United States, shall be fined under title 18, United States Code, or imprisoned not more than 10 years, or both.

---

[179] *See* note 55, *supra.*

[180] *Sic.* Sec. 242(h)(2) no longer exists. Language in the current INA §241(a)(4) is similar to that found in the former §242(h)(2).

(June 27, 1952, ch. 477, title II, ch. 8, §277, 66 Stat. 229; as amended by P.L. 100-690 (11/18/88); P.L. 101-649 (IMMACT90) (11/29/90), §§543, 603; P.L. 104-208 (IIRAIRA) (9/30/96), div. C, title III, §308.)

## Sec. 278 Importation of Alien for Immoral Purpose
**[8 U.S.C. 1328]**

The importation into the United States of any alien for the purpose of prostitution, or for any other immoral purpose, is hereby forbidden. Whoever shall, directly or indirectly, import, or attempt to import into the United States any alien for the purpose of prostitution or for any other immoral purpose, or shall hold or attempt to hold any alien for any such purpose in pursuance of such illegal importation, or shall keep, maintain, control, support, employ, or harbor in any house or other place, for the purpose of prostitution or for any other immoral purpose, any alien, in pursuance of such illegal importation, shall be fined under title 18, United States Code, or imprisoned not more than 10 years, or both. The trial and punishment of offenses under this section may be in any district to or into which such alien is brought in pursuance of importation by the person or persons accused, or in any district in which a violation of any of the provisions of this section occurs. In all prosecutions under this section, the testimony of a husband or wife shall be admissible and competent evidence against each other.

(June 27, 1952, ch. 477, title II, ch. 8, §278, 66 Stat. 230; as amended by P.L. 101-649 (IMMACT90) (11/29/90), §543.)

## Sec. 279 Jurisdiction of District Courts
**[8 U.S.C. 1329]**

The district courts of the United States shall have jurisdiction of all causes, civil and criminal, brought by the United States that arise under the provisions of this title. It shall be the duty of the United States attorney of the proper district to prosecute every such suit when brought by the United States. Notwithstanding any other law, such prosecutions or suits may be instituted at any place in the United States at which the violation may occur or at which the person charged with a violation under section 275 or 276 may be apprehended. No suit or proceeding for a violation of any of the provisions of this title shall be settled, compromised, or discontinued without the consent of the court in which it is pending and any such settlement, compromise, or discontinuance shall be entered of record with the reasons therefor. Nothing in this section shall be construed as providing jurisdiction for suits against the United States or its agencies or officers.

(June 27, 1952, ch. 477, title II, ch. 8, §279, 66 Stat. 230; as amended by P.L. 104-208 (IIRAIRA) (9/30/96), div. C, title III, §381(a) [revising §279].)

## Sec. 280 Collection of Penalties and Expenses
**[8 U.S.C. 1330]**

**(a)** Notwithstanding any other provisions of this title, the withholding or denial of clearance of or a lien upon any vessel or aircraft provided for in section 231, 234, 243(c)(2), 251, 253, 254, 255, 256, 271, 272, or 273 of this title shall not be regarded as the sole and exclusive means or remedy for the enforcement of payments of any fine, penalty or expenses imposed or incurred under such sections, but, in the discretion of the Attorney General, the amount thereof may be recovered by civil suit, in the name of the United States, from any person made liable under any of such sections.

**(b)** (1) There is established in the general fund of the Treasury a separate account which shall be known as the "Immigration Enforcement Account". Notwithstanding any other section of this title, there shall be deposited as offsetting receipts into the Immigration Enforcement Account amounts described in paragraph (2) to remain available until expended.

(2) The amounts described in this paragraph are the following:

(A) The increase in penalties collected resulting from the amendments made by sections 203(b) and 543(a) of the Immigration Act of 1990.

(B) Civil penalties collected under sections 240B(d), 274C, 274D, and 275(b).

(3) (A) The Secretary of the Treasury shall refund out of the Immigration Enforcement Account to any appropriation the amount paid out of such appropriation for expenses incurred by the Attorney General for activities that enhance enforcement of provisions of this title. Such activities include—

(i) the identification, investigation, apprehension, detention, and removal of criminal aliens;

(ii) the maintenance and updating of a system to identify and track criminal aliens, deportable aliens, inadmissible aliens, and aliens illegally entering the United States; and

(iii) for the repair, maintenance, or construction on the United States border, in areas experiencing high levels of apprehensions of illegal aliens, of structures to deter illegal entry into the United States.

(B) The amounts which are required to be refunded under subparagraph (A) shall be refunded at least quarterly on the basis of estimates made by the Attorney General of the expenses referred to in subparagraph (A). Proper adjustments shall be made in the amounts subsequently refunded under subparagraph (A) to the extent prior estimates were in excess of, or less than, the amount required to be refunded under subparagraph (A).

(C) The amounts required to be refunded from the Immigration Enforcement Account for fiscal year 1996 and thereafter shall be refunded in accordance with estimates made in the budget request of the Attorney General for those fiscal years. Any proposed changes in the amounts designated in such budget requests shall only be made after notification to the Committees on Appropriations of the House of Representatives and the Senate in accordance with section 605 of Public Law 104-134.

(D) The Attorney General shall prepare and submit annually to the Congress statements of financial condition of the Immigration Enforcement Account, including beginning account balance, revenues, withdrawals, and ending account balance and projection for the ensuing fiscal year.

(June 27, 1952, ch. 477, title II, ch. 8, §280, 66 Stat. 230; as amended by P.L. 101-649 (IMMACT90) (11/29/90); P.L. 103-416 (INTCA) (10/25/94, *effective* 4/1/95); P.L. 104-208 (IIRAIRA) (9/30/96), div. C, title III, §308(g)(4)(C), §382(a) [revising (b)(1)].)

# Chapter 9 — Miscellaneous

## Sec. 281 Nonimmigrant Visa Fees
## [8 U.S.C. 1351]

The fees for the furnishing and verification of applications for visas by nonimmigrants of each foreign country and for the issuance of visas to nonimmigrants of each foreign country shall be prescribed by the Secretary of State, if practicable, in amounts corresponding to the total of all visa, entry, residence, or other similar fees, taxes, or charges assessed or levied against nationals of the United States by the foreign countries of which such nonimmigrants are nationals or stateless residents: *Provided*, That nonimmigrant visas issued to aliens coming to the United States in transit to and from the headquarters district of the United Nations in accordance with the provisions of the Headquarters Agreement shall be gratis. Subject to such criteria as the Secretary of State may prescribe, including the duration of stay of the alien and the financial burden upon the charitable organization, the Secretary of State shall waive or reduce the fee for application and issuance of a nonimmigrant visa for any alien coming to the United States primarily for, or in activities related to, a charitable purpose involving health or nursing care, the provision of food or housing, job training, or any other similar direct service or assistance to poor or otherwise needy individuals in the United States.

(June 27, 1952, ch. 477, title II, ch. 9, §281, 66 Stat. 230; as amended by P.L. 89-236 (10/3/65); P.L. 90-609 (10/21/68); P.L. 105-54 (10/6/97).)

## Sec. 282 Printing of Reentry Permits and Blank Forms of Manifests and Crew Lists; Sale to Public
### [8 U.S.C. 1352]

(a) Reentry permits issued under section 223 shall be printed on distinctive safety paper and shall be prepared and issued under regulations prescribed by the Attorney General.

(b) The Public Printer is authorized to print for sale to the public by the Superintendent of Documents, upon prepayment, copies of blank forms of manifests and crew lists and such other forms as may be prescribed and authorized by the Attorney General to be sold pursuant to the provisions of this title.

(June 27, 1952, ch. 477, title II, ch. 9, §282, 66 Stat. 231.)

## Sec. 283 Travel Expenses and Expense of Transporting Remains of Officers and Employees Dying Outside of the United States
### [8 U.S.C. 1353]

When officers, inspectors, or other employees of the Service are ordered to perform duties in a foreign country, or are transferred from one station to another, in the United States or in a foreign country, or while performing duties in any foreign country become eligible for voluntary retirement and return to the United States, they shall be allowed their traveling expenses in accordance with such regulations as the Attorney General may deem advisable, and they may also be allowed, within the discretion and under written orders of the Attorney General, the expenses incurred for the transfer of their wives and dependent children, their household effects and other personal property, including the expenses for packing, crating, freight, unpacking, temporary storage, and drayage thereof in accordance with subchapter II of chapter 57 of title 5, United States Code. The expense of transporting the remains of such officers, inspectors, or other employees who die while in, or in transit to, a foreign country in the discharge of their official duties to their former homes in this country for interment, and the ordinary and necessary expenses of such interment and of preparation for shipment, are authorized to be paid on the written order of the Attorney General.

(June 27, 1952, ch. 477, title II, ch. 9, §283, 66 Stat. 231; as amended by P.L. 100-525 (10/24/88).)

## Sec. 284 Applicability to Members of the Armed Forces
### [8 U.S.C. 1354]

(a) Nothing contained in this title shall be construed so as to limit, restrict, deny, or affect the coming into or departure from the United States of an alien member of the Armed Forces of the United States who is in the uniform of, or who bears documents identifying him as a member of, such Armed Forces, and who is coming to or departing from the United States under official orders or permit of such Armed Forces: *Provided,* That nothing contained in this section shall be construed to give to or confer upon any such alien any other privileges, rights, benefits, exemptions, or immunities under this Act, which are not otherwise specifically granted by this Act.

**(b)**[181] If a person lawfully admitted for permanent residence is the spouse or child of a member of the Armed Forces of the United States, is authorized to accompany the member and reside abroad with the member pursuant to the member's official orders, and is so accompanying and residing with the member (in marital union if a spouse), then the residence and physical presence of the person abroad shall not be treated as—

(1) an abandonment or relinquishment of lawful permanent resident status for purposes of clause (i) of section 101(a)(13)(C); or

(2) an absence from the United States for purposes of clause (ii) of such section.

(June 27, 1952, ch. 477, title II, ch. 9, §284, 66 Stat. 232; as amended by P.L. 110-181 (1/28/07) §673 [renumbering prior section as (a) & adding (b)(1)–(2)].)

## Sec. 285 Disposal of Privileges at Immigrant Stations; Rentals; Retail Sale; Disposition of Receipts
[8 U.S.C. 1355]

**(a)** Subject to such conditions and limitations as the Attorney General shall prescribe, all exclusive privileges of exchanging money, transporting passengers or baggage, keeping eating houses, or other like privileges in connection with any United States immigrant station, shall be disposed of to the lowest responsible and capable bidder (other than an alien) in accordance with the provisions of section 3709 of the Revised Statutes, as amended (41 U.S.C. 5), and for the use of Government property in connection with the exercise of such exclusive privileges a reasonable rental may be charged. The feeding of aliens, or the furnishing of any other necessary service in connection with any United States immigrant station, may be performed by the Service without regard to the foregoing provisions of this subsection if the Attorney General shall find that it would be advantageous to the Government in terms of economy and efficiency. No intoxicating liquors shall be sold at any immigrant station.

**(b)** Such articles determined by the Attorney General to be necessary to the health and welfare of aliens detained at any immigrant station, when not otherwise readily procurable by such aliens, may be sold at reasonable prices to such aliens through Government canteens operated by the Service, under such conditions and limitations as the Attorney General shall prescribe.

**(c)** All rentals or other receipts accruing from the disposal of privileges, and all moneys arising from the sale of articles through Service-operated canteens, authorized by this section, shall be covered into the Treasury to the credit of the appropriation for the enforcement of this title.

(June 27, 1952, ch. 477, title II, ch. 9, §285, 66 Stat. 232.)

## Sec. 286 Disposition of Moneys Collected under the Provisions of this Title
[8 U.S.C. 1356]

**(a) Detention, transportation, hospitalization, and all other expenses of detained aliens; expenses of landing stations.**— All moneys paid into the Treasury to reimburse the Service for detention, transportation, hospitalization, and all other expenses of detained aliens paid from the appropriation for the enforcement of this Act, and all moneys paid into the Treasury to reimburse

---

[181] Subsection (b) applies to any application for naturalization or issuance of a certificate of citizenship pending on or after 1/28/08. P.L. 110-181, §674(d).

the Service for expenses of landing stations referred to in section 238(b) paid by the Service from the appropriation for the enforcement of this Act, shall be credited to the appropriation for the enforcement of this Act for the fiscal year in which the expenses were incurred.

**(b) Purchase of evidence.**— Moneys expended from appropriations for the Service for the purchase of evidence and subsequently recovered shall be reimbursed to the current appropriation for the Service.

**(c) Fees and administrative fines and penalties; exception.**— Except as otherwise provided in subsection (a) and subsection (b), or in any other provision of this title, all moneys received in payment of fees and administrative fines and penalties under this title shall be covered into the Treasury as miscellaneous receipts: *Provided, however,* That all fees received from applicants residing in the Virgin Islands of the United States, and in Guam, required to be paid under section 281, shall be paid over to the Treasury of the Virgin Islands and to the Treasury of Guam, respectively.

**(d) Schedule of fees.**— In addition to any other fee authorized by law, the Attorney General shall charge and collect $7 per individual for the immigration inspection of each passenger arriving at a port of entry in the United States, or for the preinspection of a passenger in a place outside of the United States prior to such arrival, aboard a commercial aircraft or commercial vessel.

**(e) Limitations of fees.**—

(1) Except as provided in paragraph (3), no fee shall be charged under subsection (d) for immigration inspection or preinspection provided in connection with the arrival of any passenger, other than aircraft passengers, whose journey originated in the following:

(A) Canada,

(B) Mexico,

(C) a State, territory or possession of the United States, or

(D) any adjacent island (within the meaning of section 101(b)(5)).

(2) No fee may be charged under subsection (d) with respect to the arrival of any passenger—

(A) who is in transit to a destination outside the United States, and

(B) for whom immigration inspection services are not provided.

(3) The Attorney General shall charge and collect $3 per individual for the immigration inspection or pre-inspection of each commercial vessel passenger whose journey originated in the United States or in any place set forth in paragraph (1): *Provided,* That this requirement shall not apply to immigration inspection at designated ports of entry of passengers arriving by ferry, or by Great Lakes vessels on the Great Lakes and connecting waterways when operating on a regular schedule. For the purposes of this paragraph, the term "ferry" means a vessel, in other than ocean or coastwise service, having provisions only for deck passengers and/or vehicles, operating on a short run on a frequent schedule between two points over the most direct water route, and offering a public service of a type normally attributed to a bridge or tunnel.

**(f) Collection.**—

(1) Each person that issues a document or ticket to an individual for transportation by a commercial vessel or commercial aircraft into the United States shall—

(A) collect from that individual the fee charged under subsection (d) at the time the document or ticket is issued; and

(B) identify on that document or ticket the fee charged under subsection (d) as a Federal inspection fee.

(2) If—

(A) a document or ticket for transportation of a passenger into the United States is issued in a foreign country; and

(B) the fee charged under subsection (d) is not collected at the time such document or ticket is issued;

the person providing transportation to such passenger shall collect such fee at the time such passenger departs from the United States and shall provide such passenger a receipt for the payment of such fee.

(3) The person who collects fees under paragraph (1) or (2) shall remit those fees to the Attorney General at any time before the date that is thirty-one days after the close of the calendar quarter in which the fees are collected, except the fourth quarter payment for fees collected from airline passengers shall be made on the date that is ten days before the end of the fiscal year, and the first quarter payment shall include any collections made in the preceding quarter that were not remitted with the previous payment. Regulations issued by the Attorney General under this subsection with respect to the collection of the fees charged under subsection (d) and the remittance of such fees to the Treasury of the United States shall be consistent with the regulations issued by the Secretary of the Treasury for the collection and remittance of the taxes imposed by subchapter C of chapter 33 of the Internal Revenue Code of 1986, but only to the extent the regulations issued with respect to such taxes do not conflict with the provisions of this section.

**(g) Provision of immigration inspection and preinspection services.**— Notwithstanding the Act of March 2, 1931, 46 Stat. 1467 (8 U.S.C. 1353b), or any other provision of law, the immigration services required to be provided to passengers upon arrival in the United States on scheduled airline flights shall be adequately provided when needed and at no cost (other than the fees imposed under subsection (d)) to airlines and airline passengers at:[182]

(1) immigration serviced airports, and

(2) places located outside of the United States at which an immigration officer is stationed for the purpose of providing such immigration services.

**(h) Disposition of receipts.**—

(1) (A) There is established in the general fund of the Treasury a separate account which shall be known as the "Immigration User Fee Account". Notwithstanding any other section of this title, there shall be deposited as offsetting receipts into the Immigration User Fee Account all fees collected under subsection (d) of this section, to remain available until expended.[183] At the end of each 2-year period, beginning with the creation of this account, the Attorney General, following a public rulemaking with opportunity for notice and comment, shall submit a report to the Congress concerning the status of the account, including any balances therein, and recommend any adjustment in the prescribed fee that

---

[182] Sec. 403(a) of the Enhanced Border Security and Visa Entry Reform Act, 2002, P.L. 107-173, deleted the requirement that services be provided within 45 minutes of presentation for inspection. Sec. 403(b) mandates staffing levels at ports of entry, to be based on a "goal" of providing services of INA §286(g) within 45 minutes of presentation for inspection.

[183] *Sic.* Extra period inserted by §671 of IIRAIRA.

may be required to ensure that the receipts collected from the fee charged for the succeeding two years equal, as closely as possible, the cost of providing these services.

(B) Notwithstanding any other provisions of law, all civil fines or penalties collected pursuant to sections 243(c), 271 and 273 of this title and all liquidated damages and expenses collected pursuant to this Act shall be deposited in the Immigration User Fee Account.

(2) (A) The Secretary of the Treasury shall refund out of the Immigration User Fee Account to any appropriation the amount paid out of such appropriation for expenses incurred by the Attorney General in providing immigration inspection and preinspection services for commercial aircraft or vessels and in—

(i) providing overtime immigration inspection services for commercial aircraft or vessels;

(ii) administration of debt recovery, including the establishment and operation of a national collections office;

(iii) expansion, operation and maintenance of information systems for nonimmigrant control and debt collection;

(iv) detection of fraudulent documents used by passengers traveling to the United States, including training of, and technical assistance to, commercial airline personnel regarding such detection;[184]

(v) providing detention and removal services for: inadmissible aliens arriving on commercial aircraft and vessels and for any alien who is inadmissible under section 212(a) who has attempted illegal entry into the United States through avoidance of immigration inspection at air or sea ports-of-entry; and

(vi) providing removal and asylum proceedings at air or sea ports-of-entry for: inadmissible aliens arriving on commercial aircraft and vessels including immigration removal proceedings resulting from presentation of fraudulent documents and failure to present documentation and for any alien who is inadmissible under section 212(a) who has attempted illegal entry into the United States through avoidance of immigration inspection at air or sea ports-of-entry.

The Attorney General shall provide for expenditures for training and assistance described in clause (iv) in an amount, for any fiscal year, not less than 5 percent of the total of the expenses incurred that are described in the previous sentence.

(B) The amounts which are required to be refunded under subparagraph (A) shall be refunded at least quarterly on the basis of estimates made by the Attorney General of the expenses referred to in subparagraph (A). Proper adjustments shall be made in the amounts subsequently refunded under subparagraph (A) to the extent prior estimates were in excess of, or less than, the amount required to be refunded under subparagraph (A).

**(i) Reimbursement.**— Notwithstanding any other provision of law, the Attorney General is authorized to receive reimbursement from the owner, operator, or agent of a private or commercial aircraft or vessel, or from any airport or seaport authority for expenses incurred by the Attorney General in providing immigration inspection services which are rendered at the request of such person or authority (including the salary and expenses of individuals employed by the Attor-

---

[184] *See* §124 of IIRAIRA. Applicable to expenses incurred during or after fiscal year 1997.

ney General to provide such immigration inspection services). The Attorney General's authority to receive such reimbursement shall terminate immediately upon the provision for such services by appropriation.

**(j) Regulations.**— The Attorney General may prescribe such rules and regulations as may be necessary to carry out the provisions of this section.

**(k) Advisory committee.**— In accordance with the provisions of the Federal Advisory Committee Act, the Attorney General shall establish an advisory committee, whose membership shall consist of representatives from the airline and other transportation industries who may be subject to any fee or charge authorized by law or proposed by the Immigration and Naturalization Service for the purpose of covering expenses incurred by the Immigration and Naturalization Service. The advisory committee shall meet on a periodic basis and shall advise the Attorney General on issues related to the performance of the inspectional services of the Immigration and Naturalization Service. This advice shall include, but not be limited to, such issues as the time periods during which such services should be performed, the proper number and deployment of inspection officers, the level of fees, and the appropriateness of any proposed fee. The Attorney General shall give substantial consideration to the views of the advisory committee in the exercise of his duties.

**(*l*) Report to Congress.**— In addition to the reporting requirements established pursuant to subsection (h), the Attorney General shall prepare and submit annually to the Congress, not later than March 31st of each year, a statement of the financial condition of the "Immigration User Fee Account" including beginning account balance, revenues, withdrawals and their purpose, ending balance, projections for the ensuing fiscal year and a full and complete workload analysis showing on a port by port basis the current and projected need for inspectors. The statement shall indicate the success rate of the Immigration and Naturalization Service in meeting the forty-five minute inspection standard and shall provide detailed statistics regarding the number of passengers inspected within the standard, progress that is being made to expand the utilization of United States citizen by-pass, the number of passengers for whom the standard is not met and the length of their delay, locational breakdown of these statistics and the steps being taken to correct any non-conformity.

**(m) Immigration examinations fee account.**— Notwithstanding any other provisions of law, all adjudication fees as are designated by the Attorney General in regulations shall be deposited as offsetting receipts into a separate account entitled "Immigration Examinations Fee Account" in the Treasury of the United States, whether collected directly by the Attorney General or through clerks of courts: *Provided, however,* That all fees received by the Attorney General from applicants residing in the Virgin Islands of the United States and in Guam, under this subsection shall be paid over to the treasury of the Virgin Islands and to the treasury of Guam: *Provided further,* That fees for providing adjudication and naturalization services may be set at a level that will ensure recovery of the full costs of providing all such services, including the costs of similar services provided without charge to asylum applicants or other immigrants. Such fees may also be set at a level that will recover any additional costs associated with the administration of the fees collected.

**(n) Reimbursement of administrative expenses; transfer of deposits to general fund of United States Treasury.**— All deposits into the "Immigration Examinations Fee Account" shall remain available until expended to the Attorney General to reimburse any appropriation the amount paid out of such appropriation for expenses in providing immigration adjudication and naturalization services and the collection, safeguarding and accounting for fees deposited in and funds reimbursed from the "Immigration Examinations Fee Account".

**(o) Annual financial reports to congress.**— The Attorney General will prepare and submit annually to Congress statements of financial condition of the "Immigration Examinations Fee

Account", including beginning account balance, revenues, withdrawals, and ending account balance and projections for the ensuing fiscal year.

**(p) Additional effective dates.**— The provisions set forth in subsections (m), (n), and (o) of this section apply to adjudication and naturalization services performed and to related fees collected on or after October 1, 1988.

**(q) Land border inspection fee account.**—

(1) (A) (i) Notwithstanding any other provision of law, the Attorney General is authorized to establish, by regulation, not more than 96 projects under which a fee may be charged and collected for inspection services provided at one or more land border points of entry. Such projects may include the establishment of commuter lanes to be made available to qualified United States citizens and aliens, as determined by the Attorney General.

(ii) This subparagraph shall take effect, with respect to any project described in clause (1)[185] that was not authorized to be commenced before the date of the enactment of the Illegal Immigration Reform and Immigrant Responsibility Act of 1996 [Sept. 30, 1996], 30 days after submission of a written plan by the Attorney General detailing the proposed implementation of such project.

(iii) The Attorney General shall prepare and submit on a quarterly basis a status report on each land border inspection project implemented under this subparagraph.

(B) The Attorney General, in consultation with the Secretary of the Treasury, may conduct pilot projects to demonstrate the use of designated ports of entry after working hours through the use of card reading machines or other appropriate technology.

(2) All of the fees collected under this subsection, including receipts for services performed in processing forms I-94, I-94W, and I-68, and other similar applications processed at land border ports of entry, shall be deposited as offsetting receipts in a separate account within the general fund of the Treasury of the United States, to remain available until expended. Such account shall be known as the Land Border Inspection Fee Account.

(3) (A) The Secretary of the Treasury shall refund, at least on a quarterly basis amounts to any appropriations for expenses incurred in providing inspection services at land border points of entry. Such expenses shall include—

(i) the providing of overtime inspection services;

(ii) the expansion, operation and maintenance of information systems for non-immigrant control;

(iii) the hire of additional permanent and temporary inspectors;

(iv) the minor construction costs associated with the addition of new traffic lanes (with the concurrence of the General Services Administration);

(v) the detection of fraudulent documents used by passengers traveling to the United States;

(vi) providing for the administration of said account.

(B) The amounts required to be refunded from the Land Border Inspection Fee Account for fiscal years 1992 and thereafter shall be refunded in accordance with estimates made

---

[185] *Sic.* Probably should be clause "(i)".

in the budget request of the Attorney General for those fiscal years: *Provided*, That any proposed changes in the amounts designated in said budget requests shall only be made after notification to the Committees on Appropriations of the House of Representatives and the Senate in accordance with section 606 of Public Law 101-162.

(4) The Attorney General will prepare and submit annually to the Congress statements of financial condition of the Land Border Immigration Fee Account, including beginning account balance, revenues, withdrawals, and ending account balance and projection for the ensuing fiscal year.

**(r) Breached bond/detention fund.—**

(1) Notwithstanding any other provision of law, there is established in the general fund of the Treasury a separate account which shall be known as the Breached Bond\Detention Fund (in this subsection referred to as the "Fund").

(2) There shall be deposited as offsetting receipts into the Fund all breached cash and surety bonds, in excess of $8,000,000, posted under this Act which are recovered by the Department of Justice, and amount described in section 245(i)(3)(b).[186]

(3) Such amounts as are deposited into the Fund shall remain available until expended and shall be refunded out of the Fund by the Secretary of the Treasury, at least on a quarterly basis, to the Attorney General for the following purposes—

(i) for expenses incurred in the collection of breached bonds, and

(ii) for expenses associated with the detention of illegal aliens.

(4) The amounts required to be refunded from the Fund for fiscal year 1998 and thereafter shall be refunded in accordance with estimates made in the budget request of the President for those fiscal years. Any proposed changes in the amounts designated in such budget requests shall only be made after Congressional reprogramming notification in accordance with the reprogramming guidelines for the applicable fiscal year.

(5) The Attorney General shall prepare and submit annually to the Congress, statements of financial condition of the Fund, including the beginning balance, receipts, refunds to appropriations, transfers to the general fund, and the ending balance.

(6) For fiscal year 1993 only, the Attorney General may transfer up to $1,000,000 from the Immigration User Fee Account to the Fund for initial expenses necessary to enhance collection efforts: *Provided,* That any such transfers shall be refunded from the Breached Bond/Detention Fund back to the Immigration User Fee Account by December 31, 1993.

**(s) H-1B nonimmigrant petitioner account.—**

(1) *In general.*— There is established in the general fund of the Treasury a separate account, which shall be known as the "H-1B Nonimmigrant Petitioner Account". Notwithstanding any other section of this title, there shall be deposited as offsetting receipts into the account all fees collected under paragraphs (9) and (11) of section 214(c).

(2) *Use of fees for job training.*— 50 percent of amounts deposited into the H-1B Nonimmigrant Petitioner Account shall remain available to the Secretary of Labor until expended for demonstration programs and projects described in section 414(c) of the American Competitiveness and Workforce Improvement Act of 1998.

---

[186] *Sic.* Probably should be section "245(i)(3)(B)".

(3) *Use of fees for low-income scholarship program.*— 30 percent of the amounts deposited into the H-1B Nonimmigrant Petitioner Account shall remain available to the Director of the National Science Foundation until expended for scholarships described in section 414(d) of the American Competitiveness and Workforce Improvement Act of 1998 for low-income students enrolled in a program of study leading to a degree in mathematics, engineering, or computer science.

(4) *National Science Foundation competitive grant program for K-12 math, science, and technology education.—*

(A) *In general.*— 10 percent of the amounts deposited into the H-1B Nonimmigrant Petitioner Account shall remain available to the Director of the National Science Foundation until expended to carry out a direct or matching grant program to support private-public partnerships in K-12 education.

(B) *Types of programs covered.*— The Director shall award grants to such programs, including those which support the development and implementation of standards-based instructional materials models and related student assessments that enable K-12 students to acquire an understanding of science, mathematics, and technology, as well as to develop critical thinking skills; provide systemic improvement in training K-12 teachers and education for students in science, mathematics, and technology; support the professional development of K-12 math and science teachers in the use of technology in the classroom; stimulate system-wide K-12 reform of science, mathematics, and technology in rural, economically disadvantaged regions of the United States; provide externships and other opportunities for students to increase their appreciation and understanding of science, mathematics, engineering, and technology (including summer institutes sponsored by an institution of higher education for students in grades 7-12 that provide instruction in such fields); involve partnerships of industry, educational institutions, and community organizations to address the educational needs of disadvantaged communities; provide college preparatory support to expose and prepare students for careers in science, mathematics, engineering, and technology; and provide for carrying out systemic reform activities under section 3(a)(1) of the National Science Foundation Act of 1950 (42 U.S.C. 1862(a)(1)).

(5) *Use of fees for duties relating to petitions.*— 5 percent of the amounts deposited into the H-1B Nonimmigrant Petitioner Account shall remain available to the Secretary of Homeland Security until expended to carry out duties under paragraphs (1) and (9) of section 214(c) related to petitions made for nonimmigrants described in section 101(a)(15)(H)(i)(b), under paragraph (1)(C) or (D) of section 204[187] of this title related to petitions for immigrants described in section 203(b).

(6) *Use of fees for application processing and enforcement.*— For fiscal year 1999, 4 percent of the amounts deposited into the H-1B Nonimmigrant Petitioner Account shall remain available to the Secretary of Labor until expended for decreasing the processing time for applications under section 212(n)(1) and for carrying out section 212(n)(2). Beginning with fiscal year 2000, 5 percent of the amounts deposited into the H-1B Nonimmigrant Petitioner Account shall remain available to the Secretary of Labor until expended for decreasing the processing time for applications under section 212(n)(1) and section 212(a)(5)(A).

---

[187] *Sic.* Probably should be "… of section 204(a) …"

**(t) Genealogy fee.—**

(1) There is hereby established the Genealogy Fee for providing genealogy research and information services. This fee shall be deposited as offsetting collections into the Examinations Fee Account. Fees for such research and information services may be set at a level that will ensure the recovery of the full costs of providing all such services.

(2) The Attorney General will prepare and submit annually to Congress statements of the financial condition of the Genealogy Fee.

(3) Any officer or employee of the Immigration and Naturalization Service shall collect fees prescribed under regulation before disseminating any requested genealogical information.

**(u) Premium fee for employment-based petitions and applications.—** The Attorney General is authorized to establish and collect a premium fee for employment-based petitions and applications. This fee shall be used to provide certain premium-processing services to business customers, and to make infrastructure improvements in the adjudications and customer-service processes. For approval of the benefit applied for, the petitioner/applicant must meet the legal criteria for such benefit. This fee shall be set at $1,000, shall be paid in addition to any normal petition/application fee that may be applicable, and shall be deposited as offsetting collections in the Immigration Examinations Fee Account. The Attorney General may adjust this fee according to the Consumer Price Index.

**(v)**[188] **Fraud prevention and detection account.—**

(1) *In general.—* There is established in the general fund of the Treasury a separate account, which shall be known as the "Fraud Prevention and Detection Account". Notwithstanding any other provision of law, there shall be deposited as offsetting receipts into the account all fees collected under paragraph (12) or (13) of section 214(c).

(2) *Use of fees to combat fraud.—*

(A) *Secretary of State.—* One-third of the amounts deposited into the Fraud Prevention and Detection Account shall remain available to the Secretary of State until expended for programs and activities at United States embassies and consulates abroad—

(i) to increase the number diplomatic security personnel assigned exclusively or primarily to the function of preventing and detecting fraud by applicants for visas described in subparagraph (H)(i), (H)(ii), or (L) of section 101(a)(15);

(ii) otherwise to prevent and detect visa fraud, including primarily fraud by applicants for visas described in subparagraph (H)(i), (H)(ii), or (L) of section 101(a)(15), in cooperation with the Secretary of Homeland Security or pursuant to the terms of a memorandum of understanding or other agreement between the Secretary of State and the Secretary of Homeland Security; and

---

[188] Added by H-1B Visa Reform Act of 2004, P.L. 108-447 (12/8/04). Sec. 426(c) of that Act states:

The amendments made by this section [including the addition of INA §286(v) by §426(b)] shall take effect on the date of enactment of this Act [12/8/04], and the fees imposed under such amendments shall apply to petitions under §214(c) of the Immigration and Nationality Act, and applications for nonimmigrant visas under §222 of such Act, filed on or after the date that is 90 days after the date of the enactment of this Act [*i.e.*, 3/8/05]. However, §430 of the Act states that the amendments made by the subtitle (excepting 426(a) but not 426(b)) take effect 90 days after the date of enactment of this Act [*i.e.*, 3/8/05]. Amended by §403(b) of REAL ID Act, P.L. 109-13 (5/11/05; *effective* 5/26/05, applicable to filings "for a fiscal year after fiscal year 2005.")

(iii) upon request by the Secretary of Homeland Security, to assist such Secretary in carrying out the fraud prevention and detection programs and activities described in subparagraph (B).

(B) *Secretary of Homeland Security.*— One-third of the amounts deposited into the Fraud Prevention and Detection Account shall remain available to the Secretary of Homeland Security until expended for programs and activities to prevent and detect fraud with respect to petitions under paragraph (1) or (2)(A) of section 214(c) to grant an alien nonimmigrant status described in subparagraph (H)(i), (H)(ii), or (L) of section 101(a)(15).

(C) *Secretary of Labor.*— One-third of the amounts deposited into the Fraud Prevention and Detection Account shall remain available to the Secretary of Labor until expended for enforcement programs and activities described in section 212(n).

(D) *Consultation.*— The Secretary of State, the Secretary of Homeland Security, and the Secretary of Labor shall consult one another with respect to the use of the funds in the Fraud Prevention and Detection Account or for programs and activities to prevent and detect fraud with respect to petitions under paragraph (1) or (2)(A) of section 214(c) to grant an alien nonimmigrant status described in section 101(a)(15)(H)(ii).

(June 27, 1952, ch. 477, title II, ch. 9, §286, 66 Stat. 232; as amended by P.L. 97-116 (12/29/81); P.L. 99-500 (10/18/86), renumbered P.L. 100-525 (10/24/88); P.L. 99-591 (10/30/86); P.L. 99-653 (11/14/86), as added by P.L. 100-525 (10/24/88); P.L. 100-71 (7/11/87); P.L. 100-459 (10/1/88); P.L. 100-525 (10/24/88); P.L. 101-162 (11/21/89); P.L. 101-515 (11/5/90); P.L. 102-232 (MTINA) (12/12/91, *effective* 4/1/92); P.L. 102-395 (10/6/92); P.L. 103-121 (10/27/93); P.L. 103-416 (INTCA) (10/25/94, *effective* 4/1/95); P.L. 104-208 (IIRAIRA) (9/30/96), div. C, title I, §122(a) [revising (q)], §124(a)(1) [adding (h)(2)(A)(iv)], title III, §308(d)(3)(A), §376(b) [adding (s)], §382(b) [revising (h)(1)(B)], title VI, §671(b)(11); P.L. 105-119 (11/26/97), title I, §110(1) [revising (r); removing (s)]; P.L. 105-277 (10/21/98), (HRIFA) div. A, §101(b), [title I, §114], (ACWIA) div. C, title IV, §414(b) [adding new (s)]; P.L. 106-113 (11/29/99), div. B, §1000(a)(1), title I, §118 [redesignating (q)(1)(A)(iii) & (iv) as (q)(1)(A)(ii) & (iii), respectively]; P.L. 106-313 (AC21) (10/17/00), title I, §110(a) [revising percentages in (s)(2), (s)(3), & (s)(6); revising (s)(4)], §113 [revising (s)(5), & revising percentages in (s)(3) & (s)(6) by "deeming" them to certain figures, "[n]otwithstanding any other provision of this Act."]; P.L. 106-553 (LIFE Act) (12/21/00), §1(a)(2), [title I, §112]; P.L. 106-554 (12/21/00), §1(a)(1), [title I, §106; P.L. 107-77 (11/28/01), title I, §109, §110; P.L. 107-173 (5/14/02), title IV, §403(a) [deleting the requirement that services be provided within 45 minutes of presentation for inspection in (g)]; P.L. 107-206 (8/2/02), title I, §202; P.L. 107-273 (11/2/02), div. C, title I, §11016(2) [revising (q)(2)]; P.L. 107-296 (11/25/02), title IV, §457 [revising (m)]; P.L. 108-7 (2/20/03), div. B, title I, §108, div. L, §107 [repealing amendment made by P.L. 107-296, §457; which also provided: "*Provided,* That no court shall have jurisdiction over any cause or claim arising under the provisions of section 457 of the Homeland Security Act of 2002 (P.L. 107-296), this section, or any regulations promulgated thereunder."]; P.L. 108-77 (9/3/03), title IV, §402(d)(2); P.L. 108-447 (12/8/04), div. J, title IV, §426(b), §427 [revising percentages in (s)]; P.L. 109-13 (REAL ID) (5/11/05), div. A, title VI, §6046 [revising (s)(6)], div. B, title IV, §403(b); P.L. 109-472 (1/11/07), §2 [revising (v)(2)(A)(i)–(ii)].)

## Sec. 287 Powers of Immigration Officers and Employees
## [8 U.S.C. 1357]

**(a) Powers without warrant.**— Any officer or employee of the Service authorized under regulations prescribed by the Attorney General shall have power without warrant—

(1) to interrogate any alien or person believed to be an alien as to his right to be or to remain in the United States;

(2) to arrest any alien who in his presence or view is entering or attempting to enter the United States in violation of any law or regulation made in pursuance of law regulating the admission, exclusion, expulsion, or removal of aliens, or to arrest any alien in the United States, if he has reason to believe that the alien so arrested is in the United States in violation of any such law or regulation and is likely to escape before a warrant can be obtained for his arrest, but the alien arrested shall be taken without unnecessary delay for examination before an officer of the Service having authority to examine aliens as to their right to enter or remain in the United States;

(3) within a reasonable distance from any external boundary of the United States, to board and search for aliens any vessel within the territorial waters of the United States and any railway car, aircraft, conveyance, or vehicle, and within a distance of twenty-five miles from any such external boundary to have access to private lands, but not dwellings, for the purpose of patrolling the border to prevent the illegal entry of aliens into the United States;

(4) to make arrests for felonies which have been committed and which are cognizable under any law of the United States regulating the admission, exclusion, expulsion, or removal of aliens, if he has reason to believe that the person so arrested is guilty of such felony and if there is likelihood of the person escaping before a warrant can be obtained for his arrest, but the person arrested shall be taken without unnecessary delay before the nearest available officer empowered to commit persons charged with offenses against the laws of the United States; and

(5) to make arrests—

(A) for any offense against the United States, if the offense is committed in the officer's or employee's presence, or

(B) for any felony cognizable under the laws of the United States, if the officer or employee has reasonable grounds to believe that the person to be arrested has committed or is committing such a felony,

if the officer or employee is performing duties relating to the enforcement of the immigration laws at the time of the arrest and if there is a likelihood of the person escaping before a warrant can be obtained for his arrest.

Under regulations prescribed by the Attorney General, an officer or employee of the Service may carry a firearm and may execute and serve any order, warrant, subpoena, summons, or other process issued under the authority of the United States. The authority to make arrests under paragraph (5)(B) shall only be effective on and after the date on which the Attorney General publishes final regulations which (i) prescribe the categories of officers and employees of the Service who may use force (including deadly force) and the circumstances under which such force may be used, (ii) establish standards with respect to enforcement activities of the Service, (iii) require that any officer or employee of the Service is not authorized to make arrests under paragraph (5)(B) unless the officer or employee has received certification as having completed a training program which covers such arrests and standards described in clause (ii), and (iv) establish an expedited, internal review process for violations of such standards, which process is consistent with standard agency procedure regarding confidentiality of matters related to internal investigations.

**(b) Administration of oath; taking of evidence.—** Any officer or employee of the Service designated by the Attorney General, whether individually or as one of a class, shall have power and authority to administer oaths and to take and consider evidence concerning the privilege of any person to enter, reenter, pass through, or reside in the United States, or concerning any matter which is material or relevant to the enforcement of this Act and the administration of the Service; and any person to whom such oath has been administered (or who has executed an unsworn declaration, certificate, verification, or statement under penalty of perjury as permitted under section 1746 of title 28, United States Code), under the provisions of this Act, who shall knowingly or willfully give false evidence or swear (or subscribe under penalty of perjury as permitted under section 1746 of title 28, United States Code) to any false statement concerning any matter referred to in this subsection shall be guilty of perjury and shall be punished as provided by section 1621, title 18, United States Code.

**(c) Search without warrant.**— Any officer or employee of the Service authorized and designated under regulations prescribed by the Attorney General, whether individually or as one of a class, shall have power to conduct a search, without warrant, of the person, and of the personal effects in the possession of any person seeking admission to the United States, concerning whom such officer or employee may have reasonable cause to suspect that grounds exist for denial of admission to the United States under this Act which would be disclosed by such search.

**(d) Detainer of aliens for violation of controlled substances laws.**— In the case of an alien who is arrested by a Federal, State, or local law enforcement official for a violation of any law relating to controlled substances, if the official (or another official)—

(1) has reason to believe that the alien may not have been lawfully admitted to the United States or otherwise is not lawfully present in the United States,

(2) expeditiously informs an appropriate officer or employee of the Service authorized and designated by the Attorney General of the arrest and of facts concerning the status of the alien, and

(3) requests the Service to determine promptly whether or not to issue a detainer to detain the alien,

the officer or employee of the Service shall promptly determine whether or not to issue such a detainer. If such a detainer is issued and the alien is not otherwise detained by Federal, State, or local officials, the Attorney General shall effectively and expeditiously take custody of the alien.

**(e) Restriction on warrantless entry in case of outdoor agricultural operations.**— Notwithstanding any other provision of this section other than paragraph (3) of subsection (a), an officer or employee of the Service may not enter without the consent of the owner (or agent thereof) or a properly executed warrant onto the premises of a farm or other outdoor agricultural operation for the purpose of interrogating a person believed to be an alien as to the person's right to be or to remain in the United States.

**(f) Fingerprinting and photographing of certain aliens.**—

(1) Under regulations of the Attorney General, the Commissioner shall provide for the fingerprinting and photographing of each alien 14 years of age or older against whom a proceeding is commenced under section 240.

(2) Such fingerprints and photographs shall be made available to Federal, State, and local law enforcement agencies, upon request.

**(g) Performance of immigration officer functions by state officers and employees.**—

(1) Notwithstanding section 1342 of title 31, United States Code, the Attorney General may enter into a written agreement with a State, or any political subdivision of a State, pursuant to which an officer or employee of the State or subdivision, who is determined by the Attorney General to be qualified to perform a function of an immigration officer in relation to the investigation, apprehension or detention of aliens in the United States (including the transportation of such aliens across State lines to detention centers), may carry out such function at the expense of the State or political subdivision and to the extent consistent with State and local law.

(2) An agreement under this subsection shall require that an officer or employee of a State or political subdivision of a State performing a function under the agreement shall have knowledge of, and adhere to, Federal law relating to the function, and shall contain a written certification that the officers or employees performing the function under the agreement have received adequate training regarding the enforcement of relevant Federal immigration laws.

(3) In performing a function under this subsection, an officer or employee of a State or political subdivision of a State shall be subject to the direction and supervision of the Attorney General.

(4) In performing a function under this subsection, an officer or employee of a State or political subdivision of a State may use Federal property or facilities, as provided in a written agreement between the Attorney General and the State or subdivision.

(5) With respect to each officer or employee of a State or political subdivision who is authorized to perform a function under this subsection, the specific powers and duties that may be, or are required to be, exercised or performed by the individual, the duration of the authority of the individual, and the position of the agency of the Attorney General who is required to supervise and direct the individual, shall be set forth in a written agreement between the Attorney General and the State or political subdivision.

(6) The Attorney General may not accept a service under this subsection if the service will be used to displace any Federal employee.

(7) Except as provided in paragraph (8), an officer or employee of a State or political subdivision of a State performing functions under this subsection shall not be treated as a Federal employee for any purpose other than for purposes of chapter 81 of title 5, United States Code, (relating to compensation for injury) and sections 2671 through 2680 of title 28, United States Code (relating to tort claims).

(8) An officer or employee of a State or political subdivision of a State acting under color of authority under this subsection, or any agreement entered into under this subsection, shall be considered to be acting under color of Federal authority for purposes of determining the liability, and immunity from suit, of the officer or employee in a civil action brought under Federal or State law.

(9) Nothing in this subsection shall be construed to require any State or political subdivision of a State to enter into an agreement with the Attorney General under this subsection.

(10) Nothing in this subsection shall be construed to require an agreement under this subsection in order for any officer or employee of a State or political subdivision of a State—

(A) to communicate with the Attorney General regarding the immigration status of any individual, including reporting knowledge that a particular alien is not lawfully present in the United States; or

(B) otherwise to cooperate with the Attorney General in the identification, apprehension, detention, or removal of aliens not lawfully present in the United States.

(h) An alien described in section 101(a)(27)(J) of the Immigration and Nationality Act who has been battered, abused, neglected, or abandoned, shall not be compelled to contact the alleged abuser (or family member of the alleged abuser) at any stage of applying for special immigrant juvenile status, including after a request for the consent of the Secretary of Homeland Security under section 101(a)(27)(J)(iii)(I) of such Act.

(June 27, 1952, ch. 477, title II, ch. 9, §287, 66 Stat. 233; as amended by P.L. 94-550 (10/18/76); P.L. 99-570 (10/27/86); P.L. 99-603 (IRCA) (11/6/86); P.L. 100-525 (10/24/88); P.L. 101-649 (IMMACT90) (11/29/90); P.L. 102-232 (MTINA) (12/12/91, *effective* 4/1/92); P.L. 104-208 (IIRAIRA) (9/30/96), div. C, title I, §133 [adding (g)(1)], title III, §308(d)(4)(L); P.L. 109-162 (1/5/06), title VIII, §826, [adding (i) (*sic.* The subsection designation (h) was not assigned at the time).]; P.L. 109-271 (8/12/06), §6 [redesignating (i) as (h)].)

### Sec. 288 Local Jurisdiction over Immigrant Stations
### [8 U.S.C. 1358]

The officers in charge of the various immigrant stations shall admit therein the proper State and local officers charged with the enforcement of the laws of the State or Territory of the United States in which any such immigrant station is located in order that such State and local officers may preserve the peace and make arrests for crimes under the laws of the States and Territories. For the purpose of this section the jurisdiction of such State and local officers and of the State and local courts shall extend over such immigrant station.

(June 27, 1952, ch. 477, title II, ch. 9, §288, 66 Stat. 234.)

### Sec. 289 Application to American Indians Born in Canada
### [8 U.S.C. 1359]

Nothing in this title shall be construed to affect the right of American Indians born in Canada to pass the borders of the United States, but such right shall extend only to persons who possess at least 50 per centum of blood of the American Indian race.

(June 27, 1952, ch. 477, title II, ch. 9, §289, 66 Stat. 234.)

### Sec. 290 Establishment of Central File; Information from Other Departments and Agencies
### [8 U.S.C. 1360]

(a) Establishment of central file.— There shall be established in the office of the Commissioner, for the use of the security and enforcement agencies of the Government of the United States, a central index, which shall contain the names of all aliens heretofore admitted or denied admission to the United States, insofar as such information is available from the existing records of the Service, and the names of all aliens hereafter admitted or denied admission to the United States, the names of their sponsors of record, if any, and such other relevant information as the Attorney General shall require as an aid to the proper enforcement of this Act.

(b) Information from other departments and agencies.— Any information in any records kept by any department or agency of the Government as to the identity and location of aliens in the United States shall be made available to the Service upon request made by the Attorney General to the head of any such department or agency.

(c) Reports on social security account numbers and earnings of aliens not authorized to work.—

(1) Not later than 3 months after the end of each fiscal year (beginning with fiscal year 1996), the Commissioner of Social Security shall report to the Committees on the Judiciary of the House of Representatives and the Senate on the aggregate quantity of social security account numbers issued to aliens not authorized to be employed, with respect to which, in such fiscal year, earnings were reported to the Social Security Administration.

(2) If earnings are reported on or after January 1, 1997, to the Social Security Administration on a social security account number issued to an alien not authorized to work in the United States, the Commissioner of Social Security shall provide the Attorney General with information regarding the name and address of the alien, the name and address of the person reporting the earnings, and the amount of the earnings. The information shall be provided in an electronic form agreed upon by the Commissioner and the Attorney General.

(d) Certification of search of service records.— A written certification signed by the Attorney General or by any officer of the Service designated by the Attorney General to make such certification, that after diligent search no record or entry of a specified nature is found to exist in the records of the Service, shall be admissible as evidence in any proceeding as evidence that the records of the Service contain no such record or entry, and shall have the same effect as the testimony of a witness given in open court.

(June 27, 1952, ch. 477, title II, ch. 9, §290, 66 Stat. 234; as amended by P.L. 100-525 (10/24/88); P.L. 104-208 (IIRAIRA) (9/30/96), div. C, title III, §308(d)(4)(M), title IV, §414(a) [revising (c)].)

### Sec. 291 Burden of Proof upon Alien
### [8 U.S.C. 1361]

Whenever any person makes application for a visa or any other document required for entry, or makes application for admission, or otherwise attempts to enter the United States, the burden of proof shall be upon such person to establish that he is eligible to receive such visa or such document, or is not inadmissible under any provision of this Act, and, if an alien, that he is entitled to the nonimmigrant, immigrant, special immigrant, immediate relative, or refugee status claimed, as the case may be. If such person fails to establish to the satisfaction of the consular officer that he is eligible to receive a visa or other document required for entry, no visa or other document required for entry shall be issued to such person, nor shall such person be admitted to the United States unless he establishes to the satisfaction of the Attorney General that he is not inadmissible under any provision of this Act. In any removal proceeding under chapter 4 against any person, the burden of proof shall be upon such person to show the time, place, and manner of his entry into the United States, but in presenting such proof he shall be entitled to the production of his visa or other entry document, if any, and of any other documents and records, not considered by the Attorney General to be confidential, pertaining to such entry in the custody of the Service. If such burden of proof is not sustained, such person shall be presumed to be in the United States in violation of law.

(June 27, 1952, ch. 477, title II, ch. 9, §291, 66 Stat. 234; as amended by P.L. 97-116 (12/29/81); P.L. 104-208 (IIRAIRA) (9/30/96), div. C, title III, §308 [revising §291].)

### Sec. 292 Right to Counsel
### [8 U.S.C. 1362]

In any removal proceedings before an immigration judge and in any appeal proceedings before the Attorney General from any such removal proceedings, the person concerned shall have the privilege of being represented (at no expense to the Government) by such counsel, authorized to practice in such proceedings, as he shall choose.

(June 27, 1952, ch. 477, title II, ch. 9, §291, 66 Stat. 234; as amended by P.L. 104-208 (IIRAIRA) (9/30/96), div. C, title III, §§308(d)(4)(O), 371(b)(9).)

### Sec. 293 Deposit of and Interest on Cash Received to Secure Immigration Bonds
### [8 U.S.C. 1363]

(a) Cash received by the Attorney General as security on an immigration bond shall be deposited in the Treasury of the United States in trust for the obligor on the bond, and shall bear interest payable at a rate determined by the Secretary of the Treasury, except that in no case shall the interest rate exceed 3 per centum per annum. Such interest shall accrue from date of deposit occurring after April 27, 1966, to and including date of withdrawal or date of breach of the immigration bond, whichever occurs first: *Provided,* That cash received by the Attorney General as security on an immigration bond, and deposited by him in the postal savings system prior to discontinuance of the system, shall accrue interest as provided in this section from the date such cash ceased to accrue interest under the system. Appropriations to the Treasury Department for interest on uninvested funds shall be available for payment of said interest.

**(b)** The interest accruing on cash received by the Attorney General as security on an immigration bond shall be subject to the same disposition as prescribed for the principal cash, except that interest accruing to the date of breach of the immigration bond shall be paid to the obligor on the bond.

(June 27, 1952, ch. 477, title II, ch. 9, §293, as added by P.L. 91-313 (7/10/70), §2.)

## Sec. 294 Undercover Investigation Authority
## [8 U.S.C. 1363a]

**(a) In general.**— With respect to any undercover investigative operation of the Service which is necessary for the detection and prosecution of crimes against the United States—

(1) sums appropriated for the Service may be used for leasing space within the United States and the territories and possessions of the United States without regard to the following provisions of law:

(A) section 3679(a) of the Revised Statutes (31 U.S.C. 1341),

(B) section 3732(a) of the Revised Statutes (41 U.S.C. 11(a)),

(C) section 305 of the Act of June 30, 1949 (63 Stat. 396; 41 U.S.C. 255),

(D) the third undesignated paragraph under the heading "Miscellaneous" of the Act of March 3, 1877 (19 Stat. 370; 40 U.S.C. 34),

(E) section 3648 of the Revised Statutes (31 U.S.C. 3324),

(F) section 3741 of the Revised Statutes (41 U.S.C. 22), and

(G) subsections (a) and (c) of section 304 of the Federal Property and Administrative Services Act of 1949 (63 Stat. 395; 41 U.S.C. 254 (a) and (c));

(2) sums appropriated for the Service may be used to establish or to acquire proprietary corporations or business entities as part of an undercover operation, and to operate such corporations or business entities on a commercial basis, without regard to the provisions of section 304 of the Government Corporation Control Act (31 U.S.C. 9102);

(3) sums appropriated for the Service, and the proceeds from the undercover operation, may be deposited in banks or other financial institutions without regard to the provisions of section 648 of title 18, United States Code, and of section 3639 of the Revised Statutes (31 U.S.C. 3302); and

(4) the proceeds from the undercover operation may be used to offset necessary and reasonable expenses incurred in such operation without regard to the provisions of section 3617 of the Revised Statutes (31 U.S.C. 3302).

The authority set forth in this subsection may be exercised only upon written certification of the Commissioner, in consultation with the Deputy Attorney General, that any action authorized by paragraph (1), (2), (3), or (4) is necessary for the conduct of the undercover operation.

**(b) Disposition of proceeds no longer required.**— As soon as practicable after the proceeds from an undercover investigative operation, carried out under paragraphs (3) and (4) of subsection (a), are no longer necessary for the conduct of the operation, the proceeds or the balance of the proceeds remaining at the time shall be deposited into the Treasury of the United States as miscellaneous receipts.

**(c) Disposition of certain corporations and business entities.**— If a corporation or business entity established or acquired as part of an undercover operation under paragraph (2) of subsection (a) with a net value of over $50,000 is to be liquidated, sold, or otherwise disposed of, the Service, as much in advance as the Commissioner or Commissioner's designee determines practicable, shall report the circumstances to the Attorney General, the Director of the Office of Management and Budget, and the Comptroller General. The proceeds of the liquidation, sale, or other disposition, after obligations are met, shall be deposited in the Treasury of the United States as miscellaneous receipts.

**(d) Financial audits.—** The Service shall conduct detailed financial audits of closed undercover operations on a quarterly basis and shall report the results of the audits in writing to the Deputy Attorney General.

(June 27, 1952, ch. 477, title II, ch. 9, §294, as added by P.L. 104-208 (IIRAIRA) (9/30/96), div. C, title II, §205(a).)

## Title III—Nationality and Naturalization (§§301–61)[189]

## Chapter 1 — Nationality at Birth and Collective Naturalization

### Sec. 301 Nationals and Citizens of United States at Birth
### [8 U.S.C. 1401]

The following shall be nationals and citizens of the United States at birth:

**(a)** a person born in the United States, and subject to the jurisdiction thereof;

**(b)** a person born in the United States to a member of an Indian, Eskimo, Aleutian, or other aboriginal tribe: *Provided*, That the granting of citizenship under this subsection shall not in any manner impair or otherwise affect the right of such person to tribal or other property;

**(c)** a person born outside of the United States and its outlying possessions of parents both of whom are citizens of the United States and one of whom has had a residence in the United States or one of its outlying possessions, prior to the birth of such person;

**(d)** a person born outside of the United States and its outlying possessions of parents one of whom is a citizen of the United States who has been physically present in the United States or one of its outlying possessions for a continuous period of one year prior to the birth of such person, and the other of whom is a national, but not a citizen of the United States;

**(e)** a person born in an outlying possession of the United States of parents one of whom is a citizen of the United States who has been physically present in the United States or one of its outlying possessions for a continuous period of one year at any time prior to the birth of such person;

**(f)** a person of unknown parentage found in the United States while under the age of five years, until shown, prior to his attaining the age of twenty-one years, not to have been born in the United States;

**(g)** a person born outside the geographical limits of the United States and its outlying possessions of parents one of whom is an alien, and the other a citizen of the United States who, prior to the birth of such person, was physically present in the United States or its outlying possessions for a period or periods totaling not less than five years, at least two of which were after attaining the age of fourteen years: *Provided*, That any periods of honorable service in the Armed Forces of the United States, or periods of employment with the United States Government or with an international organization as that term is defined in section 1 of the International Organizations Immunities Act (59 Stat. 669; 22 U.S.C. 288) by such citizen parent, or any periods during which such

---

[189] Certain 9/11 victims are entitled to posthumous citizenship "[n]otwithstanding any provision of title III." *See* §114 of P.L. 107-77, *reprinted in* Appendix M. Also, pursuant to P.L. 108-136, §1701(d), *effective* 10/1/04, the Secretaries of Homeland Security, State, and Defense "shall ensure that any applications, interviews, filings, oaths, ceremonies, or other proceedings under title III ... relating to naturalization of members of the Armed Forces are available through United States embassies, consulates, and as practicable, United States military installations overseas."

citizen parent is physically present abroad as the dependent unmarried son or daughter and a member of the household of a person (A) honorably serving with the Armed Forces of the United States, or (B) employed by the United States Government or an international organization as defined in section 1 of the International Organizations Immunities Act, may be included in order to satisfy the physical-presence requirement of this paragraph. This proviso shall be applicable to persons born on or after December 24, 1952, to the same extent as if it had become effective in its present form on that date; and

**(h)** a person born before noon (Eastern Standard Time) May 24, 1934, outside the limits and jurisdiction of the United States of an alien father and a mother who is a citizen of the United States who, prior to the birth of such person, had resided in the United States.

(June 27, 1952, ch. 477, title III, ch. 1, §301, 66 Stat. 235; as amended by P.L. 89-770 (11/6/66); P.L. 92-584 (10/27/72); P.L. 95-432 (10/10/78); P.L. 99-653 (11/14/86); P.L. 103-416 (INTCA) (10/25/94, *effective* 4/1/95), §101.)

## Sec. 302 Persons Born in Puerto Rico on or after April 11, 1899
## [8 U.S.C. 1402]

All persons born in Puerto Rico on or after April 11, 1899, and prior to January 13, 1941, subject to the jurisdiction of the United States, residing on January 13, 1941, in Puerto Rico or other territory over which the United States exercises rights of sovereignty and not citizens of the United States under any other Act, are hereby declared to be citizens of the United States as of January 13, 1941. All persons born in Puerto Rico on or after January 13, 1941, and subject to the jurisdiction of the United States, are citizens of the United States at birth.

(June 27, 1952, ch. 477, title III, ch. 1, §302, 66 Stat. 236.)

## Sec. 303 Persons Born in the Canal Zone or Republic of Panama on or after February 26, 1904
## [8 U.S.C. 1403]

**(a)** Any person born in the Canal Zone on or after February 26, 1904, and whether before or after the effective date of this Act, whose father or mother or both at the time of the birth of such person was or is a citizen of the United States, is declared to be a citizen of the United States.

**(b)** Any person born in the Republic of Panama on or after February 26, 1904, and whether before or after the effective date of this Act, whose father or mother or both at the time of the birth of such person was or is a citizen of the United States employed by the Government of the United States or by the Panama Railroad Company, or its successor in title, is declared to be a citizen of the United States.

(June 27, 1952, ch. 477, title III, ch. 1, §303, 66 Stat. 236.)

## Sec. 304 Persons Born in Alaska on or after March 30, 1867
## [8 U.S.C. 1404]

A person born in Alaska on or after March 30, 1867, except a noncitizen Indian, is a citizen of the United States at birth. A noncitizen Indian born in Alaska on or after March 30, 1867, and prior to June 2, 1924, is declared to be a citizen of the United States as of June 2, 1924. An Indian born in Alaska on or after June 2, 1924, is a citizen of the United States at birth.

(June 27, 1952, ch. 477, title III, ch. 1, §304, 66 Stat. 237.)

## Sec. 305 Persons Born in Hawaii
**[8 U.S.C. 1405]**

A person born in Hawaii on or after August 12, 1898, and before April 30, 1900, is declared to be a citizen of the United States as of April 30, 1900. A person born in Hawaii on or after April 30, 1900, is a citizen of the United States at birth. A person who was a citizen of the Republic of Hawaii on August 12, 1898, is declared to be a citizen of the United States as of April 30, 1900.

(June 27, 1952, ch. 477, title III, ch. 1, §305, 66 Stat. 237.)

## Sec. 306 Persons Living in and Born in the Virgin Islands
**[8 U.S.C. 1406]**

**(a)** The following persons and their children born subsequent to January 17, 1917, and prior to February 25, 1927, are declared to be citizens of the United States as of February 25, 1927:

(1) All former Danish citizens who, on January 17, 1917, resided in the Virgin Islands of the United States, and were residing in those islands or in the United States or Puerto Rico on February 25, 1927, and who did not make the declaration required to preserve their Danish citizenship by article 6 of the treaty entered into on August 4, 1916, between the United States and Denmark, or who, having made such a declaration have heretofore renounced or may hereafter renounce it by a declaration before a court of record;

(2) All natives of the Virgin Islands of the United States who, on January 17, 1917, resided in those islands, and were residing in those islands or in the United States or Puerto Rico on February 25, 1927, and who were not on February 25, 1927, citizens or subjects of any foreign country;

(3) All natives of the Virgin Islands of the United States who, on January 17, 1917, resided in the United States, and were residing in those islands on February 25, 1927, and who were not on February 25, 1927, citizens or subjects of any foreign country; and

(4) All natives of the Virgin Islands of the United States who, on June 28, 1932, were residing in continental United States, the Virgin Islands of the United States, Puerto Rico, the Canal Zone, or any other insular possession or territory of the United States, and who, on June 28, 1932, were not citizens or subjects of any foreign country, regardless of their place of residence on January 17, 1917.

**(b)** All persons born in the Virgin Islands of the United States on or after January 17, 1917, and prior to February 25, 1927, and subject to the jurisdiction of the United States are declared to be citizens of the United States as of February 25, 1927; and all persons born in those islands on or after February 25, 1927, and subject to the jurisdiction of the United States, are declared to be citizens of the United States at birth.

(June 27, 1952, ch. 477, title III, ch. 1, §306, 66 Stat. 237.)

## Sec. 307 Persons Living in and Born in Guam
**[8 U.S.C. 1407]**

**(a)** The following persons, and their children born after April 11, 1899, are declared to be citizens of the United States as of August 1, 1950, if they were residing on August 1, 1950, on the island of Guam or other territory over which the United States exercises rights of sovereignty:

(1) All inhabitants of the island of Guam on April 11, 1899, including those temporarily absent from the island on that date, who were Spanish subjects, who after that date continued

to reside in Guam or other territory over which the United States exercises sovereignty, and who have taken no affirmative steps to preserve or acquire foreign nationality; and

(2) All persons born in the island of Guam who resided in Guam on April 11, 1899, including those temporarily absent from the island on that date, who after that date continued to reside in Guam or other territory over which the United States exercises sovereignty, and who have taken no affirmative steps to preserve or acquire foreign nationality.

(b) All persons born in the island of Guam on or after April 11, 1899 (whether before or after August 1, 1950) subject to the jurisdiction of the United States, are hereby declared to be citizens of the United States: *Provided,* That in the case of any person born before August 1, 1950, he has taken no affirmative steps to preserve or acquire foreign nationality.

(c) Any person hereinbefore described who is a citizen or national of a country other than the United States and desires to retain his present political status shall have made, prior to August 1, 1952, a declaration under oath of such desire, said declaration to be in form and executed in the manner prescribed by regulations. From and after the making of such a declaration any such person shall be held not to be a national of the United States by virtue of this Act.

(June 27, 1952, ch. 477, title III, ch. 1, §307, 66 Stat. 237.)

### Sec. 308 Nationals but Not Citizens of the United States at Birth
### [8 U.S.C. 1408]

Unless otherwise provided in section 301 of this title, the following shall be nationals, but not citizens of the United States at birth:

(1) A person born in an outlying possession of the United States on or after the date of formal acquisition of such possession;

(2) A person born outside the United States and its outlying possessions of parents both of whom are nationals, but not citizens, of the United States, and have had a residence in the United States, or one of its outlying possessions prior to the birth of such person;

(3) A person of unknown parentage found in an outlying possession of the United States while under the age of five years, until shown, prior to his attaining the age of twenty-one years, not to have been born in such outlying possession; and

(4) A person born outside the United States and its outlying possessions of parents one of whom is an alien, and the other a national, but not a citizen, of the United States who, prior to the birth of such person, was physically present in the United States or its outlying possessions for a period or periods totaling not less than seven years in any continuous period of ten years—

(A) during which the national parent was not outside the United States or its outlying possessions for a continuous period of more than one year, and

(B) at least five years of which were after attaining the age of fourteen years.

The proviso of section 301(g) shall apply to the national parent under this paragraph in the same manner as it applies to the citizen parent under that section.

(June 27, 1952, ch. 477, title III, ch. 1, §308, 66 Stat. 238; as amended by P.L. 99-396 (8/27/86); P.L. 100-525 (10/24/88).)

### Sec. 309 Children Born Out of Wedlock
**[8 U.S.C. 1409]**

**(a)** The provisions of paragraphs (c), (d), (e), and (g) of section 301, and of paragraph (2) of section 308, shall apply as of the date of birth to a person born out of wedlock if—

(1) a blood relationship between the person and the father is established by clear and convincing evidence,

(2) the father had the nationality of the United States at the time of the person's birth,

(3) the father (unless deceased) has agreed in writing to provide financial support for the person until the person reaches the age of 18 years, and

(4) while the person is under the age of 18 years—

(A) the person is legitimated under the law of the person's residence or domicile,

(B) the father acknowledges paternity of the person in writing under oath, or

(C) the paternity of the person is established by adjudication of a competent court.

**(b)** Except as otherwise provided in section 405, the provisions of section 301(g) shall apply to a child born out of wedlock on or after January 13, 1941, and before December 24, 1952, as of the date of birth, if the paternity of such child is established at any time while such child is under the age of twenty-one years by legitimation.

**(c)** Notwithstanding the provision of subsection (a) of this section, a person born, after December 23, 1952, outside the United States and out of wedlock shall be held to have acquired at birth the nationality status of his mother, if the mother had the nationality of the United States at the time of such person's birth, and if the mother had previously been physically present in the United States or one of its outlying possessions for a continuous period of one year.

(June 27, 1952, ch. 477, title III, ch. 1, §309, 66 Stat. 238; as amended by P.L. 97-116 (12/29/81); P.L. 99-653 (11/14/86); P.L. 100-525 (10/24/88).)

## Chapter 2 — Nationality through Naturalization

### Sec. 310 Naturalization Authority
**[8 U.S.C. 1421]**

**(a) Authority in Attorney General.**— The sole authority to naturalize persons as citizens of the United States is conferred upon the Attorney General.

**(b) Court authority to administer oaths.**—

(1) *Jurisdiction.*— Subject to section 337(c)—

(A) *General jurisdiction.*— Except as provided in subparagraph (B), each applicant for naturalization may choose to have the oath of allegiance under section 337(a) administered by the Attorney General or by an eligible court described in paragraph (5). Each such eligible court shall have authority to administer such oath of allegiance to persons residing within the jurisdiction of the court.

(B) *Exclusive authority.*— An eligible court described in paragraph (5) that wishes to have exclusive authority to administer the oath of allegiance under section 337(a) to persons residing within the jurisdiction of the court during the period described in paragraph

(3)(A)(i) shall notify the Attorney General of such wish and, subject to this subsection, shall have such exclusive authority with respect to such persons during such period.

(2) *Information.*—

(A) *General information.*— In the case of a court exercising authority under paragraph (1), in accordance with procedures established by the Attorney General—

(i) the applicant for naturalization shall notify the Attorney General of the intent to be naturalized before the court, and

(ii) the Attorney General—

(I) shall forward to the court (not later than 10 days after the date of approval of an application for naturalization in the case of a court which has provided notice under paragraph (1)(B)) such information as may be necessary to administer the oath of allegiance under section 337(a), and

(II) shall promptly forward to the court a certificate of naturalization (prepared by the Attorney General).

(B) *Assignment of individuals in the case of exclusive authority.*— If an eligible court has provided notice under paragraph (1)(B), the Attorney General shall inform each person (residing within the jurisdiction of the court), at the time of the approval of the person's application for naturalization, of—

(i) the court's exclusive authority to administer the oath of allegiance under section 337(a) to such a person during the period specified in paragraph (3)(A)(i), and

(ii) the date or dates (if any) under paragraph (3)(B) on which the court has scheduled oath administration ceremonies.

If more than one eligible court in an area has provided notice under paragraph (1)(B), the Attorney General shall permit the person, at the time of the approval, to choose the court to which the information will be forwarded for administration of the oath of allegiance under this section.

(3) *Scope of exclusive authority.*—

(A) *Limited period and advance notice required.*— The exclusive authority of a court to administer the oath of allegiance under paragraph (1)(B) shall apply with respect to a person—

(i) only during the 45-day period beginning on the date on which the Attorney General certifies to the court that an applicant is eligible for naturalization, and

(ii) only if the court has notified the Attorney General, prior to the date of certification of eligibility, of the day or days (during such 45-day period) on which the court has scheduled oath administration ceremonies.

(B) *Authority of attorney general.*— Subject to subparagraph (C), the Attorney General shall not administer the oath of allegiance to a person under subsection (a) during the period in which exclusive authority to administer the oath of allegiance may be exercised by an eligible court under this subsection with respect to that person.

(C) *Waiver of exclusive authority.*— Notwithstanding the previous provisions of this paragraph, a court may waive exclusive authority to administer the oath of allegiance under section 337(a) to a person under this subsection if the Attorney General has not provided the court with the certification described in subparagraph (A)(i) within a reasonable time before the date scheduled by the court for oath administration ceremonies. Upon notification of a court's waiver of jurisdiction, the Attorney General shall promptly notify the applicant.

(4) *Issuance of certificates.*— The Attorney General shall provide for the issuance of certificates of naturalization at the time of administration of the oath of allegiance.

(5) *Eligible courts.*— For purposes of this section, the term "eligible court" means—

(A) a district court of the United States in any State, or

(B) any court of record in any State having a seal, a clerk, and jurisdiction in actions in law or equity, or law and equity, in which the amount in controversy is unlimited.

**(c) Judicial review.**— A person whose application for naturalization under this title is denied, after a hearing before an immigration officer under section 336(a), may seek review of such denial before the United States district court for the district in which such person resides in accordance with chapter 7 of title 5, United States Code. Such review shall be de novo, and the court shall make its own findings of fact and conclusions of law and shall, at the request of the petitioner, conduct a hearing de novo on the application.

**(d) Sole procedure.**— A person may only be naturalized as a citizen of the United States in the manner and under the conditions prescribed in this title and not otherwise.

(June 27, 1952, ch. 477, title III, ch. 2, §310, 66 Stat. 239; as amended by P.L. 85-508 (7/7/58); P.L. 86-3 (3/18/59); P.L. 87-301 (9/26/61); P.L. 100-525 (10/24/88); P.L. 101-649 (IMMACT90) (11/29/90), §401; P.L. 102-232 (MTINA) (12/12/91, *effective* 4/1/92), §102, §305; P.L. 103-416 (INTCA) (10/25/94, *effective* 4/1/95), §219.)

## Sec. 311 Eligibility for Naturalization
## [8 U.S.C. 1422]

The right of a person to become a naturalized citizen of the United States shall not be denied or abridged because of race or sex or because such person is married.

(June 27, 1952, ch. 477, title III, ch. 2, §311, 66 Stat. 239; as amended by P.L. 100-525 (10/24/88).)

## Sec. 312 Requirements as to Understanding the English Language, History, Principles, and Form of Government of the United States[190]
## [8 U.S.C. 1423]

**(a)** No person except as otherwise provided in this title shall hereafter be naturalized as a citizen of the United States upon his own application who cannot demonstrate—

(1) an understanding of the English language, including an ability to read, write, and speak words in ordinary usage in the English language: *Provided*, That the requirements of this paragraph relating to ability to read and write shall be met if the applicant can read or write simple words and phrases to the end that a reasonable test of his literacy shall be made and that no extraordinary or unreasonable conditions shall be imposed upon the applicant; and

(2) a knowledge and understanding of the fundamentals of the history, and of the principles and form of government, of the United States.

**(b)** (1) The requirements of subsection (a) shall not apply to any person who is unable because of

---

[190] *See* §114(d)(2) of P.L. 107-77, *reprinted in* Appendix M, for exceptions to INA §312 for certain 9/11 victims.

physical or developmental disability or mental impairment to comply therewith.

(2) The requirement of subsection (a)(1) shall not apply to any person who, on the date of the filing of the person's application for naturalization as provided in section 334, either—

(A) is over fifty years of age and has been living in the United States for periods totaling at least twenty years subsequent to a lawful admission for permanent residence, or

(B) is over fifty-five years of age and has been living in the United States for periods totaling at least fifteen years subsequent to a lawful admission for permanent residence.

(3) The Attorney General, pursuant to regulations, shall provide for special consideration, as determined by the Attorney General, concerning the requirement of subsection (a)(2) with respect to any person who, on the date of the filing of the person's application for naturalization as provided in section 334, is over sixty-five years of age and has been living in the United States for periods totaling at least twenty years subsequent to a lawful admission for permanent residence.

(June 27, 1952, ch. 477, title III, ch. 2, §312, 66 Stat. 239; as amended by P.L. 95-579 (11/2/78); P.L. 101-649 (IMMACT90) (11/29/90); P.L. 102-232 (MTINA) (12/12/91, *effective* 4/1/92); P.L. 103-416 (INTCA) (10/25/94, *effective* 4/1/95).)

## Sec. 313 Prohibition upon the Naturalization of Persons Opposed to Government or Law, or Who Favor Totalitarian Forms of Government
**[8 U.S.C. 1424]**

**(a)** Notwithstanding the provisions of section 405(b), no person shall hereafter be naturalized as a citizen of the United States—

(1) who advocates or teaches, or who is a member of or affiliated with any organization that advocates or teaches, opposition to all organized government; or

(2) who is a member of or affiliated with (A) the Communist Party of the United States; (B) any other totalitarian party of the United States; (C) the Communist Political Association; (D) the Communist or other totalitarian party of any State of the United States, of any foreign state, or of any political or geographical subdivision of any foreign state; (E) any section, subsidiary, branch, affiliate, or subdivision of any such association or party; or (F) the direct predecessors or successors of any such association or party, regardless of what name such group or organization may have used, may now bear, or may hereafter adopt, unless such alien establishes that he did not have knowledge or reason to believe at the time he became a member of or affiliated with such an organization (and did not thereafter and prior to the date upon which such organization was so registered or so required to be registered have such knowledge or reason to believe) that such organization was a Communist-front organization; or

(3) who, although not within any of the other provisions of this section, advocates the economic, international, and governmental doctrines of world communism or the establishment in the United States of a totalitarian dictatorship, or who is a member of or affiliated with any organization that advocates the economic, international, and governmental doctrines of world communism or the establishment in the United States of a totalitarian dictatorship, either through its own utterances or through any written or printed publications issued or published by or with the permission or consent of or under authority of such organizations or paid for by the funds of such organization; or

(4) who advocates or teaches or who is a member of or affiliated with any organization that advocates or teaches

(A) the overthrow by force or violence or other unconstitutional means of the Government of the United States or of all forms of law; or

(B) the duty, necessity, or propriety of the unlawful assaulting or killing of any officer or officers (either of specific individuals or of officers generally) of the Government of the United States or of any other organized government because of his or their official character; or

(C) the unlawful damage, injury, or destruction of property; or

(D) sabotage; or

(5) who writes or publishes or causes to be written or published, or who knowingly circulates, distributes, prints, or displays, or knowingly causes to be circulated, distributed, printed, published, or displayed or who knowingly has in his possession for the purpose of circulation, publication, distribution, or display, any written or printed matter, advocating or teaching opposition to all organized government, or advocating

(A) the overthrow by force, violence, or other unconstitutional means of the Government of the United States or of all forms of law; or

(B) the duty, necessity, or propriety of the unlawful assaulting or killing of any officer or officers (either of specific individuals or of officers generally) of the Government of the United States or of any other organized government, because of his or their official character; or

(C) the unlawful damage, injury, or destruction of property; or

(D) sabotage; or

(E) the economic, international, and governmental doctrines of world communism or the establishment in the United States of a totalitarian dictatorship; or

(6) who is a member of or affiliated with any organization, that writes, circulates, distributes, prints, publishes, or displays, or causes to be written, circulated, distributed, printed, published, or displayed, or that has in its possession for the purpose of circulation, distribution, publication, issue, or display, any written or printed matter of the character described in subparagraph (5).

**(b)** The provisions of this section or of any other section of this Act shall not be construed as declaring that any of the organizations referred to in this section or in any other section of this Act do not advocate the overthrow of the Government of the United States by force, violence, or other unconstitutional means.

**(c)** The provisions of this section shall be applicable to any applicant for naturalization who at any time within a period of ten years immediately preceding the filing of the application for naturalization or after such filing and before taking the final oath of citizenship is, or has been found to be within any of the classes enumerated within this section, notwithstanding that at the time the application is filed he may not be included within such classes.

**(d)** Any person who is within any of the classes described in subsection (a) solely because of past membership in, or past affiliation with, a party or organization may be naturalized without regard to the provisions of subsection (c) if such person establishes that such membership or affiliation is or was involuntary, or occurred and terminated prior to the attainment by such alien of the age of sixteen years, or that such membership or affiliation is or was by operation of law, or was for purposes of obtaining employment, food rations, or other essentials of living and where necessary for such purposes.

**(e)** A person may be naturalized under this title without regard to the prohibitions in subsections (a)(2) and (c) of this section if the person—

(1) is otherwise eligible for naturalization;

(2) is within the class described in subsection (a)(2) solely because of past membership in, or past affiliation with, a party or organization described in that subsection;

(3) does not fall within any other of the classes described in that subsection; and

(4) is determined by the Director of Central Intelligence, in consultation with the Secretary of Defense when Department of Defense activities are relevant to the determination, and with the concurrence of the Attorney General and the Secretary of Homeland Security, to have made a contribution to the national security or to the national intelligence mission of the United States.

(June 27, 1952, ch. 477, title III, ch. 2, §313, 66 Stat. 240; as amended by P.L. 100-525 (10/24/88); P.L. 101-649 (IMMACT90) (11/29/90); P.L. 102-232 (MTINA) (12/12/91, *effective* 4/1/92); P.L. 103-416 (INTCA) (10/25/94, *effective* 4/1/95); P.L. 106-120 (12/3/99), title III, §306 [adding (e)]; P.L. 108-177 (12/13/03), title III, §373 [revising (e)(4)].)

## Sec. 314 Ineligibility to Naturalization of Deserters from the Armed Forces
## [8 U.S.C. 1425]

A person who, at any time during which the United States has been or shall be at war, deserted or shall desert the military, air, or naval forces of the United States, or who, having been duly enrolled, departed, or shall depart from the jurisdiction of the district in which enrolled, or who, whether or not having been duly enrolled, went or shall go beyond the limits of the United States, with intent to avoid any draft into the military, air, or naval service, lawfully ordered, shall, upon conviction thereof by a court martial or a court of competent jurisdiction, be permanently ineligible to become a citizen of the United States; and such deserters and evaders shall be forever incapable of holding any office of trust or of profit under the United States, or of exercising any rights of citizens thereof.

(June 27, 1952, ch. 477, title III, ch. 2, §314, 66 Stat. 241.)

## Sec. 315 Citizenship Denied Alien Relieved of Service in Armed Forces Because of Alienage
## [8 U.S.C. 1426]

**(a) Permanent ineligibility.**— Notwithstanding the provisions of section 405(b) but subject to subsection (c), any alien who applies or has applied for exemption or discharge from training or service in the Armed Forces or in the National Security Training Corps of the United States on the ground that he is an alien, and is or was relieved or discharged from such training or service on such ground, shall be permanently ineligible to become a citizen of the United States.

**(b) Conclusiveness of records.**— The records of the Selective Service System or of the Department of Defense shall be conclusive as to whether an alien was relieved or discharged from such liability for training or service because he was an alien.

**(c) Service in Armed Forces of foreign country.**— An alien shall not be ineligible for citizenship under this section or otherwise because of an exemption from training or service in the Armed Forces of the United States pursuant to the exercise of rights under a treaty, if before the time of the exercise of such rights the alien served in the Armed Forces of a foreign country of which the alien was a national.

(June 27, 1952, ch. 477, title III, ch. 2, §315, 66 Stat. 242; as amended by P.L. 100-525 (10/24/88); P.L. 101-649 (IMMACT90) (11/29/90), §404.)

## Sec. 316 Requirements of Naturalization
## [8 U.S.C. 1427]

**(a) Residence.**— No person, except as otherwise provided in this title, shall be naturalized, unless such applicant,

(1) immediately preceding the date of filing his application for naturalization has resided continuously, after being lawfully admitted for permanent residence, within the United States for at least five years and during the five years immediately preceding the date of filing his application has been physically present therein for periods totaling at least half of that time, and who has resided within the State or within the district of the Service in the United States in which the applicant filed the application for at least three months,

(2) has resided continuously within the United States from the date of the application up to the time of admission to citizenship,

(3) during all the periods referred to in this subsection has been and still is a person of good moral character, attached to the principles of the Constitution of the United States, and well disposed to the good order and happiness of the United States.

**(b) Absences.**— Absence from the United States of more than six months but less than one year during the period for which continuous residence is required for admission to citizenship, immediately preceding the date of filing the application for naturalization, or during the period between the date of filing the application and the date of any hearing under section 336(a), shall break the continuity of such residence, unless the applicant shall establish to the satisfaction of the Attorney General that he did not in fact abandon his residence in the United States during such period.

Absence from the United States for a continuous period of one year or more during the period for which continuous residence is required for admission to citizenship (whether preceding or subsequent to the filing of the application for naturalization) shall break the continuity of such residence, except that in the case of a person who has been physically present and residing in the United States, after being lawfully admitted for permanent residence for an uninterrupted period of at least one year, and who thereafter, is employed by or under contract with the Government of the United States or an American institution of research recognized as such by the Attorney General, or is employed by an American firm or corporation engaged in whole or in part in the development of foreign trade and commerce of the United States, or a subsidiary thereof more than 50 per centum of whose stock is owned by an American firm or corporation, or is employed by a public international organization of which the United States is a member by treaty or statute and by which the alien was not employed until after being lawfully admitted for permanent residence, no period of absence from the United States shall break the continuity of residence if—

(1) prior to the beginning of such period of employment (whether such period begins before or after his departure from the United States), but prior to the expiration of one year of continuous absence from the United States, the person has established to the satisfaction of the Attorney General that his absence from the United States for such period is to be on behalf of such Government, or for the purpose of carrying on scientific research on behalf of such institution, or to be engaged in the development of such foreign trade and commerce or whose residence abroad is necessary to the protection of the property rights in such countries of such firm or corporation, or to be employed by a public international organization of which the United States is a member by treaty or statute and by which the alien was not employed until after being lawfully admitted for permanent residence; and

(2) such person proves to the satisfaction of the Attorney General that his absence from the United States for such period has been for such purpose.

The spouse and dependent unmarried sons and daughters who are members of the household of a person who qualifies for the benefits of this subsection shall also be entitled to such benefits during the period for which they were residing abroad as dependent members of the household of the person.

**(c) Physical presence.**— The granting of the benefits of subsection (b) of this section shall not relieve the applicant from the requirement of physical presence within the United States for the period specified in subsection (a) of this section, except in the case of those persons who are employed by, or under contract with, the Government of the United States. In the case of a person employed by or under contract with Central Intelligence Agency, the requirement in subsection (b) of an uninterrupted period of at least one year of physical presence in the United States may be complied with by such person at any time prior to filing an application for naturalization.

**(d) Moral character.**— No finding by the Attorney General that the applicant is not deportable shall be accepted as conclusive evidence of good moral character.

**(e) Determination.**— In determining whether the applicant has sustained the burden of establishing good moral character and the other qualifications for citizenship specified in subsection (a) of this section, the Attorney General shall not be limited to the applicant's conduct during the five years preceding the filing of the application, but may take into consideration as a basis for such determination the applicant's conduct and acts at any time prior to that period.

**(f) Persons making extraordinary contributions to national security.**—

(1) Whenever the Director of Central Intelligence, the Attorney General and the Commissioner of Immigration determine that an applicant otherwise eligible for naturalization has made an extraordinary contribution to the national security of the United States or to the conduct of United States intelligence activities, the applicant may be naturalized without regard to the residence and physical presence requirements of this section, or to the prohibitions of section 313 of this Act, and no residence within a particular State or district of the Service in the United States shall be required: *Provided*, That the applicant has continuously resided in the United States for at least one year prior to naturalization: *Provided further*, That the provisions of this subsection shall not apply to any alien described in clauses (i) through (v) of section 208(b)(2)(A) of this Act.

(2) An applicant for naturalization under this subsection may be administered the oath of allegiance under section 337(a) by any district court of the United States, without regard to the residence of the applicant. Proceedings under this subsection shall be conducted in a manner consistent with the protection of intelligence sources, methods and activities.

(3) The number of aliens naturalized pursuant to this subsection in any fiscal year shall not exceed five. The Director of Central Intelligence shall inform the Select Committee on Intelligence and the Committee on the Judiciary of the Senate and the Permanent Select Committee on Intelligence and the Committee on the Judiciary of the House of Representatives within a reasonable time prior to the filing of each application under the provisions of this subsection.

(June 27, 1952, ch. 477, title III, ch. 2, §316, 66 Stat. 242; as amended by P.L. 97-116 (12/29/81); P.L. 99-169 (12/4/85); P.L. 101-649 (11/29/90); P.L. 104-208, div. C, title III (9/30/96); P.L. 109-149 (12/30/05), §§518(a) [adding (g) to reduce the continuous residency requirement under (a) to 3 years for certain applicants], (b) [automatically repealing (g) on 1/1/06].)

## Sec. 317 Temporary Absence of Persons Performing Religious Duties
**[8 U.S.C. 1428]**

Any person who is authorized to perform the ministerial or priestly functions of a religious denomination having a bona fide organization within the United States, or any person who is engaged solely by a religious denomination or by an interdenominational mission organization having a bona fide organization within the United States as a missionary, brother, nun, or sister, who (1) has been lawfully admitted to the United States for permanent residence, (2) has at any time thereafter and before filing an application for naturalization been physically present and residing within the United States for an uninterrupted period of at least one year, and (3) has heretofore been or may hereafter be absent temporarily from the United States in connection with or for the purpose of performing the ministerial or priestly functions of such religious denomination, or serving as a missionary, brother, nun, or sister, shall be considered as being physically present and residing in the United States for the purpose of naturalization within the meaning of section 316(a), notwithstanding any such absence from the United States, if he shall in all other respects comply with the requirements of the naturalization law. Such person shall prove to the satisfaction of the Attorney General that his absence from the United States has been solely for the purpose of performing the ministerial or priestly functions of such religious denomination, or of serving as a missionary, brother, nun, or sister.

(June 27, 1952, ch. 477, title III, ch. 2, §317, 66 Stat. 243; as amended by P.L. 101-649 (IMMACT90) (11/29/90), §407.)

## Sec. 318 Prerequisite to Naturalization; Burden of Proof
**[8 U.S.C. 1429]**

Except as otherwise provided in this title, no person shall be naturalized unless he has been lawfully admitted to the United States for permanent residence in accordance with all applicable provisions of this Act. The burden of proof shall be upon such person to show that he entered the United States lawfully, and the time, place, and manner of such entry into the United States, but in presenting such proof he shall be entitled to the production of his immigrant visa, if any, or of other entry document, if any, and of any other documents and records, not considered by the Attorney General to be confidential, pertaining to such entry, in the custody of the Service. Notwithstanding the provisions of section 405(b), and except as provided in sections 328 and 329 no person shall be naturalized against whom there is outstanding a final finding of deportability pursuant to a warrant of arrest issued under the provisions of this or any other Act; and no application for naturalization shall be considered by the Attorney General if there is pending against the applicant a removal proceeding pursuant to a warrant of arrest issued under the provisions of this or any other Act: *Provided*, That the findings of the Attorney General in terminating removal proceedings or in canceling the removal of an alien pursuant to the provisions of this Act, shall not be deemed binding in any way upon the Attorney General with respect to the question of whether such person has established his eligibility for naturalization as required by this title.

(June 27, 1952, ch. 477, title III, ch. 2, §318, 66 Stat. 244; as amended by P.L. 90-633 (10/24/68), §4; P.L. 101-649 (11/29/90), title IV, §407; P.L. 104-208 (IIRAIRA) (9/30/96), div. C, title III, §308 [revising §318].)

## Sec. 319 Married Persons and Employees of Certain Nonprofit Organizations
**[8 U.S.C. 1430]**

**(a)** Any person whose spouse is a citizen of the United States, or any person who obtained sttus as a lawful permanent resident by reason of his or her status as a spouse or child of a United States citizen who battered him or her or subjected him or her to extreme cruelty, may be naturalized upon compliance with all the requirements of this title except the provisions of paragraph (1) of section 316(a) if such person immediately preceding the date of filing his application for naturalization has resided continuously, after being lawfully admitted for permanent residence, within the United States for at least three years, and during the three years immediately preceding the date of filing his application has been living in marital union with the citizen spouse, (except in the case of a person who has been battered or subjected to extreme cruelty by a United States citizen spouse or parent) who has been a United States citizen during all of such period, and has been physically present in the United States for periods totaling at least half of that time and has resided within the State or the district of the Service in the United States in which the applicant filed his application for at least three months.

**(b)** Any person,

(1) whose spouse is

(A) a citizen of the United States,

(B) in the employment of the Government of the United States, or of an American institution of research recognized as such by the Attorney General, or of an American firm or corporation engaged in whole or in part in the development of foreign trade and commerce of the United States, or a subsidiary thereof, or of a public international organization in which the United States participates by treaty or statute, or is authorized to perform the ministerial or priestly functions of a religious denomination having a bona fide organization within the United States, or is engaged solely as a missionary by a religious denomination or by an interdenominational mission organization having a bona fide organization within the United States, and

(C) regularly stationed abroad in such employment, and

(2) who is in the United States at the time of naturalization, and

(3) who declares before the Attorney General in good faith an intention to take up residence within the United States immediately upon the termination of such employment abroad of the citizen spouse,

may be naturalized upon compliance with all the requirements of the naturalization laws, except that no prior residence or specified period of physical presence within the United States or within a State or a district of the Service in the United States or proof thereof shall be required.

**(c)** Any person who

(1) is employed by a bona fide United States incorporated nonprofit organization which is principally engaged in conducting abroad through communications media the dissemination of information which significantly promotes United States interests abroad and which is recognized as such by the Attorney General, and

(2) has been so employed continuously for a period of not less than five years after a lawful admission for permanent residence, and

(3) who files his application for naturalization while so employed or within six months following the termination thereof, and

(4) who is in the United States at the time of naturalization, and

(5) who declares before the Attorney General in good faith an intention to take up residence within the United States immediately upon termination of such employment,

may be naturalized upon compliance with all the requirements of this title except that no prior residence or specified period of physical presence within the United States or any State or district of the Service in the United States, or proof thereof, shall be required.

(d)[191] Any person who is the surviving spouse, child, or parent of a United States citizen, whose citizen spouse, parent, or child dies during a period of honorable service in an active duty status in the Armed Forces of the United States and who, in the case of a surviving spouse, was living in marital union with the citizen spouse at the time of his death, may be naturalized upon compliance with all the requirements of this title except that no prior residence or specified physical presence within the United States, or within a State or a district of the Service in the United States shall be required. For purposes of this subsection, the terms "United States citizen" and "citizen spouse" include a person granted posthumous citizenship under section 329A.

(e)[192] (1) In the case of a person lawfully admitted for permanent residence in the United States who is the spouse of a member of the Armed Forces of the United States, is authorized to accompany such member and reside abroad with the member pursuant to the member's official orders, and is so accompanying and residing with the member in marital union, such residence and physical presence abroad shall be treated, for purposes of subsection (a) and section 316(a), as residence and physical presence in—

> (A) the United States; and

> (B) any State or district of the Department of Homeland Security in the United States.

(2) Notwithstanding any other provision of law, a spouse described in paragraph (1) shall be eligible for naturalization proceedings overseas pursuant to section 1701(d) of the National Defense Authorization Act for Fiscal Year 2004 (Public Law 108-136; 8 U.S.C. 1443a).

(June 27, 1952, ch. 477, title III, ch. 2, §319, 66 Stat. 244; as amended by P.L. 85-697 (8/20/58); P.L. 90-215 (12/18/67); P.L. 90-369 (6/29/68); P.L. 101-649 (IMMACT90) (11/29/90); P.L. 106-386 (10/28/00), div. B, title V, §1503(e); P.L. 108-136 (11/24/03), *effective* 10/1/04), div. A, title XVII, §1703(f)(1) [revising (d)]; P.L. 110-181 (1/28/08) §674 [adding (e)].)

## Sec. 320 Children Born Outside the United States and Residing Permanently in the United States; Conditions Under Which Citizenship Automatically Acquired
## [8 U.S.C. 1431]

(a) A child born outside of the United States automatically becomes a citizen of the United States when all of the following conditions have been fulfilled:

(1) At least one parent of the child is a citizen of the United States, whether by birth or naturalization.

(2) The child is under the age of eighteen years.

(3) The child is residing in the United States in the legal and physical custody of the citizen parent pursuant to a lawful admission for permanent residence.

(b) Subsection (a) shall apply to a child adopted by a United States citizen parent if the child satisfies the requirements applicable to adopted children under section 101(b)(1).

(June 27, 1952, ch. 477, title III, ch. 2, §320, 66 Stat. 245; as amended by P.L. 95-417 (10/5/78); P.L. 97-116 (12/29/81); P.L. 99-653 (11/14/86); P.L. 100-525 (10/24/88); P.L. 106-395 (10/30/00), §101.)

---

[191] *See* P.L. 108-136 (11/24/2003), §1703(f), applicable to persons "granted posthumous citizenship under §329A of the [INA] due to death on or after 9/11/01." Other technical and conforming changes to subsection (d) made by P.L. 108-136, §1703(h), *retroactively effective* 9/11/01.

[192] Subsection (e) applies to any application for naturalization or issuance of a certificate of citizenship pending on or after 1/28/08. P.L. 110-181, §674(d).

Sec. 321 [Repealed. P.L. 106-395 (10/30/2000), title I, §103(a).]

### Sec. 322 Children Born and Residing Outside the United States; Conditions for Acquiring Certificate of Citizenship[193]
### [8 U.S.C. 1433]

**(a) In general.**— A parent who is a citizen of the United States (or, if the citizen parent has died during the preceding 5 years, a citizen grandparent or citizen legal guardian) may apply for naturalization on behalf of a child born outside of the United States who has not acquired citizenship automatically under section 320. The Attorney General shall issue a certificate of citizenship to such applicant upon proof, to the satisfaction of the Attorney General, that the following conditions have been fulfilled:

(1) At least one parent (or, at the time of his or her death, was) is[194] a citizen of the United States, whether by birth or naturalization.

(2) The United States citizen parent—

(A) has (or, at the time of his or her death, had) been physically present in the United States or its outlying possessions for a period or periods totaling not less than five years, at least two of which were after attaining the age of fourteen years; or

(B) has (or, at the time of his or her death, had) a citizen parent who has been physically present in the United States or its outlying possessions for a period or periods totaling not less than five years, at least two of which were after attaining the age of fourteen years.

(3) The child is under the age of eighteen years.

(4) The child is residing outside of the United States in the legal and physical custody of the applicant (or, if the citizen parent is deceased, an individual who does not object to the application).

(5) The child is temporarily present in the United States pursuant to a lawful admission, and is maintaining such lawful status.

**(b) Attainment of citizenship status; receipt of certificate.**— Upon approval of the application (which may be filed from abroad) and, except as provided in the last sentence of section 337(a), upon taking and subscribing before an officer of the Service within the United States to the oath of allegiance required by this Act of an applicant for naturalization, the child shall become a citizen of the United States and shall be furnished by the Attorney General with a certificate of citizenship.

**(c) Adopted children.**— Subsections (a) and (b) shall apply to a child adopted by a United States citizen parent if the child satisfies the requirements applicable to adopted children under section 101(b)(1).

**(d)**[195] In the case of a child of a member of the Armed Forces of the United States who is authorized to accompany such member and reside abroad with the member pursuant to the member's official orders, and is so accompanying and residing with the member—

(1) any period of time during which the member of the Armed Forces is residing abroad pursuant to official orders shall be treated, for purposes of subsection (a)(2)(A), as physical

---

[193] *See* §114(i) of P.L. 107-77, *reprinted in* Appendix L, for exceptions to INA §322 for certain 9/11 victims.

[194] *Sic.* Parenthetical provision probably should follow rather than precede "is."

[195] Subsection (d) applies to any application for naturalization or issuance of a certificate of citizenship pending on or after 1/28/08. P.L. 110-181, §674(d).

presence in the United States;

(2) subsection (a)(5) shall not apply; and

(3) the oath of allegiance described in subsection (b) may be subscribed to abroad pursuant to section 1701(d) of the National Defense Authorization Act for Fiscal Year 2004 (Public Law 108-136; 8 U.S.C. 1443a).

(June 27, 1952, ch. 477, title III, ch. 2, §322, 66 Stat. 246; as amended by P.L. 95-417 (10/5/78); P.L. 97-116 (12/29/81); P.L. 99-653 (11/14/86); P.L. 100-525 (10/24/88); P.L. 101-649 (IMMACT90) (11/29/90); P.L. 102-232 (MTINA) (12/12/91, *effective* 4/1/92); P.L. 103-416 (INTCA) (10/25/94, *effective* 4/1/95); P.L. 106-139 (12/7/99), §1(b)(2) [revising (a)(4)]; P.L. 106-395 (CCA) (10/30/00, *effective* 2/27/01), title I, §102(a); P.L. 107-273 (11/2/02), div. C, title I, §11030B [revising (a)]; P.L. 110-181 (1/28/08) §674 [adding (d)].)

**Sec. 323** [Repealed. P.L. 95-417 (10/5/78), §7.]

## Sec. 324 Former Citizens Regaining Citizenship
**[8 U.S.C. 1435]**

**(a) Requirements.—** Any person formerly a citizen of the United States who (1) prior to September 22, 1922, lost United States citizenship by marriage to an alien, or by the loss of United States citizenship of such person's spouse, or (2) on or after September 22, 1922, lost United States citizenship by marriage to an alien ineligible to citizenship, may if no other nationality was acquired by an affirmative act of such person other than by marriage be naturalized upon compliance with all requirements of this title, except—

(1) no period of residence or specified period of physical presence within the United States or within the State or district of the Service in the United States where the application is filed shall be required; and

(2) the application need not set forth that it is the intention of the applicant to reside permanently within the United States.

Such person, or any person who was naturalized in accordance with the provisions of section 317(a) of the Nationality Act of 1940, shall have, from and after her naturalization, the status of a native-born or naturalized citizen of the United States, whichever status existed in the case of such person prior to the loss of citizenship: *Provided*, That nothing contained herein or in any other provision of law shall be construed as conferring United States citizenship retroactively upon such person, or upon any person who was naturalized in accordance with the provisions of section 317(a) of the Nationality Act of 1940, during any period in which such person was not a citizen.

**(b) Additional requirements.—** No person who is otherwise eligible for naturalization in accordance with the provisions of subsection (a) of this section shall be naturalized unless such person shall establish to the satisfaction of the Attorney General that she has been a person of good moral character, attached to the principles of the Constitution of the United States, and well disposed to the good order and happiness of the United States for a period of not less than five years immediately preceding the date of filing an application for naturalization and up to the time of admission to citizenship, and, unless she has resided continuously in the United States since the date of her marriage, has been lawfully admitted for permanent residence prior to filing her application for naturalization.

**(c) Oath of allegiance.—**

(1) A woman who was a citizen of the United States at birth and

(A) who has or is believed to have lost her United States citizenship solely by reason of her marriage prior to September 22, 1922, to an alien, or by her marriage on or after such date to an alien ineligible to citizenship,

(B) whose marriage to such alien shall have terminated subsequent to January 12, 1941, and

(C) who has not acquired by an affirmative act other than by marriage any other nationality,

shall, from and after taking the oath of allegiance required by section 337 of this title, be a citizen of the United States and have the status of a citizen of the United States by birth, without filing an application for naturalization, and notwithstanding any of the other provisions of this title except the provisions of section 313: *Provided*, That nothing contained herein or in any other provision of law shall be construed as conferring United States citizenship retroactively upon such person, or upon any person who was naturalized in accordance with the provisions of section 317(b) of the Nationality Act of 1940, during any period in which such person was not a citizen.

(2) Such oath of allegiance may be taken abroad before a diplomatic or consular officer of the United States, or in the United States before the Attorney General or the judge or clerk of a court described in section 310(b).

(3) Such oath of allegiance shall be entered in the records of the appropriate embassy, legation, consulate, court, or the Attorney General, and, upon demand, a certified copy of the proceedings, including a copy of the oath administered, under the seal of the embassy, legation, consulate, court, or the Attorney General, shall be delivered to such woman at a cost not exceeding $5, which certified copy shall be evidence of the facts stated therein before any court of record or judicial tribunal and in any department or agency of the Government of the United States.

**(d) Persons losing citizenship for failure to meet physical presence retention requirement.—**

(1) A person who was a citizen of the United States at birth and lost such citizenship for failure to meet the physical presence retention requirements under section 301(b) (as in effect before October 10, 1978), shall, from and after taking the oath of allegiance required by section 337 be a citizen of the United States and have status of citizen of the United States by birth, without filing an application for naturalization, and notwithstanding any of the other provisions of this title except the provisions of section 313. Nothing in this subsection or any other provision of law shall be construed as conferring United States citizenship retroactively upon such person during any period in which such person was not a citizen.

(2) The provisions of paragraphs (2) and (3) of subsection (c) shall apply to a person regaining citizenship under paragraph (1) in the same manner as they apply under subsection (c)(1).

(June 27, 1952, ch. 477, title III, ch. 2, §324, 66 Stat. 246; as amended by P.L. 100-525 (10/24/88); P.L. 101-649 (IMMACT90) (11/29/90), §407; P.L. 103-416 (10/25/94), §103.)

## Sec. 325 Nationals but Not Citizens; Residence within Outlying Possessions
## [8 U.S.C. 1436]

A person not a citizen who owes permanent allegiance to the United States, and who is otherwise qualified, may, if he becomes a resident of any State, be naturalized upon compliance with the applicable requirements of this title, except that in applications for naturalization filed under the provisions of this section residence and physical presence within the United States within the meaning of this title shall include residence and physical presence within any of the outlying possessions of the United States.

(June 27, 1952, ch. 477, title III, ch. 2, §325, 66 Stat. 248; as amended by P.L. 101-649 (IMMACT90) (11/29/90), §407.)

### Sec. 326 Resident Philippine Citizens Excepted from Certain Requirements
### [8 U.S.C. 1437]

Any person who (1) was a citizen of the Commonwealth of the Philippines on July 2, 1946, (2) entered the United States prior to May 1, 1934, and (3) has, since such entry, resided continuously in the United States shall be regarded as having been lawfully admitted to the United States for permanent residence for the purpose of applying for naturalization under this title.

(June 27, 1952, ch. 477, title III, ch. 2, §326, 66 Stat. 248; as amended by P.L. 101-649 (IMMACT90) (11/29/90), §407.)

### Sec. 327 Former Citizens Losing Citizenship by Entering Armed Forces of Foreign Countries during World War II
### [8 U.S.C. 1438]

**(a) Requirements; oath; certified copies of oath.**— Any person who, (1) during World War II and while a citizen of the United States, served in the military, air, or naval forces of any country at war with a country with which the United States was at war after December 7, 1941, and before September 2, 1945, and (2) has lost United States citizenship by reason of entering or serving in such forces, or taking an oath or obligation for the purpose of entering such forces, may, upon compliance with all the provisions of title III, of this Act, except section 316(a), and except as otherwise provided in subsection (b), be naturalized by taking before the Attorney General or before a court described in section 310(b) the oath required by section 337 of this title. Certified copies of such oath shall be sent by such court to the Department of State and to the Department of Justice and by the Attorney General to the Secretary of State.

**(b) Exceptions.**— No person shall be naturalized under subsection (a) of this section unless he—

(1) is, and has been for a period of at least five years immediately preceding taking the oath required in subsection (a), a person of good moral character, attached to the principles of the Constitution of the United States and well disposed to the good order and happiness of the United States; and

(2) has been lawfully admitted to the United States for permanent residence and intends to reside permanently in the United States.

**(c) Status.**— Any person naturalized in accordance with the provisions of this section, or any person who was naturalized in accordance with the provisions of section 323 of the Nationality Act of 1940, shall have, from and after such naturalization, the status of a native-born, or naturalized, citizen of the United States, whichever status existed in the case of such person prior to the loss of citizenship: *Provided,* That nothing contained herein, or in any other provision of law, shall be construed as conferring United States citizenship retroactively upon any such person during any period in which such person was not a citizen.

**(d) Span of World War II.**— For the purposes of this section, World War II shall be deemed to have begun on September 1, 1939, and to have terminated on September 2, 1945.

**(e) Inapplicability to certain persons.**— This section shall not apply to any person who during World War II served in the armed forces of a country while such country was at war with the United States.

(June 27, 1952, ch. 477, title III, ch. 2, §327, 66 Stat. 248; as amended by P.L. 101-649 (IMMACT90) (11/29/90), §407.)

## Sec. 328 Naturalization through Service in the Armed Forces
[8 U.S.C. 1439]

**(a) Requirements.**— A person who has served honorably at any time in the Armed Forces of the United States for a period or periods aggregating one year, and who, if separated from such service, was never separated except under honorable conditions, may be naturalized without having resided, continuously immediately preceding the date of filing such person's application, in the United States for at least five years, and in the State or district of the Service in the United States in which the application for naturalization is filed for at least three months, and without having been physically present in the United States for any specified period, if such application is filed while the applicant is still in the service or within six months after the termination of such service.

**(b) Exceptions.**— A person filing an application under subsection (a) of this section shall comply in all other respects with the requirements of this title, except that—

(1) no residence within a State or district of the Service in the United States shall be required;

(2) notwithstanding section 318 insofar as it relates to deportability, such applicant may be naturalized immediately if the applicant be then actually in the Armed Forces of the United States, and if prior to the filing of the application, the applicant shall have appeared before and been examined by a representative of the Service;

(3) the applicant shall furnish to the Secretary of Homeland Security, prior to any final hearing upon his application, a certified statement from the proper executive department for each period of his service upon which he relies for the benefits of this section, clearly showing that such service was honorable and that no discharges from service, including periods of service not relied upon by him for the benefits of this section, were other than honorable (the certificate or certificates herein provided for shall be conclusive evidence of such service and discharge); and

(4) notwithstanding any other provision of law, no fee shall be charged or collected from the applicant for filing the application, or for the issuance of a certificate of naturalization upon being granted citizenship, and no clerk of any State court shall charge or collect any fee for such services unless the laws of the State require such charge to be made, in which case nothing more than the portion of the fee required to be paid to the State shall be charged or collected.

**(c) Periods when not in service.**— In the case such applicant's service was not continuous, the applicant's residence in the United States and State or district of the Service in the United States, good moral character, attachment to the principles of the Constitution of the United States, and favorable disposition toward the good order and happiness of the United States, during any period within five years immediately preceding the date of filing such application between the periods of applicant's service in the Armed Forces, shall be alleged in the application filed under the provisions of subsection (a) of this section, and proved at any hearing thereon. Such allegation and proof shall also be made as to any period between the termination of applicant's service and the filing of the application for naturalization.

**(d) Residence requirements.**— The applicant shall comply with the requirements of section 316(a) of this title, if the termination of such service has been more than six months preceding the date of filing the application for naturalization, except that such service within five years immediately preceding the date of filing such application shall be considered as residence and physical presence within the United States.

**(e) Moral character.**— Any such period or periods of service under honorable conditions, and good moral character, attachment to the principles of the Constitution of the United States, and favorable disposition toward the good order and happiness of the United States, during such service, shall be proved by duly authenticated copies of the records of the executive departments having custody of the records of such service, and such authenticated copies of records shall be accepted in lieu of compliance with the provisions of section 316(a).

**(f) Revocation.**—[196] Citizenship granted pursuant to this section may be revoked in accordance with section 340 if the person is separated from the Armed Forces under other than honorable conditions before the person has served honorably for a period or periods aggregating five years. Such ground for revocation shall be in addition to any other provided by law, including the grounds described in section 340. The fact that the naturalized person was separated from the service under other than honorable conditions shall be proved by a duly authenticated certification from the executive department under which the person was serving at the time of separation. Any period or periods of service shall be proved by duly authenticated copies of the records of the executive departments having custody of the records of such service.

**(g)** Not later than 6 months after receiving an application for naturalization filed by a current member of the Armed Forces under subsection (a), section 329(a), or section 329A, by the spouse of such member under section 319(b), or by a surviving spouse or child under section 319(d), United States Citizenship and Immigration Services shall—

(1) process and adjudicate the application, including completing all required background checks to the satisfaction of the Secretary of Homeland Security; or

(2) provide the applicant with—

(A) an explanation for its inability to meet the processing and adjudication deadline under this subsection; and

(B) an estimate of the date by which the application will be processed and adjudicated.

**(h)** The Director of United States Citizenship and Immigration Services shall submit an annual report to the Subcommittee on Immigration, Border Security, and Refugees and the Subcommittee on Homeland Security of the Senate and the Subcommittee on Immigration, Citizenship, Refugees, Border Security, and International Law and the Subcommittee on Homeland Security of the House of Representatives that identifies every application filed under subsection (a), subsection (b) or (d) of section 319, section 329(a), or section 329A that is not processed and adjudicated within 1 year after it was filed due to delays in conducting required background checks.

(June 27, 1952, ch. 477, title III, ch. 2, §328, 66 Stat. 249; as amended by P.L. 90-633 (10/24/68); P.L. 97-116 (12/29/81); P.L. 101-649 (IMMACT90) (11/29/90); P.L. 102-232 (MTINA) (12/12/91, *effective* 4/1/92); P.L. 108-136 (11/24/03, *effective* 10/1/04), div. A, title XVII, §1701(a) [revising (a), (b)(3); adding (b)(4), (f)]; P.L. 110-382 (10/9/08) [adding (g)–(h)].)

---

[196] *See* §1701(c) of the National Defense Authorization Act, P.L. 108-136 (11/24/03). Sec. 1701(c)(2) of the Act specifically states that the amendment applies to citizenship granted on or after the date of the enactment of the Act (11/24/03); *but see* §1705(a) of the Act (*reprinted in* Appendix M, *infra*), making the Act's effective date retroactive to 9/11/01.

## Sec. 329 Naturalization through Active-Duty Service in the Armed Forces during World War I, World War II, the Korean Hostilities, the Vietnam Hostilities, or in other Periods of Military Hostilities
[8 U.S.C. 1440]

(a) **Requirements.**— Any person who, while an alien or a noncitizen national of the United States, has served honorably as a member of the Selected Reserve of the Ready Reserve or in an active-duty status in the military, air, or naval forces of the United States during either World War I or during a period beginning September 1, 1939, and ending December 31, 1946, or during a period beginning June 25, 1950, and ending July 1, 1955, or during a period beginning February 28, 1961, and ending on a date designated by the President by Executive order as of the date of termination of the Vietnam hostilities, or thereafter during any other period which the President by Executive order shall designate as a period in which Armed Forces of the United States are or were engaged in military operations involving armed conflict with a hostile foreign force, and who, if separated from such service, was separated under honorable conditions, may be naturalized as provided in this section if

(1) at the time of enlistment, reenlistment, extension of enlistment, or induction such person shall have been in the United States, the Canal Zone, American Samoa, or Swains Island, or on board a public vessel owned or operated by the United States for noncommercial service, whether or not he has been lawfully admitted to the United States for permanent residence, or

(2) at any time subsequent to enlistment or induction such person shall have been lawfully admitted to the United States for permanent residence.

The executive department under which such person served shall determine whether persons have served honorably in an active-duty status, and whether separation from such service was under honorable conditions: *Provided, however,* That no person who is or has been separated from such service on account of alienage, or who was a conscientious objector who performed no military, air, or naval duty whatever or refused to wear the uniform, shall be regarded as having served honorably or having been separated under honorable conditions for the purposes of this section. No period of service in the Armed Forces shall be made the basis of an application for naturalization under this section if the applicant has previously been naturalized on the basis of the same period of service.

(b) **Exceptions.**— A person filing an application under subsection (a) of this section shall comply in all other respects with the requirements of this title, except that—

(1) he may be naturalized regardless of age, and notwithstanding the provisions of section 318 as they relate to deportability and the provisions of section 331;

(2) no period of residence or specified period of physical presence within the United States or any State or district of the Service in the United States shall be required; and

(3) service in the military, air, or naval forces of the United States shall be proved by a duly authenticated certification from the executive department under which the applicant served or is serving, which shall state whether the applicant served honorably in an active-duty status during either World War I or during a period beginning September 1, 1939, and ending December 31, 1946, or during a period beginning June 25, 1950, and ending July 1, 1955, or during a period beginning February 28, 1961, and ending on a date designated by the President by Executive order as the date of termination of the Vietnam hostilities, or thereafter during any other period which the President by Executive order shall designate as a period in which Armed Forces of

the United States are or were engaged in military operations involving armed conflict with a hostile foreign force, and was separated from such service under honorable conditions; and

(4) notwithstanding any other provision of law, no fee shall be charged or collected from the applicant for filing a petition for naturalization or for the issuance of a certificate of naturalization upon citizenship being granted to the applicant, and no clerk of any State court shall charge or collect any fee for such services unless the laws of the State require such charge to be made, in which case nothing more than the portion of the fee required to be paid to the State shall be charged or collected.

(c)[197] **Revocation.**— Citizenship granted pursuant to this section may be revoked in accordance with section 340 if the person is separated from the Armed Forces under other than honorable conditions before the person has served honorably for a period or periods aggregating five years. Such ground for revocation shall be in addition to any other provided by law, including the grounds described in section 340. The fact that the naturalized person was separated from the service under other than honorable conditions shall be proved by a duly authenticated certification from the executive department under which the person was serving at the time of separation. Any period or periods of service shall be proved by duly authenticated copies of the records of the executive departments having custody of the records of such service.

(June 27, 1952, ch. 477, title III, ch. 2, §329, 66 Stat. 250; as amended by P.L. 87-301 (9/26/61); P.L. 90-633 (10/24/68); P.L. 97-116 (12/29/81); P.L. 100-525 (10/24/88); P.L. 101-649 (IMMACT90) (11/29/90); P.L. 102-232 (MTINA) (12/12/91, *effective* 4/1/92); P.L. 105-85 (11/18/97), div. A, title X, §1080(a) [revising (a)]; P.L. 108-136 (11/24/03, *retroactively effective* 9/11/01), div. A, title XVII, §1701(b)(2) [revising (c)], §1702 [revising (a)].)

## Sec. 329A Posthumous Citizenship through Death while on Active-Duty Service in Armed Forces during World War I, World War II, the Korean Hostilities, the Vietnam Hostilities, or in other Periods of Military Hostilities
[8 U.S.C. 1440-1]

(a) **Permitting granting of posthumous citizenship.**— Notwithstanding any other provision of this title, the Secretary of Homeland Security shall provide, in accordance with this section, for the granting of posthumous citizenship at the time of death to a person described in subsection (b) if the Secretary of Homeland Security approves an application for that posthumous citizenship under subsection (c).

(b) **Noncitizens eligible for posthumous citizenship.**— A person referred to in subsection (a) is a person who, while an alien or a noncitizen national of the United States—

(1) served honorably in an active-duty status in the military, air, or naval forces of the United States during any period described in the first sentence of section 329(a),

(2) died as a result of injury or disease incurred in or aggravated by that service, and

(3) satisfied the requirements of clause (1) or (2) of the first sentence of section 329(a).

The executive department under which the person so served shall determine whether the person satisfied the requirements of paragraphs (1) and (2).

(c) **Requests for posthumous citizenship.**—

(1) *In general.*— A request for the granting of posthumous citizenship to a person described in subsection (b) may be filed on behalf of that person—

---

[197] *See* note 196, *supra*.

(A) upon locating the next-of-kin, and if so requested by the next-of-kin, by the Secretary of Defense or the Secretary's designee with the Bureau of Citizenship and Immigration Services in the Department of Homeland Security immediately upon the death of that person; or

(B) by the next-of-kin.

(2) *Approval.*— The Director of the Bureau of Citizenship and Immigration Services shall approve a request for posthumous citizenship filed by the next-of-kin in accordance with paragraph (1)(B) if—

(A) the request is filed not later than 2 years after—

(i) the date of enactment of this section [Nov. 24, 2003]; or

(ii) the date of the person's death;

whichever date is later;

(B) the request is accompanied by a duly authenticated certificate from the executive department under which the person served which states that the person satisfied the requirements of paragraphs (1) and (2) of subsection (b); and

(C) the Director finds that the person satisfied the requirement of subsection (b)(3).

**(d) Documentation of posthumous citizenship.**— If the Director of the Bureau of Citizenship and Immigration Services approves the request referred to in subsection (c), the Director shall send to the next-of-kin of the person who is granted citizenship, a suitable document which states that the United States considers the person to have been a citizen of the United States at the time of the person's death.

(June 27, 1952, ch. 477, title III, ch. 2, §329A, as added by P.L. 101-249 (3/6/90); as amended by P.L. 107-273 (11/2/02), div. C, title I, §11030(b) [revising (c)(1)(A)]; P.L. 108-136 (11/24/03, *retroactively effective* 9/11/01), div. A, title XVII, §1703(g) [removing (e)], §1704 [revising (c)–(d)].)

## Sec. 330 Constructive Residence Through Service on Certain United States Vessels
## [8 U.S.C. 1441]

Any periods of time during all of which a person who was previously lawfully admitted for permanent residence has served honorably or with good conduct, in any capacity other than as a member of the Armed Forces of the United States, (A) on board a vessel operated by the United States, or an agency thereof, the full legal and equitable title to which is in the United States; or (B) on board a vessel whose home port is in the United States, and (i) which is registered under the laws of the United States, or (ii) the full legal and equitable title to which is in a citizen of the United States, or a corporation organized under the laws of any of the several States of the United States, shall be deemed residence and physical presence within the United States within the meaning of section 316(a) of this title, if such service occurred within five years immediately preceding the date such person shall file an application for naturalization. Service on vessels described in clause (A) of this section shall be proved by duly authenticated copies of the records of the executive departments or agency having custody of the records of such service. Service on vessels described in clause (B) of this section may be proved by certificates from the masters of such vessels.

(June 27, 1952, ch. 477, title III, ch. 2, §330, 66 Stat. 251; as amended by P.L. 100-525 (10/24/88); P.L. 101-649 (IMMACT90) (11/29/90), §407; P.L. 102-232 (MTINA) (12/12/91, *effective* 4/1/92), §305.)

## Sec. 331 Alien Enemies
**[8 U.S.C. 1442]**

**(a) Naturalization under specified conditions.**— An alien who is a native, citizen, subject, or denizen of any country, state, or sovereignty with which the United States is at war may, after his loyalty has been fully established upon investigation by the Attorney General, be naturalized as a citizen of the United States if such alien's application for naturalization shall be pending at the beginning of the state of war and the applicant is otherwise entitled to admission to citizenship.

**(b) Procedure.**— An alien embraced within this section shall not have his application for naturalization considered or heard except after 90 days' notice to the Attorney General to be considered at the examination or hearing, and the Attorney General's objection to such consideration shall cause the application to be continued from time to time for so long as the Attorney General may require.

**(c) Exceptions from classification.**— The Attorney General may, in his discretion, upon investigation fully establishing the loyalty of any alien enemy who did not have an application for naturalization pending at the beginning of the state of war, except such alien enemy from the classification of alien enemy for the purposes of this title, and thereupon such alien shall have the privilege of filing an application for naturalization.

**(d) Effect of cessation of hostilities.**— An alien who is a native, citizen, subject, or denizen of any country, state, or sovereignty with which the United States is at war shall cease to be an alien enemy within the meaning of this section upon the determination by proclamation of the President, or by concurrent resolution of the Congress, that hostilities between the United States and such country, state, or sovereignty have ended.

**(e) Apprehension and removal.**— Nothing contained herein shall be taken or construed to interfere with or prevent the apprehension and removal, consistent with law, of any alien enemy at any time prior to the actual naturalization of such alien.

(June 27, 1952, ch. 477, title III, ch. 2, §331, 66 Stat. 252; as amended by P.L. 101-649 (IMMACT90) (11/29/90), §407.)

## Sec. 332 Administration
**[8 U.S.C. 1443]**

**(a) Rules and regulations governing examination of applicants.**— The Attorney General shall make such rules and regulations as may be necessary to carry into effect the provisions of this chapter and is authorized to prescribe the scope and nature of the examination of applicants for naturalization as to their admissibility to citizenship. Such examination shall be limited to inquiry concerning the applicant's residence, physical presence in the United States, good moral character, understanding of and attachment to the fundamental principles of the Constitution of the United States, ability to read, write, and speak English, and other qualifications to become a naturalized citizen as required by law, and shall be uniform throughout the United States.

**(b) Instruction in citizenship.**— The Attorney General is authorized to promote instruction and training in citizenship responsibilities of applicants for naturalization including the sending of names of candidates for naturalization to the public schools, preparing and distributing citizenship textbooks to such candidates as are receiving instruction in preparation for citizenship within or under the supervision of the public schools, preparing and distributing monthly an immigration and naturalization bulletin and securing the aid of and cooperating with official State and national organizations, including those concerned with vocational education.

**(c) Prescription of forms.**— The Attorney General shall prescribe and furnish such forms as may be required to give effect to the provisions of this chapter, and only such forms as may be so provided shall be legal. All certificates of naturalization and of citizenship shall be printed on safety paper and shall be consecutively numbered in separate series.

**(d) Administration of oaths and depositions.**— Employees of the Service may be designated by the Attorney General to administer oaths and to take depositions without charge in matters relating to the administration of the naturalization and citizenship laws. In cases where there is a likelihood of unusual delay or of hardship, the Attorney General may, in his discretion, authorize such depositions to be taken before a postmaster without charge, or before a notary public or other person authorized to administer oaths for general purposes.

**(e) Issuance of certificate of naturalization or citizenship.**— A certificate of naturalization or of citizenship issued by the Attorney General under the authority of this title shall have the same effect in all courts, tribunals, and public offices of the United States, at home and abroad, of the District of Columbia, and of each State, Territory, and outlying possession of the United States, as a certificate of naturalization or of citizenship issued by a court having naturalization jurisdiction.

**(f) Copies of records.**— Certifications and certified copies of all papers, documents, certificates, and records required or authorized to be issued, used, filed, recorded, or kept under any and all provisions of this Act shall be admitted in evidence equally with the originals in any and all cases and proceedings under this Act and in all cases and proceedings in which the originals thereof might be admissible as evidence.

**(g) Furnished quarters for photographic studios.**— The officers in charge of property owned or leased by the Government are authorized, upon the recommendation of the Attorney General, to provide quarters without payment of rent, in any building occupied by the Service, for a photographic studio, operated by welfare organizations without profit and solely for the benefit of persons seeking to comply with requirements under the immigration and nationality laws. Such studio shall be under the supervision of the Attorney General.

**(h) Public education regarding naturalization benefits.**— In order to promote the opportunities and responsibilities of United States citizenship, the Attorney General shall broadly distribute information concerning the benefits which persons may receive under this title and the requirements to obtain such benefits. In carrying out this subsection, the Attorney General shall seek the assistance of appropriate community groups, private voluntary agencies, and other relevant organizations. There are authorized to be appropriated (for each fiscal year beginning with fiscal year 1991) such sums as may be necessary to carry out this subsection.

(June 27, 1952, ch. 477, title III, ch. 2, §332, 66 Stat. 252; as amended by P.L. 101-649 (IMMACT90) (11/29/90), §406, §407; P.L. 102-232 (MTINA) (12/12/91, *effective* 4/1/92), §305.)

## Sec. 333 Photographs; number
## [8 U.S.C. 1444]

**(a)** Three identical photographs of the applicant shall be signed by and furnished by each applicant for naturalization or citizenship. One of such photographs shall be affixed by the Attorney General to the original certificate of naturalization issued to the naturalized citizen and one to the duplicate certificate of naturalization required to be forwarded to the Service.

**(b)** Three identical photographs of the applicant shall be furnished by each applicant for—

(1) a record of lawful admission for permanent residence to be made under section 249;

(2) a certificate of derivative citizenship;

(3) a certificate of naturalization or of citizenship;

(4) a special certificate of naturalization;

(5) a certificate of naturalization or of citizenship, in lieu of one lost, mutilated, or destroyed;

(6) a new certificate of citizenship in the new name of any naturalized citizen who, subsequent to naturalization, has had his name changed by order of a court of competent jurisdiction or by marriage; and

(7) a declaration of intention.

One such photograph shall be affixed to each such certificate issued by the Attorney General and one shall be affixed to the copy of such certificate retained by the Service.

(June 27, 1952, ch. 477, title III, ch. 2, §333, 66 Stat. 253; as amended by P.L. 101-649 (IMMACT90) (11/29/90), §407; P.L. 103-416 (INTCA) (10/25/94, *effective* 4/1/95), §219.)

## Sec. 334 Application for Naturalization; Declaration of Intention
## [8 U.S.C. 1445]

**(a) Evidence and form.**— An applicant for naturalization shall make and file with the Attorney General a sworn application in writing, signed by the applicant in the applicant's own handwriting, if physically able to write, which application shall be on a form prescribed by the Attorney General and shall include averments of all facts which in the opinion of the Attorney General may be material to the applicant's naturalization, and required to be proved under this title. In the case of an applicant subject to a requirement of continuous residence under section 316(a) or 319(a), the application for naturalization may be filed up to 3 months before the date the applicant would first otherwise meet such continuous residence requirement.

**(b) Who may file.**— No person shall file a valid application for naturalization unless he shall have attained the age of eighteen years. An application for naturalization by an alien shall contain an averment of lawful admission for permanent residence.

**(c) Hearings.**— Hearings under section 336(a) on applications for naturalization shall be held at regular intervals specified by the Attorney General.

**(d) Filing of application.**— Except as provided in subsection (e), an application for naturalization shall be filed in the office of the Attorney General.

**(e) Substitute filing place and administering oath other than before Attorney General.**— A person may file an application for naturalization other than in the office of the Attorney General, and an oath of allegiance administered other than in a public ceremony before the Attorney General or a court, if the Attorney General determines that the person has an illness or other disability which—

(1) is of a permanent nature and is sufficiently serious to prevent the person's personal appearance, or

(2) is of a nature which so incapacitates the person as to prevent him from personally appearing.

**(f) Declaration of intention.**— An alien over 18 years of age who is residing in the United States pursuant to a lawful admission for permanent residence may file with the Attorney General a declaration of intention to become a citizen of the United States. Such a declaration shall be filed in duplicate and in a form prescribed by the Attorney General and shall be accompanied by an application prescribed and approved by the Attorney General. Nothing in this subsection shall be construed as requiring any such alien to make and file a declaration of intention as a condition precedent to filing an application for naturalization nor shall any such declaration of intention be regarded as conferring or having conferred upon any such alien United States citizenship or nationality or the right to United States citizenship or nationality, nor shall such declaration be regarded as evidence of such alien's lawful admission for permanent residence in any proceeding, action, or matter arising under this or any other Act.

(June 27, 1952, ch. 477, title III, ch. 2, §334, 66 Stat. 254; as amended by P.L. 97-116 (12/29/81), §15; P.L. 101-649 (IMMACT90) (11/29/90), §401, §407; P.L. 102-232 (MTINA) (12/12/91, *effective* 4/1/92), §305.)

## Sec. 335 Investigation of Applicants; Examinations of Applications[198]
## [8 U.S.C. 1446]

**(a) Waiver.**— Before a person may be naturalized, an employee of the Service, or of the United States designated by the Attorney General, shall conduct a personal investigation of the person applying for naturalization in the vicinity or vicinities in which such person has maintained his actual place of abode and in the vicinity or vicinities in which such person has been employed or has engaged in business or work for at least five years immediately preceding the filing of his application for naturalization. The Attorney General may, in his discretion, waive a personal investigation in an individual case or in such cases or classes of cases as may be designated by him.

**(b) Conduct of examinations; authority of designees; record.**— The Attorney General shall designate employees of the Service to conduct examinations upon applications for naturalization. For such purposes any such employee so designated is hereby authorized to take testimony concerning any matter touching or in any way affecting the admissibility of any applicant for naturalization, to administer oaths, including the oath of the applicant for naturalization, and to require by subpoena the attendance and testimony of witnesses, including applicant, before such employee so designated and the production of relevant books, papers, and documents, and to that end may invoke the aid of any district court of the United States; and any such court may, in the event of neglect or refusal to respond to a subpoena issued by any such employee so designated or refusal to testify before such employee so designated issue an order requiring such person to appear before such employee so designated, produce relevant books, papers, and documents if demanded, and testify; and any failure to obey such order of the court may be punished by the court as a contempt thereof. The record of the examination authorized by this subsection shall be admissible as evidence in any hearing conducted by an immigration officer under section 336(a). Any such employee shall, at the examination, inform the applicant of the remedies available to the applicant under section 336.

**(c) Transmittal of record of examination.**— The record of the examination upon any application for naturalization may, in the discretion of the Attorney General, be transmitted to the Attorney General and the determination with respect thereto of the employee designated to conduct such examination shall when made also be transmitted to the Attorney General.

**(d) Determination to grant or deny application.**— The employee designated to conduct any such examination shall make a determination as to whether the application should be granted or denied, with reasons therefor.

**(e) Withdrawal of application.**— After an application for naturalization has been filed with the Attorney General, the applicant shall not be permitted to withdraw his application, except with the consent of the Attorney General. In cases where the Attorney General does not consent to the withdrawal of the application, the application shall be determined on its merits and a final order

---

[198] *See* §114(d)(4) of P.L. 107-77, *reprinted in* Appendix M, *infra*, for provisions relating to certain 9/11 victims.

determination made accordingly. In cases where the applicant fails to prosecute his application, the application shall be decided on the merits unless the Attorney General dismisses it for lack of prosecution.

**(f) Transfer of application.**— An applicant for naturalization who moves from the district of the Service in the United States in which the application is pending may, at any time thereafter, request the Service to transfer the application to any district of the Service in the United States which may act on the application. The transfer shall not be made without the consent of the Attorney General. In the case of such a transfer, the proceedings on the application shall continue as though the application had originally been filed in the district of the Service to which the application is transferred.

(June 27, 1952, ch. 477, title III, ch. 2, §335, 66 Stat. 255; as amended by P.L. 97-116 (12/29/81); P.L. 100-525 (10/24/88); P.L. 101-649 (IMMACT90) (11/29/90); P.L. 102-232 (MTINA) (12/12/91, *effective* 4/1/92).)

**Sec. 336 Hearings on Denials of Applications for Naturalization**
**[8 U.S.C. 1447]**

**(a) Request for hearing before immigration officer.**— If, after an examination under section 335, an application for naturalization is denied, the applicant may request a hearing before an immigration officer.

**(b) Request for hearing before District Court.**— If there is a failure to make a determination under section 335 before the end of the 120-day period after the date on which the examination is conducted under such section, the applicant may apply to the United States district court for the district in which the applicant resides for a hearing on the matter. Such court has jurisdiction over the matter and may either determine the matter or remand the matter, with appropriate instructions, to the Service to determine the matter.

**(c) Appearance of Attorney General.**— The Attorney General shall have the right to appear before any immigration officer in any naturalization proceedings for the purpose of cross-examining the applicant and the witnesses produced in support of the application concerning any matter touching or in any way affecting the applicant's right to admission to citizenship, and shall have the right to call witnesses, including the applicant, produce evidence, and be heard in opposition to, or in favor of, the granting of any application in naturalization proceedings.

**(d) Subpena of witnesses.**— The immigration officer shall, if the applicant requests it at the time of filing the request for the hearing, issue a subpena for the witnesses named by such applicant to appear upon the day set for the hearing, but in case such witnesses cannot be produced upon the hearing other witnesses may be summoned upon notice to the Attorney General, in such manner and at such time as the Attorney General may by regulation prescribe. Such subpenas may be enforced in the same manner as subpenas under section 335(b) may be enforced.

**(e) Change of name.**— It shall be lawful at the time and as a part of the administration by a court of the oath of allegiance under section 337(a) for the court, in its discretion, upon the bona fide prayer of the applicant included in an appropriate petition to the court, to make a decree changing the name of said person, and the certificate of naturalization shall be issued in accordance therewith.

(June 27, 1952, ch. 477, title III, ch. 2, §336, 66 Stat. 257; as amended by P.L. 91-136 (12/5/69); P.L. 97-116 (12/29/81); P.L. 100-525 (10/24/88); P.L. 101-649 (IMMACT90) (11/29/90), §407; P.L. 102-232 (MTINA) (12/12/91, *effective* 4/1/92), §305.)

## Sec. 337 Oath of Renunciation and Allegiance
## [8 U.S.C. 1448]

**(a) Public ceremony.**— A person who has applied for naturalization shall, in order to be and before being admitted to citizenship, take in a public ceremony before the Attorney General or a court with jurisdiction under section 310(b) an oath

(1) to support the Constitution of the United States;

(2) to renounce and abjure absolutely and entirely all allegiance and fidelity to any foreign prince, potentate, state, or sovereignty of whom or which the applicant was before a subject or citizen;

(3) to support and defend the Constitution and the laws of the United States against all enemies, foreign and domestic;

(4) to bear true faith and allegiance to the same; and

(5)  (A) to bear arms on behalf of the United States when required by the law, or

(B) to perform noncombatant service in the Armed Forces of the United States when required by the law, or

(C) to perform work of national importance under civilian direction when required by the law.

Any such person shall be required to take an oath containing the substance of clauses (1) through (5) of the preceding sentence, except that a person who shows by clear and convincing evidence to the satisfaction of the Attorney General that he is opposed to the bearing of arms in the Armed Forces of the United States by reason of religious training and belief shall be required to take an oath containing the substance of clauses (1) through (4) and clauses (5)(B) and (5)(C), and a person who shows by clear and convincing evidence to the satisfaction of the Attorney General that he is opposed to any type of service in the Armed Forces of the United States by reason of religious training and belief shall be required to take an oath containing the substance of clauses (1) through (4) and clause (5)(C). The term "religious training and belief" as used in this section shall mean an individual's belief in a relation to a Supreme Being involving duties superior to those arising from any human relation, but does not include essentially political, sociological, or philosophical views or a merely personal moral code. In the case of the naturalization of a child under the provisions of section 322 of this title the Attorney General may waive the taking of the oath if in the opinion of the Attorney General the child is unable to understand its meaning. The Attorney General may waive the taking of the oath by a person if in the opinion of the Attorney General the person is unable to understand, or to communicate an understanding of, its meaning because of a physical or developmental disability or mental impairment. If the Attorney General waives the taking of the oath by a person under the preceding sentence, the person shall be considered to have met the requirements of section 316(a)(3) with respect to attachment to the principles of the Constitution and well disposition to the good order and happiness of the United States.

**(b) Hereditary titles or orders of nobility.**— In case the person applying for naturalization has borne any hereditary title, or has been of any of the orders of nobility in any foreign state, the applicant shall in addition to complying with the requirements of subsection (a) of this section, make under oath in the same public ceremony in which the oath of allegiance is administered, an express renunciation of such title or order of nobility, and such renunciation shall be recorded as a part of such proceedings.

**(c) Expedited judicial oath administration ceremony.**— Notwithstanding section 310(b), an individual may be granted an expedited judicial oath administration ceremony or administrative naturalization by the Attorney General upon demonstrating sufficient cause. In determining whether to grant an expedited judicial oath administration ceremony, a court shall consider special circumstances (such as serious illness of the applicant or a member of the applicant's immediate family, permanent disability sufficiently incapacitating as to prevent the applicant's personal appearance at the scheduled ceremony, developmental disability or advanced age, or exigent circumstances relating to travel or employment). If an expedited judicial oath administration ceremony is impracticable, the court shall refer such individual to the Attorney General who may provide for immediate administrative naturalization.

**(d) Rules and regulations.**— The Attorney General shall prescribe rules and procedures to ensure that the ceremonies conducted by the Attorney General for the administration of oaths of allegiance under this section are public, conducted frequently and at regular intervals, and are in keeping with the dignity of the occasion.

(June 27, 1952, ch. 477, title III, ch. 2, §337, 66 Stat. 258; as amended by P.L. 97-116 (12/29/81); P.L. 101-649 (IMMACT90) (11/29/90); P.L. 102-232 (MTINA) (12/12/91, *effective* 4/1/92); P.L. 106-448 (11/6/00), §1 [adding last paragraph to (a)].)

### Sec. 338 Certificate of Naturalization; Contents
[8 U.S.C. 1449]

A person admitted to citizenship in conformity with the provisions of this title shall be entitled upon such admission to receive from the Attorney General a certificate of naturalization, which shall contain substantially the following information: Number of application for naturalization; number of certificate of naturalization; date of naturalization; name, signature, place of residence, autographed photograph, and personal description of the naturalized person, including age, sex, marital status, and country of former nationality; location of the district office of the Service in which the application was filed and the title, authority, and location of the official or court administering the oath of allegiance; statement that the Attorney General, having found that the applicant had complied in all respects with all of the applicable provisions of the naturalization laws of the United States, and was entitled to be admitted a citizen of the United States of America, thereupon ordered that the applicant be admitted as a citizen of the United States of America; attestation of an immigration officer; and the seal of the Department of Justice.

(June 27, 1952, title III, ch. 2, §338, 66 Stat. 259; as amended by P.L. 101-649 (IMMACT90) (11/29/90), title IV, §407; P.L. 102-232 (MTINA) (12/12/91, *effective* 4/1/92), §305; P.L. 103-416 (INTCA) (10/25/94, *effective* 4/1/95), §104, §219.)

### Sec. 339 Functions and Duties of Clerks and Records of Declarations of Intention and Applications for Naturalization
[8 U.S.C. 1450]

**(a)** The clerk of each court that administers oaths of allegiance under section 337 shall—

(1) Deliver to each person administered the oath of allegiance by the court pursuant to section 337(a) the certificate of naturalization prepared by the Attorney General pursuant to section 310(b)(2)(A)(ii),

(2) forward to the Attorney General a list of applicants actually taking the oath at each scheduled ceremony and information concerning each person to whom such an oath is administered by the court, within 30 days after the close of the month in which the oath was administered,

(3) forward to the Attorney General certified copies of such other proceedings and orders instituted in or issued out of the court affecting or relating to the naturalization of persons as may be required from time to time by the Attorney General, and

(4) be responsible for all blank certificates of naturalization received by them from time to time from the Attorney General and shall account to the Attorney General for them whenever required to do so.

No certificate of naturalization received by any clerk of court which may be defaced or injured in such manner as to prevent its use as herein provided shall in any case be destroyed, but such certificates shall be returned to the Attorney General.

**(b)** Each district office of the Service in the United States shall maintain, in chronological order, indexed, and consecutively numbered, as part of its permanent records, all declarations of intention and applications for naturalization filed with the office.

(June 27, 1952, ch. 477, title III, ch. 2, §339, 66 Stat. 259; as amended by P.L. 101-649 (IMMACT90) (11/29/90), §407; P.L. 102-232 (MTINA) (12/12/91, *effective* 4/1/92), §102.)

## Sec. 340 Revocation of Naturalization
## [8 U.S.C. 1451]

**(a) Concealment of material evidence; refusal to testify.**— It shall be the duty of the United States attorneys for the respective districts, upon affidavit showing good cause therefor, to institute proceedings in any district court of the United States in the judicial district in which the naturalized citizen may reside at the time of bringing suit, for the purpose of revoking and setting aside the order admitting such person to citizenship and canceling the certificate of naturalization on the ground that such order and certificate of naturalization were illegally procured or were procured by concealment of a material fact or by willful misrepresentation, and such revocation and setting aside of the order admitting such person to citizenship and such canceling of certificate of naturalization shall be effective as of the original date of the order and certificate, respectively: *Provided,* That refusal on the part of a naturalized citizen within a period of ten years following his naturalization to testify as a witness in any proceeding before a congressional committee concerning his subversive activities, in a case where such person has been convicted of contempt for such refusal, shall be held to constitute a ground for revocation of such person's naturalization under this subsection as having been procured by concealment of a material fact or by willful misrepresentation. If the naturalized citizen does not reside in any judicial district in the United States at the time of bringing such suit, the proceedings may be instituted in the United States District Court for the District of Columbia or in the United States district court in the judicial district in which such person last had his residence.

**(b) Notice to party.**— The party to whom was granted the naturalization alleged to have been illegally procured or procured by concealment of a material fact or by willful misrepresentation shall, in any such proceedings under subsection (a) of this section, have sixty days' personal notice, unless waived by such party, in which to make answer to the petition of the United States; and if such naturalized person be absent from the United States or from the judicial district in which such person last had his residence, such notice shall be given either by personal service upon him or by publication in the manner provided for the service of summons by publication or upon absentees by the laws of the State or the place where such suit is brought.

**(c) Membership in certain organizations; prima facie evidence.**— If a person who shall have been naturalized after December 24, 1952 shall within five years next following such naturalization become a member of or affiliated with any organization, membership in or affiliation with which at the time of naturalization would have precluded such person from naturalization under the provisions of section 313, it shall be considered prima facie evidence that such person was not attached to the principles of the Constitution of the United States and was not well disposed to the good order and happiness of the United States at the time of naturalization, and, in the absence of countervailing evidence, it shall be sufficient in the proper proceeding to authorize the revocation and setting aside of the order admitting such person to citizenship and the cancellation of the certificate of naturalization as having been obtained by concealment of a material fact or by willful misrepresentation, and such revocation and setting aside of the order admitting such person to citizenship and such canceling of certificate of naturalization shall be effective as of the original date of the order and certificate, respectively.

**(d) Applicability to citizenship through naturalization of parent or spouse.**— Any person who claims United States citizenship through the naturalization of a parent or spouse in whose case there is a revocation and setting aside of the order admitting such parent or spouse to citizenship under the provisions of subsection (a) of this section on the ground that the order and certificate of naturalization were procured by concealment of a material fact or by willful misrepresentation shall be deemed to have lost and to lose his citizenship and any right or privilege of citizenship which he may have, now has, or may hereafter acquire under and by virtue of such naturalization of such parent or spouse, regardless of whether such person is residing within or without the United States at the time of the revocation and setting aside of the order admitting such parent or spouse to citizenship. Any person who claims United States citizenship through the naturalization of a parent or spouse in whose case there is a revocation and setting aside of the order admitting such parent or spouse to citizenship and the cancellation of the certificate of naturalization under the provisions of subsection (c) of this section, or under the provisions of section 329(c) of this title on any ground other than that the order and certificate of naturalization were procured by concealment of a material fact or by willful misrepresentation, shall be deemed to have lost and to lose his citizenship and any right or privilege of citizenship which would have been enjoyed by such person had there not been a revocation and setting aside of the order admitting such parent or spouse to citizenship and the cancellation of the certificate of naturalization, unless such person is residing in the United States at the time of the revocation and setting aside of the order admitting such parent or spouse to citizenship and the cancellation of the certificate of naturalization.

**(e) Citizenship unlawfully procured.**— When a person shall be convicted under section 1425 of title 18 of the United States Code of knowingly procuring naturalization in violation of law, the court in which such conviction is had shall thereupon revoke, set aside, and declare void the final order admitting such person to citizenship, and shall declare the certificate of naturalization of such person to be canceled. Jurisdiction is hereby conferred on the courts having jurisdiction of the trial of such offense to make such adjudication.

**(f) Cancellation of certificate of naturalization.**— Whenever an order admitting an alien to citizenship shall be revoked and set aside or a certificate of naturalization shall be canceled, or both, as provided in this section, the court in which such judgment or decree is rendered shall make an order canceling such certificate and shall send a certified copy of such order to the Attorney General. The clerk of court shall transmit a copy of such order and judgment to the Attorney General. A person holding a certificate of naturalization or citizenship which has been canceled as provided by this section shall upon notice by the court by which the decree of cancellation was made, or by the Attorney General, surrender the same to the Attorney General.

**(g) Applicability to certificates of naturalization and citizenship.**— The provisions of this section shall apply not only to any naturalization granted and to certificates of naturalization and citizenship issued under the provisions of this title, but to any naturalization heretofore granted by any court, and to all certificates of naturalization and citizenship which may have been issued heretofore by any court or by the Commissioner based upon naturalization granted by any court, or by a designated representative of the Commissioner under the provisions of section 702 of the Nationality Act of 1940, as amended, or by such designated representative under any other Act.

**(h) Power to correct, reopen, alter, modify, or vacate order.**— Nothing contained in this section shall be regarded as limiting, denying, or restricting the power of the Attorney General to correct, reopen, alter, modify, or vacate an order naturalizing the person.

(June 27, 1952, ch. 477, title III, ch. 2, §340, 66 Stat. 260; Sept. 3, 1954, ch. 1263, §18, 68 Stat. 1232; as amended by P.L. 87-301 (9/26/61); P.L. 99-653 (11/14/86); P.L. 100-525 (10/24/88); P.L. 101-649 (IMMACT90) (11/29/90); P.L. 102-232 (MTINA) (12/12/91, *effective* 4/1/92); P.L. 103-416 (INTCA) (10/25/94, *effective* 4/1/95), §104(b) [repealing (d)].)

## Sec. 341 Certificates of Citizenship or U.S. Non-Citizen National Status; Procedure[199] [8 U.S.C. 1452]

**(a) Application to Attorney General for certificate of citizenship; proof; oath of allegiance.**— A person who claims to have derived United States citizenship through the naturalization of a parent or through the naturalization or citizenship of a husband, or who is a citizen of the United States by virtue of the provisions of section 1993 of the United States Revised Statutes, or of section 1993 of the United States Revised Statutes, as amended by section 1 of the Act of May 24, 1934 (48 Stat. 797), or who is a citizen of the United States by virtue of the provisions of subsection (c), (d), (e), (g), or (i) of section 201 of the Nationality Act of 1940, as amended (54 Stat. 1138; 8 U.S.C. 601), or of the Act of May 7, 1934 (48 Stat. 667), or of paragraph (c), (d), (e), or (g) of section 301 of this title, or under the provisions of the Act of August 4, 1937 (50 Stat. 558), or under the provisions of section 203 or 205 of the Nationality Act of 1940 (54 Stat. 1139; 8 U.S.C. 603, 605), or under the provisions of section 303 of this title, may apply to the Attorney General for a certificate of citizenship. Upon proof to the satisfaction of the Attorney General that the applicant is a citizen, and that the applicant's alleged citizenship was derived as claimed, or acquired, as the case may be, and upon taking and subscribing before a member of the Service within the United States to the oath of allegiance required by this Act of an applicant for naturalization, such individual shall be furnished by the Attorney General with a certificate of citizenship, but only if such individual is at the time within the United States.

**(b) Application to Secretary of State for certificate of non-citizen national status; proof; oath of allegiance.**— A person who claims to be a national, but not a citizen, of the United States may apply to the Secretary of State for a certificate of non-citizen national status. Upon—

(1) proof to the satisfaction of the Secretary of State that the applicant is a national, but not a citizen, of the United States, and

(2) in the case of such a person born outside of the United States or its outlying possessions, taking and subscribing, before an immigration officer within the United States or its outlying possessions, to the oath of allegiance required by this Act of a petitioner for naturalization,

the individual shall be furnished by the Secretary of State with a certificate of non-citizen national status, but only if the individual is at the time within the United States or its outlying possessions.

(June 27, 1952, ch. 477, title III, ch. 2, §341, 66 Stat. 263; as amended by P.L. 97-116 (12/29/81); P.L. 99-396 (8/27/86); P.L. 99-653 (11/14/86); P.L. 100-525 (10/24/88); P.L. 102-232 (MTINA) (12/12/91, *effective* 4/1/92); P.L. 103-416 (INTCA) (10/25/94, *effective* 4/1/95) [repealing (c)].)

---

[199] *See* §114(h) of P.L. 107-77, *reprinted in* Appendix L, *infra*, for exceptions to INA §341 for certain 9/11 victims.

## Sec. 342 Cancellation of Certificates Issued by the Attorney General, the Commissioner or a Deputy Commissioner; Action Not to Affect Citizenship Status
**[8 U.S.C. 1453]**

The Attorney General is authorized to cancel any certificate of citizenship, certificate of naturalization, copy of a declaration of intention, or other certificate, document or record heretofore issued or made by the Commissioner or a Deputy Commissioner or hereafter made by the Attorney General if it shall appear to the Attorney General's satisfaction that such document or record was illegally or fraudulently obtained from, or was created through illegality or by fraud practiced upon, him or the Commissioner or a Deputy Commissioner; but the person for or to whom such document or record has been issued or made shall be given at such person's last-known place of address written notice of the intention to cancel such document or record with the reasons therefor and shall be given at least sixty days in which to show cause why such document or record should not be canceled. The cancellation under this section of any document purporting to show the citizenship status of the person to whom it was issued shall affect only the document and not the citizenship status of the person in whose name the document was issued.

(June 27, 1952, ch. 477, title III, ch. 2, §342, 66 Stat. 263.)

## Sec. 343 Documents and Copies Issued by the Attorney General
**[8 U.S.C. 1454]**

**(a)** If any certificate of naturalization or citizenship issued to any citizen or any declaration of intention furnished to any declarant is lost, mutilated, or destroyed, the citizen or declarant may make application to the Attorney General for a new certificate or declaration. If the Attorney General finds that the certificate or declaration is lost, mutilated, or destroyed, he shall issue to the applicant a new certificate or declaration. If the certificate or declaration has been mutilated, it shall be surrendered to the Attorney General before the applicant may receive such new certificate or declaration. If the certificate or declaration has been lost, the applicant or any other person who shall have, or may come into possession of it is hereby required to surrender it to the Attorney General.

**(b)** The Attorney General shall issue for any naturalized citizen, on such citizen's application therefor, a special certificate of naturalization for use by such citizen only for the purpose of obtaining recognition as a citizen of the United States by a foreign state. Such certificate when issued shall be furnished to the Secretary of State for transmission to the proper authority in such foreign state.

**(c)** If the name of any naturalized citizen has, subsequent to naturalization, been changed by order of any court of competent jurisdiction, or by marriage, the citizen may make application for a new certificate of naturalization in the new name of such citizen. If the Attorney General finds the name of the applicant to have been changed as claimed, the Attorney General shall issue to the applicant a new certificate and shall notify the naturalization court of such action.

**(d)** The Attorney General is authorized to make and issue certifications of any part of the naturalization records of any court, or of any certificate of naturalization or citizenship, for use in complying with any statute, State or Federal, or in any judicial proceeding. No such certification shall be made by any clerk of court except upon order of the court.

(June 27, 1952, ch. 477, title III, ch. 2, §343, 66 Stat. 263; as amended by P.L. 100-525 (10/24/88).)

## Sec. 344 Fiscal Provisions
**[8 U.S.C. 1455]**

**(a)** The Attorney General shall charge, collect, and account for fees prescribed by the Attorney General pursuant to section 9701 of title 31, United States Code for the following:

(1) Making, filing, and docketing an application for naturalization, including the hearing on such application, if such hearing be held, and a certificate of naturalization, if the issuance of such certificate is authorized by Attorney General.

(2) Receiving and filing a declaration of intention, and issuing a duplicate thereof.

**(b)** Notwithstanding the provisions of this Act or any other law, no fee shall be charged or collected for an application for declaration of intention or a certificate of naturalization in lieu of a declaration or a certificate alleged to have been lost, mutilated, or destroyed, submitted by a person who was a member of the military or naval forces of the United States at any time after April 20, 1898, and before July 5, 1902; or at any time after April 5, 1917, and before November 12, 1918; or who served on the Mexican border as a member of the Regular Army or National Guard between June 1916 and April 1917; or who has served or hereafter serves in the military, air, or naval forces of the United States after September 16, 1940, and who was not at any time during such period or thereafter separated from such forces under other than honorable conditions, who was not a conscientious objector who performed no military duty whatever or refused to wear the uniform, or who was not at any time during such period or thereafter discharged from such military, air, or naval forces on account of alienage.

**(c)** Except as provided by section 286(q)(2) or any other law, all fees collected by the Attorney General shall be deposited by the Attorney General in the Treasury of the United States except that all fees collected by the Attorney General, on or after October 1, 1988, under the provisions of this title, shall be deposited in the "Immigration Examinations Fee Account" in the Treasury of the United States established pursuant to the provisions of sections 286(m), (n), (o), and (p): *Provided, however*, That all fees received by the Attorney General from applicants residing in the Virgin Islands of the United States, and in Guam, under this title, shall be paid over to the treasury of the Virgin Islands and to the treasury of Guam, respectively.

**(d)** During the time when the United States is at war the Attorney General may not charge or collect a naturalization fee from an alien in the military, air, or naval service of the United States for filing an application for naturalization or issuing a certificate of naturalization upon admission to citizenship.

**(e)** In addition to the other fees required by this title, the applicant for naturalization shall, upon the filing of an application for naturalization, deposit with and pay to the Attorney General a sum of money sufficient to cover the expenses of subpoenaing and paying the legal fees of any witnesses for whom such applicant may request a subpoena, and upon the final discharge of such witnesses, they shall receive, if they demand the same from the Attorney General, the customary and usual witness fees from the moneys which the applicant shall have paid to the Attorney General for such purpose, and the residue, if any, shall be returned by the Attorney General to the applicant.

**(f)** (1) The Attorney General shall pay over to courts administering oaths of allegiance to persons under this title a specified percentage of all fees described in subsection (a)(1) collected by the Attorney General with respect to persons administered the oath of allegiance by the respective courts. The Attorney General, annually and in consultation with the courts, shall determine the specified percentage based on the proportion, of the total costs incurred by the Service and courts for essential services directly related to the naturalization process, which are incurred by courts.

(2) The Attorney General shall provide on an annual basis to the Committees on the Judiciary of the House of Representatives and of the Senate a detailed report on the use of the fees described in paragraph (1) and shall consult with such Committees before increasing such fees.

(June 27, 1952, ch. 477, title III, ch. 2, §344, 66 Stat. 264; as amended by P.L. 85-508 (7/7/58); P.L. 90-609 (10/21/68); P.L. 97-116 (12/29/81); P.L. 100-459 (10/1/88); P.L. 100-525 (10/24/88); P.L. 101-649 (IMMACT90) (11/29/90); P.L. 102-232 (MTINA) (12/12/91, *effective* 4/1/92); P.L. 107-273 (11/2/02), div. C, title I, §11016(1) [revising (c)].)

**Sec. 345** [Repealed. P.L. 86-682 (9/2/60, *effective* 9/1/60), §12(c).]

### Sec. 346 Publication and Distribution of Citizenship Textbooks; Use of Naturalization Fees
[8 U.S.C. 1457]

Authorization is hereby granted for the publication and distribution of the citizenship textbook described in subsection (b) of section 332 and for the reimbursement of the appropriation of the Department of Justice upon the records of the Treasury Department from the naturalization fees deposited in the Treasury through the Service for the cost of such publication and distribution, such reimbursement to be made upon statements by the Attorney General of books so published and distributed.

(June 27, 1952, ch. 477, title III, ch. 2, §346, 66 Stat. 266.)

### Sec. 347 Compilation of Naturalization Statistics and Payment for Equipment
[8 U.S.C. 1458]

The Attorney General is authorized and directed to prepare from the records in the custody of the Service a report upon those heretofore seeking citizenship to show by nationalities their relation to the numbers of aliens annually arriving and to the prevailing census populations of the foreign-born, their economic, vocational, and other classification, in statistical form, with analytical comment thereon, and to prepare such report annually hereafter. Payment for the equipment used in preparing such compilation shall be made from the appropriation for the enforcement of this Act by the Service.

(June 27, 1952, ch. 477, title III, ch. 2, §347, 66 Stat. 266.)

**Sec. 348** [Repealed.]

# Chapter 3 — Loss of Nationality

### Sec. 349 Loss of Nationality by Native-Born or Naturalized Citizen; voluntary action; burden of proof; presumptions
[8 U.S.C. 1481]

(a) A person who is a national of the United States whether by birth or naturalization, shall lose his nationality by voluntarily performing any of the following acts with the intention of relinquishing United States nationality—

    (1) obtaining naturalization in a foreign state upon his own application or upon an application filed by a duly authorized agent, after having attained the age of eighteen years; or

    (2) taking an oath or making an affirmation or other formal declaration of allegiance to a foreign state or a political subdivision thereof, after having attained the age of eighteen years; or

    (3) entering, or serving in, the armed forces of a foreign state if

        (A) such armed forces are engaged in hostilities against the United States, or

        (B) such persons serve as a commissioned or non-commissioned officer; or

    (4) (A) accepting, serving in, or performing the duties of any office, post, or employment under the government of a foreign state or a political subdivision thereof, after attaining the age of eighteen years if he has or acquires the nationality of such foreign state; or

---

[200] Repealed by P.L. 101-649 (11/29/90), title IV, §407(d)(20).

(B) accepting, serving in, or performing the duties of any office, post, or employment under the government of a foreign state or a political subdivision thereof, after attaining the age of eighteen years for which office, post, or employment an oath, affirmation, or declaration of allegiance is required; or

(5) making a formal renunciation of nationality before a diplomatic or consular officer of the United States in a foreign state, in such form as may be prescribed by the Secretary of State; or

(6) making in the United States a formal written renunciation of nationality in such form as may be prescribed by, and before such officer as may be designated by, the Attorney General, whenever the United States shall be in a state of war and the Attorney General shall approve such renunciation as not contrary to the interests of national defense; or

(7) committing any act of treason against, or attempting by force to overthrow, or bearing arms against, the United States, violating or conspiring to violate any of the provisions of section 2383 of title 18, United States Code, or willfully performing any act in violation of section 2385 of title 18, United States Code, or violating section 2384 of said title by engaging in a conspiracy to overthrow, put down, or to destroy by force the Government of the United States, or to levy war against them, if and when he is convicted thereof by a court martial or by a court of competent jurisdiction.

**(b)** Whenever the loss of United States nationality is put in issue in any action or proceeding commenced on or after the enactment of this subsection under, or by virtue of, the provisions of this or any other Act, the burden shall be upon the person or party claiming that such loss occurred, to establish such claim by a preponderance of the evidence. Any person who commits or performs, or who has committed or performed, any act of expatriation under the provisions of this or any other Act shall be presumed to have done so voluntarily, but such presumption may be rebutted upon a showing, by a preponderance of the evidence, that the act or acts committed or performed were not done voluntarily.

(June 27, 1952, ch. 477, title III, ch. 3, §349, 66 Stat. 267; Sept. 3, 1954, ch. 1256, §2, 68 Stat. 1146; as amended by P.L. 87-301 (9/26/61); P.L. 94-412 (9/14/76); P.L. 95-432 (10/10/78); P.L. 97-116 (12/29/81); P.L. 99-653 (11/14/86) [striking (b)]; P.L. 100-525 (10/24/88) [adding new (b)].)

## Sec. 350 [Repealed.][201]

## Sec. 351 Restrictions on Loss of Nationality
## [8 U.S.C. 1483]

**(a)** Except as provided in paragraphs (6) and (7) of section 349(a) of this title, no national of the United States can lose United States nationality under this Act while within the United States or any of its outlying possessions, but loss of nationality shall result from the performance within the United States or any of its outlying possessions of any of the acts or the fulfillment of any of the conditions specified in this chapter if and when the national thereafter takes up a residence outside the United States and its outlying possessions.

**(b)** A national who within six months after attaining the age of eighteen years asserts his claim to United States nationality, in such manner as the Secretary of State shall by regulation prescribe, shall not be deemed to have lost United States nationality by the commission, prior to his eighteenth birthday, of any of the acts specified in paragraphs (3) and (5) of section 349(a) of this title.

(June 27, 1952, ch. 477, title III, ch. 3, §351, 66 Stat. 269; as amended by P.L. 97-116 (12/29/81); P.L. 99-653 (11/14/86); P.L. 100-525 (10/24/88); P.L. 103-416 (INTCA) (10/25/94, *effective* 4/1/95), §105; P.L. 104-208 (IIRAIRA) (9/30/96), div. C, title VI, §671.)

---

[201] Repealed by P.L. 95-432 (10/10/78), §1

**Secs. 352–55** [Repealed.][202]

### Sec. 356 Nationality Lost Solely from Performance of Acts or Fulfillment of Conditions
**[8 U.S.C. 1488]**

The loss of nationality under this chapter shall result solely from the performance by a national of the acts or fulfillment of the conditions specified in this chapter.

(June 27, 1952, ch. 477, title III, ch. 3, §356, 66 Stat. 272.)

### Sec. 357 Application of Treaties; Exceptions
**[8 U.S.C. 1489]**

Nothing in this title shall be applied in contravention of the provisions of any treaty or convention to which the United States is a party and which has been ratified by the Senate before December 25, 1952: *Provided, however,* That no woman who was a national of the United States shall be deemed to have lost her nationality solely by reason of her marriage to an alien on or after September 22, 1922, or to an alien racially ineligible to citizenship on or after March 3, 1931, or, in the case of a woman who was a United States citizen at birth, through residence abroad following such marriage, notwithstanding the provisions of any existing treaty or convention.

(June 27, 1952, ch. 477, title III, ch. 3, §357, 66 Stat. 272; as amended by P.L. 100-525 (10/24/88).)

## Chapter 4 — Miscellaneous

### Sec. 358 Certificate of Diplomatic or Consular Officer of the United States as to Loss of American Nationality
**[8 U.S.C. 1501]**

Whenever a diplomatic or consular officer of the United States has reason to believe that a person while in a foreign state has lost his United States nationality under any provision of chapter 3 of this title, or under any provision of chapter IV of the Nationality Act of 1940, as amended, he shall certify the facts upon which such belief is based to the Department of State, in writing, under regulations prescribed by the Secretary of State. If the report of the diplomatic or consular officer is approved by the Secretary of State, a copy of the certificate shall be forwarded to the Attorney General, for his information, and the diplomatic or consular office in which the report was made shall be directed to forward a copy of the certificate to the person to whom it relates. Approval by the Secretary of State of a certificate under this section shall constitute a final administrative determination of loss of United States nationality under this Act, subject to such procedures for administrative appeal as the Secretary may prescribe by regulation, and also shall constitute a denial of a right or privilege of United States nationality for purposes of section 360.

(June 27, 1952, ch. 477, title III, ch. 4, §358, 66 Stat. 272; as amended by P.L. 103-416 (INTCA) (10/25/94, *effective* 4/1/95), §106.)

---

[202] Repealed by P.L. 95-432 (10/10/78), §2.

### Sec. 359 Certificate of Nationality Issued by Secretary of State for Person Not a Naturalized Citizen of United States for Use in Proceedings of a Foreign State
[8 U.S.C. 1502]

The Secretary of State is hereby authorized to issue, in his discretion and in accordance with rules and regulations prescribed by him, a certificate of nationality for any person not a naturalized citizen of the United States who presents satisfactory evidence that he is an American national and that such certificate is needed for use in judicial or administrative proceedings in a foreign state. Such certificate shall be solely for use in the case for which it was issued and shall be transmitted by the Secretary of State through appropriate official channels to the judicial or administrative officers of the foreign state in which it is to be used.

(June 27, 1952, ch. 477, title III, ch. 4, §359, 66 Stat. 273.)

### Sec. 360 Denial of Rights and Privileges as National
[8 U.S.C. 1503]

**(a) Proceedings for declaration of United States nationality.**— If any person who is within the United States claims a right or privilege as a national of the United States and is denied such right or privilege by any department or independent agency, or official thereof, upon the ground that he is not a national of the United States, such person may institute an action under the provisions of section 2201 of title 28, United States Code, against the head of such department or independent agency for a judgment declaring him to be a national of the United States, except that no such action may be instituted in any case if the issue of such person's status as a national of the United States

(1) arose by reason of or in connection with any removal proceeding under the provisions of this or any other act, or

(2) is in issue in any such removal proceeding.

An action under this subsection may be instituted only within five years after the final administrative denial of such right or privilege and shall be filed in the district court of the United States for the district in which such person resides or claims a residence, and jurisdiction over such officials in such cases is hereby conferred upon those courts.

**(b) Application for certificate of identity; appeal.**— If any person who is not within the United States claims a right or privilege as a national of the United States and is denied such right or privilege by any department or independent agency, or official thereof, upon the ground that he is not a national of the United States, such person may make application to a diplomatic or consular officer of the United States in the foreign country in which he is residing for a certificate of identity for the purpose of traveling to a port of entry in the United States and applying for admission. Upon proof to the satisfaction of such diplomatic or consular officer that such application is made in good faith and has a substantial basis, he shall issue to such person a certificate of identity. From any denial of an application for such certificate the applicant shall be entitled to an appeal to the Secretary of State, who, if he approves the denial, shall state in writing his reasons for his decision. The Secretary of State shall prescribe rules and regulations for the issuance of certificates of identity as above provided. The provisions of this subsection shall be applicable only to a person who at some time prior to his application for the certificate of identity has been physically present in the United States, or to a person under sixteen years of age who was born abroad of a United States citizen parent.

**(c) Application for admission to United States under certificate of identity; revision of determination.**— A person who has been issued a certificate of identity under the provisions of subsection (b), and while in possession thereof, may apply for admission to the United States at any port of entry, and shall be subject to all the provisions of this Act relating to the conduct of proceedings involving aliens seeking admission to the United States. A final determination by the Attorney General that any such person is not entitled to admission to the United States shall be subject to review by any court of competent jurisdiction in habeas corpus proceedings and not otherwise. Any person described in this section who is finally denied admission to the United States shall be subject to all the provisions of this Act relating to aliens seeking admission to the United States.

(June 27, 1952, ch. 477, title II, ch. 9, §290, 66 Stat. 234; as amended by P.L. 104-208 (IIRAIRA) (9/30/96), div. C, title III, §308 [revising (a) & (c)].)

## Sec. 361 Cancellation of United States Passports and Consular Reports of Birth
[8 U.S.C. 1504]

**(a)** The Secretary of State is authorized to cancel any United States passport or Consular Report of Birth, or certified copy thereof, if it appears that such document was illegally, fraudulently, or erroneously obtained from, or was created through illegality or fraud practiced upon, the Secretary. The person for or to whom such document has been issued or made shall be given, at such person's last known address, written notice of the cancellation of such document, together with the procedures for seeking a prompt post-cancellation hearing. The cancellation under this section of any document purporting to show the citizenship status of the person to whom it was issued shall affect only the document and not the citizenship status of the person in whose name the document was issued.

**(b)** For purposes of this section, the term "Consular Report of Birth" refers to the report, designated as a "Report of Birth Abroad of a Citizen of the United States", issued by a consular officer to document a citizen born abroad.

(June 27, 1952, ch. 477, title III, ch. 4, §361, as added by P.L. 103-416 (INTCA) (10/25/94, *effective* 4/1/95), §107.)

## Title IV — Refugee Assistance (§§401–14)

### Chapter 1 — Miscellaneous

**Sec. 401** [Repealed.][203]

**Secs. 402–03** [Omitted.][204]

### Sec. 404 Authorization of Appropriations
[8 U.S.C. 1101, note]

**(a)** There are authorized to be appropriated such sums as may be necessary to carry out the provisions of this Act (other than chapter 2 of title IV).

**(b)** (1) There are authorized to be appropriated (for fiscal year 1991 and any subsequent fiscal year) to an immigration emergency fund, to be established in the Treasury, an amount sufficient to provide for a balance of $35,000,000 in such fund, to be used to carry out paragraph (2) and to provide for an increase in border patrol or other enforcement activities of the Service and for reimbursement of State and localities in providing assistance as requested by the Attorney General in meeting an immigration emergency, except that no amounts may be

---

[203] Repealed by P.L. 91-510 (10/26/70).
[204] Sec. 402 of the INA amended a number of non-INA statutes. Sec. 403 repealed a large number of statutes.

withdrawn from such fund with respect to an emergency unless the President has determined that the immigration emergency exists and has certified such fact to the Judiciary Committees of the House of Representatives and of the Senate.

(2)  (A) Funds which are authorized to be appropriated by paragraph (1), subject to the dollar limitation contained in subparagraph (B), shall be available, by application for the reimbursement of States and localities providing assistance as required by the Attorney General, to States and localities whenever—

(i) a district director of the Service certifies to the Commissioner that the number of asylum applications filed in the respective district during a calendar quarter exceeds by at least 1,000 the number of such applications filed in that district during the preceding calendar quarter,[205]

(ii) the lives, property, safety, or welfare of the residents of a State or locality are endangered, or

(iii) in any other circumstances as determined by the Attorney General.

In applying clause (i), the providing of parole at a point of entry in a district shall be deemed to constitute an application for asylum in the district.

(B) Not more than $20,000,000 shall be made available for all localities under this paragraph.

(C) For purposes of subparagraph (A), the requirement of paragraph (1) that an immigration emergency be determined shall not apply.

(D) A decision with respect to an application for reimbursement under subparagraph (A) shall be made by the Attorney General within 15 days after the date of receipt of the application.

(P.L. 101-649 (IMMACT90) (11/29/90) §705(a) [revising (b)(1), adding (b)(2)]; P.L. 102-232 (MTINA) (12/12/91, *effective* 4/1/92), §308(d) [revising (b)(2)(A)].)

## Sec. 405 Savings Clauses
[8 U.S.C. 1101, note]

(a) Nothing contained in this Act, unless otherwise specifically provided therein, shall be construed to affect the validity of any declaration of intention, petition for naturalization, certificate of naturalization, certificate of citizenship, warrant of arrest, order or warrant of deportation, order of exclusion, or other document or proceeding which shall be valid at the time this Act shall take effect; or to affect any prosecution, suit, action, or proceedings, civil or criminal, brought, or any status, condition, right in process of acquisition, act, thing, liability, obligation, or matter, civil or criminal, done or existing, at the time this Act shall take effect; but as to all such prosecutions, suits, actions, proceedings, statutes, conditions, rights, acts, things, liabilities, obligations, or matters the statutes or parts of statutes repealed by this Act are, unless otherwise specifically provided therein, hereby continued in force and effect. When an immigrant, in possession of an unexpired immigrant visa issued prior to the effective date of this Act, makes application for admission, his admissibility shall be determined under the provisions of law in effect on the date of the issuance of such visa. An application for suspension of deportation under section 19 of the Immigration Act of 1917, as amended, or for adjustment of status under section 4 of the Dis-

---

[205] Sec. 705(b) of P.L. 101-649 (IMMACT90) (11/29/90), provides that INA §404(b)(2)(A)(i), as amended, applies with respect to increases in the number of asylum applications filed in a calendar quarter beginning on or after 1/1/89.

placed Persons Act of 1948, as amended, which is pending on the date of enactment of this Act, shall be regarded as a proceeding within the meaning of this subsection.

**(b)** Except as otherwise specifically provided in title III, any petition for naturalization heretofore filed which may be pending at the time this Act shall take effect shall be heard and determined in accordance with the requirements of law in effect when such petition was filed.

**(c)** Except as otherwise specifically provided in this Act, the repeal of any statute by this Act shall not terminate nationality heretofore lawfully acquired nor restore nationality heretofore lost under any law of the United States or any treaty to which the United States may have been a party.

**(d)** Except as otherwise specifically provided in this Act, or any amendment thereto, fees, charges and prices for purposes specified in title V of the Independent Offices Appropriation Act, 1952 (Public Law 137, Eighty-second Congress, approved August 31, 1951), may be fixed and established in the manner and by the head of any Federal Agency as specified in that Act.

**(e)** This Act shall not be construed to repeal, alter, or amend section 231(a) of the Act of April 30, 1946 (60 Stat. 148; 22 U.S.C. 1281(a)), the Act of June 20, 1949 (Public Law 110, section 8, Eighty-first Congress, first session; 63 Stat. 208), the Act of June 5, 1950 (Public Law 535, Eighty-first Congress, second session), nor title V of the Agricultural Act of 1949, as amended (Public Law 78, Eighty-second Congress, first session).

### Sec. 406 Separability
### [8 U.S.C. 1101, note]

If any particular provision of this Act, or the application thereof to any person or circumstance, is held invalid, the remainder of the Act and the application of such provision to other persons or circumstances shall not be affected thereby.

### Sec. 407 Effective Date
### [8 U.S.C. 1101, note]

Except as provided in subsection (k) of section 401, this Act shall take effect at 12:01 ante meridian United States Eastern Standard Time on the one hundred eightieth day immediately following the date of its enactment.[206]

## Chapter 2 — Refugee Assistance

### Sec. 411 Office of Refugee Resettlement; Establishment; Appointment of Director; Functions
### [8 U.S.C. 1521]

**(a)** There is established, within the Department of Health and Human Services, an office to be known as the Office of Refugee Resettlement (hereinafter in this chapter referred to as the "Office"). The head of the Office shall be a Director (hereinafter in this chapter referred to as the "Director"), to be appointed by the Secretary of Health and Human Services (hereinafter in this chapter referred to as the "Secretary").

**(b)** The function of the Office and its Director is to fund and administer (directly or through arrangements with other Federal agencies), in consultation with the Secretary of State, programs of the Federal Government under this chapter.[207]

---

[206] The Act took effect on 12/24/52.

(June 27, 1952, ch. 477, title IV, ch. 2, §411, as added by P.L. 96-212 (3/17/80); as amended by P.L. 103-236 (4/30/94) [revising reference "Secretary of State" to "U.S. Coordinator for Refugee Affairs"].)

## Sec. 412 Authorization for Programs for Domestic Resettlement of and Assistance to Refugees [8 U.S.C. 1522]

### (a) Conditions and considerations.—

(1) (A) In providing assistance under this section, the Director shall, to the extent of available appropriations,

(i) make available sufficient resources for employment training and placement in order to achieve economic self-sufficiency among refugees as quickly as possible,

(ii) provide refugees with the opportunity to acquire sufficient English language training to enable them to become effectively resettled as quickly as possible,

(iii) insure that cash assistance is made available to refugees in such a manner as not to discourage their economic self-sufficiency, in accordance with subsection (e)(2), and

(iv) insure that women have the same opportunities as men to participate in training and instruction.

(B) It is the intent of Congress that in providing refugee assistance under this section—

(i) employable refugees should be placed on jobs as soon as possible after their arrival in the United States;

(ii) social service funds should be focused on employment-related services, English-as-a-second-language training (in non-work hours where possible), and case-management services; and

(iii) local voluntary agency activities should be conducted in close cooperation and advance consultation with State and local governments.

(2) (A) The Director and the Federal agency administering subsection (b)(1), shall consult regularly (not less often than quarterly) with State and local governments and private nonprofit voluntary agencies concerning the sponsorship process and the intended distribution of refugees among the States and localities before their placement in those States and localities.

(B) The Director shall develop and implement, in consultation with representatives of voluntary agencies and State and local governments, policies and strategies for the placement and resettlement of refugees within the United States.

(C) Such policies and strategies, to the extent practicable and except under such unusual circumstances as the Director may recognize, shall—

(i) insure that a refugee is not initially placed or resettled in an area highly impacted (as determined under regulations prescribed by the Director after consultation with such agencies and governments) by the presence of refugees or comparable populations unless the refugee has a spouse, parent, sibling, son, or daughter residing in that area,

---

[207] Paragraph (1) of §162(n) of the Foreign Relations Authorization Act, Fiscal Years 1994 and 1995 (P.L. 103-236 (4/30/94)) substituted a reference to the Secretary of State for a reference to the U.S. Coordinator for Refugee Affairs; paragraphs (2) and (3) of that section deleted subsequent references in §412 & §413 to the Coordinator.

(ii) provide for a mechanism whereby representatives of local affiliates of voluntary agencies regularly (not less often than quarterly) meet with representatives of State and local governments to plan and coordinate in advance of their arrival the appropriate placement of refugees among the various States and localities, and

(iii) take into account—

(I) the proportion of refugees and comparable entrants in the population in the area,

(II) the availability of employment opportunities, affordable housing, and public and private resources (including educational, health care, and mental health services) for refugees in the area,

(III) the likelihood of refugees placed in the area becoming self-sufficient and free from long-term dependence on public assistance, and

(IV) the secondary migration of refugees to and from the area that is likely to occur.

(D) With respect to the location of placement of refugees within a State, the Federal agency administering subsection (b)(1) shall, consistent with such policies and strategies and to the maximum extent possible, take into account recommendations of the State.

(3) In the provision of domestic assistance under this section, the Director shall make a periodic assessment, based on refugee population and other relevant factors, of the relative needs of refugees for assistance and services under this chapter and the resources available to meet such needs. The Director shall compile and maintain data on secondary migration of refugees within the United States and, by State of residence and nationality, on the proportion of refugees receiving cash or medical assistance described in subsection (e). In allocating resources, the Director shall avoid duplication of services and provide for maximum coordination between agencies providing related services.

(4) (A) No grant or contract may be awarded under this section unless an appropriate proposal and application (including a description of the agency's ability to perform the services specified in the proposal) are submitted to, and approved by, the appropriate administering official. Grants and contracts under this section shall be made to those agencies which the appropriate administering official determines can best perform the services. Payments may be made for activities authorized under this chapter in advance or by way of reimbursement. In carrying out this section, the Director, the Secretary of State, and any such other appropriate administering official are authorized—

(i) to make loans, and

(ii) to accept and use money, funds, property, and services of any kind made available by gift, devise, bequest, grant, or otherwise for the purpose of carrying out this section.

(B) No funds may be made available under this chapter (other than under subsection (b)(1)) to States or political subdivisions in the form of block grants, per capita grants, or similar consolidated grants or contracts. Such funds shall be made available under separate grants or contracts—

(i) for medical screening and initial medical treatment under subsection (b)(5),

(ii) for services for refugees under subsection (c)(1),

(iii) for targeted assistance project grants under subsection (c)(2), and

(iv) for assistance for refugee children under subsection (d)(2).

(C) The Director may not delegate to a State or political subdivision his authority to review or approve grants or contracts under this chapter or the terms under which such grants or contracts are made.

(5) Assistance and services funded under this section shall be provided to refugees without regard to race, religion, nationality, sex, or political opinion.

(6) As a condition for receiving assistance under this section, a State must—

(A) submit to the Director a plan which provides—

(i) a description of how the State intends to encourage effective refugee resettlement and to promote economic self-sufficiency as quickly as possible,

(ii) a description of how the State will insure that language training and employment services are made available to refugees receiving cash assistance,

(iii) for the designation of an individual, employed by the State, who will be responsible for insuring coordination of public and private resources in refugee resettlement,

(iv) for the care and supervision of and legal responsibility for unaccompanied refugee children in the State, and

(v) for the identification of refugees who at the time of resettlement in the State are determined to have medical conditions requiring, or medical histories indicating a need for, treatment or observation and such monitoring of such treatment or observation as may be necessary;

(B) meet standards, goals, and priorities, developed by the Director, which assure the effective resettlement of refugees and which promote their economic self-sufficiency as quickly as possible and the efficient provision of services; and

(C) submit to the Director, within a reasonable period of time after the end of each fiscal year, a report on the uses of funds provided under this chapter which the State is responsible for administering.

(7) The Secretary, together with the Secretary of State with respect to assistance provided by the Secretary of State under subsection (b), shall develop a system of monitoring the assistance provided under this section. This system shall include—

(A) evaluations of the effectiveness of the programs funded under this section and the performance of States, grantees, and contractors;

(B) financial auditing and other appropriate monitoring to detect any fraud, abuse, or mismanagement in the operation of such programs; and

(C) data collection on the services provided and the results achieved.

(8) The Attorney General shall provide the Director with information supplied by refugees in conjunction with their applications to the Attorney General for adjustment of status, and the Director shall compile, summarize, and evaluate such information.

(9) The Secretary, the Secretary of Education, the Attorney General, and the Secretary of State may issue such regulations as each deems appropriate to carry out this chapter.

(10) For purposes of this chapter, the term "refugee" includes any alien described in section 207(c)(2).

## (b) Program of initial resettlement.—

(1)  (A) For—

(i) fiscal years 1980 and 1981, the Secretary of State is authorized, and

(ii) fiscal year 1982 and succeeding fiscal years, the Director (except as provided in subparagraph (B)) is authorized,

to make grants to, and contracts with, public or private nonprofit agencies for initial resettlement (including initial reception and placement with sponsors) of refugees in the United States. Grants to, or contracts with, private nonprofit voluntary agencies under this paragraph shall be made consistent with the objectives of this chapter, taking into account the different resettlement approaches and practices of such agencies. Resettlement assistance under this paragraph shall be provided in coordination with the Director's provision of other assistance under this chapter. Funds provided to agencies under such grants and contracts may only be obligated or expended during the fiscal year in which they are provided (or the subsequent fiscal year or such subsequent fiscal period as the Federal contracting agency may approve) to carry out the purposes of this subsection.

(B) If the President determines that the Director should not administer the program under this paragraph, the authority of the Director under the first sentence of subparagraph (A) shall be exercised by such officer as the President shall from time to time specify.[208]

(2) The Director is authorized to develop programs for such orientation, instruction in English, and job training for refugees, and such other education and training of refugees, as facilitates their resettlement in the United States. The Director is authorized to implement such programs, in accordance with the provisions of this section, with respect to refugees in the United States. The Secretary of State is authorized to implement such programs with respect to refugees awaiting entry into the United States.

(3) The Secretary is authorized to make arrangements (including cooperative arrangements with other Federal agencies) for the temporary care of refugees in the United States in emergency circumstances, including the establishment of processing centers, if necessary, without regard to such provisions of law (other than the Renegotiation Act of 1951 and section 414(b) of this chapter) regulating the making, performance, amendment, or modification of contracts and the expenditure of funds of the United States Government as the Secretary may specify.

(4) The Secretary shall—

(A) assure that an adequate number of trained staff are available at the location at which the refugees enter the United States to assure that all necessary medical records are available and in proper order;

(B) provide for the identification of refugees who have been determined to have medical conditions affecting the public health and requiring treatment;

(C) assure that State or local health officials at the resettlement destination within the United States of each refugee are promptly notified of the refugee's arrival and provided with all applicable medical records; and

---

[208] The President has specified the Secretary of State. *See* letter of 1/13/81, from Pres. Carter to the Speaker of the House and President of the Senate, 17 *Weekly Compil. of Pres. Docs.*, p. 2880.

(D) provide for such monitoring of refugees identified under subparagraph (B) as will insure that they receive appropriate and timely treatment.

The Secretary shall develop and implement methods for monitoring and assessing the quality of medical screening and related health services provided to refugees awaiting resettlement in the United States.

(5) The Director is authorized to make grants to, and enter into contracts with, State and local health agencies for payments to meet their costs of providing medical screening and initial medical treatment to refugees.

(6) The Comptroller General shall directly conduct an annual financial audit of funds expended under each grant or contract made under paragraph (1) for fiscal year 1986 and for fiscal year 1987.

(7) Each grant or contract with an agency under paragraph (1) shall require the agency to do the following:

(A) To provide quarterly performance and financial status reports to the Federal agency administering paragraph (1).

(B) (i) To provide, directly or through its local affiliate, notice to the appropriate county or other local welfare office at the time that the agency becomes aware that a refugee is offered employment and to provide notice to the refugee that such notice has been provided, and

(ii) upon request of such a welfare office to which a refugee has applied for cash assistance, to furnish that office with documentation respecting any cash or other resources provided directly by the agency to the refugee under this subsection.

(C) To assure that refugees, known to the agency as having been identified pursuant to paragraph (4)(B) as having medical conditions affecting the public health and requiring treatment, report to the appropriate county or other health agency upon their resettlement in an area.

(D) To fulfill its responsibility to provide for the basic needs (including food, clothing, shelter, and transportation for job interviews and training) of each refugee resettled and to develop and implement a resettlement plan including the early employment of each refugee resettled and to monitor the implementation of such plan.

(E) To transmit to the Federal agency administering paragraph (1) an annual report describing the following:

(i) The number of refugees placed (by county of placement) and the expenditures made in the year under the grant or contract, including the proportion of such expenditures used for administrative purposes and for provision of services.

(ii) The proportion of refugees placed by the agency in the previous year who are receiving cash or medical assistance described in subsection (e).

(iii) The efforts made by the agency to monitor placement of the refugees and the activities of local affiliates of the agency.

(iv) The extent to which the agency has coordinated its activities with local social service providers in a manner which avoids duplication of activities and has provided notices to local welfare offices and the reporting of medical conditions of certain aliens to local health departments in accordance with subparagraphs (B)(i) and (C).

(v) Such other information as the agency administering paragraph (1) deems to be appropriate in monitoring the effectiveness of agencies in carrying out their functions under such grants and contracts.

The agency administering paragraph (1) shall promptly forward a copy of each annual report transmitted under subparagraph (E) to the Committees on the Judiciary of the House of Representatives and of the Senate,

(8) The Federal agency administering paragraph (1) shall establish criteria for the performance of agencies under grants and contracts under that paragraph, and shall include criteria relating to an agency's—

(A) efforts to reduce welfare dependency among refugees resettled by that agency,

(B) collection of travel loans made to refugees resettled by that agency for travel to the United States,

(C) arranging for effective local sponsorship and other nonpublic assistance for refugees resettled by that agency,

(D) cooperation with refugee mutual assistance associations, local social service providers, health agencies, and welfare offices,

(E) compliance with the guidelines established by the Director for the placement and resettlement of refugees within the United States, and

(F) compliance with other requirements contained in the grant or contract, including the reporting and other requirements under subsection (b)(7).

The Federal administering agency shall use the criteria in the process of awarding or renewing grants and contracts under paragraph (1).

**(c) Project grants and contracts for services for refugees.—**

(1) (A) The Director is authorized to make grants to, and enter into contracts with, public or private nonprofit agencies for projects specifically designed—

(i) to assist refugees in obtaining the skills which are necessary for economic self-sufficiency, including projects for job training, employment services, day care, professional refresher training, and other recertification services;

(ii) to provide training in English where necessary (regardless of whether the refugees are employed or receiving cash or other assistance); and

(iii) to provide where specific needs have been shown and recognized by the Director, health (including mental health) services, social services, educational and other services.

(B) The funds available for a fiscal year for grants and contracts under subparagraph (A) shall be allocated among the States based on the total number of refugees (including children and adults) who arrived in the United States not more than 36 months before the beginning of such fiscal year and who are actually residing in each State (taking into account secondary migration) as of the beginning of the fiscal year.

(C) Any limitation which the Director establishes on the proportion of funds allocated to a State under this paragraph that the State may use for services other than those described in subsection (a)(1)(B)(ii) shall not apply if the Director receives a plan (established by or in consultation with local governments) and determines that the plan provides for the maximum appropriate provision of employment-related services for, and the maximum placement of, employable refugees consistent with performance standards established under section 106 of the Job Training Partnership Act.

(2) (A) The Director is authorized to make grants to States for assistance to counties and similar areas in the States where, because of factors such as unusually large refugee populations (including secondary migration), high refugee concentrations, and high use of public assistance by refugees, there exists and can be demonstrated a specific need for supplementation of available resources for services to refugees.

(B) Grants shall be made available under this paragraph—

(i) primarily for the purpose of facilitating refugee employment and achievement of self-sufficiency,

(ii) in a manner that does not supplant other refugee program funds and that assures that not less than 95 percent of the amount of the grant award is made available to the county or other local entity.

**(d) Assistance for refugee children.—**

(1) The Secretary of Education is authorized to make grants, and enter into contracts, for payments for projects to provide special educational services (including English language training) to refugee children in elementary and secondary schools where a demonstrated need has been shown.

(2) (A) The Director is authorized to provide assistance, reimbursement to States, and grants to and contracts with public and private nonprofit agencies, for the provision of child welfare services, including foster care maintenance payments and services and health care, furnished to any refugee child (except as provided in subparagraph (B)) during the thirty-six month period beginning with the first month in which such refugee child is in the United States.

(B) (i) In the case of a refugee child who is unaccompanied by a parent or other close adult relative (as defined by the Director), the services described in subparagraph (A) may be furnished until the month after the child attains eighteen years of age (or such higher age as the State's child welfare services plan under part B of title IV of the Social Security Act prescribes for the availability of such services to any other child in that State).

(ii) The Director shall attempt to arrange for the placement under the laws of the States of such unaccompanied refugee children, who have been accepted for admission to the United States, before (or as soon as possible after) their arrival in the United States. During any interim period while such a child is in the United States or in transit to the United States but before the child is so placed, the Director shall assume legal responsibility (including financial responsibility) for the child, if necessary, and is authorized to make necessary decisions to provide for the child's immediate care.

(iii) In carrying out the Director's responsibilities under clause (ii), the Director is authorized to enter into contracts with appropriate public or private nonprofit agencies under such conditions as the Director determines to be appropriate.

(iv) The Director shall prepare and maintain a list of

(I) all such unaccompanied children who have entered the United States after April 1, 1975,

(II) the names and last known residences of their parents (if living) at the time of arrival, and

(III) the children's location, status, and progress.

**(e)**[209] **Cash assistance and medical assistance to refugees.—**

(1) The Director is authorized to provide assistance, reimbursement to States, and grants to, and contracts with, public or private nonprofit agencies for 100 per centum of the cash assistance and medical assistance provided to any refugee during the thirty-six month period beginning with the first month in which such refugee has entered the United States and for the identifiable and reasonable administrative costs of providing this assistance.

(2) (A) Cash assistance provided under this subsection to an employable refugee is conditioned, except for good cause shown—

(i) on the refugee's registration with an appropriate agency providing employment services described in subsection (c)(1)(A)(i), or, if there is no such agency available, with an appropriate State or local employment service;

(ii) on the refugee's participation in any available and appropriate social service or targeted assistance program (funded under subsection (c)) providing job or language training in the area in which the refugee resides; and

(iii) on the refugee's acceptance of appropriate offers of employment.[210]

(B) Cash assistance shall not be made available to refugees who are full-time students in institutions of higher education (as defined by the Director after consultation with the Secretary of Education).

(C) In the case of a refugee who—[211]

(i) refuses an offer of employment which has been determined to be appropriate either by the agency responsible for the initial resettlement of the refugee under subsection (b) or by the appropriate State or local employment service,

---

[209] Sec. 313(c) of the Refugee Act of 1980 (Pub. L. 96-212, 3/17/80, 94 Stat. 117) provides as follows:

(c) Notwithstanding [INA §412(e)(1)] and in lieu of any assistance which may otherwise be provided under such section with respect to Cuban refugees who entered the United States and were receiving assistance under §2(b) of the Migration and Refugee Assistance Act of 1962 before 10/1/78, the Director of the Office of Refugee Resettlement is authorized—

(1) to provide reimbursement—

(A) in fiscal year 1980, for 75 percent,

(B) in fiscal year 1981, for 60 percent,

(C) in fiscal year 1982, for 45 percent, and

(D) in fiscal year 1983, for 25 percent,

of the non-Federal costs of providing cash and medical assistance (other than assistance described in paragraph (2) to such refugees, and

(2) to provide reimbursement in any fiscal year for 100 percent of the non-Federal costs associated with such Cuban refugees with respect to whom supplemental security income payments were being paid as of September 30, 1978, under title XVI of the Social Security Act.

[210] For aliens who enter the U.S. as refugees before 4/1/87, the following sentence (which was stricken by §9(a)(1) of the Refugee Assistance Extension Act, 1986 (P.L. 99-605, 11/6/86)) applies:

"Such cash assistance provided to such a refugee shall be terminated (after opportunity for an administrative hearing) with the month in which the refugee refuses such an appropriate offer of employment or refuses to participate in such an available and appropriate social service program."

[211] This subparagraph applies to aliens who enter the U.S. as refugees on or after 4/1/87, under §9(c) of the Refugee Assistance Extension Act, 1986 (P.L. 99-605, 11/6/86).

(ii) refuses to go to a job interview which has been arranged through such agency or service, or

(iii) refuses to participate in a social service or targeted assistance program referred to in subparagraph (A)(ii) which such agency or service determines to be available and appropriate,

cash assistance to the refugee shall be terminated (after opportunity for an administrative hearing) for a period of three months (for the first such refusal) or for a period of six months (for any subsequent refusal).

(3) The Director shall develop plans to provide English training and other appropriate services and training to refugees receiving cash assistance.

(4) If a refugee is eligible for aid or assistance under a State program funded under part A of title IV or under title XIX of the Social Security Act, or for supplemental security income benefits (including State supplementary payments) under the program established under title XVI of that Act, funds authorized under this subsection shall only be used for the non-Federal share of such aid or assistance, or for such supplementary payments, with respect to cash and medical assistance provided with respect to such refugee under this paragraph.

(5) The Director is authorized to allow for the provision of medical assistance under paragraph (1) to any refugee, during the one-year period after entry, who does not qualify for assistance under a State plan approved under title XIX of the Social Security Act on account of any resources or income requirement of such plan, but only if the Director determines that—

(A) this will (i) encourage economic self-sufficiency, or (ii) avoid a significant burden on State and local governments; and

(B) the refugee meets such alternative financial resources and income requirements as the Director shall establish.

(6) As a condition for receiving assistance, reimbursement, or a contract under this subsection and notwithstanding any other provision of law, a State or agency must provide assurances that whenever a refugee applies for cash or medical assistance for which assistance or reimbursement is provided under this subsection, the State or agency must notify promptly the agency (or local affiliate) which provided for the initial resettlement of the refugee under subsection (b) of the fact that the refugee has so applied.

(7) (A) The Secretary shall develop and implement alternative projects for refugees who have been in the United States less than thirty-six months, under which refugees are provided interim support, medical services, support services, and case management, as needed, in a manner that encourages self-sufficiency, reduces welfare dependency, and fosters greater coordination among the resettlement agencies and service providers. The Secretary may permit alternative projects to cover specific groups of refugees who have been in the United States 36 months or longer if the Secretary determines that refugees in the group have been significantly and disproportionately dependent on welfare and need the services provided under the project in order to become self-sufficient and that their coverage under the projects would be cost-effective.

(B) Refugees covered under such alternative projects shall be precluded from receiving cash or medical assistance under any other paragraph of this subsection or under title XIX or part A of title IV of the Social Security Act.

(C) The Secretary shall report to Congress not later than October 31, 1985, on the results of these projects and on any recommendations respecting changes in the refugee assistance program under this section to take into account such results.

(D) To the extent that the use of such funds is consistent with the purposes of such provisions, funds appropriated under section 414(a) of this Act, part A of title IV of the Social Security Act, or title XIX of such Act, may be used for the purpose of implementing and evaluating alternative projects under this paragraph.

(8) In its provision of assistance to refugees, a State or political subdivision shall consider the recommendations of, and assistance provided by, agencies with grants or contracts under subsection (b)(1).

**(f) Assistance to states and counties for incarceration of certain Cuban nationals; priority for removal and return to Cuba.—**

(1) The Attorney General shall pay compensation to States and to counties for costs incurred by the States and counties to confine in prisons, during the fiscal year for which such payment is made, nationals of Cuba who—

(A) were paroled into the United States in 1980 by the Attorney General,

(B) after such parole committed any violation of State or county law for which a term of imprisonment was imposed, and

(C) at the time of such parole and such violation were not aliens lawfully admitted to the United States—

(i) for permanent residence, or

(ii) under the terms of an immigrant or a nonimmigrant visa issued,

under this Act.

(2) For a State or county to be eligible to receive compensation under this subsection, the chief executive officer of the State or county shall submit to the Attorney General, in accordance with rules to be issued by the Attorney General, an application containing—

(A) the number and names of the Cuban nationals with respect to whom the State or county is entitled to such compensation, and

(B) such other information as the Attorney General may require.

(3) For a fiscal year the Attorney General shall pay the costs described in paragraph (1) to each State and county determined by the Attorney General to be eligible under paragraph (2); except that if the amounts appropriated for the fiscal year to carry out this subsection are insufficient to cover all such payments, each of such payments shall be ratably reduced so that the total of such payments equals the amounts so appropriated.

(4) The authority of the Attorney General to pay compensation under this subsection shall be effective for any fiscal year only to the extent and in such amounts as may be provided in advance in appropriation Acts.

(5) It shall be the policy of the United States Government that the President, in consultation with the Attorney General and all other appropriate Federal officials and all appropriate State and county officials referred to in paragraph (2), shall place top priority on seeking the expeditious removal from this country and the return to Cuba of Cuban nationals described in

paragraph (1) by any reasonable and responsible means, and to this end the Attorney General may use the funds authorized to carry out this subsection to conduct such policy.

(June 27, 1952, ch. 477, title IV, ch. 2, §412, as added by P.L. 96-212 (3/17/80); as amended by P.L. 97-363 (10/25/82); P.L. 98-164 (11/22/83); P.L. 98-473 (10/12/84); P.L. 99-605 (11/6/86); P.L. 100-525 (10/24/88); P.L. 103-236 (4/30/94); P.L. 103-416 (INTCA) (10/25/94, *effective* 4/1/95); P.L. 104-193 (8/22/96), title I, §110(s); P.L. 104-208 (IIRAIRA) (9/30/96), div. C, title VI, §671(e)(7) [revising (b)(3)–(4)].)

## Sec. 413 Congressional Reports
[8 U.S.C. 1523]

**(a)** The Secretary, shall submit a report on activities under this chapter to the Committees on the Judiciary of the House of Representatives and of the Senate not later than the January 31 following the end of each fiscal year, beginning with fiscal year 1980.

**(b)** Each such report shall contain—

(1) an updated profile of the employment and labor force statistics for refugees who have entered the United States within the five-fiscal-year period immediately preceding the fiscal year within which the report is to be made and for refugees who entered earlier and who have shown themselves to be significantly and disproportionately dependent on welfare as well as a description of the extent to which refugees received the forms of assistance or services under this chapter during that period;

(2) a description of the geographic location of refugees;

(3) a summary of the results of the monitoring and evaluation conducted under section 412(a)(7) during the period for which the report is submitted;

(4) a description of

(A) the activities, expenditures, and policies of the Office under this chapter and of the activities of States, voluntary agencies, and sponsors, and

(B) the Director's plans for improvement of refugee resettlement;

(5) evaluations of the extent to which

(A) the services provided under this chapter are assisting refugees in achieving economic self-sufficiency, achieving ability in English, and achieving employment commensurate with their skills and abilities, and

(B) any fraud, abuse, or mismanagement has been reported in the provisions of services or assistance;

(6) a description of any assistance provided by the Director pursuant to section 412(e)(5);

(7) a summary of the location and status of unaccompanied refugee children admitted to the United States; and

(8) a summary of the information compiled and evaluation made under section 412(a)(8).

(June 27, 1952, ch. 477, title IV, ch. 2, §413, as added by P.L. 96-212 (3/17/80); as amended by P.L. 97-363 (10/25/82); P.L. 99-605 (11/6/86); P.L. 100-525 (10/24/88); P.L. 103-236 (4/30/94), §162(n)(3).)

## Sec. 414 Authorization of Appropriations
[8 U.S.C. 1524]

(a) There are authorized to be appropriated for each of fiscal years 2000 through 2002 such sums as may be necessary to carry out this chapter.

(b) The authority to enter into contracts under this chapter shall be effective for any fiscal year only to such extent or in such amounts as are provided in advance in appropriation Acts.

(June 27, 1952, ch. 477, title IV, ch. 2, §414, as added by P.L. 96-212 (3/17/80); as amended by P.L. 97-363 (10/25/82); P.L. 99-605 (11/6/86); P.L. 100-525 (10/24/88); P.L. 102-110 (10/1/91); P.L. 103-37 (8/8/93), §1 [revising (a) to authorize appropriations for fiscal years 1993–1994]; P.L. 103-416 (INTCA) (10/25/94, *effective* 4/1/95), §208 [revising (a) to authorize appropriations for fiscal years 1995–1997]; P.L. 105-78 (11/13/97), title VI, §604(a) [revising (a) to authorize appropriations for fiscal years 1998–1999]; P.L. 105-136 (12/2/97), §1(a); P.L. 106-104 (11/13/99), §3 [revising (a) to authorize appropriations for fiscal years 2000–2002].)

# Title V—Alien Terrorist Removal Procedures (§§501–07)

## Sec. 501 Definitions
[8 U.S.C. 1531]

As used in this title—

(1) the term "alien terrorist" means any alien described in section 241(a)(4)(B);

(2) the term "classified information" has the same meaning as in section 1(a) of the Classified Information Procedures Act (18 U.S.C. App.);

(3) the term "national security" has the same meaning as in section 1(b) of the Classified Information Procedures Act (18 U.S.C. App.);

(4) the term "removal court" means the court described in section 502;

(5) the term "removal hearing" means the hearing described in section 504;

(6) the term "removal proceeding" means a proceeding under this title; and

(7) the term "special attorney" means an attorney who is on the panel established under section 502(e).

(June 27, 1952, ch. 477, title V, §501, as added by P.L. 104-132 (AEDPA) (4/24/96), title IV, §401(a); as amended by P.L. 104-208 (IIRAIRA) (9/30/96), div. C, title III, §308(g)(1), §354(a)(5) [revising (7), effective as if included in the enactment of subtitle A of title IV of AEDPA].)

## Sec. 502 Establishment of Removal Court
[8 U.S.C. 1532]

(a) Designation of Judges.— The Chief Justice of the United States shall publicly designate 5 district court judges from 5 of the United States judicial circuits who shall constitute a court that shall have jurisdiction to conduct all removal proceedings. The Chief Justice may, in the Chief Justice's discretion, designate the same judges under this section as are designated pursuant to section 103(a) of the Foreign Intelligence Surveillance Act of 1978 (50 U.S.C. 1803(a)).

(b) Terms.— Each judge designated under subsection (a) shall serve for a term of 5 years and shall be eligible for redesignation, except that of the members first designated—

(1) 1 member shall serve for a term of 1 year;

(2) 1 member shall serve for a term of 2 years;

(3) 1 member shall serve for a term of 3 years; and

(4) 1 member shall serve for a term of 4 years.

**(c) Chief Judge.—**

(1) *Designation.—* The Chief Justice shall publicly designate one of the judges of the removal court to be the chief judge of the removal court.

(2) *Responsibilities.—* The chief judge shall—

(A) promulgate rules to facilitate the functioning of the removal court; and

(B) assign the consideration of cases to the various judges on the removal court.

**(d) Expeditious and confidential nature of proceedings.—** The provisions of section 103(c) of the Foreign Intelligence Surveillance Act of 1978 (50 U.S.C. 1803(c)) shall apply to removal proceedings in the same manner as they apply to proceedings under that Act.

**(e) Establishment of panel of special attorneys.—** The removal court shall provide for the designation of a panel of attorneys each of whom—

(1) has a security clearance which affords the attorney access to classified information, and

(2) has agreed to represent permanent resident aliens with respect to classified information under section 504(e)(3) in accordance with (and subject to the penalties under) this title.

(June 27, 1952, ch. 477, title V, §502, as added by P.L. 104-132 (AEDPA) (4/24/96), title IV, §401(a); amended by P.L. 104-208 (IIRAIRA) (9/30/96), div. C, title III, §354(a)(4) [revising (e), effective as if included in the enactment of subtitle A of title IV of AEDPA])

**Sec. 503 Removal Court Procedure**
**[8 U.S.C. 1533]**

**(a) Application.—**

(1) *In general.—* In any case in which the Attorney General has classified information that an alien is an alien terrorist, the Attorney General may seek removal of the alien under this title by filing an application with the removal court that contains—

(A) the identity of the attorney in the Department of Justice making the application;

(B) a certification by the Attorney General or the Deputy Attorney General that the application satisfies the criteria and requirements of this section;

(C) the identity of the alien for whom authorization for the removal proceeding is sought; and

(D) a statement of the facts and circumstances relied on by the Department of Justice to establish probable cause that—

(i) the alien is an alien terrorist;

(ii) the alien is physically present in the United States; and

(iii) with respect to such alien, removal under Title II would pose a risk to the national security of the United States.

(2) *Filing.—* An application under this section shall be submitted ex parte and in camera, and shall be filed under seal with the removal court.

**(b) Right to dismiss.—** The Attorney General may dismiss a removal action under this title at any stage of the proceeding.

## (c) Consideration of application.—

(1) *Basis for decision.*— In determining whether to grant an application under this section, a single judge of the removal court may consider, ex parte and in camera, in addition to the information contained in the application—

(A) other information, including classified information, presented under oath or affirmation; and

(B) testimony received in any hearing on the application, of which a verbatim record shall be kept.

(2) *Approval of order.*— The judge shall issue an order granting the application, if the judge finds that there is probable cause to believe that—

(A) the alien who is the subject of the application has been correctly identified and is an alien terrorist present in the United States; and

(B) removal under Title II would pose a risk to the national security of the United States.

(3) *Denial of order.*— If the judge denies the order requested in the application, the judge shall prepare a written statement of the reasons for the denial, taking all necessary precautions not to disclose any classified information contained in the Government's application.

**(d) Exclusive provisions.**— If an order is issued under this section granting an application, the rights of the alien regarding removal and expulsion shall be governed solely by this title, and except as they are specifically referenced in this title, no other provisions of this Act shall be applicable.

(June 27, 1952, ch. 477, title V, §503, as added by P.L. 104-132 (AEDPA) (4/24/96), title IV, §401(a).)

## Sec. 504 Removal Hearing
[8 U.S.C. 1534]

### (a) In general.—

(1) *Expeditious hearing.*— In any case in which an application for an order is approved under section 503(c)(2), a removal hearing shall be conducted under this section as expeditiously as practicable for the purpose of determining whether the alien to whom the order pertains should be removed from the United States on the grounds that the alien is an alien terrorist.

(2) *Public hearing.*— The removal hearing shall be open to the public.

**(b) Notice.**— An alien who is the subject of a removal hearing under this title shall be given reasonable notice of—

(1) the nature of the charges against the alien, including a general account of the basis for the charges; and

(2) the time and place at which the hearing will be held.

### (c) Rights in hearing.—

(1) *Right of counsel.*— The alien shall have a right to be present at such hearing and to be represented by counsel. Any alien financially unable to obtain counsel shall be entitled to have counsel assigned to represent the alien. Such counsel shall be appointed by the judge pursuant to the plan for furnishing representation for any person financially unable to obtain adequate representation for the district in which the hearing is conducted, as provided for in section 3006A of title 18, United States Code. All provisions of that section shall apply and,

for purposes of determining the maximum amount of compensation, the matter shall be treated as if a felony was charged.

(2) *Introduction of evidence.*— Subject to the limitations in subsection (e), the alien shall have a reasonable opportunity to introduce evidence on the alien's own behalf.

(3) *Examination of witnesses.*— Subject to the limitations in subsection (e), the alien shall have a reasonable opportunity to examine the evidence against the alien and to cross-examine any witness.

(4) *Record.*— A verbatim record of the proceedings and of all testimony and evidence offered or produced at such a hearing shall be kept.

(5) *Removal decision based on evidence at hearing.*— The decision of the judge regarding removal shall be based only on that evidence introduced at the removal hearing.

**(d) Subpoenas.—**

(1) *Request.*— At any time prior to the conclusion of the removal hearing, either the alien or the Department of Justice may request the judge to issue a subpoena for the presence of a named witness (which subpoena may also command the person to whom it is directed to produce books, papers, documents, or other objects designated therein) upon a satisfactory showing that the presence of the witness is necessary for the determination of any material matter. Such a request may be made ex parte except that the judges shall inform the Department of Justice of any request for a subpoena by the alien for a witness or material if compliance with such a subpoena would reveal classified evidence or the source of that evidence. The Department of Justice shall be given a reasonable opportunity to oppose the issuance of such a subpoena.

(2) *Payment for attendance.*— If an application for a subpoena by the alien also makes a showing that the alien is financially unable to pay for the attendance of a witness so requested, the court may order the costs incurred by the process and the fees of the witness so subpoenaed to be paid from funds appropriated for the enforcement of Title II.

(3) *Nationwide service.*— A subpoena under this subsection may be served anywhere in the United States.

(4) *Witness fees.*— A witness subpoenaed under this subsection shall receive the same fees and expenses as a witness subpoenaed in connection with a civil proceeding in a court of the United States.

(5) *No access to classified information.*— Nothing in this subsection is intended to allow an alien to have access to classified information.

**(e) Discovery.—**

(1) *In general.*— For purposes of this title—

(A) the Government is authorized to use in a removal proceedings[212] the fruits of electronic surveillance and unconsented physical searches authorized under the Foreign Intelligence Surveillance Act of 1978 (50 U.S.C. 1801 *et seq.*) without regard to subsections (c), (e), (f), (g), and (h) of section 106 of that Act and discovery of information derived pursuant to such Act, or otherwise collected for national security purposes, shall not be authorized if disclosure would present a risk to the national security of the United States;

---

[212] *Sic.* Should be "in a removal proceeding" or "in removal proceedings."

(B) an alien subject to removal under this title shall not be entitled to suppress evidence that the alien alleges was unlawfully obtained; and

(C) section 3504 of title 18, United States Code, and section 1806(c) of title 50, United States Code, shall not apply if the Attorney General determines that public disclosure would pose a risk to the national security of the United States because it would disclose classified information or otherwise threaten the integrity of a pending investigation.

(2) *Protective orders.*— Nothing in this title shall prevent the United States from seeking protective orders and from asserting privileges ordinarily available to the United States to protect against the disclosure of classified information, including the invocation of the military and state secrets privileges.

(3) *Treatment of classified information.*—

(A) *Use.*— The judge shall examine, ex parte and in camera, any evidence for which the Attorney General determines that public disclosure would pose a risk to the national security of the United States or to the security of any individual because it would disclose classified information and neither the alien nor the public shall be informed of such evidence or its sources other than through reference to the summary provided pursuant to this paragraph. Notwithstanding the previous sentence, the Department of Justice may, in its discretion and, in the case of classified information, after coordination with the originating agency, elect to introduce such evidence in open session.

(B) *Submission.*— With respect to such information, the Government shall submit to the removal court an unclassified summary of the specific evidence that does not pose that risk.

(C) *Approval.*— Not later than 15 days after submission, the judge shall approve the summary if the judge finds that it is sufficient to enable the alien to prepare a defense. The Government shall deliver to the alien a copy of the unclassified summary approved under this subparagraph.

(D) *Disapproval.*—

(i) In general.— If an unclassified summary is not approved by the removal court under subparagraph (C), the Government shall be afforded 15 days to correct the deficiencies identified by the court and submit a revised unclassified summary.

(ii) Revised summary.— If the revised unclassified summary is not approved by the court within 15 days of its submission pursuant to subparagraph (C), the removal hearing shall be terminated unless the judge makes the findings under clause (iii).

(iii) Findings.— The findings described in this clause are, with respect to an alien, that—

(I) the continued presence of the alien in the United States would likely cause serious and irreparable harm to the national security or death or serious bodily injury to any person, and

(II) the provision of the summary would likely cause serious and irreparable harm to the national security or death or serious bodily injury to any person.

(E) *Continuation of hearing without summary.*— If a judge makes the findings described in subparagraph (D)(iii)—

(i) if the alien involved is an alien lawfully admitted for permanent residence, the procedures described in subparagraph (F) shall apply; and

(ii) in all cases the special removal hearing shall continue, the Department of Justice shall cause to be delivered to the alien a statement that no summary is possible, and the classified information submitted in camera and ex parte may be used pursuant to this paragraph.

(F) *Special procedures for access and challenges to classified information by special attorneys in case of lawful permanent aliens.—*

(i) In general.— The procedures described in this subparagraph are that the judge (under rules of the removal court) shall designate a special attorney to assist the alien—

(I) by reviewing in camera the classified information on behalf of the alien, and

(II) by challenging through an in camera proceeding the veracity of the evidence contained in the classified information.

(ii) Restrictions on disclosure.— A special attorney receiving classified information under clause (i)—

(I) shall not disclose the information to the alien or to any other attorney representing the alien, and

(II) who discloses such information in violation of subclause (I) shall be subject to a fine under title 18, United States Code, imprisoned for not less than 10 years nor more than 25 years, or both.

**(f) Arguments.—** Following the receipt of evidence, the Government and the alien shall be given fair opportunity to present argument as to whether the evidence is sufficient to justify the removal of the alien. The Government shall open the argument. The alien shall be permitted to reply. The Government shall then be permitted to reply in rebuttal. The judge may allow any part of the argument that refers to evidence received in camera and ex parte to be heard in camera and ex parte.

**(g) Burden of proof.—** In the hearing, it is the Government's burden to prove, by the preponderance of the evidence, that the alien is subject to removal because the alien is an alien terrorist.

**(h) Rules of evidence.—** The Federal Rules of Evidence shall not apply in a removal hearing.

**(i) Determination of deportation.—** If the judge, after considering the evidence on the record as a whole, finds that the Government has met its burden, the judge shall order the alien removed and detained pending removal from the United States. If the alien was released pending the removal hearing, the judge shall order the Attorney General to take the alien into custody.

**(j) Written order.—** At the time of issuing a decision as to whether the alien shall be removed, the judge shall prepare a written order containing a statement of facts found and conclusions of law. Any portion of the order that would reveal the substance or source of information received in camera and ex parte pursuant to subsection (e) shall not be made available to the alien or the public.

**(k) No right to ancillary relief.—** At no time shall the judge consider or provide for relief from removal based on—

(1) asylum under section 208;

(2) by[213] withholding of removal under section 241(b)(3);

---

[213] *Sic.* The word "by" probably should not be included.

(3) cancellation of removal under section 240A;

(4) voluntary departure under section 244(e);

(5) adjustment of status under section 245; or

(6) registry under section 249.

(*l*) **Report on terrorist removal proceedings.**— Not later than 3 months from the date of the enactment of this subsection,[214] the Attorney General shall submit to Congress a report concerning the effect and efficacy of alien terrorist removal proceedings, including the reasons why proceedings pursuant to this section have not been used by the Attorney General in the past and the effect on the use of these proceedings after the enactment of the USA PATRIOT Act of 2001 (Public Law 107-56).

(June 27, 1952, ch. 477, title V, §504, as added by P.L. 104-132 (AEDPA) (4/24/96), title IV, §401(a); amended by P.L. 104-208 (IIRAIRA) (9/30/96), div. C, title III, §308(g)(7)(B), §354(a)(1) [revising (e)–(f), (j), effective as if included in the enactment of subtitle A of title IV of AEDPA], §357 [revising (k), effective as if included in the enactment of subtitle A of title IV of AEDPA]; P.L. 107-108 (12/28/01), title III, §313 [adding (*l*)].)

## Sec. 505 Appeals
## [8 U.S.C. 1535]

**(a) Appeal of denial of application for removal proceedings.**—

(1) *In general.*— The Attorney General may seek a review of the denial of an order sought in an application filed pursuant to section 503. The appeal shall be filed in the United States Court of Appeals for the District of Columbia Circuit by notice of appeal filed not later than 20 days after the date of such denial.

(2) *Record on appeal.*— The entire record of the proceeding shall be transmitted to the Court of Appeals under seal, and the Court of Appeals shall hear the matter ex parte.

(3) *Standard of review.*— The Court of Appeals shall—

(A) review questions of law de novo; and

(B) set aside a finding of fact only if such finding was clearly erroneous.

**(b) Appeal of determination regarding summary of classified information.**—

(1) *In general.*— The United States may take an interlocutory appeal to the United States Court of Appeals for the District of Columbia Circuit of—

(A) any determination by the judge pursuant to section 504(e)(3); or

(B) the refusal of the court to make the findings permitted by section 504(e)(3).

(2) *Record.*— In any interlocutory appeal taken pursuant to this subsection, the entire record, including any proposed order of the judge, any classified information and the summary of evidence, shall be transmitted to the Court of Appeals. The classified information shall be transmitted under seal. A verbatim record of such appeal shall be kept under seal in the event of any other judicial review.

**(c) Appeal of decision in hearing.**—

---

[214] Subsection enacted 12/28/01.

(1) *In general.*— Subject to paragraph (2), the decision of the judge after a removal hearing may be appealed by either the alien or the Attorney General to the United States Court of Appeals for the District of Columbia Circuit by notice of appeal filed not later than 20 days after the date on which the order is issued. The order shall not be enforced during the pendency of an appeal under this subsection.

(2) *Automatic appeals in cases of permanent resident aliens in which no summary provided.*—

(A) *In general.*— Unless the alien waives the right to a review under this paragraph, in any case involving an alien lawfully admitted for permanent residence who is denied a written summary of classified information under section 504(e)(3) and with respect to which the procedures described in section 504(e)(3)(F) apply, any order issued by the judge shall be reviewed by the Court of Appeals for the District of Columbia Circuit.

(B) *Use of special attorney.*— With respect to any issue relating to classified information that arises in such review, the alien shall be represented only by the special attorney designated under section 504(e)(3)(F)(i) on behalf of the alien.

(3) *Transmittal of record.*— In an appeal or review to the Court of Appeals pursuant to this subsection—

(A) the entire record shall be transmitted to the Court of Appeals; and

(B) information received in camera and ex parte, and any portion of the order that would reveal the substance or source of such information, shall be transmitted under seal.

(4) *Expedited appellate proceeding.*— In an appeal or review to the Court of Appeals under this subsection—

(A) the appeal or review shall be heard as expeditiously as practicable and the court may dispense with full briefing and hear the matter solely on the record of the judge of the removal court and on such briefs or motions as the court may require to be filed by the parties;

(B) the Court of Appeals shall issue an opinion not later than 60 days after the date of the issuance of the final order of the district court;

(C) the court shall review all questions of law de novo; and

(D) a finding of fact shall be accorded deference by the reviewing court and shall not be set aside unless such finding was clearly erroneous, except that in the case of a review under paragraph (2) in which an alien lawfully admitted for permanent residence was denied a written summary of classified information under section 504(c)(3),[215] the Court of Appeals shall review questions of fact de novo.

**(d) Certiorari.**— Following a decision by the Court of Appeals pursuant to subsection (c), the alien or the Attorney General may petition the Supreme Court for a writ of certiorari. In any such case, any information transmitted to the Court of Appeals under seal shall, if such information is also submitted to the Supreme Court, be transmitted under seal. Any order of removal shall not be stayed pending disposition of a writ of certiorari, except as provided by the Court of Appeals or a Justice of the Supreme Court.

**(e) Appeal of detention order.**—

---

[215] *Sic.* Probably should be §504(e)(3).

(1) *In general.*— Sections 3145 through 3148 of title 18, United States Code, pertaining to review and appeal of a release or detention order, penalties for failure to appear, penalties for an offense committed while on release, and sanctions for violation of a release condition shall apply to an alien to whom section 507(b)(1) applies. In applying the previous sentence—

(A) for purposes of section 3145 of such title an appeal shall be taken to the United States Court of Appeals for the District of Columbia Circuit; and

(B) for purposes of section 3146 of such title the alien shall be considered released in connection with a charge of an offense punishable by life imprisonment.

(2) *No review of continued detention.*— The determinations and actions of the Attorney General pursuant to section 507(b)(2)(C) shall not be subject to judicial review, including application for a writ of habeas corpus, except for a claim by the alien that continued detention violates the alien's rights under the Constitution. Jurisdiction over any such challenge shall lie exclusively in the United States Court of Appeals for the District of Columbia Circuit.

(June 27, 1952, ch. 477, title V, §505, as added by P.L. 104-132 (AEDPA) (4/24/96), title IV, §401(a); as amended by P.L. 104-208 (IIRAIRA) (9/30/96), div. C, title III, §354(a)(3) [revising (c), effective as if included in the enactment of subtitle A of title IV of AEDPA].)

## Sec. 506 Custody and Release Pending Removal Hearing
## [8 U.S.C. 1536]

### (a) Upon filing application.—

(1) *In general.*— Subject to paragraphs (2) and (3), the Attorney General may—

(A) take into custody any alien with respect to whom an application under section 503 has been filed; and

(B) retain such an alien in custody in accordance with the procedures authorized by this title.

(2) *Special rules for permanent resident aliens.*—

(A) *Release hearing.*— An alien lawfully admitted for permanent residence shall be entitled to a release hearing before the judge assigned to hear the removal hearing. Such an alien shall be detained pending the removal hearing, unless the alien demonstrates to the court that the alien—

(i) is a person lawfully admitted for permanent residence in the United States;

(ii) if released upon such terms and conditions as the court may prescribe (including the posting of any monetary amount), is not likely to flee; and

(iii) will not endanger national security, or the safety of any person or the community, if released.

(B) *Information considered.*— The judge may consider classified information submitted in camera and ex parte in making a determination whether to release an alien pending the removal hearing.

(3) *Release if order denied and no review sought.*—

(A) *In general.*— Subject to subparagraph (B), if a judge of the removal court denies the order sought in an application filed pursuant to section 503, and the Attorney General does not seek review of such denial, the alien shall be released from custody.

(B) *Application of regular procedures.*— Subparagraph (A) shall not prevent the arrest and detention of the alien pursuant to Title II.

**(b) Conditional release if order denied and review sought.—**

(1) *In general.*— If a judge of the removal court denies the order sought in an application filed pursuant to section 503 and the Attorney General seeks review of such denial, the judge shall release the alien from custody subject to the least restrictive condition, or combination of conditions, of release described in section 3142(b) and clauses (i) through (xiv) of section 3142(c)(1)(B) of title 18, United States Code, that—

(A) will reasonably assure the appearance of the alien at any future proceeding pursuant to this title; and

(B) will not endanger the safety of any other person or the community.

(2) *No release for certain aliens.*— If the judge finds no such condition or combination of conditions, as described in paragraph (1), the alien shall remain in custody until the completion of any appeal authorized by this title.

(June 27, 1952, ch. 477, title V, §503, as added by P.L. 104-132 (AEDPA) (4/24/96), title IV, §401(a).)

## Sec. 507 Custody and Release after Removal Hearing
[8 U.S.C. 1537]

**(a) Release.—**

(1) *In general.*— Subject to paragraph (2), if the judge decides that an alien should not be removed, the alien shall be released from custody.

(2) *Custody pending appeal.*— If the Attorney General takes an appeal from such decision, the alien shall remain in custody, subject to the provision of section 3142 of title 18, United States Code.

**(b) Custody and removal.—**

(1) *Custody.*— If the judge decides that an alien shall be removed, the alien shall be detained pending the outcome of any appeal. After the conclusion of any judicial review thereof which affirms the removal order, the Attorney General shall retain the alien in custody and remove the alien to a country specified under paragraph (2).

(2) *Removal.—*

(A) *In general.*— The removal of an alien shall be to any country which the alien shall designate if such designation does not, in the judgment of the Attorney General, in consultation with the Secretary of State, impair the obligation of the United States under any treaty (including a treaty pertaining to extradition) or otherwise adversely affect the foreign policy of the United States.

(B) *Alternate countries.*— If the alien refuses to designate a country to which the alien wishes to be removed or if the Attorney General, in consultation with the Secretary of State, determines that removal of the alien to the country so designated would impair a treaty obligation or adversely affect United States foreign policy, the Attorney General shall cause the alien to be removed to any country willing to receive such alien.

(C) *Continued detention.*— If no country is willing to receive such an alien, the Attorney General may, notwithstanding any other provision of law, retain the alien in custody. The

Attorney General, in coordination with the Secretary of State, shall make periodic efforts to reach agreement with other countries to accept such an alien and at least every 6 months shall provide to the attorney representing the alien at the removal hearing a written report on the Attorney General's efforts. Any alien in custody pursuant to this subparagraph shall be released from custody solely at the discretion of the Attorney General and subject to such conditions as the Attorney General shall deem appropriate.

(D) *Fingerprinting.*— Before an alien is removed from the United States pursuant to this subsection, or pursuant to an order of removal because such alien is inadmissible under section 212(a)(3)(B), the alien shall be photographed and fingerprinted, and shall be advised of the provisions of section 276(b).

**(c) Continued detention pending trial.—**

(1) *Delay in removal.*— The Attorney General may hold in abeyance the removal of an alien who has been ordered removed, pursuant to this title, to allow the trial of such alien on any Federal or State criminal charge and the service of any sentence of confinement resulting from such a trial.

(2) *Maintenance of custody.*— Pending the commencement of any service of a sentence of confinement by an alien described in paragraph (1), such an alien shall remain in the custody of the Attorney General, unless the Attorney General determines that temporary release of the alien to the custody of State authorities for confinement in a State facility is appropriate and would not endanger national security or public safety.

(3) *Subsequent removal.*— Following the completion of a sentence of confinement by an alien described in paragraph (1), or following the completion of State criminal proceedings which do not result in a sentence of confinement of an alien released to the custody of State authorities pursuant to paragraph (2), such an alien shall be returned to the custody of the Attorney General who shall proceed to the removal of the alien under this title.

**(d) Application of certain provisions relating to escape of prisoners.**— For purposes of sections 751 and 752 of title 18, United States Code, an alien in the custody of the Attorney General pursuant to this title shall be subject to the penalties provided by those sections in relation to a person committed to the custody of the Attorney General by virtue of an arrest on a charge of a felony.

**(e) Rights of aliens in custody.—**

(1) *Family and attorney visits.*— An alien in the custody of the Attorney General pursuant to this title shall be given reasonable opportunity, as determined by the Attorney General, to communicate with and receive visits from members of the alien's family, and to contact, retain, and communicate with an attorney.

(2) *Diplomatic contact.*— An alien in the custody of the Attorney General pursuant to this title shall have the right to contact an appropriate diplomatic or consular official of the alien's country of citizenship or nationality or of any country providing representation services therefore. The Attorney General shall notify the appropriate embassy, mission, or consular office of the alien's detention.

(June 27, 1952, ch. 477, title V, §507, as added by P.L. 104-132 (4/24/96), title IV, §401; as amended P.L. 104-208 (IIRAIRA) (9/30/96), div. C, title III, §308(d)(4)(Q) [revising (b)(2)].)

# APPENDICES

# APPENDIX A
# 8 USC Provisions Not in INA

## Sec. 1182d Denial of visas to confiscators of American property

**(a) Denial of visas.** Except as otherwise provided in section 6091 of title 22, and subject to subsection (b) of this section, the Secretary of State may deny the issuance of a visa to any alien who—

> (1) through the abuse of position, including a governmental or political party position, converts or has converted for personal gain real property that has been confiscated or expropriated, a claim to which is owned by a national of the United States, or who is complicit in such a conversion; or

> (2) induces any of the actions or omissions described in paragraph (1) by any person.

**(b) Exceptions.** Subsection (a) of this section shall not apply to—

> (1) any country established by international mandate through the United Nations; or

> (2) any territory recognized by the United States Government to be in dispute.

**(c) Reporting requirement.** Not later than 6 months after October 21, 1998, and every 12 months thereafter, the Secretary of State shall submit to the Speaker of the House of Representatives and to the chairman of the Committee on Foreign Relations of the Senate a report, including—

> (1) a list of aliens who have been denied a visa under this subsection; and

> (2) a list of aliens who could have been denied a visa under subsection (a) of this section but were issued a visa and an explanation as to why each such visa was issued.

(P.L. 105-277 (10/21/98), div. G, subdiv. B, title XXII, §2225.)


## Sec. 1182e Denial of entry into United States of foreign nationals engaged in establishment or enforcement of forced abortion or sterilization policy

**(a) Denial of entry.** Notwithstanding any other provision of law, the Secretary of State may not issue any visa to, and the Attorney General may not admit to the United States, any foreign national whom the Secretary finds, based on credible and specific information, to have been directly involved in the establishment or enforcement of population control policies forcing a woman to undergo an abortion against her free choice or forcing a man or woman to undergo sterilization against his or her free choice, unless the Secretary has substantial grounds for believing that the foreign national has discontinued his or her involvement with, and support for, such policies.

**(b) Exceptions.** The prohibitions in subsection (a) of this section shall not apply in the case of a foreign national who is a head of state, head of government, or cabinet level minister.

**(c) Waiver.** The Secretary of State may waive the prohibitions in subsection (a) of this section with respect to a foreign national if the Secretary—

> (1) determines that it is important to the national interest of the United States to do so; and

> (2) provides written notification to the appropriate congressional committees containing a justification for the waiver.

(P.L. 106-113 (11/29/99), div. B, §1000 [div. A, title VIII, §801].)

### Sec. 1182f Denial of entry into United States of Chinese and other nationals engaged in coerced organ or bodily tissue transplantation

**(a) Denial of entry.** Notwithstanding any other provision of law and except as provided in subsection (b) of this section, the Secretary shall direct consular officers not to issue a visa to any person whom the Secretary finds, based on credible and specific information, to have been directly involved with the coercive transplantation of human organs or bodily tissue, unless the Secretary has substantial grounds for believing that the foreign national has discontinued his or her involvement with, and support for, such practices.

**(b) Exception.** The prohibitions in subsection (a) of this section do not apply to an applicant who is a head of state, head of government, or cabinet-level minister.

**(c) Waiver.** The Secretary may waive the prohibitions in subsection (a) of this section with respect to a foreign national if the Secretary—

(1) determines that it is important to the national interest of the United States to do so; and

(2) not later than 30 days after the issuance of a visa, provides written notification to the appropriate congressional committees containing a justification for the waiver.

(P.L. 107-228 (9/30/02), div. A, title II, §232.)

### Sec. 1184a Philippine Traders as nonimmigrants

Upon a basis of reciprocity secured by agreement entered into by the President of the United States and the President of the Philippines, a national of the Philippines, and the spouse and children of any such national if accompanying or following to join him, may, if otherwise eligible for a visa and if otherwise admissible into the United States under the Immigration and Nationality Act [8 U.S.C. 1101 *et seq.*] (66 Stat. 163), be considered to be classifiable as a nonimmigrant under section 101(a)(15)(E) of said Act if entering solely for the purposes specified in subsection (i) or (ii) of said section.

(June 18, 1954, ch. 323, 68 Stat. 264.)

### Sec. 1252c Authorizing State and local law enforcement officials to arrest and detain certain illegal aliens

**(a) In general.** Notwithstanding any other provision of law, to the extent permitted by relevant State and local law, State and local law enforcement officials are authorized to arrest and detain an individual who—

(1) is an alien illegally present in the United States; and

(2) has previously been convicted of a felony in the United States and deported or left the United States after such conviction, but only after the State or local law enforcement officials obtain appropriate confirmation from the Immigration and Naturalization Service of the status of such individual and only for such period of time as may be required for the Service to take the individual into Federal custody for purposes of deporting or removing the alien from the United States.

**(b) Cooperation.** The Attorney General shall cooperate with the States to assure that information in the control of the Attorney General, including information in the National Crime Information Center, that would assist State and local law enforcement officials in carrying out duties under subsection (a) of this section is made available to such officials.

(P.L. 104-132 (4/24/96), title IV, §439.)

**Sec. 1255b Adjustment of status of certain nonimmigrants to that of persons admitted for permanent residence. Notwithstanding any other provision of law—**

**(a) Application.** Any alien admitted to the United States as a nonimmigrant under the provisions of either section 101(a)(15)(A)(i) or (ii) or 101(a)(15)(G)(i) or (ii) of the Immigration and Nationality Act [8 U.S.C. 1101(a)(15)(A)(i), (ii), (G)(i), (ii)], who has failed to maintain a status under any of those provisions, may apply to the Attorney General for adjustment of his status to that of an alien lawfully admitted for permanent residence.

**(b) Record of admission.** If, after consultation with the Secretary of State, it shall appear to the satisfaction of the Attorney General that the alien has shown compelling reasons demonstrating both that the alien is unable to return to the country represented by the government which accredited the alien or the member of the alien's immediate family and that adjustment of the alien's status to that of an alien lawfully admitted for permanent residence would be in the national interest, that the alien is a person of good moral character, that he is admissible for permanent residence under the Immigration and Nationality Act [8 U.S.C. 1101 *et seq.*], and that such action would not be contrary to the national welfare, safety, or security, the Attorney General, in his discretion, may record the alien's lawful admission for permanent residence as of the date the order of the Attorney General approving the application for adjustment of status is made.

**(c) Report to the Congress; resolution not favoring adjustment of status; reduction of quota.** A complete and detailed statement of the facts and pertinent provisions of law in the case shall be reported to the Congress with the reasons for such adjustment of status. Such reports shall be submitted on the first day of each calendar month in which Congress is in session. The Secretary of State shall, if the alien was classifiable as a quota immigrant at the time of his entry, reduce by one the quota of the quota area to which the alien is chargeable under section 202 of the Immigration and Nationality Act [8 U.S.C. 1152] for the fiscal year then current or the next following year in which a quota is available. No quota shall be so reduced by more than 50 per centum in any fiscal year.

**(d) Limitations.** The number of aliens who may be granted the status of aliens lawfully admitted for permanent residence in any fiscal year, pursuant to this section, shall not exceed fifty.

(P.L. 85-316 (9/11/57), §13; P.L. 97-116 (12/29/81), §17; P.L. 100-525 (10/24/88), §9(kk); P.L. 103-416 (10/25/94), title II, §207; P.L. 104-208 (IIRAIRA) (9/30/96), div. C, title VI, §671.)

**Sec. 1353a Officers and employees; overtime services; extra compensation; length of working day.**

The Attorney General shall fix a reasonable rate of extra compensation for overtime services of immigration officers and employees of the Immigration and Naturalization Service who may be required to remain on duty between the hours of five o'clock postmeridian and eight o'clock antemeridian, or on Sundays or holidays, to perform duties in connection with the examination and landing of passengers and crews of steamships, trains, airplanes, or other vehicles, arriving in the United States from a foreign port by water, land, or air, such rates to be fixed on a basis of one-half day's additional pay for each two hours or fraction thereof of at least one hour that the overtime extends beyond five o'clock postmeridian (but not to exceed two and one-half days' pay for the full period from five o'clock postmeridian to eight o'clock antemeridian) and two additional days' pay for Sunday and holiday duty; in those ports where the customary working hours are other than those heretofore mentioned, the Attorney General is vested with authority to regulate the hours of such employees so as to agree with the prevailing working hours in said ports, but nothing contained in this section shall be construed in any manner to affect or alter the length of a working day for such employees or the overtime pay herein fixed.

(Mar. 2, 1931, ch. 368, Sec. 1, 46 Stat. 1467; Ex. Ord. No. 6166 (6/10/33), §14; 1940 Reorg. Plan No. V, *effective* (6/14/40) 5 F.R. 2223; (6/27/52), ch. 477, title IV, §402.)

### Sec. 1353b Extra compensation; payment

The said extra compensation shall be paid by the master, owner, agent, or consignee of such vessel or other conveyance arriving in the United States from a foreign port to the Attorney General, who shall pay the same to the several immigration officers and employees entitled thereto as provided in this section and section 1353a of this title. Such extra compensation shall be paid if such officers or employees have been ordered to report for duty and have so reported, whether the actual inspection or examination of passengers or crew takes place or not: *Provided,* That this section shall not apply to the inspection at designated ports of entry of passengers arriving by international ferries, bridges, or tunnels, or by aircraft, railroad trains, or vessels on the Great Lakes and connecting waterways, when operating on regular schedules.

(Mar. 2, 1931, ch. 368, §2, 46 Stat. 1467; 1940 Reorg. Plan No. V, *effective* (6/14/40), 5 F.R. 2223.)

### Sec. 1353c Immigration officials; service in foreign contiguous territory.

Nothing in section 209 of title 18 relative to augmenting salaries of Government officials from outside sources shall prevent receiving reimbursements for services of immigration officials incident to the inspection of aliens in foreign contiguous territory and such reimbursement shall be credited to the appropriation, "Immigration and Naturalization Service—Salaries and Expenses."

(Mar. 4, 1921, ch. 161, §1, 41 Stat. 1424; (9/3/54), ch. 1263, §6.)

### Sec. 1353d Disposition of money received as extra compensation.

Moneys collected on or after July 1, 1941, as extra compensation for overtime service of immigration officers and employees of the Immigration Service pursuant to sections 1353a and 1353b of this title, shall be deposited in the Treasury of the United States to the credit of the appropriation for the payment of salaries, field personnel of the Immigration and Naturalization Service, and the appropriation so credited shall be available for the payment of such compensation.

(Aug. 22, 1940, ch. 688, 54 Stat. 858; (6/27/52), ch. 477, title IV, §402.)

### Sec. 1364 Triennial comprehensive report on immigration.

(a) Triennial report. The President shall transmit to the Congress, not later than January 1, 1989, and not later than January 1 of every third year thereafter, a comprehensive immigration-impact report.

(b) Details in each report. Each report shall include—

 (1) the number and classification of aliens admitted (whether as immediate relatives, special immigrants, refugees, or under the preferences classifications, or as nonimmigrants), paroled, or granted asylum, during the relevant period;

 (2) a reasonable estimate of the number of aliens who entered the United States during the period without visas or who became deportable during the period under section 237 of the Immigration and Nationality Act [8 U.S.C. 1227]; and

 (3) a description of the impact of admissions and other entries of immigrants, refugees, asylees, and parolees into the United States during the period on the economy, labor and housing markets, the educational system, social services, foreign policy, environmental quality and resources, the rate, size, and distribution of population growth in the United States,

and the impact on specific States and local units of government of high rates of immigration resettlement.

**(c) History and projections.** The information (referred to in subsection (b) of this section) contained in each report shall be—

(1) described for the preceding three-year period, and

(2) projected for the succeeding five-year period, based on reasonable estimates substantiated by the best available evidence.

**(d) Recommendations.** The President also may include in such report any appropriate recommendations on changes in numerical limitations or other policies under title II of the Immigration and Nationality Act [8 U.S.C. 1151 *et seq.*] bearing on the admission and entry of such aliens to the United States.

(P.L. 99-603 (11/6/86), title IV, §401; P.L. 104-208 (IIRAIRA) (9/30/96), div. C, title III, §308.)

## Sec. 1365 Reimbursement of States for costs of incarcerating illegal aliens and certain Cuban nationals.

**(a) Reimbursement of States.** Subject to the amounts provided in advance in appropriation Acts, the Attorney General shall reimburse a State for the costs incurred by the State for the imprisonment of any illegal alien or Cuban national who is convicted of a felony by such State.

**(b) Illegal aliens convicted of a felony.** An illegal alien referred to in subsection (a) of this section is any alien who is any alien convicted of a felony who is in the United States unlawfully and—

(1) whose most recent entry into the United States was without inspection, or

(2) whose most recent admission to the United States was as a nonimmigrant and—

(A) whose period of authorized stay as a nonimmigrant expired, or

(B) whose unlawful status was known to the Government, before the date of the commission of the crime for which the alien is convicted.

**(c) Marielito Cubans convicted of a felony.** A Marielito Cuban convicted of a felony referred to in subsection (a) of this section is a national of Cuba who—

(1) was allowed by the Attorney General to come to the United States in 1980,

(2) after such arrival committed any violation of State or local law for which a term of imprisonment was imposed, and

(3) at the time of such arrival and at the time of such violation was not an alien lawfully admitted to the United States—

(A) for permanent or temporary residence, or

(B) under the terms of an immigrant visa or a nonimmigrant visa issued, under the laws of the United States.

**(d) Authorization of appropriations.** There are authorized to be appropriated such sums as are necessary to carry out the purposes of this section.

**(e) "State" defined.** The term "State" has the meaning given such term in section 1101(a)(36) of this title.

(Pub. L. 99-603 (11/6/86), title V, §501.)

### Sec. 1365a Integrated entry and exit data system

**(a) Requirement.** The Attorney General shall implement an integrated entry and exit data system.

**(b) Integrated entry and exit data system defined.** For purposes of this section, the term "integrated entry and exit data system" means an electronic system that—

(1) provides access to, and integrates, alien arrival and departure data that are—

(A) authorized or required to be created or collected under law;

(B) in an electronic format; and

(C) in a data base of the Department of Justice or the Department of State, including those created or used at ports of entry and at consular offices;

(2) uses available data described in paragraph (1) to produce a report of arriving and departing aliens by country of nationality, classification as an immigrant or nonimmigrant, and date of arrival in, and departure from, the United States;

(3) matches an alien's available arrival data with the alien's available departure data;

(4) assists the Attorney General (and the Secretary of State, to the extent necessary to carry out such Secretary's obligations under immigration law) to identify, through on-line searching procedures, lawfully admitted nonimmigrants who may have remained in the United States beyond the period authorized by the Attorney General; and

(5) otherwise uses available alien arrival and departure data described in paragraph (1) to permit the Attorney General to make the reports required under subsection (e) of this section.

**(c) Construction.**

(1) *No additional authority to impose documentary or data collection requirements.* Nothing in this section shall be construed to permit the Attorney General or the Secretary of State to impose any new documentary or data collection requirements on any person in order to satisfy the requirements of this section, including—

(A) requirements on any alien for whom the documentary requirements in section 1182(a)(7)(B) of this title have been waived by the Attorney General and the Secretary of State under section 1182(d)(4)(B) of this title; or

(B) requirements that are inconsistent with the North American Free Trade Agreement.

(2) *No reduction of authority.* Nothing in this section shall be construed to reduce or curtail any authority of the Attorney General or the Secretary of State under any other provision of law.

**(d) Deadlines.**

(1) *Airports and seaports.* Not later than December 31, 2003, the Attorney General shall implement the integrated entry and exit data system using available alien arrival and departure data described in subsection (b)(1) of this section pertaining to aliens arriving in, or departing from, the United States at an airport or seaport. Such implementation shall include ensuring that such data, when collected or created by an immigration officer at an airport or seaport, are entered into the system and can be accessed by immigration officers at other airports and seaports.

(2) *High-traffic land border ports of entry.* Not later than December 31, 2004, the Attorney General shall implement the integrated entry and exit data system using the data described in paragraph (1) and available alien arrival and departure data described in subsection (b)(1) of

this section pertaining to aliens arriving in, or departing from, the United States at the 50 land border ports of entry determined by the Attorney General to serve the highest numbers of arriving and departing aliens. Such implementation shall include ensuring that such data, when collected or created by an immigration officer at such a port of entry, are entered into the system and can be accessed by immigration officers at airports, seaports, and other such land border ports of entry.

(3) *Remaining data.* Not later than December 31, 2005, the Attorney General shall fully implement the integrated entry and exit data system using all data described in subsection (b)(1) of this section. Such implementation shall include ensuring that all such data are available to immigration officers at all ports of entry into the United States.

**(e) Reports.**

(1) *In general.* Not later than December 31 of each year following the commencement of implementation of the integrated entry and exit data system, the Attorney General shall use the system to prepare an annual report to the Committees on the Judiciary of the House of Representatives and of the Senate.

(2) *Information.* Each report shall include the following information with respect to the preceding fiscal year, and an analysis of that information:

(A) The number of aliens for whom departure data was collected during the reporting period, with an accounting by country of nationality of the departing alien.

(B) The number of departing aliens whose departure data was successfully matched to the alien's arrival data, with an accounting by the alien's country of nationality and by the alien's classification as an immigrant or nonimmigrant.

(C) The number of aliens who arrived pursuant to a nonimmigrant visa, or as a visitor under the visa waiver program under section 1187 of this title, for whom no matching departure data have been obtained through the system or through other means as of the end of the alien's authorized period of stay, with an accounting by the alien's country of nationality and date of arrival in the United States.

(D) The number of lawfully admitted nonimmigrants identified as having remained in the United States beyond the period authorized by the Attorney General, with an accounting by the alien's country of nationality.

**(f) Authority to provide access to system.**

(1) *In general.* Subject to subsection (d) of this section, the Attorney General, in consultation with the Secretary of State, shall determine which officers and employees of the Departments of Justice and State may enter data into, and have access to the data contained in, the integrated entry and exit data system.

(2) *Other law enforcement officials.* The Attorney General, in the discretion of the Attorney General, may permit other Federal, State, and local law enforcement officials to have access to the data contained in the integrated entry and exit data system for law enforcement purposes.

**(g) Use of task force recommendations.** The Attorney General shall continuously update and improve the integrated entry and exit data system as technology improves and using the recommendations of the task force established under section 3 of the Immigration and Naturalization Service Data Management Improvement Act of 2000.

**(h) Authorization of appropriations.** There are authorized to be appropriated to carry out this section such sums as may be necessary for fiscal years 2001 through 2008.

(P.L. 104-208 (IIRAIRA) (9/30/96), div. C, title I, §110; P.L. 105-259 (10/15/98), §1; P.L. 105-277 (10/21/98), div. A, §101 [title I, §116]; P.L. 106-215 (6/15/00), §2.)

### Sec. 1365b Biometric entry and exit data system

**(a) Finding.** Consistent with the report of the National Commission on Terrorist Attacks Upon the United States, Congress finds that completing a biometric entry and exit data system as expeditiously as possible is an essential investment in efforts to protect the United States by preventing the entry of terrorists.

**(b) Definition.** In this section, the term "entry and exit data system" means the entry and exit system required by applicable sections of—

(1) the Illegal Immigration Reform and Immigrant Responsibility Act of 1996 (Public Law 104-208);

(2) the Immigration and Naturalization Service Data Management Improvement Act of 2000 (Public Law 106-205[1]);

(3) the Visa Waiver Permanent Program Act (Public Law 106-396);

(4) the Enhanced Border Security and Visa Entry Reform Act of 2002 (Public Law 107-173); and

(5) the Uniting and Strengthening America by Providing Appropriate Tools Required to Intercept and Obstruct Terrorism (USA PATRIOT ACT) Act of 2001 (Public Law 107-56).

**(c) Plan and report.**

(1) *Development of plan.* The Secretary of Homeland Security shall develop a plan to accelerate the full implementation of an automated biometric entry and exit data system.

(2) *Report.* Not later than 180 days after December 17, 2004, the Secretary shall submit a report to Congress on the plan developed under paragraph (1), which shall contain—

(A) a description of the current functionality of the entry and exit data system, including—

(i) a listing of ports of entry and other Department of Homeland Security and Department of State locations with biometric entry data systems in use and whether such screening systems are located at primary or secondary inspection areas;

(ii) a listing of ports of entry and other Department of Homeland Security and Department of State locations with biometric exit data systems in use;

(iii) a listing of databases and data systems with which the entry and exit data system are interoperable;

(iv) a description of—

(I) identified deficiencies concerning the accuracy or integrity of the information contained in the entry and exit data system;

---

[1] *Sic.* Probably should read "106-215".

(II) identified deficiencies concerning technology associated with processing individuals through the system; and

(III) programs or policies planned or implemented to correct problems identified in subclause (I) or (II); and

(v) an assessment of the effectiveness of the entry and exit data system in fulfilling its intended purposes, including preventing terrorists from entering the United States;

(B) a description of factors relevant to the accelerated implementation of the biometric entry and exit data system, including—

(i) the earliest date on which the Secretary estimates that full implementation of the biometric entry and exit data system can be completed;

(ii) the actions the Secretary will take to accelerate the full implementation of the biometric entry and exit data system at all ports of entry through which all aliens must pass that are legally required to do so; and

(iii) the resources and authorities required to enable the Secretary to meet the implementation date described in clause (i);

(C) a description of any improvements needed in the information technology employed for the biometric entry and exit data system;

(D) a description of plans for improved or added interoperability with any other databases or data systems; and

(E) a description of the manner in which the Department of Homeland Security's US-VISIT program—

(i) meets the goals of a comprehensive entry and exit screening system, including both entry and exit biometric; and

(ii) fulfills the statutory obligations under subsection (b) of this section.

**(d) Collection of biometric exit data.** The entry and exit data system shall include a requirement for the collection of biometric exit data for all categories of individuals who are required to provide biometric entry data, regardless of the port of entry where such categories of individuals entered the United States.

**(e) Integration and interoperability.**

(1) *Integration of data system.* Not later than 2 years after December 17, 2004, the Secretary shall fully integrate all databases and data systems that process or contain information on aliens, which are maintained by—

(A) the Department of Homeland Security, at—

(i) the United States Immigration and Customs Enforcement;

(ii) the United States Customs and Border Protection; and

(iii) the United States Citizenship and Immigration Services;

(B) the Department of Justice, at the Executive Office for Immigration Review; and

(C) the Department of State, at the Bureau of Consular Affairs.

(2) *Interoperable component.* The fully integrated data system under paragraph (1) shall be an interoperable component of the entry and exit data system.

(3) *Interoperable data system.* Not later than 2 years after December 17, 2004, the Secretary shall fully implement an interoperable electronic data system, as required by section 202 of the Enhanced Border Security and Visa Entry Reform Act (8 U.S.C. 1722) to provide current and immediate access to information in the databases of Federal law enforcement agencies and the intelligence community that is relevant to determine—

(A) whether to issue a visa; or

(B) the admissibility or deportability of an alien.

**(f) Maintaining accuracy and integrity of entry and exit data system.**

(1) *Policies and procedures.*

(A) *Establishment.* The Secretary of Homeland Security shall establish rules, guidelines, policies, and operating and auditing procedures for collecting, removing, and updating data maintained in, and adding information to, the entry and exit data system that ensure the accuracy and integrity of the data.

(B) *Training.* The Secretary shall develop training on the rules, guidelines, policies, and procedures established under subparagraph (A), and on immigration law and procedure. All personnel authorized to access information maintained in the databases and data system shall receive such training.

(2) *Data collected from foreign nationals.* The Secretary of Homeland Security, the Secretary of State, and the Attorney General, after consultation with directors of the relevant intelligence agencies, shall standardize the information and data collected from foreign nationals, and the procedures utilized to collect such data, to ensure that the information is consistent and valuable to officials accessing that data across multiple agencies.

(3) *Data maintenance procedures.* Heads of agencies that have databases or data systems linked to the entry and exit data system shall establish rules, guidelines, policies, and operating and auditing procedures for collecting, removing, and updating data maintained in, and adding information to, such databases or data systems that ensure the accuracy and integrity of the data and for limiting access to the information in the databases or data systems to authorized personnel.

(4) *Requirements.* The rules, guidelines, policies, and procedures established under this subsection shall—

(A) incorporate a simple and timely method for—

(i) correcting errors in a timely and effective manner;

(ii) determining which government officer provided data so that the accuracy of the data can be ascertained; and

(iii) clarifying information known to cause false hits or misidentification errors;

(B) include procedures for individuals to—

(i) seek corrections of data contained in the databases or data systems; and

(ii) appeal decisions concerning data contained in the databases or data systems;

(C) strictly limit the agency personnel authorized to enter data into the system;

(D) identify classes of information to be designated as temporary or permanent entries, with corresponding expiration dates for temporary entries; and

(E) identify classes of prejudicial information requiring additional authority of supervisory personnel before entry.

(5) *Centralizing and streamlining correction process*

(A) *In general.* The President, or agency director designated by the President, shall establish a clearinghouse bureau in the Department of Homeland Security, to centralize and streamline the process through which members of the public can seek corrections to erroneous or inaccurate information contained in agency databases, which is related to immigration status, or which otherwise impedes lawful admission to the United States.

(B) *Time schedules.* The process described in subparagraph (A) shall include specific time schedules for reviewing data correction requests, rendering decisions on such requests, and implementing appropriate corrective action in a timely manner.

**(g) Integrated biometric entry-exit screening system.** The biometric entry and exit data system shall facilitate efficient immigration benefits processing by—

(1) ensuring that the system's tracking capabilities encompass data related to all immigration benefits processing, including—

(A) visa applications with the Department of State;

(B) immigration related filings with the Department of Labor;

(C) cases pending before the Executive Office for Immigration Review; and

(D) matters pending or under investigation before the Department of Homeland Security;

(2) utilizing a biometric based identity number tied to an applicant's biometric algorithm established under the entry and exit data system to track all immigration related matters concerning the applicant;

(3) providing that—

(A) all information about an applicant's immigration related history, including entry and exit history, can be queried through electronic means; and

(B) database access and usage guidelines include stringent safeguards to prevent misuse of data;

(4) providing real-time updates to the information described in paragraph (3)(A), including pertinent data from all agencies referred to in paragraph (1); and

(5) providing continuing education in counterterrorism techniques, tools, and methods for all Federal personnel employed in the evaluation of immigration documents and immigration-related policy.

**(h) Entry-exit system goals.** The Department of Homeland Security shall operate the biometric entry and exit system so that it—

(1) serves as a vital counterterrorism tool;

(2) screens travelers efficiently and in a welcoming manner;

(3) provides inspectors and related personnel with adequate real-time information;

(4) ensures flexibility of training and security protocols to most effectively comply with security mandates;

(5) integrates relevant databases and plans for database modifications to address volume increase and database usage; and

(6) improves database search capacities by utilizing language algorithms to detect alternate names.

**(i) Dedicated specialists and front line personnel training.** In implementing the provisions of subsections (g) and (h) of this section, the Department of Homeland Security and the Department of State shall—

(1) develop cross-training programs that focus on the scope and procedures of the entry and exit data system;

(2) provide extensive community outreach and education on the entry and exit data system's procedures;

(3) provide clear and consistent eligibility guidelines for applicants in low-risk traveler programs; and

(4) establish ongoing training modules on immigration law to improve adjudications at our ports of entry, consulates, and embassies.

**(j) Compliance status reports.** Not later than 1 year after December 17, 2004, the Secretary of Homeland Security, the Secretary of State, the Attorney General, and the head of any other department or agency subject to the requirements of this section, shall issue individual status reports and a joint status report detailing the compliance of the department or agency with each requirement under this section.

**(k) Expediting registered travelers across international borders.**

(1) *Findings.* Consistent with the report of the National Commission on Terrorist Attacks Upon the United States, Congress makes the following findings:

(A) Expediting the travel of previously screened and known travelers across the borders of the United States should be a high priority.

(B) The process of expediting known travelers across the borders of the United States can permit inspectors to better focus on identifying terrorists attempting to enter the United States.

(2) *Definition.* In this subsection, the term "registered traveler program" means any program designed to expedite the travel of previously screened and known travelers across the borders of the United States.

(3) *Registered travel program.*

(A) *In general.* As soon as is practicable, the Secretary shall develop and implement a registered traveler program to expedite the processing of registered travelers who enter and exit the United States.

(B) *Participation.* The registered traveler program shall include as many participants as practicable by—

(i) minimizing the cost of enrollment;

(ii) making program enrollment convenient and easily accessible; and

(iii) providing applicants with clear and consistent eligibility guidelines.

(C) *Integration.* The registered traveler program shall be integrated into the automated biometric entry and exit data system described in this section.

(D) *Review and evaluation.* In developing the registered traveler program, the Secretary shall—

(i) review existing programs or pilot projects designed to expedite the travel of registered travelers across the borders of the United States;

(ii) evaluate the effectiveness of the programs described in clause (i), the costs associated with such programs, and the costs to travelers to join such programs;

(iii) increase research and development efforts to accelerate the development and implementation of a single registered traveler program; and

(iv) review the feasibility of allowing participants to enroll in the registered traveler program at consular offices.

(4) *Report.* Not later than 1 year after December 17, 2004, the Secretary shall submit to Congress a report describing the Department's progress on the development and implementation of the registered traveler program.

(*l*) **Authorization of appropriations.** There are authorized to be appropriated to the Secretary, for each of the fiscal years 2005 through 2009, such sums as may be necessary to carry out the provisions of this section.

(P.L. 108-458 (12/17/04), title VII, §7208.)

## Sec. 1366 Annual report on criminal aliens.

Not later than 12 months after September 30, 1996, and annually thereafter, the Attorney General shall submit to the Committees on the Judiciary of the House of Representatives and of the Senate a report detailing—

(1) the number of illegal aliens incarcerated in Federal and State prisons for having committed felonies, stating the number incarcerated for each type of offense;

(2) the number of illegal aliens convicted of felonies in any Federal or State court, but not sentenced to incarceration, in the year before the report was submitted, stating the number convicted for each type of offense;

(3) programs and plans underway in the Department of Justice to ensure the prompt removal from the United States of criminal aliens subject to removal; and

(4) methods for identifying and preventing the unlawful reentry of aliens who have been convicted of criminal offenses in the United States and removed from the United States.

(P.L. 104-208 (IIRAIRA) (9/30/96), div. C, title III, §332.)

## Sec. 1367 Penalties for disclosure of information

(a) **In general.** Except as provided in subsection (b) of this section, in no case may the Attorney General, or any other official or employee of the Department of Justice, the Secretary of Homeland Security, the Secretary of State, or any other official or employee of the Department of Homeland Security or Department of State (including any bureau or agency of either of such Departments)—

(1) make an adverse determination of admissibility or deportability of an alien under the Immigration and Nationality Act [8 U.S.C. 1101 *et seq.*] using information furnished solely by—

(A) a spouse or parent who has battered the alien or subjected the alien to extreme cruelty,

(B) a member of the spouse's or parent's family residing in the same household as the alien who has battered the alien or subjected the alien to extreme cruelty when the spouse or parent consented to or acquiesced in such battery or cruelty,

(C) a spouse or parent who has battered the alien's child or subjected the alien's child to extreme cruelty (without the active participation of the alien in the battery or extreme cruelty),

(D) a member of the spouse's or parent's family residing in the same household as the alien who has battered the alien's child or subjected the alien's child to extreme cruelty when the spouse or parent consented to or acquiesced in such battery or cruelty and the alien did not actively participate in such battery or cruelty,

(E) in the case of an alien applying for status under section 101(a)(15)(U) of the Immigration and Nationality Act [8 U.S.C. 1101(a)(15)(U)], the perpetrator of the substantial physical or mental abuse and the criminal activity,

(F) in the case of an alien applying for status under section 101(a)(15)(T) of the Immigration and Nationality Act (8 U.S.C. 1101(a)(15)(T)), under section 107(b)(1)(E)(i)(II)(bb) of the Trafficking Victims Protection Act of 2000 (22 U.S.C. 7105), under section 244(a)(3) of the Immigration and Nationality Act (8 U.S.C. 1254a(a)(3)), as in effect prior to March 31, 1999, or as a VAWA self-petitioner (as defined in section 101(a)(51) of the Immigration and Nationality Act (8 U.S.C. 1101(a)(51)), the trafficker or perpetrator, unless the alien has been convicted of a crime or crimes listed in section 241(a)(2) of the Immigration and Nationality Act [8 U.S.C. 1227(a)(2)]; or

(2) permit use by or disclosure to anyone (other than a sworn officer or employee of the Department, or bureau or agency thereof, for legitimate Department, bureau, or agency purposes) of any information which relates to an alien who is the beneficiary of an application for relief under paragraph (15)(T), (15)(U), or (51) of section 101(a) of the Immigration and Nationality Act or section 240A(b)(2) of such Act.

The limitation under paragraph (2) ends when the application for relief is denied and all opportunities for appeal of the denial have been exhausted.

## (b) Exceptions

(1) The Attorney General may provide, in the Attorney General's discretion, for the disclosure of information in the same manner and circumstances as census information may be disclosed by the Secretary of Commerce under section 8 of title 13.

(2) The Attorney General may provide in the discretion of the Attorney General for the disclosure of information to law enforcement officials to be used solely for a legitimate law enforcement purpose.

(3) Subsection (a) of this section shall not be construed as preventing disclosure of information in connection with judicial review of a determination in a manner that protects the confidentiality of such information.

(4) Subsection (a)(2) of this section shall not apply if all the battered individuals in the case are adults and they have all waived the restrictions of such subsection.

(5) The Attorney General is authorized to disclose information, to Federal, State, and local public and private agencies providing benefits, to be used solely in making determinations of eligibility for benefits pursuant to section 1641(c) of this title.

(6) Subsection (a) of this section may not be construed to prevent the Attorney General and the Secretary of Homeland Security from disclosing to the chairmen and ranking members of the Committee on the Judiciary of the Senate or the Committee on the Judiciary of the House of Representatives, for the exercise of congressional oversight authority, information on closed cases under this section in a manner that protects the confidentiality of such information and that omits personally identifying information (including locational information about individuals).

(7) Government entities adjudicating applications for relief under subsection (a)(2) of this section, and government personnel carrying out mandated duties under section 101(i)(1) of the Immigration and Nationality Act [8 U.S.C. 1101(i)(1)], may, with the prior written consent of the alien involved, communicate with nonprofit, nongovernmental victims' service providers for the sole purpose of assisting victims in obtaining victim services from programs with expertise working with immigrant victims. Agencies receiving referrals are bound by the provisions of this section. Nothing in this paragraph shall be construed as affecting the ability of an applicant to designate a safe organization through whom governmental agencies may communicate with the applicant.

**(c) Penalties for violations.** Anyone who willfully uses, publishes, or permits information to be disclosed in violation of this section or who knowingly makes a false certification under section 239(e) of the Immigration and Nationality Act [8 U.S.C. 1229(e)] shall be subject to appropriate disciplinary action and subject to a civil money penalty of not more than $5,000 for each such violation.

**(d) Guidance.** The Attorney General and the Secretary of Homeland Security shall provide guidance to officers and employees of the Department of Justice or the Department of Homeland Security who have access to information covered by this section regarding the provisions of this section, including the provisions to protect victims of domestic violence from harm that could result from the inappropriate disclosure of covered information.

(P.L. 104-208 (IIRAIRA) (9/30/96), div. C, title III, §308; P.L. 105-33 (8/5/97), title V, §5572; P.L. 106-386 (10/28/00), div. B, title V, §1513; P.L. 109-162 (1/5/06), title VIII, §817.)

### Sec. 1368 Increase in INS detention facilities; report on detention space

**(a) Increase in detention facilities.** Subject to the availability of appropriations, the Attorney General shall provide for an increase in the detention facilities of the Immigration and Naturalization Service to at least 9,000 beds before the end of fiscal year 1997.

**(b) Report on detention space**

(1) *In general.* Not later than 6 months after September 30, 1996, and every 6 months thereafter, the Attorney General shall submit a report to the Committees on the Judiciary of the House of Representatives and of the Senate estimating the amount of detention space that will be required, during the fiscal year in which the report is submitted and the succeeding fiscal year, to detain—

(A) all aliens subject to detention under section 1226(c) of this title and section 1231(a) of this title;

(B) all inadmissible or deportable aliens subject to proceedings under section 1228 of this title or section 1225(b)(2)(A) or 1229a of this title; and

(C) other inadmissible or deportable aliens in accordance with the priorities established by the Attorney General.

(2) *Estimate of number of aliens released into the community*

(A) *Criminal aliens*

(i) In general. The first report submitted under paragraph (1) shall include an estimate of the number of criminal aliens who, in each of the 3 fiscal years concluded prior to the date of the report—

(I) were released from detention facilities of the Immigration and Naturalization Service (whether operated directly by the Service or through contract with other persons or agencies); or

(II) were not taken into custody or detention by the Service upon completion of their incarceration.

(ii) Aliens convicted of aggravated felonies. The estimate under clause (i) shall estimate separately, with respect to each year described in such clause, the number of criminal aliens described in such clause who were convicted of an aggravated felony.

(B) *All inadmissible or deportable aliens.* The first report submitted under paragraph (1) shall also estimate the number of inadmissible or deportable aliens who were released into the community due to a lack of detention facilities in each of the 3 fiscal years concluded prior to the date of the report notwithstanding circumstances that the Attorney General believed justified detention (for example, a significant probability that the released alien would not appear, as agreed, at subsequent exclusion or deportation proceedings).

(C) *Subsequent reports.* Each report under paragraph (1) following the first such report shall include the estimates under subparagraphs (A) and (B), made with respect to the 6-month period immediately preceding the date of the submission of the report.

(P.L. 104-208 (IIRAIRA) (9/30/96), div. C, title III, §308, §386.)

## Sec. 1369 Treatment of expenses subject to emergency medical services exception

**(a) In general.** Subject to such amounts as are provided in advance in appropriation Acts, each State or political subdivision of a State that provides medical assistance for care and treatment of an emergency medical condition (as defined in subsection (d) of this section) through a public hospital or other public facility (including a nonprofit hospital that is eligible for an additional payment adjustment under section 1395ww of title 42) or through contract with another hospital or facility to an individual who is an alien not lawfully present in the United States is eligible for payment from the Federal Government of its costs of providing such services, but only to the extent that such costs are not otherwise reimbursed through any other Federal program and cannot be recovered from the alien or another person.

**(b) Confirmation of immigration status required.** No payment shall be made under this section with respect to services furnished to an individual unless the immigration status of the individual has been verified through appropriate procedures established by the Secretary of Health and Human Services and the Attorney General.

**(c) Administration.** This section shall be administered by the Attorney General, in consultation with the Secretary of Health and Human Services.

**(d) "Emergency medical condition" defined.** For purposes of this section, the term "emergency medical condition" means a medical condition (including emergency labor and delivery) manifesting itself by acute symptoms of sufficient severity (including severe pain) such that the absence of immediate medical attention could reasonably be expected to result in—

(1) placing the patient's health in serious jeopardy,

(2) serious impairment to bodily functions, or

(3) serious dysfunction of any bodily organ or part.

**(e) Effective date.** Subsection (a) of this section shall apply to medical assistance for care and treatment of an emergency medical condition furnished on or after January 1, 1997.

(P.L. 104-208 (IIRAIRA) (9/30/96), div. C, title V, §562.)

## Sec. 1370 Reimbursement of States and localities for emergency ambulance services

Subject to the availability of appropriations, the Attorney General shall fully reimburse States and political subdivisions of States for costs incurred by such a State or subdivision for emergency ambulance services provided to any alien who—

**(1)** is injured while crossing a land or sea border of the United States without inspection or at any time or place other than as designated by the Attorney General; and

**(2)** is under the custody of the State or subdivision pursuant to a transfer, request, or other action by a Federal authority.

(P.L. 104-208 (IIRAIRA) (9/30/96), div. C, title V, §563.)

## Sec. 1371 Reports

Not later than 180 days after the end of each fiscal year, the Attorney General shall submit a report to the Inspector General of the Department of Justice and the Committees on the Judiciary of the House of Representatives and of the Senate describing the following:

**(1) Public charge deportations.** The number of aliens deported on public charge grounds under section 1227(a)(5) of this title during the previous fiscal year.

**(2) Indigent sponsors.** The number of determinations made under section 1631(e) of this title during the previous fiscal year.

**(3) Reimbursement actions.** The number of actions brought, and the amount of each action, for reimbursement under section 1183a of this title (including private collections) for the costs of providing public benefits.

(P.L. 104-208 (IIRAIRA) (9/30/96), div. C, title V, §565.)

## Sec. 1372 Program to collect information relating to nonimmigrant foreign students and other exchange program participants

**(a) In general.**

(1) *Program.* The Attorney General, in consultation with the Secretary of State and the Secretary of Education, shall develop and conduct a program to collect from approved institutions of higher education, other approved educational institutions, and designated exchange visitor programs in the United States the information described in subsection (c) of this section with respect to aliens who—

(A) have the status, or are applying for the status, of nonimmigrants under subparagraph (F), (J), or (M) of section 1101(a)(15) of this title; and

(B) are nationals of the countries designated under subsection (b) of this section.

(2) *Deadline.* The program shall commence not later than January 1, 1998.

(3) *Aliens for whom a visa is required.* The Attorney General, in consultation with the Secretary of State, shall establish an electronic means to monitor and verify—

(A) the issuance of documentation of acceptance of a foreign student by an approved institution of higher education or other approved educational institution, or of an exchange visitor program participant by a designated exchange visitor program;

(B) the transmittal of the documentation referred to in subparagraph (A) to the Department of State for use by the Bureau of Consular Affairs;

(C) the issuance of a visa to a foreign student or an exchange visitor program participant;

(D) the admission into the United States of the foreign student or exchange visitor program participant;

(E) the notification to an approved institution of higher education, other approved educational institution, or exchange visitor program sponsor that the foreign student or exchange visitor participant has been admitted into the United States;

(F) the registration and enrollment of that foreign student in such approved institution of higher education or other approved educational institution, or the participation of that exchange visitor in such designated exchange visitor program, as the case may be; and

(G) any other relevant act by the foreign student or exchange visitor program participant, including a changing of school or designated exchange visitor program and any termination of studies or participation in a designated exchange visitor program.

(4) *Reporting requirements.* Not later than 30 days after the deadline for registering for classes for an academic term of an approved institution of higher education or other approved educational institution for which documentation is issued for an alien as described in paragraph (3)(A), or the scheduled commencement of participation by an alien in a designated exchange visitor program, as the case may be, the institution or program, respectively, shall report to the Immigration and Naturalization Service any failure of the alien to enroll or to commence participation.

**(b) Covered countries.** The Attorney General, in consultation with the Secretary of State, shall designate countries for purposes of subsection (a)(1)(B) of this section. The Attorney General shall initially designate not less than 5 countries and may designate additional countries at any time while the program is being conducted.

**(c) Information to be collected.**

(1) *In general.* The information for collection under subsection (a) of this section with respect to an alien consists of—

(A) the identity and current address in the United States of the alien;

(B) the nonimmigrant classification of the alien and the date on which a visa under the classification was issued or extended or the date on which a change to such classification was approved by the Attorney General;

(C) in the case of a student at an approved institution of higher education, or other approved educational institution, the current academic status of the alien, including whether the alien is maintaining status as a full-time student or, in the case of a participant in a designated exchange visitor program, whether the alien is satisfying the terms and conditions of such program;

(D) in the case of a student at an approved institution of higher education, or other approved educational institution, any disciplinary action taken by the institution against the alien as a result of the alien's being convicted of a crime or, in the case of a participant in a designated exchange visitor program, any change in the alien's participation as a result of the alien's being convicted of a crime; and[2]

(E) the date of entry and port of entry;

(F) the date of the alien's enrollment in an approved institution of higher education, other approved educational institution, or designated exchange visitor program in the United States;

(G) the degree program, if applicable, and field of study; and

(H) the date of the alien's termination of enrollment and the reason for such termination (including graduation, disciplinary action or other dismissal, and failure to re-enroll).

(2) *FERPA.* The Family Educational Rights and Privacy Act of 1974 [20 USC Sec. 1232g] shall not apply to aliens described in subsection (a) of this section to the extent that the Attorney General determines necessary to carry out the program under subsection (a) of this section.

(3) *Electronic collection.* The information described in paragraph (1) shall be collected electronically, where practicable.

(4) *Computer software.*

(A) *Collecting institutions.* To the extent practicable, the Attorney General shall design the program in a manner that permits approved institutions of higher education, other approved educational institutions, and designated exchange visitor programs to use existing software for the collection, storage, and data processing of information described in paragraph (1).

(B) *Attorney general.* To the extent practicable, the Attorney General shall use or enhance existing software for the collection, storage, and data processing of information described in paragraph (1).

(5) *Reporting requirements.* The Attorney General shall prescribe by regulation reporting requirements by taking into account the curriculum calendar of the approved institution of higher education, other approved educational institution, or exchange visitor program.

---

[2] *Sic.* The word "and" probably should not appear.

**(d) Participation by institutions of higher education and exchange visitor programs.**

(1) *Condition.* The information described in subsection (c) of this section shall be provided by institutions of higher education, other approved educational institutions, or exchange visitor programs as a condition of—

(A) in the case of an approved institution of higher education, or other approved educational institution, the continued approval of the institution under subparagraph (F) or (M) of section 1101(a)(15) of this title; and

(B) in the case of an approved institution of higher education or a designated exchange visitor program, the granting of authority to issue documents to an alien demonstrating the alien's eligibility for a visa under subparagraph (F), (J), or (M) of section 1101(a)(15) of this title.

(2) *Effect of failure to provide information.* If an approved institution of higher education, other approved educational institution, or a designated exchange visitor program fails to provide the specified information, such approvals and such issuance of visas shall be revoked or denied.

**(e) Funding.**

(1) *In general.* Beginning on April 1, 1997, the Attorney General shall impose on, and collect from, each alien described in paragraph (3), with respect to whom the institution or program is required by subsection (a) of this section to collect information, a fee established by the Attorney General under paragraph (4) at a time prior to the alien being classified under subparagraph (F), (J), or (M) of section 1101(a)(15) of this title.

(2) *Remittance.* The fees collected under paragraph (1) shall be remitted by the alien pursuant to a schedule established by the Attorney General for immediate deposit and availability as described under section 1356(m) of this title.

(3) *Aliens described.* An alien referred to in paragraph (1) is an alien who seeks nonimmigrant status under subparagraph (F), (J), or (M) of section 1101(a)(15) of this title (other than a nonimmigrant under section 1101(a)(15)(J) of this title who seeks to come to the United States as a participant in a program sponsored by the Federal Government).

(4) *Amount and use of fees.*

(A) *Establishment of amount.* The Attorney General shall establish the amount of the fee to be imposed on, and collected from, an alien under paragraph (1). Except as provided in subsection (g)(2) of this section, the fee imposed on any individual may not exceed $100, except that, in the case of an alien admitted under section 1101(a)(15)(J) of this title as an au pair, camp counselor, or participant in a summer work travel program, the fee shall not exceed $40, except that, in the case of an alien admitted under section 1101(a)(15)(J) of this title as an au pair, camp counselor, or participant in a summer work travel program, the fee shall not exceed $35. The amount of the fee shall be based on the Attorney General's estimate of the cost per alien of conducting the information collection program described in this section.

(B) *Use.* Fees collected under paragraph (1) shall be deposited as offsetting receipts into the Immigration Examinations Fee Account (established under section 1356(m) of this title) and shall remain available until expended for the Attorney General to reimburse any appropriation the amount paid out of which is for expenses in carrying out this section. Such expenses include, but are not necessarily limited to, those incurred by the Secretary of State in connection with the program under subsection (a) of this section.

416                                                    *American Immigration Lawyers Association*

(5) *Proof of payment.* The alien shall present proof of payment of the fee before the granting of—

(A) a visa under section 1202 of this title or, in the case of an alien who is exempt from the visa requirement described in section 1182(d)(4) of this title, admission to the United States; or

(B) change of nonimmigrant classification under section 1258 of this title to a classification described in paragraph (3).

(6) *Implementation.* The provisions of section 553 of title 5 (relating to rule-making) shall not apply to the extent the Attorney General determines necessary to ensure the expeditious, initial implementation of this section.

**(f) Joint report.** Not later than 4 years after the commencement of the program established under subsection (a) of this section, the Attorney General, the Secretary of State, and the Secretary of Education shall jointly submit to the Committees on the Judiciary of the Senate and the House of Representatives a report on the operations of the program and the feasibility of expanding the program to cover the nationals of all countries.

**(g) Worldwide applicability of the program.**

(1) *Expansion of program.* Not later than 12 months after the submission of the report required by subsection (f) of this section, the Attorney General, in consultation with the Secretary of State and the Secretary of Education, shall commence expansion of the program to cover the nationals of all countries.

(2) *Revision of fee.* After the program has been expanded, as provided in paragraph (1), the Attorney General may, on a periodic basis, revise the amount of the fee imposed and collected under subsection (e) of this section in order to take into account changes in the cost of carrying out the program.

**(h) Definitions.** As used in this section:

(1) *Approved institution of higher education.* The term "approved institution of higher education" means a college or university approved by the Attorney General, in consultation with the Secretary of Education, under subparagraph (F), (J), or (M) of section 1101(a)(15) of this title.

(2) Designated exchange visitor program. The term "designated exchange visitor program" means a program that has been—

(A) designated by the Secretary of State for purposes of section 1101(a)(15)(J) of this title; and

(B) selected by the Attorney General for purposes of the program under this section.

(3) *Other approved educational institution.* The term "other approved educational institution" includes any air flight school, language training school, or vocational school, approved by the Attorney General, in consultation with the Secretary of Education and the Secretary of State, under subparagraph (F), (J), or (M) of section 1101(a)(15) of this title.

(P.L. 104-208 (IIRAIRA) (9/30/96), div. C, title VI, §641; P.L. 106-396 (10/30/00), title IV, §404, §405, & §406; P.L. 106-553 (12/21/00), §1 [title I, §110]; P.L. 107-56 (10/26/01), title IV, §416; P.L. 107-173 (5/14/02), title V, §501.)

## Sec. 1373 Communication between government agencies and the Immigration and Naturalization Service

**(a) In general.** Notwithstanding any other provision of Federal, State, or local law, a Federal, State, or local government entity or official may not prohibit, or in any way restrict, any government entity or official from sending to, or receiving from, the Immigration and Naturalization Service information regarding the citizenship or immigration status, lawful or unlawful, of any individual.

**(b) Additional authority of government entities.** Notwithstanding any other provision of Federal, State, or local law, no person or agency may prohibit, or in any way restrict, a Federal, State, or local government entity from doing any of the following with respect to information regarding the immigration status, lawful or unlawful, of any individual:

(1) Sending such information to, or requesting or receiving such information from, the Immigration and Naturalization Service.

(2) Maintaining such information.

(3) Exchanging such information with any other Federal, State, or local government entity.

**(c) Obligation to respond to inquiries.** The Immigration and Naturalization Service shall respond to an inquiry by a Federal, State, or local government agency, seeking to verify or ascertain the citizenship or immigration status of any individual within the jurisdiction of the agency for any purpose authorized by law, by providing the requested verification or status information.

(P.L. 104-208 (IIRAIRA) (9/30/96), div. C, title VI, §642.)

## Sec. 1374 Information regarding female genital mutilation

**(a) Provision of information regarding female genital mutilation.** The Immigration and Naturalization Service (in cooperation with the Department of State) shall make available for all aliens who are issued immigrant or nonimmigrant visas, prior to or at the time of entry into the United States, the following information:

(1) Information on the severe harm to physical and psychological health caused by female genital mutilation which is compiled and presented in a manner which is limited to the practice itself and respectful to the cultural values of the societies in which such practice takes place.

(2) Information concerning potential legal consequences in the United States for (A) performing female genital mutilation, or (B) allowing a child under his or her care to be subjected to female genital mutilation, under criminal or child protection statutes or as a form of child abuse.

**(b) Limitation.** In consultation with the Secretary of State, the Commissioner of Immigration and Naturalization shall identify those countries in which female genital mutilation is commonly practiced and, to the extent practicable, limit the provision of information under subsection (a) of this section to aliens from such countries.

**(c) "Female genital mutilation" defined.** For purposes of this section, the term "female genital mutilation" means the removal or infibulation (or both) of the whole or part of the clitoris, the labia minora, or labia majora.

(P.L. 104-208 (IIRAIRA) (9/30/96), div. C, title VI, §644.)

## Sec. 1375a Domestic violence information and resources for immigrants and regulation of international marriage brokers

**(a) Information for K Nonimmigrants on Legal Rights and Resources for Immigrant Victims of Domestic Violence.—**

(1) *In general.—* The Secretary of Homeland Security, in consultation with the Attorney General and the Secretary of State, shall develop an information pamphlet, as described in

paragraph (2), on legal rights and resources for immigrant victims of domestic violence and distribute and make such pamphlet available as described in paragraph (5). In preparing such materials, the Secretary of Homeland Security shall consult with nongovernmental organizations with expertise on the legal rights of immigrant victims of battery, extreme cruelty, sexual assault, and other crimes.

(2) *Information pamphlet.*— The information pamphlet developed under paragraph (1) shall include information on the following:

(A) The K nonimmigrant visa application process and the marriage-based immigration process, including conditional residence and adjustment of status.

(B) The illegality of domestic violence, sexual assault, and child abuse in the United States and the dynamics of domestic violence.

(C) Domestic violence and sexual assault services in the United States, including the National Domestic Violence Hotline and the National Sexual Assault Hotline.

(D) The legal rights of immigrant victims of abuse and other crimes in immigration, criminal justice, family law, and other matters, including access to protection orders.

(E) The obligations of parents to provide child support for children.

(F) Marriage fraud under United States immigration laws and the penalties for committing such fraud.

(G) A warning concerning the potential use of K nonimmigrant visas by United States citizens who have a history of committing domestic violence, sexual assault, child abuse, or other crimes and an explanation that such acts may not have resulted in a criminal record for such a citizen.

(H) Notification of the requirement under subsection (d)(3)(A) that international marriage brokers provide foreign national clients with background information gathered on United States clients from searches of Federal and State sex offender public registries and collected from United States clients regarding their marital history and domestic violence or other violent criminal history, but that such information may not be complete or accurate because the United States client may not have a criminal record or may not have truthfully reported their marital or criminal record.

(3) *Summaries.*— The Secretary of Homeland Security, in consultation with the Attorney General and the Secretary of State, shall develop summaries of the pamphlet developed under paragraph (1) that shall be used by Federal officials when reviewing the pamphlet in interviews under subsection (b).

(4) *Translation.*—

(A) *In general.*— In order to best serve the language groups having the greatest concentration of K nonimmigrant visa applicants, the information pamphlet developed under paragraph (1) shall, subject to subparagraph (B), be translated by the Secretary of State into foreign languages, including Russian, Spanish, Tagalog, Vietnamese, Chinese, Ukrainian, Thai, Korean, Polish, Japanese, French, Arabic, Portuguese, Hindi, and such other languages as the Secretary of State, in the Secretary's discretion, may specify.

(B) *Revision.*— Every 2 years, the Secretary of Homeland Security, in consultation with the Attorney General and the Secretary of State, shall determine at least 14 specific languages into which the information pamphlet is translated based on the languages spoken by the greatest concentrations of K nonimmigrant visa applicants.

(5) *Availability and distribution.*— The information pamphlet developed under paragraph (1) shall be made available and distributed as follows:

(A) *Mailings to k nonimmigrant visa applicants.*—

(i) The pamphlet shall be mailed by the Secretary of State to each applicant for a K nonimmigrant visa at the same time that the instruction packet regarding the visa application process is mailed to such applicant. The pamphlet so mailed shall be in the primary language of the applicant or in English if no translation into the applicant's primary language is available.

(ii) The Secretary of Homeland Security shall provide to the Secretary of State, for inclusion in the mailing under clause (i), a copy of the petition submitted by the petitioner for such applicant under subsection (d) or (r) of section 214 of such Act (8 U.S.C. 1184).

(iii) The Secretary of Homeland Security shall provide to the Secretary of State any criminal background information the Secretary of Homeland Security possesses with respect to a petitioner under subsection (d) or (r) of section 214 of such Act (8 U.S.C. 1184). The Secretary of State, in turn, shall share any such criminal background information that is in government records or databases with the K nonimmigrant visa applicant who is the beneficiary of the petition. The visa applicant shall be informed that such criminal background information is based on available records and may not be complete. The Secretary of State also shall provide for the disclosure of such criminal background information to the visa applicant at the consular interview in the primary language of the visa applicant. Nothing in this clause shall be construed to authorize the Secretary of Homeland Security to conduct any new or additional criminal background check that is not otherwise conducted in the course of adjudicating such petitions.

(B) *Consular access.*— The pamphlet developed under paragraph (1) shall be made available to the public at all consular posts. The summaries described in paragraph (3) shall be made available to foreign service officers at all consular posts.

(C) *Posting on federal websites.*— The pamphlet developed under paragraph (1) shall be posted on the websites of the Department of State and the Department of Homeland Security, as well as on the websites of all consular posts processing applications for K nonimmigrant visas.

(D) *International marriage brokers and victim advocacy organizations.*— The pamphlet developed under paragraph (1) shall be made available to any international marriage broker, government agency, or nongovernmental advocacy organization.

(6) *Deadline for pamphlet development and distribution.*—The pamphlet developed under paragraph (1) shall be distributed and made available (including in the languages specified under paragraph (4)) not later than 120 days after the date of the enactment of this Act.

**(b) Visa and Adjustment Interviews.**—

(1) *Fiancé(e)s, spouses and their derivatives.*— During an interview with an applicant for a K nonimmigrant visa, a consular officers shall—

(A) provide information, in the primary language of the visa applicant, on protection orders or criminal convictions collected under subsection (a)(5)(A)(iii);

(B) provide a copy of the pamphlet developed under subsection (a)(1) in English or another appropriate language and provide an oral summary, in the primary language of the visa applicant, of that pamphlet; and

(C) ask the applicant, in the primary language of the applicant, whether an international marriage broker has facilitated the relationship between the applicant and the United States petitioner, and, if so, obtain the identity of the international marriage broker from the applicant and confirm that the international marriage broker provided to the applicant the information and materials required under subsection (d)(3)(A)(iii).

(2) *Family-based applicants.*— The pamphlet developed under subsection (a)(1) shall be distributed directly to applicants for family-based immigration petitions at all consular and adjustment interviews for such visas. The Department of State or Department of Homeland Security officer conducting the interview shall review the summary of the pamphlet with the applicant orally in the applicant's primary language, in addition to distributing the pamphlet to the applicant in English or another appropriate language.

**(c) Confidentiality.**— In fulfilling the requirements of this section, no official of the Department of State or the Department of Homeland Security shall disclose to a nonimmigrant visa applicant the name or contact information of any person who was granted a protection order or restraining order against the petitioner or who was a victim of a crime of violence perpetrated by the petitioner, but shall disclose the relationship of the person to the petitioner.

**(d) Regulation of International Marriage Brokers.**—

(1) *Prohibition on marketing children.*— An international marriage broker shall not provide any individual or entity with the personal contact information, photograph, or general information about the background or interests of any individual under the age of 18.

(2) *Requirements of international marriage brokers with respect to mandatory collection of background information.*—

(A) *In general.*—

(i) Search of sex offender public registries.— Each international marriage broker shall search the National Sex Offender Public Registry or State sex offender public registry, as required under paragraph (3)(A)(i).

(ii) Collection of background information.— Each international marriage broker shall also collect the background information listed in subparagraph (B) about the United States client to whom the personal contact information of a foreign national client would be provided.

(B) *Background information.*— The international marriage broker shall collect a certification signed (in written, electronic, or other form) by the United States client accompanied by documentation or an attestation of the following background information about the United States client:

(i) Any temporary or permanent civil protection order or restraining order issued against the United States client.

(ii) Any Federal, State, or local arrest or conviction of the United States client for homicide, murder, manslaughter, assault, battery, domestic violence, rape, sexual assault, abusive sexual contact, sexual exploitation, incest, child abuse or neglect, torture, trafficking, peonage, holding hostage, involuntary servitude, slave trade, kidnapping, abduction, unlawful criminal restraint, false imprisonment, or stalking.

(iii) Any Federal, State, or local arrest or conviction of the United States client for—

(I) solely, principally, or incidentally engaging in prostitution;

(II) a direct or indirect attempt to procure prostitutes or persons for the purpose of prostitution; or

(III) receiving, in whole or in part, of the proceeds of prostitution.

(iv) Any Federal, State, or local arrest or conviction of the United States client for offenses related to controlled substances or alcohol.

(v) Marital history of the United States client, including whether the client is currently married, whether the client has previously been married and how many times, how previous marriages of the client were terminated and the date of termination, and whether the client has previously sponsored an alien to whom the client was engaged or married.

(vi) The ages of any of the United States client's children who are under the age of 18.

(vii) All States and countries in which the United States client has resided since the client was 18 years of age.

(3) *Obligation of international marriage brokers with respect to informed consent.*—

(A) *Limitation on sharing information about foreign national clients.*— An international marriage broker shall not provide any United States client or representative with the personal contact information of any foreign national client unless and until the international marriage broker has—

(i) performed a search of the National Sex Offender Public Registry, or of the relevant State sex offender public registry for any State not yet participating in the National Sex Offender Public Registry in which the United States client has resided during the previous 20 years, for information regarding the United States client;

(ii) collected background information about the United States client required under paragraph (2);

(iii) provided to the foreign national client—

(I) in the foreign national client's primary language, a copy of any records retrieved from the search required under paragraph (2)(A)(i) or documentation confirming that such search retrieved no records;

(II) in the foreign national client's primary language, a copy of the background information collected by the international marriage broker under paragraph (2)(B); and

(III) in the foreign national client's primary language (or in English or other appropriate language if there is no translation available into the client's primary language), the pamphlet developed under subsection (a)(1); and

(iv) received from the foreign national client a signed, written consent, in the foreign national client's primary language, to release the foreign national client's personal contact information to the specific United States client.

(B) *Confidentiality.*— In fulfilling the requirements of this paragraph, an international marriage broker shall disclose the relationship of the United States client to individuals who were issued a protection order or restraining order as described in clause (i) of paragraph (2)(B), or of any other victims of crimes as described in clauses (ii) through (iv) of such paragraph, but shall not disclose the name or location information of such individuals.

(C) *Penalty for misuse of information.*— A person who knowingly discloses, uses, or causes to be used any information obtained by an international marriage broker as a result of the obligations imposed on it under paragraph (2) and this paragraph for any purpose other than the disclosures required under this paragraph shall be fined in accordance with title 18, United States Code, or imprisoned not more than 1 year, or both. These penalties are in addition to any other civil or criminal liability under Federal or State law which a person may be subject to for the misuse of that information, including to threaten, intimidate, or harass any individual. Nothing in this section shall prevent the disclosure of such information to law enforcement or pursuant to a court order.

(4) *Limitation on disclosure.*— An international marriage broker shall not provide the personal contact information of any foreign national client to any person or entity other than a United States client. Such information shall not be disclosed to potential United States clients or individuals who are being recruited to be United States clients or representatives.

(5) *Penalties.*—

(A) *Federal civil penalty.*—

(i) *Violation.*— An international marriage broker that violates (or attempts to violate) paragraph (1), (2), (3), or (4) is subject to a civil penalty of not less than $5,000 and not more than $25,000 for each such violation.

(ii) Procedures for imposition of penalty.— A penalty may be imposed under clause (i) by the Attorney General only after notice and an opportunity for an agency hearing on the record in accordance with subchapter II of chapter 5 of title 5, United States Code (popularly known as the Administrative Procedure Act).

(B) *Federal criminal penalty.*— In circumstances in or affecting interstate or foreign commerce, an international marriage broker that, within the special maritime and territorial jurisdiction of the United States, violates (or attempts to violate) paragraph (1), (2), (3), or (4) shall be fined in accordance with title 18, United States Code, or imprisoned for not more than 5 years, or both.

(C) *Additional remedies.*— The penalties and remedies under this subsection are in addition to any other penalties or remedies available under law.

(6) *Nonpreemption.*— Nothing in this subsection shall preempt—

(A) any State law that provides additional protections for aliens who are utilizing the services of an international marriage broker; or

(B) any other or further right or remedy available under law to any party utilizing the services of an international marriage broker.

(7) *Effective date.*—

(A) *In general.*— Except as provided in subparagraph (B), this subsection shall take effect on the date that is 60 days after the date of the enactment of this Act.

(B) *Additional time allowed for information pamphlet.*— The requirement for the distribution of the pamphlet developed under subsection (a)(1) shall not apply until 30 days after the date of its development and initial distribution under subsection (a)(6).

**(e) Definitions.**— In this section:

(1) *Crime of violence.*— The term "crime of violence" has the meaning given such term in section 16 of title 18, United States Code.

(2) *Domestic violence.*— The term "domestic violence" has the meaning given such term in section 3 of this Act.

(3) *Foreign national client.*— The term "foreign national client" means a person who is not a United States citizen or national or an alien lawfully admitted to the United States for permanent residence and who utilizes the services of an international marriage broker. Such term includes an alien residing in the United States who is in the United States as a result of utilizing the services of an international marriage broker and any alien recruited by an international marriage broker or representative of such broker.

(4) *International marriage broker.*—

(A) *In general.*— The term "international marriage broker" means a corporation, partnership, business, individual, or other legal entity, whether or not organized under any law of the United States, that charges fees for providing dating, matrimonial, matchmaking services, or social referrals between United States citizens or nationals or aliens lawfully admitted to the United States as permanent residents and foreign national clients by providing personal contact information or otherwise facilitating communication between individuals.

(B) *Exceptions.*— Such term does not include—

(i) a traditional matchmaking organization of a cultural or religious nature that operates on a nonprofit basis and otherwise operates in compliance with the laws of the countries in which it operates, including the laws of the United States; or

(ii) an entity that provides dating services if its principal business is not to provide international dating services between United States citizens or United States residents and foreign nationals and it charges comparable rates and offers comparable services to all individuals it serves regardless of the individual's gender or country of citizenship.

(5) *K nonimmigrant visa.*— The term "K nonimmigrant visa" means a nonimmigrant visa under clause (i) or (ii) of section 101(a)(15)(K) of the Immigration and Nationality Act (8 U.S.C. 1101(a)(15)(K)).

(6) *Personal contact information.*—

(A) *In general.*— The term "personal contact information" means information, or a forum to obtain such information, that would permit individuals to contact each other, including—

(i) the name or residential, postal, electronic mail, or instant message address of an individual;

(ii) the telephone, pager, cellphone, or fax number, or voice message mailbox of an individual; or

(iii) the provision of an opportunity for an in-person meeting.

(B) *Exception.*— Such term does not include a photograph or general information about the background or interests of a person.

(7) *Representative.*— The term "representative" means, with respect to an international marriage broker, the person or entity acting on behalf of such broker. Such a representative may be a recruiter, agent, independent contractor, or other international marriage broker or other person conveying information about or to a United States client or foreign national client, whether or not the person or entity receives remuneration.

(8) *State.*— The term "State" includes the District of Columbia, Puerto Rico, the Virgin Islands, Guam, American Samoa, and the Northern Mariana Islands.

(9) *United States.*— The term "United States", when used in a geographic sense, includes all the States.

(10) *United States client.*— The term "United States client" means a United States citizen or other individual who resides in the United States and who utilizes the services of an international marriage broker, if a payment is made or a debt is incurred to utilize such services.

## (f) GAO Study and Report.—

(1) *Study.*— The Comptroller General of the United States shall conduct a study—

(A) on the impact of this section and section 832 on the K nonimmigrant visa process, including specifically—

(i) annual numerical changes in petitions for K nonimmigrant visas;

(ii) the annual number (and percentage) of such petitions that are denied under subsection (d)(2) or (r) of section 214 of the Immigration and Nationality Act (8 U.S.C. 1184), as amended by this Act;

(iii) the annual number of waiver applications submitted under such a subsection, the number (and percentage) of such applications granted or denied, and the reasons for such decisions;

(iv) the annual number (and percentage) of cases in which the criminal background information collected and provided to the applicant as required by subsection (a)(5)(A)(iii) contains one or more convictions;

(v) the annual number and percentage of cases described in clause (iv) that were granted or were denied waivers under section 214(d)(2) of the Immigration and Nationality Act, as amended by this Act;

(vi) the annual number of fiancé(e) and spousal K nonimmigrant visa petitions or family-based immigration petitions filed by petitioners or applicants who have previously filed other fiancé(e) or spousal K nonimmigrant visa petitions or family-based immigration petitions;

(vii) the annual number of fiancé(e) and spousal K nonimmigrant visa petitions or family-based immigration petitions filed by petitioners or applicants who have concurrently filed other fiancé(e) or spousal K nonimmigrant visa petitioners or family-based immigration petitions; and

(viii) the annual and cumulative number of petitioners and applicants tracked in the multiple filings database established under paragraph (4) of section 214(r) of the Immigration and Nationality Act, as added by this Act;

(B) regarding the number of international marriage brokers doing business in the United States, the number of marriages resulting from the services provided, and the extent of compliance with the applicable requirements of this section;

(C) that assesses the accuracy and completeness of information gathered under section 832 and this section from clients and petitioners by international marriage brokers, the Department of State, or the Department of Homeland Security;

(D) that examines, based on the information gathered, the extent to which persons with a history of violence are using either the K nonimmigrant visa process or the services of international marriage brokers, or both, and the extent to which such persons are providing accurate and complete information to the Department of State or the Department of Homeland Security and to international marriage brokers in accordance with subsections (a) and (d)(2)(B); and

(E) that assesses the accuracy and completeness of the criminal background check performed by the Secretary of Homeland Security at identifying past instances of domestic violence.

(2) *Report.*— Not later than 2 years after the date of enactment of this Act, the Comptroller General shall submit to the Committee on the Judiciary of the Senate and the Committee on the Judiciary of the House of Representatives a report setting forth the results of the study conducted under paragraph (1).

(3) *Data collection.*— The Secretary of Homeland Security and the Secretary of State shall collect and maintain the data necessary for the Comptroller General of the United States to conduct the study required by paragraph (1).

(P.L. 109-162 (1/5/06), title VIII, subtitle D, §833.)

## Sec. 1376 Data on nonimmigrant overstay rates

**(a) Collection of data.** Not later than the date that is 180 days after April 27, 1998, the Attorney General shall implement a program to collect data, for each fiscal year, regarding the total number of aliens within each of the classes of nonimmigrant aliens described in section 1101(a)(15) of this title whose authorized period of stay in the United States terminated during the previous fiscal year, but who remained in the United States notwithstanding such termination.

**(b) Annual report.** Not later than June 30, 1999, and not later than June 30 of each year thereafter, the Attorney General shall submit an annual report to the Congress providing numerical estimates, for each country for the preceding fiscal year, of the number of aliens from the country who are described in subsection (a) of this section.

(P.L. 105-173 (4/27/98), §2.)

## Sec. 1377 Collection of data on detained asylum seekers

**(a) In general.** The Attorney General shall regularly collect data on a nation-wide basis with respect to asylum seekers in detention in the United States, including the following information:

(1) The number of detainees.

(2) An identification of the countries of origin of the detainees.

(3) The percentage of each gender within the total number of detainees.

(4) The number of detainees listed by each year of age of the detainees.

(5) The location of each detainee by detention facility.

(6) With respect to each facility where detainees are held, whether the facility is also used to detain criminals and whether any of the detainees are held in the same cells as criminals.

(7) The number and frequency of the transfers of detainees between detention facilities.

(8) The average length of detention and the number of detainees by category of the length of detention.

(9) The rate of release from detention of detainees for each district of the Immigration and Naturalization Service.

(10) A description of the disposition of cases.

**(b) Annual reports.** Beginning October 1, 1999, and not later than October 1 of each year thereafter, the Attorney General shall submit to the Committee on the Judiciary of each House of Congress a report setting forth the data collected under subsection (a) of this section for the fiscal year ending September 30 of that year.

**(c) Availability to public.** Copies of the data collected under subsection (a) of this section shall be made available to members of the public upon request pursuant to such regulations as the Attorney General shall prescribe.

(P.L. 105-277 (10/21/98), div. A, §101 [title IX, §903].)

### Sec. 1378 Collection of data on other detained aliens

**(a) In general.** The Attorney General shall regularly collect data on a nationwide basis on aliens being detained in the United States by the Immigration and Naturalization Service other than the aliens described in section 1377 of this title, including the following information:

(1) The number of detainees who are criminal aliens and the number of detainees who are noncriminal aliens who are not seeking asylum.

(2) An identification of the ages, gender, and countries of origin of detainees within each category described in paragraph (1).

(3) The types of facilities, whether facilities of the Immigration and Naturalization Service or other Federal, State, or local facilities, in which each of the categories of detainees described in paragraph (1) are held.

**(b) Length of detention, transfers, and dispositions.** With respect to detainees who are criminal aliens and detainees who are noncriminal aliens who are not seeking asylum, the Attorney General shall also collect data concerning—

(1) the number and frequency of transfers between detention facilities for each category of detainee;

(2) the average length of detention of each category of detainee;

(3) for each category of detainee, the number of detainees who have been detained for the same length of time, in 3-month increments;

(4) for each category of detainee, the rate of release from detention for each district of the Immigration and Naturalization Service; and

(5) for each category of detainee, the disposition of detention, including whether detention ended due to deportation, release on parole, or any other release.

**(c) Criminal aliens.** With respect to criminal aliens, the Attorney General shall also collect data concerning—

(1) the number of criminal aliens apprehended under the immigration laws and not detained by the Attorney General; and

(2) a list of crimes committed by criminal aliens after the decision was made not to detain them, to the extent this information can be derived by cross-checking the list of criminal aliens not detained with other databases accessible to the Attorney General.

**(d) Annual reports.** Beginning on October 1, 1999, and not later than October 1 of each year thereafter, the Attorney General shall submit to the Committee on the Judiciary of each House of Congress a report setting forth the data collected under subsections (a), (b), and (c) of this section for the fiscal year ending September 30 of that year.

**(e) Availability to public.** Copies of the data collected under subsections (a), (b), and (c) of this section shall be made available to members of the public upon request pursuant to such regulations as the Attorney General shall prescribe.

(P.L. 105-277 (10/21/98), div. A, §101 [title IX, §904].)

## Sec. 1379 Technology standard to confirm identity

**(1) In general.** The Attorney General and the Secretary of State jointly, through the National Institute of Standards and Technology (NIST), and in consultation with the Secretary of the Treasury and other Federal law enforcement and intelligence agencies the Attorney General or Secretary of State deems appropriate and in consultation with Congress, shall within 15 months after October 26, 2001, develop and certify a technology standard, including appropriate biometric identifier standards, that can be used to verify the identity of persons applying for a United States visa or such persons seeking to enter the United States pursuant to a visa for the purposes of conducting background checks, confirming identity, and ensuring that a person has not received a visa under a different name or such person seeking to enter the United States pursuant to a visa.

**(2) Interoperable.** The technology standard developed pursuant to paragraph (1), shall be the technological basis for a cross-agency, cross-platform electronic system that is a cost-effective, efficient, fully interoperable means to share law enforcement and intelligence information necessary to confirm the identity of such persons applying for a United States visa or such person seeking to enter the United States pursuant to a visa.

**(3) Accessible.** The electronic system described in paragraph (2), once implemented, shall be readily and easily accessible to—

(A) all consular officers responsible for the issuance of visas;

(B) all Federal inspection agents at all United States border inspection points; and

(C) all law enforcement and intelligence officers as determined by regulation to be responsible for investigation or identification of aliens admitted to the United States pursuant to a visa.

**(4) Report.** Not later than one year after October 26, 2001, and every 2 years thereafter, the Attorney General and the Secretary of State shall jointly, in consultation with the Secretary of Treasury, report to Congress describing the development, implementation, efficacy, and privacy implications of the technology standard and electronic database system described in this section.

**(5) Funding.** There is authorized to be appropriated to the Secretary of State, the Attorney General, and the Director of the National Institute of Standards and Technology such sums as may be necessary to carry out the provisions of this section.

(P.L. 107-56 (10/26/01), title IV, §403; P.L. 107-173 (5/14/02), title II, §201, §202.)

### Sec. 1380 Maintenance of statistics by the Department of Homeland Security

**(a) In general.** The Department of Homeland Security shall maintain statistics regarding petitions filed, approved, extended, and amended with respect to nonimmigrants described in section 1101(a)(15)(L) of this title, including the number of such nonimmigrants who are classified on the basis of specialized knowledge and the number of nonimmigrants who are classified on the basis of specialized knowledge in order to work primarily at offsite locations.

**(b) Applicability.** Subsection (a) of this section shall apply to petitions filed on or after the effective date of this subtitle.

(P.L. 108-447 (12/8/04), div. J, title IV, §414.)

### Sec. 1381 Secretary of Labor Report

Not later than January 31 of each year, the Secretary of Labor shall report to the Committees on the Judiciary of the Senate and the House of Representatives on the investigations undertaken based on—

**(1)** the authorities described in clauses (i) and (ii) of section 1182(n)(2)(G) of this title; and

**(2)** the expenditures by the Secretary of Labor described in section 1356(v)(2)(D) of this title.

(P.L. 108-447 (12/8/04), div. J, title IV, §424.)

### Sec. 1401a Birth abroad before 1952 to service parent

Section 1401(g) of this title shall be considered to have been and to be applicable to a child born outside of the United States and its outlying possessions after January 12, 1941, and before December 24, 1952, of parents one of whom is a citizen of the United States who has served in the Armed Forces of the United States after December 31, 1946, and before December 24, 1952, and whose case does not come within the provisions of section 201(g) or (i) of the Nationality Act of 1940.

(Mar. 16, 1956, ch. 85, 70 Stat. 50; P.L. 97-116 (12/29/81), §18.)

### Sec. 1440e Exemption from naturalization fees for aliens naturalized through service during Vietnam hostilities or other subsequent period of military hostilities; report by clerks of courts to Attorney General

Notwithstanding any other provision of law, no clerk of a United States court shall charge or collect a naturalization fee from an alien who has served in the military, air, or naval forces of the United States during a period beginning February 28, 1961, and ending on the date designated by the President by Executive order as the date of termination of the Vietnam hostilities, or thereafter during any other period which the President by Executive order shall designate as a period in which Armed Forces of the United States are or were engaged in military operations involving armed conflict with a hostile foreign force, and who is applying for naturalization during such periods under section 329 of the Immigration and Nationality Act, as amended by this Act [8 U.S.C. 1440], for filing a petition for naturalization or issuing a certificate of naturalization upon his admission to citizenship, and no clerk of any State court shall charge or collect any fee for such services unless the laws of the State require such charge to be made, in which case nothing more than the portion of the fee required to be paid to the State shall be charged or collected. A report of all transactions under this section shall be made to the Attorney General as in the case of other reports required of clerks of courts by title III of the Immigration and Nationality Act [8 U.S.C. 1401 *et seq.*].

(P.L. 90-633 (10/24/68), §3.)

### Sec. 1443a Naturalization proceedings overseas for members of the Armed Forces

Notwithstanding any other provision of law, the Secretary of Homeland Security, the Secretary of State, and the Secretary of Defense shall ensure that any applications, interviews, filings, oaths, ceremonies, or other proceedings under title III of the Immigration and Nationality Act (8 U.S.C. 1401 *et seq.*) relating to naturalization of members of the Armed Forces are available through United States embassies, consulates, and as practicable, United States military installations overseas.

(P.L. 108-136 (11/24/03), div. A, title XVII, §1701.)

# APPENDIX B
# IIRAIRA §110, as amended
# (Entry/Exit Data System)

*(P.L. 104-208 (IIRAIRA), as amended by P.L. 105-259 (Automated Entry-Exit Control System), P.L. 105-277 (Omnibus Consolidated Appropriations), and P.L. 106-215 (INS Data Management Improvement Act)*[3]

## §110 Integrated entry and exit data system
## [8 U.S.C. §1365a]

(a) Requirement.— The Attorney General shall implement an integrated entry and exit data system.

(b) Integrated entry and exit data system defined.— For purposes of this section, the term "integrated entry and exit data system" means an electronic system that—

(1) provides access to, and integrates, alien arrival and departure data that are—

(A) authorized or required to be created or collected under law;

(B) in an electronic format; and

(C) in a data base of the Department of Justice or the Department of State, including those created or used at ports of entry and at consular offices;

(2) uses available data described in paragraph (1) to produce a report of arriving and departing aliens by country of nationality, classification as an immigrant or nonimmigrant, and date of arrival in, and departure from, the United States;

---

[3] Sec. 302 of the Enhanced Border Security and Visa Entry Reform Act (P.L. 107-173), imposes requirements on the Attorney General, INS, and State Department. Section 414 of the USA PATRIOT Act, P.L. 107-56 also affects IIRAIRA §110. It provides as follows:

Sec. 414. Visa Integrity and Security.

(a) Sense of Congress Regarding the Need to Expedite Implementation of Integrated Entry and Exit Data System

(1) Sense of Congress—In light of the terrorist attacks perpetrated against the United States on September 11, 2001, it is the sense of the Congress that—

(A) the Attorney General, in consultation with the Secretary of State, should fully implement the integrated entry and exit data system for airports, seaports, and land border ports of entry, as specified in section 110 of the Illegal Immigration Reform and Immigrant Responsibility Act of 1996 (8 U.S.C. 1365a), with all deliberate speed and as expeditiously as practicable; and

(B) the Attorney General, in consultation with the Secretary of State, the Secretary of Commerce, the Secretary of the Treasury, and the Office of Homeland Security, should immediately begin establishing the Integrated Entry and Exit Data System Task Force, as described in section 3 of the Immigration and Naturalization Service Data Management Improvement Act of 2000 (Public Law 106-215).

(2) Authorization of Appropriations—There is authorized to be appropriated such sums as may be necessary to fully implement the system described in paragraph (1)(A).

(b) Development of the System—In the development of the integrated entry and exit data system under section 110 of the Illegal Immigration Reform and Immigrant Responsibility Act of 1996 (8 U.S.C. 1365a), the Attorney General and the Secretary of State shall particularly focus on—

(1) the utilization of biometric technology; and

(2) the development of tamper-resistant documents readable at ports of entry.

(c) Interface with Law Enforcement Databases—The entry and exit data system described in this section shall be able to interface with law enforcement databases for use by Federal law enforcement to identify and detain individuals who pose a threat to the national security of the United States.

(d) [repealed by §201(b)(2) of Enhanced Border Security and Visa Entry Reform Act of 2002, P.L. 107-173.]

(3) matches an alien's available arrival data with the alien's available departure data;

(4) assists the Attorney General (and the Secretary of State, to the extent necessary to carry out such Secretary's obligations under immigration law) to identify, through on-line searching procedures, lawfully admitted nonimmigrants who may have remained in the United States beyond the period authorized by the Attorney General; and

(5) otherwise uses available alien arrival and departure data described in paragraph (1) to permit the Attorney General to make the reports required under subsection (e).

(c) Construction.—

(1) No additional authority to impose documentary or data collection requirements.— Nothing in this section shall be construed to permit the Attorney General or the Secretary of State to impose any new documentary or data collection requirements on any person in order to satisfy the requirements of this section, including—

(A) requirements on any alien for whom the documentary requirements in section 212(a)(7)(B) of the Immigration and Nationality Act (8 U.S.C. 1182(a)(7)(B)) have been waived by the Attorney General and the Secretary of State under section 212(d)(4)(B) of such Act (8 U.S.C. 1182(d)(4)(B)); or

(B) requirements that are inconsistent with the North American Free Trade Agreement.

(2) No reduction of authority.— Nothing in this section shall be construed to reduce or curtail any authority of the Attorney General or the Secretary of State under any other provision of law.

(d) Deadlines.—

(1) Airports and seaports.— Not later than December 31, 2003, the Attorney General shall implement the integrated entry and exit data system using available alien arrival and departure data described in subsection (b)(1) pertaining to aliens arriving in, or departing from, the United States at an airport or seaport. Such implementation shall include ensuring that such data, when collected or created by an immigration officer at an airport or seaport, are entered into the system and can be accessed by immigration officers at other airports and seaports.

(2) High-traffic land border ports of entry.— Not later than December 31, 2004, the Attorney General shall implement the integrated entry and exit data system using the data described in paragraph (1) and available alien arrival and departure data described in subsection (b)(1) pertaining to aliens arriving in, or departing from, the United States at the 50 land border ports of entry determined by the Attorney General to serve the highest numbers of arriving and departing aliens. Such implementation shall include ensuring that such data, when collected or created by an immigration officer at such a port of entry, are entered into the system and can be accessed by immigration officers at airports, seaports, and other such land border ports of entry.

(3) Remaining data.— Not later than December 31, 2005, the Attorney General shall fully implement the integrated entry and exit data system using all data described in subsection (b)(1). Such implementation shall include ensuring that all such data are available to immigration officers at all ports of entry into the United States.

(e) Reports.—

(1) In general.— Not later than December 31 of each year following the commencement of implementation of the integrated entry and exit data system, the Attorney General shall use the system to prepare an annual report to the Committees on the Judiciary of the House of Representatives and of the Senate.

(2) Information.— Each report shall include the following information with respect to the preceding fiscal year, and an analysis of that information:

(A) The number of aliens for whom departure data was collected during the reporting period, with an accounting by country of nationality of the departing alien.

(B) The number of departing aliens whose departure data was successfully matched to the alien's arrival data, with an accounting by the alien's country of nationality and by the alien's classification as an immigrant or nonimmigrant.

(C) The number of aliens who arrived pursuant to a nonimmigrant visa, or as a visitor under the visa waiver program under section 217 of the Immigration and Nationality Act (8 U.S.C. 1187), for whom no matching departure data have been obtained through the system or through other means as of the end of the alien's authorized period of stay, with an accounting by the alien's country of nationality and date of arrival in the United States.

(D) The number of lawfully admitted nonimmigrants identified as having remained in the United States beyond the period authorized by the Attorney General, with an accounting by the alien's country of nationality.

(f) Authority to Provide Access to System.—

(1) In general.— Subject to subsection (d), the Attorney General, in consultation with the Secretary of State, shall determine which officers and employees of the Departments of Justice and State may enter data into, and have access to the data contained in, the integrated entry and exit data system.

(2) Other law enforcement officials.— The Attorney General, in the discretion of the Attorney General, may permit other Federal, State, and local law enforcement officials to have access to the data contained in the integrated entry and exit data system for law enforcement purposes.

(g) Use of Task Force Recommendations.— The Attorney General shall continuously update and improve the integrated entry and exit data system as technology improves and using the recommendations of the task force established under section 3 of the Immigration and Naturalization Service Data Management Improvement Act of 2000.

(h) Authorization of Appropriations.— There are authorized to be appropriated to carry out this section such sums as may be necessary for fiscal years 2001 through 2008.

# IIRAIRA §309
## (Effective Date and Transition Rules)

**Sec. 309 Effective Dates; Transition.**

(a) In general.— Except as provided in this section and sections 303(b)(2), 306(c), 308(d)(2)(D), or 308(d)(5) of this division, this subtitle and the amendments made by this subtitle shall take effect on the first day of the first month beginning more than 180 days after the date of the enactment of this Act (in this title referred to as the "title III-A effective date").

(b) Promulgation of Regulations.— The Attorney General shall first promulgate regulations to carry out this subtitle by not later than 30 days before the title III-A effective date.

(c) Transition for Aliens in Proceedings.—

(1) General rule that new rules do not apply.— Subject to the succeeding provisions of this subsection, in the case of an alien who is in exclusion or deportation proceedings before the title III-A effective Date—

(A) the amendments made by this subtitle shall not apply, and

(B) the proceedings (including judicial review thereof) shall continue to be conducted without regard to such amendments.

(2) Attorney General option to elect to apply new procedures.— In a case described in paragraph (1) in which an evidentiary hearing under section 236 or 242 and 242B of the Immigration and Nationality Act has not commenced as of the title III-A effective date, the Attorney General may elect to proceed under chapter 4 of title II of such Act (as amended by this subtitle). The Attorney General shall provide notice of such election to the alien involved not later than 30 days before the date any evidentiary hearing is commenced. If the Attorney General makes such election, the notice of hearing provided to the alien under section 235 or 242(a) of such Act shall be valid as if provided under section 239 of such Act (as amended by this subtitle) to confer jurisdiction on the immigration judge.

(3) Attorney General option to terminate and reinitiate proceedings.— In the case described in paragraph (1), the Attorney General may elect to terminate proceedings in which there has not been a final administrative decision and to reinitiate proceedings under chapter 4 of title II the Immigration and Nationality Act (as amended by this subtitle). Any determination in the terminated proceeding shall not be binding in the reinitiated proceeding.

(4) Transitional changes in judicial review.— In the case described in paragraph (1) in which a final order of exclusion or deportation is entered more than 30 days after the date of the enactment of this Act, notwithstanding any provision of section 106 of the Immigration and Nationality Act (as in effect as of the date of the enactment of this Act) to the contrary—

(A) in the case of judicial review of a final order of exclusion, subsection (b) of such section shall not apply and the action for judicial review shall be governed by the provisions of subsections (a) and (c) of such in the same manner as they apply to judicial review of orders of deportation;

(B) a court may not order the taking of additional evidence under section 2347(c) of title 28, United States Code;

(C) the petition for judicial review must be filed not later than 30 days after the date of the final order of exclusion or deportation;

(D) the petition for review shall be filed with the court of appeals for the judicial circuit in which the administrative proceedings before the special inquiry officer or immigration judge were completed;

(E) there shall be no appeal of any discretionary decision under section 212(c), 212(h), 212(i), 244, or 245 of the Immigration and Nationality Act (as in effect as of the date of the enactment of this Act);

(F) service of the petition for review shall not stay the deportation of an alien pending the court's decision on the petition, unless the court orders otherwise; and

(G) there shall be no appeal permitted in the case of an alien who is inadmissible or deportable by reason of having committed a criminal offense covered in section 212(a)(2) or section 241(a)(2)(A)(iii), (B), (C), or (D) of the Immigration and Nationality Act (as in effect as of the date of the enactment of this Act), or any offense covered by section 241(a)(2)(A)(ii) of such Act (as in effect on such date) for which both predicate offenses are, without regard to their date of commission, otherwise covered by section 241(a)(2)(A)(i) of such Act (as so in effect).

(5) Transitional rule with regard to suspension of deportation.— Paragraphs (1) and (2) of section 240A(d) of the Immigration and Nationality Act (relating to continuous residence or physical presence) shall apply to notices to appear issued before, on, or after the date of the enactment of this Act.

(6) Transition for certain family unity aliens.— The Attorney General may waive the application of section 212(a)(9) of the Immigration and Nationality Act, as inserted by section 301(b)(1) of this division, in the case of an alien who is provided benefits under the provisions of section 301(b)(1) of the Immigration Act of 1990 (relating to family unity).

(7) Limitation on suspension of deportation.— The Attorney General may not suspend the deportation and adjust the status under section 244 of the Immigration and Nationality Act of more than 4,000 aliens in any fiscal year (beginning after the date of the enactment of this Act). The previous sentence shall apply regardless of when an alien applied for such suspension and adjustment.

(d) Transitional References.— For purposes of carrying out the Immigration and Nationality Act, as amended by this subtitle—

(1) any reference in section 212(a)(1)(A) of such Act to the term "inadmissible" is deemed to include a reference to the term "excludable", and

(2) any reference in law to an order of removal shall be deemed to include a reference to an order of exclusion and deportation or an order of deportation.

(e) Transition.— No period of time before the date of the enactment of this Act shall be included in the period of 1 year described in section 212(a)(6)(B)(i)[4] of the Immigration and Nationality Act (as amended by section 301(c)).

---

[4] *Sic.* This reference to subparagraph 212(a)(6)(B)(i) as added by §301(c) of IIRAIRA makes no sense since there is no "period of 1 year described" in that clause (i). The section it apparently was intending to reference is INA §212(a)(9)(B)(i) as that section was amended by §301(b)(1) of IIRAIRA. *See supra* §301(b)(3) of IIRAIRA, which is set forth in the footnote for INA §212(a)(9)(B) in this document.

# IIRAIRA §641, as amended
## (Student Monitoring)

*(P.L. 104-208 (IIRAIRA), as amended by P.L. 106-396 (Visa Waiver Permanent Program Act),*
*P.L. 106-553 (LIFE Act), P.L. 107-56 (USA PATRIOT Act), and*
*P.L. 107-173 (Enhanced Border Security & Visa Entry Reform Act))*[5]

**§641 Program to collect information relating to nonimmigrant foreign students and other exchange program participants**
**[8 U.S.C. §1372]**

(a) In general—

(1) Program— The Attorney General, in consultation with the Secretary of State and the Secretary of Education, shall develop and conduct a program to collect from approved institutions of higher education, other approved educational institutions, and designated exchange visitor programs in the United States the information described in subsection (c) with respect to aliens who—

(A) have the status, or are applying for the status, of nonimmigrants under subparagraph (F), (J), or (M) of section 101(a)(15) of the Immigration and Nationality Act; and

(B) are nationals of the countries designated under subsection (b) of this section.

(2) Deadline— The program shall commence not later than January 1, 1998.

(3)[6] Aliens for Whom a Visa is Required.— The Attorney General, in consultation with the Secretary of State, shall establish an electronic means to monitor and verify—

(A) the issuance of documentation of acceptance of a foreign student by an approved institution of higher education or other approved educational institution, or of an exchange visitor program participant by a designated exchange visitor program;

(B) the transmittal of the documentation referred to in subparagraph (A) to the Department of State for use by the Bureau of Consular Affairs;

(C) the issuance of a visa to a foreign student or an exchange visitor program participant;

(D) the admission into the United States of the foreign student or exchange visitor program participant;

(E) the notification to an approved institution of higher education, other approved educational institution, or exchange visitor program sponsor that the foreign student or exchange visitor participant has been admitted into the United States;

---

[5] The USA PATRIOT Act, §416(a), also provides "The Attorney General, in consultation with the Secretary of State, shall fully implement and expand the program established by [IIRAIRA §641(a)]." Section 416(b) provides "For each alien with respect to whom information is collected under [IIRAIRA §641], the Attorney General, in consultation with the Secretary of State, shall include information on the date of entry and port of entry.".

[6] Added by §501(a)(1) of the Enhanced Border Security and Visa Entry Reform Act, 2002, P.L. 107-173.

(F) the registration and enrollment of that foreign student in such approved institution of higher education or other approved educational institution, or the participation of that exchange visitor in such designated exchange visitor program, as the case may be; and

(G) any other relevant act by the foreign student or exchange visitor program participant, including a changing of school or designated exchange visitor program and any termination of studies or participation in a designated exchange visitor program.

(4)[7] Reporting Requirements.— Not later than 30 days after the deadline for registering for classes for an academic term of an approved institution of higher education or other approved educational institution for which documentation is issued for an alien as described in paragraph (3)(A), or the scheduled commencement of participation by an alien in a designated exchange visitor program, as the case may be, the institution or program, respectively, shall report to the Immigration and Naturalization Service any failure of the alien to enroll or to commence participation.

(b) Covered countries— The Attorney General, in consultation with the Secretary of State, shall designate countries for purposes of subsection (a)(1)(B). The Attorney General shall initially designate not less than 5 countries and may designate additional countries at any time while the program is being conducted.

(c) Information to be collected—

(1)[8] In general— The information for collection under subsection (a) of this section with respect to an alien consists of—

(A) the identity and current address in the United States of the alien;

(B) the nonimmigrant classification of the alien and the date on which a visa under the classification was issued or extended or the date on which a change to such classification was approved by the Attorney General;

(C) in the case of a student at an approved institution of higher education, or other approved educational institution, the current academic status of the alien, including whether the alien is maintaining status as a full-time student or, in the case of a participant in a designated exchange visitor program, whether the alien is satisfying the terms and conditions of such program;

(D) in the case of a student at an approved institution of higher education, or other approved educational institution, any disciplinary action taken by the institution against the alien as a result of the alien's being convicted of a crime or, in the case of a participant in a designated exchange visitor program, any change in the alien's participation as a result of the alien's being convicted of a crime; and

(E) the date of entry and port of entry;

(F) the date of the alien's enrollment in an approved institution of higher education, other approved educational institution, or designated exchange visitor program in the United States;

(G) the degree program, if applicable, and field of study; and

---

[7] *Id.*

[8] Amended by §501(a)(2) of the Enhanced Border Security and Visa Entry Reform Act of 2002, P.L. 107-173.

(H) the date of the alien's termination of enrollment and the reason for such termination (including graduation, disciplinary action or other dismissal, and failure to reenroll).

(2) FERPA— The Family Educational Rights and Privacy Act of 1974 (20 U.S.C. 1232g) shall not apply to aliens described in subsection (a) to the extent that the Attorney General determines necessary to carry out the program under subsection (a).

(3) Electronic collection— The information described in paragraph (1) shall be collected electronically, where practicable.

(4) Computer software—

(A) Collecting institutions— To the extent practicable, the Attorney General shall design the program in a manner that permits approved institutions of higher education, other approved educational institutions, and designated exchange visitor programs to use existing software for the collection, storage, and data processing of information described in paragraph (1).

(B) Attorney General— To the extent practicable, the Attorney General shall use or enhance existing software for the collection, storage, and data processing of information described in paragraph (1).

(5)[9] Reporting Requirements.— The Attorney General shall prescribe by regulation reporting requirements by taking into account the curriculum calendar of the approved institution of higher education, other approved educational institution, or exchange visitor program.

(d) Participation by institutions of higher education and exchange visitor programs—

(1) Condition— The information described in subsection (c) shall be provided by institutions of higher education, or other approved educational institution, other approved educational institutions, or exchange visitor programs as a condition of—

(A) in the case of an approved institution of higher education, the continued approval of the institution under subparagraph (F) or (M) of section 101(a)(15) of the Immigration and Nationality Act; and (B) in the case of an approved institution of higher education or a designated exchange visitor program, the granting of authority to issue documents to an alien demonstrating the alien's eligibility for a visa under subparagraph (F), (J), or (M) of section 101(a)(15) of such Act.

(2) Effect of failure to provide information— If an approved institution of higher education, other approved educational institution, or a designated exchange visitor program fails to provide the specified information, such approvals and such issuance of visas shall be revoked or denied.

(e) Funding—

(1) In general— Beginning on April 1, 1997, the Attorney General shall impose on, and collect from, each alien described in paragraph (3), with respect to whom the institution or program is required by subsection (a) to collect information, a fee established by the Attorney General under paragraph (4) at a time prior to the alien being classified under subparagraph (F), (J), or (M) of section 101(a)(15) of the Immigration and Nationality Act.

---

[9] Added by §501(a)(3) of the Enhanced Border Security and Visa Entry Reform Act, 2002, P.L. 107-173.

(2) Remittance— The fees collected under paragraph (1) shall be remitted by the alien pursuant to a schedule established by the Attorney General for immediate deposit and availability as described under section 286(m) of the Immigration and Nationality Act.

(3) Aliens described— An alien referred to in paragraph (1) is an alien who seeks nonimmigrant status under subparagraph (F), (J), or (M) of section 101(a)(15) of the Immigration and Nationality Act (other than a nonimmigrant under section 101(a)(15)(J) of such Act who seeks to come to the United States as a participant in a program sponsored by the Federal Government).

(4) Amount and use of fees—

(A) Establishment of amount— The Attorney General shall establish the amount of the fee to be imposed on, and collected from, an alien under paragraph (1). Except as provided in subsection (g)(2), the fee imposed on any individual may not exceed $100, except that, in the case of an alien admitted under section 101(a)(15)(J) of the Immigration and Nationality Act as an au pair, camp counselor, or participant in a summer work travel program, the fee shall not exceed $40. The amount of the fee shall be based on the Attorney General's estimate of the cost per alien of conducting the information collection program described in this section.

(B) Use— Fees collected under paragraph (1) shall be deposited as offsetting receipts into the Immigration Examinations Fee Account (established under section 286(m) of the Immigration and Nationality Act) and shall remain available until expended for the Attorney General to reimburse any appropriation the amount paid out of which is for expenses in carrying out this section. Such expenses include, but are not necessarily limited to, those incurred by the Secretary of State in connection with the program under subsection (a).

(5) Proof of payment— The alien shall present proof of payment of the fee before the granting of—

(A) a visa under section 222 of the Immigration and Nationality Act or, in the case of an alien who is exempt from the visa requirement described in section 212(d)(4) of the Immigration and Nationality Act, admission to the United States; or

(B) change of nonimmigrant classification under section 248 of the Immigration and Nationality Act to a classification described in paragraph (3).

(6) Implementation— The provisions of section 553 of title 5, United States Code (relating to rule-making) shall not apply to the extent the Attorney General determines necessary to ensure the expeditious, initial implementation of this section.

(f) Joint report— Not later than 4 years after the commencement of the program established under subsection (a) of this section, the Attorney General, the Secretary of State, and the Secretary of Education shall jointly submit to the Committees on the Judiciary of the Senate and the House of Representatives a report on the operations of the program and the feasibility of expanding the program to cover the nationals of all countries.

(g) Worldwide applicability of program—

(1) Expansion of program— Not later than 12 months after the submission of the report required by subsection (f), the Attorney General, in consultation with the Secretary of State and the Secretary of Education, shall commence expansion of the program to cover the nationals of all countries.

(2) Revision of fee— After the program has been expanded, as provided in paragraph (1), the Attorney General may, on a periodic basis, revise the amount of the fee imposed and collected under subsection (e) in order to take into account changes in the cost of carrying out the program.

(h) Definitions— As used in this section:

(1) Approved institution of higher education— The term "approved institution of higher education" means a college or university approved by the Attorney General, in consultation with the Secretary of Education, under subparagraph (F), (J), or (M) of section 101(a)(15) of the Immigration and Nationality Act.

(2) Designated exchange visitor program— The term "designated exchange visitor program" means a program that has been—

(A) designated by the Secretary of State for purposes of section 101(a)(15)(J) of the Immigration and Nationality Act; and

(B) selected by the Attorney General for purposes of the program under this section.

(3) Other approved educational institution.— The term "other approved educational institution" includes any air flight school, language training school, or vocational school, approved by the Attorney General, in consultation with the Secretary of Education and the Secretary of State, under subparagraph (F), (J), or (M) of section 101(a)(15) of the Immigration and Nationality Act.

# Nicaraguan Adjustment & Central American Relief Act
# (NACARA), as amended

*(P.L. 105-100 (NACARA), as amended by P.L. 105-139 (NACARA),*
*P.L. 106-386 (Victims of Trafficking and Violence Protection Act, 2000),*
*P.L. 106-554 (LIFE Act), and P.L. 109-162(VAWA & DOJ Reauthorization Act))*

105th Congress
At the First Session

Begun and held at the City of Washington on Tuesday, the seventh day of January, one thousand nine hundred and ninety-seven

An Act

Making appropriations for the government of the District of Columbia and other activities chargeable in whole or in part against the revenues of said District for the fiscal year ending September 30, 1998, and for other purposes.

Be it enacted by the Senate and House of Representatives of the United States of America in Congress assembled, That the following sums are appropriated, out of any money in the Treasury not otherwise appropriated, for the District of Columbia for the fiscal year ending September 30, 1998, and for other purposes, namely:

## Title II—Clarification of Eligibility for Relief
## from Removal and Deportation for Certain Aliens

**Sec. 201. Short Title—This title may be cited as the "Nicaraguan Adjustment and Central American Relief Act."**

**Sec. 202. Adjustment of Status of Certain Nicaraguans and Cubans.**

(a) Adjustment of Status

(1) In general— The status of any alien described in subsection (b) shall be adjusted by the Attorney General to that of an alien lawfully admitted for permanent residence, if the alien—

(A) applies for such adjustment before April 1, 2000; and

(B) is otherwise admissible to the United States for permanent residence, except in determining such admissibility the grounds for inadmissibility specified in paragraphs (4), (5), (6)(A), (7)(A), and (9)(B) of section 212(a) of the Immigration and Nationality Act shall not apply.

(2) Rules in applying certain provisions.— In the case of an alien described in subsection (b) or (d) who is applying for adjustment of status under this section—

(A) the provisions of section 241(a)(5) of the Immigration and Nationality Act shall not apply; and

(B) the Attorney General may grant the alien a waiver of the grounds of inadmissibility under subparagraphs (A) and (C) of section 212(a)(9) of such Act.

In granting waivers under subparagraph (B), the Attorney General shall use standards used in granting consent under subparagraphs (A)(iii) and (C)(ii) of such section 212(a)(9).

(3) Relationship of Application to Certain Orders— An alien present in the United States who has been ordered excluded, deported, removed, or ordered to depart voluntarily from the United States under any provision of the Immigration and Nationality Act may, notwithstanding such order, apply for adjustment of status under paragraph (1). Such an alien may not be required, as a condition of submitting or granting such application, to file a separate motion to reopen, reconsider, or vacate such order. If the Attorney General grants the application, the Attorney General shall cancel the order. If the Attorney General renders a final administrative decision to deny the application, the order shall be effective and enforceable to the same extent as if the application had not been made.

(b) Aliens Eligible for Adjustment of Status

(1) In general— The benefits provided by subsection (a) shall apply to any alien who is a national of Nicaragua or Cuba and who has been physically present in the United States for a continuous period, beginning not later than December 1, 1995, and ending not earlier than the date the application for adjustment under such subsection is filed, except an alien shall not be considered to have failed to maintain continuous physical presence by reason of an absence, or absences, from the United States for any periods in the aggregate not exceeding 180 days.

(2) Proof of Commencement of Continuous Presence— For purposes of establishing that the period of continuous physical presence referred to in paragraph (1) commenced not later than December 1, 1995, an alien—

(A) shall demonstrate that the alien, prior to December 1, 1995—

(i) applied to the Attorney General for asylum;

(ii) was issued an order to show cause under section 242 or 242B of the Immigration and Nationality Act (as in effect prior to April 1, 1997);

(iii) was placed in exclusion proceedings under section 236 of such Act (as so in effect);

(iv) applied for adjustment of status under section 245 of such Act;

(v) applied to the Attorney General for employment authorization;

(vi) performed service, or engaged in a trade or business, within the United States which is evidenced by records maintained by the Commissioner of Social Security; or

(vii) applied for any other benefit under the Immigration and Nationality Act by means of an application establishing the alien's presence in the United States prior to December 1, 1995; or

(B) shall make such other demonstration of physical presence as the Attorney General may provide for by regulation.

(c) Stay of Removal; Work Authorization

(1) In general— The Attorney General shall provide by regulation for an alien subject to a final order of deportation or removal to seek a stay of such order based on the filing of an application under subsection (a).

(2) During Certain Proceedings— Notwithstanding any provision of the Immigration and Nationality Act, the Attorney General shall not order any alien to be removed from the United States, if the alien is in exclusion, deportation, or removal proceedings under any provision of

such Act and has applied for adjustment of status under subsection (a), except where the Attorney General has rendered a final administrative determination to deny the application.

(3) Work Authorization— The Attorney General may authorize an alien who has applied for adjustment of status under subsection (a) to engage in employment in the United States during the pendency of such application and may provide the alien with an "employment authorized" endorsement or other appropriate document signifying authorization of employment, except that if such application is pending for a period exceeding 180 days, and has not been denied, the Attorney General shall authorize such employment.

(d) Adjustment of Status for Spouses and Children

(1) In general— The status of an alien shall be adjusted by the Attorney General to that of an alien lawfully admitted for permanent residence, if—

(A) the alien is a national of Nicaragua or Cuba;

(B) the alien—

(i) is the spouse, child, or unmarried son or daughter of an alien whose status is adjusted to that of an alien lawfully admitted for permanent residence under subsection (a), except that in the case of such an unmarried son or daughter, the son or daughter shall be required to establish that the son or daughter has been physically present in the United States for a continuous period beginning not later than December 1, 1995, and ending not earlier than the date on which the application for adjustment under this subsection is filed; or

(ii) was, at the time at which an alien filed for adjustment under subsection (a), the spouse or child of an alien whose status is adjusted, or was eligible for adjustment, to that of an alien lawfully admitted for permanent residence under subsection (a), and the spouse, child, or child of the spouse has been battered or subjected to extreme cruelty by the alien that filed for adjustment under subsection (a);

(C) the alien applies for such adjustment and is physically present in the United States on the date the application is filed;

(D) the alien is otherwise admissible to the United States for permanent residence, except in determining such admissibility the grounds for inadmissibility specified in paragraphs (4), (5), (6)(A), (7)(A), and (9)(B) of section 212(a) of the Immigration and Nationality Act shall not apply; and

(E) applies for such adjustment before April 1, 2000, or, in the case of an alien who qualifies under subparagraph (B)(ii), applies for such adjustment during the 18-month period beginning on the date of enactment of the Violence Against Women and Department of Justice Reauthorization Act of 2005.

(2) Proof of Continuous Presence— For purposes of establishing the period of continuous physical presence referred to in paragraph (1)(B), an alien—

(A) shall demonstrate that such period commenced not later than December 1, 1995, in a manner consistent with subsection (b)(2); and

(B) shall not be considered to have failed to maintain continuous physical presence by reason of an absence, or absences, from the United States for any period in the aggregate not exceeding 180 days.

(3) Procedure— In acting on an application under this section with respect to a spouse or child who has been battered or subjected to extreme cruelty, the Attorney General shall apply section 204(a)(1)(J).[10]

(e) Availability of Administrative Review— The Attorney General shall provide to applicants for adjustment of status under subsection (a) the same right to, and procedures for, administrative review as are provided to—

(1) applicants for adjustment of status under section 245 of the Immigration and Nationality Act; or

(2) aliens subject to removal proceedings under section 240 of such Act.

(f) Limitation on Judicial Review— A determination by the Attorney General as to whether the status of any alien should be adjusted under this section is final and shall not be subject to review by any court.

(g) No Offset in Number of Visas Available— When an alien is granted the status of having been lawfully admitted for permanent residence pursuant to this section, the Secretary of State shall not be required to reduce the number of immigrant visas authorized to be issued under any provision of the Immigration and Nationality Act.

(h) Application of Immigration and Nationality Act Provisions— Except as otherwise specifically provided in this section, the definitions contained in the Immigration and Nationality Act shall apply in the administration of this section. Nothing contained in this section shall be held to repeal, amend, alter, modify, affect, or restrict the powers, duties, functions, or authority of the Attorney General in the administration and enforcement of such Act or any other law relating to immigration, nationality, or naturalization. The fact that an alien may be eligible to be granted the status of having been lawfully admitted for permanent residence under this section shall not preclude the alien from seeking such status under any other provision of law for which the alien may be eligible.

## Sec. 203. Modification of Certain Transitional Rules

(a) Transitional Rules With Regard to Suspension of Deportation—

(1) In general— Section 309(c)(5) of the Illegal Immigration Reform and Immigrant Responsibility Act of 1996 (Public Law 104-208; division C; 110 Stat. 3009-627) is amended to read as follows:

(5) Transitional Rules With Regard to Suspension of Deportation—

(A) In general— Subject to subparagraphs (B) and (C), paragraphs (1) and (2) of section 240A(d) of the Immigration and Nationality Act (relating to continuous residence or physical presence) shall apply to orders to show cause (including those referred to in section 242B(a)(1) of the Immigration and Nationality Act, as in effect before the title III-A effective date), issued before, on, or after the date of the enactment of this Act.

(B) Exception for Certain Orders— In any case in which the Attorney General elects to terminate and reinitiate proceedings in accordance with paragraph (3) of this sub-

---

[10] The amendment to NACARA §202(d)(3) made by P.L. 109-162, §815(b) [changing "204(a)(1)(H)" to "204(a)(1)(J)"] takes effect, pursuant to §815(c), "as if included in the enactment of [VAWA, div. B of P.L. 106-386]."

section, paragraphs (1) and (2) of section 240A(d) of the Immigration and Nationality Act shall not apply to an order to show cause issued before April 1, 1997.

(C) Special Rule for Certain Aliens Granted Temporary Protection From Deportation—

(i) In general— For purposes of calculating the period of continuous physical presence under section 244(a) of the Immigration and Nationality Act (as in effect before the title III-A effective date) or section 240A of such Act (as in effect after the title III-A effective date), subparagraph (A) and paragraphs (1) and (2) of section 240A(d) of the Immigration and Nationality Act shall not apply in the case of an alien, regardless of whether the alien is in exclusion or deportation proceedings before the title III-A effective date, who has not been convicted at any time of an aggravated felony (as defined in section 101(a) of the Immigration and Nationality Act) and—

(I) was not apprehended after December 19, 1990, at the time of entry, and is—

(aa) a Salvadoran national who first entered the United States on or before September 19, 1990, and who registered for benefits pursuant to the settlement agreement in American Baptist Churches, et al. v. Thornburgh (ABC), 760 F. Supp. 796 (N.D. Cal. 1991) on or before October 31, 1991, or applied for temporary protected status on or before October 31, 1991; or

(bb) a Guatemalan national who first entered the United States on or before October 1, 1990, and who registered for benefits pursuant to such settlement agreement on or before December 31, 1991;

(II) is a Guatemalan or Salvadoran national who filed an application for asylum with the Immigration and Naturalization Service on or before April 1, 1990;

(III) is the spouse or child (as defined in section 101(b)(1) of the Immigration and Nationality Act) of an individual, at the time a decision is rendered to suspend the deportation, or cancel the removal, of such individual, if the individual has been determined to be described in this clause (excluding this subclause and subclause (IV));

(IV) is the unmarried son or daughter of an alien parent, at the time a decision is rendered to suspend the deportation, or cancel the removal, of such alien parent, if—

(aa) the alien parent has been determined to be described in this clause (excluding this subclause and subclause (III)); and

(bb) in the case of a son or daughter who is 21 years of age or older at the time such decision is rendered, the son or daughter entered the United States on or before October 1, 1990; or

(V) is an alien who entered the United States on or before December 31, 1990, who filed an application for asylum on or before December 31, 1991, and who, at the time of filing such application, was a national of the Soviet Union, Russia, any republic of the former Soviet Union, Latvia, Estonia,

Lithuania, Poland, Czechoslovakia, Romania, Hungary, Bulgaria, Albania, East Germany, Yugoslavia, or any state of the former Yugoslavia.

(ii) Limitation On Judicial Review— A determination by the Attorney General as to whether an alien satisfies the requirements of this clause (i) is final and shall not be subject to review by any court. Nothing in the preceding sentence shall be construed as limiting the application of section 242(a)(2)(B) of the Immigration and Nationality Act (as in effect after the title III-A effective date) to other eligibility determinations pertaining to discretionary relief under this Act.

(2) Conforming Amendment— Subsection (c) of section 309 of the Illegal Immigration Reform and Immigrant Responsibility Act of 1996 (Public Law 104-208; division C; 110 Stat. 3009-625) is amended by striking the subsection designation and the subsection heading and inserting the following:

(c) Transition for Certain Aliens—.

(b) Special Rule for Cancellation of Removal— Section 309 of the Illegal Immigration Reform and Immigrant Responsibility Act of 1996 (Public Law 104-208; 110 Stat. 3009-625) is amended by adding at the end the following:

(f) Special Rule for Cancellation of Removal—

(1) In general— Subject to the provisions of the Immigration and Nationality Act (as in effect after the title III-A effective date), other than subsections (b)(1), (d)(1), and (e) of section 240A of such Act (but including section 242(a)(2)(B) of such Act), the Attorney General may, under section 240A of such Act, cancel removal of, and adjust to the status of an alien lawfully admitted for permanent residence, an alien who is inadmissible or deportable from the United States, if the alien applies for such relief, the alien is described in subsection (c)(5)(C)(i) of this section, and—

(A) the alien—

(i) is not inadmissible or deportable under paragraph (2) or (3) of section 212(a) or paragraph (2), (3), or (4) of section 237(a) of the Immigration and Nationality Act and is not an alien described in section 241(b)(3)(B)(i) of such Act;

(ii) has been physically present in the United States for a continuous period of not less than 7 years immediately preceding the date of such application;

(iii) has been a person of good moral character during such period; and

(iv) establishes that removal would result in extreme hardship to the alien or to the alien's spouse, parent, or child, who is a citizen of the United States or an alien lawfully admitted for permanent residence; or

(B) the alien—

(i) is inadmissible or deportable under section 212(a)(2), 237(a)(2) (other than 237(a)(2)(A)(iii)), or 237(a)(3) of the Immigration and Nationality Act;

(ii) is not an alien described in section 241(b)(3)(B)(i) or 101(a)(43) of such Act;

(iii) has been physically present in the United States for a continuous period of not less than 10 years immediately following the commission of an act, or the assumption of a status, constituting a ground for removal;

(iv) has been a person of good moral character during such period; and

(v) establishes that removal would result in exceptional and extremely unusual hardship to the alien or to the alien's spouse, parent, or child, who is a citizen of the United States or an alien lawfully admitted for permanent residence.

(2) Treatment of Certain Breaks In Presence— Section 240A(d)(2) shall apply for purposes of calculating any period of continuous physical presence under this subsection, except that the reference to subsection (b)(1) in such section shall be considered to be a reference to paragraph (1) of this section.

(c) Motions to Reopen Deportation or Removal Proceedings— Section 309 of the Illegal Immigration Reform and Immigrant Responsibility Act of 1996 (Public Law 104-208; 110 Stat. 3009-625), as amended by subsection (b), is further amended by adding at the end the following:

(g) Motions to Reopen Deportation or Removal Proceedings— Notwithstanding any limitation imposed by law on motions to reopen removal or deportation proceedings (except limitations premised on an alien's conviction of an aggravated felony (as defined in section 101(a) of the Immigration and Nationality Act)), any alien who has become eligible for cancellation of removal or suspension of deportation as a result of the amendments made by section 203 of the Nicaraguan Adjustment and Central American Relief Act may file one motion to reopen removal or deportation proceedings to apply for cancellation of removal or suspension of deportation. The Attorney General shall designate a specific time period in which all such motions to reopen are required to be filed. The period shall begin not later than 60 days after the date of the enactment of the Nicaraguan Adjustment and Central American Relief Act and shall extend for a period not to exceed 240 days.

(d) Temporary Reduction in Diversity Visas—

(1) Beginning in fiscal year 1999, subject to paragraph (2), the number of visas available for a fiscal year under section 201(e) of the Immigration and Nationality Act shall be reduced by 5,000 from the number of visas otherwise available under that section for such fiscal year.

(2) In no case shall the reduction under paragraph (1) for a fiscal year exceed the amount by which—

(A) one-half of the total number of individuals described in subclauses (I), (II), (III), and (IV) of section 309(c)(5)(C)(i) of the Illegal Immigration Reform and Immigrant Responsibility Act of 1996 who have adjusted their status to that of aliens lawfully admitted for permanent residence under the Nicaraguan Adjustment and Central American Relief Act as of the end of the previous fiscal year; exceeds—

(B) the total of the reductions in available visas under this subsection for all previous fiscal years.

(e) Temporary Reduction in Other Workers' Visas—

(1) Beginning in the fiscal year following the fiscal year in which a visa has been made available under section 203(b)(3)(A)(iii) of the Immigration and Nationality Act for all aliens who are the beneficiary of a petition approved under section 204 of such Act as of the date of the enactment of this Act for classification under section 203(b)(3)(A)(iii) of such Act, subject to paragraph (2), visas available under section 203(b)(3)(A)(iii) of that Act shall be reduced by 5,000 from the number of visas otherwise available under that section for such fiscal year.

(2) In no case shall the reduction under paragraph (1) for a fiscal year exceed the amount by which—

(A) the number computed under subsection (d)(2)(A); exceeds—

(B) the total of the reductions in available visas under this subsection for all previous fiscal years.

(f) Effective Date— The amendments made by this section to the Illegal Immigration Reform and Immigrant Responsibility Act of 1996 shall take effect as if included in the enactment of such Act.

## Sec. 204. Limitation on Cancellations of Removal and Suspensions of Deportation

(a) Annual Limitation— *[omitted herewith; see codification at INA §240A(e)—ed.]*

(b) Cancellation of Removal and Adjustment of Status for Certain Nonpermanent Residents— *[omitted herewith; see codification at INA §240A(b)—ed.]*

(c) Recordation of Date— *[omitted herewith; see codification at INA §240A(b)(3)—ed.]*

(d) April 1 Effective Date for Aggregate Limitation— Section 309(c)(7) of the Illegal Immigration Reform and Immigrant Responsibility Act of 1996 (Public Law 104-208; division C; 110 Stat. 3009-627) is amended to read as follows:

(7) Limitation On Suspension of Deportation— After April 1,1997, the Attorney General may not suspend the deportation and adjust the status under section 244 of the Immigration and Nationality Act (as in effect before the title III-A effective date) of any alien in any fiscal year, except in accordance with section 240A(e) of such Act. The previous sentence shall apply regardless of when an alien applied for such suspension and adjustment.

(e) Effective Date— The amendments made by this section shall take effect as if included in the enactment of the Illegal Immigration Reform and Immigrant Responsibility Act of 1996 (Public Law 104-208; 110 Stat. 3009-546).

Speaker of the House of Representatives.
Vice President of the United States and President of the Senate.

# Haitian Refugee Immigration Fairness Act
## (HRIFA), as amended

*(P.L. 105-277 (HRIFA-Title IX), as amended by P.L. 106-386 (Victims of Trafficking and Violence Protection Act, 2000) and 109-162 (VAWA & DOJ Reauthorization Act))*

**Sec. 901. Short Title.** This title may be cited as the "Haitian Refugee Immigration Fairness Act of 1998".

**Sec. 902. Adjustment of Status of Certain Haitian Nationals.**

(a) Adjustment of Status.—

(1) In general.— The status of any alien described in subsection (b) shall be adjusted by the Attorney General to that of an alien lawfully admitted for permanent residence, if the alien—

(A) applies for such adjustment before April 1, 2000; and

(B) is otherwise admissible to the United States for permanent residence, except that, in determining such admissibility, the grounds for inadmissibility specified in paragraphs (4), (5), (6)(A), (7)(A), and (9)(B) of section 212(a) of the Immigration and Nationality Act shall not apply.

(2) Inapplicability of Certain Provisions.— In the case of an alien described in subsection (b) or (d) who is applying for adjustment of status under this section—

(A) the provisions of section 241(a)(5) of the Immigration and Nationality Act shall not apply; and

(B) the Attorney General may grant the alien a waiver of the grounds of inadmissibility under subparagraphs (A) and (C) of section 212(a)(9) of such Act.

In granting waivers under subparagraph (B), the Attorney General shall use standards used in granting consent under subparagraphs (A)(iii) and (C)(ii) of such section 212(a)(9).

(3) Relationship of application to certain orders.— An alien present in the United States who has been ordered excluded, deported, removed, or ordered to depart voluntarily from the United States under any provision of the Immigration and Nationality Act may, notwithstanding such order, apply for adjustment of status under paragraph (1). Such an alien may not be required, as a condition on submitting or granting such application, to file a separate motion to reopen, reconsider, or vacate such order. If the Attorney General grants the application, the Attorney General shall cancel the order. If the Attorney General makes a final decision to deny the application, the order shall be effective and enforceable to the same extent as if the application had not been made.

(b) Aliens Eligible for Adjustment of Status.— The benefits provided by subsection (a) shall apply to any alien who is a national of Haiti who—

(1) was present in the United States on December 31, 1995, who—

(A) filed for asylum before December 31, 1995,

(B) was paroled into the United States prior to December 31, 1995, after having been identified as having a credible fear of persecution, or paroled for emergent reasons or reasons deemed strictly in the public interest, or

(C) was a child (as defined in the text above subparagraph (A) of section 101(b)(1) of the Immigration and Nationality Act (8 U.S.C. 1101(b)(1)) at the time of arrival in the United States and on December 31, 1995, and who—

(i) arrived in the United States without parents in the United States and has remained without parents in the United States since such arrival,

(ii) became orphaned subsequent to arrival in the United States, or

(iii) was abandoned by parents or guardians prior to April 1, 1998 and has remained abandoned since such abandonment; and

(2) has been physically present in the United States for a continuous period beginning not later than December 31, 1995, and ending not earlier than the date the application for such adjustment is filed, except that an alien shall not be considered to have failed to maintain continuous physical presence by reason of an absence, or absences, from the United States for any period or periods amounting in the aggregate to not more than 180 days.

(c) Stay of Removal.—

(1) In general.— The Attorney General shall provide by regulation for an alien who is subject to a final order of deportation or removal or exclusion to seek a stay of such order based on the filing of an application under subsection (a).

(2) During certain proceedings.— Notwithstanding any provision of the Immigration and Nationality Act, the Attorney General shall not order any alien to be removed from the United States, if the alien is in exclusion, deportation, or removal proceedings under any provision of such Act and has applied for adjustment of status under subsection (a), except where the Attorney General has made a final determination to deny the application.

(3) Work authorization.— The Attorney General may authorize an alien who has applied for adjustment of status under subsection (a) to engage in employment in the United States during the pendency of such application and may provide the alien with an "employment authorized" endorsement or other appropriate document signifying authorization of employment, except that if such application is pending for a period exceeding 180 days, and has not been denied, the Attorney General shall authorize such employment.

(d) Adjustment of Status for Spouses and Children.—

(1) In general.— The status of an alien shall be adjusted by the Attorney General to that of an alien lawfully admitted for permanent residence, if—

(A) the alien is a national of Haiti;

(B) (i) the alien is the spouse, child, or unmarried son or daughter of an alien who is or was eligible for classification under subsection (a), except that, in the case of such an unmarried son or daughter, the son or daughter shall be required to establish that the son or daughter has been physically present in the United States for a continuous period beginning not later than December 1, 1995, and ending not earlier than the date on which the application for such adjustment is filed;

(ii) at the time of filing of the application for adjustment under subsection (a), the alien is the spouse or child of an alien who is or was eligible for classification under subsection (a) and the spouse, child, or child of the spouse has been battered or sub-jected to extreme cruelty by the individual described in subsection (a); and

(iii) in acting on applications under this section with respect to spouses or children who have been battered or subjected to extreme cruelty, the Attorney General shall apply the provisions of section 204(a)(1)(J).

(C) the alien applies for such adjustment and is physically present in the United States on the date the application is filed; and

(D) the alien is otherwise admissible to the United States for permanent residence, except that, in determining such admissibility, the grounds for inadmissibility specified in paragraphs (4), (5), (6)(A), (7)(A), and (9)(B) of section 212(a) of the Immigration and Nationality Act shall not apply.

(2) Proof of continuous presence.— For purposes of establishing the period of continuous physical presence referred to in paragraph (1)(B), an alien shall not be considered to have failed to maintain continuous physical presence by reason of an absence, or absences, from the United States for any period or periods amounting in the aggregate to not more than 180 days.

(e) Availability of Administrative Review.— The Attorney General shall provide to applicants for adjustment of status under subsection (a) the same right to, and procedures for, administrative review as are provided to—

(1) applicants for adjustment of status under section 245 of the Immigration and Nationality Act; or

(2) aliens subject to removal proceedings under section 240 of such Act.

(f) Limitation on Judicial Review.— A determination by the Attorney General as to whether the status of any alien should be adjusted under this section is final and shall not be subject to review by any court.

(g) No Offset in Number of Visas Available.— When an alien is granted the status of having been lawfully admitted for permanent resident pursuant to this section, the Secretary of State shall not be required to reduce the number of immigrant visas authorized to be issued under any provision of the Immigration and Nationality Act.

(h) Application of Immigration and Nationality Act Provisions.— Except as otherwise specifically provided in this title, the definitions contained in the Immigration and Nationality Act shall apply in the administration of this section. Nothing contained in this title shall be held to repeal, amend, alter, modify, effect, or restrict the powers, duties, functions, or authority of the Attorney General in the administration and enforcement of such Act or any other law relating to immigration, nationality, or naturalization. The fact that an alien may be eligible to be granted the status of having been lawfully admitted for permanent residence under this section shall not preclude the alien from seeking such status under any other provision of law for which the alien may be eligible.

(i) Adjustment of Status Has No Effect On Eligibility for Welfare and Public Benefits.— No alien whose status has been adjusted in accordance with this section and who was not a qualified alien on the date of enactment of this Act may, solely on the basis of such adjusted status, be considered to be a qualified alien under section 431(b) of the Personal Responsibility and Work Opportunity Rec-onciliation Act of 1996 (8 U.S.C. 1641(b)), as amended by section 5302 of the Balanced Budget Act of 1997 (Public Law 105-33; 111 Stat. 598), for purposes of determining the alien's eligibility for supplemental security income benefits under title XVI of the Social Security Act (42 U.S.C. 1381 *et seq.*) or medical assistance under title XIX of such Act (42 U.S.C. 1396 *et seq.*).

(j) Period of Applicability.— Subsection (i) shall not apply after October 1, 2003.

(k) Not later than 6 months after the date of the enactment of this Act, and every 6 months thereafter (until all applications for adjustment of status under this section have been finally adjudicated), the Comptroller General of the United States shall submit to the Committees on the Judiciary and the Committees on Appropriations of the United States House of Representatives and the United States Senate a report containing the following:

(1)  (A) The number of aliens who applied for adjustment of status under subsection (a), including a breakdown specifying the number of such applicants who are described in subparagraph (A), (B), or (C) of subsection (b)(1), respectively.

(B) the number of aliens described in subparagraph (A) whose status was ajusted under this section, including a breakdown described in the subparagraph.

(2)  (A) The number of aliens who applied for adjustment of status under subsection (d), including a breakdown specifying the number of such applicants who are sponsors, children, or unmarried sons or daughters described in such subsection, respectively.

(B) The number of aliens described in subparagraph (A) whose status was adjusted under this section, including a breakdown described in the subparagraph.

## Sec. 903. Collection of Data on Detained Asylum Seekers.

(a) In general.— The Attorney General shall regularly collect data on a nation-wide basis with respect to asylum seekers in detention in the United States, including the following information:

(1) The number of detainees.

(2) An identification of the countries of origin of the detainees.

(3) The percentage of each gender within the total number of detainees.

(4) The number of detainees listed by each year of age of the detainees.

(5) The location of each detainee by detention facility.

(6) With respect to each facility where detainees are held, whether the facility is also used to detain criminals and whether any of the detainees are held in the same cells as criminals.

(7) The number and frequency of the transfers of detainees between detention facilities.

(8) The average length of detention and the number of detainees by category of the length of detention.

(9) The rate of release from detention of detainees for each district of the Immigration and Naturalization Service.

(10) A description of the disposition of cases.

(b) Annual Reports.— Beginning October 1, 1999, and not later than October 1 of each year thereafter, the Attorney General shall submit to the Committee on the Judiciary of each House of Congress a report setting forth the data collected under subsection (a) for the fiscal year ending September 30 of that year.

(c) Availability to Public.— Copies of the data collected under subsection (a) shall be made available to members of the public upon request pursuant to such regulations as the Attorney General shall prescribe.

## Sec. 904. Collection of Data on Other Detained Aliens.

(a) In general.— The Attorney General shall regularly collect data on a nationwide basis on aliens being detained in the United States by the Immigration and Naturalization Service other than the aliens described in section 903, including the following information:

(1) The number of detainees who are criminal aliens and the number of detainees who are noncriminal aliens who are not seeking asylum.

(2) An identification of the ages, gender, and countries of origin of detainees within each category described in paragraph (1).

(3) The types of facilities, whether facilities of the Immigration and Naturalization Service or other Federal, State, or local facilities, in which each of the categories of detainees described in paragraph (1) are held.

(b) Length of Detention, Transfers, and Dispositions.— With respect to detainees who are criminal aliens and detainees who are noncriminal aliens who are not seeking asylum, the Attorney General shall also collect data concerning—

(1) the number and frequency of transfers between detention facilities for each category of detainee;

(2) the average length of detention of each category of detainee;

(3) for each category of detainee, the number of detainees who have been detained for the same length of time, in 3-month increments;

(4) for each category of detainee, the rate of release from detention for each district of the Immigration and Naturalization Service; and

(5) for each category of detainee, the disposition of detention, including whether detention ended due to deportation, release on parole, or any other release.

(c) Criminal Aliens.— With respect to criminal aliens, the Attorney General shall also collect data concerning—

(1) the number of criminal aliens apprehended under the immigration laws and not detained by the Attorney General; and

(2) a list of crimes committed by criminal aliens after the decision was made not to detain them, to the extent this information can be derived by cross-checking the list of criminal aliens not detained with other databases accessible to the Attorney General.

(d) Annual Reports.— Beginning on October 1, 1999, and not later than October 1 of each year thereafter, the Attorney General shall submit to the Committee on the Judiciary of each House of Congress a report setting forth the data collected under subsections (a), (b), and (c) for the fiscal year ending September 30 of that year.

(e) Availability to Public.— Copies of the data collected under subsections (a), (b), and (c) shall be made available to members of the public upon request pursuant to such regulations as the Attorney General shall prescribe.

# APPENDIX G
## Hmong Veterans' Naturalization Act, as amended

*(P.L. 106-207 (Hmong Veterans' Naturalization Act, 2000), as amended by
P.L. 106-415 (Extension for Hmong Veterans' Naturalization Act, 2000)
and P.L. 107-77 (DOJ, DOS, and DOJ Appropriations Act))*

### Sec. 1. Short Title.

This Act may be cited as the "Hmong Veterans' Naturalization Act of 2000".

### Sec. 2. Exemption From English Language Requirement for Certain Aliens Who Served With Special Guerrilla Units or Irregular Forces in Laos.

The requirement of paragraph (1) of section 312(a) of the Immigration and Nationality Act (8 U.S.C. 1423(a)(1)) shall not apply to the naturalization of any person—

(1) who—

(A) was admitted into the United States as a refugee from Laos pursuant to section 207 of the Immigration and Nationality Act (8 U.S.C. 1157); and

(B) served with a special guerrilla unit, or irregular forces, operating from a base in Laos in support of the United States military at any time during the period beginning February 28, 1961, and ending September 18, 1978;

(2) who—

(A) satisfies the requirement of paragraph (1)(A); and

(B) was the spouse of a person described in paragraph (1) on the day on which such described person applied for admission into the United States as a refugee; or

(3) who—

(A) satisfies the requirement of paragraph (1)(A); and

(B) is the surviving spouse of a person described in paragraph (1)(B) which described person was killed or died in Laos, Thailand, or Vietnam.

### Sec. 3. Special Consideration Concerning Civics Requirement for Certain Aliens Who Served With Special Guerrilla Units or Irregular Forces in Laos.

The Attorney General shall provide for special consideration, as determined by the Attorney General, concerning the requirement of paragraph (2) of section 312(a) of the Immigration and Nationality Act (8 U.S.C. 1423(a)(2)) with respect to the naturalization of any person described in paragraph (1), (2), or (3) of section 2 of this Act.

### Sec. 4. Documentation of Qualifying Service.

A person seeking an exemption under section 2 or special consideration under section 3 shall submit to the Attorney General documentation of their, or their spouse's, service with a special guerrilla unit, or irregular forces, described in section 2(1)(B), in the form of—

(1) original documents;

(2) an affidavit of the serving person's superior officer;

(3) two affidavits from other individuals who also were serving with such a special guerrilla unit, or irregular forces, and who personally knew of the person's service; or

(4) other appropriate proof.

## Sec. 5.  Determination of Eligibility for Exemption and Special Consideration.

(a) In determining a person's eligibility for an exemption under section 2 or special consideration under section 3, the Attorney General—

(1) shall review the refugee processing documentation for the person, or, in an appropriate case, for the person and the person's spouse, to verify that the requirements of section 2 relating to refugee applications and admissions have been satisfied;

(2) shall consider the documentation submitted by the person under section 4;

(3) may request an advisory opinion from the Secretary of Defense regarding the person's, or their spouse's, service in a special guerrilla unit, or irregular forces, described in section 2(1)(B); and

(4) may consider any documentation provided by organizations maintaining records with respect to Hmong veterans or their families.

(b) The Secretary of Defense shall provide any opinion requested under paragraph (3) to the extent practicable, and the Attorney General shall take into account any opinion that the Secretary of Defense is able to provide.

## Sec. 6.  Deadline for Application and Payment of Fees.

This Act shall apply to a person only if the person's application for naturalization is filed, as provided in section 334 of the Immigration and Nationality Act (8 U.S.C. 1445), with appropriate fees not later than 36 months after the date of the enactment of this Act.  In the case of a person described in section 2(3), the application referred to in the preceding sentence, and appropriate fees, shall be filed not later than 36 months after the date of the enactment of this sentence.

## Sec. 7.  Limitation on Number of Beneficiaries.

Notwithstanding any other provision of this Act, the total number of aliens who may be granted an exemption under section 2 or special consideration under section 3, or both, may not exceed 45,000.

Approved May 26, 2000.

# Selected Uncodified* Provisions of the
# American Competitiveness in the 21st Century Act (AC21)

*(P.L. 106-313 (AC21), as amended by P.L. 107-273 (21st Century DOJ
Appropriations Authorization Act) and P.L. 109-13 (REAL ID Act, 2005))*

## Sec. 102. Temporary Increase in Visa Allotments.

* * *

(b) Additional Visas for Fiscal Years 1999 and 2000—

(1) In general—

(A) Notwithstanding section 214(g)(1)(A)(ii) of the Immigration and Nationality Act (8 U.S.C. 1184(g)(1)(A)(ii)), the total number of aliens who may be issued visas or otherwise provided nonimmigrant status under section 101(a)(15)(H)(i)(b) of such Act in fiscal year 1999 is increased by a number equal to the number of aliens who are issued such a visa or provided such status during the period beginning on the date on which the limitation in such section 214(g)(1)(A)(ii) is reached and ending on September 30, 1999.

(B) In the case of any alien on behalf of whom a petition for status under section 101(a)(15)(H)(I)(b) is filed before September 1, 2000, and is subsequently approved, that alien shall be counted toward the numerical ceiling for fiscal year 2000 notwithstanding the date of the approval of the petition. Notwithstanding section 214(g)(1)(A)(iii) of the Immigration and Nationality Act, the total number of aliens who may be issued visas or otherwise provided nonimmigrant status under section 101(a)(15)(H)(i)(b) of such Act in fiscal year 2000 is increased by a number equal to the number of aliens who may be issued visas or otherwise provided nonimmigrant status who filed a petition during the period beginning on the date on which the limitation in such section 214(g)(1)(A)(iii) is reached and ending on August 31, 2000.

(2) Effective Date— Paragraph (1) shall take effect as if included in the enactment of section 411 of the American Competitiveness and Workforce Improvement Act of 1998 (as contained in title IV of division C of the Omnibus Consolidated and Emergency Supplemental Appropriations Act, 1999; Public Law 105-277).

## Sec. 104. Limitation on Per Country Ceiling with Respect to Employment-Based Immigrants.

* * *

(c) One-Time Protection Under Per Country Ceiling— Notwithstanding section 214(g)(4) of the Immigration and Nationality Act (8 U.S.C. 1184(g)(4)), any alien who—

(1) is the beneficiary of a petition filed under section 204(a) of that Act for a preference status under paragraph (1), (2), or (3) of section 203(b) of that Act; and

---

* Subsections omitted herein directly amend the INA, and are thus incorporated in the main text of the book.

(2) is eligible to be granted that status but for application of the per country limitations applicable to immigrants under those paragraphs, may apply for, and the Attorney General may grant, an extension of such nonimmigrant status until the alien's application for adjustment of status has been processed and a decision made thereon.

## Sec. 106. Special Provisions in Cases of Lengthy Adjudications.

(a)[11] Exemption from Limitation.— The limitation contained in section 214(g)(4) of the Immigration and Nationality Act (8 U.S.C. 1184(g)(4)) with respect to the duration of authorized stay shall not apply to any nonimmigrant alien previously issued a visa or otherwise provided nonimmigrant status under section 101(a)(15)(H)(i)(b) of such Act (8 U.S.C. 1101(a)(15)(H)(i)(b)), if 365 days or more have elapsed since the filing of any of the following:

(1) Any application for labor certification under section 212(a)(5)(A) of such Act (8 U.S.C. 1182(a)(5)(A)), in a case in which certification is required or used by the alien to obtain status under section 203(b) of such Act (8 U.S.C. 1153(b)).

(2) A petition described in section 204(b) of such Act (3 U. S.C. 1154(b)) to accord the alien a status under section 203(b) of such Act.

(b)[12] Extension of H1-B Worker Status— The Attorney General shall extend the stay of an alien who qualifies for an exemption under subsection (a) in one-year increments until such time as a final decision is made—

(1) to deny the application described in subsection (a)(1), or, in a case in which such application is granted, to deny a petition described in subsection (a)(2) filed on behalf of the alien pursuant to such grant;

(2) to deny the petition described in subsection (a)(2); or

(3) to grant or deny the alien's application for an immigrant visa or for adjustment of status to that of an alien lawfully admitted for permanent residence.

* * *

(d)[13] Recapture of Unused Employment-Based Immigrant Visas—

(1) In general— Notwithstanding any other provision of law, the number of employment-based visas (as defined in paragraph (3)) made available for a fiscal year (beginning with fiscal year 2001) shall be increased by the number described in paragraph (2). Visas made available under this subsection shall only be available in a fiscal year to employment-based immigrants under paragraph (1), (2), or (3) of section 203(b) of the Immigration and Nationality Act and any such visa that is made available due to the difference between the number of employment-based visas that were made available in fiscal year 2001, 2002, 2003, or 2004 and the number of such visas that were actually used in such fiscal year shall be available only to employment-based immigrants (and their family members accompanying or following to join under section 203(d) of such Act (8 U.S.C. 1153(d))) whose immigrant worker petitions were approved based on schedule A, as defined in section 656.5 of title 20, Code of Federal Regulations, as promulgated by the Secretary of Labor.

---

[11] Amended by §11030A(a) of P.L. 107-273 (11/2/02).

[12] Amended by §11030A(b) of P.L. 107-273 (11/2/02).

[13] Amended by §502 of P.L. 109-13 (5/11/05).

(2) Number Available—

(A) In general— Subject to subparagraph (B), the number described in this paragraph is the difference between the number of employment-based visas that were made available in fiscal year 1999 through 2004 and the number of such visas that were actually used in such fiscal years.

(B) (i) Reduction— The number described in subparagraph (A) shall be reduced, for each fiscal year after fiscal year 2001, by the cumulative number of immigrant visas actually used under paragraph (1) for previous fiscal years.

(ii) Maximum.— The total number of visas made available under paragraph (1) from unused visas from the fiscal years 2001 through 2004 may not exceed 50,000.

(C) Construction— Nothing in this paragraph shall be construed as affecting the application of section 201(c)(3)(C) of the Immigration and Nationality Act (8 U.S.C. 1151(c)(3)(C)).

(3) Employment-Based Visas Defined— For purposes of this subsection, the term "employment-based visa" means an immigrant visa which is issued pursuant to the numerical limitation under section 203(b) of the Immigration and Nationality Act (8 U.S.C. 1153(b)).

## Sec. 107. Extension of Certain Requirements and Authorities Through Fiscal Year 2002.

\* \* \*

(b) Department of Labor Investigative Authorities— Section 413(e)(2) of the American Competitiveness and Workforce Improvement Act of 1998 (as contained in title IV of division C of Public Law 105-277) is amended by striking "September 30, 2001" and inserting "September 30, 2003".

## Sec. 114. Exclusion of Certain "J" Nonimmigrants From Numerical Limitations Applicable to "H-1B" Nonimmmigrants.

The numerical limitations contained in section 102 of this title shall not apply to any nonimmigrant alien granted a waiver that is subject to the limitation contained in paragraph (1)(B) of the first section 214(*l*) of the Immigration and Nationality Act (relating to restrictions on waivers).

## Selected Uncodified Provisions of the
## Legal Immigration and Family Equity Act (LIFE Act),

*(P.L. 106-553 (LIFE Act), as amended by P.L. 106-554 (LIFE Act Amendments))*

**Sec. 1104. Adjustment of Statuof Certain Class Action Participants Who Entered Before January 1, 1982, to That of Person Admitted for Lawful Residence**

[Sec. 1104 of P.L. 106-553, as amended by Sec. 1503 of P.L. 106-554]

(a) In general— In the case of an eligible alien described in subsection (b), the provisions of section 245A of the Immigration and Nationality Act (8 U.S.C. 1255a), as modified by subsection (c), shall apply to the alien.

(b) Eligible Aliens Described— An alien is an eligible alien described in this subsection if, before October 1, 2000, the alien filed with the Attorney General a written claim for class membership, with or without a filing fee, pursuant to a court order issued in the case of—

(1) *Catholic Social Services, Inc. v. Meese, vacated sub nom. Reno v. Catholic Social Services, Inc.*, 509 U.S. 43 (1993);

(2) *League of United Latin American Citizens v. INS, vacated sub nom. Reno v. Catholic Social Services, Inc.*, 509 U.S. 43 (1993); or

(3) *Zambrano v. INS, vacated sub nom. Immigration and Naturalization Service v. Zambrano*, 509 U.S. 918 (1993).

(c) Modifications to Provisions Governing Adjustment of Status— The modifications to section 245A of the Immigration and Nationality Act that apply to an eligible alien described in subsection (b) of this section are the following:

(1) Temporary Resident Status— Subsection (a) of such section 245A shall not apply.

(2) Adjustment to Permanent Resident Status— In lieu of paragraphs (1) and (2) of subsection (b) of such section 245A, the Attorney General shall be required to adjust the status of an eligible alien described in subsection (b) of this section to that of an alien lawfully admitted for permanent residence if the alien meets the following requirements:

(A) Application Period— The alien must file with the Attorney General an application for such adjustment during the 12-month period beginning on the date on which the Attorney General issues final regulations to implement this section.

(B) Continuous Unlawful Residence—

(i) In general— The alien must establish that the alien entered the United States before January 1, 1982, and that he or she has resided continuously in the United States in an unlawful status since such date and through May 4, 1988. In determining whether an alien maintained continuous unlawful residence in the United States for purposes of this subparagraph, the regulations prescribed by the Attorney General under section 245A(g) of the Immigration and Nationality Act that were most recently in effect before the date of the enactment of this Act shall apply.

(ii) Nonimmigrants— In the case of an alien who entered the United States as a nonimmigrant before January 1, 1982, the alien must establish that the alien's period of authorized stay as a nonimmigrant expired before such date through the passage of time or the alien's unlawful status was known to the Government as of such date.

(iii) Exchange Visitors— If the alien was at any time a nonimmigrant exchange alien (as defined in section 101(a)(15)(J) of the Immigration and Nationality Act (8 U.S.C. 1101(a)(15)(J)), the alien must establish that the alien was not subject to the two-year foreign residence requirement of section 212(e) of such Act or has fulfilled that requirement or received a waiver thereof.

(iv) Cuban and Haitian Entrants— For purposes of this section, an alien in the status of a Cuban and Haitian entrant described in paragraph (1) or (2)(A) of section 501(e) of Public Law 96-422 shall be considered to have entered the United States and to be in an unlawful status in the United States.

(C) Continuous Physical Presence—

(i) In general— The alien must establish that the alien was continuously physically present in the United States during the period beginning on November 6, 1986, and ending on May 4, 1988, except that—

(I) an alien shall not be considered to have failed to maintain continuous physical presence in the United States for purposes of this subparagraph by virtue of brief, casual, and innocent absences from the United States; and

(II) brief, casual, and innocent absences from the United States shall not be limited to absences with advance parole.

(ii) Admissions— Nothing in this section shall be construed as authorizing an alien to apply for admission to, or to be admitted to, the United States in order to apply for adjustment of status under this section or section 245A of the Immigration and Nationality Act.

(D) Admissible as Immigrant— The alien must establish that the alien—

(i) is admissible to the United States as an immigrant, except as otherwise provided under section 245A(d)(2) of the Immigration and Nationality Act;

(ii) has not been convicted of any felony or of three or more misdemeanors committed in the United States;

(iii) has not assisted in the persecution of any person or persons on account of race, religion, nationality, membership in a particular social group, or political opinion; and

(iv) is registered or registering under the Military Selective Service Act, if the alien is required to be so registered under that Act.

(E) Basic Citizenship Skills—

(i) In general— The alien must demonstrate that the alien either—

(I) meets the requirements of section 312(a) of the Immigration and Nationality Act (8 U.S.C. 1423(a)) (relating to minimal understanding of ordinary English and a knowledge and understanding of the history and government of the United States); or

(II) is satisfactorily pursuing a course of study (recognized by the Attorney General) to achieve such an understanding of English and such a knowledge and understanding of the history and government of the United States.

(ii) Exception for Elderly or Developmentally Disabled Individuals— The Attorney General may, in the discretion of the Attorney General, waive all or part of the requirements of clause (i) in the case of an alien who is 65 years of age or older or who is developmentally disabled.

(iii) Relation to Naturalization Examination— In accordance with regulations of the Attorney General, an alien who has demonstrated under clause (i)(I) that the alien meets the requirements of section 312(a) of the Immigration and Nationality Act may be considered to have satisfied the requirements of that section for purposes of becoming naturalized as a citizen of the United States under title III of such Act.

(3) Temporary Stay of Removal, Authorized Travel, and Employment During Pendency of Application— In lieu of subsections (b)(3) and (e)(2) of such section 245A, the Attorney General shall provide that, in the case of an eligible alien described in subsection (b) of this section who presents a prima facie application for adjustment of status to that of an alien lawfully admitted for permanent residence under such section 245A during the application period described in paragraph (2)(A), until a final determination on the application has been made—

(A) the alien may not be deported or removed from the United States;

(B) the Attorney General shall, in accordance with regulations, permit the alien to return to the United States after such brief and casual trips abroad as reflect an intention on the part of the alien to adjust to lawful permanent resident status and after brief temporary trips abroad occasioned by a family obligation involving an occurrence such as the illness or death of a close relative or other family need; and

(C) the Attorney General shall grant the alien authorization to engage in employment in the United States and provide to that alien an "employment authorized" endorsement or other appropriate work permit.

(4) Applications— Paragraphs (1) through (4) of subsection (c) of such section 245A shall not apply.

(5) Confidentiality of Information— Subsection (c)(5) of such section 245A shall apply to information furnished by an eligible alien described in subsection (b) pursuant to any application filed under such section 245A or this section, except that the Attorney General (and other officials and employees of the Department of Justice and any bureau or agency thereof) may use such information for purposes of rescinding, pursuant to section 246(a) of the Immigration and Nationality Act (8 U.S.C. 1256(a)), any adjustment of status obtained by the alien.

(6) Use of Fees for Immigration-Related Unfair Employment Practices— Notwithstanding subsection (c)(7)(C) of such section 245A, no application fee paid to the Attorney General pursuant to this section by an eligible alien described in subsection (b) of this section shall be available in any fiscal year for the purpose described in such subsection (c)(7)(C).

(7) Temporary Stay of Removal and Work Authorization for Certain Applicants Before Application Period— In lieu of subsection (e)(1) of such section 245A, the Attorney General shall provide that in the case of an eligible alien described in subsection (b) of this section who is apprehended before the beginning of the application period described in paragraph (2)(A) and who can establish a prima facie case of eligibility to have his status adjusted under such section 245A pursuant to this section (but for the fact that he may not apply for such adjustment until the beginning of such period), until the alien

has had the opportunity during the first 30 days of the application period to complete the filing of an application for adjustment, the alien—

(A) may not be deported or removed from the United States; and

(B) shall be granted authorization to engage in employment in the United States and be provided an "employment authorized" endorsement or other appropriate work permit.

(8) Jurisdiction of Courts— Effective as of November 6, 1986, subsection (f)(4)(C) of such section 245A shall not apply to an eligible alien described in subsection (b) of this section.

(9) Public Welfare Assistance— Subsection (h) of such section 245A shall not apply.

(10) Conforming Application of Consent Provision.— In addition to the waivers provided in subsection (d)(2) of such section 245A of the Immigration and Nationality Act, the Attorney General may grant the alien a waiver of the grounds of inadmissibility under subparagraphs (A) and (C) of section 212(a)(9) of such Act (8 U.S.C. 1182(a)(9)). In granting such waivers, the Attorney General shall use standards used in granting consent under subparagraphs (A)(iii) and (C)(ii) of such section.

(d) Applications from Abroad— The Attorney General shall establish a process under which an alien who has become eligible to apply for adjustment of status to that of an alien lawfully admitted for permanent residence as a result of the enactment of this section and who is not physically present in the United States may apply for such adjustment from abroad.

(e) Deadline for Regulations— The Attorney General shall issue regulations to implement this section not later than 120 days after the date of the enactment of this Act.

(f) Administrative and Judicial Review— The provisions of subparagraphs (A) and (B) of section 245A(f)(4) of the Immigration and Nationality Act (8 U.S.C. 1255a(f)(4)) shall apply to administrative or judicial review of a determination under this section or of a determination respecting an application for adjustment of status under section 245A of the Immigration and Nationality Act filed pursuant to this section.

(g) Inapplicability of Removal Order Reinstatement.— Section 241(a)(5) of the Immigration and Nationality Act shall not apply with respect to an alien who is applying for adjustment of status under this section.

(h) Definition— For purposes of this section, the term "such section 245A" means section 245A of the Immigration and Nationality Act (8 U.S.C. 1255a).

## Sec. 1504. Application of Family Unity Provisions to Spouses and Unmarried Children of Certain Life Act Beneficiaries.

[Sec. 1504 of P.L. 106-554]

(a) Immigration Benefits.— Except as provided in subsection (d), in the case of an eligible spouse or child (as described in subsection (b)), the Attorney General—

(1) shall not remove the alien on a ground specified in paragraph (1)(A), (1)(B), (1)(C), or (3)(A) of section 237(a) of the Immigration and Nationality Act (8 U.S.C. 1227(a)), other than so much of paragraph (1)(A) of such section as relates to a ground of inadmissibility described in paragraph (2) or (3) of section 212(a) of such Act (8 U.S.C. 1182(a)); and

(2) shall authorize the alien to engage in employment in the United States during the period of time in which protection is provided under paragraph (1) and shall provide the alien with

an "employment authorized" endorsement or other appropriate document signifying authorization of employment.

(b) Eligible Spouses and Children.— For purposes of this section, the term "eligible spouse or child" means an alien who is the spouse or unmarried child of an alien described in section 1104(b) of the Legal Immigration Family Equity Act if the spouse or child—

(1) entered the United States before December 1, 1988; and

(2) resided in the United States on such date.

(c) Process for Relief for Eligible Spouses and Children Outside the United States.— If an alien has obtained lawful permanent resident status under section 1104 of the Legal Immigration Family Equity Act and the alien has an eligible spouse or child who is no longer physically present in the United States, the Attorney General shall establish a process under which the eligible spouse or child may be paroled into the United States in order to obtain the benefits of subsection (a) unless the Attorney General finds that the spouse or child would be inadmissible or deportable on any ground, other than a ground for which the alien would not be subject to removal under subsection (a)(1). An alien so paroled shall not be treated as paroled into the United States for purposes of section 201(c)(4) of the Immigration and Nationality Act (8 U.S.C. 1151(c)(4)).

(d) Exception.— An alien is not eligible for the benefits of this section if the Attorney General finds that—

(1) the alien has been convicted of a felony or three or more misdemeanors in the United States; or

(2) the alien is described in section 241(b)(3)(B) of the Immigration and Nationality Act (8 U.S.C. 1231(b)(3)(B)).

(e) Application of Definitions.— Except as otherwise specifically provided in this section, the definitions contained in the Immigration and Nationality Act shall apply in the administration of this section.

### Sec. 1505. Miscellaneous Amendments to Various Adjustment and Relief Acts.

[Sec. 1505 of P.L. 106-554]

(a) Nicaraguan Adjustment and Central American Relief Act.—

(1) In general.— *[omitted here; incorporated in NACARA §202(a). See Appendix E.]*

(2) Permitting Motion to Reopen.— Notwithstanding any time and number limitations imposed by law on motions to reopen exclusion, removal, or deportation proceedings (except limitations premised on an alien's conviction of an aggravated felony (as defined by section 101(a) of the Immigration and Nationality Act)), a national of Cuba or Nicaragua who has become eligible for adjustment of status under the Nicaraguan Adjustment and Central American Relief Act as a result of the amendments made by paragraph (1), may file one motion to reopen exclusion, deportation, or removal proceedings to apply for such adjustment under that Act. The scope of any proceeding reopened on this basis shall be limited to a determination of the alien's eligibility for adjustment of status under that Act. All such motions shall be filed within 180 days of the date of the enactment of this Act.

(b) Haitian Refugee Immigration Fairness Act of 1998.—

(1) Inapplicability of Certain Provisions.— *[omitted here; incorporated in HRIFA as §902(a)(2). See Appendix E.]*

(2) Permitting Motion to Reopen.— Notwithstanding any time and number limitations imposed by law on motions to reopen exclusion, removal, or deportation proceedings (except limitations premised on an alien's conviction of an aggravated felony (as defined by section 101(a) of the Immigration and Nationality Act)), a national of Haiti who has become eligible for adjustment of status under the Haitian Refugee Immigration Fairness Act of 1998 as a result of the amendments made by paragraph (1), may file one motion to reopen exclusion, deportation, or removal proceedings to apply for such adjustment under that Act. The scope of any proceeding reopened on this basis shall be limited to a determination of the alien's eligibility for adjustment of status under that Act. All such motions shall be filed within 180 days of the date of the enactment of this Act.

(c) Section 309 of IIRIRA.— Section 309 of the Illegal Immigration Reform and Immigrant Responsibility Act of 1996 is amended by adding at the end the following new subsection:

(h) Relief and Motions to Reopen.-—

(1) Relief.— An alien described in subsection (c)(5)(C)(i) who is otherwise eligible for—

(A) suspension of deportation pursuant to section 244(a) of the Immigration and Nationality Act, as in effect before the title III-A effective date; or

(B) cancellation of removal, pursuant to section 240A(b) of the Immigration and Nationality Act and subsection (f) of this section; shall not be barred from applying for such relief by operation of section 241(a)(5) of the Immigration and National Act, as in effect after the title III-A effective date.

(2) Additional Motion to Reopen Permitted.— Notwithstanding any limitation imposed by law on motions to reopen removal or deportation proceedings (except limitations premised on an alien's conviction of an aggravated felony (as defined by section 101(a) of the Immigration and Nationality Act)), any alien who is described in subsection (c)(5)(C)(i) and who has become eligible for cancellation of removal or suspension of deportation as a result of the enactment of paragraph (1) may file one motion to reopen removal or deportation proceedings in order to apply for cancellation of removal or suspension of deportation. The scope of any proceeding reopened on this basis shall be limited to a determination of the alien's eligibility for cancellation of removal or suspension of deportation. The Attorney General shall designate a specific time period in which all such motions to reopen are required to be filed. The period shall begin not later than 60 days after the date of the enactment of this subsection and shall extend for a period not to exceed 240 days.

(3) Construction.— Nothing in this subsection shall preclude an alien from filing a motion to reopen pursuant to section 240(b)(5)(C)(ii) of the Immigration and Nationality Act, or section 242B(c)(3)(B) of such Act (as in effect before the title III-A effective date).

## Title IV, Subtitle C of the Uniting and Strengthening America by Providing Appropriate Tools Required to Intercept and Obstruct Terrorism (USA PATRIOT) Act, 2001

*P.L. 107-56*

## Subtitle C—Preservation of Immigration Benefits for Victims of Terrorism

### SEC. 421. SPECIAL IMMIGRANT STATUS.

(a) IN GENERAL— For purposes of the Immigration and Nationality Act (8 U.S.C. 1101 *et seq.*), the Attorney General may provide an alien described in subsection (b) with the status of a special immigrant under section 101(a)(27) of such Act (8 U.S.C. 1101(a)(27)), if the alien—

(1) files with the Attorney General a petition under section 204 of such Act (8 U.S.C. 1154) for classification under section 203(b)(4) of such Act (8 U.S.C. 1153(b)(4)); and

(2) is otherwise eligible to receive an immigrant visa and is otherwise admissible to the United States for permanent residence, except in determining such admissibility, the grounds for inadmissibility specified in section 212(a)(4) of such Act (8 U.S.C. 1182(a)(4)) shall not apply.

(b) ALIENS DESCRIBED—

(1) PRINCIPAL ALIENS— An alien is described in this subsection if—

(A) the alien was the beneficiary of—

(i) a petition that was filed with the Attorney General on or before September 11, 2001—

(I) under section 204 of the Immigration and Nationality Act (8 U.S.C. 1154) to classify the alien as a family-sponsored immigrant under section 203(a) of such Act (8 U.S.C. 1153(a)) or as an employment-based immigrant under section 203(b) of such Act (8 U.S.C. 1153(b)); or

(II) under section 214(d) (8 U.S.C. 1184(d)) of such Act to authorize the issuance of a nonimmigrant visa to the alien under section 101(a)(15)(K) of such Act (8 U.S.C. 1101(a)(15)(K)); or

(ii) an application for labor certification under section 212(a)(5)(A) of such Act (8 U.S.C. 1182(a)(5)(A)) that was filed under regulations of the Secretary of Labor on or before such date; and

(B) such petition or application was revoked or terminated (or otherwise rendered null), either before or after its approval, due to a specified terrorist activity that directly resulted in—

(i) the death or disability of the petitioner, applicant, or alien beneficiary; or

(ii) loss of employment due to physical damage to, or destruction of, the business of the petitioner or applicant.

(2) SPOUSES AND CHILDREN—

(A) IN GENERAL— An alien is described in this subsection if—

(i) the alien was, on September 10, 2001, the spouse or child of a principal alien described in paragraph (1); and

(ii) the alien—

(I) is accompanying such principal alien; or

(II) is following to join such principal alien not later than September 11, 2003.

(B) CONSTRUCTION— For purposes of construing the terms 'accompanying' and 'following to join' in subparagraph (A)(ii), any death of a principal alien that is described in paragraph (1)(B)(i) shall be disregarded.

(3) GRANDPARENTS OF ORPHANS— An alien is described in this subsection if the alien is a grandparent of a child, both of whose parents died as a direct result of a specified terrorist activity, if either of such deceased parents was, on September 10, 2001, a citizen or national of the United States or an alien lawfully admitted for permanent residence in the United States.

(c) PRIORITY DATE— Immigrant visas made available under this section shall be issued to aliens in the order in which a petition on behalf of each such alien is filed with the Attorney General under subsection (a)(1), except that if an alien was assigned a priority date with respect to a petition described in subsection (b)(1)(A)(i), the alien may maintain that priority date.

(d) NUMERICAL LIMITATIONS— For purposes of the application of sections 201 through 203 of the Immigration and Nationality Act (8 U.S.C. 1151–1153) in any fiscal year, aliens eligible to be provided status under this section shall be treated as special immigrants described in section 101(a)(27) of such Act (8 U.S.C. 1101(a)(27)) who are not described in subparagraph (A), (B), (C), or (K) of such section.

## SEC. 422. EXTENSION OF FILING OR REENTRY DEADLINES.

(a) AUTOMATIC EXTENSION OF NONIMMIGRANT STATUS—

(1) IN GENERAL— Notwithstanding section 214 of the Immigration and Nationality Act (8 U.S.C. 1184), in the case of an alien described in paragraph (2) who was lawfully present in the United States as a nonimmigrant on September 10, 2001, the alien may remain lawfully in the United States in the same nonimmigrant status until the later of—

(A) the date such lawful nonimmigrant status otherwise would have terminated if this subsection had not been enacted; or

(B) 1 year after the death or onset of disability described in paragraph (2).

(2) ALIENS DESCRIBED—

(A) PRINCIPAL ALIENS— An alien is described in this paragraph if the alien was disabled as a direct result of a specified terrorist activity.

(B) SPOUSES AND CHILDREN— An alien is described in this paragraph if the alien was, on September 10, 2001, the spouse or child of—

(i) a principal alien described in subparagraph (A); or

(ii) an alien who died as a direct result of a specified terrorist activity.

(3) AUTHORIZED EMPLOYMENT— During the period in which a principal alien or alien spouse is in lawful nonimmigrant status under paragraph (1), the alien shall be provided an

"employment authorized" endorsement or other appropriate document signifying authorization of employment not later than 30 days after the alien requests such authorization.

(b) NEW DEADLINES FOR EXTENSION OR CHANGE OF NONIMMIGRANT STATUS—

(1) FILING DELAYS— In the case of an alien who was lawfully present in the United States as a nonimmigrant on September 10, 2001, if the alien was prevented from filing a timely application for an extension or change of nonimmigrant status as a direct result of a specified terrorist activity, the alien's application shall be considered timely filed if it is filed not later than 60 days after it otherwise would have been due.

(2) DEPARTURE DELAYS— In the case of an alien who was lawfully present in the United States as a nonimmigrant on September 10, 2001, if the alien is unable timely to depart the United States as a direct result of a specified terrorist activity, the alien shall not be considered to have been unlawfully present in the United States during the period beginning on September 11, 2001, and ending on the date of the alien's departure, if such departure occurs on or before November 11, 2001.

(3) SPECIAL RULE FOR ALIENS UNABLE TO RETURN FROM ABROAD—

(A) PRINCIPAL ALIENS— In the case of an alien who was in a lawful nonimmigrant status on September 10, 2001, but who was not present in the United States on such date, if the alien was prevented from returning to the United States in order to file a timely application for an extension of nonimmigrant status as a direct result of a specified terrorist activity—

(i) the alien's application shall be considered timely filed if it is filed not later than 60 days after it otherwise would have been due; and

(ii) the alien's lawful nonimmigrant status shall be considered to continue until the later of—

(I) the date such status otherwise would have terminated if this subparagraph had not been enacted; or

(II) the date that is 60 days after the date on which the application described in clause (i) otherwise would have been due.

(B) SPOUSES AND CHILDREN— In the case of an alien who is the spouse or child of a principal alien described in subparagraph (A), if the spouse or child was in a lawful nonimmigrant status on September 10, 2001, the spouse or child may remain lawfully in the United States in the same nonimmigrant status until the later of—

(i) the date such lawful nonimmigrant status otherwise would have terminated if this subparagraph had not been enacted; or

(ii) the date that is 60 days after the date on which the application described in subparagraph (A) otherwise would have been due.

(4) CIRCUMSTANCES PREVENTING TIMELY ACTION—

(A) FILING DELAYS— For purposes of paragraph (1), circumstances preventing an alien from timely acting are—

(i) office closures;

(ii) mail or courier service cessations or delays; and

    (iii) other closures, cessations, or delays affecting case processing or travel necessary to satisfy legal requirements.

    (B) DEPARTURE AND RETURN DELAYS— For purposes of paragraphs (2) and (3), circumstances preventing an alien from timely acting are—

    (i) office closures;

    (ii) airline flight cessations or delays; and

    (iii) other closures, cessations, or delays affecting case processing or travel necessary to satisfy legal requirements.

(c) DIVERSITY IMMIGRANTS—

    (1) WAIVER OF FISCAL YEAR LIMITATION— Notwithstanding section 203(e)(2) of the Immigration and Nationality Act (8 U.S.C. 1153(e)(2)), an immigrant visa number issued to an alien under section 203(c) of such Act for fiscal year 2001 may be used by the alien during the period beginning on October 1, 2001, and ending on April 1, 2002, if the alien establishes that the alien was prevented from using it during fiscal year 2001 as a direct result of a specified terrorist activity.

    (2) WORLDWIDE LEVEL— In the case of an alien entering the United States as a lawful permanent resident, or adjusting to that status, under paragraph (1) or (3), the alien shall be counted as a diversity immigrant for fiscal year 2001 for purposes of section 201(e) of the Immigration and Nationality Act (8 U.S.C. 1151(e)), unless the worldwide level under such section for such year has been exceeded, in which case the alien shall be counted as a diversity immigrant for fiscal year 2002.

    (3) TREATMENT OF FAMILY MEMBERS OF CERTAIN ALIENS— In the case of a principal alien issued an immigrant visa number under section 203(c) of the Immigration and Nationality Act (8 U.S.C. 1153(c)) for fiscal year 2001, if such principal alien died as a direct result of a specified terrorist activity, the aliens who were, on September 10, 2001, the spouse and children of such principal alien shall, until June 30, 2002, if not otherwise entitled to an immigrant status and the immediate issuance of a visa under subsection (a), (b), or (c) of section 203 of such Act, be entitled to the same status, and the same order of consideration, that would have been provided to such alien spouse or child under section 203(d) of such Act as if the principal alien were not deceased and as if the spouse or child's visa application had been adjudicated by September 30, 2001.

    (4) CIRCUMSTANCES PREVENTING TIMELY ACTION— For purposes of paragraph (1), circumstances preventing an alien from using an immigrant visa number during fiscal year 2001 are—

    (A) office closures;

    (B) mail or courier service cessations or delays;

    (C) airline flight cessations or delays; and

    (D) other closures, cessations, or delays affecting case processing or travel necessary to satisfy legal requirements.

(d) EXTENSION OF EXPIRATION OF IMMIGRANT VISAS—

    (1) IN GENERAL— Notwithstanding the limitations under section 221(c) of the Immigration and Nationality Act (8 U.S.C. 1201(c)), in the case of any immigrant visa issued to an alien

that expires or expired before December 31, 2001, if the alien was unable to effect entry into the United States as a direct result of a specified terrorist activity, then the period of validity of the visa is extended until December 31, 2001, unless a longer period of validity is otherwise provided under this subtitle.

(2) CIRCUMSTANCES PREVENTING ENTRY— For purposes of this subsection, circumstances preventing an alien from effecting entry into the United States are—

(A) office closures;

(B) airline flight cessations or delays; and

(C) other closures, cessations, or delays affecting case processing or travel necessary to satisfy legal requirements.

(e) GRANTS OF PAROLE EXTENDED—

(1) IN GENERAL— In the case of any parole granted by the Attorney General under section 212(d)(5) of the Immigration and Nationality Act (8 U.S.C. 1182(d)(5)) that expires on a date on or after September 11, 2001, if the alien beneficiary of the parole was unable to return to the United States prior to the expiration date as a direct result of a specified terrorist activity, the parole is deemed extended for an additional 90 days.

(2) CIRCUMSTANCES PREVENTING RETURN— For purposes of this subsection, circumstances preventing an alien from timely returning to the United States are—

(A) office closures;

(B) airline flight cessations or delays; and

(C) other closures, cessations, or delays affecting case processing or travel necessary to satisfy legal requirements.

(f) VOLUNTARY DEPARTURE— Notwithstanding section 240B of the Immigration and Nationality Act (8 U.S.C. 1229c), if a period for voluntary departure under such section expired during the period beginning on September 11, 2001, and ending on October 11, 2001, such voluntary departure period is deemed extended for an additional 30 days.

## SEC. 423. HUMANITARIAN RELIEF FOR CERTAIN SURVIVING SPOUSES AND CHILDREN.

(a) TREATMENT AS IMMEDIATE RELATIVES—

(1) SPOUSES— Notwithstanding the second sentence of section 201(b)(2)(A)(i) of the Immigration and Nationality Act (8 U.S.C. 1151(b)(2)(A)(i)), in the case of an alien who was the spouse of a citizen of the United States at the time of the citizen's death and was not legally separated from the citizen at the time of the citizen's death, if the citizen died as a direct result of a specified terrorist activity, the alien (and each child of the alien) shall be considered, for purposes of section 201(b) of such Act, to remain an immediate relative after the date of the citizen's death, but only if the alien files a petition under section 204(a)(1)(A)(ii) of such Act within 2 years after such date and only until the date the alien remarries. For purposes of such section 204(a)(1)(A)(ii), an alien granted relief under the preceding sentence shall be considered an alien spouse described in the second sentence of section 201(b)(2)(A)(i) of such Act.

(2) CHILDREN—

(A) IN GENERAL— In the case of an alien who was the child of a citizen of the United States at the time of the citizen's death, if the citizen died as a direct result of a specified terrorist activity, the alien shall be considered, for purposes of section 201(b) of the Immigration and Nationality Act (8 U.S.C. 1151(b)), to remain an immediate relative after the date of the citizen's death (regardless of changes in age or marital status thereafter), but only if the alien files a petition under subparagraph (B) within 2 years after such date.

(B) PETITIONS— An alien described in subparagraph (A) may file a petition with the Attorney General for classification of the alien under section 201(b)(2)(A)(i) of the Immigration and Nationality Act (8 U.S.C. 1151(b)(2)(A)(i)). For purposes of such Act, such a petition shall be considered a petition filed under section 204(a)(1)(A) of such Act (8 U.S.C. 1154(a)(1)(A)).

(b) SPOUSES, CHILDREN, UNMARRIED SONS AND DAUGHTERS OF LAWFUL PERMANENT RESIDENT ALIENS—

(1) IN GENERAL— Any spouse, child, or unmarried son or daughter of an alien described in paragraph (3) who is included in a petition for classification as a family-sponsored immigrant under section 203(a)(2) of the Immigration and Nationality Act (8 U.S.C. 1153(a)(2)) that was filed by such alien before September 11, 2001, shall be considered (if the spouse, child, son, or daughter has not been admitted or approved for lawful permanent residence by such date) a valid petitioner for preference status under such section with the same priority date as that assigned prior to the death described in paragraph (3)(A). No new petition shall be required to be filed. Such spouse, child, son, or daughter may be eligible for deferred action and work authorization.

(2) SELF-PETITIONS— Any spouse, child, or unmarried son or daughter of an alien described in paragraph (3) who is not a beneficiary of a petition for classification as a family-sponsored immigrant under section 203(a)(2) of the Immigration and Nationality Act may file a petition for such classification with the Attorney General, if the spouse, child, son, or daughter was present in the United States on September 11, 2001. Such spouse, child, son, or daughter may be eligible for deferred action and work authorization.

(3) ALIENS DESCRIBED— An alien is described in this paragraph if the alien—

(A) died as a direct result of a specified terrorist activity; and

(B) on the day of such death, was lawfully admitted for permanent residence in the United States.

(c) APPLICATIONS FOR ADJUSTMENT OF STATUS BY SURVIVING SPOUSES AND CHILDREN OF EMPLOYMENT-BASED IMMIGRANTS—

(1) IN GENERAL— Any alien who was, on September 10, 2001, the spouse or child of an alien described in paragraph (2), and who applied for adjustment of status prior to the death described in paragraph (2)(A), may have such application adjudicated as if such death had not occurred.

(2) ALIENS DESCRIBED— An alien is described in this paragraph if the alien—

(A) died as a direct result of a specified terrorist activity; and

(B) on the day before such death, was—

(i) an alien lawfully admitted for permanent residence in the United States by reason of having been allotted a visa under section 203(b) of the Immigration and Nationality Act (8 U.S.C. 1153(b)); or

(ii) an applicant for adjustment of status to that of an alien described in clause (i), and admissible to the United States for permanent residence.

(d) WAIVER OF PUBLIC CHARGE GROUNDS— In determining the admissibility of any alien accorded an immigration benefit under this section, the grounds for inadmissibility specified in section 212(a)(4) of the Immigration and Nationality Act (8 U.S.C. 1182(a)(4)) shall not apply.

## SEC. 424. "AGE-OUT" PROTECTION FOR CHILDREN.

For purposes of the administration of the Immigration and Nationality Act (8 U.S.C. 1101 *et seq.*), in the case of an alien—

(1) whose 21st birthday occurs in September 2001, and who is the beneficiary of a petition or application filed under such Act on or before September 11, 2001, the alien shall be considered to be a child for 90 days after the alien's 21st birthday for purposes of adjudicating such petition or application; and

(2) whose 21st birthday occurs after September 2001, and who is the beneficiary of a petition or application filed under such Act on or before September 11, 2001, the alien shall be considered to be a child for 45 days after the alien's 21st birthday for purposes of adjudicating such petition or application.

## SEC. 425. TEMPORARY ADMINISTRATIVE RELIEF.

The Attorney General, for humanitarian purposes or to ensure family unity, may provide temporary administrative relief to any alien who—

(1) was lawfully present in the United States on September 10, 2001;

(2) was on such date the spouse, parent, or child of an individual who died or was disabled as a direct result of a specified terrorist activity; and

(3) is not otherwise entitled to relief under any other provision of this subtitle.

## SEC. 426. EVIDENCE OF DEATH, DISABILITY, OR LOSS OF EMPLOYMENT.

(a) IN GENERAL— The Attorney General shall establish appropriate standards for evidence demonstrating, for purposes of this subtitle, that any of the following occurred as a direct result of a specified terrorist activity:

(1) Death.

(2) Disability.

(3) Loss of employment due to physical damage to, or destruction of, a business.

(b) WAIVER OF REGULATIONS— The Attorney General shall carry out subsection (a) as expeditiously as possible. The Attorney General is not required to promulgate regulations prior to implementing this subtitle.

## SEC. 427. NO BENEFITS TO TERRORISTS OR FAMILY MEMBERS OF TERRORISTS.

Notwithstanding any other provision of this subtitle, nothing in this subtitle shall be construed to provide any benefit or relief to—

(1) any individual culpable for a specified terrorist activity; or

(2) any family member of any individual described in paragraph (1).

## SEC. 428. DEFINITIONS.

(a) APPLICATION OF IMMIGRATION AND NATIONALITY ACT PROVISIONS— Except as otherwise specifically provided in this subtitle, the definitions used in the Immigration and Nationality Act (excluding the definitions applicable exclusively to title III of such Act) shall apply in the administration of this subtitle.

(b) SPECIFIED TERRORIST ACTIVITY— For purposes of this subtitle, the term 'specified terrorist activity' means any terrorist activity conducted against the Government or the people of the United States on September 11, 2001.

## APPENDIX K
## Division C, Title I, Subtitle B of the
## 21st Century Department of Justice Appropriations Authorization Act

*P.L. 107-273*

## SUBTITLE B—EB-5 AMENDMENTS

## Chapter 1—Immigration Benefits

## SEC. 11031. REMOVAL OF CONDITIONAL BASIS OF PERMANENT RESIDENT STATUS FOR CERTAIN ALIEN ENTREPRENEURS, SPOUSES, AND CHILDREN.

(a) IN GENERAL.— In lieu of the provisions of section 216A(c)(3) of the Immigration and Nationality Act (8 U.S.C. 1186b(c)(3)), subsection (c) shall apply in the case of an eligible alien described in subsection (b)(1).

(b) ELIGIBLE ALIENS DESCRIBED.—

(1) IN GENERAL.— An alien is an eligible alien described in this subsection if the alien—

(A) filed, under section 204(a)(1)(H) of the Immigration and Nationality Act (8 U.S.C. 1154(a)(1)(H)) (or any predecessor provision), a petition to accord the alien a status under section 203(b)(5) of such Act (8 U.S.C. 1153(b)(5)) that was approved by the Attorney General after January 1, 1995, and before August 31, 1998;

(B) pursuant to such approval, obtained the status of an alien entrepreneur with permanent resident status on a conditional basis described in section 216A of such Act (8 U.S.C. 1186b); and

(C) timely filed, in accordance with section 216A(c)(1)(A) of such Act (8 U.S.C. 1186b(c)(1)(A)) and before the date of the enactment of this Act, a petition requesting the removal of such conditional basis.

(2) REOPENING PETITIONS PREVIOUSLY DENIED.—

(A) IN GENERAL.— In the case of a petition described in paragraph (1)(C) that was denied under section 216A(c)(3)(C) of the Immigration and Nationality Act (8 U.S.C. 1186b(c)(3)(C)) before the date of the enactment of this Act, upon a motion to reopen such petition filed by the eligible alien not later than 60 days after such date, the Attorney General shall make determinations on such petition pursuant to subsection (c).

(B) PETITIONERS ABROAD.— In the case of such an eligible alien who is no longer physically present in the United States, the Attorney General shall establish a process under which the alien may be paroled into the United States if necessary in order to obtain the determinations under subsection (c), unless the Attorney General finds that—

(i) the alien is inadmissible or deportable on any ground; or

(ii) the petition described in paragraph (1)(C) was denied on the ground that it contains a material misrepresentation in the facts and information described in section 216A(d)(1) of the Immigration and Nationality Act (8 U.S.C. 1186b(d)(1)) and alleged in the petition with respect to a commercial enterprise.

**EB-5 Amendments**

Div C, Tit. I, Subtit. B (21st Century DOJ Appropriations)

**Additional Provisions**

(C) DEPORTATION OR REMOVAL PROCEEDINGS.— In the case of such an eligible alien who was placed in deportation or removal proceedings by reason of the denial of the petition described in paragraph (1)(C), a motion to reopen filed under subparagraph (A) shall be treated as a motion to reopen such proceedings. The Attorney General shall grant such motion notwithstanding any time and number limitations imposed by law on motions to reopen such proceedings, except that the scope of any proceeding reopened on this basis shall be limited to whether any order of deportation or removal should be vacated, and the alien granted the status of an alien lawfully admitted for permanent residence (unconditionally or on a conditional basis), by reason of the determinations made under subsection (c). An alien who is inadmissible or deportable on any ground shall not be granted such status, except that this prohibition shall not apply to an alien who has been paroled into the United States under subparagraph (B).

(c) DETERMINATIONS ON PETITIONS.—

(1) INITIAL DETERMINATION.—

(A) IN GENERAL.— With respect to each eligible alien described in subsection (b)(1), the Attorney General shall make a determination, not later than 180 days after the date of the enactment of this Act, whether—

(i) the petition described in subsection (b)(1)(C) contains any material misrepresentation in the facts and information described in section 216A(d)(1) of the Immigration and Nationality Act (8 U.S.C. 1186b(d)(1)) and alleged in the petition with respect to a commercial enterprise (regardless of whether such enterprise is a limited partnership and regardless of whether the alien entered the enterprise after its formation);

(ii) subject to subparagraphs (B) and (C), such enterprise created full-time jobs for not fewer than 10 United States citizens or aliens lawfully admitted for permanent residence or other immigrants lawfully authorized to be employed in the United States (other than the eligible alien and the alien's spouse, sons, or daughters), and those jobs exist or existed on any of the dates described in subparagraph (D); and

(iii) on any of the dates described in subparagraph (D), the alien is in substantial compliance with the capital investment requirement described in section 216A(d)(1)(B) of the Immigration and Nationality Act (8 U.S.C. 1186b(d)(1)(B)).

(B) INVESTMENT UNDER PILOT IMMIGRATION PROGRAM.— For purposes of subparagraph (A)(ii), an investment that satisfies the requirements of section 610(c) of the Departments of Commerce, Justice, and State, the Judiciary, and Related Agencies Appropriations Act, 1993 (8 U.S.C. 1153 note), as in effect on the date of the enactment of this Act, shall be deemed to satisfy the requirements of such subparagraph.

(C) EXCEPTION FOR TROUBLED BUSINESSES.— In the case of an eligible alien who has made a capital investment in a troubled business (as defined in 8 CFR 204.6(e), as in effect on the date of the enactment of this Act), in lieu of the determination under subparagraph (A)(ii), the Attorney General shall determine whether the number of employees of the business, as measured on any of the dates described in subparagraph (D), is at no less than the pre-investment level.

(D) DATES.— The dates described in this subparagraph are the following:

(i) The date on which the petition described in subsection (b)(1)(C) is filed.

(ii) 6 months after the date described in clause (i).

(iii) The date on which the determination under subparagraph (A) or (C) is made.

(E) REMOVAL OF CONDITIONAL BASIS IF FAVORABLE DETERMINATION.—
If the Attorney General renders an affirmative determination with respect to clauses (ii)
and (iii) of subparagraph (A), and if the Attorney General renders a negative determination with respect to clause (i) of such subparagraph, the Attorney General shall so notify
the alien involved and shall remove the conditional basis of the alien's status (and that
of the alien's spouse and children if it was obtained under section 216A of the Immigration and Nationality Act (8 U.S.C. 1186b)) effective as of the second anniversary of the
alien's lawful admission for permanent residence.

(F) REQUIREMENTS RELATING TO ADVERSE DETERMINATIONS.—

(i) NOTICE.— If the Attorney General renders an adverse determination with
respect to clause (i), (ii), or (iii) of subparagraph (A), the Attorney General shall so
notify the alien involved. The notice shall be in writing and shall state the factual
basis for any adverse determination. The Attorney General shall provide the alien
with an opportunity to submit evidence to rebut any adverse determination. If the
Attorney General reverses all adverse determinations pursuant to such rebuttal, the
Attorney General shall so notify the alien involved and shall remove the conditional
basis of the alien's status (and that of the alien's spouse and children if it was obtained under section 216A of the Immigration and Nationality Act (8 U.S.C.
1186b)) effective as of the second anniversary of the alien's lawful admission for
permanent residence.

(ii) CONTINUATION OF CONDITIONAL BASIS IF CERTAIN ADVERSE
DETERMINATIONS.— If the Attorney General renders an adverse determination
with respect to clause (ii) or (iii) of subparagraph (A), and the eligible alien's rebuttal does not cause the Attorney General to reverse such determination, the Attorney
General shall continue the conditional basis of the alien's permanent resident status
(and that of the alien's spouse and children if it was obtained under section 216A of
the Immigration and Nationality Act (8 U.S.C. 1186b)) for a 2-year period.

(iii) TERMINATION IF ADVERSE DETERMINATION.— If the Attorney
General renders an adverse determination with respect to subparagraph (A)(i), and
the eligible alien's rebuttal does not cause the Attorney General to reverse such determination, the Attorney General shall so notify the alien involved and, subject to
subsection (d), shall terminate the permanent resident status of the alien (and that of
the alien's spouse and children if it was obtained on a conditional basis under section 216A of the Immigration and Nationality Act (8 U.S.C. 1186b)).

(iv) ADMINISTRATIVE AND JUDICIAL REVIEW.— An alien may seek
administrative review of an adverse determination made under subparagraph (A) by
filing a petition for such review with the Board of Immigration Appeals. If the
Board of Immigration Appeals denies the petition, the alien may seek judicial review. The procedures for judicial review under this clause shall be the same as the
procedures for judicial review of a final order of removal under section 242(a)(1) of
the Immigration and Nationality Act (8 U.S.C. 1252(a)(1)). During the period in
which an administrative or judicial appeal under this clause is pending, the Attorney
General shall continue the conditional basis of the alien's permanent resident status
(and that of the alien's spouse and children if it was obtained under section 216A of
the Immigration and Nationality Act (8 U.S.C. 1186b)).

**EB-5 Amendments**                                                    **Additional Provisions**

Div C, Tit. I, Subtit. B (21st Century DOJ Appropriations)

(2) SECOND DETERMINATION.—

(A) AUTHORIZATION TO CONSIDER INVESTMENTS IN OTHER COMMER-CIAL ENTERPRISES.— In determining under this paragraph whether to remove a conditional basis continued under paragraph (1)(F)(ii) with respect to an alien, the Attorney General shall consider any capital investment made by the alien in a commercial enterprise (regardless of whether such enterprise is a limited partnership and regardless of whether the alien entered the enterprise after its formation), in the United States, regardless of whether that investment was made before or after the determinations under paragraph (1) and regardless of whether the commercial enterprise is the same as that considered in the determinations under such paragraph, if facts and information with respect to the investment and the enterprise are included in the petition submitted under subparagraph (B).

(B) PETITION.— In order for a conditional basis continued under paragraph (1)(F)(ii) for an eligible alien (and the alien's spouse and children) to be removed, the alien must submit to the Attorney General, during the period described in subparagraph (C), a petition which requests the removal of such conditional basis and which states, under penalty of perjury, the facts and information described in subparagraphs (A) and (B) of section 216A(d)(1) of the Immigration and Nationality Act (8 U.S.C. 1186b(d)(1)) with respect to any commercial enterprise (regardless of whether such enterprise is a limited partnership and regardless of whether the alien entered the enterprise after its formation) which the alien desires to have considered under this paragraph, regardless of whether such enterprise was created before or after the determinations made under paragraph (1).

(C) PERIOD FOR FILING PETITION.—

(i) 90-DAY PERIOD BEFORE SECOND ANNIVERSARY.— Except as provided in clause (ii), the petition under subparagraph (B) must be filed during the 90-day period before the second anniversary of the continuation, under paragraph (1)(F)(ii), of the conditional basis of the alien's lawful admission for permanent residence.

(ii) DATE PETITIONS FOR GOOD CAUSE.— Such a petition may be considered if filed after such date, but only if the alien establishes to the satisfaction of the Attorney General good cause and extenuating circumstances for failure to file the petition during the period described in clause (i).

(D) TERMINATION OF PERMANENT RESIDENT STATUS FOR FAILURE TO FILE PETITION.—

(i) IN GENERAL.— In the case of an alien with permanent resident status on a conditional basis under paragraph (1)(F)(ii), if no petition is filed with respect to the alien in accordance with subparagraph (B), the Attorney General shall terminate the permanent resident status of the alien (and the alien's spouse and children if it was obtained on a conditional basis under section 216A of the Immigration and Nationality Act (8 U.S.C. 1186b)) as of the second anniversary of the continuation, under paragraph (1)(F)(ii), of the conditional basis of the alien's lawful admission for permanent residence.

(ii) HEARING IN REMOVAL PROCEEDING.— In any removal proceeding with respect to an alien whose permanent resident status is terminated under clause (i), the burden of proof shall be on the alien to establish compliance with subparagraph (B).

(E) DETERMINATIONS AFTER PETITION.— If a petition is filed by an eligible alien in accordance with subparagraph (B), the Attorney General shall make a determination, within 90 days of the date of such filing, whether—

(i) the petition contains any material misrepresentation in the facts and information alleged in the petition with respect to the commercial enterprises included in such petition;

(ii) all such enterprises, considered together, created full-time jobs for not fewer than 10 United States citizens or aliens lawfully admitted for permanent residence or other immigrants lawfully authorized to be employed in the United States (other than the eligible alien and the alien's spouse, sons, or daughters), and those jobs exist on the date on which the determination is made, except that—

(I) this clause shall apply only if the Attorney General made an adverse determination with respect to the eligible alien under paragraph (1)(A)(ii);

(II) the provisions of subparagraphs (B) and (C) of paragraph (1) shall apply to a determination under this clause in the same manner as they apply to a determination under paragraph (1)(A)(ii); and

(III) if the Attorney General determined under paragraph (1)(A)(ii) that any jobs satisfying the requirement of such paragraph were created, the number of those jobs shall be subtracted from the number of jobs otherwise needed to satisfy the requirement of this clause; and

(iii) considering all such enterprises together, on the date on which the determination is made, the eligible alien is in substantial compliance with the capital investment requirement described in section 216A(d)(1)(B) of the Immigration and Nationality Act (8 U.S.C. 1186b(d)(1)(B)), except that—

(I) this clause shall apply only if the Attorney General made an adverse determination with respect to the eligible alien under paragraph (1)(A)(iii); and

(II) if the Attorney General determined under paragraph (1)(A)(iii) that any capital amount was invested that could be credited towards compliance with the capital investment requirement described in section 216A(d)(1)(B) of the Immigration and Nationality Act (8 U.S.C. 1186b(d)(1)(B)), such amount shall be subtracted from the amount of capital otherwise needed to satisfy the requirement of this clause.

(F) REMOVAL OF CONDITIONAL BASIS IF FAVORABLE DETERMINATION.— If the Attorney General renders an affirmative determination with respect to clauses (ii) and (iii) of subparagraph (E), and if the Attorney General renders a negative determination with respect to clause (i) of such subparagraph, the Attorney General shall so notify the alien involved and shall remove the conditional basis of the alien's status (and that of the alien's spouse and children if it was obtained under section 216A of the Immigration and Nationality Act (8 U.S.C. 1186b)) effective as of the second anniversary of the continuation, under paragraph (1)(F)(ii), of the conditional basis of the alien's lawful admission for permanent residence.

(G) REQUIREMENTS RELATING TO ADVERSE DETERMINATIONS.—

(i) NOTICE.— If the Attorney General renders an adverse determination under subparagraph (E), the Attorney General shall so notify the alien involved. The notice shall be in writing and shall state the factual basis for any adverse determination. The Attorney General shall provide the alien with an opportunity to submit evidence to rebut any adverse determination. If the Attorney General reverses all adverse determinations pursuant to such rebuttal, the Attorney General shall so notify the alien involved and shall remove the conditional basis of the alien's status (and that of the alien's spouse and children if it was obtained under section 216A of the Immigration and Nationality Act (8 U.S.C. 1186b)) effective as of the second anniversary of the continuation, under paragraph (1)(F)(ii), of the conditional basis of the alien's lawful admission for permanent residence.

(ii) TERMINATION IF ADVERSE DETERMINATION.— If the eligible alien's rebuttal does not cause the Attorney General to reverse each adverse determination under subparagraph (E), the Attorney General shall so notify the alien involved and, subject to subsection (d), shall terminate the permanent resident status of the alien (and that of the alien's spouse and children if it was obtained on a conditional basis under section 216A of the Immigration and Nationality Act (8 U.S.C. 1186b)).

(d) HEARING IN REMOVAL PROCEEDING.— Any alien whose permanent resident status is terminated under paragraph (1)(F)(iii) or (2)(G)(ii) of subsection (c) may request a review of such determination in a proceeding to remove the alien. In such proceeding, the burden of proof shall be on the Attorney General.

(e) CLARIFICATION WITH RESPECT TO CHILDREN.— In the case of an alien who obtained the status of an alien lawfully admitted for permanent residence on a conditional basis before the date of the enactment of this Act by virtue of being the child of an eligible alien described in subsection (b)(1), the alien shall be considered to be a child for purposes of this section regardless of any change in age or marital status after obtaining such status.

(f) DEFINITION OF FULL-TIME.— For purposes of this section, the term "full-time" means a position that requires at least 35 hours of service per week at any time, regardless of who fills the position.

## SEC. 11032. CONDITIONAL PERMANENT RESIDENT STATUS FOR CERTAIN ALIEN ENTREPRENEURS, SPOUSES, AND CHILDREN.

(a) IN GENERAL.— With respect to each eligible alien described in subsection (b), the Attorney General or the Secretary of State shall approve the application described in subsection (b)(2) and grant the alien (and any spouse or child of the alien, if the spouse or child is eligible to receive a visa under section 203(d) of the Immigration and Nationality Act (8 U.S.C. 1153(d))) the status of an alien lawfully admitted for permanent residence on a conditional basis under section 216A of such Act (8 U.S.C. 1186b). Such application shall be approved not later than 180 days after the date of the enactment of this Act.

(b) ELIGIBLE ALIENS DESCRIBED.— An alien is an eligible alien described in this subsection if the alien—

(1) filed, under section 204(a)(1)(H) of the Immigration and Nationality Act (8 U.S.C. 1154(a)(1)(H)) (or any predecessor provision), a petition to accord the alien a status under section 203(b)(5) of such Act (8 U.S.C. 1153(b)(5)) that was approved by the Attorney General after January 1, 1995, and before August 31, 1998;

(2) pursuant to such approval, timely filed before the date of the enactment of this Act an application for adjustment of status under section 245 of such Act (8 U.S.C. 1255) or an application for an immigrant visa under section 203(b)(5) of such Act (8 U.S.C. 1153(b)(5)); and

(3) is not inadmissible or deportable on any ground.

(c) TREATMENT OF CERTAIN APPLICATIONS.—

(1) REVOCATION OF APPROVAL OF PETITIONS.— If the Attorney General revoked the approval of a petition described in subsection (b)(1), such revocation shall be disregarded for purposes of this section if it was based on a determination that the alien failed to satisfy section 203(b)(5)(A)(ii) of the Immigration and Nationality Act (8 U.S.C. 1153(b)(5)(A)(ii)).

(2) APPLICATIONS NO LONGER PENDING.—

(A) IN GENERAL.— If an application described in subsection (b)(2) is not pending on the date of the enactment of this Act, the Attorney General shall disregard the circumstances leading to such lack of pendency and treat it as reopened, if such lack of pendency is due to a determination that the alien—

(i) failed to satisfy section 203(b)(5)(A)(ii) of the Immigration and Nationality Act (8 U.S.C. 1153(b)(5)(A)(ii)); or

(ii) departed the United States without advance parole.

(B) APPLICANTS ABROAD.— In the case of an eligible alien who filed an application for adjustment of status described in subsection (b)(2), but who is no longer physically present in the United States, the Attorney General shall establish a process under which the alien may be paroled into the United States if necessary in order to obtain adjustment of status under this section.

(d) RECORDATION OF DATE; REDUCTION OF NUMBERS.— Upon the approval of an application under subsection (a), the Attorney General shall record the alien's lawful admission for permanent residence on a conditional basis as of the date of such approval and the Secretary of State shall reduce by one the number of visas authorized to be issued under sections 201(d) and 203(b)(5) of the Immigration and Nationality Act (8 U.S.C. 1151(d) and 1153(b)(5)) for the fiscal year then current.

(e) REMOVAL OF CONDITIONAL BASIS.—

(1) PETITION.— In order for a conditional basis established under this section for an alien (and the alien's spouse and children) to be removed, the alien must satisfy the requirements of section 216A(c)(1) of the Immigration and Nationality Act (8 U.S.C. 1186b(c)(1)), including the submission of a petition in accordance with subparagraph (A) of such section. Such petition may include the facts and information described in subparagraphs (A) and (B) of section 216A(d)(1) of the Immigration and Nationality Act (8 U.S.C. 1186b(d)(1)) with respect to any commercial enterprise (regardless of whether such enterprise is a limited partnership and regardless of whether the alien entered the enterprise after its formation) in the United States in which the alien has made a capital investment at any time.

(2) DETERMINATION.— In carrying out section 216A(c)(3) of the Immigration and Nationality Act (8 U.S.C. 1186b(c)(3)) with respect to an alien described in paragraph (1), the Attorney General, in lieu of the determination described in such section 216A(c)(3), shall make a determination, within 90 days of the date of such filing, whether—

(A) the petition described in paragraph (1) contains any material misrepresentation in the facts and information alleged in the petition with respect to the commercial enterprises included in the petition;

(B) subject to subparagraphs (B) and (C) of section 11031(c)(1), all such enterprises, considered together, created full-time jobs for not fewer than 10 United States citizens or aliens lawfully admitted for permanent residence or other immigrants lawfully authorized to be employed in the United States (other than the alien and the alien's spouse, sons, or daughters), and those jobs exist or existed on either of the dates described in paragraph (3); and

(C) considering the alien's investments in such enterprises on either of the dates described in paragraph (3), or on both such dates, the alien is or was in substantial compliance with the capital investment requirement described in section 216A(d)(1)(B) of the Immigration and Nationality Act (8 U.S.C. 1186b(d)(1)(B)).

(3) DATES.— The dates described in this paragraph are the following:

(A) The date on which the application described in subsection (b)(2) was filed.

(B) The date on which the determination under paragraph (2) is made.

(f) CLARIFICATION WITH RESPECT TO CHILDREN.— In the case of an alien who was a child on the date on which the application described in subsection (b)(2) was filed, the alien shall be considered to be a child for purposes of this section regardless of any change in age or marital status after such date.

## SEC. 11033. REGULATIONS.

The Immigration and Naturalization Service shall promulgate regulations to implement this chapter not later than 120 days after the date of enactment of this Act. Until such regulations are promulgated, the Attorney General shall not deny a petition filed or pending under section 216A(c)(1)(A) of the Immigration and Nationality Act (8 U.S.C. 1186b(c)(1)(A)) that relates to an eligible alien described in section 11031, or on an application filed or pending under section 245 of such Act (8 U.S.C. 1255) that relates to an eligible alien described in section 11032. Until such regulations are promulgated, the Attorney General shall not initiate or proceed with removal proceedings under section 240 of the Immigration and Nationality Act (8 U.S.C. 1229a) that relate to an eligible alien described in section 11031 or 11032.

## SEC. 11034. DEFINITIONS.

Except as otherwise provided, the terms used in this chapter shall have the meaning given such terms in section 101(b) of the Immigration and Nationality Act (8 U.S.C. 1101(b)).

# Rules of Procedure and Statement of Policy for Private Immigration Bills

U.S. HOUSE OF REPRESENTATIVES

## COMMITTEE ON THE JUDICIARY

### SUBCOMMITTEE ON IMMIGRATION AND CLAIMS

### ONE HUNDRED TENTH CONGRESS

## RULES OF PROCEDURE AND STATEMENT OF POLICY FOR PRIVATE IMMIGRATION BILLS

1. All requests for consideration of a private immigration bill shall commence with a letter to the Chairman of the Subcommittee from the author of such bill outlining the relevant facts in the case and attaching thereto all pertinent documents. Documentation will not be accepted if submitted by anyone other than the author of the bill. The following must be submitted in triplicate:

(a) Date and place of birth of each beneficiary; addresses and telephone numbers of each beneficiary presently in the United States.

(b) Dates of all entries (legal and illegal) and departures from the United States, along with the type of visas used for admission; consulate where each beneficiary obtained a visa for entry to the United States; consulate where each beneficiary will be seeking a visa if one is made available.

(c) Status of all petitions and proceedings with the Department of Homeland Security, including nonimmigrant or immigrant petitions that have been filed by the beneficiaries or on their behalf.

(d) Names, addresses, and telephone numbers of interested parties in the United States.

(e) Names, addresses, dates and places of birth, and immigration or citizenship status of all close relatives.

(f) Occupations, recent employment records, and salaries of all beneficiaries.

(g) Copies of all immigration related letters to and from agencies of the United States.

(h) Copies of all administrative and judicial decisions involving the beneficiaries' case.

(i) A signed statement by each beneficiary, or the beneficiary's guardian, that he or she desires the relief sought by the bill.

(j) An explanation as to how the failure to obtain the relief sought in the private bill will result in extreme hardship to the beneficiary or each beneficiary's U.S. citizen spouse, parent or child.

(k) A signed statement by the author of the bill confirming that the author has met personally with the beneficiary or with members of the beneficiary's family

(l) In support of any private bill relating to adoption, the following additional information must accompany the request for Subcommittee action.

(1) Home-study of the prospective parents;

481

(2) Evidence of child support; and

(3) Statement detailing ages and occupations of natural parents and brothers and sisters.

(m) In support of a private bill on behalf of a doctor or nurse, the following additional information must accompany the request for Subcommittee action:

(1) Evidence of passage of the Federal Licensing Examination, or its equivalent, for doctors, and the Commission on Graduates of Foreign Nursing School Exam (CGFNS) for nurses.

(2) Evidence of employment by the doctor or the nurse in a health manpower shortage area, or a recommendation by a U.S. Government Agency indicating the doctor or nurse's services are needed.

(3) Evidence of substantial community ties over a long period of time. Extensive periods of employment give the Subcommittee some assurance there is every likelihood the doctor or nurse would remain employed in the area and provide medical services.

(4) Documentation as to a potential employer's efforts to recruit U.S. citizens for the position. Such information shall include salary levels of other doctors or nurses on staff and an explanation as to recruitment techniques on employment of the beneficiary.

(n) In support of a private bill waiving grounds of exclusion or deportation relating to criminal activity, the following addition documents, if available, will be required.

(1) All records relating to offenses, including state, and local police records; and

(2) An affidavit from the beneficiary describing his or her criminal record in full.

(o) Private bills concerning beneficiaries who are receiving medical treatment will require documentation as to the availability of similar medical treatment in the beneficiary's home country.

2. Each private bill must provide that the beneficiaries must apply for the benefits of the enacted law within a specified period of time, which shall be not more than two years from the date of enactment of the private law.

3. No private bill shall be scheduled for Subcommittee action until all administrative and judicial remedies are exhausted.

4. The Subcommittee will not intervene in deportation proceedings and will not request stays of deportation on behalf of beneficiaries of private bills, except as indicated in Rule 5.

5. The Subcommittee may, at a formal meeting, entertain a motion to request that the Department of Homeland Security provide the Subcommittee with a departmental report on a beneficiary of a private bill. In the past, the Department of Homeland Security has honored requests for departmental reports by staying deportation until final action is taken on the private bill. Only those cases designed to prevent extreme hardship to the beneficiary or a U.S. citizen spouse, parent, or child will merit a request for a report.

6. The Subcommittee may request reports on private bills from appropriate Federal agencies or Departments and shall await receipt of such reports before taking final action.

7. Only the author of a private bill shall be permitted to testify before the Subcommittee on behalf of the private bill. All requests to testify shall be addressed in writing to the Chairman of the Subcommittee.

8. Action on a private bill shall not be deferred more than once due to the failure of the author to appear and testify at a duly noticed hearing.

9. The Subcommittee shall take no further action on a private bill that has been tabled by the full Judiciary Committee.

10. Each of the following types of private bills shall be subject to a point of order unless its consideration is agreed to by a two-thirds vote of the Subcommittee:

(a) Bills not in compliance with these Rules.

(b) Bills that waive the two-year foreign residence requirement for doctors.

(c) Bills that waive any law regarding naturalization.

## STATEMENT OF POLICY

In considering private immigration bills, the Subcommittee reviews only those cases that are of such an extraordinary nature that an exception to the law is needed. It is the policy of the Subcommittee generally to act favorably on only those private bills that meet certain precedents.

Members intending to introduce a private immigration bill are strongly encouraged to seek the technical drafting assistance of the Subcommittee staff (or the Office of Legislative Counsel) prior to introducing a private immigration bill. This will facilitate consideration of the bill by avoiding the need for Subcommittee amendments.

The following sets forth common types of private immigration bills and the criteria for reviewing them.

### A. Adoption

Existing law provides for the immigration of foreign born adopted children if the adoption takes place while the child is under the age of 16 and (1) the child is an "orphan" as defined by immigration law, or (2) the child has resided with the adoptive parents two years. Favorable precedents exist if the child is young and there has been a longstanding parent-child relationship.

### B. Doctors and Nurses

The Immigration and Nationality Act provides for the admission of foreign doctors and nurses who have passed certain exams prior to seeking immigrant status.

In past years, a number of private bills were introduced on behalf of foreign medical graduates. The legislative history relating to this group indicates many doctors enter the United States as nonimmigrants with the intention of remaining permanently. Legislation enacted in 1976 and 1977 sought to tighten the law requiring the return of such doctors to their home country.

The Subcommittee is dismayed to find that doctors who are beneficiaries of private laws often seek more lucrative employment upon gaining permanent residence, thereby leaving medically underserved areas without any medical assistance. Because of these experiences, the Subcommittee views doctor bills unsympathetically.

### C. Drugs and Criminal Activity

In the case of a beneficiary who has been convicted of a deportable crime the Subcommittee will wish to review testimony and affidavits relating to the beneficiary's behavior subsequent to any criminal conviction. Such information is helpful in making a determination as to whether legislation will serve the best interests of the community. In this regard, letters of reference, bank records, and employment records are particularly helpful.

## D. Medical Cases

The Subcommittee will be reluctant to schedule bills on behalf of persons who entered the United States for the purpose of seeking medical treatment. This type of admission is available to accommodate persons seeking advanced medical treatment in the United States. Many cases have come to the attention of the Subcommittee in which persons obtained admission to the United States for medical reasons and decided to try to stay here permanently. This undermines the intent of the original admission and jeopardizes continuance of the program.

The Subcommittee's reluctance to schedule such bills is based on the premise that persons may seek all available medical assistance while in the United States, but upon completion of any medical treatment the purpose of the visa expires and the alien must return home.

It is therefore the policy of the Subcommittee that advisory opinions be sought by the author from such organizations as the World Health Organization and the Pan American Health Organization as to the availability of adequate medical treatment in the alien's home country.

## E. Deferred Action and Parole Cases

The Subcommittee will be reluctant to schedule any bill on behalf of an alien who is in "deferred" status or has been paroled into the United States indefinitely. It is the Subcommittee's understanding that the Department of Homeland Security reserves the conferral of such status to cases of a particularly compelling nature. In view of this, the Subcommittee will view such cases unsympathetically.

## F. Waiver of Exclusions

1. HEALTH— All bills waiving the grounds of exclusion for mental or physical infirmities will require the posting of a bond. There are few favorable precedents for cases in this category. In order to obtain the best possible information, the Subcommittee will require all medical records as well as information from government agencies concerning possible public charge aspects of the case.

2. DRAFT EVADERS— There are few precedents for favorable action on behalf of aliens who seek permanent residency to avoid conscription. It will be the Subcommittee's policy to continue to view such bills unsympathetically.

3. FRAUD— The Subcommittee has been extremely reluctant to act favorably on cases involving visa fraud. It will be the policy of the subcommittee to adhere closely to precedents in such cases.

## G. Naturalization

The Subcommittee will require that any bill expediting naturalization be accompanied by evidence indicating that such action would be in the national interest, as opposed to personal interest. There are few precedents for favorable action on bills waiving any naturalization requirements or granting posthumous or honorary citizenship. It is the Subcommittee's intent generally to view unfavorably legislation of this type. More appropriate mechanisms for rewarding individuals may be in the form of medals, awards, or ceremonies.

The Subcommittee is extremely concerned by requests to expedite citizenship on behalf of athletes seeking to compete in national, international, or Olympic games. The Subcommittee does not believe U.S. citizenship should be provided because of a person's athletic ability.

There are few instances of favorable action on behalf of individuals who renounce U.S. citizenship. The Subcommittee will adhere to precedents in such cases.

*H. Bills Tabled in a Previous Congress*

The Subcommittee has often been confronted with request for reconsideration of private bills that were tabled by the full Committee in previous Congresses. The Subcommittee believes that each bill is given sufficient review during the meetings of the Subcommittee and that authors are afforded ample time to present the merits of the case. Repetitious consideration of these cases detrimentally affects other private bills and reflects poorly on the integrity of the private bill process. For these reasons, the Subcommittee will be reluctant to reconsider its prior action absent new evidence or information not available at the time of initial consideration by the Subcommittee.

# APPENDIX M
## Posthumous Benefits for 9/11 Victims

*Provisions not codified in the INA.*[*]
*See also USA PATRIOT Act provisions in Appendix J*

*(P.L. 107-77, §114; P.L. 108-136, §§1703, 1705)*

**Sec. 114 [Pub. L. 107-77]**

(a) Notwithstanding any provision of title III of the Immigration and Nationality Act (8 U.S.C. 1401 *et seq.*), the Attorney General shall provide, in accordance with this section, for the granting of posthumous citizenship, as of September 10, 2001, to a person described in subsection (b), if the Attorney General approves an application for such citizenship filed under subsection (e).

(b) A person referred to in subsection (a) is a person who—

(1) while an alien or a noncitizen national of the United States, died as a result of an injury incurred in one or more of the events described in subsection (c);

(2) was not culpable for any of such events; and

(3) on September 11, 2001, had pending an application for naturalization filed with the Attorney General by the person.

(c) (1) The events described in this subsection are the following:

(A) The hijacking of American Airlines Flight 11 on September 11, 2001, the crash of that aircraft into the World Trade Center in New York, New York, and the subsequent destruction that resulted.

(B) The hijacking of United Airlines Flight 175 on such date, the crash of that aircraft into the World Trade Center in New York, New York, and the subsequent destruction that resulted.

(C) The hijacking of American Airlines Flight 77 on such date, the crash of that aircraft into the Pentagon in Arlington, Virginia, and the subsequent destruction that resulted.

(D) The hijacking of United Airlines Flight 93 on such date, and the crash of that aircraft in Stony Creek Township, Pennsylvania.

(2) Any person who died as a result of an injury incurred while assisting in the emergency response to an event described in paragraph (1) (such as military personnel, law enforcement officers, firefighters, emergency management personnel, search and rescue personnel, medical personnel, engineers and other personnel providing technical assistance, and volunteers) shall be considered to have died as a result of an injury incurred in such event.

(d) (1) Unless otherwise provided by this section, no person may be granted posthumous citizenship under this section who would not otherwise have been eligible for naturalization

---

[*] Provisions in the statutes that directly amend the Immigration & Nationality Act (INA) are incorporated therein, and are not included here.

on the date of the person's death. Unless otherwise provided by this section, any provision of law that specifically bars or prohibits a person from being naturalized as a citizen of the United States shall be applied to the granting of posthumous citizenship under this section.

(2) Notwithstanding section 312 of the Immigration and Nationality Act (8 U.S.C. 1423), or any similar provision of law requiring that a person demonstrate an understanding of the English language or a knowledge and understanding of the fundamentals of the history, and of the principles and form of government, of the United States in order to be naturalized, no such demonstration shall be required for the granting of posthumous citizenship under this section.

(3) No oath of renunciation or allegiance shall be required for the granting of posthumous citizenship under this section.

(4) To the maximum extent practicable, the investigation and examination described in section 335 of the Immigration and Nationality Act (8 U.S.C. 1446) shall be conducted with respect to an application described in subsection (b)(3) in the same manner as they otherwise would have been conducted if the subject of the application had not died.

(e) A request for the granting of posthumous citizenship to a person described in subsection (b) may be filed on behalf of the person only by the next of kin (as defined by the Attorney General) or another representative (as defined by the Attorney General), and must be filed not later than 2 years after the later of—

(1) the date of the enactment of this section; or

(2) the date of the person's death.

(f) If the Attorney General approves such a request to grant a person posthumous citizenship, the Attorney General shall send to the individual who filed the request a suitable document which states that the United States considers the person to have been a citizen of the United States as of September 10, 2001.

(g) Nothing in this section shall be construed as providing for any benefits under the Immigration and Nationality Act for any spouse, son, daughter, or other relative of a person granted posthumous citizenship under this section.

(h) (1) Notwithstanding section 341 of the Immigration and Nationality Act (8 U.S.C. 1452), the Attorney General shall provide, in accordance with this subsection, for the furnishing of a certificate of citizenship to a person described in paragraph (4), if the Attorney General approves under paragraph (3) an application for such certificate described in paragraph (2).

(2) An application described in this paragraph is an application for a certificate of citizenship that was—

(A) filed with the Attorney General under such section 341 by a person who subsequently died as a result of an injury incurred in one or more of the events described in section 114(c) and who was not culpable for any of such events; and

(B) pending on September 11, 2001.

(3) The Attorney General shall consider an application described in paragraph (2) pursuant to the standards under such section 341 and shall approve the application if the applicant would have been eligible to receive a certificate of citizenship on September 11, 2001, if the applicant had not died, except that the requirements of such section relating to the oath of allegiance and presence within the United States shall not apply.

(4) A request for a certificate of citizenship under this subsection may be filed only by the next of kin (as defined by the Attorney General) or another representative (as defined by the Attorney General) of the applicant described in paragraph (2), and must be filed not later than 2 years after the later of—

    (A) the date of the enactment of this section; or

    (B) the date of the applicant's death.

(i) (1) Notwithstanding section 322 of the Immigration and Nationality Act (8 U.S.C. 1433), the Attorney General shall provide, in accordance with this subsection, for the furnishing of a certificate of citizenship to a parent described in paragraph (2), if, upon the request of the parent, the Attorney General approves under paragraph (3) an application for naturalization described in paragraph (2).

(2) An application described in this paragraph is an application for naturalization that was—

    (A) filed with the Attorney General under such section 322 by a parent of a child who subsequently died as a result of an injury incurred in one or more of the events described in section 114(c) and who was not culpable for any of such events; and

    (B) pending on September 11, 2001.

(3) The Attorney General shall consider an application described in paragraph (2) pursuant to the standards under such section 322 and shall approve the application if the child would have been eligible to receive a certificate of citizenship on September 11, 2001, if the child had not died, except that the requirements of such section relating to the oath of allegiance shall not apply.

---

## §1703 [Pub. L. 108-136]. EXTENSION OF POSTHUMOUS BENEFITS TO SURVIVING SPOUSES, CHILDREN, AND PARENTS

(a) TREATMENT AS IMMEDIATE RELATIVES.—

(1) SPOUSES.— Notwithstanding the second sentence of section 201(b)(2)(A)(i) of the Immigration and Nationality Act (8 U.S.C. 1151(b)(2)(A)(i)), in the case of an alien who was the spouse of a citizen of the United States at the time of the citizen's death and was not legally separated from the citizen at the time of the citizen's death, if the citizen served honorably in an active duty status in the military, air, or naval forces of the United States and died as a result of injury or disease incurred in or aggravated by combat, the alien (and each child of the alien) shall be considered, for purposes of section 201(b) of such Act, to remain an immediate relative after the date of the citizen's death, but only if the alien files a petition under section 204(a)(1)(A)(ii) of such Act within 2 years after such date and only until the date the alien remarries. For purposes of such section 204(a)(1)(A)(ii), an alien granted relief under the preceding sentence shall be considered an alien spouse described in the second sentence of section 201(b)(2)(A)(i) of such Act.

(2) CHILDREN.—

    (A) IN GENERAL.— In the case of an alien who was the child of a citizen of the United States at the time of the citizen's death, if the citizen served honorably in an active duty status in the military, air, or naval forces of the United States and died as a result of injury or disease incurred in or aggravated by combat, the alien shall be considered, for purposes of section 201(b) of the Immigration and Nationality Act (8 U.S.C. 1151(b)), to remain an immediate relative after the date of the citizen's death (regardless of changes in age or marital status thereafter), but only if the alien files a petition under subparagraph (B) within 2 years after such date.

(B) PETITIONS.— An alien described in subparagraph (A) may file a petition with the Secretary of Homeland Security for classification of the alien under section 201(b)(2)(A)(i) of the Immigration and Nationality Act (8 U.S.C. 1151(b)(2)(A)(i)). For purposes of such Act, such a petition shall be considered a petition filed under section 204(a)(1)(A) of such Act (8 U.S.C. 1154(a)(1)(A)).

(3) PARENTS.—

(A) IN GENERAL.— In the case of an alien who was the parent of a citizen of the United States at the time of the citizen's death, if the citizen served honorably in an active duty status in the military, air, or naval forces of the United States and died as a result of injury or disease incurred in or aggravated by combat, the alien shall be considered, for purposes of section 201(b) of the Immigration and Nationality Act (8 U.S.C. 1151(b)), to remain an immediate relative after the date of the citizen's death (regardless of changes in age or marital status thereafter), but only if the alien files a petition under subparagraph (B) within 2 years after such date.

(B) PETITIONS.— An alien described in subparagraph (A) may file a petition with the Secretary of Homeland Security for classification of the alien under section 201(b)(2)(A)(i) of the Immigration and Nationality Act (8 U.S.C. 1151(b)(2)(A)(i)). For purposes of such Act, such a petition shall be considered a petition filed under section 204(a)(1)(A) of such Act (8 U.S.C. 1154(a)(1)(A)).

(C) EXCEPTION.— Notwithstanding section 201(b)(2)(A)(i) of the Immigration and Nationality Act (8 U.S.C. 1151(b)(2)(A)(i)), for purposes of this paragraph, a citizen described in subparagraph (A) does not have to be 21 years of age for a parent to benefit under this paragraph.

(b) APPLICATIONS FOR ADJUSTMENT OF STATUS BY SURVIVING SPOUSES, CHILDREN, AND PARENTS.—

(1) IN GENERAL.— Notwithstanding subsections (a) and (c) of section 245 of the Immigration and Nationality Act (8 U.S.C. 1255), any alien who was the spouse, child, or parent of an alien described in paragraph (2), and who applied for adjustment of status prior to the death described in paragraph (2)(B), may have such application adjudicated as if such death had not occurred.

(2) ALIEN DESCRIBED.— An alien is described in this paragraph if the alien—

(A) served honorably in an active duty status in the military, air, or naval forces of the United States;

(B) died as a result of injury or disease incurred in or aggravated by combat; and

(C) was granted posthumous citizenship under section 329A of the Immigration and Nationality Act (8 U.S.C. 1440-1).

(c) SPOUSES AND CHILDREN OF LAWFUL PERMANENT RESIDENT ALIENS.—

(1) TREATMENT AS IMMEDIATE RELATIVES.—

(A) IN GENERAL.— A spouse or child of an alien described in paragraph (3) who is included in a petition for classification as a family-sponsored immigrant under section 203(a)(2) of the Immigration and Nationality Act (8 U.S.C. 1153(a)(2)) that was filed by such alien, shall be considered (if the spouse or child has not been admitted or approved for lawful permanent residence by such date) a valid petitioner for immediate relative status under section 201(b)(2)(A)(i) of the Immigration and Nationality Act (8 U.S.C. 1151(b)(2)(A)(i)). Such spouse or child shall be eligible for deferred action, advance parole, and work authorization.

(B) PETITIONS.— An alien spouse or child described in subparagraph (A) may file a petition with the Secretary of Homeland Security for classification of the alien under section 201(b)(2)(A)(i) of the Immigration and Nationality Act (8 U.S.C. 1151(b)(2)(A)(i)). For purposes of such Act, such a petition shall be considered a petition filed under section 204(a)(1)(A) of such Act (8 U.S.C. 1154(a)(1)(A)).

(2) SELF-PETITIONS.— Any spouse or child of an alien described in paragraph (3) who is not a beneficiary of a petition for classification as a family-sponsored immigrant may file a petition for such classification under section 201(b)(2)(A)(i) of the Immigration and Nationality Act (8 U.S.C. 1151(b)(2)(A)(i)) with the Secretary of Homeland Security, but only if the spouse or child files a petition within 2 years after such date. Such spouse or child shall be eligible for deferred action, advance parole, and work authorization.

(3) ALIEN DESCRIBED.— An alien is described in this paragraph if the alien—

(A) served honorably in an active duty status in the military, air, or naval forces of the United States;

(B) died as a result of injury or disease incurred in or aggravated by combat; and

(C) was granted posthumous citizenship under section 329A of the Immigration and Nationality Act (8 U.S.C. 1440-1).

(d) PARENTS OF LAWFUL PERMANENT RESIDENT ALIENS.—

(1) SELF-PETITIONS.— Any parent of an alien described in paragraph (2) may file a petition for classification under section 201(b)(2)(A)(i) of the Immigration and Nationality Act (8 U.S.C. 1151(b)(2)(A)(i)), but only if the parent files a petition within 2 years after such date. For purposes of such Act, such petition shall be considered a petition filed under section 204(a)(1)(A) of such Act (8 U.S.C. 1154(a)(1)(A)). Such parent shall be eligible for deferred action, advance parole, and work authorization.

(2) ALIEN DESCRIBED.— An alien is described in this paragraph if the alien—

(A) served honorably in an active duty status in the military, air, or naval forces of the United States;

(B) died as a result of injury or disease incurred in or aggravated by combat; and

(C) was granted posthumous citizenship under section 329A of the Immigration and Nationality Act (8 U.S.C. 1440-1).

(e) WAIVER OF GROUND FOR INADMISSIBILITY.— In determining the admissibility of any alien accorded an immigration benefit under this section for purposes of the Immigration and

Nationality Act, the ground for inadmissibility specified in section 212(a)(4) of such Act (8 U.S.C. 1182(a)(4)) shall not apply.

(f)–(h) [incorporated in INA; omitted here]

### §1705 [Pub. L. 108-136] EFFECTIVE DATE.

(a) IN GENERAL.— Except as provided in subsection (b), this title and the amendments made by this title shall take effect as if enacted on September 11, 2001.

(b) EXCEPTION.— The amendments made by sections 1701(b) (relating to naturalization fees) and 1701(d) (relating to naturalization proceedings overseas) shall take effect on October 1, 2004.

# INDEX

*References in roman (nonitalic) type are to INA sections.*
*References in italics are to appendices. References to 8 USC citations*
*not in INA (App. A) are of the form 8:1182d.*

## A

**A visas (foreign diplomats)**
adjustment of status, 247; *8:1255b*
definitions, 101(a)(9), (a)(11), (a)(15)(A)
deportation, approval by DOS, 237(b)
failure to maintain status, *8:1255b*
registration, special regulations and
forms, 263(b)
removal proceedings, 102(1)
**abduction of children,** *see* Inadmissibility
**aboriginal tribes**
Generally, 301(b)
**abortion**
forced abortion or sterilization policy,
denial of visa and entry, *8:1182e*
**abuse of children**
*see also* Battered women and children
Adam Walsh Act, 204(a)(1)(A)(viii)
aging-out, extension when abuse is reason
for untimely filing, 204(a)(1)(D)(v)
definition of, 214(r)(5)
deportation, 237(a)(2)(E)(i)
**AC21,** *see* American Competitiveness in
21st Century Act
**Adam Walsh Child Protection and**
**Safety Act of 2006**
crimes committed against minors, admission prohibited, 204(a)(1)(A)(viii)
**addicts,** *see* Drug abusers and addicts
**address**
central address file, 239(a)(3)
in notice to appear, 239(a)(1)(F), (a)(2)(B)
requirement to report change, 265
affidavits of support, 213A(d)
deportability, 237(a)(3)(A)
in absentia orders, 240(b)(5)
misdemeanor, 266(b)
**adjustment of status**
Generally, 245–50
approval of adjustment, 245(b)
Armed Forces, service in, 245(g)
asylum, 208(d)(3)
authority to adjust status, 245(a)
conditional residents, 245(d), (f)
crewmen, 245(c)(1); 245(i); 248(a)(1)
criminal investigations, persons assisting
in, 245(m)
distress, removal of aliens who have
fallen into, 250
employment, acceptance of unauthorized, 245(c)(2); 245(i)
employment-based immigrants, 245(k)
fee for application, 245(i)(1), (i)(3)
waiver for trafficking victims, 245(l)(7)
fiancées and fiancés, change of nonimmigrant classification, 248(a)(1)

flexibility of job, long-delayed applicants, 204(j)
diplomats, adjustment from LPR to
A nonimmigrant status, 247
fee waiver for VAWA self-petitioners,
245(l)(7)
good moral character, waiver of requirement for trafficking victims, 245(l)(6)
Guam, visitor for business or pleasure,
245(c)(4); 245(i); 248(a)(4)
immediate relatives, 203(g)
investor, adjustment of LPR to E nonimmigrant status, 247
legalization, *see* Legalization
LIFE Act, 214(q)(3); *App. I*
marriage during removal proceeding,
245(e)
naturalization, 246(b)
occupational status, adjustment back to
A, E, or G nonimmigrant status, 247
physical presence in U.S., 245(i)(1), (k)
record of adjustment, 245(b), (j)(3)
refugees, *see* Refugees
registry, *see* Registry
rescission of status, 246
special agricultural workers, *see* Special
agricultural workers
special immigrant juveniles, 245(h)
temporary protected status, 244(f)(4)
terrorists, 245(c)(6); 245(i); 504(k)(5)
time for rescission of status, 246(a)
traders, adjustment to E status, 247
Philippine traders, *8:1184a*
trafficking in persons, persons subjected
to, 245(l)
transit without visa, aliens in, 245(c)(3);
245(i); 248(a)(1)
VAWA self-petitioner, 245(a)
victims of crime, 245(l)
visa-waiver nonimmigrants, 245(c)(4)
witnesses, 245(c)(5); 245(i), (j);
248(a)(1)
**administrative review**
agricultural labor or services, expedited
appeals, 218(e)
asylum, 208(d)(5)(A)(iv)
document fraud, 274C(d)(4)
inspection by immigration officers,
235(b)(1)(B)(iii)(III), (b)(1)(C)
legalization, *see* Legalization
removal proceedings, *see* Removal proceedings
special agricultural workers, 210(e)(1)–(2)
temporary protected status, 244(b)(5)
unlawful employment, 274A(e)(7)
**administrator**
defined, 101(a)(1)
internal security officers, liaison with, 105

**admission**
*see also* Inadmissibility; Inspections;
Parole; Passports
burden of proof, 291
Canadian citizen, admission under free
trade agreements, 214(e)
defined, 101(a)(13)
documentary requirements, 211
duration of status, 214(a)(2)
fee on employer, 214(c)(9)
legalization, continuous lawful residence, 245A(a)(2)(B)
Mexican citizen, admission under free
trade agreement, 214(c)(2)–(5)
nonimmigrants, generally, 214
numerical restrictions, 214(g), (k);
*App. H (AC21)*
presumption of immigrant status,
214(b)
records of admission, 240C
refugees, 207(c); 211(c)
registration, waiver of fingerprinting,
262(c)
returning resident immigrants, 211(b)
terrorism sponsoring countries, aliens
from, 214(c)(4)(F)
unexpired immigrant visa, 211(a)(1)
withdrawal of application for admission,
235(a)(4)
**adopted children**
birth of child and residence outside U.S.,
322(c)
in definition of child, 101(b)(1)(E)
inadmissibility, vaccine-preventable diseases, 212(a)(1)(C)
naturalization, birth and residence outside U.S., 321(c)
**adult education programs**
F visas, 214(m)(1)(A), 214(m)(2)
**AFDC benefits**
special agricultural workers, temporary
disqualification, 210(f)
**affidavits of support**
Generally, 213A
demonstration of means, 213A(f)(6)
employment-based, 212(a)(4)(D)
family-sponsored, 212(a)(4)(C)
notice of change of address, 213A(d)
reimbursement, 213A(b)
**aged persons,** *see* Elderly persons
**aggravated felonies,** *see* Removal
**aging-out**
abuse as reason for not timely filing, extension possible, 204(a)(1)(D)(v)
Child Status Protection Act, 201(f);
203(h); 204(k)

**chargeability rules**
numerical limitations, 202(b), (c)

**children and minors**
*see also* Family-sponsored immigration
abuse, *see* Abuse of children; Battered
women and children
adopted, *see* Adopted children
Armed Forces dependents, residence
abroad with service member,
285(b); 319(e); 322(d)
asylum
treatment of child of alien, 208(b)(3)
unaccompanied minors, 208(a)(2)(E),
(b)(3)(C)
Child Nutrition Act, temporary disqualification from welfare benefits following legalization, 245A(h)(4)(B)
Child Status Protection Act, 201(f);
203(h); 204(k)
conditional residents, *see* Conditional
permanent resident status
crimes committed against minors, inadmissibility, 204(a)(1)(A)(viii)
definition, 101(a)(51)(b)
illegitimate children, 309
inadmissibility, *see* Inadmissibility
loss of nationality, 351(b)
N visas (parents and children of certain
special immigrants), 101(a)(15)(N)
naturalization, *see* Naturalization
permanent residents, numerical limitations, 202(a)(4)
recruitment or use of child soldiers
as deportability ground, 237(a)(4)(F)
as inadmissibility ground, 212(a)(3)(G)
refugee, child of, 207(c)(2)
resettlement of and assistance to refugees, 412(a)(4)(b)(iv), (d)
rules for determining status, 203(h)
special immigrant juveniles,
101(a)(27)(J); 245(h)

**Chile**
U.S.–Chile Free Trade Agreement,
101(a)(15)(E); 101(a)(15)(H)(i)(b1);
212(t)[first]; 214(c)(11)(A);
214(g)(8); 214(j)(2)

**CIA**, *see* Central Intelligence Agency

**citizenship**, *see* Former citizens; Legalization; Loss of Nationality; Nationality;
Naturalization

**class actions**
inspection by immigration officers, judicial review, 242(e)(1)(B)

**classified information**
terrorists, 504(d)(5), (e)(3); 505(b)

**collateral attack**
inspection by immigration officers,
235(b)(1)(D)
removal proceedings, asylum,
235(b)(1)(D)

**collective bargaining agreements**
D visas, longshore work, 258(c), (d)

**Commissioner of INS**
liaison with internal security officers, 105
powers and duties, 103

**common carriers**, *see* Transportation and
transportation lines

**communicable diseases**
crewmen, 253; 255
inadmissibility, 212(a)(1)

**Communists**
naturalization, 313; 340(c)

**concealment**
naturalization, revocation of, 340(a), (b)
smuggling of aliens, 274(a)(1)(A)(iii)

**conditional permanent resident status**
Generally, 216; 216A
adjustment of status, 245(d), (f)
contents of petition, 216(d)(1); 216a(d)(1)
definitions, 216A(f); 216(g)
deportation, 237(a)(1)(D), (c)
entrepreneurs and their spouses and children, 216A
hardship waiver, 216(c)(4)
inadmissibility waivers, treatment of,
216(f)
interview for removal of conditional
status, 216(c)–(d); 216A(c)–(d)
marriage, status based on, 216(b)(2),
(c)(2)(B), (c)(3)(D)
naturalization, treatment for purposes of,
216A(e); 216(e)
notice of requirements, 216(a)(2);
216A(a)(2)
petition for removal of conditional
status, 216(c)–(d); 216A(c)–(d)
termination of status
adverse determination, 216(c)(3)(C);
216A(c)(3)(C)
failure to file petition or have interview,
216(c)(2); 216A(c)(2)
improper entrepreneurship status,
216A(b)
improper marriage, 216(b)

**confidentiality of information**
abuse, disclosure and use of information
given by perpetrator, *8:1367*
legalization, applications, 245A(c)(4)–(5)
registration, 264(b)
special agricultural workers, applications
for adjustment, 210(b)(5), (b)(6)
temporary protected status, 244(c)(6)
visas, 222(f)

**confiscators of American property**
denial of visa, *8:1182d*

**conspiracy**
deportation, 237(a)(2)(D)
smuggling of aliens, 274(a)(1)(A)(v)

**Constitution, principles of**
naturalization, 316(a)(3); 324(b); 327(b);
328(c), (e); 340(c)

**consular processing**, *see* Visas

**consuls**, *see* A visas

**contagious diseases**, *see* Communicable
diseases

**continuous residence**
Armed Forces, spouses and children of,
284(b); 319(e); 322(b)
cancellation of removal, 240A(d)
legalization, *see* Legalization
naturalization, 316(a)–(b); 319; 322
registry, 249(b)
temporary protected status, 244(c)(4)

**convictions**
defined, 101(a)(48)(A)
multiple convictions
grounds of deportability, 237(a)(2)(A)(ii)
grounds of inadmissibility, 212(a)(2)(B)
proof of, removal proceedings,
240(c)(3)(B)–(C)
for unlawful procurement of naturalization, 340(e)

**costs and expenses**
*see also* Fees; Fines and penalties
B visas (temporary visits for business or
pleasure), 212(q)
D visas, *see* D visas (crewmen)
detention pending removal, payment of
costs of, 241(c)(2)(B), (b)(3)
disposition of moneys collected, 286(a)
incarceration, 241(i)(2)
remains of immigration officers and
border patrol agents, transportation
of, 283, 295
removal proceedings, *see* Removal proceedings
reimbursement to state for expenses
for incarceration, *8:1365*
for emergency medical services,
*8:1369–70*
travel expenses, 283
voluntary departure, 241(e)(3)(C)

**counsel, right to**, *see* Attorneys

**counterfeiting and forgery**
Generally, 274C(a)(1), (a)(2)
passports, 101(a)(43)(P)
registration certificates and receipt cards,
266(d)
travel documentation, 215(a)(6), (a)(7)
unlawful employment, counterfeit-
resistant documents, 274A(d)(2)(B)

**crewmen**, *see* D visas

**crimes and offenses**
aggravated felonies, *see* Removal
arrest and detention, 236(c)–(d); 241(a)(6)
asylum, ineligibility for,
208(b)(2)(A)(ii)–(iii)
certificate of registration, failure to possess, 264(e)
deportation, *see* Removal
document fraud, *see* Document fraud
drug offenses, *see* Drug offenses
fines, *see* Fines and penalties
inadmissibility, *see* Inadmissibility
incarceration, *see* Arrest and detention
legalization, *see* Legalization
penalties, *see* Fines and penalties
reentry of removed alien, 276(b)(1), (c)

# E

# F

# Q

# R

**R visas (religious organizations)**
defined, 101(a)(15)(R)

**race discrimination**
naturalization, 311

**railroads**
prevention of unauthorized landing by
aliens, 271(a), (c)(1)

**reentry and reentry permits**
Generally, 223
applications, 223(a)
duration of permit, 223(b)(3)
good faith, 223(b)(2)
issuance of permit, 223(b)
port of entry, presentation of permit at,
223(d)
printing of reentry permits, 277; 282
removed alien, reentry of, 276
criminal offenses, removal for,
276(b)(1), (c)
drug offenses, crimes against the person
or felonies, removal for, 276(b)(1)
fine or imprisonment, 276
public charge, removal as, 276(b)(4)
terrorist activities, removal for,
276(b)(3)
validity of deportation order, challenge
to, 276(d)
surrender of permit, 223(d)
use of permit, 223(c)
visa, acceptance in lieu of, 223(e)

**Refugee Education Assistance Act**
legalization, temporary disqualification
from receiving public welfare,
245A(h)(5)

**refugees**
*see also* Asylum
Generally, 207; 209
adjustment of status, 209
inadmissibility, inapplicability, or
waiver of grounds for, 209(c)
admissions, 207(c); 211(c)
assistance to refugees, *see* Resettlement
of and assistance to refugees
child of refugee, admission of, 207(c)(2)
consultation, President of U.S., 207(d)–(e)
defined, 101(a)(42)
humanitarian concerns, 207(c)
inadmissibility, *see* Inadmissibility
numerical limitations, 201(b)(1)(B);
207(a)–(b)
reports, 207(d)–(e)
resettlement of refugees, *see* Resettlement of and assistance to refugees
spouse of refugee, admission of,
207(c)(2)
termination of status, 207(c)(4)
training, 207(f)

**registered nurses**, *see* H-1C visas

**registration**
Generally, 261–66
address, notice of, 265; 266(b)

alien registration receipt card,
264(d), (e)
application for registration, requirement
of, 262; 266(a)
border-crossing identification cards, special regulations and forms for holders of, 263(a)(2)
certificate of registration, 264(d), (e)
change of address, notice of, 265
confidentiality of records, 264(b)
crewmen, special regulations and forms
for, 263(a)(1)
crimes and offenses
address or change of address, failure to
give notice of, 266(b)
application for registration and fingerprinting, failure to make or be,
266(a)
counterfeit certificates and receipt
cards, 266(d)
fraud and false statements, 266(c)
criminal probation or parole in U.S.,
special regulations and forms for
aliens on, 263(a)(5)
fingerprinting, 262
foreign diplomats, special regulations
and forms, 263(b)
forms and procedures, 264
guardians of aliens, 262(b)
institutions, regulations and forms for
aliens confined in, 263(a)(3)
international organizations, special regulations and forms, 263(b)
oath, submission of information under,
264(c)
parents of aliens, 262(b)
removal order, regulations and forms for
aliens subject to, 263(a)(4)
Social Security number, 264(f)
visas, 221(b); 261

**registry**
Generally, 249
continuous residence, 249(b)
inadmissibility, ineligibility based on,
249
moral character, 249(c)
terrorist activities, ineligibility based on,
249(d); 504(k)(6)

**reimbursement**
fees, 286(i)

**reinstatement**
removal orders against aliens illegally
reentering, 241(a)(5)

**religion and religious workers**, *see* Employment-based immigration; Naturalization; R visas

**religious freedom**
violations by foreign government officials, inadmissibility, 212(a)(2)(G)

**religious organizations**
faith-based defense to alien-smuggling
charge, 274(a)(1)(C)
R visas, 101(a)(15)(R)

**removal**
*see also* Inadmissibility
Generally, 239–43
administrative review
asylum, 235(b)(1)(B)(iii)(III), (b)(1)(C)
security and related grounds, 235(c)(2)
aggravated felonies, 237(a)(2)(A)(iii)
defined, 101(a)(43)
expedited removal, *see in this heading*
Expedited removal
alternative countries to which alien may
be removed, 241(b)(1)(C), (b)(2)(D)
armed forces of foreign state, recruitment
or use of child soldiers, 237(a)(4)(F)
ambassadors, 102(1)
asylum, *see* asylum
authority of immigration judge,
240(b)(1)
burden of proof, 240(c)(2), (c)(3)
threat to life or freedom of alien,
241(b)(3)(C)
cancellation of removal, *see* Cancellation
of removal
central address files, initiation of proceedings, 239(a)(3)
change in time or place of proceedings,
notice of, 239(a)(2)
change of address, failure to give notice
of, 237(a)(3)(A), (c)
charges, 240(a)(2)
classes of deportable aliens, 237(a)
criminal-offenses grounds, 237(a)(2)
attempted crimes, 237(a)(2)(D)
child abuse, 237(a)(2)(E)(i)
conspiracy or attempt, 237(a)(2)(D)
domestic violence, 237(a)(2)(E)(i), (a)(7)
drug offenses, 237(a)(2)(B)
espionage, 237(a)(2)(D)(i), (a)(4)(A)(i)
firearm offenses, 237(a)(2)(C)
high speed flight, 237(a)(2)(A)(iv)
immoral purpose, importation of alien
for, 237(a)(2)(D)(iv)
Military Selective Service Act, Trading
with Enemy Act, 237(a)(2)(D)(iii)
moral turpitude, crimes of,
237(a)(2)(A)(i)
multiple convictions, 237(a)(2)(A)(ii)
protection orders, violation of,
237(a)(2)(E)(ii)
sabotage, 237(a)(2)(D)(i), (a)(4)(A)(i)
sedition, 237(a)(2)(D)(i)
sex offender's failure to register,
237(a)(2)(A)(v)
stalking, 237(a)(2)(E)(i)
travel documentation, 237(a)(2)(D)(iv)
treason, 237(a)(2)(D)(i)
waiver, 237(a)(2)(A)(vi)
clearance of vessels and aircraft, penalties, 243(c)(2)
collateral attack, asylum, 235(b)(1)(D)
commencement of time for removal,
241(a)(1)(B)
conduct of proceeding, 240(b)
construction of statute, 241(h)